JEAN-JACQUES
ROUSSEAU

JEAN-JACQUES
ROUSSEAU

Restless Genius

LEO DAMROSCH

HOUGHTON MIFFLIN COMPANY
BOSTON · NEW YORK

To Joyce Van Dyke

For information about permission to reproduce selections from
this book, write to Permissions, Houghton Mifflin Company,
215 Park Avenue South, New York, New York 10003.

Visit our Web site: www.houghtonmifflinbooks.com.

Library of Congress Cataloging-in-Publication Data
Damrosch, Leopold.
Jean-Jacques Rousseau : restless genius / Leo Damrosch.
p.   cm.
Includes bibliographical references and index.
ISBN-13: 978-0-618-44696-4
ISBN-10: 0-618-44696-6
1. Rousseau, Jean-Jacques, 1712–1778. 2. Authors,
French — 18th century — Biography. I. Title.
PQ2043.D36 2005 848'.509 — dc22 2005013579

Book design by Victoria Hartman

Printed in the United States of America

QUM 10 9 8 7 6 5 4 3 2

Contents

Illustrations

Introduction

JEAN-JACQUES ROUSSEAU was a teenage dropout who ran away from a hated apprenticeship, spent the next twenty years in apparent idleness punctuated by occasional low-level jobs, and until he was well into his thirties seemed to have no future whatsoever. But then, unexpectedly even to those who knew him best, he became one of the most influential writers of his time and, as it would eventually turn out, of the modern world. Rousseau's triumph was the more surprising since, unlike most famous writers then or later, he did not go to school for a single day and was essentially self-taught. In a series of amazingly original books, of which *The Social Contract* is the best known, he developed a political theory that deeply influenced the American Founding Fathers and the French revolutionaries, helped to invent modern anthropology, and advanced a concept of education that remains challenging and inspiring to this day. His *Confessions* virtually created the genre of autobiography as we know it, tracing lifelong patterns of feeling to formative experiences and finding a deep unity of the self beneath apparent contradictions; modern psychology owes him an immense debt.

But although his influence was great, Rousseau founded no school of disciples, and he came to regret that he had ever published a word. And even at their most compelling, his books are filled with paradoxes that many people, then and later, have regarded as contradictions. Although he argued in *The Social Contract* for a community in which each individual would be satisfyingly united with "the general will," his theory can seem disturbingly prophetic of modern totalitarianism. He held that children should be allowed to develop and learn according to their natural bent, but in *Émile* this goal is attained by a tutor who cunningly manipulates his pupil's responses, and Rousseau consigned his own children to a foundling home as soon as they were born. And even though he made a brilliant case for social equality, he formed close friendships with aristocrats and endorsed a view of female subservience that was old-fashioned even in his own time.

To say that Rousseau's contemporaries were aware of the paradoxes in his writing would be putting it mildly. It was the constant theme of reviewers, from his first publications in the early 1750s to his posthumous works, which came out in the 1780s. The usual line was that his compelling prose style veiled the hollowness of his paradoxes and that other writers, notably Voltaire, were much deeper thinkers. Rousseau himself was well aware of these criticisms, but the impulse behind all of his work was a determination to confront the contradictions that seem inseparable from our experience. It is easy to think up theories that get rid of contradictions, but not so easy to get rid of the contradictions themselves. Since his time, two centuries of further reflection have of course brought new ways of answering his questions. As Jean Starobinski has said, "It took Kant to think Rousseau's thoughts, and Freud to think Rousseau's feelings." But the questions remain as important as ever, and Freud himself stands directly in the line that leads from Rousseau. As for Voltaire, it seems obvious today that he was a witty and prolific popularizer whose ideas were largely derivative. It was Rousseau who was the most original genius of his age — so original that most people at the time could not begin to appreciate how powerful his thinking was.

Rousseau put it very well in *Émile:* "I would rather be a man of paradoxes than a man of prejudices." Prejudices are the shared assumptions that make it easy to get along with one's social group and to feel at home in the world. Rousseau wanted to go behind the assumptions that society equips us with, in order to understand why it is so hard to be at peace with ourselves and others. Many writers have insisted that their lives were none of their readers' business. Not so Rousseau. He thought of his writings as the direct product of life experience; conversely, his insights into personality and motivation illuminate his great theoretical works, in which passion burns on every page.

As powerful as Rousseau's legacy as a thinker has been, it is still more his example that has influenced those who have come after, including many who have never read him. Above all he is a questing personality, unwilling to settle for what life seems to have dealt him and yearning for something deeper than mere success, which he achieved and then rejected. "I found in myself," he wrote when he was fifty, "an inexplicable void that nothing was able to fill, a certain longing of the heart for another kind of enjoyment of which I had no idea, and of which I nevertheless felt the need." He believed that his example would be valuable to his fellow human beings, his *semblables,* as he called them, and I hope that this new attempt to tell his story will confirm that belief.

Any biographer of Rousseau faces a challenge in the ambiguity as well as the richness of the autobiographical material. He devoted fully one-third of the *Confessions* to the first twenty years of his life, a period that any of his predecessors or contemporaries would have dismissed in a few pages. Today we take it for granted that a person's early experiences are crucially important, and it is no exaggeration to say that it was Rousseau who taught us to think so. But most of what we know about those years in his life comes from his own recollections recorded long afterward, when he had become a celebrated novelist and told his story novelistically, as indeed any good autobiographer must. This, too, was something Rousseau understood very well. Although he did declare that "no one can write a man's life but himself; his inner way of being and his true life are known only to him," he went on to say, "In writing his life he disguises it, and in the name of his life, he gives us his apologia." In his last years he was even able to recognize that the only truth he could really report was the truth about his own efforts at self-understanding. "The 'Know Thyself' of the temple at Delphi was not such an easy maxim to follow as I believed when I wrote my *Confessions.*" Many of the incidents and relationships he describes invite interpretations that modify his, or even contradict them. But it remains true that we can attempt such interpretations only because Rousseau himself grasped the significance of the evidence he provided, and began to forge tools with which to understand his own motives and behavior.

Beneath all the issues of evidence and interpretation lies the deepest issue of all, Rousseau's personality and its relation to his achievement. He stands as the type of the lonely and questing spirit, but loneliness is not necessarily attractive, and many people have found his personality exasperating. He was unreliable and temperamental, highly demanding of those around him, with a noble self-image that clashed with his everyday behavior. He was a difficult friend, a disappointing lover, and an impossible employee. Yet it is precisely from his disappointments, frustrations, and psychic conflicts that his deepest insights emerged, and his writings rise like mountain peaks above the routine of daily living. He was a prodigious genius, but for many years his genius was deeply buried, and his struggle to understand and liberate it was inseparable from the insights he gave to the world.

Years of exploring Rousseau's writings with students at every level, from freshman seminars to adult education classes, have convinced me that his ideas remain fresh and powerful, and also that the way they emerged from his life is a story that deserves to be told. His deepest concern was with the painful dissonance between inner feelings and outward social pressures, and he came to see that versions of that personal dissonance haunt our culture at large. His myth of a lost state of nature, his dream of a social contract fully shared by all of its members, his anxieties about sexual politics, and his yearning for psychic wholeness — all of these were rooted in his own experience, and he knew it. Much in his life was baffling and distressing, which provoked him to an ever deeper quest for meaning, and despite an increasing drift into paranoia toward the end, his writings are triumphant in their sanity and wisdom.

My intention is to integrate the story of Rousseau's extraordinarily original writings with the story of the tumultuous life that produced them, to use wherever possible his own words and those of others who knew him, to make the insights of modern scholarship available for the general reader, and to suggest why his ideas have had such electrifying effects. The standard biography in English, by the political scientist Maurice Cranston, is exhaustively detailed, but almost willfully ignores the stranger aspects of Rousseau's experience. In addition, because Cranston died before finishing his third and final volume, the last ten years of Rousseau's life are not covered at all. And most important, he makes almost no mention of the interpretations of brilliant scholars who have thrown light on Rousseau's motives and conflicts. In French the standard biography, by Raymond Trousson, is much more generously informed but assumes the prior familiarity with Rousseau that is normal in the French educational system, and it has not been translated.

A biographer of Rousseau has extraordinary resources to work with. The *Oeuvres Complètes,* annotated by leading scholars, fill ten thousand pages in the magnificent Pléiade edition. The *Correspondance Complète* fills fifty volumes and includes hundreds of texts and documents by Rousseau's contemporaries in addition to his own letters, a single-handed feat of scholarship by the late R. A. Leigh that is awe-inspiring in its range, completeness, and sustained intelligence. I have used this edition, on matters of interpretation as well as of detail, much more extensively than previous writers have done, and my gratitude is immense. More recently, two invaluable reference works have appeared, the comprehensive *Dictionnaire de Jean-Jacques Rousseau* and the chronology *Jean-Jacques Rousseau au Jour le Jour,* both edited by Raymond Trousson and Frédéric S. Eigeldinger.

In addition, I have drawn on hundreds of articles and books on Rousseau, and while I have tried not to clog the notes with references, I indicate specific debts whenever I am aware of them. Some of these works are well known, such as Jean Starobinski's *Jean-Jacques Rousseau: La Transparence et l'Obstacle* (translated as *Jean-Jacques Rousseau: Transparency and Obstruction*), after fifty years still the finest single study of Rousseau, and Arthur Melzer's splendid overview of Rousseau's thought, *The Natural Goodness of Man.* Others are less familiar but have also been immensely helpful, for example Pierre-Paul Clément's psychological study, *Jean-Jacques Rousseau: De l'Éros Coupable à l'Éros Glorieux;* Benoît Mély's examination of Rousseau's finances and relationships with patrons, *Jean-Jacques Rousseau: Un Intellectuel en Rupture;*

and Frédéric S. Eigeldinger's exploration of events and relationships at a crucial period, *"Des Pierres dans mon Jardin": Les Années Neuchâtelois de J. J. Rousseau et la Crise de 1765*. Above all, however, I have tried to let Rousseau speak in his own voice. I have given my own translations throughout, since short passages suffer from being quoted in varying styles with different notions of fidelity to the originals.

I

The Loneliness of a Gifted Child

"I WAS BORN IN GENEVA in 1712," Rousseau wrote in his *Confessions,* "son of Isaac Rousseau *citoyen* and Suzanne Bernard *citoyenne.*" He was always proud of that citizenship, and when he became a prominent writer in Paris he signed himself *Jean-Jacques Rousseau, Citoyen de Genève.* But by then he had abjured the Protestant faith and thereby lost his citizenship rights in Geneva. Still later his books would be publicly burned there, and a standing warrant lodged for his arrest if ever he should return.

The birth on June 28 was inauspicious. "I was born almost dying," he claimed without further explanation; "they had little hope of saving me." And a true disaster made his birth "the first of my misfortunes." Three days after he was baptized in the great cathedral on July 4, his mother died of puerperal fever. Half a century later, when he wrote his treatise on child development, Rousseau declared that a small child has no way of understanding death. "He has not been shown the art of affecting grief that he doesn't feel; he has not feigned tears at anyone's death, because he doesn't know what it is to die." But his own early experience was of being required to grieve for a mother whom he resembled disturbingly and had somehow killed, and this burden of guilt haunted his later life. If he was indeed born almost dying, he may well have felt that it would have been better if he had died in her place.

EIGHTEENTH-CENTURY GENEVA

A view from the northern shore of Lac Léman, showing the great cathedral dominating the city and the peak of the Salève rising beyond. The village of Bossey,
where Rousseau went to live at the age of ten, is close to the Salève; the lake dis-
charges into the Rhône, out of sight to the right.

Throughout his life he tended to see motherhood in a sentimental light;
in middle age he wrote solemnly to a young man seeking advice, "A son
who quarrels with his mother is always wrong . . . The right of mothers
is the most sacred I know, and in no circumstances can it be violated
without crime."

There was a lot Rousseau seems never to have known about his
parents, including their ages; he thought his father was fifteen years
younger than he actually was. He was even less well informed about his
ancestors. Like many Genevan families, the first Rousseaus immigrated
from France when Protestants began to be persecuted there. Didier
Rousseau, Jean-Jacques' great-great-great-grandfather, arrived in Geneva in 1549 and went into business as a wine merchant. He had been a
bookseller in Paris and may well have gotten into trouble, as his famous
descendant did two centuries later, for subversive publications. It would
be pleasant to think that Jean-Jacques was proud of this ancestor who

had accepted exile for his beliefs, but there is no evidence that he ever heard of him.

Didier's descendants became industrious tradespeople and artisans, leaving little trace in official records, but Jean-Jacques' father, Isaac, was an interesting character. He took up watchmaking as a trade, not surprisingly, since his grandfather, father, and brothers were all watchmakers. But he also loved music and played the violin well, and as a young man he abandoned the workshop to become a dancing master. Dancing was no longer forbidden by the Calvinist theocracy of Geneva, but it was not in good repute, and the Consistory — a committee of pastors and laymen that oversaw morals — limited it to foreign residents who refused to give it up. After a short time Isaac ended this dubious experiment and returned to the family trade, in which he eventually qualified as a master craftsman. Over the years, however, his volatile temper repeatedly got him into trouble. In 1699 he provoked a quarrel with some English officers who drew their swords and threatened him; it was he who was punished, since the authorities were anxious to propitiate foreigners. A similar incident would one day result in his virtual disappearance from his son's life.

As Jean-Jacques understood it, his own origin was a sad chapter in a great romance. His mother's family was socially superior to the Rousseaus and disapproved of the daughter's alliance with a humble watchmaker, even though the pair had been inseparable since early childhood. According to the story in the *Confessions,* Suzanne advised Isaac to travel in order to forget her, but he returned more passionate than ever. She had remained chaste, they swore eternal fidelity, "and heaven blessed their vow." Meanwhile Suzanne's brother Gabriel fell in love with Isaac's sister Théodora, who insisted on a joint wedding, and so it was that "love arranged everything, and the two weddings took place on the same day."

The facts that can be extracted from the records tell a rather different story. Suzanne's father, Jacques Bernard, had been jailed for fornication, and a year later was required to pay the expenses of an illegitimate child by a second mistress. He then married a third woman, Anne-Marie Marchard, and Suzanne was born six months later. When Suzanne was only nine her father died, in his early thirties, and the family took care afterward to erase his memory as much as possible. The kindly pastor Samuel Bernard, who raised her, and whom Jean-Jacques always believed to be her father (he died eleven years before the boy's birth), was actually her uncle.

Suzanne was good-looking, musically talented, and evidently a spirited young woman. In 1695, when she was twenty-three, she was summoned before the Consistory to be rebuked for permitting a married man named Vincent Sarrasin to visit her. Equally provocatively, she showed an interest in the theater, which was illegal in Geneva except for street performances. One day in the Place Molard, "near the theater where they sell medicines and play farces and comedies, the maiden lady Bernard was seen dressed as a man or a peasant." Further inquiry established that she was disguised as a peasant woman, not as a man, and according to witnesses she claimed she wanted to see the farces without being recognized by her would-be lover, Sarrasin. She herself swore that none of this ever happened, but the Consistory delivered a stern verdict: "Persuaded, notwithstanding her denial, that we are well informed as to the truth of the said disguise, for which we have censured her severely, . . . we exhort her solemnly to have no commerce at all with M. Vincent Sarrasin."

Eight years later, when she was thirty-one, Suzanne married Isaac Rousseau. This was not particularly late by the standards of the time. The age of majority was twenty-five, and in France as well as Geneva the average marriage age was twenty-eight, reflecting insistence on financial security and serving as well to hold down the birth rate. But the twin weddings Jean-Jacques evoked in the *Confessions* were a fairy tale. Isaac's sister did marry Suzanne's brother, but that happened five years earlier, barely a week before the birth of their child, a circumstance that provoked a stern condemnation by the Consistory. The infant died immediately, and this too was a story that Jean-Jacques never heard anything about. Instead he was encouraged by his family to harbor a highly romantic idea of his parents' and their siblings' irresistible attraction and triumph over obstacles.

Isaac and Suzanne began their married life in comfortable circumstances, in the Bernards' elegant house at Grande Rue No. 40 in the fashionable upper town. It was customary for daughters to receive generous dowries and for sons to get smaller sums but to be established in a trade that would support their families. Isaac Rousseau had 1,500 florins from his father, equivalent to 750 French livres, not a fortune but not insignificant either: a family could get by on 200 livres per year and could live comfortably on 1,000. Suzanne, meanwhile, brought 6,000 florins, along with a piece of land in the Jura, a walnut wardrobe, a green leather writing case, and six coffee spoons. Nine months later their first son, François, was born.

Before long the family found itself in financial difficulty, in part because of a general economic downturn, and it seems likely that Suzanne's mother, with whom they were living, made life increasingly disagreeable for her improvident son-in-law. At any rate, only three months after François' birth, Isaac departed for Constantinople, where he became watchmaker to the sultan. (That at least was his story; there is no evidence to confirm that he was so employed.) His departure was not quite so extraordinary as it might seem today, since Genevans were described by a contemporary as "the greatest vagabonds in the world," and in Isaac's immediate family one uncle lived in London, another in Hamburg, and a brother in Amsterdam; his brother-in-law lived in Venice and died in South Carolina, and a cousin traveled to Persia. Still, as Raymond Trousson comments, Constantinople was a long way to go to get away from a mother-in-law. While there, Isaac lived in a Genevan community whose Calvinist pastor mentioned him in a letter to his colleagues at home (praising them for "shining the torch of your piety and erudition in the midst of the shadows of the Papacy"). We know almost nothing of what Suzanne's life was like while Isaac was away, but Jean-Jacques believed she was happy. He recorded an impromptu poem she was said to have made up when walking with her sister-in-law, about the husbands who were also brothers and the wives who were also sisters, and he especially relished the story that the senior French diplomat in Geneva lost his heart to her, though without ever compromising her virtue.

A year after his mother-in-law's death in 1710, Isaac Rousseau, having been absent for fully six years, finally came home, attracted no doubt by the 10,000 florins that Suzanne had inherited. Jean-Jacques was born nine months later and named after a wealthy godfather, who unfortunately died soon afterward. Then came the shocking loss entered in the official records: "On Thursday 7 July 1712, at eleven in the morning, Suzanne Bernard, wife of M. Isaac Rousseau, citizen and master watchmaker, aged thirty-nine, died of continued fever in the Grande Rue." All told, they had spent only two years of married life together.

Isaac stayed on in his late wife's house, and his unmarried youngest sister, also named Suzanne, moved in to help with François and the new baby. As an adult Jean-Jacques could only guess at what his earliest years were like, for although he more than anyone else taught the world to pay attention to early childhood experiences, "I don't know what I did before the age of five or six." Looking back through the clouds of the troubled times that were to follow, he imagined it had been an era of idyllic contentment. "The children of kings could not have been cared for with more zeal than I was during my first years, idolized by everyone around me." Certainly he formed a close bond with his aunt Suzon, as he called her. In *The Confessions* he praised her as "a maiden lady full of graces, intelligence, and good sense" and fondly remembered his happiness watching her embroider and listening to her sing. "Her cheerfulness, her sweetness, and her pleasant face have left such strong impressions on me that I still see her manner, her expression, her attitude; I recall her little affectionate sayings; I could say how she was dressed and how she wore her hair, not forgetting the two curls that her black hair made on her temples, after the fashion of those days." He was especially grateful for the love of music she inspired in him, singing a prodigious number of songs "with a small, very sweet voice." In later life it always moved him to tears to sing one of them in particular, a pastoral air about the dangers of love, and he admitted that he avoided trying to locate the original words. "I'm almost certain that the pleasure I get from remembering this air would fade if I got proof that others sang it besides my poor aunt Suzon."

Jean-Jacques would not have understood at first that Suzon was not his actual mother. Sixty years later, when she was past eighty and he had become famous, she dictated a letter to him (her eyesight was probably failing) in which she said that she always had "a maternal tenderness" for him, and signed herself "your affectionate and tender friend and aunt." In another letter the friend who transcribed her message added, "We've talked about you as the dearest object of her affection." In the *Confessions* Rousseau would say, "Dear aunt, I forgive you for having kept me alive, and it grieves me not to be able to give you, at the end of your days, the tender care you lavished on me at the beginning of mine." A few years later, when she died at the age of ninety-three, he paid a further tribute: "It is through her that I'm still attached to something of value on this earth, and no matter what people do, so long as I retain that I will continue to love life."

There was another female figure in the boy's life: his nursemaid or *mie,* Jacqueline Faramand, a cobbler's daughter only sixteen years older than himself. Long afterward a Genevan whose father had likewise been cared for by Jacqueline said that she was adored for her kind heart, generosity, and gaiety. He remembered her saying that when the little Jean-Jacques unluckily tore a book and was locked up for several days in a garret, "the good Jacqueline was his sole consoler during that time." After Rousseau became a celebrity he wrote to tell her that he had never ceased to love her, adding rather grimly that she too was to blame for his continued existence. "I often say to myself amidst my sufferings that if my good Jacqueline had not taken such pains to preserve me when I was little, I would not have suffered such great misfortunes after I grew up."

When François was twelve and Jean-Jacques five, a drastic change occurred. Increasingly pressed for cash, Isaac sold his wife's house for the impressive sum of 31,500 florins. Supposedly the money was to be held in trust for the two boys until they reached the age of twenty-five, and Isaac was to live on the interest in the meantime, but over the years he managed to get his hands on most of the principal as well. The family moved down the hill and across the Rhône to the rue de Coutance in the artisans' quarter of Saint-Gervais. Geneva was a small city at the time, with about 20,000 inhabitants (Lyon had 100,000 and Paris at least half a million). The distance between the two houses was not great, but there was a potent symbolic distinction between the upper and lower town, the inhabitants *du haut* and *du bas,* and this move was a painful descent from the privileged heights of the Bernard family, who had never cared much for their Rousseau in-laws.

Isaac, Suzon, and the two boys occupied the fourth of five stories in an apartment house in a neighborhood of watchmakers, engravers, and silversmiths. Isaac's bedroom and workshop faced the street in order to get the best light for his exacting trade. On the other side, looking out on what is today the rue Rousseau, were a large kitchen and a bedroom that Jean-Jacques probably shared with Suzon. As it happens, the rue Rousseau got its later name from a misunderstanding. After the French Revolution his admirers preferred not to believe that he had been born in the fashionable upper town, and they installed a plaque — reverently viewed by such pilgrims as Stendhal, Dumas, Ruskin, and Dostoevski — on a different house in Saint-Gervais, one that had belonged to David Rousseau, his cold and ungenerous grandfather, with whom he seems to have had virtually no relationship.

Many of Geneva's Protestant refugees from France had been skilled craftsmen, and the little city grew wealthy from trades such as watchmaking and jewelry, in a system by which bankers supplied raw materials and distributed work among a host of small workshops. Two men out of every ten, in fact, were watchmakers. Jean-Jacques always liked to think of himself as *un homme du peuple,* and his familiarity with skilled labor contributed to his scorn for "those important persons who are called artists rather than artisans, work solely for the idle and rich, and put an arbitrary price on their baubles." The artisan class was particularly proud of its intellectual abilities. "A Genevan watchmaker," Rousseau wrote, "is a man who can be introduced everywhere; a Parisian watchmaker is only fit to talk about watches." And indeed a British visitor commented, "Even the lower class of people are exceedingly well informed, and there is perhaps no city in Europe where learning is more universally diffused"; another at midcentury noticed that Genevan workmen were fond of reading the works of Locke and Montesquieu.

The artisans of Geneva not only read about politics, they lived it, in a campaign of resistance to the privileged class that governed Geneva and would one day commit Rousseau's *Social Contract* to the flames. It has recently been demonstrated that the block in Saint-Gervais where the Rousseaus lived had more political agitators than any other. Even foreigners were struck by the open displays of class feeling, as an English aristocrat commented half a century later when he climbed nearby Mont Salève and was offended there by "a gang of bandylegged watchmakers, smoking their pipes, and scraping their fiddles, and snapping their fingers, with all that insolent vulgarity so characteristic of the Ruebasse portion of the Genevese community."

ISAAC ROUSSEAU
This rather disquieting portrait, a miniature on ivory, fails to capture Isaac's sentimentality but does full justice to his suspicious and quarrelsome side. Maurice Cranston, ungenerously perhaps, sees "a puffy, shapeless, bucolic sort of face, with small dark eyes and pursed lips, all bespeaking a commonplace character."

Above all it was his father's example that inspired Jean-Jacques. Isaac Rousseau had plenty of faults: he was self-centered, quarrelsome, unreliable, and capable of abandoning his family with unconcern. These are not attractive traits, and Jean-Jacques suffered their consequences. But Isaac was also energetic, imaginative, and affectionate, a lover of music, books, and ideas. Most of all, his gifted son saw him as a companion, very different from the stern authority figures of Calvinist tradition, which included most of the relatives on the Bernard side. Isaac encouraged, or at least permitted, Jean-Jacques to develop in his own way, and made him feel like an equal as they shared their rather eccentric reading of the romantic novels left by his mother. These books — the best known is *Astraea* by Honoré d'Urfé — had been hugely popular in the previous century but were falling out of favor by the time Jean-Jacques encountered them, and would soon be supplanted by a more realistic kind of fiction. At first, when he was only six or seven, he and Isaac read together to help the boy practice his reading, "but soon our interest was so lively that we took turns reading them without a pause, and spent the nights like that. We could never stop before the end of the volume. Sometimes my father, hearing the swallows in the morning, would say all shamefaced, "'Let's go to bed; I'm more of a child than you are.'" As Rousseau later realized, precocious reading "gave me bizarre and romantic notions of human life, which experience and reflection have never been able to cure me of." It also gave him something else of immense value: a deep intuitive sense of literary style, of rhythm and emphasis and memorable phrasing. This early immersion in literature was crucial to his later development as one of the great masters of French prose. (He had less experience of poetry, and was never much good at it.)

From time to time Isaac gave his son instruction of various kinds, for example bewildering the boy with a lecture on Copernican astronomy that helped convince him in retrospect that children are not ready to understand abstractions. Practical illustrations were more successful. "My first and best lessons in cosmography were received at a watchmaker's workbench with a polishing ball stuck with pins as the only instruments." As for books, when the novels gave out, an altogether different kind of reading took their place. His mother's uncle, the minister, had left a collection of ancient and modern classics, and the boy read these aloud to his father as he worked. Plutarch became his particular favorite. To him Plutarch's *Lives of Noble Greeks and Romans* was another kind of novel, displaying history not as a series of events — something he never took much interest in at any time — but as the noble actions of a series of heroes. Once again the imaginative boy found himself vicariously exalted. "Constantly occupied with Rome and Athens, living so to speak with these great men, and son of a father whose love of the fatherland was his strongest passion, I inflamed myself with their example. I believed myself to be Greek or Roman; I would become the character whose life I was reading." Once at the table he went so far as to alarm the family by holding his hand over a flaming chafing dish, in imitation of a brave Roman named Scaevola who allowed his hand to be burned off. His love for "my master and comforter Plutarch" never waned; a friend said that he knew Plutarch by heart and could have found his way in the streets of Athens better than in Geneva.

In some ways the Geneva of Rousseau's youth was the closest thing to a classical city-state in the modern world. Surrounded by powerful and often threatening neighbors, it had preserved its independence and would not become part of Switzerland until 1814, a full century after Rousseau's birth. In theory Geneva was governed democratically by a General Council of all male citizens, who were a minority of the total population; the majority were immigrants called "inhabitants," their descendants were "natives," and all lacked the rights of citizenship. In practice, however, the city was controlled by a small group of wealthy families that made up the Council of Two Hundred, which in turn delegated actual power to a twenty-five-member executive known as the Little Council. No Rousseau was ever elected to the Council of Two Hundred, which would have implied elevation to the *haute bourgeoisie.*

Living in the workers' quarter with a father who loved to debate politics, Rousseau grew up believing in the sovereignty of the people but well aware that the governing oligarchy made a mockery of it. "A sovereign that never performs an act of sovereignty is an imaginary being," said the patriot Pierre Fatio in 1707, calling for democratic reform. The Little Council had him shot. One positive result of the Fatio affair was that the authorities were induced to publish the *Edicts of the Republic of Geneva,* in effect admitting that until then citizens had no way to read the laws they were supposed to obey. Isaac Rousseau was in Constantinople at the time and missed the excitement, but his father, David, supported Fatio's protest and was disciplined as a result.

In later life Rousseau settled on a sentimental picture of his father, "the virtuous citizen from whom I received my being," meditating at his workbench on the sublime insights of political thought. "I see Tacitus, Plutarch, and Grotius mingled before him with the tools of his trade; I see at his side a cherished son receiving, with all too little profit, the tender instruction of the best of fathers." In the end no one could say that Rousseau failed to profit from this early instruction. What he learned was that Geneva had betrayed the city-state ideal, and *The Social Contract* would be founded on a profound theory of the sovereignty of the people. Like the hero of his novel *Julie,* Rousseau was a *roturier,* a commoner, and when he proudly signed himself "citizen of Geneva" he was asserting membership in a *patrie* or fatherland. For as a writer said in 1736, "Today there is more true nobility in a Swiss *roturier* who is citizen of a fatherland than in a Turkish basha who is subservient to a master."

In his mid-forties, writing in praise of an idealized Geneva, Rousseau recalled a memorable incident in his childhood when a group of citizen soldiers finished their maneuvers in a volunteer militia.

> Most of them gathered after the meal in the Place Saint-Gervais and began dancing all together, officers and soldiers, around the fountain, onto which drummers, fifers, and torch-carriers had climbed . . . The women couldn't remain at their windows for long, and they came down. Wives came to see their husbands, servants brought

THE PLACE DE COUTANCE AT SAINT-GERVAIS

An early-eighteenth-century view of the principal square in Rousseau's boyhood neighborhood, with market stalls for the produce that arrived in carts and wheelbarrows from the countryside. It was around this fountain that the militia danced in a scene that Rousseau later made famous.

wine, and even the children, awakened by the noise, ran around half-dressed among their fathers and mothers. The dance was suspended, and there was only embracing, laughter, toasts, caresses . . . My father, hugging me, was overcome by trembling in a way that I can still feel and share. "Jean-Jacques," he said to me, "love your country. Do you see these good Genevans? They are all friends, they are all brothers, joy and concord reign in their midst."

What Rousseau did not say but expected his readers to understand was that throughout Europe militias were thought of as embodiments of popular spirit, in contrast to the mercenary armies of their rulers. Indeed, the citizen bands of Geneva were regarded with great suspicion by the oligarchy. But as a boy he was most impressed by the mood of spontaneous celebration, and he relished the all too rare experience of belonging to a group. Eventually his native city would remember this

THE SITE OF ROUSSEAU'S BOYHOOD HOME
The inscription just above the department store entrance reads: ON THIS SITE
USED TO STAND THE HOUSE WHERE JEAN-JACQUES ROUSSEAU LIVED AS A CHILD
FROM 1718 TO 1722. In larger letters is his father's pronouncement on the evening
of the militia dancing: JEAN-JACQUES, LOVE YOUR COUNTRY.

---

moment with civic pride, and today the site of his childhood home bears
an enormous stone plaque engraved with his father's solemn injunction,
"*Jean-Jacques, aime ton pays.*" But since Geneva would condemn Rousseau as an enemy of the state before it eventually resurrected him as a
patron saint, it is symbolically appropriate that the house itself is gone.
It was demolished in the 1960s during a period of urban renewal, and
the plaque is an incongruous megalith on the façade of a department
store.

Notwithstanding the tender nostalgia with which Rousseau recalled
his early years, there is reason to believe that the period was more
troubling than he wanted to remember. François was six when Isaac
returned from Constantinople, and seven when Jean-Jacques' arrival
caused his mother's death; his resentment of his younger brother would
surely have been apparent. Still more disturbingly, Isaac Rousseau, even
while claiming to dote on his younger son, subjected him to emotional

blackmail. "Never did he hug me without my feeling, in his sighs and convulsive embraces, a bitter regret mingled with his caresses . . . 'Ah!' he would say, groaning, 'give her back to me, console me for her, fill up the void she has left in my soul.'" Moreover, he would imply, alarmingly, that the boy's chief merit was that he looked like the lost Suzanne, and would exclaim, "Would I love you like this if you were only my son?" Interestingly, Jean-Jacques resembled Isaac as well as Suzanne. A Genevan who met him when he was in his forties remarked, "I recognized him on the spot, by his look of his late father, who was one of my friends."

The family as the boy perceived it was essentially sexless, with parent figures who were brother and sister, not mates. He had to admit that his father was "a man of pleasure," but he managed to believe that Isaac observed the strictest chastity and devoted his life to grieving for his lost wife. With this idealized example before him, Jean-Jacques was a good little boy, but François became a very bad boy indeed. In the *Confessions* Rousseau says rather vaguely that François "took up the life of a libertine, even before he was old enough really to be one." Official records show that at thirteen, when François had been bound as an apprentice watchmaker, he was committed to a house of correction "at the request of his father on account of his *libertinage*" (which would have meant unruly behavior of all kinds, not necessarily sexual). François made so little progress in his trade that four years later, humiliatingly, he had to be apprenticed all over again to a different master.

What Jean-Jacques remembered most vividly about family life in those early years was his own privileged position, along with a gratifying conviction that he could inspire affection in his brother (whose name he neglects to mention in the *Confessions*). "I scarcely saw him at all, and I can barely say that I made his acquaintance, but I didn't fail to love him tenderly, and he loved me too, so far as a rascal can love anything." When he developed a theory of childhood Rousseau took it for granted that affection between siblings could only be casual and shallow. "The child knows no attachments except those of habit; he loves his sister as he does his watch." Given the trade that Isaac followed and François bungled, the watch was an interesting example to choose.

On one memorable occasion Jean-Jacques had a chance to play the hero on his brother's behalf. "I remember that once when my father was punishing him roughly and angrily, I threw myself impetuously between them, embracing him tightly. I covered him like that with my body, receiving the blows that were intended for him, and kept up that posture so well that in the end my father let him off, whether because he was disarmed by my cries and tears or because he didn't want to treat me worse than him." The incident made so deep an impression that Rousseau re-created it in his novel *Julie,* with fascinating transpositions: there an enraged father beats the young heroine mercilessly while her self-sacrificing mother interposes and receives the blows. Perhaps little Jean-Jacques was trying to appease François' resentment for all the ways he had made his life worse, or perhaps he had learned that accepting punishment was a way to extort affection. In the novel the father remorsefully kisses his daughter's hand and calls her his dear girl, and she fondly declares as she relates the incident, "I would be only too happy to be beaten every day at the same price, and no treatment could be so harsh that a single one of his caresses wouldn't efface it from the depths of my heart." For little Jean-Jacques, already predisposed perhaps to feelings that today would be called masochistic, it had been an opportunity to insinuate himself into an exciting emotional scene and to take his place literally at the center.

In later years Rousseau needed to believe that his early childhood had been a paradise of security. "My father, my aunt, my *mie,* our friends, our neighbors, all those around me didn't obey me, to be sure, but they loved me, and I loved them likewise. My desires were so little aroused and so little contradicted that it never occurred to me to have any." The worst thing he could remember doing was mischievously urinating into the cooking pot of a disagreeable old woman named Mme Clot, who lived next door. Admittedly, most of this period of his life remains a blank; a chronology of his life that runs to four hundred pages has only two entries for the year 1720:

> Rousseau and his father read the historians and moralists from the library of his uncle, pastor Samuel Bernard.
> Rousseau pisses in the cooking pot of Mme Clot.

To the improbable claim that his desires were never contradicted, however, one should add what his alter ego Saint-Preux says in *Julie:* "Is there any being on earth weaker, more impoverished, more at the mercy of everything around it, with so great a need for pity, love, and protection, as a child?"

Two other anecdotes survive, not included in the *Confessions* but recorded by Rousseau elsewhere, and both calculated to illustrate self-sacrificing generosity. On one occasion when he was visiting an uncle's textile workshop, his fingers were crushed in a roller by a careless cousin. He was confined to bed for three weeks, unable to use his hand for two months, and permanently scarred, but he stoutly protected his cousin by claiming that a rock had fallen on his fingers. Another time he was playing the mallet game *mail* (what the English called pall-mall) and got into a quarrel with a friend who whacked him on the head so violently "that if he had been any stronger, he would have knocked my brains out." Once again the other boy was aghast and repentant, and once again Jean-Jacques was in a position to forgive nobly.

However much Rousseau may have wanted to remember those early years as idyllic, it is clear that he felt plenty of anxiety about who he was and how much he was valued. Whenever he wrote about childhood, he seemed determined to minimize affective relationships. His character Julie, though an ideal mother, makes the extraordinary claim that a child of four or five is virtually incapable of emotional response, so that "our children are dear to us for a long time before they are able to feel it and love us in return." Still more strikingly, in *Émile* the father is relegated to obscurity, and the tutor who raises Émile never expects love or even affection — he is thus the opposite of the unstable and emotionally demanding Isaac Rousseau — while the boy is brought up with the understanding that he is "indifferent to everything outside himself, like all other children, and takes no interest in anyone."

Idyllic or not, the period at the rue de Coutance came to a sudden and shocking end. Isaac had a passion for hunting rabbits and fowl in the fields outside the city, and would return in the evening weary, bramble-torn, and happy. "I remember the pounding heart my father experienced at the flight of the first partridge, and the transports of joy with which he would find a hare he had been seeking for a whole day." But in 1722, when Jean-Jacques had just turned ten, Isaac got into a disastrous quarrel as a result of one of these excursions. Near the village of Meyrin just outside Geneva, a former army captain named Pierre Gautier noticed two men trampling a field of his that had not yet been mowed. One of them was Isaac Rousseau. According to Gautier's later testimony, when he told them to leave, Isaac threatened him with his gun. The aggrieved landowner hurried to the village to get reinforcements, but when he came back with some farmers the trespassers had vanished.

Four months later, however (the exact date is recorded, October 9), Gautier was in Geneva on business and became aware of a man staring at him meaningfully, who then said angrily, "You're having a good look at me; do you want to buy me?" It was Isaac, who reminded Gautier of the incident in the fields, grabbed him by the arm, and exclaimed, "Don't say another word; let's go out of town and settle this with the sword." In fact it was unusual for artisans to wear swords; Isaac apparently did so as a sign that he had been unjustly reduced to the plebeian world of Saint-Gervais. It was all the more infuriating, therefore, when Gautier retorted cuttingly that he had drawn his sword many times but used only sticks on people of an inferior social class. Isaac thereupon wounded Gautier on the cheek before bystanders could separate them. When a magistrate looked into the case the next day, several witnesses reported that Isaac had repeatedly shouted, "Listen, you'd better remember this: I am Rousseau!" Nevertheless, well aware that some of Gautier's relatives were magistrates, he failed to show up at the hearing, and when an officer went to arrest him a week later he was nowhere to be found.

Isaac's own story, as Jean-Jacques heard it, was that he gave Gautier a bloody nose but never actually drew his sword, and that he chose to leave Geneva forever rather than yield on a point of honor. Since the authorities waited an entire week to arrest him, it seems likely that they anticipated his flight and regarded exile rather than prison as the best solution, ridding the city permanently of a hot-tempered and insubordinate character. In later life Rousseau emphasized the political aspect of the affair, regarding his father as a heroic victim of class injustice. He liked to tell the story of a group of bourgeois who were talking and laughing in the street when an aristocrat, suspecting that the joking was aimed at him, demanded furiously, "Why are you laughing while I'm passing by?" One of the men replied, "So why are you passing by while we're laughing?"

But at the time, what Jean-Jacques must have felt most deeply was an astonishing abandonment, by his mother figure as well as his father. Isaac settled in the lakeside town of Nyon, fifteen miles from Geneva in the Vaud territory governed by Berne, and Suzon accompanied him there; she married a local man and stayed for the rest of her life. Jean-Jacques made occasional visits to Nyon, but Isaac showed little interest in him from then on, and Suzon seems to have pretty much disappeared from his life. Left with two unwanted boys on their hands, the Bernard family took prompt action. François was bound over to a demanding new master, with whom he would be expected to live, and Jean-Jacques and his cousin Abraham Bernard were sent to board with a pastor in the village of Bossey, three miles beyond the city walls.

2

The End of Innocence

BOSSEY WAS A PLEASANT village just three miles outside of Geneva, close enough that the tower of the cathedral could be seen from the windows of Jean-Jacques' new home The village was surrounded by meadows, which intoxicated the city boy, but social relations were less satisfactory. When he was writing *Émile* and wanted to illustrate the inferiority of urban children, he claimed that the village children considered him a complete idiot when he first got there, for trying to catch up with a galloping horse and for throwing a stone at Mont Salève, a mile away. Both examples seem preposterous, but they confirm Jean-Jacques' perception of not fitting in, which would torment him throughout his life. And it is conceivable that in addition to severe shortsightedness, he had some sort of perceptual disability; these examples don't sound like mere city-boy confusion.

Rousseau's guardians for the next two years, whom he may well have never seen before, were the pastor Lambercier, coincidentally also named Jean-Jacques, and his sister Gabrielle. The ménage from the rue de Coutance was curiously duplicated, with an unmarried man and his unmarried sister, close in ages respectively to Isaac Rousseau and Suzon. The little parish had not always been tranquil; a decade earlier there were rumors that the pastor and his sister had had improper relations and even that she had given birth to a child, but a formal investigation dismissed the reports as groundless. As with the family scandals that scholars have uncovered, it is far from clear that Rousseau ever heard of this one. He recalled an atmosphere of strict virtue in which, for example, an excellent servant was dismissed for making a mildly ribald remark.

François stayed on in Geneva, making a botch of his new apprenticeship, and soon disappeared for parts unknown. He seems to have written his father a few letters from Fribourg during the next year, but when those dried up, Jean-Jacques became, as he rather complacently put it, "an only son." For the first time, however, he had a companion his own age, the son of his uncle Gabriel Bernard, a former military engineer who was then employed in fortifying Geneva. The two boys were doubly cousins, born from the unions of two pairs of siblings. Abraham, lanky and scrawny, was "as gentle in spirit as he was feeble in body," and from the start the boys depended on each other for emotional security. "Each of us needed a comrade; to separate us was practically to annihilate us." It was unfortunately the case that Abraham was better treated than Jean-Jacques, "because, separated from my father, I was nothing but a poor orphan." However, it is worth noting that at no point in his account of life at Bossey does Rousseau say that he found it painful to be separated from his father. It may well have been a relief to escape the emotional sway that Isaac exerted over his sensitive and impressionable son. Losing tender aunt Suzon was another matter.

M. Lambercier was engaged to teach the boys Latin "and all the petty jumble that goes with it under the name of education." Jean-Jacques was the better student and would whisper answers to Abraham and help with his themes. What he liked best about his studies was their modest scope. "M. Lambercier was a very reasonable man, and without neglecting our instruction, he didn't burden us with excessive work. The proof that he did well in this is that in spite of my aversion to constraint, I have never recalled my hours of study with distaste, and if I didn't learn much from him, what I did learn I learned without difficulty, and I have forgotten none of it." To remember it without distaste is a fairly lukewarm tribute, but Lambercier's rather casual tutoring was the last instruction Rousseau would ever receive. Later on he was embarrassed by the shortcomings in his education, but as he became aware of the gaps he worked energetically to fill them, and throughout his life he was hungry for knowledge in a way that conventionally educated people seldom are.

Lessons apart, Rousseau was always moved to nostalgia when recalling those days. "I can still see the maid or the valet working in the room, a swallow coming in through the window, a fly alighting on my hand, while I was reciting my lesson; I can see the entire arrangement of the room where we were, M. Lambercier's study on the right, a print showing all of the popes, a barometer, and a big calendar; and in a high garden behind the house, raspberry bushes that shaded the window and sometimes strayed inside."

Religious instruction was naturally provided as well, and Rousseau remembered gratefully that he had been "raised with gentleness in the home of a minister who was full of virtue and religion," acknowledging that Lambercier gave him "maxims, some might say prejudices, that have never entirely deserted me." He had already formed a strong impression of religion in Geneva, whose Calvinism, once so militant that the city was known as the Protestant Rome, was becoming relatively liberal in doctrine if not in observance. Services were still held several times every day of the week, and Sundays were marathons of religious observance, but people chatted freely in church, children ran in and out, and only the sermons elicited a reasonable degree of attentiveness. These were notable not for theology but for the denunciation of lax morals, abhorrence of Catholicism (why did Lambercier have those popes' portraits, anyway?), and pride in the spiritual eminence of their city. A scholar who has studied hundreds of these sermons comments that they exhibit a uniform and wearisome austerity: "No matter who opened his mouth, it was always the same voice crying in the wilderness." As a boy, Rousseau imagined that he would one day become a preacher, and he and Abraham made up sermons. With his love of music, he was particularly moved by the psalms that formed an important part of Calvinist worship. "When I hear our psalms sung in four parts," he later wrote, "I always begin by being seized and transported by that full and lively harmony, and when the opening chords are well intoned they move me almost to shivering."

Insofar as formal doctrine was taught, Rousseau was not especially receptive. He mentions reciting the catechism, whose language still retained the ferocity of Calvin's day, but in a way that shows he mainly wanted to avoid mistakes. "When I happened to hesitate, nothing troubled me more than to see signs of uneasiness and pain on Mlle Lambercier's face." In *Émile* he remarked, "If I had to depict exasperating stupidity, I would show a pedant teaching the catechism to children, and if I wanted to drive a child crazy, I would force him to explain what he was saying." And in fact Lambercier's critics, in their complaint to the religious authorities, had mentioned that "he treats as stupid all the children who don't respond as they should, and his sister makes the same censures too." Still, Rousseau felt that Lambercier's influence was positive, and "far from getting bored during the sermon, I never came away without being inwardly moved, and without making resolutions to live well, which I rarely neglected so long as I remembered them."

The village church was once the scene of a bad fright. One evening Jean-Jacques incautiously boasted that unlike his cousin he wasn't afraid of the dark, and to teach him a lesson Lambercier sent him to retrieve a Bible that had been left in the pulpit. Though he had no light he trotted cheerfully enough through the cemetery, but in the total darkness of the church he fell into a panic, blundered about among the pews until he finally located the door, and then dashed home. When he got there he heard laughter and talk about coming to rescue him, and this immediately calmed him down. He hurried back to the church, found the Bible without difficulty, and delivered it proudly, "flustered, but palpitating with joy at having gotten back before the help that was intended for me." He eventually related the story in *Émile* to show that children need not succumb to irrational fears: "I give it as proof that nothing is more reassuring to someone who is afraid of the shadows of the night than to hear company laughing and chatting tranquilly in a neighboring room." But he never forgot the terror in the echoing darkness, and in middle age, when he had come to believe that a vast conspiracy was organized against him, he recalled a more general dread of the unknown in his earliest years. "I was never scared during my childhood by the most hideous object, but a face hidden under a white sheet could throw me into convulsions."

What Rousseau remembered most vividly from the time at Bossey were a few incidents that he described in the *Confessions* as crucial in his psychic development. No previous writer of memoirs would have included stories like these, and it was he who literally taught the world to think of such experiences as forming the personality. The first is the famous *fessée,* or spanking. One day the boys had committed some minor offense and were both spanked by Mlle Lambercier. To his surprise Jean-Jacques enjoyed it, though he had never felt pleasure in being punished by her brother. "I found in the pain, in the shame even, a mixture of sensuality that left me desiring more than fearing to experience it again from the same hand." Contemporary readers of the *Confessions* found the story trivial and embarrassing, but in modern times it has not lacked for commentary. One writer suggests that to derive pleasure from punishment was the perfect revenge of the guilty child: you insist on beating me, very well, I want to be beaten. Another observes that according to an old proverb, *Qui aime bien, châtie bien* — "He who loves well, punishes well" — and conjectures that Jean-Jacques, too little loved by his own relatives, understood the truism the other way around and took the spanking for a sign of affection. In any event the sequel was discouraging. "The second time was also the last, for Mlle Lambercier doubtless perceived by some sign that the punishment wasn't serving its purpose and declared that she would give it up — it was too tiring. Until then we had slept in her room, and in winter sometimes even in her bed. Two days later they made us sleep in another room, and from then on I had the honor, which I could well have done without, of being treated by her as a big boy." Growing up thus meant a loss of physical intimacy, and a realization that if he revealed a sensual pleasure it would be immediately withdrawn.

That flagellation might be arousing was no novel insight in the eighteenth century, when plenty of libertines enjoyed it. A police report noted that the philosopher Helvétius, whom Rousseau later knew in Paris and disliked, could perform his conjugal duty only if one of his wife's maids stood by simultaneously flogging him. As Philippe Lejeune suggests in a brilliant analysis of the *fessée,* what Rousseau learned from Mlle Lambercier was something very different, that in future he could experience the thrill of being reproved without actual physical contact, an erotic charge that was all the more intense for being taboo and withheld. "To be at the knees of an imperious mistress," he says in the *Confessions,* "to obey her orders, to have to beg her pardon, have been for me the sweetest delights" (his word is *jouissances,* which then as now could connote sexual pleasure). In an earlier draft he was still more specific: "I had an affection for acts of submission, confusing the posture of a suppliant lover with that of a penitent schoolboy."

Of course this memorable episode can hardly have been, as Rousseau later assumed, the sole cause of a lifelong orientation. "Who would believe," he says, "that this childhood punishment, received at the age of eight from a maiden lady of thirty, would have determined my tastes, my desires, my passions, my *me,* for the rest of my life?" Actually Mlle Lambercier was forty and Jean-Jacques eleven, which throws a rather different light on the event, but in any case it must have brought latent feelings to the surface. He had always felt guilty, at some deep level, for existing at all, and as Pierre-Paul Clément suggests, masochistic behavior might authorize him to experience pleasure by making sure that a stylized enactment of punishment came first. In any event, his originality in formulating the question cannot be overestimated. "Is Jean-Jacques' posterior," Cocteau asked, "the rising sun of Freud?" (He added, "I see rather the Romantic *clair de lune.*") Freud would certainly be able to account for Rousseau's interest in another incident that afforded symbolic revenge, in which "the derrière of Mlle Lambercier, by an unlucky tumble at the end of the meadow, was fully displayed before the king of Sardinia, who was passing by." But Rousseau preferred to believe that at the time he was merely alarmed "for a person whom I loved like a mother, and perhaps even more." Having lost both Suzanne Rousseaus, he sought a substitute in Mlle Lambercier, but it does not appear that she was much interested in playing that role.

However Rousseau's masochistic tendencies were formed, he was clearly uneasy about ordinary sexuality from an early age. By the time he arrived at Bossey he was already associating sex with prostitution and with the copulation of animals, as a remarkable observation in the *Confessions* makes clear: "I couldn't look at a debauched person without disdain, even dread; my aversion to debauchery went that far ever since I was walking one day to the Petit Sacconex through a sunken road, and saw holes in the earth on both sides in which I was told those people did their coupling. Also what I had seen of dogs doing that always came into my mind when I thought of them, and the very memory of it made my gorge rise." Lejeune remarks that a psychoanalyst would have plenty to say about the cavities in the earth, and Clément notes that Rousseau refers to the dogs not as *chiens* but as *chiennes,* bitches. All his life he would find female sexuality particularly disturbing.

Another experience at Bossey taught a different but equally powerful lesson. A maid left some combs near the chimney to dry, and when she came back the teeth of one were broken. Jean-Jacques appeared to be the only person who had gone into the room, but he denied it stoutly, and eventually his uncle Gabriel was summoned to punish him for lying. For good measure Abraham was thrashed at the same time for some other offense. "Almost fifty years have passed since this incident," Rousseau says in the *Confessions,* "and I'm not afraid today to be punished all over again for the same crime. I declare before the face of Heaven that I was innocent of it. I neither broke nor touched the comb, I never went near the chimney, I didn't even think of it." He and his cousin sat up in bed afterward and shouted "Carnifex, carnifex," the Latin for "executioner"; evidently Lambercier had at least managed to teach them some Latin. The chastisement was exceptionally brutal, leaving him "in pieces," as he says. We happen to know that Gabriel Bernard, who administered the beating, was a violent man who got into trouble for striking people and throwing their furniture into the street, and on one occasion was warned that he would go to jail if he did it again.

Throughout his life Rousseau longed in vain to feel open, or "transparent" as he called it, to other people, a longing that forms the central theme of Jean Starobinski's great book *Transparency and Obstruction.* But already he was learning that appearances can make one look guilty even when innocent. The people he trusted most condemned him as a liar, there was no way to make them believe the truth, and an uncle he disliked meted out harsh correction with an air of virtue. In *Émile* he would argue that a child cannot possibly grasp the moral rules he is expected to obey. "Devoid of all morality in his actions, he cannot do anything that is morally bad and that deserves either punishment or reprimand." Children have a natural instinct for self-preservation, and they have not yet really internalized the rules they may happen to break. Fearing punishment, they will say whatever they can to avert it. "It follows from this that children's lies are all the work of their masters, and that to want to teach them to tell the truth is nothing else than to teach them to lie." Is it possible that Rousseau really did break that comb?

One other anecdote from Bossey seems more encouraging. Jean-Jacques and Abraham had taken part in a ceremony, perhaps intended to be playful, that accompanied the planting of a walnut tree beside the house. A moat was dug around the tree to hold water, and the boys got the idea of diverting some of the water to a tiny willow sapling of their own. In excited secrecy they laboriously lined a trench with wooden supports, covered it over, and were met with success. Their triumph was brief, however, for Lambercier heard their cries of joy and detected the theft of water from his beloved walnut. He immediately smashed their construction with a pickax, "shouting at the top of his lungs, 'An aqueduct! an aqueduct!' and striking pitiless blows on all sides, each one of which pierced our hearts." But this time there was no punishment. The boys heard Lambercier afterward bellowing with laughter as he told his sister about it, and the whole episode flattered Jean-Jacques' Roman fantasies. "To have been able to make an aqueduct with our own hands, to have put a willow cutting in competition with a big tree, seemed to me the height of glory, about which I was a better judge at ten than Caesar was at thirty." The aqueduct story caught the fancy of readers of the *Confessions* and was the subject of many engravings. A century later an enterprising cabinetmaker sold pieces of the Lambercier walnut tree with documentary authentication. And perhaps the pastor did see something unusual in his young charge; Rousseau supposedly said long afterward (though the anecdote comes at secondhand) that Lambercier told him "he would either be a very great man and acquire a great reputation, or else he would come to a bad end."

By this time the cousins were becoming accomplished at concealment and mendacity, and as Rousseau remembered it they no longer took pleasure even in the countryside. It was time for them to leave, in any case, for they were reaching the age of apprenticeship. We know that they were still in Bossey on August 23, 1724, since the date when the king of Sardinia passed through (and was treated to a view of Mlle Lambercier's derrière) is recorded. Sometime that fall they were sum-

"AN AQUEDUCT!"
A late-eighteenth-century
illustration for the
Confessions, showing the
boys' shock and
resentment in a way that
reflects Rousseau's theme
of the discovery of
injustice. Taking the
experience of childhood
seriously was very much
his message from *Émile*
onward, and pictures such
as this testify to a growing
public response.

moned back to Geneva, where they lived for half a year with Abraham's family in the elegant heights of the Grande Rue, where Jean-Jacques had been born. Looking back, he believed that he had spent two or three years there, which suggests how strongly he appreciated the temporary freedom. He and Abraham remained inseparable during that winter, making kites and drums and popguns, using and damaging watchmaker's tools, trying to paint pictures but producing a mess, and acting out plays with homemade marionettes. In later years he liked to think of his boyhood companions in Geneva as free spirits who engaged with all their might in wrestling, running, and boxing, and who got hurt often enough, "but afterward embraced through their tears." In truth, however, the cousins kept pretty much to themselves, and when they occasionally took walks the other boys would set upon them, jeering at the mild and awkward Abraham with cries of *"Barnâ bredanna"* ("bridled ass" in the local dialect), an allusion to the ass Bernard in the

Roman de Renard. Jean-Jacques would take the bait and rush furiously to his cousin's defense, but they soon concluded that it was best to stay at home except when the bullies were in school.

This period was also notable for developments in Rousseau's understanding of relations between the sexes. Though he does not comment on it, he found himself for the first time in the kind of household that most children grow up in. After having lived with adults who were siblings and presumed to be celibate — first Isaac Rousseau and aunt Suzon, then the Lamberciers — he found himself now living with a husband and wife, and sexual tensions were painfully evident. "My uncle, a man of pleasure, occupied himself very little with us, and my aunt, to console herself for her husband's infidelities, became devout." As for Rousseau, he formed two brief but potent relationships that struck him afterward as reflecting permanent facets of his personality. Apparently he seldom went to Nyon to visit his father, but on one occasion he was smitten by a young woman of twenty-two named Charlotte Vulson, who amused herself by permitting the thirteen-year-old boy to be her little escort. "I gave myself with all my heart, or rather all my head, for it was only through it that I was in love, even if to the point of madness, and my transports, agitations, and frenzies created scenes that would make one weak with laughter." In effect he was casting her as the lofty, unattainable lady of the old romances he had inherited from his mother, who was the most unattainable lady of all. But after pretending to favor Jean-Jacques over other admirers, and even paying him an affectionate visit in Geneva, Mlle Vulson shocked him by getting engaged to a lawyer; the real purpose of her Geneva trip had been to pick out her wedding clothes. Rousseau vowed never to speak to her again, as indeed he refused to do many years later when his father pointed her out to him when they were boating on the lake at Nyon.

The other relationship was very different. An imperious girl of his own age known as Goton (a contraction of "Margoton" or Marguerite) enjoyed playing the schoolmistress with him and was even willing to administer the correction for which he yearned. Rousseau was captivated by her combination of audacity and reserve. "She permitted herself the greatest liberties with me, without ever permitting me any with her; she treated me exactly like a child." For a while, imploring her attentions on his knees, he experienced "the supreme happiness," but she betrayed him to her friends, and the girls in the street would murmur as he went by, *"Goton tic tac Rousseau,"* which he took to refer to the spankings. With Mlle Vulson he played at chivalrous devotion; with Goton "all my senses were overwhelmed" and he felt as if he would expire from palpitations. In later comments he showed great insight into the complementary nature of these relationships. "They have nothing in common, although they are both very violent: one is sensual, or from temperament, and the other is platonic, or from opinion." A perennially reiterated pattern was being established: with Vulson, a chaste passion that was openly avowed but essentially imaginary; with Goton, sensual gratification that was shameful and doomed to disappointment. With Vulson he was trying to act like a precocious, if ridiculous, adult; with Goton he was a bad boy being punished, but at the hands of a juvenile dominatrix from whom he actually had nothing to fear.

Soon it was time to enter the world of work. Abraham was to become a civil engineer like his father, and there was some thought at first of preparing Jean-Jacques for the ministry, but he had no money to pay for the necessary studies and was apprenticed instead to Jean-Louis Masseron, the city notary or registrar. His uncle suggested that he might one day become a *grapignan,* a contemptuous term for a prosecutor, but he loathed going to the office in the imposing hôtel de ville down the street; Masseron and his clerks found him intolerably dull-witted, and he was soon dismissed. Preparation for an artisan's career was now inevitable. There seems to have been doubt that he could master the skills of a watchmaker, so on April 26, 1725, he was apprenticed in a less exacting trade to a young engraver named Abel Ducommun for a term of five years. The contract survives in a big folio volume in the state archives of Geneva. Gabriel Bernard, acting on behalf of his brother-in-law Isaac Rousseau, undertakes to pay Ducommun three livres of silver and two louis of gold, to keep Jean-Jacques supplied with clothing, and to guarantee his faithful service throughout the five years. For his part, "the said M. Ducommun promises to teach the said apprentice Rousseau the said profession of engraver, and the circumstances and dependencies with which it is involved, without hiding or concealing any of it, provided always that the said apprentice is able to understand it, and he is likewise charged with boarding and domiciling the said apprentice during the said time, and with bringing him up and instructing him in

the fear of God and in good morals, as is proper for a *père de famille.*"
The document was duly attested by witnesses, one of whom, a cabinetmaker named Crapoix, "did not sign, not knowing how to write." Neither Ducommun nor Bernard, as it turned out, would be able to fulfill
his share of the bargain.

For the first year Ducommun lived in the rue de Ville Neuve
(known today as the rue des Étuves) in the Saint-Gervais quarter, just
around the corner from Rousseau's old home in the rue des Coutances.
A year later he married and moved his establishment across the river to
the rue de la Poissonerie, close to the Place Molard, where a big market
was held every Wednesday and Saturday, and where Suzanne Rousseau
had gotten into trouble long before for dressing as a peasant. Historians
have ascertained that No. 18, on the allée du Four de la Marjolaine (the
street's later name), had twenty-one residents on its five floors. Ducommun's widowed mother was a grocer as well as a landlady, and there
were also a goldsmith and a lacemaker; the houses on either side included people who made vinegar, clothes, shoes, watches, and lanterns.
All of the artisans except Mme Ducommun were "inhabitants" or "natives" who lacked the rights of citizenship.

Once again Jean-Jacques had come down the hill and down in the
world. A Swedish traveler some years later complained of dunghills in
front of the doors "that give off a frightful odor," and the best the authorities could do was to insist that they be cleaned up once a week,
adding that pigs should be slaughtered in the neighborhood abattoirs
and not in the public streets. Still, Rousseau remembered with pleasure
the commercial bustle in his new environment. "What first strikes every
foreigner entering Geneva is the atmosphere of life and activity. All are
busy, all are in motion, all are hurrying about their work and affairs. I
don't know that any other small city in the world offers a like spectacle.
Visit the Saint-Gervais district: all the watchmaking of Europe seems
gathered there. Walk through the Molard and the *rues basses:* a grand
system of commerce, piles of packages, barrels flung about in confusion,
an odor of the Indies and of drugs that makes you imagine a seaport."
Lac Léman, surrounded by picturesque mountains, is indeed large
enough to seem almost a sea, and for the rest of his life Rousseau always
preferred to live near mountains and water. In Paris thirty years later,
he nostalgically described Geneva as having "a charming situation, a

temperate climate, a fertile countryside, and the most delightful appearance beneath the heavens." And although he lamented having to give up the fields of Bossey, the countryside was not far away; as recently as the 1950s roosters could be heard crowing in some parts of the city.

Ducommun, however, seems to have been a disastrous choice to play the part of a *père de famille*. He was just twenty, and coarse and violent to boot; marriage did nothing to soften him. Curiously, Rousseau had nothing to say about Ducommun's wife, though he lived with the couple for nearly two years after their marriage. As for the work, he rather liked it at first, since he had a talent for drawing and enjoyed handling the engraver's tools. But soon Ducommun's harshness "tarnished all the brightness of my childhood, numbed my loving and lively character, and reduced me in spirit just as much as in fortune to my true rank of apprentice." On his occasional visits to Nyon, his father was disappointed in him. Women no longer found him charming, and he was ashamed even to encounter the Lamberciers, whom he never saw again. Indeed he never saw Bossey again either. In 1754, when he was forty-two, he returned to Geneva for a happy four-month visit, but in spite of a sentimental desire to see how the walnut tree had grown, he never found time to go out to Bossey. "I must have had a great tendency to degenerate," he concluded ruefully when describing his apprenticeship. "I was bold in my father's house, free in M. Lambercier's, discreet in my uncle's; I became fearful at my master's, and from then on I was a lost child."

Another unwelcome change occurred: in March 1726, when Jean-Jacques was not quite fourteen, Isaac Rousseau remarried in Nyon. Jean-Jacques disliked his stepmother and chose to believe that his father could never really have loved her. He even made the extravagant claim that at the very end, thirty-five years after the loss of Suzanne, Isaac "died in the arms of a second wife, but with the name of the first on his lips, and with her image in the depths of his heart." It is barely conceivable that someone reported the dying words to him, but he certainly had no way of seeing into the depths of his father's heart; by then they had been estranged for many years.

As for the apprenticeship itself, it was almost bound to be unpleasant. Apprentices throughout Europe hated the petty tyranny and privations imposed by their masters and by the adult journeymen who came in to work by the day. Jean-Jacques was never an overt rebel, but as he said of himself near the end of his life, "His strength is not in action but in resistance." Here his resistance took the form of slipshod work and minor thievery, inspired at first (so he claims) by a journeyman who got him to steal some asparagus and sell it in the Place Molard. Before long he was stealing from his master too, and he was caught red-handed in a rather ludicrous attempt to extract apples from a locked bin with a collection of pokers and boards. He also got back at Ducommun by sneaking into a private workroom and secretly using the best tools and designs to engrave chivalric medals of his own invention. "I believed I was stealing his talent along with his productions." Once again the outcome was unfortunate; Ducommun caught him, accused him of trying to counterfeit money, and gave him a sound beating.

Rousseau's account in the *Confessions* has created an image of Ducommun as a Dickensian ogre, but the youthful master must have had good reason to be exasperated by his apprentice's pilfering and indifference to work. As for Jean-Jacques, nothing could have prepared him for the "great human desert," as Lejeune calls it, of the years of apprenticeship. His father had decamped and remarried, his Bernard relatives treated him with disdain, the Lamberciers vanished once their job was finished, he seldom saw his cousin Abraham, and what passed for friendship now was nothing more than a cynical journeyman getting a naive boy to pilfer vegetables. Stealing Ducommun's apples and appropriating his tools was a way of making himself free of the household, as if he were at home instead of in the workplace. But Ducommun always found out, and it came to seem normal to transgress and get caught. "I judged that to beat me as a rascal authorized me to be one. I found that stealing and being beaten went together, and made a sort of condition in which if I fulfilled the part that depended on me, I could let my master take care of the other."

It was apprenticeship itself that shocked Rousseau, after a childhood of relative indulgence. When parents paid a handsome sum for a son to be bound to a master, they expected that he would learn discipline and obedience as well as a trade, and few youths welcomed this drastic change in their lives. At almost the same moment as Rousseau, the cocky extrovert Benjamin Franklin was running away from a hated apprenticeship to his own brother in Boston; as he later wrote, "I fancy his harsh and tyrannical treatment of me might be a means of impressing me with that aversion to arbitrary power that has stuck to me through my whole life." Rousseau likewise abhorred tyranny, but unlike Franklin he developed a loathing for any labor imposed by others. He could work with intense application, but only at self-appointed tasks. When he came to theorize about primitive humans he imagined them superbly idle, with "mortal hatred for continuous labor." Even in the throes of composing his greatest books he never escaped "my lazy habit of working by fits and starts."

Lonely and insecure, Rousseau was developing a lifelong tendency to imagine that people were staring at him. If he went into a bakery he would leave without buying anything because he thought the women behind the counter were laughing at "the little gourmand"; at a fruit seller's he would admire the fragrant pears out of the corner of his eye but go away flushed with shame after suspecting that some distant person, blurry in his shortsighted vision, might be a servant who knew him. Saint Augustine never got over his guilt caused by a boyhood raid on a pear orchard; Rousseau couldn't bring himself to lay hands on a pear. And maybe that was the point. "I went home in the end like a fool, devoured by covetousness, having money in my pocket to satisfy it but not daring to buy a thing." Thou shalt not covet, says the commandment; he averted guilt by refusing to gratify his yearning, and projected his guilty feelings on to the imagined hostility of everyone around him.

The one means of escape in this depressing existence was a renewed interest in reading. Rousseau discovered a lending library run by a disreputable woman known as La Tribu and devoured her books indiscriminately, even selling his clothes when necessary to pay the modest advances she required. "Good and bad alike, I never made a choice, I read them all with equal avidity. I read at the workbench, I read while carrying messages, I read at the toilet, I lost myself for hours on end, my head was turned by reading, I did nothing else but read. My master spied on me, he surprised me, he beat me, he took away my books." Nothing could cure him, and Rousseau came to believe that he paid a high price for the relief of vicarious living. "This love of imaginary objects, and this facility for occupying myself with them, ended by disgusting me with everything that surrounded me, and determined that taste for solitude that has remained with me ever since." The only reading he shied away from was the kind most adolescent boys would have sought. When La Tribu offered indecent novels he always refused them, "as much from disgust as from shame," and he claims that his "modest disposition" kept him from looking at any until he was thirty.

By the spring of 1728 Rousseau could stand it no longer. "I reached my sixteenth year restless, discontented with everything and with myself, without the tastes of my station in life, without the pleasures of my age, consumed by desires whose object I didn't know, weeping with no cause for tears, sighing without knowing for what." Soon enough an opportunity to escape appeared. It was not uncommon for people to take Sunday excursions outside the city, in part to avoid the intensive religious observances that were otherwise required, but they had to be careful to return before evening curfew. Like many European cities, Geneva looked like a fortress — the definition of a city in the *Encyclopédie* was "a space enclosed by walls" — and its gates were locked and guarded every night. Twice already Jean-Jacques had arrived too late to get in and had been severely punished by his master the next day. On March 14 he and some companions ran panting to the drawbridge but were once again shut out, through the malice of "an accursed captain named M. Minutoli," who raised the bridge half an hour early. They had to spend the night outside, probably staying with farmers who had been kind to them in the past. The other apprentices merely laughed at their plight, but Rousseau resolved never to return to Geneva, and in all likelihood he had dreamed of escaping for some time. What he may not have realized was that he was reenacting his brother François' pattern. Rejected by his father and family, he had become a lazy, dishonest apprentice and was now taking flight.

Later on, when Rousseau developed the habit of looking for omens in his life, the premature lifting of the drawbridge came to seem "the sinister and fatal augury of the inescapable fate that commenced for me at that moment." At the time, however, it was a thrilling break for freedom. He was not quite sixteen, and he had no money and not much in the way of skills, but he somehow harbored a conviction that he was an exceptional person and bound to succeed. "Free and my own master, I believed I could do everything and achieve everything; I had only to leap to rise up and fly through the air. I was entering the vast space of

STATUE OF ROUSSEAU ON THE ÎLE ROUSSEAU

The bronze statue by James Pradier was erected in 1838 on the tiny Île Rousseau, which was constructed where Lac Léman empties into the Rhône. Rousseau gazes meditatively over the lake he loved.

the world with perfect safety, and my merit was going to fill it up." Behind him were a brutal master, a tedious trade, and censorious relatives who made him feel unwanted and unappreciated. Before him lay a vision that was all the more intoxicating because it had yet to take shape. He might go anywhere; he might become anything.

Much later, when he had become an international celebrity, he liked to imagine that it would have been far better if he had never left Geneva at all. "I would have spent a sweet and peaceful life in the bosom of my religion, my fatherland, my family, and my friends. I would have been a good Christian, good citizen, good father, good friend, good workman, good man in all things." But as Marcel Raymond says, this was a retrospective illusion that he caressed without ever really believing it. More accurate was a self-assessment at the very end of his life: "I have never really been fitted for civil society, where everything is discomfort, obligation, and duty. My independent nature has always made me incapable of enduring the constraints that are necessary for anyone who wants to live among men."

In 1838 a tiny island was created out of landfill in the old marsh area where the outflow from Lac Léman rushes into a narrow passage that becomes the Rhône. This is the Île Rousseau, on which a fine bronze statue of an alert Rousseau, pen suspended in hand, gazes out over the lake. The inscription reads JEAN-JACQUES ROUSSEAU: CITOYEN DE GENÈVE. He did indeed sign himself in that fashion for many years, but when his books were being burned and he was under sentence of arrest if he should ever return, he pointedly renounced his citizenship. Perhaps it is appropriate that the statue has its back to the city.

3

"I Desired a Happiness
of Which I Had No Idea"

THE MORNING AFTER the gates of Geneva closed on him, Rousseau sent a message to his cousin Abraham asking him to help or even to accompany him. Abraham duly showed up, bringing as a gift a small sword that Rousseau had admired, but he encouraged Jean-Jacques to depart in a way that made him suspect the Bernard family were glad to be rid of him. "He was a boy of the upper town; I was a mean apprentice and nothing more than a child of Saint-Gervais." It was the last time Rousseau ever saw Abraham, who left home soon afterward and disappeared. The die was cast, or so Jean-Jacques chose to believe. If the Bernards were unwilling to fetch him back, he was free to fulfill an unknown but perhaps thrilling destiny. He always needed to feel that he was pushed into doing something, so that it wasn't really his fault: the malicious captain had locked him out, and now his relatives were rejecting him. If he jumped, it was because he was pushed.

The nearby countryside was hardly unknown territory. Rousseau mentions in the *Confessions* that he spent several days close to the city "lodging with farmers I knew, all of whom received me with more kindness than city people would have shown." He was already accustomed to indulging in escapist fantasies while wandering in the fields, as he told a friend long afterward in describing a curious instance of

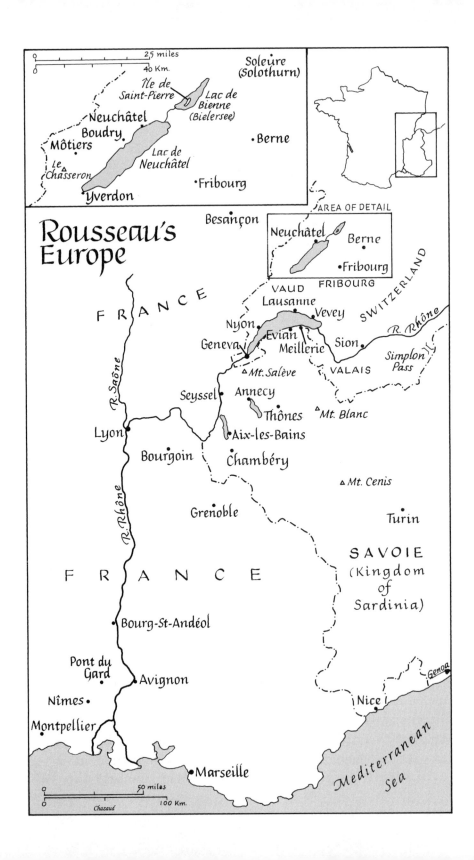

Rousseau's Europe

Inset map (top left):

25 miles
40 Km.

Soleure
(Solothurn)

Île de
Saint-Pierre

Lac de
Bienne
(Bielersee)

Neuchâtel
Boudry
Môtiers

•Berne

Le
Chasseron

Lac de
Neuchâtel

•Fribourg

Yverdon

Inset map (right): AREA OF DETAIL

Neuchâtel

Berne

•Fribourg

Inset map (detail):

Besançon

Neuchâtel

Berne

•Fribourg

FRIBOURG

Main map:

VAUD

Lausanne

SWITZERLAND

Nyon

Vevey

R. Rhône

Geneva

Evian
Meillerie

Sion

VALAIS

Simplon
Pass

FRANCE

R. Saône

△ Mt. Salève

Seyssel

Annecy

Thônes

△ Mt. Blanc

Lyon

Aix-les-Bains

Bourgoin

Chambéry

R. Rhône

△ Mt. Cenis

Grenoble

Turin

FRANCE

SAVOIE
(Kingdom
of
Sardinia)

Bourg-St-Andéol

Pont du
Gard

Avignon

Genoa

Nîmes •

Nice

Montpellier

Marseille

Mediterranean
Sea

50 miles
100 Km.

Chazaud

déjà vu. Once, at the age of fourteen, when he was outside the city and lost in thought, he was suddenly startled to perceive a château and its inhabitants. "Many years later I found myself in a château with the same gates, people, faces, and activity, so perfectly similar that I gave a great cry of astonishment." The fantasy of being a prince in disguise, a sort of male Cinderella, was a potent one, and Rousseau now strolled along like the hero of a fairy tale in search of his appointed château. "I was content to be the favorite of the lord and lady, lover of the maiden, friend of the brother, and protector of the neighborhood; I wouldn't need anything more than that."

That was the fantasy, but the step he actually took was hardly a leap in the dark. After passing a couple of days in casual meandering, he called upon an elderly priest named Benoît de Pontverre in the village of Confignon, a few miles west of Geneva (and a suburb of the city today). In the *Confessions* he implies disingenuously that mere curiosity took him there, but he had to be aware that Pontverre was an energetic agent of the Counter-Reformation and had gained numerous converts to Catholicism. The duchy of Savoie, which was not yet part of France but was governed from Turin, was very much Catholic territory.

Rousseau describes Pontverre in the *Confessions* as "a sort of missionary who imagined that nothing could be better for the good of the faith than to make libels against the ministers of Geneva." Whether he knew it or not, a pamphlet of Pontverre's, years before, had retailed some of the scandalous accusations against the Lamberciers in Bossey. But he cheerfully accepted his host's dinner and excellent wine, a treat he was fully expecting, since priests outside Geneva were well known for regaling potential converts. Despite the Protestant pastors' strenuous efforts to make him fear Catholicism, whenever he heard bells ringing for mass or vespers, "they made me recall a luncheon, a snack, fresh butter, fruits, dairy products." (Bells were illegal within the city, where they were regarded as tools of popish superstition.)

At dinner theological topics naturally came up, and Rousseau claims that he humored the priest complacently. In retrospect he thought of him as a genial old duffer who was inept at argument, but Pontverre undoubtedly knew very well what he was doing. After flattering the lad's theological acumen, he recommended a benevolent lady in the cathedral town of Annecy who might take him under her protection. To Annecy, therefore, he went.

It was common in those days for young artisans to travel about for years, picking up jobs in various places as they mastered their craft. Rousseau was unusual, not in taking to the road, but in abandoning his trade with no apparent desire to find a new one. Annecy was just twenty-five miles to the south, and he made a leisurely three-day trip of it. In the *Confessions* he claims that he paused from time to time to sing romantically under windows, but that is the kind of novelistic detail that need not be taken at face value. On March 21, 1728, he entered Annecy; the date is known because it was Palm Sunday. At the house of the kindly Catholic lady, Mme de Warens, he was told that she had left for church, and he caught up with her breathlessly in the street, carrying a letter of introduction from Pontverre and another of his own composition.

Expecting a person of advanced years and somber aspect, Rousseau was staggered by what met his eyes. Pontverre had neglected to mention that Mme de Warens was young and uncommonly attractive. Rousseau fell head over heels. "I saw a face steeped in charm, beautiful blue eyes full of sweetness, a dazzling complexion, and the outline of an enchanting bosom. Nothing escaped the rapid glance of the young proselyte, and I became hers in that moment." His carefully composed letter spoke for him even as he continued to devour her attractions. "She smilingly took the letter that I gave her with a trembling hand, opened it, glanced over M. de Pontverre's letter, returned to mine, read it straight through, and would have read it again if her footman had not told her that it was time to go in. 'Ah, my child,' she said in a tone that made me quiver, 'you are very young to be wandering around the country; really it's a shame.' Without waiting for me to reply she added, 'Go and wait for me at my house; tell them to give you something for breakfast; after mass I will come and talk with you.'" There was no need to speak; his trembling eagerness told her all she needed to know.

Afterward Rousseau was able to appreciate that he, in turn, must have struck the lady as an interesting object, and he stressed the almost feminine delicacy of his appearance. "Without being what one calls a handsome boy, I had a nice little figure: I had a handsome foot, a slender leg, an open manner, animated features, an attractive mouth, black eyebrows and hair, and eyes that were small and somewhat deep set but sparkling with the fire that burned in my blood." At the time, however, "I knew nothing of all that," and no doubt his naiveté added to his charm. A manuscript draft adds that the attractive mouth contained bad teeth, rather spoiling the picture, but probably on this occasion he was too awestruck to smile. In the eighteenth century nothing much could be done about dental problems, and in middle age he would mention with disgust his "horrible teeth." But in any case he was something of a pretty boy, and must have struck Mme de Warens the way Saint-Preux struck Julie in his novel *Julie:* "A rather timid demeanor, even a bit self-conscious when he is cool-headed, but seething and swept away by passion."

Rousseau rightly regarded this as the most important meeting of his life. The rootless, unemployed youth had found a patron who would eventually become his friend, surrogate mother, and even lover, and under her influence his talents would flourish and his ambitions grow. In the *Confessions* he expressed his feeling that the spot where they met should be enclosed with a railing of gold, and posterity has indeed provided one, gilt if not gold, erected in 1928 on the two-hundredth anniversary of the encounter.

Françoise-Louise-Eléonore de la Tour, baroness de Warens, was twenty-nine years old. Two years earlier she had abruptly left her home and husband near Lausanne and had sought the protection of the king of Sardinia, who governed the Savoie. At that point she converted to Catholicism, settled in Annecy, and accepted a pension from the king in return for working for the Catholic cause. Rousseau spent the next three days at her house, but he probably learned very little about her, concentrating on her visible charms. On further inspection he noted that "she had a tender and caressing manner, a very sweet gaze, an angelic smile, a mouth the same size as my own, and ash-blonde hair of an uncommon beauty to which she gave a careless turn that made it very piquant. She was small in stature, short even, and a bit stocky in the waist, but without deformity. It would be impossible to see a more beautiful head, a more beautiful bosom, more beautiful hands, or more beautiful arms." Just as Saint-Preux later represented his youthful self, Mme de Warens, neither too reticent nor too seductive, would reappear as Saint-Preux's lover Julie, "blonde, with a sweet expression,

THE FATEFUL MEETING PLACE

A somber and aged Rousseau presides over the spot where his life changed. The gilt railing protects a seat (or an altar?) with the inscription ON THE MORNING OF PALM SUNDAY, 1728, JEAN-JACQUES ROUSSEAU HERE MET MME DE WARENS.

tender, modest and enchanting; natural grace without the slightest affectation." To this Rousseau added, in directions for the illustrator of the novel, "her bosom covered like a modest girl, not like a devout woman." Women's breasts, especially when half-hidden but suggestively implied, would always be the focus of his erotic imagination, and when he received the artist's sketches of his heroine and her cousin he wrote disapprovingly to a Genevan friend, "In all of the pictures I find that Julie and Claire are too flat-chested. Swiss women are not like that. You're probably not unaware that the women of our country have larger breasts than Parisiennes." Unfortunately, none of the alleged portraits of Mme de Warens are likely to be authentic, but there can be no doubt that she combined exactly the qualities Rousseau most admired in a woman: as Raymond Trousson puts it, "a lot of heart in a lot of *poitrine.*"

Smitten though he was, Rousseau was unable to bask for long in the smiles of this new patron, for she soon made a decision for him: he would travel to Turin, the capital of the Savoie, with a married couple who were going that way, and at a hospice there he would complete his conversion. Rousseau believed that she was inspired to send him away by a ponderous *manant,* or yokel, who happened to be devouring dinner with them one day. But with a reputation to protect, Mme de Warens would have had qualms about allowing an attractive youth to remain in her care, and it is likely that she had sent other converts to the Turin hospice in the past. In effect it was her job, and Pontverre probably counted on her to do it. Certainly she had no trouble obtaining money for the trip from her friend the bishop of Annecy. But as usual, Rousseau preferred to believe that he was the passive subject of chance or fate. "It is a series of ricochets," Trousson comments; "he went to Confignon out of curiosity, to Annecy to have a destination, to Turin on account of a yokel."

For a youth not yet sixteen who had never been more than a few miles from home, the trip was an exciting prospect but also an intimidating one. Ten days had passed since he left Geneva, and he still thought, and perhaps even hoped, that his family would fetch him home. He eventually learned that his uncle Gabriel Bernard had delayed for a few days before going in search of his nephew, reached Confignon shortly after Jean-Jacques had left for Annecy, and then returned home, sending to Nyon for his brother-in-law Isaac. Five days later, accompanied by a favorite hunting companion named Rival, Isaac Rousseau finally arrived in Annecy and learned that his son had departed for Turin the previous day. What happened next caused resentment that the passage of forty years did nothing to diminish when he recounted it in the *Confessions.* "These gentlemen saw Mme de Warens and contented themselves with lamenting my fate with her, instead of following and catching up with me, as they could easily have done since they were on horseback and I was on foot . . . It seemed that my closest relatives were conspiring with my stars to deliver me to the fate that awaited me."

How to explain this betrayal? When Isaac himself had fled from Geneva six years before, he was a victim of his own volatile temper but also of class injustice. His failure to stay in close touch with his son thereafter was harder to understand. And now, when the boy could have expected his father to rescue him from his own rashness, he turned around and went home. The explanation Jean-Jacques arrived at was that Isaac couldn't resist the temptation to hold on to the income from his dead wife's inheritance, which otherwise would have gone to his sons. François had already removed himself from the picture, and now Jean-Jacques was doing the same. The still more painful implication was that Suzanne Rousseau's bequest would go not to her own sons but to the second wife in Nyon.

There was an additional financial consideration that Jean-Jacques seems to have paid no attention to, then or later. Because he ran away after completing only three years of the five-year apprenticeship to which he was legally bound, a settlement had to be worked out, and it was duly signed by Ducommun, Isaac, his friend Rival, and two witnesses on March 30, five days after Isaac returned home from Annecy. The document stipulated that if Jean-Jacques were to return within four months, he should resume his apprenticeship from that date, but that otherwise "the said act of apprenticeship will be null and void," and Isaac would have to pay Ducommun an indemnity of twenty-five écus, which was approximately the annual wage of a household servant. It seems likely that all concerned thought it best to end the business in this way. Rousseau always ascribed the coolness of his uncle's family to the widening social gap between them, but he seems not to have considered that they must have been disturbed by Ducommun's reports of his laziness and dishonesty, and neither Gabriel nor Isaac could have felt optimistic about forcing him to return to Ducommun.

After three days in Annecy, then, Jean-Jacques set out for Turin, in the company of the "yokel" Sabran and his wife. For them his company was literally a godsend, since the bishop's financial contribution would defray their traveling costs. Going on foot, they could hardly move rapidly — not that coach travel would have been much faster, since even in well-traveled regions the roads were more like rural trails than highways. Besides that, Mme Sabran was rather portly and in no particular hurry. She and her boisterous husband proved to be agreeable companions, though at night Rousseau was often awakened from slumber by strange noises whose meaning was still a mystery to him. Daydreaming of future favors from Mme de Warens and relishing the pleasant countryside, he felt freed from all care. "Young, vigorous, filled with health, security, and confidence in myself and others, I was in that brief but precious moment in life when its expansive fullness extends our being, so to speak, through all our sensations, and embellishes the whole of nature in our eyes with the charm of our existence." This feeling of complete happiness in the present moment was something Rousseau would value increasingly as the years went by, and he would one day diagnose its absence as the fundamental flaw of modern civilization.

As he often did when recalling happy times, Rousseau thought the journey had been much more rapid than it was, a mere week, but we know that he left Annecy on March 24 and arrived in Turin on April 12, so it took almost three weeks to cover the 150 miles. After a relatively easy southward stage, they had to turn southeast, make a gradual ascent up the Maurienne valley, with precipitous cliffs on either side, and then climb steeply to the snow-covered Mont Cenis pass at an altitude of nearly seven thousand feet. Even well-to-do travelers had to go on foot at that point or else hire porters to carry them over the summit in sedan chairs, as Horace Walpole and Edward Gibbon did some years later. The final stretch was the easiest, down to the Susa valley, which opens into the fertile northern Italian plain.

Turin at that time was an opulent city of sixty thousand, undergoing a surge of magnificent new construction under Victor Amadeus II, whose duchy of Savoie had enlarged itself into the kingdom of Sicily and then of Sardinia (known in the nineteenth century as Piedmont). Joseph Addison, visiting Turin twenty years earlier, admired its cleanliness and noted that "the court of Turin is reckoned the most splendid and polite of any in Italy." That is not to say that everything was opulent; Thomas Gray (author later of the famous "Elegy") found it a pleasant city but ramshackle by English standards: "The houses are of brick plastered, which is apt to want repairing; the windows of oiled paper, which is apt to be torn; and everything very slight, which is apt to tumble down." But for Rousseau Turin was a revelation: three times as big as Geneva, taking its tone from an elegant court, and foreign without being forbidding. French was widely understood, though he soon picked up the Piedmontese dialect, and indeed the region's affinity with France has always been strong. An industrial magnate at the beginning of the twenty-first century could still say, "For anyone like myself who was born in the Piedmont and heard, from childhood on, the patois being spoken along the valleys that lead from Turin toward the Savoie

THE DOOR OF THE
HOSPICE IN TURIN
The massive door "was
closed on my heels with a
double turn of the lock as
soon as I went through it."
By the time he emerged,
Rousseau would be a
Protestant no more.

and Chambéry, France is much more than a nation at the front door: it is a natural bond, a spontaneous affinity."

There was no chance to explore the city, for Rousseau was immediately taken to the Hospice of the Catechumens, the term for persons receiving religious instruction. As soon as he entered the big barred door — it is still there today, though the building is now an apartment house and wine shop — it was ostentatiously locked behind him, and he was effectively a prisoner until the priests of the Confraternity of the Holy Spirit should determine that his conversion was complete. His first impression was of some extremely unprepossessing fellow converts, "four or five fearful bandits who looked more like the Devil's troops than like aspirants to become the children of God." It soon became apparent that these characters, two of whom called themselves Moors, were professional converts who traveled from place to place for the free food and lodging that went along with the process. Soon some female catechumens joined them, and they struck Rousseau as "the worst sluts and vilest man-chasers who ever stank up the Lord's sheepfold." One of them nonetheless caught his fancy, a pretty girl with "mischievous eyes that sometimes met mine," but that was as far as it went, since they were never allowed to speak to each other. Rousseau suspected that the girl's unusually long stay in the hospice showed that the priests had their own uses for her. The registry in which his arrival was recorded, with his name in the form "Rosso," allows us to recover the names of his fellow catechumens. The villainous "Moors" were a pair of Jews named Ruben Abraham and Len Isaac; a third Jew, Neve Abraham, had already converted to Calvinism in Geneva and was now reaping the modest rewards of a second conversion to Catholicism. The flirtatious girl whose eyes met Rousseau's was also a Jew, Judith Komès. She was eighteen, and the oldest of the group was twenty-two.

However dubious the whole business was, the clergy took their task seriously, and an old priest set to work to instruct Rousseau. Since the young Genevan had some theological knowledge and was inconveniently eager to argue, he was soon turned over to a younger and brighter priest, who bandied quotations from Saint Augustine and Saint Gregory. As he had done with Pontverre, Rousseau tactfully refrained from exerting his full intellectual force, or at least that is how he preferred to remember it. At no time in his life did he show the slightest interest in religious dogma, but he relished the discovery that his mental agility could challenge that of an experienced proselytizer; beyond that, it was convenient not to have to leave the hospice too soon. Even so, it was in his interest to yield. "Feeling that I was, so to speak, at his mercy, I thought it best that, however young I might be, I had better not push him too far." Though he doesn't exactly say so, it was a major step to desert Calvinism in favor of the enemy it routinely denounced as the Whore of Babylon. Strictly speaking, this was not apostasy, since he had not yet been confirmed and admitted to communion in Geneva, which would have happened later that year. All the same, it was a striking repudiation of the culture in which he had been raised, and in his unfinished last work he was still brooding about his defection. He settled on his favorite explanation of submission to external pressure: "Still a child and left to myself, enticed by caresses, seduced by vanity, lured by hope, forced by necessity, I became a Catholic."

The most memorable experience at the hospice was a disturbing one, a sexual overture by one of the self-styled Moors, ugly, filthy, and rank with tobacco, who pressed affectionate kisses on Rousseau and attempted to share his bed. Though Rousseau did his best to fend him off, he could not prevent some confused grappling that ended, to his surprise and bewilderment, with the sudden spurting of "something sticky and whitish" from the Moor, which made him rush away "more agitated, more troubled, more frightened even than I had ever been in my life, and ready to be sick." The spectacle was so new to him that he claims he mistook it for an epileptic fit, but when he eventually grasped what was going on, it confirmed the sexual revulsion he had felt as a boy when he passed the holes in the ground where people were copulating like dogs. "Truly I know nothing more hideous for anyone in a calm state to see than that obscene and filthy comportment, and that frightful face inflamed with the most brutal lust. I have never seen another man besides that one in such a state, but if we are like that in our transports when we're with women, their eyes would have to be bewitched not to regard us with horror." A logical conclusion might be that men are not actually so very horrible and that female sexuality cooperates with theirs, but Rousseau was never willing to accept that. The episode of the lecherous Moor, accordingly, only served to strengthen his chivalric idealization of women. "It seemed to me that I owed them tender sentiments and the homage of my person as reparation for the offenses of my sex."

For the rest of his life Rousseau was alarmed by any hint of homosexuality, which has prompted numerous interpreters to suspect him of homosexual feelings that had to be repressed. It is true that he often experienced powerful infatuations with admired male companions. But in any case the sexual act itself was alarming to him, and he combined passionate emotion with physical timidity. He may not have been so profoundly revolted by the incident as a British scholar once suggested: "In the hospice sexual vice in its most hideous, abnormal forms was brutally thrust upon him." But he was certainly more squeamish about sex in general, not just homosexuality, than most of the Enlightenment figures who were his contemporaries. Voltaire, for instance, quite casually told Alexander Pope and his mother that when he was at school the Jesuits "buggered me to such a degree that I shall never get over it as long as I live." Most disillusioning of all for Rousseau was the attitude of the hospice authorities. The old *intendante,* or mother superior, told him to keep quiet about it, but at least he heard her muttering under her breath, *"Can maledit, brutta bestia"* ("the damned dirty beast!"). Still worse was the male administrator who told him blandly that he was making a fuss over nothing, and even hinted that he might have enjoyed it.

In due course it was decided that Rousseau was ready to be released from the hospice. In the *Confessions* he claimed to have stayed there for more than two months, presumably detained because his skill in argument baffled the priests, but the records show unmistakably that he abjured the Protestant faith on April 21, nine days after his arrival, and was baptized only two days later. It seems highly unlikely that he would have been kept on for weeks, let alone months, after that. Perhaps he was embarrassed, forty years later, to admit that the authorities found him so troublesome that they got rid of him with unprecedented haste, or at best that his conversion was so prompt that little time was needed for it. The other catechumens in fact stayed a good deal longer than he did, and as his modern editors comment, the register indicates that far from resisting the priests' instruction, he was converted in record time. Very likely his complaints about the Moor's advances sealed the decision to discharge him. (Of course, it is possible that the hospice register is inaccurate. The original volume was destroyed during a bombing attack in the Second World War, but a facsimile of the relevant page suggests that dates were filled in rather casually and at intervals, and it has been suggested that a scribe might have mistaken the date.)

The vicar general of the Holy Office of the Inquisition examined Rousseau on his new faith and apparently was not entirely satisfied with the answers. Normally a Protestant baptism was accepted as valid, but it was ordered that Rousseau be rebaptized. His formal act of baptism survives in the registry of the church of San Giovanni, where he was given the additional name Franco in honor of a lady who served as godmother pro forma: "Giovanni Giacomo Franco Rosso, son of Isaac of Geneva, sixteen years of age, having previously abjured the doctrine of Calvin, received the sacrament of baptism the twenty-third of April 1728. Godparents: Giuseppe Andrea Ferrero and Francesca Cristina Rocca." Afterward he remembered with particular resentment that the

inquisitor asked whether his mother was damned. He replied diplo-
matically that he hoped God had enlightened her in her final hour. Or
at least he liked to believe he said that; it has been suggested that the
question would have been unlikely at such a time, and that it may actually have been asked earlier and the other way around. Carrying the
burden of having caused his mother's death, he might have asked anxiously about the state of her soul, and been told reassuringly that God
could enlighten people at the moment of death.

It was over. "They advised me to live as a good Christian and be
faithful to grace; they wished me good luck, they closed the door on me,
and everyone disappeared." Rousseau suddenly faced the reality that he
was entirely on his own. Far from launching him on a fine new life, the
journey to Turin had left him friendless and low on cash, with just a
few francs collected at the baptismal ceremony. The Sabrans had consumed all the money from the bishop in Annecy. Still, it was exhilarating to be free.

After wandering about the city for a while, he bought some milk
curds known as *giuncata* — all his life he retained the Swiss fondness
for milk products — and two *grissini,* or baguettes, of "that excellent
Piedmontese bread that I like better than any other; for my five or six
sous I made one of the best dinners I've ever had in my life." This may
well have been the first time in his life that he was free to choose his
own meals, and he greatly enjoyed it. "I brought to it the greatest possible sensuality. My pears, my *giuncata,* my cheese, my *grissini,* and some
glasses of a strong wine from Montferrat that you could cut with a
knife, made me the happiest of gourmands." Throughout the *Confessions* there are numerous reminiscences of eating, and the editors rightly
say that if Rousseau always preferred simple meals, his was "a voluptuous frugality."

It was time to find a place to stay, and someone suggested a rooming
house whose landlady took in unemployed servants at one sou per
night. "We all slept in the same room, the mother, the children, and the
guests . . . On the whole she was a good woman, swearing like a cart-
driver, always slovenly and unkempt, but kindhearted and obliging,
who became friendly with me and even was useful to me." Rousseau
was learning the valuable lesson that women found him appealing and
were glad to help him.

He continued to stroll around Turin, taking in the celebration of mass every morning at the royal court in order to hear the superb music there, and soon caught another woman's eye. He had started going into shops to offer his only talent, engraving initials or coats of arms on tableware, but had met with no success. One young and pretty shopkeeper, however, got him to tell "my little story," fed him breakfast, and gave him some small tasks to do. "She was an extremely piquant brunette" named Mme Basile, about whom nothing is known except what Rousseau relates. Her husband was away on a trip, which was encouraging, but had left his surly clerk as watchdog, which was not. Nonetheless Mme Basile permitted Rousseau frequent visits, and as always he was attracted as much by female paraphernalia as by the woman herself. "With avid eyes I devoured everything that I could see without being detected: the flowers on her dress, the tip of her pretty foot, the firm white arm that appeared in the space between her glove and cuff, and the space that sometimes showed itself between her throat and her scarf . . . By gazing at everything I could see and at more than that too, my eyes got blurry, my chest was constricted, my breathing grew more difficult by the moment and harder to control, and all I could do was soundlessly release my awkward sighs in the silence we often found ourselves in." When she did speak, Mme Basile seemed perfectly calm, but he did not fail to notice that her bosom rose and fell in an interesting way.

These pleasingly stifled encounters continued for some time, always under the baleful glare of the clerk, until one day Rousseau was bold enough to follow the lady into a back room, where he found her embroidering by a window with her back to him. Impulsively, he threw himself on his knees at the doorway and stretched out his arms, assuming that he was unseen, "but there was a mirror on the mantel that betrayed me. I don't know what effect this transport had on her; she didn't look at me or speak to me at all, but half-turning her head, she pointed to the mat at her feet with a simple movement of her finger." They both remained motionless, at least in the final version of the story in the *Confessions*. In an earlier draft he had added, "If I had the temerity to place my hand several times on her knee, it was done so lightly that in my simplicity I believed she didn't feel it." He was filled with confused excitement but unsure what her gesture meant, and Mme

Basile did nothing to clarify the situation. In any case the tableau was interrupted by the sound of the maid arriving. He kissed her hand fiercely and felt it press his lips in return, and then he hurried out. When he returned to the shop, the clerk was more threatening than ever and the delicious moment could not be repeated.

When he wrote the *Confessions,* Rousseau baffled his readers by including what seemed to be trivial and embarrassing details like the incident with Mme Basile and the spanking by Mlle Lambercier. It is remarkable not only that he recounted such episodes but that he refrained from explaining them away. What he had come to understand, with extraordinary originality, was that experiences that strangely haunt the memory can be a key to understanding personality. The young Rousseau, nourished by romantic fiction, saw himself as a prince in disguise, and awestruck silence was an appropriate response to an enchanting lady, especially if she seemed to impose it. In *Émile* he recalled an anecdote about a sixteenth-century lover whose mistress commanded him to be silent and who never said a word for two years, resuming only when she uttered the word "Speak." "Is there not something grand and heroic in that love?" Rousseau asked. "What woman today could count on a similar silence for a single day, even if she were to repay it with the greatest prize she has to offer?" Mme Basile was not obliged to repay with anything.

As he remembered the incident, the mirror was the most important thing. He could adore her from a distance, she could see him without looking at him, and when she pointed to the floor the gesture was decisive and yet mysterious. Was she commanding him to assume the position for chastisement — which would have rejoiced his masochistic imagination — or was she inviting him to kneel in homage before proceeding to further delights? The moment remained a permanent freeze-frame in memory, perfect because it led nowhere and did not have to yield to potential embarrassment and disappointment. And of course we know it not as an actual event but as an artistic re-creation in the *Confessions,* as unalterable as the lovers on Keats's urn, "for ever panting and for ever young."

The idyll soon turned to comedy or farce, when M. Basile unexpectedly came home and surprised the household at dinner. He was big, loud, and flashily dressed, and he demanded insultingly to know who "that little boy" at the table was. Clearly the clerk had tipped him off. Mme Basile's confessor, a genial Jacobin monk, was present and made a speech in defense of her honor, but M. Basile was implacable. Rousseau was ejected, and when he hung about the shop later on, the clerk brandished his yardstick in a threatening manner. The relationship, such as it was, was over, but he stored it up in memory as revealing something profound in his own nature. "Nothing I have felt in the possession of women is worth the two minutes that I passed at her feet without daring so much as to touch her dress. No, there are no gratifications like the ones that can be given by a virtuous woman one loves. Everything is a favor with her. A little sign with the finger, a hand pressed lightly against my mouth, were the sole favors I ever received from Mme Basile, and the memory of those slight favors still transports me as I think of them."

D. H. Lawrence used to preach against sex in the head, but that is where Rousseau's sex life nearly always took place. If it produced frustration, it also provided satisfactions that were the more reliable for dispensing with the need for another person's cooperation. It was at this time — he had just turned sixteen — that he belatedly discovered the physical reality of sexual pleasure. "My restless temperament finally declared itself, and its first eruption, very involuntary, gave me fears for my health that depict better than anything else the innocence I had lived in until then." He seems not to have thought of masturbation as sinful, but to have distrusted it instead as a "dangerous supplement that betrays nature" by encouraging escapist fantasy, "disposing, so to speak, of the whole female sex at one's pleasure." Even the simple possibility of sexual release, he later came to believe, would never occur to someone whose imagination had not been stimulated by the artifices of society. "I am persuaded that a solitary person who grew up in a desert without books, instruction, and women would die a virgin at whatever age he might reach." It wasn't sexual acts that haunted his imagination, but those glimpses of arms and breasts half hidden and half revealed.

By now Rousseau was completely penniless and even had to sell the little sword Abraham had given him. It was time to get a job. His landlady knew of a noblewoman who might have a position for him, and he went eagerly to inquire about it. He was disappointed to find that he would be a lowly footman or lackey. Still worse, he would have to wear livery, though at least it was simple in design and could be mistaken for ordinary clothing. But it was a job, and he accepted it. His new employer was the comtesse de Vercellis, in her late fifties and widowed for thirty years, who spoke excellent French. She was afflicted with cancer and could no longer write, so she needed someone to take letters from dictation. Literacy among servants was not common, and she was pleased to find that Rousseau performed this duty well.

As he got to know the comtesse, Rousseau was moved by her stoicism in the face of death, but she failed to play the role of sympathetic lady that he was coming to expect, instead questioning him peremptorily about himself and showing no feeling of her own toward him. After five months she succumbed to her illness, and Rousseau happened to be present when she died. The event left a deep impression on him, both for its solemnity and for its tragicomic conclusion. "Her life had been that of a woman of intelligence and good sense; her death was that of a sage. I can say that she made the Catholic religion attractive to me by the serenity of soul with which she fulfilled its duties . . . She didn't take to her bed until the final two days, and never ceased to converse calmly with everyone. Finally, no longer talking, and already in the death agony, she gave a big fart. 'Good,' she said, turning over, 'a woman who farts isn't dead.' Those were her last words."

Rather strangely, considering how briefly he had been there, Rousseau expected the comtesse to remember him in her will and was indignant to learn that it did not mention him. In the *Confessions* he complained that a couple of favored servants named Lorenzini schemed to keep him out of her sight during her last days, preventing him from getting the bequest that other servants received, though her nephew the comte de la Roque (in Italian, della Rocca) did give him thirty livres. At the early age of sixteen, his tendency to suspect conspiracy was already active. But in fact the will was registered when he had been in service for only a month, and it provided that all of the servants should get the same thirty livres that he did. As for the Lorenzinis, they had been trusted stewards and confidants for twenty years, and would hardly have appreciated a teenage newcomer underfoot as they worked to put her affairs in order at the end.

What Rousseau really wanted was acknowledgment of his intrinsic worth, which those many hours of questioning and of secretarial labor might have made the comtesse perceive. "She judged me less by what I was than by what she had made me, and by seeing nothing more in me than a lackey, she prevented me from seeming like anything else." The lackey's painful experience was forming the consciousness that would one day dazzle the world with the *Discourse on Inequality* and the *Social Contract.*

An incident that occurred immediately after the comtesse de Vercellis' death produced another of those unforgettable moments that imprinted themselves in Rousseau's memory and gave rise to extraordinary insights. While the dead woman's belongings were being collected and sorted, he noticed a little silver ribbon that appealed to him, and he pilfered it. The inventory was comprehensive, the ribbon was missed, the servants' belongings were searched, and it was found in his room. There followed an inquisition in front of the whole household at which he was forced to explain himself. After hesitating, he blurted out that a pretty young cook named Marion, toward whom he felt an attraction, had given him the ribbon. Marion was accordingly brought in, and Rousseau describes with bitter self-reproach what happened next. "They showed her the ribbon, and I accused her insolently. She was dumbfounded and said nothing; she threw me a glance that would have disarmed devils, but my barbarous heart resisted it . . . With an infernal impudence I repeated my declaration, and told her to her face that she had given me the ribbon. The poor girl began to cry, and said only these words to me: 'Ah, Rousseau! I believed you were a good fellow! You are making me very unhappy, and yet I wouldn't want to be in your place.'"

In the end Marion was judged likelier than Rousseau to be guilty, and they were both dismissed. Later on, though he never learned anything further about her, he was tortured by the fear that she might have been unable to get a good job afterward and have come to a miserable end as a result of his impulsive action. For forty years, he says in the *Confessions,* he was so tormented by guilt that he was never able to tell the story to a single person. And indeed, if he did finally manage to confess it to his readers, it was the lapse of nearly half a century that made it possible. As Lejeune says, "One can find the strength to open this walled-up door only when no one is waiting behind it."

As for the theft itself, it is easy to imagine the anxiety and distress that prompted it. Just sixteen, Rousseau had been abandoned by his family and was about to lose his job in a foreign city where he had no connections and no prospects. On top of that, he was disappointed and hurt to receive virtually nothing from the lady he had admired, and it is not surprising that he privately helped himself to a little reward. Thieving was not new to him, and as an apprentice in Geneva he had grown accustomed to lying about it. What was shocking now was the terror of public shame in a noble household where he had enjoyed some favor, followed by the discovery that he could brazenly accuse an innocent person and get away with it.

As Starobinski has noticed, the story of the ribbon is a mirror image of the story of the broken comb at Bossey, confirming a gap between outward appearance and inner reality. There Rousseau had been the accused innocent whose sincere defense was not believed; now he was guilty, but his insincere defense was believed, or at least accepted. Interpreters have stressed psychoanalytic explanations for what Rousseau did, and one may well suspect that the choice of a ribbon was not accidental. He was always aroused by the conventional props of femininity, especially when they suggested upper-class elegance, and he perhaps imagined dressing Marion up as a lady. (He greatly regretted that Mme Sabran made off with "a little ribbon glazed with silver that Mme de Warens had given me for my little sword.") It is even conceivable that Marion had seemed unresponsive to him and that unconscious aggression inspired him to accuse her.

Interpretations like these depend on ways of thinking that did not exist in Rousseau's time. He himself saw the episode as an instance of the power of socially induced shame to overcome even the keenest feelings of guilt. He thought that if only the comte de la Roque had taken him aside and questioned him in a kindly way, he would have confessed everything, but he found the accusing stares intolerable. "The presence of everybody was stronger than my repentance. I didn't fear punishment much, I feared only shame; but I feared that more than death, more than crime, more than anything in the world . . . I saw only the horror of being recognized, declared publicly — while I was present — to be a thief, liar, and calumniator." All his life Rousseau longed to be truly known. But being known would be desirable only if he had nothing to hide. What if he were indeed a thief, as the incident of the ribbon seemed to confirm? Then it would be disastrous to be recognized;

better not to be known. The heart of Rousseau's later thinking lies in this little incident, which no other writer of the time would have been likely to relate. To liberate the authentic self from socially induced hypocrisy and deception would become his mission, and no one knew better than he how hard it would be to achieve.

For the next several weeks Rousseau returned to his old rooming house while he hunted for work. The enforced idleness had one very positive result: it allowed him to cultivate the acquaintance of a priest in his late thirties, the abbé Jean-Claude Gaime, who came from a farm in the Savoie, had been educated in Annecy, and was now tutor to a nobleman's children. The term *abbé* was in widespread and ambiguous usage at that time: it could mean the abbot in charge of a monastery, or a priest who had income from a monastery to which he did not belong, or even a person with a nominal religious position but no actual duties. In Paris Rousseau would get to know many worldly abbés of the third type who were scarcely religious at all. Gaime was a priest of the second type, and he made a profound impression on the lonely and insecure youth, who visited him often in the months to come.

Gaime's counsel as Rousseau describes it in the *Confessions* may seem judicious to the point of platitude: "He made me feel that enthusiasm for sublime virtues was of little use in society; that in reaching too high one was subject to falls; that steadiness in small duties, always well fulfilled, required no less strength than heroic actions; and that it was far better to have men's esteem all the time than their admiration occasionally." What the priest was really teaching Rousseau, however, was that his combination of romantic fantasy and practical fecklessness was not serving him well and that he needed to make better sense of his life. If this advice had been didactically given, he would doubtless have ignored it, but Gaime accompanied it with the greatest gift of all: he made Rousseau feel that he understood him and believed in him. Not since his aunt Suzon left for Nyon had anyone treated him like that, and Gaime was a wise, thoughtful, well-read person whom he could genuinely look up to. "I have a loving soul, and I have always become attached to people less because of the good they have done me than because of what they have wanted to do for me, and it's certain that my instinct hardly ever deceives me in this. Accordingly I became truly fond of M. Gaime, I was so to speak his second disciple, and for that time at least this did me the inestimable good of turning me aside from the slide into vice, toward which my idleness was leading me."

In addition, Gaime gave religious instruction, and by contrast with the priests at the hospice he was mild and tolerant. In the *Confessions* Rousseau says that Gaime was cautious in expressing views that might seem heretical, but in *Émile* he goes much further, re-creating him as the Savoyard vicar, whose skepticism about dogma caused great scandal when the book was published. It is clear that what made the greatest impression was not so much Gaime's arguments and advice as the living example of an emotional faith. "The good priest had spoken vehemently," Rousseau says of the Savoyard vicar; "he was moved, and so was I. I believed I was hearing the divine Orpheus singing the first hymns and teaching men the worship of the gods." In *Émile* Rousseau gives an impressive account of the stages of a psychological rescue. "To protect the young unfortunate from this moral death that was so near to him, he began by reawakening self-love and self-esteem in him . . . To detach him imperceptibly from his idle and vagabond life, he had him copy extracts from selected books, and, pretending to have need of these extracts, he nourished in him the noble feeling of gratitude. He instructed him indirectly through these books: he made him regain a good enough opinion of himself to believe that he was not useless for anything good."

During these weeks Rousseau was subject to yearnings that were the more painful for being obscure. "I was restless, distracted, and dreamy; I wept, I sighed, I desired a happiness of which I had no idea, and of which I nonetheless felt the lack." His fantasies about women continued to take their old form, and he longed for a quarter of an hour's discipline at the hands of another Goton. Fixated on spanking, he felt a compulsion to expose his rear end to strangers, and one day he actually did so near a well where a group of young women were collected. "What they saw wasn't the obscene object, I didn't even dream of that; it was the ridiculous one. The foolish pleasure I took in exposing it to their eyes cannot be described." The response, however, was unsatisfactory (though it's not obvious what a satisfactory one would have been — a gang spank, perhaps). Some of the women laughed, some screamed, and Rousseau rushed away.

The sequel was both ludicrous and nightmarish. In his haste he got lost in a labyrinth of subterranean alleyways, heard pursuers following him, and in a dead-end passage was confronted by "a big man with a big mustache, a big hat, and a big saber." With surprising presence of mind, Rousseau persuaded this supremely masculine avenger to let him go by claiming to be a young foreigner of high birth who was mentally disturbed and had run away from his family. The story was true in a way, the high birth aside, and the man may actually have believed him, though some days later when they encountered each other again the mustached man remarked ironically, "'I'm a prince, I'm a prince'; as for me, I'm a fool, but don't let his highness come back here again." Still, Rousseau was grateful, since he was walking with a young abbé at the time and felt that the man had generously refrained from revealing the details of what had happened. At any rate it put a good scare into him "and made me well-behaved for a long time."

Rousseau had left the comtesse de Vercellis' household at the end of December, and a couple of months later her nephew the comte de la Roque unexpectedly did him a favor. A distinguished nobleman of eighty, the comte de Gouvon, needed a footman and was willing to employ him. Gouvon was the head of the family of Solar or Solaro, whose impressive town house survives to this day (Mme de Vercellis' house was demolished long ago). Once again Rousseau was given secretarial work, and soon the comte's son, the abbé Gouvon, who was well educated and destined for a bishopric, recognized his potential and began to tutor him in literature and languages. There was a long-established tradition in Italy of developing the talents of young men who would remain attached to their patrons, and the family doubtless had this in mind.

One incident stood out in Rousseau's mind as especially significant, and he made it the subject of a brilliant set piece in the *Confessions* that has attracted much commentary. The daughter of the house, Pauline-Gabrielle de Breil, was a pretty girl exactly his own age, and although she had black hair he even managed to assimilate her to his preferred category of beauty: she had "that air of softness of blondes that my heart has never been able to resist," not to mention that her dress showed off her bosom to advantage. As a servant he was of course not supposed to notice her looks, but he worshiped her in reverent silence, shocked that the rest of the servants discussed her charms in coarse language.

Waiting at table, he would watch eagerly for the chance to dart forward and change her plate, but "I had the mortification to be nothing to her; she didn't even notice I was there." One night, however, at a particularly fancy dinner, he got his chance. One of the guests declared that the heraldic motto of the house of Solaro, *Tel fiert qui ne tue pas,* contained a mistake in spelling, since *fier* ("proud") has no final *t.* The old comte de Gouvon noticed that the young lackey Rousseau smiled at this, and invited him to speak. Drawing perhaps on knowledge acquired when he invented armorial medals as an engraver's apprentice, Rousseau then astonished the company by explaining that the old French *fiert* came from the Latin *ferit,* "he strikes," rather than from *ferus,* "proud, threatening." The motto thus meant "Such a one who strikes but doesn't kill" rather than "Such a one who is proud but doesn't kill."

It was as if a piece of furniture had spoken up. There was an amazed silence followed by applause, and Rousseau saw, or thought he saw, that Mlle de Breil suddenly glanced at him with respect. It has been suggested that he may even have had in mind a possible implication of the motto, "That which wounds without killing is love," which would have underlined his own role as a lovelorn prince in disguise. It all passed away in an instant, however. In his agitation he spilled the water Mlle de Breil asked him to pour, she went back to ignoring him, and when she encountered him later hanging about her antechamber, she asked him coldly what he was doing there.

Looking back on the episode, Rousseau saw it as full of meaning. During the eighteenth century servants were regarded, as countless novels make clear, as a potentially treacherous fifth column within the walls. Accusations of theft followed by sudden departures were common, and in both the Vercellis and Gouvon households, Rousseau had plenty of opportunity to see the dishonesty and selfishness of his fellow servants. Here, however, his true worth had been almost magically revealed. "This was one of those all too rare moments that replace things in their natural order and avenge reviled merit for the insults of fortune." Indeed, the incident was prophetic of Rousseau's as yet unsuspected intellectual vocation, for one day he would make the dynamics of inequality the basis of a radical theory of society. The momentary triumph at the dinner table, indeed, was a confirmation of the class system, since it was stage-managed by a comte who enjoyed owning an unexpectedly gifted footman. In later life Rousseau would make a point of insisting — even to friends who felt hurt when he rejected their assistance — that nobody would ever be able to own him. And although he would form important friendships with people of rank and wealth, he would also say grimly, "I hate the great, I hate their high status, their harshness, their pettiness, and all their vices, and I would hate them even more if I despised them less."

During his time at the Palazzo Solaro, Rousseau continued to see the abbé Gaime, and in the account of the Savoyard vicar he described setting out with him on a summer's day for a serious talk. "He took me outside the city to a high hill beneath which flowed the Po, whose course one could follow along the fertile banks that it bathed. In the distance, the immense chain of the Alps crowned the countryside. The rays of the rising sun were already grazing the plain, projecting on the fields long shadows of trees, hills, and houses, and enriching with a thousand variations of light the most beautiful tableau that could strike the eye." All his life Rousseau loved mountainous landscapes like the one surrounding Geneva: not the high peaks themselves, but the pastoral world at their feet. And all his life he connected this love of nature with religious emotion, in a way that would one day become widely familiar but was still unusual in his day. In fact, he did more than any other single person to inspire that response in the Romantic writers and readers who came after him.

Rousseau certainly could have continued to live in Turin indefinitely, ending up perhaps as a trusted functionary of the Gouvons. But he never liked having to satisfy the expectations of other people, and he had not forgotten Mme de Warens, with whom he sometimes corresponded (unfortunately, no letters have survived). As usual, he didn't so much take a decision as wait for something to happen. A fellow apprentice from Geneva turned up, a lively but empty-headed fellow named Bâcle. This was either Pierre Bâcle, two years younger than Rousseau, or his brother Étienne, who was two years older — not that it matters much, since nothing else is known about either of them. Rousseau developed quite a crush on Bâcle, who was full of jokes and charmingly irresponsible, and was soon spending so much time with him that he had to be warned to remember his duties. This only provoked him to further delinquency; as he later acknowledged, he was finding discipline confining and needed an excuse to quit. Bâcle was about to return to Geneva, which meant that Rousseau could travel with him as far as Annecy. "I remembered with delight how charming that same journey had seemed to me in coming. What would it not be when, with all the attractions of independence, I would make the trip with a companion of my own age, good-humored and much to my own taste, without bother, duty, or constraint?" The result of his behavior was inevitable, as he wanted it to be. The steward gave him notice, and the elderly comte de Gouvon's grandson made one last, kindly attempt to reason with him. Rousseau replied coldly that he had already been fired and could not consider staying; he was hustled out of the house by the shoulders, and his stay in Turin was over. It was September 1729, a year and a half since he had left Annecy. He had recently turned seventeen.

4

Rousseau Finds a Mother

SOMETIME IN THE SUMMER of 1729 Rousseau set off from Turin with Bâcle. The abbé de Gouvon had given him a scientific toy called a Hero fountain, after its inventor, Hero of Alexandria, in which air pressure caused water to spurt in a surprising way, and the youths persuaded themselves that people along the road would pay to gape at this marvel. Just after the Mont Cenis pass they accidentally broke their exhibit before it had attracted any cash, but they trotted on in high spirits all the same. As they approached Annecy, however, Rousseau began to think seriously about the reception he was likely to meet from Mme de Warens, who had urged him to be worthy of the Gouvons' patronage, and to fear what she would think of his frivolous companion.

It turned out that neither concern was a problem. Bâcle recognized that he wasn't wanted, said cheerfully "There, you're home," turned on his heel, and disappeared forever. As for Mme de Warens, her reception could not have been more encouraging. All his life Rousseau was subject to incendiary bursts of emotion: "Feelings come and fill up my soul more suddenly than a lightning flash, but instead of enlightening me they burn and dazzle me." When it was a woman who provoked the burning, and it often was, she was bound to appreciate the tribute. "I trembled at the first sound of her voice, I threw myself at her feet, and in a transport of joy I pressed my mouth on her hand. As for her, I don't know whether she had heard any news of me, but I saw little surprise in her face, and no ill humor. 'Poor *petit,*' she said to me in a caressing tone, 'so you're here again? I knew very well that you were too young for that journey; I'm relieved that at least it didn't turn out as badly as I feared.'" To Rousseau's joy she actually declared that he would live in her home, and a bit later he overheard her remarking, "They can say what they like, but since providence has sent him back to me, I'm determined not to abandon him."

Years later Rousseau described the characteristic feelings of adolescence: "A change in mood, frequent fits of anger, and a continual agitation of mind make the child almost impossible to control . . . He doesn't acknowledge his guide, and is no longer willing to be governed." The engraver Ducommun had been no guide at all; the abbé Gaime was a wise counselor but detached from Rousseau's daily life; and the Gouvons were well intentioned but coercive. What he longed for was to be guided not by authority but by affection, and that is what he found in Mme de Warens. She continued to call him *petit* — she had no children of her own — and soon he was calling her Maman. They regarded these names as perfectly normal; indeed, as a youthful dependent he could hardly call her by her first name, and "Madame" would have been too formal. It seems, moreover, that "Maman" was a common term of address for the mistress of a household in the Savoie. But Rousseau understood clearly that it was more than that as well. After losing Suzon he had yearned for a mother, and now he had found one.

Because Mme de Warens became the most important person in Rousseau's emotional life, and because the portrait he left of her is so vivid, we naturally want to know more about her. A surprising amount of information has survived, partly because she came from a distinguished family and partly because the separation from her husband left a documentary trail. She was born in the small town of Vevey, on the northeastern shore of Lac Léman, in 1699. Like Jean-Jacques, she had no memory of her mother, who died in childbirth when she was only a year old, at which time she was committed to the care of affectionate aunts. In later life she used the name Louise, but she had been christened Françoise-Louise-Eléanore de la Tour and was known in the family as Françoise, perhaps to avoid confusion with an aunt Louise. Some traits of her character can probably be traced to a rather hit-or-miss upbringing: a love of reading with only a slender foundation of formal instruction, a marked dislike of household management and economy, and a fondness for an entourage of obsequious social inferiors, like the farmers' daughters who were her playmates at her aunts' country home.

When the girl was ten, another death intervened, the loss of the aunt Louise who was her mother figure, as Suzon was Rousseau's, and she was sent back to her father, who by then had remarried and sired two sons. Nothing was stable for long in her life; her father died shortly afterward. She didn't get along well with her stepmother, and at twelve she was sent to live with a lady in Lausanne, the nearest large town, where her legal guardians provided for lessons in the usual female accomplishments, notably playing music and singing, which she loved for the rest of her life and would share with the highly receptive Jean-Jacques.

Lonely and unsure of her future, such a girl might well look forward to marriage, and she didn't have long to wait. Sébastien-Isaac de Loÿs had fought in the Swedish army against Russia before returning to his native Lausanne, where he remained an officer in the service of the government in Berne, to which the Vaud region east of Geneva belonged. The marriage was initially suggested by his father, but when the young man met the proposed bride he was "seized by a violent passion," according to his own later testimony, and they were married in 1713. He was twenty-five and she was fourteen (girls as young as twelve could be legally married); it appears that her guardians were anxious to see her provided for.

Money was in fact an issue from the very start, as it would continue to be to the end of her days. The groom's father wanted legal assurances limiting his own financial responsibility, and the bride's guardians were so dubious about the arrangement that they refused to sign the contract. A judge had to replace the guardians with the aged clergyman François Magny, who had been her mentor in a pietist faith that preferred inward spirituality to dogmatic correctness. The young M. de Loÿs, incidentally, had not yet taken the name of Warens, the German spelling of the Vaudois village of Vuarens, whose seigneury he later acquired, after going to court to force his own father to relinquish it.

The marriage began well enough, with a continual round of social engagements that elicited reproofs from Magny, to which his young disciple returned the curiously ambiguous defense, "I do things with an indifference that sometimes surprises me." They also made regular sojourns in the countryside to supervise the grape harvest, an activity romanticized later by Rousseau in his account of Julie and her husband on their estate. For a time the couple lived in Lausanne, but in 1724 they went back to Vevey, where Mme de Warens embarked on the first of her entrepreneurial adventures, which were to cause great trouble for the rest of her life. The town council agreed to provide a building rent-free for a factory that would manufacture silk stockings — why she hit on this plan is not known — and although her husband did his best to stay clear of the whole sorry adventure, he found himself borrowing increasingly large sums of money to cover its costs. The factory lost money right away and kept on losing it, and he was legally responsible for its debts. One necessary retrenchment was especially sad: the childless couple had been raising as their own the children of two impoverished families, and they had to be sent away.

Mme de Warens's health began to suffer under the strain — she seems to have been a lifelong hypochondriac who nonetheless had genuine health problems — and in 1725 she traveled to Aix-les-Bains in the Savoie for a rest cure. While there, she thought of a way out of the tangled mess, and it seems obvious that she had had enough of the marriage as well. The following summer she persuaded a doctor to recommend that she take the waters again, this time at Évian, just across Lac Léman. As soon as she got there she declared her conversion to Catholicism, threw herself upon the protection of the king of Sardinia, who was there at the time, and fled to Annecy, in his province of the Savoie. She was twenty-seven, and had already been married for half her life.

Several years later her husband wrote a long account to his brother (from London, where he had gone to escape disgrace and bankruptcy) that is filled with painful details. The deserter, as he calls her — *ma déserteuse* — helped him lock up the family silver before she set out for Évian, but afterward she transferred nearly all of it surreptitiously to a trunk, which the servant who had to carry it remembered as uncommonly heavy. She managed to get away in addition with a large part of the goods from the stocking factory, an ample supply of linens, and all of her jewelry. Claiming that traveling during the heat of the day would be oppressive, she embarked in a boat shortly after midnight, "evidently finding," as her husband observed, "that nothing suited a work of darkness better than darkness itself." Shortly afterward he crossed the lake himself to visit her at Évian. She showered him with affection but did her best to keep him from talking to other people, and she had tears in her eyes when he left for home. He claimed to have learned later that when her servant girl commented, "Madame, you have a good husband," she replied dryly, "If you think so, take him, he'll soon be without a wife."

Once news of her departure for Annecy reached him, he hastened on horseback to Geneva, where he hoped to intercept her baggage, but it was protected by the official seal of the king of Sardinia and he was unable to touch it. Victor Amadeus was clearly taking an interest in the attractive convert, and had even provided her with an armed guard for the journey to Annecy. Thwarted at Geneva, her husband returned to Vevey and soon received a letter from the *déserteuse* affirming her new religious conviction and piously hoping that the Holy Spirit would enlighten him similarly. Even then he didn't give up but agreed to visit her in Annecy, where she unnerved him by receiving him in bed, bursting into tears, and beseeching his pardon. It was soon apparent, however, that her chief interest was financial, and by the time he left four days later he concluded that she was "a veritable actress." He never saw her again, and neither of them could have imagined that two years later she would meet a wandering teenager who would make her famous in world literature. Famous, indeed, under her husband's name, for although he soon obtained a divorce, it could not be recognized in Catholic Savoie. There was no justification, however, for her continuing to style herself the baroness de Warens, since in 1728 he was forced to sell the seigneury of Warens to pay off the debts she had left him with.

Rousseau eventually got a general idea of this history, but not a very accurate one, since he was convinced that Mme de Warens had nobly given up fortune and security to follow her conscience. That was certainly the interpretation accepted by Bishop Michel Gabriel de Bernex of Annecy (officially titled the bishop of Geneva, from which his predecessors had been exiled), who soon became her friend. In 1732 Bernex extolled her work with Protestant converts and declared, "She left her family, her ample possessions, and all that she had most dear in the world to embrace our holy religion, to the edification of the entire diocese." Rousseau told the same story ten years later, claiming that she just happened to be in Évian, attended a Catholic service there out of curiosity, was converted on the spot by the eloquence of Bernex, and promptly "abandoned a great fortune and brilliant rank in her country in order to follow the voice of the Lord and yield unreservedly to Providence." When she was confirmed in Annecy two months later, the bishop preached with even greater eloquence about her sacrifice, and "all the numerous assembly melted with weeping, and the women came to kiss her awash in tears."

Certainly we might suspect hypocrisy, conscious or unconscious, in this dramatic conversion. As Maurice Cranston comments, "For her, the principle of 'guidance by inner light' was often a signal to follow the most intense of her inner sentiments." After her death her friend François-Joseph de Conzié wrote his own account of the episode in Évian, which he had witnessed as a member of the royal entourage: she fell to her knees before Bishop Bernex, caught him by the cassock in full sight of the king, and cried out emotionally, "*In manus tuas domine commendo spiritum meum*" ("Into thy hands, O Lord, I commend my spirit"). Conzié recalled that while some people hailed her as a repentant Magdalen, others were convinced it was a staged performance to escape her husband and the financial wreckage she had saddled him with. But she assured Conzié earnestly that her commitment was real and that long after her conversion she was tortured by doubts about abandoning her religion and her husband.

All of this was two years in the past when Rousseau met Mme de Warens, but there was something else, of more immediate interest, that he didn't know. Living in the house with her was a young man named Claude Anet, officially a valet, but in reality her *intendant* and *homme de confiance,* her steward and right-hand man. And Anet was a good deal more to her than that. Back in Vevey, he had been the nephew of her gardener, and it appears that he was very much in love with his uncle's employer, for at the age of twenty he gave up everything to follow her to Annecy and renounced Protestantism along with her. He also shared her bed, but Rousseau managed not to know that for a long time. What was obvious was that Mme de Warens relished her independence, and there may well be an echo of her views in *Julie* when the heroine's cousin Claire feels relief at being widowed and comments that women have to enter slavery as a preliminary to being their own masters later on.

The side of Mme de Warens's character that Rousseau responded to was generous, playful, and affectionate. But he was baffled by another side of her, which he interpreted only as an unworldly tendency to throw money away on ill-conceived projects. He never grasped how worldly she really was. In addition to assisting converts to the Catholic faith, she seems to have done some sort of covert work for the government, though it has proved impossible to discover anything about it. The best guess is that as an attractive and well-spoken young woman, she made herself useful transmitting confidential messages to highly placed persons in Paris and elsewhere. In addition, she was a gambler who liked to take chances, and she persisted in risky schemes to make money. When one project after another fell short, the stakes kept going up. For his part Rousseau was content to remain in adoring ignorance. "When she was pondering her projects she would often fall into reverie. Very well, I let her dream; I kept silent, I gazed at her, and I was the happiest of men."

Claude Anet, meanwhile, was an efficient household manager, and she needed one. In addition to her moneymaking ventures, some of which involved concocting herbal medicines, assisted by Anet, she kept an open table for anyone who happened to drop in — curiously, she could hardly bear the smell of food, and although plump she ate sparingly — and she maintained a cook, a housemaid, and a gardener, as well as a pair of men who were hired as needed to carry her sedan chair. As Rousseau soon grasped, "That's quite a lot for two thousand livres of income . . . Unfortunately, economy was never her favorite virtue; she got into debt, she made payments, money went back and forth, and it all went on like that."

The house itself was charming, with a view across a stream to fields and orchards. This was the first time since he lived in Bossey that Rousseau was able to see anything but walls and roofs from his bedroom. As for Annecy, on the northern shore of the lake of that name, it was by modern standards a small town, with a population of five thousand. It had an impressive castle, a number of churches and convents — Rousseau loved the sound of their bells — and canals that brought a regular traffic of grain and wine. "It has the lake at its head and sewers at its feet, and its intestines are usually irrigated," one citizen approvingly remarked. The Savoie was mainly agricultural, but the farmers could extract only a meager living from the rocky soil and had to import a good deal of their grain from France. Thomas Gray a few years later was struck by the contrast between the prosperity of Geneva and the poverty of the Savoie: "You meet with nothing in it but meager, ragged, barefooted peasants, with their children, in extreme misery and nastiness." Rousseau was not unaware of the poverty, but living in town he didn't have to confront it directly, and the picturesque landscape fed his fantasy of happy peasants at home in the natural world. Twenty years later he drafted a few pages of a short story that began, "I was born in the mountains of the Savoie. My father was a good peasant, rich enough to live at ease in his condition, and poor enough not to be exposed to the torments of covetousness, for one can't desire very keenly what one believes impossible to obtain."

In the first months of living with Mme de Warens, Rousseau was abjectly in her thrall, though anxious not to admit the extent to which the attraction was sexual. "She was the tenderest of mothers to me, never seeking her own pleasure but always my good, and if the senses did enter into my attachment to her, they didn't alter its nature, but only made it more exquisite, intoxicating me with the charm of having a young and pretty *maman* whom it was delicious to caress. I say 'caress' in the literal sense, for it never occurred to her to withhold kisses and the most tender of maternal caresses from me, and it never entered my heart to abuse them." Probably no one had ever kissed or caressed Rousseau after childhood, not counting the foul attentions of the Moor in the hospice, and as for the spanking in Bossey and its sequel at the hands of Goton, those were the opposite of caresses. He began to behave like someone desperately in love. He needed to be with Mme de Warens constantly and was filled with rage whenever she had visitors, which was often. "As soon as anyone arrived, man or woman, it didn't matter which, I would go out grumbling, unable to bear being a third party with her. I would go and count the minutes in her antechamber, cursing these eternal visitors a thousand times." In a manuscript draft of the *Confessions* he gave an interesting explanation for his distress when he was separated from her: "I was always in fear that someone might speak to her and make her disgusted with me, that something that was done or said might separate us." The insecurity is obvious: people might inform her about behavior of his that could give offense, without his even understanding how he had offended. Still deeper was the ineradicable fear of being abandoned without warning by those he loved.

However innocent Rousseau may have felt the caresses to be, his behavior when alone was passionate to the point of fetishism. He would kiss his bed, which had once been hers, furniture that she had touched with her hand, "and even the floor, on which I would prostrate myself while thinking that she had walked on it." And if she was finicky about her food, that could hardly be said of her young admirer. "One day at the table, when she had just put a morsel in her mouth, I cried out that I saw a hair on it; she replaced the morsel on her plate, and I seized it greedily and swallowed it."

All of this homage was highly agreeable to Mme de Warens, who was not above stimulating it flirtatiously and then bursting into helpless laughter at Rousseau's jealous fury. "If some new importunate person turned up during our quarrel, she knew how to take advantage of it for her own amusement by prolonging the visit maliciously, throwing me glances meanwhile for which I would gladly have beaten her." It was he, of course, who needed to be beaten, but apparently that possibility never arose. Still, the endless teasing was exhilarating, not least when he complained about the nasty taste of the medicines she and Claude Anet were forever concocting. "In spite of my resistance and my horrible grimaces, in spite of myself and my teeth, when I saw those pretty smeared fingers approaching my mouth, I simply had to open up and suck them."

Rousseau's life was not all frivolity. M. Gaime and the abbé Gouvon had already introduced him to good books; now he found himself reading with profit under the guidance of an intelligent woman whom he adored. He began with a rather motley collection that she happened to possess: Voltaire's historical epic *The Henriad,* literary essays by Charles de Saint-Évremond, an important treatise on international law by Samuel Pufendorf, and a French translation of the *Spectator* essays of Joseph Addison. Every one of these books had value for his intellectual development. From Voltaire, whom he greatly admired from that time forward, he learned clarity and accuracy of expression. Saint-Évremond's drama criticism, though old-fashioned, stimulated his interest in plays, which he had never seen until he went to Turin. Pufendorf got him thinking about political questions that would become central to his life's work, and indeed there is a trenchant critique of Pufendorf in *The Social Contract*. The *Spectator* was a widely appreciated model of urbane social commentary mingled with popularized philosophy; at almost exactly the same time, the young Benjamin Franklin was patterning his own writing on it. Mme de Warens especially enjoyed the unillusioned but even-tempered picture of human behavior in the *Characters* of La Bruyère, which they read aloud together, and if the moralizing sometimes grew tedious, "I would recover my patience by kissing her mouth or her hands from time to time."

Rousseau had no wish to change this agreeable way of life, but Mme de Warens did. Her plan was to find some profession suitable to his talents and to give him a start in the world. What exactly that might be was far from obvious, but sometime in the autumn of 1729, when Rousseau had been in Annecy for two or three months, a distant relative of hers offered advice. This was Paul-Bernard d'Aubonne, a former colonel at Berne and something of a confidence man, who had done time in the Bastille for a financial speculation that went bad and was now on his way to Turin to sell the court a plan for a lottery. He stayed on in Annecy rather longer than he intended, because he happened to fall in love with the wife of an official there, which gave him time to interest himself in Rousseau's future. After questioning the youth at length, he delivered an unflattering verdict. "Despite what my exterior appearance and animated features might seem to promise, I was, if not absolutely inept, at any rate a boy of small intelligence, lacking in ideas, practically without accomplishments, in a word very limited in all respects, so that the honor of someday becoming a village priest would be the highest fortune I could aspire to." It is easy to see why Mme de Warens, dependent on the church for financial support, would have welcomed the suggestion of such a path for Jean-Jacques. And for a brief time he dreamed of becoming a wise and learned priest like M. Gaime, who had been educated at that very seminary in Annecy.

The next step was to do something about the gaps in Rousseau's education, particularly the feebleness of his Latin, which must be addressed before he could study for the priesthood. For this Mme de Warens enlisted the superior of the seminary, a good-natured priest named Aimé Gros, who often visited the house and enjoyed the task of tightening her bodice laces while she ran from one task to another. Gros was a Lazarist, a member of a teaching order named after the College of St. Lazare in Paris, and Rousseau thought highly of him: "a good little man, half blind, lean and gray, the most amusing and least pedantic Lazarist I have known, which in truth is not saying much." Gros not only undertook to help him gain admission, but secured the necessary fees from the bishop, and now there was no turning back. "I went to the seminary as I would have gone to be tortured. What a gloomy house a seminary is, especially for someone who is leaving the house of a charming woman!"

The experiment did not last long. Rousseau had two teachers there, of very different aspect. The first was another Lazarist, with greasy hair, a face that looked like gingerbread, and a voice like a buffalo, whose attempts to teach him Latin went nowhere. M. Gros took pity on Rousseau and transferred him to a young abbé named Gâtier, who reminded him very much of M. Gaime. "What was strongly marked in him was a sensitive, affectionate, and loving soul; in his large blue eyes there was a mixture of sweetness, tenderness, and sadness that compelled one to be interested in him." But despite his fondness for Gâtier, Rousseau still did poorly in his studies. Having never experienced formal instruction, he found it impossible to follow a curriculum, and his efforts to pay attention only made matters worse. "For fear of making the person speaking to me impatient, I pretend to understand, he keeps on going, and I understand nothing. My mind wants to go at its own pace, it can't submit to someone else's." What nobody at the time could have guessed was that this disability was actually a source of strength. Once he finally became his own teacher, Rousseau would turn out to be a brilliant pupil.

Perhaps the stay at the seminary would have continued longer if M. Gâtier had remained there, but after a couple of months it was time for the seminarian to be ordained and depart for a parish. Sometime later he fell in love with a young woman, had a child with her, and was harshly punished with imprisonment and expulsion from the priesthood. At least that was what Rousseau believed, though the records of the school Gâtier went on to head suggest nothing of the kind. True or not, the story contributed to the portrait of the Savoyard vicar in *Émile,* in which Rousseau comments bitterly that priests were expected to sleep with married women whose lapses could be conveniently covered up, not to fall in love with virgins. He repeated the thought in *Julie,* denouncing the purpose of clerical celibacy as "not so much to forbid them to have wives as to command them to content themselves with other men's."

After at most two months in the seminary (the dates are unclear) it was agreed that although Rousseau was a well-meaning lad, he had no discernible abilities, and he was sent home to Mme de Warens. As it turned out, the clergy of Annecy whom he met at her house had a positive influence of a different kind. In Geneva, a typical sermon the year he left extolled the Reformation for saving the faithful from the horrors of Catholicism: "Let us think, my dear brothers, of the gloomy state we would still find ourselves in without this happy revolution: without this grace we would still be slaves of the pope, slaves of the Court of Rome, slaves of a throng of monks, ignorant, idle, debauched, and greedy, who would seek only to suck us dry." Rousseau found the slaves of the pope far more charming and encouraging than the stern pastors of Geneva had been, and in Mme de Warens's circle he was constantly in contact with intelligent priests and monks who enjoyed conversation and music. She regarded them as brothers, and they in turn treated Jean-Jacques with familial indulgence; some years later he wrote to her, "Allow me to send a thousand kind regards to all our friends, and to all my uncles."

In fact he was receiving an informal education. In a small provincial town it was the clergy who read most widely, and they subscribed to the *Mercure de France,* a journal of conservative tendency that praised Voltaire for his poetry, ignored his skeptical *Philosophical Letters,* and offered a regular diet of edifying verses and paraphrases of the Psalms. In 1735 Rousseau himself became a subscriber to the *Mercure de France,* and he was still reading it fourteen years later, when a chance encounter with one of its announcements provoked the most decisive turn in his career.

One memorable incident occurred while Rousseau was still at the seminary. When he was paying a visit to Mme de Warens one day, a fire broke out next door and everyone hurried to rescue the valuables. Rousseau himself rushed about wildly, hurling furniture out of windows, and would have flung a big mirror too if someone hadn't stopped him. Bishop Bernex knelt down in the garden and got everyone to pray, and at that very moment the wind shifted and the house was saved. Years later, after Bernex's death, his colleagues began to collect evidence for his possible beatification, and Rousseau agreed to provide an eyewitness testimonial to the miracle. Still later, when his own religious views were exciting controversy, one of his enemies discovered the document and made satirical use of it, and in the *Confessions* Rousseau admitted that loyalty to Bernex had made him assert more than he really knew. The bishop led prayers and the wind changed, but of course it might have been a coincidence. What is more interesting is the genuine religious conviction that Rousseau remembered. "So far as I can recall my thinking, which was sincerely Catholic at that time, I was in good faith. The love of the marvelous that is so natural to the human heart, my veneration for this virtuous prelate, and secret pride at having perhaps contributed myself to the miracle, all helped to seduce me."

Almost by chance, a new path suggested itself. Mme de Warens was fond of music and had little concerts in her house once a week. Rousseau too loved music, and she had begun to teach him to read it, though he found the process daunting. In addition to his struggles to grasp musical notation, he seems always to have been a slow reader, and it is possible to suspect some degree of dyslexia, which no one at the time would have understood. When he entered the seminary he took with him a cantata by the contemporary composer Clerambault and laboriously managed to memorize one of the airs, and this accomplishment so struck Mme de Warens that she thought it worth encouraging. (In a draft of the *Confessions* he admits wryly that she undertook it *faute de mieux* — for want of anything better.) The music master of the cathedral, a cheerful young man named Jacques-Louis-Nicholas Le Maître, whom she playfully called her kitten, agreed to give Rousseau instruction for a modest fee, so he moved into Le Maître's house.

He spent six months there, learning (as usual) more slowly than might have been expected, but relishing the change from the glum seminary. Mme de Warens's maid, a young woman about his own age named Anne-Marie Merceret, was an organist's daughter with musical ability, and Le Maître had them sing duets together. Rousseau also made some progress on the recorder, and he glowed with pride when Le Maître wrote a little solo for him to play in church. In later years he remembered it as a happy time, calm and unconflicted, that embedded itself in his memory with a Proustian fullness. "In the various situations I've found myself in, some have been marked by such a feeling of well-being that when I remember them I am affected as if I were still there. Not only do I recall the times, the places, and the people, but all the surrounding objects as well, the temperature of the air, its scent, its color, a certain local impression that can be felt only there, and the vivid memory of it carries me there all over again." As with the songs of aunt Suzon, he was moved most of all by melody. "I've always kept a tender affection for a certain air, 'Conditor alme syderum,' that goes in iambics, because one Sunday in Advent I heard from my bed this hymn being sung before daybreak on the cathedral steps."

Rousseau liked Le Maître but didn't feel particularly drawn to him. Then one cold February night someone more compelling burst upon the scene. There was a knock on Le Maître's door, and a stocky, rather oddly built young man, dressed in clothes that had once been expensive but were now in tatters, announced himself as a musician from Paris (though he had a Provençal accent) who happened to be passing through. His name was Venture de Villeneuve, he knew all the fine ladies and noble lords in Paris, and to every remark or question he responded with a risqué quip that made everyone laugh. It seemed improbable that this braggart actually knew any music, but he offered to sing in the cathedral the next day, and to everyone's surprise he performed superbly, hardly bothering to glance at the score beforehand. Rousseau fell for him instantly.

Everything about Venture was captivating for a shy, awkward teenager who didn't know how to talk to women and had barely acquired the rudiments of music. "Bantering, playful, irrepressible, seductive in conversation, always smiling but never laughing, he would say the grossest things in the most elegant way and make them pass. Even the most modest women were amazed at what they would accept from him. In vain they would feel that they ought to take offense; they didn't have the power to do it." Rousseau adds that Venture's actual conquests were entirely among "fallen girls," which he ascribes to mysteriously bad luck. No doubt Venture preferred to flirt with impunity while avoiding compromising entanglements. Mme de Warens disapproved of him highly, fearing that his libertinism would infect Jean-Jacques, but her warnings had no effect. "I loved to see him and hear him, everything he did was charming to me, and everything he said seemed like an oracle."

Early in April another unexpected change occurred. Though Le Maître was well respected for his work with the choir, he was in the habit of drinking too much wine, a great deal too much, in fact, and he frequently took umbrage at slights from the haughtier members of the clergy. After one such offense he decided to decamp without warning just before Easter, so as to take revenge on the cathedral at a time when they most needed him. Mme de Warens tried to dissuade Le Maître, but finding him obdurate, she was a loyal friend and conspired to help him get away with a heavy box of music — in a striking parallel to her own getaway from Vevey — that contained his own work but also some scores that belonged to the cathedral. Rousseau was deputed to accompany Le Maître to Lyon, a formidable journey of close to a hundred miles along winding mountain roads. In the dark of night he and Claude Anet staggered along with the chest to the next village, where a donkey was hired.

At that point Anet returned to Annecy, while Le Maître and Rousseau pressed on westward to Seyssel, across the border in France, where they felt so safe from pursuit that they amused themselves by persuading the local curé that they were traveling on official cathedral business. After enjoying his hospitality, they traveled on to Belley, where Le Maître conducted the Easter music to great applause; they spent the better part of a week there. At last they arrived in Lyon and settled down in an inn to wait for the chest of music, which they had consigned to a boat on the Rhône. But here an emergency occurred. On the road Le Maître had several times suffered from epileptic seizures and now, on a street in Lyon, he had a massive one, foaming at the mouth and falling helpless to the ground. Rousseau was terrified, perhaps as much by the scrape he had gotten himself into as by Le Maître's condition, and on the spur of the moment he fled. After telling some passersby the name of the sick man's inn, "I turned the corner of the street and disappeared." For poor Le Maître, the sequel was even more disastrous, since the authorities seized his chest of music when it arrived in Lyon and he lost his entire life's work.

Ashamed of his treachery but desperate to see Maman again, Rousseau hurried back to Annecy, and to his amazement found her gone. She had departed for Paris with only Anet as a companion, on a mission whose purpose Rousseau never did find out. It was rumored that she had been sent to the French court, by either the bishop or the king, to conduct some sort of secret negotiation. Scholars have combed the surviving records and have not learned much. The one thing known for certain is that her relative d'Aubonne was mixed up in it somehow and that he joined her at Seyssel on the way to Paris. The best guess is that d'Aubonne was hoping to promote a revolution in the Vaud, Mme de Warens's native district, that might return it to Catholic rule. A corroborating piece of evidence is a letter in the state archives of Turin, sent from Paris by the Sardinian ambassador to the senate of the Savoie, which warns that Mme de Warens should be watched during her return from Lyon "without however giving her the least suspicion of it," to make sure she was really heading back to Annecy and not to Switzerland, where she might well say or do something that would expose the plot.

The royal agent in Seyssel, meanwhile, wrote to say that she had been seen getting into the Paris coach wearing a mask and accompanied by two men, one of whom he recognized as d'Aubonne (the other must have been Anet) and that he feared for her loyalty to Catholicism. "Word has reached me that her conduct is problematic. It may be that she is a Catholic in good faith, but it may also be that she is looking behind her, like Lot's wife." The surveillance continued for some weeks, in due course establishing her loyalty to King Victor Amadeus and revealing that she and d'Aubonne had had some kind of falling out. On September 2 the king himself wrote to his ambassador to urge that "the secret of our own involvement must be inviolably kept, and since circumstances are not proper for the execution of a project of this nature, we do not think it advisable to consider it at this time." The circumstances were certainly not proper, for the very next day, for reasons that remain unclear, the king abdicated his throne.

Rousseau was utterly ignorant of these mysterious schemes. But what exactly had Mme de Warens intended by sending him off with Le Maître on their dubious escapade? In all likelihood she expected him to remain with Le Maître indefinitely; this was not the last time that she would show signs of wanting him to move on. Rousseau himself later decided that her chief motive was to detach him from Venture, but dispatching him with an alcoholic musician and a box of stolen manuscripts seems a strange way of going about it. More likely her main idea was to rid herself of responsibility for him. Certainly Anet was happy to lend a hand, packing up the manuscripts and helping to carry them out of town, and giving no hint to Rousseau of the imminent Paris trip.

Finding himself all alone in Annecy, Rousseau was at a loss. Because of his complicity in Le Maître's escape, he didn't dare go to the bishop, who might otherwise have helped him. He couldn't stay in Mme de Warens's house, since it had been left in the care only of the housemaid, Merceret, and his presence there with an unmarried woman would have caused a scandal. So he looked up Venture, who was boarding with a cobbler, and moved in with him. Merceret, meanwhile, took quite a fancy to him, as did several of her friends. One of them, a convert from Geneva named Esther Giraud, was especially direct, but she met with no success. "When she pushed her dry black muzzle, smeared with Spanish tobacco, into my face, I could barely keep from spitting at it." Esther Giraud's station in life was likewise unappealing, since she was a humble *contrepointière* who made curtains and repaired upholstery.

Soon the perfect opportunity for romance presented itself. On a fine day around the end of June, just after his eighteenth birthday, Rousseau was strolling in the countryside and was hailed by two young women on horseback, roughly his own age, who were timorous about crossing a stream. He had met them before and recognized them as Claudine Galley, whose mother owned an estate some distance from Annecy, and her friend Marie-Anne de Graffenried. Gallantly he led the horses through the stream, expecting that the charming girls would then take their leave, but after they conferred with each other in low voices, Mlle de Graffenried cried, "No no, you don't escape us like that! You got wet in our service, and in good conscience we should get you dry. You will please to come with us, we're taking you prisoner." Mlle Galley added, "Prisoner of war, get on the horse behind her, we want to take charge of you."

For Rousseau this was an incomparable stroke of luck. He needed to be passive and let women make the moves, and in later life he tended to prefer threesomes; the playful cooperation of these two spared him anxiety about an intimidating encounter with just one. His only remaining worry was that Mlle Galley's mother would object, and when they informed him that she was not at home, he felt an electric thrill. He gladly mounted Mlle de Graffenried's horse, although when she invited him to confirm how fiercely her heart was beating ("for fear of falling," she demurely claimed), he couldn't bring himself to verify it but kept his arms tightly clasped around her waist. Exciting as this was, he was sorry not to be on the other horse, for Mlle Galley was even more attractive, "at once delicate and well formed, which is the perfect stage for a girl."

Rousseau had plenty of time to hold Mlle de Graffenried's waist, since the estate was in Thônes, a good twelve miles from Annecy. In due course they arrived and enjoyed a pleasingly rustic meal on benches in the kitchen of the tenant farmer. They then went out to the orchard to pick some cherries for dessert, a scene that Rousseau describes so tenderly in the *Confessions* that it became famous as the idyll of the cherries. "I climbed the tree and threw down bunches of cherries, whose stones they threw back at me among the branches. Once Mlle Galley, opening her apron and holding her head back, presented herself so well, and my aim was so good, that a bunch fell into her bosom. What laughter! I said to myself, 'If only my lips were cherries! how gladly would I cast them there!'" All that happened, however, was a kiss on Mlle Galley's hand, "which she gently withdrew, gazing at me in a way that was not at all offended."

They returned to Annecy, and that was the end of it, but the moment stayed with Rousseau forever. He had done nothing to embarrass himself, the attraction was implicit rather than overt, and it was an innocent and very temporary ménage à trois. Mlle de Graffenried, whose German name reflected her origins in Berne, had been expelled from that city for what Rousseau vaguely calls "some youthful folly." But Rousseau was not after follies, and what he especially appreciated was a liberation from social constraints that avoided embarrassment and shame. "Not a single equivocal word or jest was uttered, and we didn't have to impose this decency on ourselves; it came all by itself, and we took the tone that our hearts gave us." When Rousseau returned home he took care not to tell Venture anything about his day.

Back in Annecy, Rousseau tried hanging about outside the house where the young ladies were staying, but didn't encounter anyone. He then commissioned their friend Esther Giraud to carry a letter to them and was thrilled to get a reply, which however he does not describe. He never saw either of them again, and so they vanish from history, having entered it momentarily on the strength of an eloquent reminiscence by a great writer. (The records show that some years later Mlle de Graffen-ried entered a convent and that Mlle Galley married a Savoyard senator thirty years her senior.)

Esther Giraud, understandably jealous, saw a way to get Rousseau out of town if she couldn't have him for herself. Her friend Merceret was increasingly uneasy at the long and unexplained absence of her employer, Mme de Warens, and began to think of returning home to Fribourg, in the Bernese region. She needed a companion, since a young woman would be ill advised to travel alone, and Mlle Giraud urged her to take Rousseau. He too was feeling far from secure, with no way to reach Mme de Warens and no idea when she might return. Besides, he was absolutely broke, with no prospects for employment, and Merceret promised to pay his expenses. So the decision was taken, rather casually and accidentally, like most decisions in Rousseau's life, and in early July 1730, less than a week after the episode of the cherries, he and Merceret said goodbye to Annecy.

5

A Year of Wandering

It MIGHT SEEM that Rousseau was in a very disheartening position in the summer of 1730. He had gotten mixed up in a dubious escapade with the unstable Le Maître, had extricated himself shamefully from that, and had returned to Annecy only to find that his adored Maman had disappeared without a word. Now he was hitting the road with no concrete plans whatsoever. Yet far from being distressed, he seems to have been positively elated. In one way or another he had been a dependent all his life. Now he was ready to try his wings, and he didn't much care where he flew.

First there was the relationship with Anne-Marie Merceret to consider. Rousseau couldn't help noticing that she was highly attentive to him; she made sure they always slept in the same room, and she even picked up his tone of voice in a flattering way. He also found her quite attractive. Yet he claims that shyness and inexperience prevented him from responding as she hoped. "I couldn't imagine how a girl and boy could ever arrive at sleeping together; I believed it would take centuries to bring about that terrifying arrangement. If poor Merceret counted on some recompense for defraying my expenses, she was disappointed, and we reached Fribourg exactly as we had left Annecy." By the end of the trip her ardor had understandably cooled. Her father greeted Rousseau unenthusiastically, and he said goodbye without emotion. As he always did in such cases, he later fantasized about the pleasant, peaceful life he might have led in Fribourg as the organist's son-in-law, but the fantasy was not a compelling one.

On the way to Fribourg their route took them through Nyon, where he felt obligated to call upon "my good father," apparently without advance notice. It is impossible to know what their infrequent encounters were really like, since Jean-Jacques was committed to believing that a deep affection between them never waned. His account of this reunion, however, is notably vague. "At my appearance his soul opened itself to the paternal feelings that filled it. What tears we shed as we embraced!" After this sentimental display they settled down to discuss what Jean-Jacques ought to do, and it was obvious that Isaac had no interest in having him stay in Nyon. Apparently he frowned on what he took to be an improper connection with Merceret, and when his wife invited her stepson to stay for dinner her sugary tone was obviously insincere. Jean-Jacques thanked them, said he would drop in again sometime, and departed, "well contented to have seen my father and to have dared to do my duty."

This moderately cheerful picture, however, was the fruit of selective reminiscence. An abject letter survives from about a year later, apparently written with no intervening contact of any kind, that throws a very different light on the meeting in Nyon. "In spite of the unhappy assurances you have given that you no longer regard me as your son, I dare to appeal to you again as the best of all fathers, and whatever may be the just causes of hatred that you have against me, the rights of an unhappy and repentant son should efface them in your heart, and the lively and sincere pain I feel at having misused your paternal tenderness ought to restore me in the rights that blood gives me. You are still my dear father." It is not clear what Jean-Jacques' offenses were, but they presumably included abandoning his faith and his apprenticeship. Whatever the reasons, his father's rejection was so painful that he never allowed himself to acknowledge it, and he made the heroine of his novel say, after her father has beaten her so ferociously as to draw blood, "A father's heart feels that it is made to pardon, and to have no need of being pardoned."

Up to this point in Rousseau's life, a certain number of documents in the archives of Geneva, Turin, and Annecy can supplement what he relates in the *Confessions*. For the next year, however, from the summer of 1730 to the summer of 1731, the sole evidence is his own account and the copies he made in a notebook of a couple of letters written at the time. Emotionally it was a turbulent period, marked by repeated changes of place, humiliating failures to make a living, and a prevailing mood of loneliness. But the time was far from wasted. Rousseau found that he could indeed live on his own, and that he had charm and resourcefulness enough to extricate himself from each successive setback. His *Wanderjahr* would take him over much of western Switzerland and even to Paris, and it would have a happy ending, reunion at last with his beloved Mme de Warens.

Having left Merceret in Fribourg with small regret, Rousseau headed, more or less at random, for Lausanne. "I badly needed to arrive, wherever it might be, and the closer the better." Lausanne is a good forty miles from Fribourg, however, and traveling on foot, he must have been on the road for some days. Halfway there he used up the last of his money, and at a village inn he had to offer his jacket in lieu of payment. The innkeeper said he had never stripped a guest and agreed to let him come back later to pay. In this unprepossessing condition he reached Lausanne, which he claims to have chosen mainly because it commands an especially fine view of Lac Léman. A year before, when his money ran out in Turin, he had managed to find work, first with Mme de Vercellis and then with the Gouvons. This time he had no intention of being a lackey, especially in a provincial town that had none of the glamour of Turin. But he did possess a skill of sorts, or believed that he did. He had learned something about music. Musicians got paid for teaching pupils. Venture had turned up unannounced in Annecy and supported himself with music. Might he not do the same?

The first thing was to find a place to stay, which was accomplished when a kindly innkeeper named Perrotet agreed to board him cheaply and to wait to be paid. Rousseau now felt ready to write to his father, who sent on a parcel of belongings he had left in Nyon. A fragmentary letter, the first of Rousseau's that we have, also survives from this time, but it sheds little light; he wrote in injured self-defense to an unnamed cousin (not Abraham Bernard) to explain why a debt had gone unpaid.

Rousseau was so intoxicated with the idea of emulating Venture that he decided to compose an original piece of music for a concert sponsored by a local lawyer named Treytorrens. His story would be that he came from Paris, and he went so far as to give himself a new name, Vaussore de Villeneuve, using an anagram of "Rousseau" (with V for U) that echoed the name of his hero Venture de Villeneuve. The only drawback was that, unlike Venture, Vaussore knew very little about music. Nonetheless, he set confidently to work, and in two weeks had completed his piece and distributed scores to the musicians. After explaining exactly how he wanted them to interpret it, he raised his baton. A fearful cacophony burst forth, revealing his utter incompetence; the musicians amused themselves by scraping as harshly as possible, while the audience covered their ears. Sweating and all but paralyzed with embarrassment, Rousseau forced himself to keep going to the end of the piece, which completed the disaster. He had inserted an engaging minuet tune that Venture had taught him "together with the bass." (As a music historian comments, this remark shows that he was unable to compose the accompaniment for himself, as was routinely expected at the time.) He had remembered the piece because of the obscene words that went with it, and as it turned out, he wasn't the only one who knew the words. The audience exploded in laughter. "Everyone congratulated me on my taste for a song; they assured me that this minuet would make me much talked of, and that I deserved to be sung everywhere. I need not describe my anguish or admit that I well deserved it."

Given the distance in time and the studied irony of Rousseau's account in the *Confessions,* there is no way of knowing what really happened. How could everyone have been taken in until the last minute? More likely his ineptitude was obvious and the musicians went along with him as a joke. Starobinski interprets the ghastly concert as an example of magical thinking, an attempt at bypassing the normal expedients of study and practice by transforming himself into a clone of Venture. What Rousseau found inspiring in Venture was the embodiment of talent in a charismatic person, someone for whom making music was second nature and whose technical mastery seemed to have cost no labor at all. If he could absorb Venture's *mana,* then surely music would flow freely for him too. So the shy, unprepossessing, musically incompetent teenager became the Parisian composer Vaussore de Villeneuve.

Predictably, Vaussore acquired hardly any pupils, and the few who did present themselves were either stupid or malicious. "I was called into only one house, where a little snake of a girl gave herself the pleasure of showing me a lot of music of which I couldn't read a note, and then demonstrating how it should be performed." Someone wormed the secret of his identity out of him and spread it all over town, and it seems that people actually treated him sympathetically, but Rousseau was lonely and miserable. He wrote occasionally to the pretty girls of the cherry episode, but he admits that he allowed the connection to dry up.

Of Mme de Warens there was no news at all. To cheer himself up, Rousseau made a pilgrimage to the village of Vevey, where she once lived, though he didn't dare ask which house had been hers for fear of hearing something discreditable about her. Instead he indulged his ability to feel sentimental sorrow in natural settings, especially those that included water. "During this trip to Vevey, while following that beautiful shore, I gave myself to the sweetest melancholy . . . I was touched, I sighed and wept like a child. Pausing to weep at my ease, seated on a big rock, how often did I amuse myself by watching my tears fall into the water?"

In after years Rousseau made the environs of Vevey the setting for *Julie,* and, as with many other places where the unwanted, rootless youth stayed briefly, it would one day become a point of civic pride to commemorate his presence. A marble plaque on the Auberge de la Clef proclaims: JEAN-JACQUES ROUSSEAU SLEPT HERE IN 1730 and adds a quotation from the *Confessions:* "I went to Vevey and lodged at the Key . . . I acquired a love for that town that has followed me through all my travels." The inscription omits the rest of what he said: "During two days I was there without seeing anyone."

At some point that autumn, Rousseau left Lausanne and traveled north, apparently at random once again, to Neuchâtel, on the lake of that name. He knew no one there, and not only was he penniless but he still owed money to the innkeeper Perrotet, who had kept him going in Lausanne. It is hard to avoid thinking that he was marking time in the hope that his father would relent and send for him, but as Trousson remarks, there would be no fatted calf for this prodigal son. He must have been even more hopeful that Mme de Warens would invite him back, but no word came from her.

By dint of pretending to be a musician, Rousseau actually made a bit of progress. "I was gradually learning music by teaching it." He acquired some paying pupils, bought a violet suit in keeping with his new profession, and even repaid the debt to Perrotet. Still, it was a hand-to-mouth existence, and he was more than ready for a change. As he was sitting down to a frugal meal in an inn at Boudry, near Neuchâtel, an opportunity came. He overheard someone speaking in a Levantine lingua franca that nobody there could understand, he addressed the stranger in Italian, which he had learned to speak in Turin, the man embraced him joyously, and he had a new employer. This curious character called himself the Reverend Father Athanasius Paulus, of the Greek Orthodox order of Saints Peter and Paul in Jerusalem. He claimed to hold the office of archimandrite, or abbot, of his order, on whose behalf he was collecting money for the restoration of the Holy Sepulcher. His qualifications included a long beard, a purple robe, some letters patent from the czarina of Russia and the Holy Roman Emperor, and an inability to speak any northern European language. Since an Italian-speaking interpreter was just what he needed, an arrangement was easily struck: "I didn't ask for anything, and he promised a lot." The very next day this odd couple took to the road together.

Their first stop was at Fribourg, where the authorities made a modest contribution to their cause and granted them permission for a month-long stay to collect further donations. A few days later, however, the permission was withdrawn, no doubt because suspicions had arisen. Rousseau says nothing, incidentally, about seeing Merceret again in Fribourg. Next they moved on to Berne, where the young interpreter found himself involved in lengthy explanations with the representatives of the legislature. Much to his alarm, he was called upon to make a speech before the entire senate, and to his own amazement he carried it off fluently. "That was the only time in my life that I spoke in public and before a sovereign body, and it was also, perhaps, the only time I ever spoke boldly and well." As the *porte-parole* for someone else, he could speak with confidence, like a stutterer whose awkwardness vanishes when he plays a role onstage. But what Rousseau wanted above all was to be heard and known for himself, and eventually he would think deeply about the obstacles that prevented him from doing so.

The appeal for funds at Berne was more successful than at Fribourg, for the official register contains the entry, "The cashier will pay ten écus to Father Athanasius Paulus, a Greek monk who is taking up a collection for the ransom of Christian slaves." The archimandrite now began to think of heading into Germany before returning to his putative home in the east, harvesting donations along the way, and from Berne they continued northward to Soleure (Soluthurn in German). There they paid a call on the French ambassador to the Swiss Confederation, the marquis de Bonac, and this proved fatal to the fundraising scheme. The ambassador quickly exposed Rousseau's claim to be a Parisian (apparently he was still calling himself Vaussore), and as a former ambassador to Constantinople he had no difficulty unmasking the fraudulent archimandrite. Rousseau, who was always eager to pour out his heart to anyone who would listen — he may well have found the Catholic confessional congenial — freely told his whole story, and the ambassador promised to help him, giving orders meanwhile that he should have no further contact with his bearded friend. Rousseau had become rather fond of the jolly impostor, who had treated him to excellent meals along the way, but he seems not to have been much distressed when the caper ended. In fact he had to feel relief, for a distinguished French ambassador was a much more prepossessing patron than an itinerant confidence man. He also received a hint that he later remembered as prophetic: a then-famous poet named Jean-Baptiste Rousseau had once stayed in the very room he was given, and the ambassador's secretary suggested that if he worked hard on his writing, he might someday be known as Rousseau the Second. Inspired by this oracle, Rousseau tried his hand at some verses, which were not only feeble in themselves but gave no promise of ever surpassing Rousseau the First. It would be in prose, not poetry, that he would one day excel.

The dates of these events are far from clear. Probably Rousseau gave his music lessons, such as they were, in Neuchâtel during the winter of 1730–31 and encountered the archimandrite in early April. By the end of that month the archimandrite was gone and the marquis de Bonac was considering what to do with Rousseau. At some point Bishop Bernex in Annecy wrote to the ambassador on his behalf. De Bonac was willing to help, and decided to place Rousseau as tutor to a young gentleman in Paris. In the *Confessions* he remembers going directly there, but we know that in fact he returned to Neuchâtel for some weeks and endured fresh humiliations.

From this period two painful letters (or drafts of letters) survive, copied into a notebook that later came into Mme de Warens's possession. In the first, Rousseau wrote to someone in Annecy, almost certainly the spurned Esther Giraud, lamenting that he had offended Mme de Warens and begging for help in effecting a reconciliation. Word had evidently reached him that he was believed to have renounced Catholicism, for he declares, "Be assured, Mademoiselle, that my religion is deeply engraved on my heart and that nothing could efface it. I won't boast here of the constancy with which I have refused to return to my home." And it was true that he had remained loyal to the new faith; in Lausanne he would walk six miles to an outlying village in order to attend Catholic services. If his correspondent was indeed Mlle Giraud, it was hardly tactful to add that "the charming Mlle de Graffenried is still in my thoughts, and I burn with impatience for news of her. If she should still be in Annecy, do me the kindness of asking whether she would accept a letter from my hand." Rousseau concluded with a frank acknowledgment of financial distress, adding disingenuously that he hoped Mme de Warens would never hear of it, and lamented, "I don't know how to get out of here, and I don't know how to stay, since I will not do anything base."

To his father, in the letter already quoted in part, Rousseau wrote with greater abjectness and desperation: "The misfortunes that have long overwhelmed me expiate only too fully the crimes of which I feel guilty, and if it's true that my faults are enormous, my penitence surpasses them . . . Your eyes would fill with tears if you knew my true situation in full." Mentioning that he had "left here somewhat inconsiderately" — a far from explicit reference to the archimandrite escapade — he had to admit that he had lost all his pupils and was absolutely broke. But along with the pleading, there was a characteristic note of pride and superiority. "I will grovel no longer, and this trade is unworthy of me." To this he added mysteriously, "If I have several times refused a dazzling fortune it is because I value obscure liberty more than brilliant slavery." What this might have meant is impossible to say. Perhaps he had had some prospect of an advantageous marriage, or perhaps he was just trying to impress his father. It didn't work, and there is no evidence of any response to the pathetic conclusion: "My dear father, honor me with a reply in your own hand, which will be the first letter I will have received from you since I left Geneva. Give me the pleasure at least of kissing that dear handwriting, and do me the favor of making haste, for I am in a most pressing crisis."

The ambassador's proposal to go to Paris was Rousseau's only available solution, and he gratefully embraced it. Once again he traveled on foot, as he always preferred to do, politely declining whenever someone in a carriage offered him a lift. This was the longest journey he had yet undertaken, three hundred miles, and it took him two weeks. His future employer was a colonel in the Swiss Guards and his uncle Bernard was a military engineer, and since he himself hoped for an appointment as a cadet, he indulged in fantasies of heroism despite his shortsighted vision, "with myself in the midst of the fire and smoke, calmly giving orders with my spyglass in my hand." Whatever might come of the military dream, and he must have known that nothing would, he was about to achieve the goal of every French-speaking provincial of talent: entry into Paris. He had a generous gift of 100 francs from the ambassador, with a promise of more if needed, and the future seemed limitless.

The impression Paris actually made on Rousseau was not at all what he was expecting, especially by contrast with his memories of Turin. "Entering by the faubourg Saint-Marceau, I saw nothing but dirty stinking little streets, ugly dark houses, and an air of filth and poverty, with beggars, carters, menders of old clothes, and people selling herbal tea and old hats." The Saint-Marceau suburb was, in truth, notoriously grubby. Voltaire compared it in *Candide* to the nastiest villages in Westphalia. In fact the city as a whole would have been off-putting for anyone used to pleasant provincial towns. The great avenues of modern Paris were far in the future, and the narrow streets were crowded and malodorous, owing especially to a foul stench that emanated from the many cemeteries in the heart of town (in Geneva they were outside the walls). Above all, Paris was enormous. Estimates of its population, always imprecise because of inadequate record keeping in those days, ran from six hundred thousand to a million, at least thirty times as large as the Geneva of Rousseau's youth.

Far from launching a brilliant career, this first stay in Paris was short-lived and discouraging. Rousseau hastened to visit the Opéra and Versailles and found that neither came up to his romantic expectations. As for his new employer, a sour and miserly officer named Godard or

Gaudard, it turned out that what he really wanted was an unpaid valet rather than a tutor, and Rousseau had had his fill of being a valet. He had a recommendation from Soleure to a kindly lady named Mme de Merveilleux, who promised to find him some advantageous connection, but nothing came of it, and his money was running out. The only reason to linger in Paris was the hope that Mme de Warens might still be there, but when Mme de Merveilleux made inquiries it appeared that she had left some time before, perhaps for the Savoie, perhaps for Turin. Rousseau had no trouble deciding to leave. From his brief and colorless account of this period it is hard to tell how long he was in Paris, but it cannot have been more than a couple of months.

All in all, the year of wandering had been a continuing series of disappointments. Since the summer of 1730 Rousseau had lived successively in Lausanne, Neuchâtel, and Paris, none of which left him with any affection, and had seen all of his personal relationships wither away. Whatever hope he had entertained of a heartwarming reconciliation with his father was dispelled, and Mme de Warens was not only out of reach but was known to be displeased with him. He apparently made no new friends along the way. Three potential patrons took an interest in him, but the spurious archimandrite departed after a few weeks, the ambassador at Soleure was only briefly helpful, and Gaudard was mean-spirited and repulsive. Still, Rousseau had become a marginally competent musician and had proved that he could live on his own. In June 1731 he turned nineteen.

Sometime in August Rousseau was on the road again, and despite all of these disappointments, he remembered the journey as a happy one. In fact sedentary life always depressed him, and the physical rhythm of tramping along the highway felt liberating and even inspiring. Gaston Bachelard makes a comment about long-distance walking that applies remarkably well to Rousseau: "The *grands timides* are great walkers; they win symbolic victories at each step, and compensate for their timidity with every blow of the walking stick." Of this time Rousseau wrote, "Never have I thought, existed, and lived so fully, been so fully myself, if I can put it like that, than during those journeys I made alone and on foot. There is something in walking that animates and enlivens my thoughts; I can scarcely think at all when I stay in one place, my body has to be in motion if my mind is to be." As he freely admitted, these episodes were especially gratifying because they were an escape from ordinary obligations. "The remoteness of everything that makes me feel my dependence, and of everything that would recall my situation to me, all of this sets my soul free and lends great boldness to my thoughts."

What is remarkable is that the thoughts that emerged from this kind of daydreaming, "reverie" as Rousseau would later call it, gradually condensed into powerful ideas. Sitting at a desk in front of a book, he always felt confined and stupid. On the road his mind could expand. "I never foresaw that I would have ideas; they come when they please, not when it pleases me. They don't come at all, or they come in a crowd, they overwhelm me with their number and power." Above all, the unknown future opened invitingly before him, just as it did when he first put Geneva behind him. "I felt that a new paradise was waiting for me outside the door, and I thought only of going to seek it."

In Auxerre, Rousseau paused to send the ungenerous Gaudard a little satire that he had written in Paris: "So you believed, old geezer, that I was insane enough to want to educate your nephew?" In the *Confessions,* where he quotes this squib with relish, he adds piously that he lacked the hatred to be a satirist but could have been a mordant one if he had wanted. It was a modest enough revenge, but at least he got to say what he really thought. "I still laugh sometimes when I think of the grimaces he must have made when he read this panegyric that depicted him perfectly."

One other incident from this journey to Annecy stayed in Rousseau's memory. He was in no hurry to get anywhere, and often wandered off the main road to look at interesting sights. On one occasion he got hopelessly lost, became desperately hungry and thirsty, and stopped at a peasant's house to ask for something to eat and drink. The man who greeted him appeared to be living in the most abject poverty and gave him only some coarse bread and skim milk, but then, after sizing up the newcomer, he opened a trap door and brought out good bread, a ham, and a bottle of wine, to which he added a generous omelet. His explanation was that government spies were always on the lookout for evaders of the tax known as the *taille* and that he would be done for if they knew his real condition. Rousseau claims to have had no suspicion of that kind of injustice before this encounter, and declares that it inspired "that inextinguishable hatred that has grown in my heart against the vexations the unhappy populace experience, and against their oppressors." He had already encountered plenty of injustice himself, of course, but now he was beginning to see that it had a structural basis. It was not merely unkind behavior by individuals like his Geneva master Ducommun; injustice was fundamental to the way society functioned. And indeed, as late as the 1880s a historian of taxation could comment sternly, "What does all of this prove against the *taille*? Only this, that Rousseau's peasant was nothing more than a miser and bad citizen who concealed his real circumstances and feigned poverty in order to make others pay his share." It would have been hard to determine what a fair share was, since the *taille* was arbitrarily assessed and widely feared, and did not apply to noblemen or town-dwelling bourgeois.

The city of Lyon lay on the way to the Savoie, and Rousseau had a good reason for stopping there. He still had no idea where Mme de Warens was or whether she would permit his return, and in Lyon, during his brief stay with Le Maître, he had met a friend of hers named Mlle du Châtelet, who boarded as a layperson in a convent there. He sought out this lady, who knew that Mme de Warens was back in the Savoie and promised to write to her on his behalf. Although he was once again penniless, he thought it best to follow her advice and stay in Lyon for a while.

It was early September, the weather was mild, and although Rousseau had found cheap lodgings he sometimes spent the night outdoors. On one occasion a man sat down next to him, started a conversation, and after a few minutes suggested casually that they might masturbate together. There was nothing threatening about his manner, but Rousseau's deepest anxieties were aroused. In horror he leaped up, ran down to the river as fast as he could, "and didn't stop until I had passed the wooden bridge, trembling as if I had just committed a crime. I was subject to the same vice myself, but this memory cured me of it for a long time."

Another warm evening produced a still more distressing experience. A charming abbé stopped to speak with him, expressed concern that he was sleeping in the open, and offered him a place to stay. That night the abbé made overtures, but he was tactful and cautious, and after Rousseau told him about his revulsion toward the Moor in Turin, the matter proceeded no further. The next morning, however, the abbé's landlady showed obvious disgust at what she assumed had taken place, and instead of serving breakfast she and her daughters made a point of spilling water on Rousseau, pulling away the chair he was about to sit on, and jabbing a pointed heel into his foot. He could not fail to grasp what they were driving at and was relieved to get away from the abbé as soon as he could. As before, the notion of homosexuality triggered horror and disgust, and he claims that on account of this rather inconclusive experience he always regarded Lyon as the one city in Europe "where the most appalling corruption reigns."

Rousseau's happiest memories from his stay in Lyon were, characteristically, of nature and music. He particularly enjoyed a night spent by one of the rivers that enclose the city (either the Rhône or the Saône, he couldn't remember which). Thirty-five years later he recalled it in the style of poetic prose that helped to inspire all of Europe with a taste for natural description: "It had been very hot that day, and the evening was charming. The dew moistened the withered grass, there was no wind, it was a tranquil night. The air was cool without being chilly, and the setting sun had left a red haze whose reflection made the water rosy; the trees in the terraced gardens were full of nightingales calling to each other. I strolled along in a kind of ecstasy, opening up my senses and my heart to enjoying all this, only sighing a little with regret that I was enjoying it alone." He was absorbed, he says, in "a sweet reverie," a state that would become his favorite release from work, anxiety, and even conscious thought. The last book he ever wrote, unfinished at the time of his death, would be *Les Rêveries du Promeneur Solitaire,* "the reveries of the solitary walker."

The other happy memory followed soon after. Rousseau fell asleep under the trees while nightingales sang above, and awoke the next morning refreshed but ravenously hungry. Tramping cheerfully back into town, he gaily sang a cantata that he knew by heart, a musical setting of a poem by his namesake, Jean-Baptiste Rousseau. A monk named Rolichon heard him singing, questioned him about his musical knowledge, and took him home to the monastery to spend several agreeable days copying music and devouring excellent meals that were highly welcome, "for I was as skinny as a stick." It turned out that this Rolichon (about whom nothing else is known) was passionately fond of music and had an enormous collection of scores, and since Rousseau had taught himself music by laborious copying, he seemed ideally suited for the job. In fact, however, he made a mess of it, with so many omissions and mistakes that the monk had to tell him the result was completely useless. Rousseau himself ascribed his blunders to inattention, but if he really did suffer from dyslexia, the struggle to read and write accurately may actually have forced him to concentrate his mind more strenuously than other people do. Voltaire and Diderot, both brilliant students in their schooldays, could assimilate vast amounts of printed matter confidently and fast; Rousseau read and thought slowly, tenaciously, and deeply.

Rolichon cheerfully forgave the bungled copying and gave Rousseau three francs, which he badly needed. A few days after that he was overjoyed to learn that Mme de Warens had written to her friend in Lyon, wanted him to come back to her, and had even found a job for him. She also promised to send money for his traveling expenses, and while waiting for that to arrive he chatted with Mlle du Châtelet through the grill of the convent. "She was neither young nor pretty," but intelligent and well read, and she got him to read Lesage's picaresque novel *Gil Blas.* Although something of a picaresque character himself in those days, Rousseau didn't care for it much. "I needed novels with grand emotions." Indeed, on his way to Lyon from Paris he had intended to make a detour to visit the setting of Honoré d'Urfé's *Astraea,* one of the romantic novels of his boyhood, but changed his mind when he learned that it had become a locality of decidedly unromantic blacksmiths and their forges.

After several weeks in Lyon, he set out for the Savoie. The destination this time was Mme de Warens's new home in Chambéry, the provincial capital, thirty miles south of Annecy. When Rousseau reached the final range of hills before the valley in which the town lies, he took a route through a narrow gorge known as Les Échelles, or "the ladders" (he misremembered it in the *Confessions* as the Pas de l'Échelle, the name of a path on Mont Salève near Geneva). Here the ancient Romans had built a road, some of whose paving stones survive to this day, and long afterward the dukes of Savoie had improved it with stone walls against the flooding of the stream. For a modern visitor, the strongest impression is of the human labor that has shaped and civilized this rocky defile, as confirmed by an imposing monument at its entrance (it was there in Rousseau's time) boasting that nature's barriers have been overcome to make a passageway for commerce. For Rousseau it was the wildness of the scene that mattered. "Never has a flat countryside, however beautiful it may be, seemed beautiful to my eyes. I must have torrents, boulders, fir trees, dark woods, mountains, rough paths that are hard to climb and descend, and precipices alongside that make me really afraid." Standing on the masonry parapet leading up to the gorge, he dropped stones over the edge to watch them bound away, and lost himself in reverie. "Well supported on the parapet, I leaned forward and stayed like that for hours on end, glimpsing from time to time the foam and blue water whose roaring I could hear through the cries of the crows and birds of prey that flew from crag to crag and from bush to bush, a hundred fathoms below me."

The parapet is gone today because of yet another event in the long historical sequence: during the Second World War, French military engineers blew it up for fear the Germans might use it. But one can still stand where Rousseau stood, with the duke of Savoie's pompous monument at one's back, and look out over the valley below. It is a pretty scene, typical of the Alpine foothills, but the dizzying precipice, the roaring water, and the screaming birds existed mainly in Rousseau's mind; from memories of that kind he created an awe at natural grandeur that would inspire generations of nature lovers. Wordsworth was writing as an heir of Rousseau when he evoked his own experience of the Alps:

> . . . a blue chasm, a fracture in the vapour,
> A deep and gloomy breathing-place through which
> Mounted the roar of waters, torrents, streams
> Innumerable, roaring with one voice.

Soon afterward Rousseau made the final descent into Chambéry. He found his way to Mme de Warens's house, and there he experienced the long-awaited reunion, though it was a curiously impersonal one. She was not alone but had with her Don Antoine Petitti, the *intendant général,* or chief financial officer, of the Savoie. "Without speaking to me, she took me by the hand and introduced me to him with that charm that opened all hearts to her. 'Here he is, Monsieur, this poor young man,' she said; 'be so good as to patronize him as long as he deserves it, and I will have no further anxiety about him for the rest of his life.'" After this solemn speech she turned at last to Rousseau. "'My child,' she said to me, 'you belong to the king; give thanks to Monsieur the Intendant who is giving you your bread.'" The new king, Charles-Emmanuel III, intended to reform taxation and was planning a comprehensive survey of all the land and properties in the Savoie. Rousseau was to be a clerk in the office that would carry it out, and for the first time in his life he would have a respectable job. As to his relationship with Maman, what that would be remained to be seen.

6

―――――――

In Maman's House

IT IS NOT EXACTLY CLEAR why Mme de Warens had moved from Annecy to Chambéry, but it may well have had to do with her need to remain in close contact with the court on which her income depended. When Victor Amadeus abdicated in favor of his son Charles-Emmanuel, continuation of her pension was in jeopardy, and she traveled to Turin to make sure that the new king would honor the commitment. She had lived in Annecy because it was the ecclesiastical center; she moved to Chambéry because it was the political center. But as might have been predicted from the confusion of her Paris trip and the suspicions of her employers, her days as a government agent were over, though she managed to hold on to her pension.

Chambéry was an attractive town, nestled in a fertile valley surrounded by limestone peaks. Its situation reflects the traditional description of the counts of Savoie as "doorkeepers of the Alps." The town was enclosed within walls thirty feet high and had an imposing castle. A contemporary visitor declared, "It surpasses every other town in the Savoie in grandeur and beauty." With a population of ten thousand, twice the size of Annecy, it was dominated by civil servants and lawyers and had numerous tradesmen of all sorts; in 1740 there were fifty shoemakers and cobblers. And it was a busy commercial center, with markets three days a week that sold grain, wood, produce, and cattle. The

CHAMBÉRY

A view of Chambéry in the 1780s, little changed from Rousseau's time there, showing the compact town with its imposing castle at the far left, the sheer limestone ridge that rises on the far side of the valley, and fashionably dressed citizens taking their evening stroll in the hills.

streets were none too clean, with hundreds of noisy, smelly pigs living within the walls.

Above all this bustle and dirt presided a network of wealthy families who, even when they farmed rural estates, kept town houses, where they spent the winter months in a busy social round. As a particular sign of affluence these mansions had glass in their windows, while most houses still had to settle for oilpaper or turpentine-soaked cloth. In due course Rousseau would find his way into many of the mansions as a music teacher or invited guest. As Mme de Warens's dependent, he was placed well above the working class, which occupied a world of its own beneath the level of the bureaucracy and local dignitaries. During the time Rousseau was there, as we learn from other sources, a female laborer was caught stealing a pruning hook and was tied to a column in the public square. Passersby hurried to watch "as if it had been a play" and pelted her with eggs and mud until she was unrecognizable; when she was released she plunged into the river to get clean and tragically vanished forever. It is worth noting also that literacy was far from general. In 1720 only one man in five in the Savoie was able to sign his name to a marriage contract, and only one woman in ten could do so. Bizarre phonetic spelling was common, too. *"Trais cous eis demis de pismon quean eisle ceist tans nas le cheis ele le 13 ceittansbre,"* wrote the wife of a leading citizen ("Trois sous et demi de Piémont quand elle s'est en allée chez elle le 13 septembre").

The one disappointment for Rousseau was Mme de Warens's new home, which still exists today at 13 rue de Boigne. Even the grandest town houses in Chambéry were forbidding from the outside, presenting blank façades to the street; one entered through narrow passageways that opened into murky courtyards. To gain the favor of a treasury official who had hitherto been hostile to her, Mme de Warens shrewdly rented from him a house so unappealing that it had been standing empty. Whatever its usefulness in securing her financial situation, it was sadly unlike the house in Annecy. "No more garden, no more brook, no more countryside. The house she occupied was dark and gloomy, and my room was the darkest and gloomiest of all. A wall for a view, a cul-de-sac for a street, not much air, not much light, not much space, crickets, rats, rotten planks; this did not make for a pleasant home."

All the same, Rousseau reveled in being at last *"chez moi,* that is to say, *chez* Maman."* And it was a relief to discover that his desperate infatuation had abated. When he looked back later at the changing relationship, he saw it as taking the form, familiar in French literature, of a distinction between happiness and pleasure. Pleasure is intense but short-lived; happiness is milder but more enduring. "In Annecy I was intoxicated, in Chambéry I no longer was. I still loved her as passionately as possible, but I loved her more for herself and less for me, or at least I sought my happiness more than my pleasure with her." She began to take an interest in his talents and development, and he felt increasingly secure. One of the older Rousseau scholars spoke accurately, if sentimentally, when he referred to this period as "the fertile years when maternal wings incubated an unknown genius."

A somewhat less romantic impression of the relationship was recorded many years later by François-Joseph de Conzié, a cultivated aristocrat five years older than Rousseau whose aunt was mother superior of the Annecy convent in which Mme de Warens had received instruction as a convert. After the publication of the *Confessions* had made her widely known, Conzié wrote down a description that confirms her charm and also her increasing girth.

> She was of middle height, but not in a favorable sense, inasmuch as she was extremely stout, which rounded her shoulders somewhat and made her alabaster bosom rather bulky, but she easily made you forget these defects with her expression of frankness and engaging gaiety. Her laugh was charming, her coloring was of lily and rose, and the vivacity of her eyes expressed the liveliness of her mind and gave uncommon energy to everything she said. Without the slightest pretentiousness — far from it — everything about her breathed sincerity, humaneness, and kindness. There was not the least suspicion of wanting to seduce by her wit any more than by her looks, which indeed she neglected too much.

As for young Rousseau, he struck Conzié as humbly subservient. "I went to her house every day and often dined there with Jean-Jacques, whose education she had already undertaken, behaving toward him like a tender and benevolent mother, mingled from time to time with the attitude of a patron, to which Jean-Jacques always responded with docility and even submission." Although Conzié liked Rousseau, he formed a critical view of his temperament. "As I saw him daily and he talked freely with me, I have no doubt as to his decided taste for solitude, and, I may say, his innate disdain for men [*hommes,* people in general], with a fixed tendency to condemn their faults and weaknesses. He nursed inwardly a constant mistrust of their integrity."

The ménage in which Rousseau was finding his place was a complicated one. Even if he failed to grasp that Claude Anet was secretly Mme de Warens's lover, there was no ignoring his importance in the household. Anet was just six years older than Rousseau, and after a two-year apprenticeship with a cabinetmaker had been living with Mme de Warens as her confidant and manager. Rousseau fell easily into regarding Anet as an older brother or even a father. "Although he was as young as she was, he was so mature and serious that he regarded us almost as two children who needed indulgence." This perception of the ménage effectively desexualizes it, but Anet was suspicious of the young interloper and kept him under constant surveillance. "I didn't dare forget myself in front of him . . . I didn't dare to do anything that he might seem to disapprove." One alarming incident, however, could hardly be ignored. Not long after Rousseau arrived, Anet and Mme de Warens had a quarrel, after which Anet swallowed enough laudanum to kill himself. Mme de Warens found out in time to make him vomit it up, but in the scramble to revive him, she confessed the true nature of the relationship to Rousseau. Surprisingly, he never connected Anet's suicide attempt with his own arrival.

Rousseau was no longer free to spend his days at home, for he had an office job to report to and an obligation to deserve the patronage Mme de Warens had secured for him. He was employed in the *cadastre,* the land registry, which was no sleepy bureaucratic department but part of a concerted effort by monarchs throughout Europe to ascertain landowners' income in order to regularize and increase taxation. The previous king, Victor Amadeus, had already instituted a registry in his Piedmont territories, and in 1728 the program was extended to the Savoie. The establishment of the Chambéry *cadastre,* with a work force of some two hundred surveyors and clerks, was immediately recognized there as an aggressive action, invading fiscal privileges that the nobility and clergy had long enjoyed. In its very first year there was a scandal when the windows of a corrupt police chief from Turin were broken by gunshots in the night. During the inquiry that followed, the leading families of Chambéry took every opportunity to undermine one another, revealing the less attractive side of what one writer calls "the closed field of a narrow, jealous, and secretive provincial life."

The survey work was not without incidental rewards. One duty of the bureau was to produce superb colored maps, and through friends who worked in that department Rousseau developed a taste for watercolors and began painting flowers and landscapes. His own job, however, was entirely clerical and computational. With his haphazard education, he lacked the necessary skill in arithmetic, so he bought some textbooks and had no difficulty learning what he needed. As with everything, he had to do it for himself, not at a teacher's direction, and he discovered a good deal about himself in the process. "Reflection joined with practice produces clear ideas, and one then invents shortcuts that flatter one's self-esteem. The accuracy gratifies the mind, and it helps one to carry out with pleasure a task that is unrewarding in itself." With his tendency to romantic daydreaming and emotional flights, Rousseau found it reassuring that he could master a systematic discipline if he had to.

Still, there was no denying that the job, laboriously recording each of the properties in the remote district of Sainte-Foy-en-Tarentaise, was stupefyingly repetitive. "Occupied eight hours a day doing disagreeable work with still more disagreeable people, imprisoned in a gloomy office that stank with the bad breath and sweat of all those boors, most of them unkempt and dirty, I sometimes felt overwhelmed to the point of vertigo by the strain, the smell, the constraint, and the boredom." Rousseau had never held any employment for long. After eight months at the *cadastre,* a much briefer period than the two years he later remembered it as being, he was ready to hand in his resignation. Undoubtedly it did feel like two years. To those who knew him, and especially to Mme de Warens, it looked as if he was incapable of holding a job. To Rousseau himself it felt very different. A deep impulse urged him to escape from every commitment that might lead to a conventional career. He didn't yet know what he wanted, but he knew very well what he didn't want. Only in middle age would he fully grasp that externally imposed obligations of every kind were hateful to him. A profound idleness — not the same thing as laziness — was his true disposition, and "the smallest duties of social life are intolerable to it; a word to be spoken, a letter to write, a visit to make, are tortures for me as soon as they become necessary." Putting it in more positive terms, as he did at the end of his life, "in everything imaginable, it quickly becomes impossible for me to do anything I can't do with pleasure."

The psychobiographer Erik Erikson writes about the tendency of geniuses to begin with conventional career expectations but then to drop out in a temporary "moratorium" that baffles their friends. Rousseau is an extreme case, since his life to that point was one long moratorium and would remain so for another decade. Looking back over the time at Chambéry, which extended with one interruption from 1731 to 1742, he was struck by a surprising sameness from year to year. "I will have few events to relate, since my life was as simple as it was sweet, and this uniformity was exactly what I most needed to finish forming my character, which continual troubles had prevented from acquiring a fixed form." The paucity of memorable events was real enough, but the uniformity and sweetness were a retrospective ideal. It was indeed a crucial time in Rousseau's development, but it was marked by complex relationships and painful anxieties. And if he wanted to believe, in the conventional terms of the day, that he was establishing a fixed and predictable character, his deepest intuitions suggested something very different. What the *Confessions* seek to reveal, with their emphasis on intense and confusing emotional episodes, is an elusive core of self that underlies apparent contradictions and can never be fixed and predictable. The concept of personality in its modern sense did not yet exist, but Rousseau, more perhaps than any other thinker, would prepare the way for its invention.

If he was to leave the *cadastre,* Rousseau would have to find a new source of income; he proposed to be a musician. Mme de Warens was far from enthusiastic, reminding him of the proverb *Qui bien chante et bien danse fait un métier qui peu avance,* "One with skill at song and dance pursues a trade that won't advance." In reply he pointed out that his current job would have to end when the survey was finished, that he needed to develop a skill to live by, and that music was his consuming passion. This she could see for herself. Indeed, he was devoting so much time to it that she feared he would get fired in any case. So she reluctantly agreed, and in June 1732, shortly before his twentieth birthday, he was again unemployed and a full-time presence in the house. But for once his plan was not just a fantasy, for he was well on the way to making himself a real musician, and music would always remain at the center of his life. In his last years he told a friend that it was as necessary to him as bread.

At this point, apparently, Mme de Warens made yet another effort to get Rousseau to move on. He was sent to Besançon to study with the choir director there, the abbé Blanchard, who had once taught Venture de Villeneuve. Blanchard received him warmly and complimented him on his singing, but it soon emerged that the cathedral chapter had reprimanded him for absences and misconduct and that he was about to depart for Paris. Rousseau wrote to Mme de Warens to outline his options. He could go to Paris with Blanchard or, alternatively, he could try to make contact with the marquis de Bonac, who had been helpful to him when he left the archimandrite in Soleure. What he did not want was to stay in Besançon after Blanchard left, and he proposed instead to return home and support himself as a music teacher, trusting that he had skills enough to do better than he had in Neuchâtel. "I have decided, therefore, to return in a few days to Chambéry, where I will enjoy teaching for a period of two years; this will help me to continue to improve. I don't want to stop at this point and pass for a simple musician, which would one day do me considerable harm. Be so good as to write to me, Madame, to say whether I will be well received, and whether I will get any pupils." The letter is signed with scrupulous formality: "I await, Madame, with submission, the honor of your command, and I am, Madame, with respectful esteem, J.-J. Rousseau." In writing to Mme de Warens, and very possibly in conversation as well, he always used the formal *vous* and not the familiar *tu*.

So Rousseau returned to Chambéry and devoted himself to his art. He pored over challenging works of music theory by the great Jean Philippe Rameau, whom years later he would meet in Paris, and he committed half a dozen cantatas to memory; when he wrote the *Confessions* he remarked that he still knew almost every note of a couple of them, "Sleeping Loves" and "Love Stung by a Bee." Best of all, he was among congenial friends who knew how to enjoy the pleasures of life even if they were men of the church. Historians tell us that a lot of wine was drunk on social occasions in Chambéry, where it was remarked that "one hardly knows how to have a good time without a bottle of wine in one's hand," and a bishop estimated that the per capita consumption was at least two liters per day.

Rousseau soon became friendly with an Italian harpischordist, the abbé Palais (the name is a gallicized version of Palazzo), who stimulated his interest in harmony, and the two of them encouraged Mme de Warens to host a monthly concert at which Rousseau would act as conductor. She herself played the harpsichord and sang. The cellist was another Italian named Canevas or Canavazzo, one of the many Piedmontese who got jobs in the *cadastre* when its survey work began. Another musician was an intelligent monk, rather worldly and very entertaining, named Philibert Caton. Caton's fate was distressing. His colleagues resented his position in society, accused him falsely of financial misconduct, and got him ejected from his position as head of a monastery, "and after having been the delight of the most agreeable social circles, he died of grief on a mean bed, at the bottom of some cell or dungeon, missed and lamented by all the honorable people who had known him, and who found no other fault in him than being a monk." It used to be thought that Rousseau invented this tale out of anticlerical spite, but research has shown that Caton was indeed forced out of his position by a pair of scheming rivals, one of whom later accused the other of having "persecuted the late Father Caton and hounded him to his grave."

For Rousseau it was a heady time. After years of being a lonely outsider, he was now accepted into a delightful social milieu. "There I was, thrown all at once into the midst of the *beau monde,* sought after in the best houses, and received everywhere with a gracious and flattering welcome. Well-dressed and agreeable young ladies waited for me and received me eagerly, I saw only charming objects, and I smelled nothing but roses and orange blossoms. We sang, chatted, laughed, and amused ourselves, and I left one place only in order to go to another and do the same things there." Years later he remembered the Savoyards as "the best and most sociable people I know," and Chambéry as the best of all possible towns. "If there is a little city in the world where one can enjoy the sweetness of life in an agreeable and secure society, it is Chambéry." When he wrote that, to be sure, he had been successively rejected by the French, the Genevans, and the Swiss, and was in the process of becoming disillusioned with the English.

Almost every one of Rousseau's pupils struck him as appealing and pretty, so he found himself losing his heart all over town. A young Frenchwoman in a convent seemed lazy and dull at first but turned out to possess a risqué wit. Another girl, a lively brunette of fifteen, unnerved him by receiving him *en déshabillé,* with her hair loosely done up and a flower put in for his benefit. An older unmarried woman ("with impossible names," Trousson remarks), Gasparde-Balthazarde de Challes, was more amply endowed and very good-natured, and her sister, "the most beautiful woman in Chambéry," had an eight-year-old niece who needed lessons. It was probably to this child's mother that Rousseau wrote with elaborate courtesy to say that through some misunderstanding he had not been paid for sixteen lessons, "but if you still see any difficulties after this explanation, I willingly renounce this little sum." Yet another pupil, Françoise Sophie de Menthon, only fourteen, was an ash-blonde, the type that appealed to Rousseau most, and she had a scar on her breast "that sometimes attracted my attention, and soon not just for the scar." Her mother, however, was a waspishly witty countess who encouraged her admirers to write libels that sometimes landed them in jail, and Rousseau was fortunate not to attract her interest. She did furnish a pleasing scene on one social occasion when she pulled off Mme de Warens's scarf in order to expose a rat-shaped birthmark on her bosom that a joker had claimed was there. "But instead of the big rat, the gentleman saw only a very different object that was no easier to forget than it had been to reveal, which didn't at all accomplish the countess's intention."

Chambéry was virtually a harem for Jean-Jacques, or would have been if he had been able to act on his desires. In *Julie* the young tutor becomes the lover of his pupil; in Chambéry the young music teacher came and went in a pleasant haze of flirtation and innuendo, without ever going any further. But Mme de Warens regarded the whole business with uneasiness, especially when he began to give lessons to a grocer's daughter named Péronne Lard, "the very model for a Greek statue, and I could call her the most beautiful girl I ever saw if there could be true beauty without life or soul. Her indolence, coldness, and insensibility were unbelievable." The problem was not Mlle Lard but her mother, who had a face marked by smallpox and perpetually reddened eyes, but was extremely forthcoming and always greeted Rousseau with a kiss on the mouth. He duly reported her advances to Mme de Warens, who concluded that Mme Lard "would make it a point of honor to leave me less stupid than she found me, and would find one way or another of making herself understood."

Mme de Warens then arrived at a startling decision. She and Rousseau had been in the habit of strolling in a garden she had rented outside the town. In the fall of 1732 she arranged for them to spend an entire day there undisturbed. It soon became clear that she was carefully outlining the conditions under which she would give herself to him, and she proposed giving him a week to think it over, for which he was grateful. "The novelty of these ideas had struck me so, and I felt such an upheaval in my own ideas, that I needed time to deal with them." At any rate, that was how he remembered it thirty years later, but one may well wonder what the encounter was actually like. Mme de Warens's stipulations probably concerned the triangular relationship with Claude Anet, whose outward calm masked a volatile temperament and who was bound to be jealous. She must also have been concerned to ensure secrecy, since if Rousseau did get involved with other women in town he might betray details of her private life that would ruin her standing with the church. And as he himself acknowledged, "she always believed that nothing attached a man to a woman so firmly as possession." But it seems improbable that she planned to give him a week to think it over when she staged this secluded tryst in the garden, which conveniently contained a little summerhouse with a bed in it. More likely her overtures were met with such alarm that she backed off and gave her reluctant swain time to collect himself.

The week passed and the promised event arrived, but it was far from unconflicted. "For the first time I saw myself in the arms of a woman, and a woman I adored. Was I happy? No, I tasted pleasure, but I know not what invincible sadness poisoned its charm. I felt as if I had committed incest. Two or three times, pressing her with rapture in my arms, I flooded her bosom with my tears." This was his surrogate Maman, and he was greatly rattled by the turn the relationship had taken. Moreover, his ideal of womanhood entailed a purity that excluded sexuality, and he was not prepared to see Mme de Warens in this new light. It was surely for this reason that he always insisted she had no erotic feelings toward him or anyone else, and slept with him solely to protect him from misbehaving with other women. He also laid stress on her story that early in her marriage a certain M. de Tavel had seduced her not with passion but with specious arguments.

The nature and significance of this newly sexual relationship has attracted endless commentary, all of it hampered by the fact that we have no evidence except what Rousseau himself has given us. Accordingly, it has become something of a Rorschach picture onto which critics have been free to project their own values. A French writer at the beginning of the last century considered it an ideal love story, in which a promising lad meets an intelligent and beautiful woman who initiates him into mysterious delights. "What a dream, what a destiny, what felicity! This was the lot of Jean-Jacques." The English have been less approving. Cranston says grudgingly that Mme de Warens "was totally without the instincts of a harlot," while another writer suggests that she was "a sexually promiscuous and frigid woman who took a certain perverse pleasure in seducing an innocent youth." Rousseau may have been innocent in the sense that he was inexperienced, but his imagination was a riot of erotic longings, and there is no reason to credit his insistence that "since she wasn't very sensual and never sought sexual pleasure at all, she didn't experience its delights and never had the remorse." This claim has often been taken at face value, but Olivier Marty is surely right to say, "One can well believe that there were few delights with Rousseau. Did he never ask himself whether Mme de Warens really expected nothing for herself when she invited a lad of twenty into her bed?"

It is far from clear how often they slept together in the years that followed, but at any rate Rousseau never felt easy about it. "With Maman my pleasure was always disturbed by a feeling of sadness, by a secret clenching of the heart that I could overcome only with difficulty, and instead of congratulating myself on possessing her, I reproached myself for defiling her." In this her equableness was actually a drawback. He retained his Calvinist anxieties about sex, and if Maman was spared the remorse, that meant he got a double share of it. Things might have gone better if she had behaved passionately and overwhelmed his inhibitions, but by offering herself so coolly she made him feel that he was degrading a madonna who should never have descended from her pedestal. Earlier, kissing the bed she had slept in, he could enjoy her in imagination without the complexities of real experience, but now he was trapped in an ambiguous situation from which he longed to escape.

Again it was imagination that came to the rescue; Rousseau fantasized about other women while he was in bed with Mme de Warens. "The need for love devoured me in the midst of gratification. I had a tender mother, a dear friend, but I needed a mistress; I imagined one in her place . . . If I had believed I was holding Maman in my arms, my embraces would have been no less lively, but all of my desire would have been extinguished." Rather sadly he adds, "Ah, if a single time in my life I had ever tasted all the delights of love in their fullness, I doubt that my frail existence could have stood it; I would have died in the act." What he needed was to be loved passionately and romantically, and instead he was loved mildly and affectionately. Having taken the place of the mother he never knew, Mme de Warens fell far short of being the ideal lover he might never find.

Meanwhile the triangular relationship continued to generate more tension than Rousseau later cared to remember. "I don't know whether Claude Anet was aware of our intimacy. I have reason to believe it was not concealed from him. He was a very perceptive fellow, but very discreet, who never said what he didn't think, but didn't always say what he did think. Without giving me the slightest indication that he knew, he acted as if he did." In short the awkwardness was obvious, although Mme de Warens did her best to allay it by telling both men how much she loved them, and by promoting sentimental scenes of harmony. "How many times did she touch our hearts and make us embrace in tears, by telling us how necessary we both were to her happiness!"

The situation wasn't made any easier by an ever more extravagant series of moneymaking schemes. Anet, the gardener's nephew, was devoted to botany and had already made himself indispensable in the concoction of herbal remedies. A new opportunity seemed to present itself when the chief doctor of the Savoie, François Grossy, moved to Chambéry. Though sarcastic and irritable, Grossy took to Anet, and Mme de Warens conceived the idea that a college of pharmacy should be established with Grossy as its patron and Anet as its lecturer. But the project was derailed by a tragic event. As Rousseau understood it, in March 1734 Grossy sent Anet up into the high Alps to find a rare plant called *génipi* that grew only there, and the exertion and cold somehow caused him to succumb to pleurisy. Despite the best efforts of Grossy and Mme de Warens, "on the fifth day he died in our arms after suffering the cruelest agony." Rousseau adds rather complacently, "During that time he had no religious exhortations except my own, and I lavished them on him with such grief and zeal that if he was in a condition to understand me, they must have been some consolation for him."

Unfortunately for the story of the fatal search for *génipi,* in March the mountains would have been deep in snow, and scholars have surmised that Anet's death was in fact a suicide. As Clément points out, it is easy to imagine that Mme de Warens was bitterly aware of her own guilt in Anet's death and invented the story of the mountain expedition to forestall suspicion. Rousseau knew almost nothing of botany at the time, so he may well have believed it, but it does seem astonishing that he never called to mind Anet's suicide attempt the previous year. Not only that, he was so tactless as to ask for the distinguished black suit that

Anet had often worn. He must have felt that by donning Anet's clothes he could take over his role — Vaussore all over again — but Mme de Warens's torrent of tears put an end to that idea.

Throughout his life Rousseau claimed to be utterly unacquainted with jealousy and, strangely, he has been taken at his word. It seems far more likely that he was deeply jealous of Anet but didn't allow himself to admit it, and that just as with his father, he painted a highly idealized picture of the relationship. One curious incident in *Julie,* written a quarter of a century later, does suggest an impulse toward revenge. The hero, Saint-Preux, performs an act of generosity toward a young man who is betrothed to Julie's former servant and who, remarkably, bears the name "Claude Anet." In thus patronizing the fictional Anet, Saint-Preux exhibits his own virtue by obeying Julie's command, even though it means losing a rare opportunity for a sexual encounter with her, and she congratulates him on his noble sacrifice. Rousseau's revenge is completed when the servant girl reappears later on and reports that Anet has gone bad, neglecting his work and abandoning her and her child.

Not much else can be reliably dated from these years, except for the occasional brief intrusion of events from the outside world. Such an occasion was the appearance in Chambéry of a French army in 1733, in consequence of the War of the Polish Succession. The army was on its way to Italy, where it hoped to defeat the forces of the Holy Roman Empire and deliver the territory of Milan to the king of Sardinia. Rousseau, always impressionable, was temporarily intoxicated with martial glory and devoured books of military history, and he even claimed that his lifelong partiality to France was due to this encounter. Also, in a document from that year he mentions having written to his father about a portion of his mother's inheritance that he hoped to recover. The letter itself is lost, but we have his description of his father's response as a true gasconade or bluster, "all the worse because it's me he does it to, *c'est bien moi qu'il gasconne.*" At the time he was staying at a monastery in Cluses, in the Arve valley, east of Annecy, where a hospitable priest was treating him with a milk cure — bathing in milk and drinking lots of it — for an acute inflammation of some kind. He seems to have enjoyed the stay, remarking happily, "The reverend father has told me firmly that I mustn't leave until it pleases him, and that I will be well and truly lactified."

Only a month after Claude Anet's death, Mme de Warens had another upsetting loss. Her friend and patron Bishop Bernex died, and she was deeply affected, although Rousseau certainly exaggerated when he later wrote in a testimonial to Bernex's piety, "After the death of this prelate, Mme de Warens devoted herself entirely to solitude and retirement, saying that after having lost her father, there was nothing left to attach her to this world." More immediately, the bishop's death was a serious blow to her financial condition, since her pension from the church now dried up, just when she was suffering exasperating delays in the payment of her pension from the king. In this emergency an attempt was made to enlist Rousseau as Anet's successor in household management, and a notebook still exists that the two of them filled with laborious calculations. But although he was alarmed at the financial hemorrhaging, he totally lacked Anet's discipline and authority, and he could think of nothing better to do than to hide small sums where Mme de Warens wouldn't find them. It was with a sense of relief that he occasionally got away, commissioned to carry out various little negotiations in Lyon and Besançon. Meanwhile Mme de Warens tried to get legal rights to some of her husband's property in Lausanne, but not surprisingly she failed. On top of it all, she had an unspecified illness so serious that she was moved to make her will (it has not survived). Happily, however, the king responded favorably to her pleas, and the pension was paid; at the end of the year she wrote to him in suitably fervent language: "I ardently pray, Sire, that heaven will continue to bestow its precious benedictions on your majesty and on your victorious arms."

The next year, 1735, seems to have been more cheerful, and for the first time we have a fair amount of documentary evidence apart from the *Confessions*. But this only serves to confirm that our knowledge of Rousseau's early life is much more fragmentary than it might seem. He wrote the *Confessions* with a novelist's skill, and he told his story so compellingly that one is seldom provoked to wonder what he left out. But whenever evidence does exist, it hints at incidents that are otherwise entirely invisible. There are drafts of three letters to Isaac Rousseau in a notebook, with plenty of crossings-out and revisions, referring obscurely to errors that ought to be pardoned, to "this aberration," and to some new step Jean-Jacques had taken. Whatever that step was, it must have occasioned concern, since he quickly adds that the trip he took was only a short one and that he had written to Mme de Warens before leaving "to forestall any anxiety on her part." Some have guessed that an otherwise unaccounted-for visit to Besançon may have been involved, during which Rousseau's trunk was confiscated because the customs officers found a satire in it that someone had given him and claimed that he was under suspicion of spreading irreligion in France, which was a crime. In this letter Rousseau also thanks his father for having finally, after long delay, written a reply to Mme de Warens.

> For six months, what else have I asked of you than to show a little appreciation for Mme de Warens's many favors, for the benefits her goodness constantly heaps upon me? But what have you done? Instead of this, you have neglected the first duty of politeness and propriety toward her. If you're doing it solely to upset me, you're infinitely in the wrong. You are dealing with a lady who is kind in a thousand ways and deserving of respect for a thousand virtues, and who is not of a rank or situation to be despised. I have always observed that whenever she has had the honor to write to the greatest lords of the court, and even to the king, her letters were answered with perfect punctuality.

From this reproof one might infer not just that Isaac resented Mme de Warens's proselytizing for Catholicism, but that her dubious sexual reputation was known in the region where he lived. It was less than ten years since she had fled from her husband in Vevey, thirty miles from Nyon; Isaac probably had suspicions about her relationship with his son and had made inquiries about her. It seems likely also that there were rumors in Chambéry itself, though her social standing and connections in the church kept them from damaging her privileged position. Some years later Rousseau wrote an indignant letter to a lady who had apparently made facetious references to Mme de Warens's behavior. The letter is mostly about a quarrel over money, but Rousseau's equivocal relationship with his patron must also have been in question, because he defends her virtue indignantly and also makes a point of describing her as his godmother, which she was not. "Since she has nothing to hide in her conduct, she has nothing to fear from the talk of her enemies . . . A large number of persons of merit and distinction know that I have the honor to be the godson of Mme de Warens, who has had the kindness to bring me up and to inspire in me feelings of uprightness and probity that are worthy of her." Similarly, her friend Conzié protested too much when he said, "This baroness, doubtless finding the town of Annecy too small for her projects and ideas, came to settle in Chambéry, but this was not in order to elude the vigilance of her pious instructors, for her conduct until then had always been exempt from all suspicion, free even from the calumny that commonly pursues newcomers who are intelligent and good-looking." When Conzié called her conduct free from suspicion "until then," he surely implied that attitudes changed later on.

In a third letter to his father, Rousseau acknowledges, in response to continued promptings, that it is high time for him to find a profession or trade, but he then reviews rather somberly the possibilities that seem available. The church and the law are out, for lack of money to pay for training, and so is commerce, for which some capital would be necessary. For that matter, even the humbler trades require an expensive apprenticeship, and it is now too late for that. "It's true that I know something of the engraver's trade, but leaving aside that it was never to my taste, it's certain that I didn't learn enough to be able to support myself, and no master would take me on without being paid." As he sees it, only three realistic courses are open to him. One is to continue to teach music, for which there is plenty of demand and not much competition in provincial towns. Another is to become a secretary to some eminent person, employing the gift for writing well that he has discovered he possesses. And the third is to take a job as *gouverneur* or tutor to a young gentleman. Rousseau did in fact try his hand at all three means of livelihood in the years to come, but the real path to the future lay in a direction that he may already have begun to guess. "I have undertaken a system of study that I have divided under two principal headings: the first, everything that serves to enlighten the mind and fill it with useful and agreeable knowledge; the second, methods for training the heart in wisdom and virtue. Mme de Warens has had the goodness to furnish me with books, and I've tried to make as much progress as possible, and to dispose my time in such a way that nothing will be without its use." He began to order books of his own, ranging from mathematics to Latin classics, and he took out a subscription to the *Mercure de France,* which expanded his awareness of contemporary books and ideas.

The remark about wisdom and virtue was not just a routine platitude. Rousseau was interested in philosophy, but he also took religion seriously, in the relaxed and tolerant form that Mme de Warens espoused. Her family's mentor in Vevey had been the pietist pastor and mystic François Magny, and her aunts had been called before the local consistory to explain their unorthodox views, which emphasized the inner spirit and tended to ignore the Calvinist preoccupation with predestination and sin. An eighteenth-century Genevan liturgy still required believers to declare "that we are miserable sinners, born in corruption, inclined to evil, incapable by ourselves of doing good." Mme de Warens's formal statement when she embraced Catholicism was much more optimistic: "I avow that Our Lord has given his church the power to absolve sins, however enormous they may be, and to grant indulgences whose use is very salutary for Christians." In her permissive understanding of religion, very much as in the views of the abbés Gaime and Gâtier, Rousseau found relief from the rigid teachings of his boyhood, in which nature was vile, human impulses were usually sinful, and willpower must rigorously dominate feeling.

Embracing this new attitude enthusiastically, Rousseau read Saint François de Sales and became, as he later said, "devout almost in the manner of Fénelon." Fénelon he already admired as the author of *Telemachus,* a high-minded narrative of virtue and moral integrity; François de Sales, who had been bishop of Geneva in exile in Annecy, taught that direct intuition of the divine is preferable to conscious thought. As Starobinski observes, in a secularized form this belief would undergird Rousseau's idealized picture of human happiness. And whereas Enlightenment thinkers like Voltaire and Diderot identified religion with an oppressive institutional church, Rousseau saw it as inner experience. Eventually he would reject most of the dogmas of orthodox religion, but the boy who played at being a preacher in Geneva survived in the man who would lecture the world on personal authenticity and social justice. It seems appropriate that in after years the street in front of the seminary in Annecy was sometimes named for Saint François de Sales and sometimes for Rousseau, depending on the preferences of the time.

Life at Chambéry seemed to be settling into a routine, agreeable enough from day to day but giving little indication of progress in any particular direction. "I passed two or three years like this between music, medical potions, projects, and journeys, drifting endlessly from one thing to another, trying to settle on something without knowing what, but gradually drawn toward study, seeing literary people, hearing them talk about literature, sometimes joining in the talk myself, and picking up the jargon of books more than any knowledge of their contents." Mme de Warens's friend Conzié was a great fan of Voltaire, and Rousseau eagerly read the master's works with him, striving to imitate his elegance of style. Various other people broadened Rousseau's experience. He made the acquaintance of Jean-Vincent Gauffecourt, a Geneva watchmaker's son like himself but a generation older, whose unaffected friendliness was irresistible. "No matter how reserved one might be, from the first sight one couldn't help being as familiar with him as if one had known him for twenty years, and I, who found it so hard to be at my ease with new faces, was like that with him from the very start." They remained friends for life. A very different character was an ugly and insinuating parasite named Gabriel Bagueret, who wanted to ingratiate himself with Mme de Warens's favorite in order to get access to her purse and who taught Rousseau to play chess. He may not have realized that Bagueret, an accomplished rascal who had been in trouble with the law in numerous countries, was some sort of secret agent for the king and had probably made contact with Mme de Warens in that capacity. But Rousseau discovered that he loved chess, and for some months he was completely obsessed with it. He had a real talent for the game, but he could play well only if he relied on intuition and not memory. Laborious attempts to memorize openings and combinations got him nowhere.

Still less successful were Mme de Warens's attempts to provide Rousseau with the skills of a gentleman. There were dancing lessons, but he could never learn not to tramp on his heels; there were fencing lessons, but after months of practice the instructor could still knock the foil out of his hand whenever he felt like it. Even in music he was aware that his progress was slow. By now he had quite a solid grasp of the fundamentals, but because he could never learn to sight-read with ease, more accomplished musicians were always skeptical of his abilities. On one occasion a visiting young marquis contrived to test his knowledge and was kind enough to acknowledge that he passed the test, but on another occasion he was given no part in a public concert because he was thought unequal to the challenge.

Marking time in this way, failing conspicuously to fill Anet's managerial role, and well aware that Mme de Warens was exasperated by his fecklessness, Rousseau took refuge in illness. His symptoms were feverishness and chest pains, which may have had an organic cause but probably had a psychosomatic component too. "Feeling myself growing weaker, I became more tranquil and lost something of my passion for traveling. As I became more sedentary I was overtaken not by boredom but by melancholy; vapors took the place of passions, my languor turned into sadness; I wept and sighed at nothing, I felt my life slipping away without ever having tasted it . . . In the end I fell completely ill." In the eighteenth century, "melancholy" and its attendant "vapors" indicated serious emotional disturbance, which today would be known as depression. It is interesting that Mme de Warens herself complained constantly of ill health and often visited spas in search of relief; the pharmacopoeia of herbal remedies she produced may well have been intended first of all for her own use.

By adopting the role of a childlike invalid, Rousseau found a way to justify his passivity and to encourage Mme de Warens to be his Maman again. The strategy succeeded. She nursed him tenderly, she talked and wept with him, and it seemed that "I became completely her work, completely her child, and more so than if she had been my real mother." In a sense it was true. She was a voluntary mother, a mother who chose him when she didn't have to, with whom he had joined himself at just the stage when he would have been separating emotionally from a birth mother. And now as an invalid he could enjoy spiritual closeness relieved of erotic anxiety, "not the possession of love, but a more essential kind that did not depend on the senses, on sex, on age, or on appearance, but rather on everything by which one is oneself, and which one can lose only by ceasing to be." But however concerned Mme de Warens may have been about Rousseau's health, it seems highly unlikely that she felt the unqualified commitment that he did, or that she would have approved of what he wrote to his father from Besançon: "I intend to beg Mme de Warens to be so kind as to allow me to pass the rest of my days with her, and that until the end of my life I may render her all the service that lies in my power."

As Rousseau's health began to improve, she prescribed a milk cure such as he had previously undergone in the valley of the Arve. For this a stay in the country would be beneficial, especially since the cramped and gloomy house in Chambéry was getting both of them down. They had given up renting the little garden, partly to save money and partly because plants had lost their appeal after Anet's death, so it was necessary to look elsewhere for a rural retreat. Soon Mme de Warens engaged a charming house in the hills just outside of town, easily reached on foot "but as isolated and solitary as if it had been a hundred leagues away." The little valley in which it lay was known as Les Charmettes.

7

The Idyll of Les Charmettes

THE HANDSOME STONE HOUSE at Les Charmettes — the name derives from a forest of hornbeams, or *charmes,* rather than from any seductive qualities of the site — is one of the few dwellings Rousseau lived in that can still be visited. Today it is maintained as a museum in his honor, and a visitor can see the little alcove bed he is supposed to have used, Mme de Warens's grander bedroom, and an altar next to it where a priest would sometimes come to say mass. A lease survives that Mme de Warens signed on July 6, 1738, with a Captain Noëray, who owned the house and land, but she had already made an oral agreement to use the house during the summer season, which she did in 1735 and again in 1736. In those years a certain Jean Girod held the lease for the farm, which produced modest quantities of wheat, rye, barley, broad beans, and buckwheat. For livestock there were two oxen, two cows, two heifers, ten sheep, and a dozen fowl. Girod inhabited a barnlike structure, while Mme de Warens had the furnished house. In 1737, inspired by the idea of doing some farming herself, she briefly rented another farm nearby, but in 1738 Girod quit and she was able to sign the lease to farm the Noëray property as well as to live in the house.

Writing under the spell of nostalgia, Rousseau made the time he spent at Les Charmettes an idyll of unequaled tranquility. In the late *Reveries* he remembered it as a golden age in which a loving Maman lib-

Les Charmettes from above

Unchanged externally since Rousseau's time, the house stands by itself near the road that mounts the hill, with the town of Chambéry in the distance. Getting there on foot was a taxing climb for the portly Mme de Warens.

LES CHARMETTES

Mme de Warens had the corner bedroom on the second floor, overlooking the valley, and Rousseau a smaller bedroom adjoining it. The window at the far right was hers, the one next to it Rousseau's. The plaque between the ground-floor windows contains commemorative verses by the French revolutionary Hérault de Séchelles: "Retreat where Jean-Jacques lived, you recall to me his genius, his solitude, his pride, his misfortunes, and his madness. He dared to devote his life to fame and to truth, and he was forever persecuted, whether by envy or by himself."

---

erated him to be "perfectly free, and better than free, because I was subjected only by my affections and did only what I wanted to do." In the *Confessions* he had been even more eloquent, re-creating emotional fullness with the very rhythm of his sentences. "Here begins the brief happiness of my life; here come the peaceful but rapid moments that have given me the right to say I have lived. Precious moments that I miss so much, ah! begin again for me your pleasant course; flow more slowly in my memory, if that is possible, than you actually did in your fleeting succession." He conceived of this time as one of true happiness, as opposed to transitory pleasure, such that it didn't really matter what he was doing at any given time.

If all of that consisted in doings, in actions, in words, I would be able to describe and render it to some extent; but how can I say what was never said, or done, or even thought, but tasted and felt, so that I can name no object for my happiness except the feeling itself? I got up with the sun and was happy, I took a walk and was happy, I saw Maman and was happy, I left her and was happy, I roamed the woods and hills, I wandered in the valleys, I read, I was idle, I worked in the garden, I gathered fruit, I helped around the house, and happiness followed me everywhere. It wasn't in any single thing one could identify, it was entirely in myself, and it couldn't leave me for a single moment.

For a while the country air seemed to improve Rousseau's health, but that was not to last. He gave up wine at meals, of which he had been fond, and began consuming large quantities of water, and his own diagnosis was that the hard mountain water somehow ruined his stomach. This had the effect of confirming his recently acquired commitment to hypochondria. "No longer able to digest anything, I understood that I had no hope of being cured." His generalized state of debility was perhaps not dramatic enough to arouse Mme de Warens's concern, and it was duly followed by a crisis. One morning his heart began to pound so violently that he could feel his arteries throbbing, and his ears were deafened by buzzing, whistling, and gurgling sounds. Terrified, he took to his bed while a doctor was sent for, but the suggested treatment, evidently involving strong cathartics, since he describes it as disgusting, did no good at all. In those days the medical profession relied on rules of thumb that went back to ancient Greece and were as likely to do harm as good. As late as 1799 George Washington met his end when his doctors treated a sore throat by draining a third of the blood from his body. And doctors were not plentiful. At the time Rousseau lived in Chambéry there were only four in a town of ten thousand, and in the Savoie as a whole the average was one doctor for every twenty thousand inhabitants. Moreover, the practice of medicine was bizarrely divided: physicians were not allowed to work with their hands or to shed blood (apparently deriving from their original status as clerics in the Middle Ages), while barber-surgeons, who were regarded as greatly inferior to physicians, were forbidden to give opinions about internal medicine.

Whatever the cause of Rousseau's illness — and the tinnitus, which never entirely left him, was very likely a real organic disorder — it had its advantages, and not just in giving Maman reason to fuss over him. He believed that the onset of these frightening symptoms heralded a welcome release from the frustrations of sexual desire. "This accident, which ought to have killed my body, killed only my passions, and I give thanks every day to heaven for the fortunate effect it produced on my soul. I can well say that I did not begin to live until I regarded myself as a dead man." The conviction of imminent death, to which he constantly referred for the rest of his life, was liberating rather than distressing. "That time during which I lived always in retirement and always ill was the time in my life when I was least lazy and least bored." Eventually he was even able to admit that he tended to use illness manipulatively. To an admirer who provided him with a country retreat, he acknowledged frankly that he demanded a lot from his friends: "As a sick man I have a right to the consideration that humaneness owes to weakness and to the whims of a man who suffers."

When the grape harvest was over and cold weather came, it was time to return to the gloomy house in Chambéry. "Doubting that I would ever see spring again, I believed I was saying farewell forever to Les Charmettes. I didn't leave until I had kissed the ground and the trees, and I looked back repeatedly as we went away." Back in town Rousseau settled into the role of full-time invalid. The more alarming symptoms had abated, but he suffered from insomnia and lassitude, dismissed his music pupils, and lay about all day. Fortunately, the doctor who looked after him, Jean-Baptiste Salomon, understood very well that he needed stimulation more than medicine, and engaged him in conversation about philosophy and science. Soon Rousseau was devouring books that might help him to keep up with Salomon, who was a disciple of Descartes, and he "read and reread a hundred times" a guidebook entitled *Conversations on the Sciences* by Père Bernard Lamy that sought to unite scientific inquiry with religious faith. This work was far from up-to-date, having been published half a century before, but it was clear, concise, and invaluable for a groping autodidact. By "sciences" Lamy meant learning in all its aspects, including literature and history, and what seems to have impressed Rousseau most was his emphasis on learning by doing rather than by memorizing information as students normally did. "After having known everything in their youth," Lamy wrote, "they no longer know anything once their masters have left them. But when one has exerted oneself personally in the quest for truth, one's heart is always where the foundation of all the sciences lies." For Rousseau the experience of self-education was intoxicating. In his mid-twenties, he wasn't just repairing gaps in his knowledge, he was learning how to think. In addition, his newfound passion for ideas had the practical result that Salomon must have anticipated: "I no longer thought about my ills and was far less affected by them."

Springtime brought further relief. For the rest of Rousseau's life it would always be in winter that he would agonize about his health. "The joy with which I saw the first buds is indescribable. For me, to see the springtime again was to revive in paradise. Scarcely had the snow begun to melt than we left our dungeon, and we were at Les Charmettes early enough to hear the first songs of the nightingale. After that I no longer believed I was dying, and really it is remarkable that I have never suffered serious illness in the country." True, he still felt too weak to work, and the slightest effort with a spade was enough to make his head pound. Instead he tended the beehives and the dovecote, befriending the birds to the point that they would perch trustingly on his arms and head. "I have always taken particular pleasure in taming animals, especially those that are timid and wild. It seemed delightful to me to inspire them with a confidence that I have never abused. I wanted them to love me in freedom." It could be added that the birds stayed in the dovecote because that was where they were fed, and that their fate was to be eaten in their turn.

Debilitated though he claimed to be, Rousseau was always able to take long walks in the hills above Les Charmettes. He formed the habit of getting up before sunrise, ascending a path that overlooked Chambéry, and offering morning prayers "to the author of that lovely nature whose beauties lay before my eyes." He would then return to the house by a circuitous route and watch for the moment when Mme de Warens's shutters opened and he could hasten to greet her. It must have been a servant who opened the shutters, because he would find her still in bed and half asleep and would seize the opportunity for an embrace "as pure as it was tender, its very innocence giving it a charm that is never joined to sensual pleasure." He certainly wanted it that way, and as his editors comment, "It is probable that his illness and the 'extreme weakness' resulting from it had permitted him to recover this 'innocence.'"

He and Mme de Warens would have breakfast and chat, and then attend to the activities of the farm, in which a number of workers were employed. Occasionally they took excursions into the hills. Rousseau especially remembered a long outing on August 25, the feast day of Saint Louis, her patron saint, which included coffee made outdoors over a fire of twigs and dinner shared with peasants who welcomed them into their house. Rousseau claims to have cried out in ecstasy, "Maman, Maman, this day has been promised me for a long time, and I can see nothing that could go beyond it. Thanks to you my happiness is at its height, may it never more decline!" But this pinnacle of happiness must have been attained at the very outset of the time at Les Charmettes, for he mentions that on this occasion they were exploring the slope next to the house, "which we had not yet visited."

The chronology of these years is far from clear, since Rousseau tended to merge all of his happy memories into a continuous state of being. The situation was more complex than that, and not least because he continued to fall short in two respects that mattered a lot to Mme de Warens: he was totally incompetent to manage the farm, and his embraces were all too chaste. A rival soon appeared, whose advent was so distressing to Rousseau that he gives a very misleading account in the *Confessions* and describes it as occurring much later than it actually did. The new young man, Jean-Samuel-Rodolphe Wintzenried, was the son of the keeper of the castle of Chillon at the eastern end of Lac Léman. Four years younger than Rousseau, he had a rather similar story: he had left home at sixteen to seek adventures and in 1731 had passed through Chambéry, where he met Mme de Warens and converted to Catholicism. In the summer of 1737 he turned up again and soon assumed the twin duties of estate manager and lover, which had been badly neglected since the death of Claude Anet.

Rousseau found Wintzenried intolerable. He was big and blond, loud and confident, fond of boasting of the husbands he had cuckolded when working for a wigmaker, and more than willing to run the farm. "He was as noisy as I was quiet, and he made himself seen, and still more heard, at the plow, the hayfield, the woods, the stable, and the farmyard all at the same time. The only thing he neglected was the garden, because the work there was too peaceful and didn't make any noise. His greatest pleasure was to load wood and cart it around, and to saw it or split it. He was always to be seen with an ax or a pick in his hand, and you would hear him running around, banging, and yelling his head off." Rousseau thought it pitiable that Mme de Warens was taken in by his bustle and uproar, but in truth she desperately needed someone to assume Anet's responsibilities; as her loyal friend Conzié said long afterward, she was hopelessly given to "ruinous projects."

For the next twenty years Mme de Warens found Wintzenried indispensable, and in fact he was widely recognized as a person of ability, especially when he and his employer later extended their efforts into the challenging field of mining in the Maurienne valley to the south. In 1757 a Chambéry administrator described him as altogether different from the buffoon Rousseau made him out to be: "He has wit and vivacity, and shows taste and intelligence in everything relating to the exploitation of mines and the excavation of coal. He expresses himself well, speaks readily, and knows how to give value to everything he does." Rousseau tried to regain control of the situation by establishing himself as the newcomer's mentor, as Anet had formerly been his, but in vain; a mentor was the last thing Wintzenried wanted.

As for Wintzenried's responsibilities in the bedroom, Rousseau felt deeply wounded but had no wish to compete, especially when Mme de Warens made the humiliating suggestion that they share her favors, as he and Anet had done. "Never have the purity, truthfulness, and force of my feelings for her, never have the sincerity and decency of my soul been more apparent to me than at that moment. I threw myself at her feet, embraced her knees, and drenched them with floods of tears. 'No, Maman,' I cried passionately, 'I love you too much to defile you; my possessing you is too precious to be shared.'" He added sententiously, or so he liked to remember, "May I perish a thousand times before I taste pleasure that degrades the one I love." This was the high-flown romantic language of his mother's novels, but in fact he was experiencing a violent upheaval, "a sudden and complete *bouleversement* in my entire being." It was the same term he used to describe how he had felt as a child when he was punished for the broken comb: "What a *bouleversement* in his heart, in his brain, and in the whole of his little intellectual and moral being!"

What hurt the most was that Mme de Warens had replaced Rousseau not just with a new lover, a role he never much cared for, but with a new son; she actually required him to address Wintzenried as "brother." And his understanding of their relationship was very different from hers, as he eventually came to see. "The abstinence that I had imposed on myself, and that she had pretended to approve, is one of the things women do not forgive, whatever face they may put on it . . . Take the most sensible, most philosophical, and least sensual of women, and the most inexcusable offense that can be committed, even by the man she cares least about in other respects, is to have the opportunity to enjoy her and not to take it."

At about this time, probably just before the arrival of Wintzenried, a terrifying accident occurred. On the day before his twenty-fifth birthday in June 1737, Rousseau was attempting a science experiment to produce sympathetic ink, invisible when used but visible after being treated with a "sympathetic" chemical. He mixed quicklime and arsenic sulfide with water, corked the mixture in a bottle, and panicked when the chemicals quickly started to effervesce. Before he could open the bottle, it exploded. He was temporarily blinded, and he swallowed some of the toxic mixture. Convinced that he was about to die, he immediately dictated a formal will, which was signed by six witnesses. The notary testified that Rousseau himself was unable to sign because he couldn't open his eyes. In this document Rousseau bequeaths everything he has, after his debts have been paid, to Mme de Warens (he inexplicably calls her the countess of Warens), and adds with obvious guilt that if he should be fortunate enough to survive, he will pay her two thousand Savoyard livres within six months "for his lodging and support which the said lady has given him during the past ten years." Notably, the document begins by emphasizing loyalty to Catholicism in the strongest terms:

> Considering the certainty of death and the uncertainty of its hour, and that he is prepared to account to God for his actions, he has made his testament as follows; and first he has prepared himself by

making the sign of the cross upon his body and by declaring, in the name of the Father, the Son, and the Holy Spirit, that he commends his soul to God his creator, beseeching him that through the merits of our Lord Jesus Christ, and through the intercession of the most holy Virgin and of his patron saints Jean and Jacques, he will have mercy upon him and receive his soul into his holy paradise; and he affirms his intention to live and die in the holy faith of the holy Catholic, Apostolic, and Roman Church.

Rousseau recovered quickly, and now an encouraging financial prospect beckoned. Twenty-five was the age of majority in Geneva, and at long last he was in a position to claim whatever was left of his mother's inheritance. The French resident in the city was an elderly gentleman named Pierre de la Closure, who had nursed a gallant but supposedly unrequited passion for Rousseau's mother when Isaac Rousseau was in Constantinople. On Rousseau's previous visits to Geneva "he often talked to me about my mother, for whom his heart had not lost affection in spite of death and the passage of time," and Rousseau counted on getting his help. His own apostasy from Protestantism made it technically illegal for him to reside in the city, so he took lodgings outside the walls and waited anxiously, "shut up in my inn like a regular prisoner," as he wrote to Mme de Warens. In an aggrieved tone he added, "Just to complete my happiness, Madame, I've had no news whatever of you." What mainly interested her was the status of the inheritance, because she had made up her mind to demand some repayment for all those years of support. Rousseau was cheered when Jacques Barrillot, a bookseller who agreed to act on his behalf, assured him that La Closure was intervening personally and that the affair would soon have a happy ending. And he did indeed secure rights to 6,500 florins, his half of the 13,000 that Suzanne Rousseau's sons were to inherit when they came of age. Although François' fate was unknown, it had to be assumed that he might someday return to reclaim his share; in the meantime Isaac Rousseau continued to collect the interest on it. The rest of the original inheritance of 30,000 florins had mysteriously evaporated. Rousseau says that after spending part of the windfall on books, he hastened to give the rest of it to Mme de Warens, and that "she received it with that simplicity of beautiful souls who, since they do such things without effort, regard them without admiration." Most of the money, he admits, then went to his own expenses.

While Rousseau was at Geneva, a civil war threatened to break out between conservatives, who supported the ruling oligarchy, and liberals, who asserted the rights of citizens. He was particularly struck by the fact that the kindly bookseller Barrillot, "who used to call me his grandson," and his son were on opposite sides. "I saw father and son emerge fully armed from the same house, the one to go up to the hôtel de ville, the other to return to his own quarter, certain of seeing each other face to face two hours later with the risk of cutting each other's throats." The crisis soon blew over, but Rousseau vowed then, he says, never to get involved in civil war if he should someday move back to Geneva.

During the same visit, Rousseau did something less admirable. Visiting his aunt Bernard, he was allowed to look through the papers of his uncle Gabriel, the stern relative who had been summoned to beat him in Bossey and who was now working as a military engineer in Charleston, South Carolina. Rousseau got his hands on a document containing secret information concerning the fortifications of Geneva, and he says it occurred to him to give it to the head of the customs bureau in Chambéry "to prove to him that I was connected to notables in Geneva who were privy to state secrets." More likely he knew that the information would be transmitted to Turin and that he was betraying his native city, quite possibly in a spirit of revenge. Nothing ever came of it, and the incident is known only because he mentions it in the *Confessions*. It does suggest, however, that Mme de Warens still hoped to resume her career as a secret agent. Certainly it seems a suspicious sign that a year later, after learning of Gabriel Bernard's death, Rousseau wrote to his aunt to say that he would be happy to receive any remaining papers. Moreover, the copy he made of this letter is surrounded by notes and sketches concerning fortifications. For that matter, what was the invisible ink intended for?

Thirty years later, after he had become an international celebrity, Rousseau received a letter from a woman who remembered seeing him on this occasion at his aunt Clermonde Fazy's. "We regarded attentively a young man who seemed to be a stranger to his own country and even to his relatives, through a fatal destiny that had led him ever since birth in painful and disagreeable paths. We parted from you with tears in our eyes, without speaking to you or showing our sympathy for your misfortunes." She added perceptively that if he had stayed in Geneva he might never have become known. "The strange singularity of your fate was the motive and instrument that developed talents buried deep in your soul."

When Rousseau returned to Chambéry, the house and farm at Les Charmettes were still infested by Wintzenried and no longer felt like home. It was time to fall ill again. This time the symptoms were clearly psychosomatic, and he himself acknowledged that like other people of keen sensibility, he was subject to the vapors. He had palpitations, felt suffocated when he tried to walk fast, got dizzy when he bent over, and was too weak to pick up even the lightest object. He then undertook the time-honored expedient of the hypochondriac, which was to ransack medical textbooks in search of a diagnosis. Of course he became convinced that he was suffering from every disease known to man, and the doctors regarded him as a *malade imaginaire.* At length he concluded that he had a polyp on the heart, which an eighteenth-century writer defines as "a mass of coagulable lymph filling up some of the large cavities of the heart." Dr. Salomon claimed to be persuaded by this suggestion, and encouraged Rousseau to make a long journey to Montpellier to consult an expert on that particular condition. No doubt he was exasperated with Rousseau's unceasing anxiety and happy to get rid of him. Mme de Warens likewise urged him to make the trip. She had her own reasons for wanting him out of town, and perhaps out of her life as well.

Close to the Mediterranean coast and well to the west of Avignon and Nîmes, Montpellier was more than two hundred miles from Chambéry, a considerable journey for someone who believed he was at death's door. Rousseau set out on horseback from Chambéry on September 11; two days later, having reached Grenoble, he wrote rather stiffly to Mme de Warens to assert his emotional rights: "Allow me, Madame, to take the liberty again of recommending that you take care of your health. Are you not my dear Maman, do I not have the right to take the liveliest interest in it, and do you not need to be encouraged constantly to pay more attention to it?" As if changing the subject, he then described a performance of Voltaire's *Alzire* at which he became short of breath and his palpitations got worse, an account clearly intended to underline the contrast between himself and Wintzenried, whom he regarded as a coarse philistine. "Why, Madame, are there hearts that feel the great, the sublime, the moving, while others seem made only to grovel in the baseness of their emotions?" He concluded, rather pompously, that he had better not see any more tragedies, since they were so dangerous to his health. There was also a characteristic expression of injured pride. A gentleman to whom he delivered a letter from Mme de Warens insulted him by giving him a tip; after accepting it meekly he handed the money to the doorman on his way out. "I don't know if I did well, but my soul would have to change its form before I could bring myself to do otherwise."

Finding horseback too exhausting, at Grenoble Rousseau secured a place in one of a group of carriages that were heading toward Avignon. Several ladies in the party began to take an interest in the shy but attractive invalid, particularly a woman of forty-four named Mme de Larnage, who was on her way home to Bourg-Saint-Andéol, north of Avignon. For some reason — he claims it was embarrassment at revealing that he was a recent convert — Rousseau took it into his head to identify himself as an English Jacobite, an adherent of the exiled Stuart pretender to the throne, and on a whim he called himself M. Dudding. The choice of alias was not altogether bizarre. Jacobites were well known and welcome in Avignon and Montpellier, it was not unlikely that one would be traveling in that part of France, and the pose allowed Rousseau to cast himself as a romantic exile. Unfortunately, he didn't know a word of English, and he immediately began to dread being exposed, especially when a malicious marquis de Torignan (more accurately Taulignan) attempted to draw him out on the subject of the pretender.

It soon became clear that Mme de Larnage had designs on Rousseau, though first she had to overcome his hypersensitivity to ridicule, since he was convinced that she and Taulignan were slyly mocking him. In fact the elderly Taulignan was dropping sarcastic innuendos about her obvious preference for Rousseau. When he began to grasp what she had in mind, he was paralyzed with shyness and behaved more awkwardly than ever, but she solved that problem by taking him for a walk, pressing his arm against her side, and kissing him warmly on the mouth. They had time for several nights together before their paths diverged, not to mention daylong dalliance in the carriage, and he gratefully yielded to the ministrations of an older woman whose only concern was mutual pleasure. Not coincidentally, his illness evaporated. "*Voilà* Mme de Larnage, who took me over, and it was farewell to poor Jean-Jacques, or rather farewell to fever, vapors, and the polyp, all of which departed when I was with her, except for certain remaining palpitations that she had no wish to cure me of." More surprisingly, he experienced complete gratification. "Proud of being a man and proud of my good fortune, I abandoned myself to my senses with joy and confidence, and shared in the effect I had on hers. I was sufficiently myself to contemplate my triumph with as much vanity as sensuality, and to gain thereby the power to redouble it." For four or five days "I gorged myself, I grew intoxicated on the sweetest delights. I tasted them pure, strong, and with no mixture of pain. These were the first and only ones I have ever enjoyed, and I can say that I owe it to Mme de Larnage not to have died without ever experiencing pleasure."

The most curious aspect of the whole affair was that it was absurdly pretending to be Dudding that allowed Rousseau to feel free. "She had given me that confidence whose absence has nearly always prevented me from being myself." The idea of no longer being oneself was conventional enough. In Fénelon's *Telemachus,* when the hero falls in love with a comely nymph, "a budding passion, of which he himself was not aware, made him no longer the same man." But a moralist like Fénelon took it for granted that Telemachus in love was betraying his true self. Rousseau's originality was to grasp that both of his roles, the timorous Jean-Jacques and also the passionate Dudding, reflected a deeper unity that he needed to understand. He was always inhibited with women and fearful that his advances, however timid, might be taken as brutally aggressive. Mme de Warens was more alarming than encouraging, since despite her overt advances he was convinced that he was somehow defiling her. Now at last a complete stranger showed frank desire, a masterful Venus taking her pleasure from a stricken Adonis. As Starobinski observes, his exhibitionism and masochism had been stratagems by which to remain passive and let someone else be active, but women never seemed to figure out what was expected of them or, if they did, found Rousseau ridiculous. Now at last, incapacitated by illness and concealed behind the mask of Dudding, he could submit to the advances of a woman who knew exactly what she wanted. Perhaps she even gave him the chastisement he longed for. True, he declared in the *Confessions* that he could never bring himself to ask for it, but perhaps she intuited his wish without being asked.

When it was time to part, Rousseau continued on to Montpellier with a promise to visit Mme de Larnage in her home (she had been separated from her husband for two years) after his medical treatment. Along the way he made a detour to see the Pont du Gard, the magnificent Roman aqueduct that carries drinking water for Nîmes over the gorge of the Gard, and he was even more impressed than he expected. "The echoing of my footsteps beneath those immense vaults made me believe I was hearing the strong voices of those who had built them. I felt lost like an insect in that immensity. But even as I felt myself grow smaller, a *je ne sais quoi* elevated my soul, and I said to myself as I sighed, 'Why was I not born a Roman!'" At Bossey, M. Lambercier had exclaimed, "An aqueduct! an aqueduct!" while demolishing Rousseau's childish construction. Now he stood in veneration before a real aqueduct, which symbolized the victory of virtue over pleasure, as Roman thoughts replaced erotic ones. "I spent several hours in rapt contemplation. When I came to myself I was distracted and dreamy, and this reverie was not favorable to Mme de Larnage. She had taken care to warn me against the girls of Montpellier, but not against the Pont du Gard. One never thinks of everything."

In his new state of well-being Rousseau found the journey pleasurable in every way. "At an inn a few leagues before reaching Montpellier," he told a friend with satisfaction forty years later, "they served us an excellent dinner of game, fish, and fruit. The cheap price, the agreeable company, and the beauty of the landscape and the season made us decide to let the coach go without us. We stayed there three days, to enjoy ourselves. I have never eaten better." At Montpellier Rousseau rented a room in the rue Basse (today the rue J.-J. Rousseau), and began taking his meals in a boardinghouse run by an Irish doctor named Thomas Fitzmaurice, who undertook to supervise his dietary regimen. Next he consulted the eminent physician Antoine Fizes, who not surprisingly concluded that he was a hypochondriac. Years later Rousseau told a friend that the famous doctor "Fitse" (presumably Fizes rather than Fitzmaurice) "regarded me with a smile, and slapping me on the shoulder, 'My good friend,' he said, 'drink a good glass of wine for me from time to time.' He called the vapors 'the malady of happy people.'"

Since he still had some money left from his mother's inheritance, Rousseau was able to live comfortably enough for a while. He spent his days hanging about with medical students, placing small bets on their games of mall, and dining in taverns. Afterward he remembered the stay as lasting two months, but in fact it was at least twice that long, and not nearly so cheerful as he described it in the *Confessions*. He wrote at the time to a correspondent in Chambéry, "Montpellier is a large and populous city divided into an immense labyrinth of dirty streets, tortuous and barely six feet wide, lined alternately with magnificent mansions and miserable hovels full of mud and dung . . . The women are of two classes. The ladies spend the morning putting on makeup, the afternoon playing cards, and the night in debauchery, unlike the bourgeois women whose only occupation is the last of those." Not even the surrounding countryside pleased him. "I don't love arid lands," he wrote on a later occasion, "and Provence doesn't attract me much."

To Mme de Warens, Rousseau complained that she was neglecting to answer his letters, and he threatened that unless he heard from her soon he would return to Chambéry as early as December, despite her demand that he stay away until the feast of Saint John the following June. His money was running low, and his health was terrible because of fogs from the sea and "bad air" in general. Moreover, "The food is worthless, it's worthless I tell you, and I'm not joking. The wine is too strong, and always unpleasant; the bread is passable, in truth, but there is no beef or butter. There is nothing to eat except bad mutton and lots of ocean fish, all cooked in stinking oil. You would find it impossible to taste the soup or the ragouts that they serve in my *pension* without throwing up." He might, he suggested, stop off on the way home for a cure of asses' milk at a pretty town where there was "good company" he had met on the road — a deliberately opaque allusion to Mme de Larnage — but what he really wanted was to regain his old position in Mme de Warens's home and heart. "In God's name, arrange things so that I won't die of despair! I agree to everything, I submit to everything, except this sole condition, which I can't possibly consent to, even if I were to be prey to the most miserable fate. Ah, my dear Maman, are you then no longer my dear Maman? Have I lived some months too long?"

The unacceptable condition, perhaps, was a demand that he leave her household for good. He closed with a mysterious hint that no one has been able to elucidate: "You know there is one circumstance in which I would accept the thing with heartfelt joy. But that circumstance is unique. You understand me."

In February he started home, breaking his promise to visit Mme de Larnage, with whom he had been corresponding regularly (the letters are lost). The rationalization he came up with was that she had an attractive fifteen-year-old daughter with whom he was bound to fall in love, and he congratulated himself on passing the standard test of French classical literature: "For the first time in my life I tasted the interior satisfaction of saying to myself, 'I deserve my own esteem, I know how to prefer my duty to my pleasure.'" The real reason, as he must have known, was that everything that had made their encounter delicious would be fatally altered if a real relationship were established. So Mme de Larnage disappears from history, having acquired accidental immortality along with Bâcle, Mme Basile, the abbé Gaime, and many others who crossed Rousseau's path, because she happened to spend a few nights with a young stranger on the road.

The long-awaited return to Maman was disappointing in the extreme. Rousseau had written to say when he would arrive, and finding himself ahead of schedule he dawdled along the way to make sure of a joyful welcome at the appointed hour. No one seemed to be around when he reached Les Charmettes, which filled him with alarm, but he encountered the maid, who greeted him calmly enough. As for Mme de Warens, she was with Wintzenried, and she received him with a blandness that shocked him. "I went upstairs and saw her at last, that dear Maman whom I loved with such tenderness, force, and purity. I ran to her and threw myself at her feet. 'Ah, there you are, *petit!*' she said, embracing me. 'Did you have a good trip?'"

Rousseau had been told to stay away until June, he had returned in February, and there was nothing for it but to let him stay. The idyll was over, however. His endless dependency was increasingly exasperating to Mme de Warens, and the mutual devotion he dreamed of had evaporated. For the next year and a half he lived alone at Les Charmettes, even in the depths of winter, while she stayed mainly at her house in town, and Wintzenried came and went in connection with the management of the farm. As he rose in status, the new favorite adopted an impressive name that filled Rousseau with scorn: "Since the name of Wintzenried seemed insufficiently noble to him, he gave it up for that of Monsieur de Courtilles." The scorn was hardly justified, since Wintzenried came from the town of Courtilles in the Vaud, where his birth certificate identifies him as the son of "Monsieur the château-keeper and justice Wintzenried de Courtilles." It must have been especially painful to cosign with Wintzenried (or rather De Courtilles) a legal deposition swearing that Mme de Warens's valet had been caught with his pockets full of stolen chestnuts, beans, and wheat. As Cranston observes, Rousseau used to steal from employers himself (and in fact would do so again) but was now "enacting the role of policeman, with a fellow adventurer he despised, at the expense of a poor valet."

Much of the time Rousseau was reduced to communicating with Mme de Warens by post, as if she were in some remote country rather than a couple of miles away. At times he tried to be playful, as when he told her, in laboriously facetious verse, "Madame, receive the news of the taking of four rats. Four rats are no bagatelle, so I'm not in jest. With great zeal I dispatch these verses that will murmur to you, 'Madame, receive the news of the taking of four rats.'" At other times he indulged in overt sarcasm. "Since you have settled yourself in town, has the whim never taken you, my dear Maman, to undertake one day a little journey into the country? If my good genius should inspire you to do it, you will oblige me by giving me notice three or four months in advance, so that I can prepare myself to receive you and give you due honors *chez moi.*" It should have been *chez nous,* and it no longer was.

Two weeks later Rousseau was penitent, writing as "the most tender of sons" to his "dearest Maman," and regretting that he had offended her by quarreling with Wintzenried. Noting that she had promised to forgive him by Easter, ten days hence, he complained that he had not been permitted to see her for more than a month, and added, "I am sure that when a heart like yours has loved someone as much as I remember being loved by you, it is impossible for it to reach such a state of harshness that motives of religion would be needed to reconcile it. I take this to be a little mortification that you impose on me even while pardoning me, knowing that a full understanding of your true feelings will sweeten the bitterness." It was far too late for that, and forty years later he was able to admit it. "Ah, if only I had been as sufficient for her heart as she was for mine!" He may also have come to understand that the idyll always had an element of illusion. Clément suggests the relevance of a passage in the sequel to *Émile,* after Émile's wife has betrayed him: "Why was it not given to me to pass whole centuries in that all too pleasant state, to love her, to respect her, to cherish her, to groan under her tyranny, to want to sway her without ever succeeding, to demand, implore, and desire endlessly, and never to obtain anything?" Such a state was not given to Rousseau because Mme de Warens wanted an energetic companion and lover, not an abject dependent.

By now, what Rousseau had at Les Charmettes wasn't Maman at all, but the double solace of nature and books. Lonely and wounded, he immersed himself in both, and his intellectual career at last began to take shape. He had already developed a taste for learning, which now became a substitute for relationships. "To read while eating," he later wrote, "has always been my fancy in default of a tête-à-tête. It compensates for the social life I lack. I devour alternately a page and a mouthful; it's as if my book were dining with me." For guidance he relied on journeyman textbooks, mostly by priests, that would have been despised by the advanced thinkers of the day, but like Lamy's *Conversations* they helped orient his thinking. During the next two years he consumed an impressive range of classics, ancient and modern. Conzié, who had already inspired him with enthusiasm for Voltaire's brilliant style, generously shared his large personal library. Among many other authors, Rousseau read the Latin poets Virgil, Horace, and Juvenal; the Roman historians; the philosophers Plato, Descartes, Locke, and Leibniz; the essayists Montaigne, Saint-Évremond, and La Bruyère; the novels of Marivaux and Prévost; the plays of Racine and Voltaire. He also tried, without much success, to improve his knowledge of languages. "I don't know why my stubbornness in these vain and continual efforts didn't end by making me stupid. I had to learn and relearn Virgil's *Eclogues* twenty times, and now I don't know one word of them. I lost multitudes of books or broke up sets through my habit of taking them with me to the dovecote, garden, orchard, and vineyard. When I was occupied with something else I would lay my book under a tree or on a hedge, forget to retrieve it, and find it two weeks later moldy or ravaged by ants and slugs." Italian would be the only foreign language Rousseau ever learned well. At various times in his life he would make hopeless stabs at Greek, grapple repeatedly with Latin, and acquire a passable reading knowledge of English without being able to speak it. He never even considered learning German.

Rousseau therefore read ancient and foreign writers in French translation. Better-educated scholars would have regarded this practice as amateurish, but it allowed him to respond imaginatively to what the writers were saying instead of struggling to construe their meaning. And the method of study he developed was remarkable. Noticing that authors were in perpetual disagreement, he realized that he was in no position to adjudicate among them. "While reading each writer, I made a rule for myself to adopt and follow all of his ideas without adding my own or anyone else's, and without ever disputing with him. I said to myself, I'll start by collecting a storehouse of ideas, true or false, but distinct, and wait until my head is sufficiently equipped to compare and choose among them." This may sound naive, but it contrasts strikingly with the usual procedure of formal education, which is to interpret everything through a preferred system or theory, and to do it in such a way as to win a teacher's approval. Rousseau was doing his best to grasp intellectual positions in themselves, and when he came to critique them later on, he knew them intimately.

To be sure, this was not the most efficient way to learn, as he was the first to admit. "If there are advantages to studying alone, there are also great drawbacks, and above all incredible difficulty. I know this better than anyone." But he had something most conventional students do not, a true hunger to learn. "To know nothing at almost twenty-five, and to want to learn everything, is to commit oneself to making the best use of one's time." The ultimate benefit was inestimable: it was by far the most effective way to find his own ideas and his own voice. As a friend of his observed much later, "Men of genius are formed in the provinces, far from academies." And Rousseau somehow knew, or at least suspected, that he really did possess genius.

In the late 1730s, when Rousseau was plunging into these studies, mathematics and physics were still the most highly admired disciplines in Paris, and accordingly he spent many hours teaching himself geometry, algebra, and even calculus. It is striking, however, that abstract thought exasperated him, and that just as when he played chess, his imagination was visual rather than analytical. When he attempted to master Cartesian geometry, "It seemed to me that to solve a problem in geometry by equations was like playing a tune by turning a crank. The first time I succeeded in proving that the square of a binomial was composed of the square of each of its parts and twice the product of the one times the other, I couldn't believe it until I had drawn the diagram, notwithstanding the accuracy of my multiplication." He even sent the *Mercure de France* a long letter (which didn't get published) about a controversy concerning the shape of the earth, remarking archly, "A diagram would make all of this more intelligible, but I omit it so as not to shock the eyes of the ladies who read this journal." He also studied astronomy, though his poor eyesight made observation difficult, and his attempts to learn the stars led to a ludicrous incident. He had set up a planisphere at eye level, lit from below by a flickering candle, and to keep warm had put on a floppy hat and a dressing gown of Maman's that was too short for him (it bore the expressive name *pet-en-l'air* — "fart in the air"). Some farmers coming up the road took him for a magician casting spells and spread the alarm, but fortunately two Jesuit friends were able to reassure them. He doesn't comment on his motives for appropriating the dressing gown.

Chambéry was a Jesuit stronghold, which was a good thing for Rousseau, because he needed help resisting the alarming theology of their mortal enemies the Jansenists, who held that the vast majority of the human race had been predestined to damnation since the beginning of time. It was during this period that he read the *Pensées* of the great Pascal, who wrote that "the 'me' is hateful," that "all men naturally hate each other," and that Christianity was the one true religion because "no other religion has proposed to men that they should hate themselves." Naturally enough, reading Jansenist works inspired Rousseau with a fear of damnation, "and if Maman had not tranquilized my soul, that terrifying doctrine would have ended by overwhelming me." In effect the Calvinism of his boyhood was surfacing again in Jansenist guise. But the anxiety was only temporary; he staged a preposterous test by throwing a stone at a tree to provoke a sign from heaven: if he hit the tree he would be among the saved, if he missed he would be damned. He did hit the tree, "which in truth was not difficult, since I had taken care to choose one that was very big and very close. After that I never doubted my salvation again." More efficacious than the omen of the tree, of course, was the untroubled confidence of Mme de Warens's faith, which has been aptly called "a Catholicism without sin."

During these years Rousseau also began to imagine that he might have a future as a writer. His most interesting effort was a play called *Narcissus, or the Self-Lover,* but it is known today only in a much revised later form. He also began a very conventional tragedy entitled *Iphis,* set in ancient Greece and intended for the Royal Academy of Music; it was to have a chorus of gods and goddesses, a chorus of warriors, and a chorus of dancing furies. Only a few pages of *Iphis* still exist, since he had the good sense, as he says in the *Confessions,* to throw it into the fire. In 1737 his name appeared in print for the first time when the *Mercure de France* published a song "set to music by M. Rousseau of Chambéry." The text, however, in which a rose laments that her butterfly lover has deserted her for a grapevine and accuses Bacchus of provoking his inconstancy, may well have been by someone else.

Rousseau's most ambitious piece of writing during this period was a carefully revised poem, over two hundred lines long, entitled *The Orchard of Mme de Warens,* which he had privately printed in 1739. It gives no hint of literary genius, being filled, as a critic remarks, with "stale and colorless epithets" that have the effect of uninspired padding. All the same, it is a fascinating piece, combining praise of Mme de Warens, whom "I dare to call by the tender name of Mother," with a good deal of injured self-assertion. The poem begins on a note of innocence ("Orchard dear to my heart, abode of innocence, honoring the finest days that heaven has granted me") and ends on one of virtue ("The ills that overwhelm my body are but occasions to affirm my virtue"). In between these high-minded declarations, some lines that did not appear in the printed version suggest that malicious tongues have been gossiping about Mme de Warens's relationship with her young protégé, but that her only real fault is excessive generosity. As for Rousseau himself, he has cheerfully accepted a solitary life, sometimes laughing at human woes with Montaigne and La Bruyère, sometimes inspired by Socrates and "the divine Plato" to follow in the footsteps of the severe Cato. There follows an ostentatious catalogue of his program of study in his lonely retreat, which manages to be an expression of ambition and a veiled reproach all at the same time.

Rousseau did not choose solitude so much as solitude chose him. His notebook from those years contains the heavily revised draft of a letter that purports to congratulate an unnamed young gentleman on withdrawing from worldly pleasures. "I tell you frankly, I have often regretted that a mind as sound as yours, and a soul as fine, should have been made for nothing but gallantry, cards, and champagne. You were born, my dear sir, for a better occupation." No addressee is indicated, and the piece was surely an earnest exercise rather than an actual letter. However much he might dream of worldly success, Rousseau was trying to convince himself that solitude and obscurity were even better. "The tumult of cities and the world's din are far from suited to this examination . . . Let us retreat to the country, and seek there a repose and contentment that are not to be found amidst assemblies and diversions." His religious ideas tended toward renunciation in the same vein. An unpublished poem of his, "In Praise of the Monks of the Grande Chartreuse," describes the monks as freed from earthly cares in their isolated Alpine retreat, "floating always in the purest joy," an ideal for Rousseau to emulate as he struggles to overcome "the thousand stabs of remorse that tear at my soul, fearing to be delivered one day to fire and to devils." He had once composed a morning prayer to recite in unison with Mme de Warens, which gave thanks to God for blessing their union. Now he wrote another prayer declaring that his conscience was weighed down with guilt and his pleasures had turned to "odious bitterness," and asking God's help in pardoning those who had injured him.

Other documents from this period give glimpses of more practical matters, most of them discouraging. Mme de Warens, whose finances were in terrible shape, demanded that Rousseau find some way to support himself, but he persisted in believing that his health made work impossible. In an attempt to recover the half of his mother's inheritance still being held in trust for his brother, François, he wrote in March 1739 to the French chargé d'affaires in Geneva, asking him to intercede with the authorities there. He assembled a long list of reasons why he should have the money: François had not been heard from for almost twenty years; there had been reports that he had changed his name in Germany and died there, which his tendency to poor health made probable; even if he was still living, he had made no attempt to recover his inheritance in the nine years since he reached his majority (actually it was seven

years, as Rousseau knew very well). This letter got no results, if indeed
it was ever sent.

Another idea was to write to the governor of the duchy of Savoie to
beg for a pension that would relieve Mme de Warens of financial responsibility for Rousseau. She labored carefully with him over this
document, which stresses his piety and his decrepitude in a shameless
manner.

> I left my fatherland of Geneva very young, abandoning my rights in
> order to enter into the bosom of the Church . . . While still a child I
> fell into the hands of the late Monseigneur the bishop of Geneva,
> and I tried, by the ardor and assiduity of my studies, to deserve the
> flattering opinion the worthy prelate had of me. Madame the baron-
> ess of Warens was so good as to respond to his request that she take
> charge of my education . . . I have been afflicted with a languor that
> has brought me today almost to the grave . . . And finally, to com-
> plete my distress, I have succumbed to a malady that has disfigured
> me. Henceforth I will be shut in, all but unable even to get out of
> bed, until it shall please God to dispose of what remains of my short
> but wretched life.

The disfiguring disease seems to have been a complete fiction, unless
it was temporary scarring from the chemical explosion. Rousseau may
have wanted to imply that it was smallpox without actually saying so. In
a separate letter to Mme de Warens he mentions needing to give some
explanation of "that accursed trip to Besançon, whose purpose I thought
best to disguise a bit for my own good." But whatever did happen on
that occasion, they evidently decided to omit any reference to it. Not
that it mattered, for this appeal went unanswered, as did a completely
implausible proposal that he be granted a monopoly for the transport of
merchandise between Italy and the Savoie by way of the Mont Cenis
pass, where he had made his journey to Turin a decade before. Perhaps
the proposal was never sent.

So Mme de Warens continued to search for a means of support for
Rousseau, and in the fall of 1739 she found one. He was to go to Lyon
and serve as tutor for a wealthy family there, and he felt obligated to accept. After ten years, his stay with Maman was at an end; he would always remember it as the most important stage in his life.

8

Broadening Horizons: Lyon and Paris

Rousseau was now twenty-seven, and at long last Mme de Warens had found him a promising position. His new employer was Jean Bonnot de Mably, the provost general of police in the region around Lyon. Mably was forty-four, a cultivated man who wanted his sons to receive a progressive education, and thanks to some friends of Mme de Warens in Grenoble, Rousseau had been recommended for the task. The occasion seemed so propitious that Isaac Rousseau wrote a fulsome letter to Mme de Warens, declaring that she had a beautiful soul and must not deny it, and expressing relief that his son finally had employment that could "rescue him from inaction." Isaac added that Jean-Jacques would do well to desist from experiments in chemistry. The fact that these had stopped after the near-blinding three years before suggests that there hadn't been much communication between father and son.

For his own part, Jean-Jacques felt a good deal of trepidation. He was well aware that he lacked social graces, but he longed to be accepted as an equal rather than as an employee. Before leaving Chambéry he wrote earnestly to Mably that he was eager to make himself welcome in the new household, and in a manner that may have seemed both presumptuous and poignant, he declared his emotional need: "I will try to deserve your treating me like a father, and to fulfill toward you all the duties of a respectful son. Having left my own country as a youth, I have no ties on earth except to a benefactress and mother by adoption." From Grenoble, where he stopped to thank Mme de Warens's friends, Rousseau wrote sadly to her that it felt like a thousand years since he had left. He was careful to convey greetings "with all my heart" to Monsieur de Courtilles and signed the letter with a touching alternation of affection and formality: "I have the honor to be, with profound respect and the most tender gratitude, Madame my very dear Maman, your very humble and very obedient servant and son, J.-J. Rousseau."

Lyon seems not to have interested Rousseau much. It was quite a metropolis, with a hundred thousand inhabitants, most of whom were employed in the textile trades, especially in silk. Despite its size it was something of a backwater, "a town without a history" as a modern historian says, "a sort of forgotten city." Although the merchant and professional class to which Mably belonged was affluent, for everyone else poverty and famine were ever-present. Workers' revolts were a constant threat and sometimes a reality, and a shockingly high percentage of infants, perhaps as many as two-thirds, died in the care of wet nurses; eighteenth-century visitors described Lyon as a tomb of humanity. Only a continual influx from the countryside prevented the population from declining; people kept arriving not because life in the city was good, but because rural subsistence was even worse.

In later years Rousseau was keenly concerned with such inequities, and he may well have reflected on them at this time, but his immediate goal was to ingratiate himself with patrons who could help him rise in the world. Lyon had a flourishing academy, not a school but a reading club where gentlemen met to discuss ideas and to listen to each other's papers on topics of interest. Verse letters were a popular genre at the time, and Rousseau wrote one to a member of the academy named Charles Bordes, proclaiming that Lyon's manufactures miraculously reconciled the artistic god Apollo with Plutus, the god of wealth. Lyon, he declared, was the ornament of France and treasure of the universe, and within its walls all arts were welcomed. The ones he especially had in mind were the elegant textiles, but he made no reference to the backbreaking labor that produced them. Only in later years could he write,

"I don't care for those stupid trades in which the workers, without industry and practically automatons, never exercise their hand at anything but the same task. Weavers, stocking-makers, stonecutters — what's the use of employing men of sense in those trades? It's only one machine managing another." Mme de Warens, he would have recalled, had run a disastrously unsuccessful stocking factory before fleeing from her husband.

Rousseau and Bordes later broke off relations, but other members of the group would remain lasting friends. Jacques David was an accomplished musician who gave Rousseau valuable instruction and encouraged him to compose an operatic drama called *The Discovery of the New World,* in which Columbus and his Spaniards bring the blessings of civilization to the West Indies, with a promise of even more civilized Frenchmen to follow. The "noble and generous" former mayor Camille Perrichon shared his extensive collection of books, and Gabriel Parisot, a doctor and intellectual, remained in Rousseau's memory "the best and best-acting of men." In the "Epistle to Parisot," written at this time, Rousseau addresses him as a father and acknowledges that his own proud Geneva republicanism must be unlearned. He declares in pedestrian verse, "I was a base child abandoned by fate, destined perhaps to perish in the mire, a conceited runt whose farcical pride mingled childhood with romance in a ridiculous way."

Ten years later Rousseau would proudly sign himself "Citizen of Geneva" and ponder the origins of inequality, but in Lyon he was determined to honor rank and privilege. "I will renounce forever those fierce maxims, the bitter, premature fruits of my native prejudice . . . I have learned to respect an illustrious nobility that knows how to add luster to virtue. It would not be good for society if there were less inequality between the ranks." In fact, his chief goal during this period seems to have been to repudiate the Genevan in himself, which he was beginning to see as an obstacle to getting ahead in the world. "Even if, in my vain obsession, I should play the great declaimer, the new Don Quixote, destiny has determined the stations of life on earth and will certainly not alter them on my account." Jean Guéhenno catches the note of ambiguity well: "He was glimpsing, and at the same time refuting, a part that he might one day play, the Don Quixote of equality."

Most of Rousseau's time was spent in the Mably household on the rue Saint-Dominique in the center of town, and here too he made valuable connections. Rousseau's employer and two brothers shared the surname Bonnot, although he and his brother Gabriel chose to be called after their property at Mably. Gabriel, who would become well known in intellectual circles as the abbé de Mably, had just published a treatise comparing Roman institutions of government with French ones and celebrating the progress of civilization. Another family property, at Condillac, gave its name to a third brother, Étienne, who was already engaged in the philosophical studies that would make him famous as the abbé de Condillac. In Paris a few years later, he would prove an invaluable ally when Rousseau was struggling to get established. Conversing with Mably, Condillac, Parisot, Bordes, and their friends, Rousseau found himself in a stimulating intellectual milieu, and the studies he had put himself through in Chambéry suddenly came to life. The great movement known as the Enlightenment was getting under way, reaching out from Paris into the provinces, and he was excited by its power. A decade later he would become one of its most visible and controversial figures.

Jean Bonnot de Mably had four sons, two of whom were barely out of infancy and were not Rousseau's responsibility. The other two were distressingly different in temperament and ability, and he quickly realized that he would have his hands full. The older boy, François-Paul-Marie, known as Monsieur de Sainte-Marie after yet another family property, had just turned six. Rousseau describes him as "good looking, with an outgoing spirit, lively, careless, playful, and mischievous in a cheerful way." At least he was intelligent, though not much inclined to study or to discipline of any kind. His brother Jean-Antoine, known as Monsieur de Condillac, was not yet five and a truly daunting challenge, "stupid, idle, stubborn as a mule, and incapable of learning a thing." It was obvious that Rousseau was not cut out to be a tutor, and in retrospect he acknowledged that each pupil managed to frustrate him in his own way. The elder wore him down with endless arguments, while the younger drove him to fury with stolid resistance. By turns Rousseau tried reasoning, displays of emotion, and rage, and all three approaches were counterproductive. "I could see through everything but prevent nothing, I didn't succeed in anything, and whatever I did was exactly what I should not have done."

Fortunately, Mably was a kindly man who seemed willing to keep Rousseau on indefinitely, and he had a genuine interest in the philosophy of education. Some months after beginning the job, Rousseau drafted an impressive "Memorandum to Monsieur de Mably on the Education of Monsieur His Son," together with a shorter "Project for the Education of Monsieur de Sainte-Marie," based on progressive theories of the day. By contrast with the usual curriculum, Latin was to be minimized and scholastic philosophy omitted altogether, while modern history and natural science would be emphasized. Rousseau was already beginning to understand that children resist learning unless they can be persuaded, in ways that are inevitably different for different temperaments, to want it for themselves. Right in the middle of the soberly argued "Memorandum" comes an altogether unexpected question that is prophetic of his entire life's work: "Nothing is more depressing than the general fate of men. And yet they feel in themselves a consuming desire to become happy, and it makes them feel at every moment that they were born to be happy. So why are they not?"

The "Memorandum" is interesting as well for its poignant revelation of Rousseau's self-image at the time. He has no doubt, he says, about his qualifications to give instruction. "I avow in good faith that few men my age have read as much as I." He even claims that he is incapable of neglecting his duties — a pious hope at best. But with bitter self-knowledge he adds:

> I feel all too strongly what I lack in certain respects. A constrained and embarrassed manner, dry and charmless conversation, and foolish and ridiculous bashfulness are faults that I will find it hard to correct. Three great obstacles always oppose my efforts to do so. The first is an invincible tendency to melancholy, which torments my spirit in spite of myself. Whether from temperament or from the habit of being unhappy, I carry a source of unhappiness in myself . . . The second obstacle is an insurmountable bashfulness that puts me out of countenance and robs me of freedom of mind, even with people who are as foolish as myself . . . The third is a profound indifference to everything that is called brilliant; the opinion of others hardly affects me at all.

It is an unsparing self-portrait, and on the whole an accurate one. What no one could have foreseen was that these very characteristics, handicaps as they certainly were in ordinary life, would be inseparable from Rousseau's greatness as a thinker and writer.

Little more is known of the time Rousseau spent in Lyon, and his account in the *Confessions* is brief and colorless. He does relate one anecdote that confirms the experience of isolation. He would often go out to get some pastry for his dinner, though not until he had entered shop after shop without daring to buy anything, just as he used to do as a boy in Geneva. Then he would settle down with a book and a bottle of wine, but his wages were too slender to permit much indulgence, and he got into the habit of sneaking into M. de Mably's wine cellar and liberating an occasional bottle of "a certain very nice little white wine from Arbois." These solitary meals were pleasant enough, but the empty bottles were discovered and the key to the wine cellar was taken away. Once again he had been reduced to petty theft, and just as with Ducommun's apples, it took the form of appropriating delicacies that would have been his by right if he were not a humble employee.

Rousseau was treated generously by the Mably family, but like other employers after them, they never suspected that they had a prodigy in their midst. It was not their fault. "I'm not surprised," a friend commented long afterward, "that the provost of Lyon, at whose house, as I have heard him say, he received an education, took him for an ordinary man, because he always put himself exactly at the level of the people around him." When Rousseau collected in a notebook the handful of poems he wrote during this time, he gave it the facetious title "The Allobrogian Muse, or the Works of Tom Thumb" (in French, "Petit Poucet"), and the Latin motto he chose was probably ironic as well: *Barbarus hic ego sum quia non intelligor illis.* Written in exile by Ovid, it means "I am taken for a barbarian here because they don't understand me."

Eight years later Rousseau would use Ovid's verse again as the epigraph for the work that launched his fame, the *Discourse on the Sciences and Arts,* and by then he would understand how to use his outsider status as a strength instead of a weakness. Now, however, his amateurish attempts at verse struck a gloomy note. "Displaced by fate, betrayed by tenderness, my sufferings are as numerous as my days. I am imprudent sometimes and persecuted always, and the punishment often exceeds the frailty." Lifelong themes are evident here. A cruel fate has displaced him from his home and made him suffer, and if he endures punishment it is for frailty and not for any sin or crime. It is startling that he is already talking about being persecuted, a theme that became a full-blown obsession in later years.

Almost nothing is known of Rousseau's relations with women during this time. Inevitably, he was smitten with Mme de Mably, who was barely older than himself, but she made no response to his sighs and meaningful glances, "which I got bored with soon enough, seeing that they weren't leading to anything." At some point he became more seriously enamored of a woman named Suzanne Serre, eight years younger than himself, whom he had noticed years before, during his stay in Lyon on the way back from Paris, when she was a convent girl of eleven. In the *Confessions* he says that they made a mutual decision to part for prudential reasons: "She had nothing, and neither did I; our situations were too similar for us to be able to unite, and in the plans that occupied me, I was far from contemplating marriage . . . I have often felt since then, looking back, that even if our sacrifices to duty and virtue are painful, we are well repaid by the sweet memories they leave in the depths of our hearts."

At the time, however, he was not so philosophical. A draft of a letter has survived, almost certainly intended for Mlle Serre, in which he declares her unfit for a nun's vocation by reason of her passionate temperament, resents her preference for a rival, and complains of being neglected, with a characteristic mixture of flattery and petulance.

> I understand, Mademoiselle, that I can expect no return on your part. I am a young man with no fortune, I have nothing to offer but my heart, and this heart, as full as it can possibly be of fire and sensitivity and delicacy, is doubtless not a gift worthy of acceptance by you . . . You have treated me with incredible harshness, and if you did attain some degree of kindness toward me, you made me pay so dearly for it afterward that I would swear you intended only to torment me . . . Your heart was no less made for love than your face, and my despair is that I'm not the one who can awaken it . . . My God! If I had attained this charming possession, I would certainly have died, for how could I find the resources of soul to resist such a torrent of pleasure? If it were in my power to possess my adorable

queen for one minute, on condition of being hanged a quarter of an hour afterward, I would accept the offer with greater joy than the throne of the universe. After this I have nothing more to say to you, except that you must have been a barbarous monster to refuse me at least a little pity.

In due course Mlle Serre got engaged to a young merchant of whom her parents disapproved, and after several years she married him on the occasion of the birth of their first child. There is no way to know whether Rousseau ever sent his high-handed letter, but the thwarted romance was real enough; long afterward his aunt Suzon ended a letter with the words, "I embrace you with all my heart, and likewise Mlle Serre." She must have meant Mlle Levasseur, Rousseau's partner in later life, but evidently the name of his early flame had lodged in her memory. At some later date he scrawled heavily on the final page of the letter "*jeunesse égarée*" ("youthful aberration").

By the beginning of summer in 1741, after a year in Lyon, Rousseau had had enough of tutoring, and he and Mably agreed amicably to part. Predictably but unwisely, he returned to Chambéry and made one last attempt to reanimate the relationship with Maman, succumbing to yet another alarming illness in the hope of attracting sympathy. When he got better he wrote a poem addressed "To Fanie" (a playful nickname for Françoise, Mme de Warens's given name) in which Charon tries to make him drink the water of forgetfulness but he protests that he will never be able to forget "the divine Fanie." The poem ends with a plea for renewed love. "Charming Fanie, my ardor for you kept me from perishing. Since the god of the dead was willing to restore me to life, do not make me die!"

Equally interesting in a different way is a long letter thanking his Chambéry friend Conzié for lending him the French translation of Pope's *Essay on Man,* which Rousseau critiques with remarkable confidence and insight. Pope attempted to explain the existence of suffering by arguing, as the philosopher Leibniz had done, that since God has filled the universe with every possible kind of being, any imperfections we happen to perceive are somehow necessary for the good of the whole. Voltaire was quite taken by this argument at the time, though in *Candide* he later satirized its so-called optimism, which holds in effect that we inhabit the best of all possible worlds but that everything in it is a necessary evil. Rousseau shrewdly put his finger on the central weakness: Pope's uncritical assumption that there must be an unbroken chain of being all the way from inanimate matter up to God.

Rousseau's letter to Conzié also describes an incident in which for once he was successful in repartee, in the misanthropic vein he was trying to cultivate. When the celebrated Jacques de Vaucanson came to Lyon to show off his automaton, a mechanism that could simulate human actions, his hosts showered him with praise. "'As for myself,' I said, 'my admiration should be still less suspect, for I'm accustomed to spectacles that I dare to call even more marvelous.' They looked at me in astonishment. 'I come from a country,' I went on, 'full of well-made machines that know how to dance the quadrille and the pharaoh, swear, drink champagne, and pass the day telling lies about other fine machines that pay them back in the same way.' They burst into laughter, and what would have amused you was that two or three machines who were there laughed even harder than the rest." For Rousseau, social interaction required the intimacy of friends who knew each other well. In larger groups he always felt excluded, and the game of witty conversation seemed to him like the clattering of robots. At the end of his life he told a friend ruefully, "Wit only comes to me half an hour after other people."

For several months Rousseau stayed on at Les Charmettes, helping to draft letters in which Mme de Warens quarreled with neighbors over property rights. He was far from happy. Money had become an alarming concern, and it was time to seek support and happiness elsewhere. Finally he made up his mind to leave for good, going so far as to sell his books to raise cash. In Lyon his friend Perrichon paid for his coach ticket to Paris, Bordes and the Mably brothers provided him with letters of introduction, and like many another provincial he set out for the great city with dreams of fame.

Rousseau would see Mme de Warens just one more time, twelve years later. It is painful to realize how much significance he had always invested in encounters that apparently meant less to the women involved than they did to him. There were Mlle Vulson and little Goton in Geneva and Nyon, Mme Basile in Turin, Mlle Graffenried and Mlle Galley in the episode of the cherries, Mme de Larnage on the road to Montpellier, and Mlle Serre in Lyon. These episodes, together with

Rousseau's uneasy relations with Mme de Warens, represented the sum total of his romantic and sexual experience in his first thirty years. By a curious coincidence, Claudine Galley moved to Chambéry after her marriage in 1740 and actually lived next door to Mme de Warens, but Rousseau seems not to have known that. One cannot help imagining, as Trousson does, the encounter that might have happened but never did. "When he would go to see Maman, Jean-Jacques didn't know that a simple wall separated him from the young woman . . . Years had gone by, they had both changed. Did they sometimes cross paths without recognizing each other?"

Yet however disappointed Rousseau was by Mme de Warens's coolness, what she had given him was of inestimable value. He came to her a confused, dreamy, shiftless adolescent, mistrustful of his elders, habituated to lying and petty thievery. She gave him security and affection, if not the transcendent love he yearned for, and she believed in his talent. She also gave him the leisure and the means to educate himself, and without those gifts, his genius might never have bloomed. But no one yet suspected that he was anything more than mildly promising. In *Émile,* written after he had become a celebrity, he comments ruefully that a really original person may seem slow and dull, especially in early life. "Nothing is more difficult than to distinguish in childhood true stupidity from that apparent and deceptive stupidity that foretells powerful minds." A stupid child, he says, accepts false ideas without knowing they are false, but one with genius finds that most ideas are false even when people believe them true, and so he accepts none.

In the late summer of 1742, Rousseau was once more in Paris, and soon found lodging near the Sorbonne and the Jardin du Luxembourg, in the Hôtel St. Quentin in the rue des Cordiers — "ugly street, ugly residence, ugly room," but a good place to stay because acquaintances of his Lyon friends were there. And he had a plan for becoming rich and famous. Recalling his arduous struggle to learn to read musical scores, he hoped to devise a system of notation that would be simpler and more "natural." Conventional notation places the notes at different places on its staff of lines: middle C appears on a line below the staff, high C in a space near the top of the staff, and so on. Rousseau wanted to indicate the aural relationship between notes that repeats itself in exactly the same way with every octave. He wrote up a formal presentation of his idea, and one of his new acquaintances introduced him to the famous scientist René-Antoine de Réaumur, who in turn arranged for him to read his proposal before the Académie des Sciences. It was cordially received, but the committee appointed to examine it pointed out the obvious drawback, that the system could indicate melody but not harmony. This conclusion was seconded by the leading musician of the day, Jean Philippe Rameau, and although Rousseau was flattered to be taken seriously by the great man, a mutual dislike was born.

Still, even if Rousseau's pride was injured, he had made a start. After determining that the new system was no improvement over the usual one, the Académie nevertheless concluded with a compliment: "It appears to us that this work has been carried out with skill and expressed with great clarity, and that its author appears familiar with the subject he is treating. It is to be hoped he will continue his endeavors to make music easier." The Académie des Sciences enjoyed immense prestige at the time (more than the Académie Française, membership in which often had little to do with merit), and its deliberations were widely noticed by nonspecialists. Within a few years Rousseau would indeed be recognized as a musician, though not for his scheme of notation.

The episode was characteristic in more ways than one. It reflected Rousseau's lack of conventional training, which would have made him so familiar with the traditional staff that the system would have seemed obvious if not inevitable. With a poor memory for visual symbols, moreover, he found printed scores bewildering. For him music was melody, not the complex harmonies that the staff was invented to represent. And in the long run, as happened so many times, his oblique approach yielded insights. Ten years later he would be at the very center of a campaign to restore expressive melody to the prestige from which polyphony had displaced it. For the moment, however, music wasn't taking him far.

Still, Rousseau found it exhilarating to be in Paris, unlike his previous visit, when he knew no one and was overwhelmed by the urban clutter. Through his Lyon connections he made the acquaintance of two persons of real distinction, the playwright and novelist Marivaux and the scientist Fontenelle, both of whom treated him generously. Marivaux, whose thirty comedies are filled with stylized dialogue that gained the name of *marivaudage,* even helped him revise a play called

Narcissus that he had been working on for years, though he would not see it produced until long afterward. Fontenelle, a polymath who had been a member of both the Académie Française and the Académie des Sciences since the end of the previous century, was eighty-five years old and still in full possession of his powers. His advice took the form of an epigram that he was in the habit of presenting to young writers: "You must courageously offer your brow to laurel wreaths and your nose to blows."

Such recognition by famous writers was gratifying, but more important were the relationships Rousseau began to form among men his own age. Through Daniel Roguin, a Swiss banker from Yverdon living in Paris, he was brought to the most important friendship of his life, with Denis Diderot, another provincial eager to make a name for himself. Diderot was just a year younger than Rousseau and, like him, the son of an artisan; his father was a prosperous knife maker in Langres, in Champagne. Unlike Rousseau, however, Diderot had been a headstrong, confident youth, who as he recalled long afterward "knew better how to strike a blow with his fist than to make a bow." At sixteen he went to Paris to pursue his studies and took a master's degree at the Sorbonne. By the time Rousseau met him he had been living a bohemian existence for over a decade, picking up casual income from mathematics tutoring and odd jobs for publishers.

In personality and style Diderot was everything Rousseau was not. Rousseau was small and rather delicate, whereas Diderot was described by a contemporary as "thickset, with a build like a sedan-chair porter"; in his fifties he was still capable of hoisting a disagreeable fellow off the floor at the opera and threatening to hurl him into the pit. In his youth he had flowing blond locks that women found irresistible, or so he claimed. With a gregarious, humorous disposition, he was flamboyant and excessive in a way that the cautious Rousseau could never be. A few months after they met, Diderot traveled home to Langres to cajole his father into approving a marriage with a young woman who had no money; his father flew into a rage, Diderot demanded his inheritance, his father responded by having him imprisoned in a monastery, and Diderot escaped through a window, returning to Paris penniless and defiant.

Ever since Bâcle and Venture, Rousseau had been passionately smitten with new friends whom he temporarily perceived as doubles, in what has been compared to a walk through a hall of mirrors. But clearly he and Diderot were anything but doubles. If Rousseau was gauche and tongue-tied in conversation, Diderot was just the reverse. The abbé Morellet, who was a young, freethinking theological student when Diderot was in his forties, remembered Diderot's conversation as "brilliant in imagination, fertile in ideas, and awakening ideas in others. One allowed oneself to be carried along in it for hours on end, as if upon a gentle and limpid river in a rich countryside adorned with fine habitations." Coming from Morellet, a sharp-tongued cynic whom Voltaire liked to tease as *"Mords-les"* ("Bite 'em)," this is an impressive tribute. A German who met Diderot twenty years later remarked, "He speaks with a warmth and vehemence that almost benumbs us colder-blooded souls." He had a lifelong habit, which not everyone appreciated, of reinforcing his comments by physically grabbing his listeners to compel their attention. "He never saw me before this meeting," one young acquaintance recalled, "but when we stood he put his arms around me, and when we sat he slapped me on the thigh as though it were his own." No less a person than Catherine the Great of Russia, toward whom Diderot sought to behave with the strictest decorum, complained that "I cannot get out of my conversations with him without having my thighs bruised black and blue."

As an urbane sophisticate and man of learning, Diderot treated his new friend like a younger brother or even a pupil, and at first Rousseau was happy to oblige. By great good luck, he had arrived in Paris at a time of unusual intellectual ferment. Until recently the Académie des Sciences had dominated the scene, with the greatest prestige going to mathematicians whose achievements couldn't possibly be understood by laypersons. But during the 1740s social criticism came to the forefront, and the modern idea of the intellectual began to emerge. The great Voltaire had been celebrated until then mainly as a poet and playwright, but now his *Philosophical Letters,* which Gustave Lanson famously called "the first bomb hurled against the Ancien Régime," became an inspiration for younger writers. Prestige depended increasingly on public opinion rather than the approval of experts, and it

DENIS DIDEROT BY JEAN-ANTOINE HOUDON

Diderot's modern biographer says, "He had the look (which the sculptor Houdon caught) of a man trying hard to hear the strains of far-off music or seize the implications of some half-glimpsed but especially subtle and elusive idea." This bust was executed in 1771; when Rousseau met Diderot three decades earlier, he was even more animated and compelling. Diderot was rather vain about the difficulty artists had in capturing his personality; when a portrait by Louis-Michel Van Loo was exhibited in the Paris Salon of 1767 he wrote, "I have a mask that eludes the artist, whether because too many things are blended in it, or because the impressions of my mind succeed each other and paint themselves on my face so rapidly that the painter's eye can't capture them from one instant to the next."

---

would be Rousseau himself who triumphed most spectacularly in this way, something that would have been impossible for a slenderly educated provincial a decade or two before.

Since Rousseau always felt that his mind was sluggish in contrast to Diderot's quicksilver wit, it is fascinating to learn that when they played chess at the Café Maugis, it was invariably Rousseau who won. An observer noted, "He meditates deeply between moves, but he plays with speed, which accords with his character." And he enjoyed competition. An acquaintance who occasionally played with him later at the Café de la Régence lost regularly even when Rousseau removed his own rook as a handicap. "'Does it wound you to lose?' Rousseau asked me. 'Oh, no,' I replied, 'it's the inevitable result since there is such a marked disparity in our means of defense.' 'Well, then,' he replied ingenuously, 'in that case let's not change how we play; I like to win." Diderot was closer to Rousseau's level but got the same treatment. "Man strives for superiority, even in the smallest things. Jean-Jacques Rousseau, who always beat me at chess, refused to give me a handicap to make the game more equal. 'Does it upset you to lose?' he asked me. 'No,' I said, 'but I would make a better defense, and you would enjoy the game more.' 'That may be,' he replied. 'All the same, let's leave things as they are.'" The *frères ennemis,* as they have been aptly called, were competitive from the start.

By now Rousseau's slender stock of cash was nearly gone, and he was casting about for something to do. A Jesuit mathematician named Castel, whom he remembered as "crazy, but a good man at bottom," suggested that he try a different tactic. "Since the musicians and the *savants* aren't singing in unison with you, change your tune and go to see the women . . . Nothing is done in Paris except through women." This was congenial advice for Rousseau, especially since Castel added helpfully that the game should not be carried too far: "They are like curves of which wise men are the asymptotes: they constantly approach them but never touch." This advice led to his introduction to the stratospheric world of the salons, weekly gatherings presided over by celebrated hostesses. But if he was aware that "*entrée* into a wealthy house was an open door to fortune," his clumsy shyness was a grave handicap, and for the rest of his life he regarded the brittle glamour of the salons with something close to loathing. And in reality, salon conversations were not always as brilliant as later generations wanted to believe. Voltaire, the wittiest of men, included an acerbic sketch of a typical Parisian supper in *Candide:* "First silence, then an indistinguishable noise of words, then witticisms, most of them insipid, false news, bad reasoning, a little politics, and a great deal of malicious gossip."

Our best insight into Rousseau's feelings at this time comes not from the *Confessions* but from *Julie,* in which Saint-Preux describes at length his first experience of Paris. What shocks him above all is the universal insincerity. He complains to Julie that a visitor must leave his soul ("if he has one") at the door along with his overcoat. In her reply, to be sure, Julie suggests that he's merely jealous, and reminds him that the Swiss are the least witty people on earth. And it is certainly true that Rousseau was ill-equipped to shine in this arena. Casanova remembered him as "entirely undistinguished either in his person or his wit" and said that "the eloquent Rousseau had neither the temperament to laugh nor the divine talent of calling forth laughter." More sympathetically, Germaine de Staël, whose parents were active in the salon culture and knew Rousseau well, commented that even in his novel he failed to make his characters witty. "One has to have great familiarity with society to foresee accurately the effect of a joke. But Rousseau, of all men in the world, was the least suited to writing gaily; everything struck him too deeply."

For his own part, Rousseau saw salon wit as desperately hollow — "biting and satiric laughter is the sorry substitute for the gaiety that no longer exists" — and he made Saint-Preux say grimly, "Woe to him who lays himself open to ridicule; its caustic imprint is ineradicable." Rousseau's own ideal was nonverbal. In a society of true friends, "a glance quicker than a flash of light, a sigh divined rather than perceived, carry the sweet feeling from one heart to another." Playing chess or discussing music and ideas, he could feel free, whereas an evening of sophisticated conversation left him, like Saint-Preux, "filled with a secret sadness, overcome by mortal disgust, and my heart empty and swollen like a ball filled with air." This was more than sour grapes; he was perceiving the in-group narcissism of a narrow band of the social spectrum that regarded itself as the world. "To be like *tout le monde,* you have to be like very few people. Those who go on foot don't belong to *le monde.* They are bourgeois, *hommes du peuple,* people from another world, and one might say that a carriage is necessary not to be driven but just to exist." To this day, *le tout-Paris* paradoxically means only the glamorous upper crust. And it struck Rousseau that the sophistication of the coterie world, in which ideals were talked about rather than acted upon, masked the social injustice on which its privilege was built, "the secret inequities by which the rich and powerful snatch away a pittance of black bread from the oppressed whom they claim to pity."

Rousseau fared better when he could converse with one or two sympathetic women instead of trying to hold his own in a larger gathering. Théodora-Élizabeth-Catherine de Broglie (aristocrats had copious names) drew him out on the subject of music, and at dinner he just happened to have his "Epistle to Parisot" in his pocket, which he read aloud, to the apparent satisfaction of his listeners. Still more stimulating was an invitation to visit Louise-Marie-Madeleine Dupin, who had married the wealthy Claude Dupin as soon as she left convent school. Now thirty-six, she presided over a brilliant salon in their mansion on the Île Saint-Louis. "When I saw her for the first time, she was still one of the most beautiful women in Paris. She received me at her toilette. She had bare arms and disheveled hair, and her dressing gown was carelessly arranged. This manner was very new to me, my poor head couldn't withstand it, I got flustered and distracted, and in short, I fell for Mme Dupin."

She affected not to notice Rousseau's agitation, talked about music, played the harpsichord and sang, and seated him next to her at dinner. He was completely in her thrall. Although her manner remained calm and rather distant, he got up his courage and wrote a poem — "Open your eyes, adorable Dupin! they have a fire that I have come to know" — which she kept for two days without acknowledgment. He had failed to grasp that despite belonging to a social class in which extramarital liaisons were normal, she was a faithful wife, and in any case would never get involved with a plebeian upstart. "The third day she returned it to me, along with a few words of advice in a cold tone that froze me. I wanted to speak, the words expired on my lips, my sudden passion was extinguished along with my hopes, and after making a formal declaration I continued to visit her just as before, but without saying anything further about it, not even with my eyes." Before long her stepson, Charles-Louis Dupin de Francueil, four years younger than Rousseau and friendly with him, advised him to stay away.

Mortified and alarmed, Rousseau hastened to write a groveling letter of the kind he already specialized in. "I have learned with the utmost pain that I have incurred your displeasure . . . If you should deign to relent, you will have the satisfaction of saving the most unfortunate of men from despair." He also wrote, in a less tragic tone, to her husband, whose patronage he still hoped to secure. "If errors of this kind seem to you to deserve any indulgence, I implore yours and that of Mme Dupin. It will suffice that the sight of me not be altogether odious for me to strive to make it bearable. My talents are extremely limited, I admit, but there are other ways in which a man can make himself liked, esteemed, and useful; this will be my sole endeavor." Rousseau could not resist adding that he was pursued by a grim fate, which was his customary way of explaining why he so often found himself doing things he didn't intend or understand. A less conflicted person like Diderot could cheerfully embrace a philosophy of determinism, in which actions result from causes over which we have no control. Rousseau argued fervently for free will, but he needed the notion of a cruel destiny to explain why he so often felt unfree.

The Dupins did relent. Mme Dupin was doubtless flattered by Rousseau's homage, and her husband was a genial man of the world who understood that nothing compromising had happened; perhaps he was flattered too. Far from ostracizing Rousseau, they gave him a job as tutor to their son, on the strength of the educational plan he had originally drawn up for M. de Mably in Lyon. Through no fault of Rousseau's, the task was impossible. The thirteen-year-old Jacques-Armand Dupin de Chenonceaux, named after the spectacularly beautiful château owned by the family, was a nasty piece of work — willful and uncooperative. When he died in disgrace at thirty-seven, a writer recalled Rousseau's brief tutorship and commented sympathetically, "He was one of the worst pupils one could possibly find." Rousseau remembered the experience as torture, and later said that he would have refused to continue after the brief trial period was over "even if Mme Dupin had given herself to me in payment."

In the long run, however, the connection with the Dupin family was invaluable. A couple of years later Rousseau accepted a secretarial position with Mme Dupin that contributed substantially to his intellectual development. And he formed a lasting friendship with her stepson Francueil, with whom he shared a passion for music; he even moved across the river to take lodgings near Francueil. In the spirit of the time, they enrolled in a course in chemistry together, but Rousseau developed pneumonia and had to drop out.

During his convalescence he began to compose an opera or "heroic ballet," *The Gallant Muses,* with "the amours of a poet" as its subject.

There were to be three acts, centered on Tasso, Ovid, and Anacreon. He also began a comedy, *The Prisoners of War,* which attempted to capitalize on French anxiety over an army trapped in Prague during the War of the Austrian Succession. Rousseau had begun to dream of being a writer, though at thirty he had not written anything of the slightest significance. As always seemed to happen when he was at loose ends, chance brought him an unexpected change in direction. Mme de Broglie (whose husband commanded the army in Prague) heard that the newly appointed French ambassador to Venice needed a secretary, and she recommended Rousseau. At first he was offered an absurdly inadequate stipend, so he declined and someone else took the job, but the new appointee quarreled with his employer and was fired before he ever got to Italy. Negotiations with Rousseau resumed, this time he accepted, and in July 1743 he was on his way to Venice.

9

The Masks of Venice

ROUSSEAU'S NEW EMPLOYER, Pierre-François, comte de Montaigu, was already on the road to Venice and had not met his new secretary, but his brother wrote to say that he had interviewed him and found him suitable: "I have a good opinion of his physiognomy and bearing." One could not say the same of the count, who was a virtual parody of a parasitic aristocrat, incredibly stupid, irascible, and swollen with self-importance. His superiors in Paris had no illusions about what they were doing when they sent him to Venice. Appointing him to an unimportant diplomatic post would do less harm than promoting him to general in the army, where he had spent thirty-seven undistinguished years. So off he went, with an official letter of instruction that bluntly outlined his role: "For many years the republic of Venice has had so little influence in the principal affairs of Europe that an ambassador resides there more from a custom of flattering them than for any important purpose."

Not only was the ambassadorship irrelevant, the secretive Venetian rulers made it impossible. They categorically refused to meet with ambassadors, who were isolated in an enclave far from the ruling doge's palace and permitted to communicate only through intermediaries; Venetian noblemen were forbidden to speak with them on pain of death. Montaigu therefore had almost no contact with the government and was reduced to passing along such scraps of casual intelligence as he was able to obtain. He wrote ineptly and spoke no Italian, so Rousseau was just what he needed.

After ordering some fancy clothes in keeping with his new status, Rousseau set off for Marseille, taking the route recommended to him as the cheapest. In the *Confessions* he remembered traveling directly to Marseille, even though he would have preferred to go by way of Chambéry "to see my poor Maman in passing." His memory seems to have been at fault, however; when Montaigu later complained that the travel costs were excessive, he objected specifically to "his trip to Chambéry." If Rousseau did make a side trip there, Mme de Warens was almost certainly absent, as had often happened before.

At the port of Toulon Rousseau picked up his passport and boarded a felucca, a small vessel that toiled along with oars as well as sails, and endured a slow and unpleasant journey along the coast to Genoa, some two hundred miles away. Unfortunately, the plague was raging at the time in Sicily, and a strict quarantine was imposed in all Italian ports. The other passengers decided to stay on board ship at Genoa, but Rousseau chose to spend his three weeks' quarantine all alone in a totally unfurnished building. He enjoyed the solitude. He slept on the floor on a pile of clothes, sat on the stairs to eat his meals, read some books he had brought along, and took the air in a cemetery outside. After two weeks he was permitted to leave, thanks to intervention by the French envoy, François Chaillou de Jonville, to whom he had written a courteous letter carefully disinfected with vinegar, garlic, and charring over a flame. At Jonville's house he made friends with his secretary, M. Dupont, who showed him around town and remained a correspondent afterward. And Jonville wrote an encouraging letter to Montaigu in Venice: "I have been charmed to make the acquaintance of M. Rousseau, and I congratulate you on having such a fine fellow, who has plenty of intelligence and talent, and joins to that a great sweetness in conversation." Rousseau always liked to exaggerate his social ineptness, but in fact many people throughout his life found him charming.

At last the quarantine was over. Rousseau was free to proceed to Venice by way of Milan and Padua, and he arrived at the beginning of September, nearly two months after leaving Paris. After introducing himself to his new employer — and getting off on the wrong foot right away, since Montaigu resented his hiring an expensive gondola for the crossing from the mainland — he moved into the embassy quarters in the Querini Palace, a rented mansion in the no longer fashionable Canareggio district, and began to explore the city. The bustle, color, and pleasure-seeking atmosphere were invigorating. He knew no one, however, and the loss of his Parisian friends made him feel something of the loneliness he had experienced during his year in Neuchâtel and Lausanne. It was in this mood that he wrote to Conzié, two weeks after reaching Venice, imploring him to send news of Mme de Warens, from whom he had heard nothing "even though since I've been here, I've written to her by an infinite number of different ways." He didn't know that because of the War of the Austrian Succession and the occupation of Chambéry by the Spanish, her pension had not been paid for a full year, and indeed would not be paid again for another four, leaving her in desperate straits.

Rousseau's relations with the ambassador, having begun badly, immediately got worse. "Two days after he arrived," Montaigu recalled, "he complained bitterly that when he was being taken in my gondola to listen to music, my servants didn't place him above them; he told me that he was the senior man in my mission." Rousseau was indignantly asserting himself, much as his father used to do, and as Guéhenno observes, "If he had never been a valet, he would not have been so much afraid of becoming one again." The crucial misunderstanding was that Montaigu thought of Rousseau as secretary to the ambassador, a personal servant, whereas Rousseau proudly styled himself "secretary to the embassy," an official in his own right. His main duty was drafting and editing routine dispatches, including weekly reports to ambassadors in other cities and to headquarters at Versailles. Some of these had to be translated into code, using a far from impenetrable system that represented each letter of the alphabet by a numeral and had standard equivalents for some of the commoner words ("Spain" was 208, "army" 506, and "honor" 592). Montaigu let Rousseau do all the work of gathering information and writing it up, though he tended to demand changes at the last possible moment.

Many of these documents survive, and they show that while Rousseau did his job well, it gave him a comprehensive view of the redundancy and general irrelevance of most of the paperwork that a government office produces. He may also have been careless at times in his rote tasks. In the *Confessions* he says he was reprimanded only once for errors, but a complaint from the foreign office in Versailles tells a different story: "The clerk for foreign affairs earnestly implores his excellency the comte de Montaigu to be so good as to advise his secretaries to be more exact in their ciphering. Their letters are harder to decipher than all of the rest from Italy. Apparently one person dictates the numerals to another, who writes them down; there are repetitions, transpositions of numerals, incomplete phrases, and numerals that are truncated or omitted." Rousseau's assistant was the embassy chaplain, the abbé de Binis; he also got help at first from the French consul, Jean Le Blond, who felt that secretarial work was beneath him and soon gave it up. Le Blond proved to be companionable, however, and Rousseau formed other friendships as well, notably with his counterpart in the Spanish embassy, Carrio or Carrion (his full name was François-Xavier de Carrion y de Ribas), with a twenty-one-year-old Spaniard named Manuel-Ignacio Altuna, and with several young Englishmen.

Thanks to Montaigu's incompetence, Rousseau acquired increasing responsibility for the affairs of the embassy, and realized that he was a good deal more capable than anyone had suspected. It went to his head, and he began to indulge in self-dramatizing role-playing that infuriated his employer. He insisted on riding in an elegantly appointed gondola that he had persuaded Montaigu to provide. (Montaigu wrote sarcastically to his brother, "I am irritated by the ill humor of Signior Rousseau, and I hope his harpsichord and gondola will sufficiently charm away his dissatisfaction.") As Leigh observes, from that time on Rousseau was quick to take offense at people who regarded themselves as his superiors even when no offense was intended, and he strove to become so independent that no one would ever be able to condescend to him again. Thin-skinned and hypersensitive, he was the true son of Isaac Rousseau. But he eventually came to understand that real independence meant freeing his consciousness from the tangled web of status and prestige, and learning not to let his self-esteem be dependent on the opinions of others.

The boring routine was punctuated from time to time by crises, minor in themselves but stimulating in the opportunities they gave to make decisions. One crisis arose when an actor named Carlo-Antonio

ROUSSEAU AS SECRETARY TO THE FRENCH AMBASSADOR IN VENICE

Rousseau had himself painted in the most opulent costume he ever wore in his life; its cost was bitterly resented by his stingy employer. The anonymous painter gives a fine impression of the dark eyes and penetrating gaze that struck everyone who met Rousseau.

Veronese and his two daughters broke a contract to perform with the Comédie Italienne at the French court, appearing instead in a theater in Venice. It was carnival time, which allowed Rousseau to enter their patron's palace wearing a mask, whereupon he dramatically identified himself. "The senator turned pale and remained dumbstruck." Rousseau threatened to have Veronese arrested if he did not leave immediately for France, and the actor capitulated. "One would hardly suspect," he says complacently in the *Confessions,* "that it is to me that the lovers of theater in Paris owed Coraline and her sister Camille."

On another occasion Rousseau was convinced that he had a chance to alter the course of history. Montaigu's only meaningful responsibility was to encourage Venice to remain neutral in the war rather than side covertly with Austria against France. In point of fact Venice did side with Austria, but Montaigu regularly reported the opposite, on the strength of empty assurances he was given. At one point the French embassy in Austria reported that a secret agent had set out from there to stir up trouble in Italy. Montaigu refused to take the warning seriously, so Rousseau took it upon himself to pass the information along to the French ambassador in Naples. This was the extent of his involvement, but it didn't prevent him from boasting later on, "It is perhaps thanks to the poor despised Jean-Jacques that the House of Bourbon owes the preservation of the Kingdom of Naples."

In later years Rousseau recalled paying little attention to the worldly attractions of Venice. Apart from "the very innocent recreations of the Piazza San Marco," the theater, and occasional sedate social visits in the company of friends, "I made my duties my sole pleasures." Pleasure and duty, however, must have overlapped more often than he chose to remember. Two hundred cafés stayed open all night, and we happen to know that he was a regular patron at one of them, since a note from a diplomatic informant mentions planning to meet him "at one o'clock tomorrow morning at his café." And it is hard to believe that the stimulating atmosphere of those *nuits blanches,* the streets crowded with vendors, dancers, priests, prostitutes, and astrologers, had no allure at all. Eighteenth-century Venice has been described as "a fabulous and half-oriental city" and "the capital of pleasure," condoning whatever it could not openly permit. The whole point of carnival, which was celebrated in several stages that occupied fully half the year, was to liberate people from constraint. "More than a disguise," a historian says, "the mask was an incognito. It was secrecy, anonymity, secure impunity; it was licensed folly." Even the doge and the papal nuncio donned masks. As for Rousseau, he wrote a few months after his arrival, "I have altered my philosophy a bit to appear like the others, so that I go to the piazzas and theaters in mask and *bautta* as proudly as if I'd worn that outfit all my life." The *bautta* was the domino, the hooded robe of masquerade.

Theater in Venice was especially compelling, and very different from what Rousseau had known in Paris. (In Geneva, of course, it was forbidden.) Goethe, who was in Venice later in the century and wished he could send his friends "a breath of the more carefree existence here," was desperately bored by a performance of a French play but delighted by the vitality of actors in Italian comedies. "During the daytime, squares, canals, gondolas, and palazzi are full of life as the buyer and the seller, the beggar and the boatman, the housewife and the lawyer offer something for sale, sing and gamble, shout and swear. In the evening these same people go to the theater to behold their actual life, presented with greater economy as make-believe interwoven with fairy stories and removed from reality by masks, yet, in its characters and manners, the life they know. They are delighted, like children, shouting, clapping, and generally making a din." The ballet, too, was different from the formal art seen in Paris. According to Goethe, "The girls considered it their duty to acquaint the audience with every beautiful part of their bodies."

Above all, Rousseau appreciated the music, which was everywhere, from gondoliers on the canals — "while listening to their *barcarolles* I realized that I had never heard singing until then" — to concerts and operas. Performances were so inexpensive that he hired a group of musicians to come to his apartment once a week and perform airs he liked while he accompanied them on the harpsichord. In his *Dictionary of Music,* published long afterward, he gave a nostalgic description of the *barcarolle:* "A type of song in the Venetian dialect that the gondoliers in Venice sing. Although the airs are made for the people, and are often composed by the gondoliers themselves, they are so melodious and charming that there is not a musician in the whole of Italy who doesn't pique himself on knowing and singing them." Rousseau added that many gondoliers knew Tasso's epic poem *Jerusalem Delivered* virtually by heart and would sing alternate stanzas from boat to boat across the lagoon on summer nights. Goethe, too, heard their performance and wrote, "The sound of their voices far away was extraordinary, a lament without sadness, and I was moved to tears."

The embassy subscribed for boxes in a number of theaters and opera houses, and Rousseau could attend whenever he liked. One day he dozed off during a performance (the name of the opera has not been traced) and was overwhelmed when he revived. "What an awakening, what ravishment, what ecstasy the moment I opened my ears and eyes! My first notion was that I must be in paradise." He obtained a copy of the piece, which began *"Conservami la bella / Che si m'accende il cor"* ("Preserve for me the beauty who so inflames my heart"), but the score was a pale echo of the original experience. "Never can that divine air be performed except in my head, as it was that day when it awakened me." As Madeline Ellis notices, Rousseau had nothing to say about operatic acting or spectacle; it was always vocal melody, bel canto, that he loved best. He heard it at its most ravishing at the church of the Mendicanti, which maintained a home for illegitimate and indigent girls that was virtually a conservatory. Accompanied by their own orchestra, they sang from behind a screen, with voices so lovely that he harbored romantic fantasies and got his friend Le Blond to arrange a visit. He was greatly disappointed. "'Come, Sophie'; she was hideous. 'Come, Cattina'; she was blind in one eye. 'Come, Bettina'; she was disfigured by smallpox. There was hardly one without some notable defect. My tormentor laughed at my cruel surprise."

Rousseau never mentions feeling religious emotions in Venice, but he did appreciate the church's encouragement of sensual beauty. In a verse letter at this time he describes attending a service after a tedious Lent and relishing the pleasures of an urbane Catholicism. "Brilliant illumination, paintings by a skillful hand, perfumes destined for the gods whose divine voluptuousness delights human nostrils before ascending to the heavens; and thou, ravishing music!" Indeed the church in Venice was highly tolerant. A popular saying was "A little Mass in the morning, a little society in the afternoon, a little woman at night," and a French visitor was startled to learn that three convents were competing fiercely for the privilege of supplying the new papal nuncio with a mistress.

Rousseau's friends had mistresses, but his inhibitions were stronger than his desires, and he reports only two brief and distressing encounters. On the first occasion, Montaigu's major-domo cajoled him into visiting a prostitute known as La Padoana, who was undeniably beautiful, "but not with the kind of beauty that pleased me." Rousseau ordered sorbet, listened to her sing, and then attempted to get away. La Padoana indignantly refused to accept the ducat she had not earned, "and with singular stupidity I relieved her of her scruples." During the ensuing weeks he was tortured by fears of venereal disease, which proved to be groundless, and a surgeon who examined him declared that his parts were formed in such an unusual way that he could never be infected. This diagnosis seems strange, to say the least, and an autopsy after Rousseau's death, undertaken in part to investigate his chronic urinary troubles, detected nothing out of the ordinary. It has been plausibly suggested that the surgeon invented this explanation to reassure a patient who was frantic with anxiety.

The other erotic encounter was more significant, and it haunted Rousseau for the rest of his life. "Whoever you may be who wish to know a man," he extravagantly asserts in the *Confessions,* "dare to read the following two or three pages, and you will know J.-J. Rousseau to the full." The episode began with a diplomatic crisis, triumphantly resolved by Rousseau of the embassy. A French ship, the *Sainte-Barbe,* commanded by a Captain Olivet, had been accidentally rammed during a sudden squall by a Slavonian ship flying the Venetian flag. The Slavonian crew then swarmed the *Sainte-Barbe* with drawn swords and wounded one of the French sailors, after which Olivet and his crew were placed under arrest. Rousseau got Montaigu to protest that France had been insulted, went out to Olivet's ship to get depositions from the crew, and successfully negotiated their release as well as the payment of damages. Montaigu's own helpful suggestion, that the Slavonian who caused the injury should have his hand cut off, was not followed up.

In gratitude Olivet invited Rousseau to a celebration aboard ship, and he took his Spanish friend Carrio along. At first Rousseau was offended because there was no cannon salute in their honor, but soon a gondola pulled alongside and an astoundingly beautiful young woman sprang out. Declaring that Rousseau looked exactly like a former lover of hers, she kissed him fiercely and had no trouble igniting him. "Her large black eyes, of an oriental cast, struck darts of fire into my heart. Although the surprise distracted me at first, sensuality overtook me so rapidly that regardless of the spectators, this beauty had to restrain me herself, for I was intoxicated, or rather in a fury." She turned out to be a courtesan named Zulietta, not more than twenty years old but obviously highly sophisticated, and high-handed in a way that Rousseau found exciting. The situation looked hopeful. Friends were encouraging him, Zulietta was even more masterful than Mme de Larnage, and the whole thing promised to be over quickly without the complications of a relationship.

Quite possibly Zulietta's imperious behavior was a canny response to signals that Rousseau himself was sending out. "She took possession of me as of a man who belonged to her, she gave me her gloves to hold, her fan, her sash, her headdress; she commanded me to go here and there, to do this and that, and I obeyed." With his fetishistic attraction to adornment, he must have especially enjoyed handling the sash and gloves. Still better, Zulietta affected complete indifference to money, which was important for Rousseau after the discouraging scene with La Padoana. At another point in the *Confessions* he says, "Women who can be bought for money would lose all their charms for me; I even doubt whether I have it in me to take advantage of them." After dinner he went with her in his gondola to buy ornaments at a nearby glassworks, and generally behaved like an adoring slave. He and Carrio then took her home, and just to emphasize her mastery, she showed them a brace of pistols. When sleeping with men who bored her, she explained, "I endure their caresses, but I don't intend to endure their insults, and I won't miss the first one who behaves like that."

Rousseau made an assignation for the following day, found Zulietta in semi-undress, and thought her superior to the houris of paradise. So long as she kept her seductive costume on, all went well. He noticed with approval that "her sleeves and bodice were edged by silk thread trimmed with rose-colored pompoms, and this seemed to me to add luster to her very beautiful skin." When she undressed, however, "I felt a mortal coldness course through my veins, my legs shook, and ready to faint, I sat down and wept like a child." Tears had been his refuge during his uneasy initiation with Mme de Warens, and they came promptly now. Lamenting that nature had inhibited his pleasure with some inexplicable poison, he began to imagine that this apparent paragon must have something wrong with her, and he scrutinized her more closely. Sure enough, he detected a hitherto hidden defect. One of her nipples was malformed, or perhaps inverted — he calls it *un téton borgne,* a blind nipple — and he suddenly grasped that "I was holding in my arms a sort of monster, cast off by nature, men, and love." Zulietta tried to reawaken his desire, but when he persisted in commenting on her defect, she walked away and said coldly, "*Zanetto, lascia le donne, e studia la matematica*" ("Little John, leave the ladies alone, and study mathematics"). When he returned the next day she had departed for Florence, leaving him wounded by his failure and her contempt.

Why did Rousseau believe that this story would display his true nature, his *naturel,* to the fullest? Did the defective nipple even exist? And supposing it was real, why did he find it so terrible? Christopher Kelly points out that he also described the one-eyed choir girl as *borgne,* and there seems to have been a connection in Rousseau's mind. The girls sang like angels but turned out to be deformed; Zulietta, conversely, had a lovely body that concealed a secret corruption, like an alluring witch. The real problem, surely, was that he felt self-conscious and ashamed in sexual situations, unable to ask for the spanking that would have truly satisfied him, and driven to explain why the desire he ought to have felt was short-circuited. If his greatest pleasure was to kneel abjectly at the feet of an imperious mistress, the freeze-frame moment when Mme Basile in Turin pointed at the floor was exactly what he needed. A pistol-carrying courtesan was not.

Years later he would make the heroine of his novel reprove her lover for permitting himself liberties after having too much to drink. "True love is always modest and doesn't seize its favors boldly; it steals them timidly. Mystery, silence, and fearful shame sharpen and conceal its sweet transports." Conversely, a high-class Italian courtesan in the novel learns to despise her way of life when she falls in love with a virtuous Englishman and unexpectedly refuses to sleep with him on that very account. "Never will you touch me! Feeling myself in your arms, I would be aware that you were holding nothing but a *fille publique,* and I would die of rage." Renouncing her charms, the Englishman in turn experiences Rousseau's own ideal of deferred enjoyment. "Happier in the pleasures he refused than the voluptuary is in the ones he tastes, he loved longer, remained free, and enjoyed life more than those do who wear it out."

But if the Zulietta story is full of implications for Rousseau's personality, it is well to remember that we know nothing about it apart from his own highly novelistic account. And the very extravagance of his challenge — "dare to read the following two or three pages" — suggests a tease or even an evasion. "Might this not be a way," his editors shrewdly ask, "to mislead the reader while claiming to supply the key to his character?" Perhaps he was so humiliated by his failure that he concocted the whole story in retrospect, including the intuition that this gorgeous creature must have some hidden defect. Or the story could be a complete red herring. Montaigu accused Rousseau of dissipation, though without giving any details, and it has been assumed that it was a mere canard. But he was in Venice for a whole year at the age of thirty-one, and perhaps he was more susceptible than he claims to the seductions of a city where, as a French visitor remarked, during carnival more women were on their backs than standing up. Montaigu himself was no ascetic. The Venetian secret service that kept an eye on foreigners reported that "he thinks only of gluttony, whores, and low dives."

After the Zulietta fiasco, Carrio, who was tired of chasing other men's mistresses and as a diplomat was prohibited from having affairs with respectable women, proposed an expedient that Rousseau says was not unusual in Venice. The two of them found a girl of eleven or twelve whose mother was willing to sell her for a modest price, and they proposed to bring her up for later enjoyment (how much later is unclear). Rousseau shows not the slightest uneasiness about this arrangement. If anyone was at fault, it was the "unworthy mother," with whom the girl continued to live. Her name was Anzoletta, and she was "blonde and sweet as a lamb; one would scarcely have believed she was Italian." She had a good voice, so they got her a spinet and a singing teacher, and they spent evenings talking and playing music in her company. Rousseau was not a pedophile, overtly at least, for nothing sexual took place. "It was necessary to wait until she matured, and we had to sow before we could reap." What they sowed was affection, and he soon developed a kind of incest anxiety, just as he had with Mme de Warens. "Gradually my heart grew attached to little Anzoletta, but with a paternal attachment . . . and I felt that when she became nubile I would have been horrified at approaching her, as if it were an abominable incest." Her fate was never put to the test, because Rousseau left Venice before anything could happen, apparently with no regrets. His one reflection was that if he and Carrio had continued in their paternal role, "far from ever corrupting her innocence, we would have been its protectors." He seems not to have known or cared what Carrio, who stayed in Venice, actually did with the girl. And it is worth noting that in all these dalliances he was characteristically passive. The major-domo brought him to La Padoana, Olivet brought him to Zulietta, and Carrio brought him to Anzoletta.

As happens so often in the story of Rousseau's life, his relations with other people are relatively well documented, but the development of his ideas, so crucial for his career as a writer and thinker, remains largely invisible. In the *Confessions* he does drop one pregnant remark about his experience of government service. When he was working on an ambitious project to be called *Political Institutions* (*The Social Contract* was the only part that he completed), he recalled how the idea first came to him in Venice, when "I had opportunities to notice the defects of that much-vaunted government." Venice was a city-state like Geneva, but the resemblance ended there. The ruling oligarchy in Geneva, in close alliance with the Calvinist ministry, promoted industry and maintained rigid control over behavior. Venice, growing steadily poorer as Geneva grew richer, relied on the pleasure industries of gambling and prostitution to forestall unrest and to protect the privileges of a parasitic nobility. "I saw that everything is connected to politics at its roots, and that from whatever angle one looks at it, a people would never be different from what the nature of their government made them." This view could, of course, have been a profoundly conservative one, but by turning it on its head, Rousseau would make it into a radical challenge. "It seemed to me that the great question of the best form of government can be reduced to this: What form of government is suited to forming the most virtuous, enlightened, and wisest people, in short the best people in the largest sense of the word?"

Rousseau's later judgment of the importance of the Venetian period can be judged from the fact that Book VII of the *Confessions* covers eight years, but nearly half of it is given to the single year in Venice, which he remembered as eighteen months. He arrived there in September 1743, and by August 1744 he had to leave. Relations with Montaigu had gotten worse and worse, since the ambassador needed his secretary to do his work for him but felt threatened as a result. In addition they had bitter quarrels over money, for the pathologically stingy Montaigu had to pay Rousseau out of his own pocket. One story (from a source other than Rousseau) was that he believed that having three shoes was just as good as having two pairs, since one shoe always wore out sooner than the other. Shrewdly, therefore, "he always had three shoes made for him at a time." Apparently they fit equally well on either foot.

What Rousseau seems not to have understood was that Montaigu's salary was a whole year overdue and that he was heavily in debt for his official expenses. He also refused to understand how exasperating his own manner must have been. Montaigu wrote indignantly to his superior, "A chair at one end of my desk didn't suit him, so he sat right down in my own armchair, and when I was dictating to him and pausing sometimes to search for a word that didn't come to me, he would generally pick up a book or gaze at me pityingly." Admittedly, there were a lot of words that didn't come to Montaigu. But much more was involved than unfortunate friction between two individuals. In his youth, Rousseau had had bitter experience of the complacent way in which privilege was taken for granted, whether in the street fight with a haughty aristocrat that provoked his father's exile from Geneva or in the kinder paternalism of the Gouvon family in Turin and the Mably family in Lyon. In Paris he had grasped all too clearly that he was regarded as a plebeian upstart by rich people who lacked his talent but had the power to make or break him. And now Montaigu, a man with rank but no abilities whatsoever, was dashing his hopes of a promising career. Guéhenno comments that the embassy experience "was almost like a deliberately arranged experiment to demonstrate the confusion and stupidity of a society in its death throes."

As early as February 1744, Montaigu told Rousseau that he was giving him six weeks' notice, but months went by. Montaigu stayed mostly in a country house he had rented on the mainland, leaving Rousseau to manage the embassy. After continued provocations on both sides — Montaigu especially infuriated Rousseau by taking away the gondola — their antagonism came to a head in August in a confrontation that threatened to turn violent. Rousseau, seeing that the relationship had broken down, had asked Montaigu's brother in Paris to recommend an honorable dismissal. When the brother duly wrote to Montaigu about it, the ambassador flew into a fury and accused Rousseau of being a spy and selling the secret of the diplomatic cipher. "I began to laugh, and asked him in a sarcastic tone if he believed there was a man in the whole of Venice stupid enough to give an écu for it. This made him foam with rage. He made a show of calling his servants to throw me out of the window." Rousseau claims that he then locked the door and suggested that the two of them have it out between themselves. This calmed Montaigu down, and Rousseau strode to the door, told him goodbye, and left the palazzo, never to return. Montaigu's own story was different. He merely mentioned to Rousseau that there had been a time when people like him would have been thrown out of windows, and stated that he would content himself with discharging him "like a bad valet for his insolence."

Montaigu demanded that the Venetian authorities expel Rousseau, which they declined to do, and he remained in the city for another two weeks, just to prove that everyone who mattered was on his side. The French consul, Le Blond, took him in, the Spanish ambassador gave him a courteous reception, and he was generally sympathized with and even feted. On August 22 he finally left Venice. It had been a heady year. His passion for Italian music would bear fruit in later life, and the discovery that he could handle responsibility was an important gain in self-esteem. Still, he was painfully aware that there was no longer any chance of the promising diplomatic career that might have developed. Already he had been an engraver's apprentice, domestic servant, seminarian, music teacher, interpreter for an itinerant monk, land office clerk, tutor, and unsuccessful composer of music. Paris awaited once more, with no obvious path to success.

Meanwhile there were Montaigu's calumnies to deal with. Rousseau wrote to his superiors in Versailles, "I shall return to Paris, it's true, weighed down by the ignominy of Monsieur the comte de Montaigu's insults, but sustained by the testimony of a clear conscience and the esteem of honest men." In the following weeks he continued to assert his case, in terms that reflected a growing belief that governments cynically serve the interests of the few. "Is there anything worse for an honest man than to see himself shamefully defamed in the eyes of the public?

. . . I have realized hopelessly that I have to submit to ridicule, and that vis-à-vis his superior, the inferior is always wrong." By the time he wrote the *Confessions,* he could put it more comprehensively. "The justice and uselessness of my complaints planted in my mind the seeds of indignation against our stupid civil institutions, in which the true public interest and real justice are always sacrificed to some apparent order that is actually destructive of all order, serving only to add the sanction of public authority to the oppression of the weak and the iniquity of the strong."

As for Montaigu, he went on making a fool of himself. Some years later Le Blond, who was still at the embassy, reported to Versailles that when some servants protested after Montaigu discharged them without pay, he began belaboring them with his cane, and they retaliated by hurling stones that struck him in the face. At about that time Montaigu was finally discharged and reluctantly entered retirement.

10

A Life Partner and a Guilty Secret

LEAVING BEHIND THE EMPTY THREATS of the comte de Montaigu, Rousseau set out for Paris, taking his time and heading first to Geneva by way of the Alps. The seventeenth-century scientist Robert Boyle wrote that there were only three ways to travel between Geneva and Italy, "by Switzerland and the Grisons, by Turin, and by Marseilles; the first is too painful because of the great quantity of snow that covereth the mountains; the second is too dangerous because of the armies that are both in Piedmont and upon the state of Milan; the third is the longest indeed but the sweetest." Rousseau had already tried the sweetest way, and now he took the painful one. After pausing to admire the Italian lakes, he continued on foot over the Simplon Pass and reached the town of Sion in the Valais after a week on the road. This was the last time he was ever in the high Alps; he made no comment on them. Though he later helped to create a cult of mountains, he preferred them as background for the cultivated landscapes lower down.

Rousseau stayed in Sion for a week, entertained by the French chargé d'affaires, the abbé Pierre de Chaignon. In the *Confessions* he says little about this visit, but it formed the basis for a romanticized image of the Valais region in his novel *Julie* that would eventually draw pilgrims from far and wide. After Rousseau left, Chaignon got a letter from Montaigu warning that Rousseau was an unscrupulous adventurer, but there is no reason to think he took it seriously; by then he had heard from a Genevan acquaintance who reported, "I drank your health with great pleasure, Monsieur, the day before yesterday with M. Rousseau; he seemed to me to be a sensible man, educated and sensitive."

Nyon lay directly on the road from Sion to Geneva, but Rousseau decided not to see his father, fearing (he says) a painful encounter with his stepmother. In Geneva, however, a bookseller friend, Emmanuel Duvillard, reproached him for this failure and persuaded him to go back to Nyon and put up at a tavern. With his friend as go-between, Rousseau was able to stage a moderately heartwarming reunion. "Duvillard went to find my poor father, who came running to embrace me. We had dinner together, and after an evening that was sweet to my heart, I returned to Geneva the next morning with Duvillard, to whom I've always been grateful for the good turn he did me on that occasion." Sweet or not, it was the last meeting between Isaac Rousseau and his son. The most memorable aspect of the visit was a chance glimpse of a woman with whom Jean-Jacques had been smitten when he was in his early teens. "Taking an excursion with him on the lake, I asked who the ladies were in a boat near our own. 'What,' my father said, smiling, 'your heart doesn't tell you? It's your former love; it's Mme Cristin — it's Mlle de Vulson.' I trembled at that almost forgotten name, but I told the boatmen to change course."

Rousseau then proceeded to Paris, arriving early in October after a journey of seven hundred miles. He wasted several weeks trying to get official acknowledgment of his mistreatment by Montaigu, which he never received, although plenty of people were willing to commiserate informally. "Everyone agreed that I was offended against, wronged, and unfortunate, that the ambassador was cruel, iniquitous, and outrageous, and that the whole affair would dishonor him forever. But so what? He was the ambassador and I was the secretary. Good order, or what they called good order, demanded that I not obtain justice, and I didn't."

With a new grudge to nurse, Rousseau began looking about for something to do. In the short run his problems were solved by renewed friendship with the young Spanish nobleman Ignacio Altuna, whom he had known in Venice and who now offered to share a comfortable apartment in the rue Saint-Honoré. They began taking meals at a table d'hôte kept by a Mme La Selle, pursued scientific studies, and even fantasized about retiring together to Altuna's estate beyond the Pyrenees. It was another of Rousseau's powerful attractions to a male companion, one who was strong-willed yet tolerant, witty yet sentimental, earnestly dedicated to acquiring knowledge, and of course good-looking. "He didn't have the Spanish coloring any more than the phlegmatic disposition. He had white skin, ruddy cheeks, and light brown hair that was almost blonde. He was tall and well built. His body was made to house his soul." Altuna especially interested Rousseau because he was at ease with women and yet apparently immune to their charms. "The flames of virtue that consumed his heart didn't allow those of the senses to be born." In short, Rousseau was projecting his own romanticized ideals onto a paragon of chastity and wisdom, a modern Galahad. After only a few months Altuna returned to his native Azcoitia, where he married, became mayor, and founded an academy of natural science.

Rousseau was once again on his own. Mobile and rootless, cut loose from ties of kinship and locality, he was very much a modern, and a fundamental aspect of his modernity is that he relied on friendship to create a personal equivalent of community. But though he yearned for intimacy in friendship, he was never much good at it. His close relationships usually turned bitter sooner or later (Altuna disappeared before that could happen), and it is fair to say that to be his friend was even harder than to be his employer. In truth, he demanded more of friendship than is humanly possible. As Stendhal remarked, "Rousseau was unhappy all his life because he sought the kind of friend of which ten or so, perhaps, have existed from Homer's time until ours." He could feel really secure only with older mentors — it is not enough to call them father figures, though they were certainly that — with whom there was no danger of jealousy and competition. In later years he would find several of them.

Very few documents survive from the years 1745 to 1749, but we do have a long letter to Mme de Warens, written in February 1745, that shows how much Rousseau had finally detached himself from her. He offers sympathy for her bad health and likewise for "my poor brother" Wintzenried, who had also been ill, and claims rather tepidly that he still hopes to end his days with her, but his view of her ongoing financial troubles is coldly realistic. In particular he demands information about "that arch-ass Keister," one of her many incompetent business associates. "I can forgive one fool for being the dupe of another, that's what they're made for, but for someone with your understanding, it's not good to be led by an animal like that." *Petit* never used to talk like that to Maman; Rousseau was now a man of experience. And in the spirit of the time, he had been studying up-to-date science, which gave him new insight into her herbal concoctions. "The more knowledge of chemistry I acquire, the more those masters who seek for secrets and potions look to me like gross imbeciles." In Paris, meanwhile, he was still trying to get justice from "my horse of an ambassador" (perhaps alluding to the horse that Caligula appointed to the Roman senate) while laboring with "many projects, and few hopes."

The letter ends with a sour account of a grandiose public celebration in honor of the dauphin's marriage to a Spanish princess. The patriotic Altuna went into ecstasies and declared that the bride was a dazzling sun who transformed everything around her into rivers of gold. As far as Rousseau could see, it was the government's determination to mount a spectacle that turned things to gold, and he was disgusted by the popular appetite for bread and circuses, so different from the spontaneous dancing in the Place Saint-Gervais when he was a boy. "I watched the rabble of Paris dancing and leaping in the superb and magnificently illuminated tents that had been set up everywhere to divert the people. Never has there been such a fête. They shook their rags, drank, and gorged so much that most of them got sick. Adieu, Maman."

Needing a place to live after his six months' stay with Altuna, in March 1745 Rousseau moved back to his old lodgings in the Saint-Quentin rooming house in the rue des Cordiers. The landlady was a person of uncertain virtue, and her tenants were boisterous and disreputable, "Irish abbés, Gascons, and others of that sort." A shy woman in her early twenties had been hired to do the laundry, and at the communal meals she became the butt of ribald humor. Her name was Thérèse Levasseur. "The first time I saw this young woman at the table, I was struck by her modest demeanor, and still more by her lively and sweet gaze, which I have never seen equaled." Rousseau chivalrously defended her, was rewarded by wordless gratitude, and became her lover, if that is the right word. They would remain together until his death thirty-three years later.

The relationship with Thérèse was essential to Rousseau in many ways. "I needed, in short, a successor for Maman. Since I could no longer live with her, I needed someone who would live with her pupil, and in whom I might find that simplicity and gentleness of heart she had found in me." So the roles were to be reversed, with Thérèse the innocent protégée, nine years younger than himself, and Rousseau the teacher. If she was not completely inexperienced sexually — she confessed tearfully to "a single slip when she was outgrowing childhood, caused by her ignorance and a seducer's wiles" — so much the better for Rousseau's status as a man of the world. "'Virginity!' I exclaimed. 'That's a fine thing to look for in Paris, and at twenty years of age! Ah, my Thérèse, I am more than happy to possess you virtuous and healthy, and not to find what I wasn't looking for anyway.'"

Rousseau's male friends (unlike some of his female ones) looked down on Thérèse, whom they regarded as stupid and narrow. Apparently she never did learn to tell time by the clock or remember the months of the calendar, and although she was literate, her spelling was bizarrely phonetic. Defending himself against his friends' condescension, Rousseau liked to imply that the relationship was merely one of convenience, and in a phrase that has attracted much commentary, since it seems to assign Thérèse a limited and extraneous role, he called her "the supplement I needed." By a supplement, apparently, he meant sexual satisfaction that remained marginal to his deeper emotional needs and might even be harmful (in *Émile* he would sternly call masturbation a "dangerous supplement" that adolescent boys must resist at all costs). But that was written twenty years after he met Thérèse, as was the unconvincing claim "From the moment I saw her until the present day, I have never felt the slightest spark of love for her . . . and the needs of the senses I satisfied with her were solely sexual, with nothing whatsoever that related to her as an individual."

The reality was very different, as his words and actions on many other occasions showed. He had grown weary of hopeless infatuations with haughty ladies, and as Clément says, "By engaging himself only halfway, he was able to avoid the trap of masochistic fascination that condemned him to intoxicating desire and passive adoration." He especially didn't want the humiliatingly dependent state he had experienced with Mme de Warens; that was something he would never repeat. And Thérèse definitely had qualities that he found attractive. His description of Marion in Turin could apply equally well to Thérèse: "Not only was Marion pretty, but she had a freshness of coloring that is found only in the mountains, and above all such an air of modesty and sweetness that one couldn't see her without loving her. Besides that, she was a good girl, virtuous, and unfailingly loyal."

Many writers at the time, while hoping for financially advantageous marriages, lived with lower-class mistresses — servants, laundresses, prostitutes — who were not averse to the Grub Street milieu. Diderot formed just such an alliance with a beautiful seamstress named Antoinette Champion, and as Rousseau says, "He had a Nanette just as I had a Thérèse; it was one more point of similarity between us." Actually, the unions were far from identical, for Diderot fell desperately in love with Nanette and married her, although he had to keep the marriage secret in order to avoid being disinherited by his father. Their marriage produced a daughter, whom Diderot greatly loved and for whom he arranged an excellent education. But in other respects it was less successful: Nanette had a ferocious temper and got into violent fights in the street, Diderot made her give up her work but allowed her no access to his social life, they quarreled constantly, and he openly kept a mistress.

Rousseau's relationship with Thérèse developed very differently. He treated her as a valued companion, and in later years he offended snobbish aristocrats by insisting that she dine with them. What he would not do was marry her, and he made that clear from the start, even while promising never to abandon her. When they finally did marry, it was to forestall malicious gossip in a small provincial town.

Almost from the start, two factors emerged to complicate the relationship. One was that Rousseau became exasperatingly entangled with Thérèse's family, and the other was that she began to bear children. He dealt with the first complication as well as he could, though it cost him no end of distress over the years; he dealt with the second so badly that it became the chief source of guilt in his life. The problem with the family was that Thérèse, with her modest laundress's wages, was virtually the sole support of numerous relatives. Her father had lost his job at the Orléans mint when it closed down and had been unemployed ever since; her imperious mother — whose husband called her the *lieute-nant-criminel,* or police chief — had been a shopkeeper but had gone bankrupt; and various shiftless siblings expected to be taken care of as well. In short, the family welcomed Rousseau as a meal ticket, and since he was lonely and insecure, he was at first glad to feel accepted. Thérèse's household "became almost my own," and that "almost" is significant. For four years, he says, he visited every evening, but continued to maintain a separate apartment for himself. How often he slept with Thérèse, and under what circumstances, is not known, and it is likewise impossible to know why he persisted in this inconvenient mode of life. He must have felt anxiety about losing his independence, and he may well have entertained thoughts of marrying up someday. Certainly he believed that Diderot made a mistake in marrying Nanette. Diderot, on the other hand, who had had a more stable and comfortable upbringing than Rousseau, evidently felt less insecure about marrying down. Incidentally, Rousseau got into the habit of calling Thérèse *tante,* "aunt," as a niece called her, which curiously echoed the chasteness of his relationship with his aunt Suzon.

Rousseau's cultivated friends deplored the connection with Thérèse and encouraged him to report her malapropisms so they could laugh at them. The abbé Morellet later said, "He could see that his friends didn't approve of the ridiculous marriage he contracted with his disgusting Thérèse." At that point, of course, it wasn't a marriage at all, and if she was disgusting, it cannot have been on physical grounds. Rousseau said she was at least as attractive as Nanette, and James Boswell, a tireless admirer of women, who met her when she was forty-three, described her as "a little, lively, neat French girl."

Not a few later commentators have found Thérèse an embarrassment as well, but they overlook Rousseau's engaging descriptions of the pleasures of ordinary existence with her. For instance, they were fond of dining overlooking the street: "The windowsill served as our table, we were breathing fresh air; we could see the neighborhood and the passers-by, and even though we were on the fourth floor, enter into the street life as we ate. Who could describe or feel the charm of those meals, composed entirely of a quarter loaf of bread, some cherries, a bit of cheese, and a half bottle of wine that we shared between us? Friendship, trust, intimacy, sweetness of soul — what delicious seasonings you contribute!" Accounts like this give substance to Rousseau's claim that "my Thérèse had the heart of an angel; our attachment grew with our intimacy, and every day we felt more strongly how much we had been made for each other." As the years went by he increasingly depended on her good sense in practical situations. "Often in Switzerland, England, and France, in the catastrophes I found myself in, she saw what I couldn't see for myself, gave me the best advice to follow, and saved me from dangers that I was blindly rushing into."

About a year after their liaison began, Thérèse revealed that she was pregnant, and a child was born at the end of 1746 or early in 1747; no record was kept of the date, and even the sex is uncertain. The infant was immediately consigned to the charitable Hôpital des Enfants-Trouvés, or foundling home, as were four more infants in subsequent years. This action seems staggering today, in light of who Rousseau was and what he became, as well as in light of his own history of abandonment as a child. But the practice was not uncommon, and he was influenced, he says, by the advice of the raffish fellows at Mme La Selle's establishment, who were accustomed to dispose of illegitimate offspring in this way. For a long time he successfully kept what he had done secret from everyone except a few friends, but by the time it came out, he had become famous as the author of a book on bringing up children, and he had a lot of explaining to do.

In Rousseau's own words, which remain the only direct evidence that exists, this is what happened.

> I made up my mind cheerfully and without the least scruples, and the only ones I had to overcome were those of Thérèse. I had the greatest difficulty in the world getting her to accept this means of preserving her honor. Her mother, who feared the inconvenience of a brat, came to my aid, and she allowed herself to be overcome. A discreet and trustworthy midwife named Mlle Gouin was chosen, who lived at the Pointe St. Eustache, and when Thérèse's time came, she was taken there by her mother for the birth. I went to see her several times, and I took with me a cipher that I had written in duplicate on two cards, one of which was placed in the child's clothes. He was then deposited by the midwife at the Enfants-Trouvés office in the way that was customary. The following

year there came the same inconvenience and the same expedient, except that the cipher was neglected. I didn't reflect any further, and the mother didn't approve any more fully; she groaned but obeyed.

The cipher was supposed to make identification possible if parents ever wanted to reclaim a child, but when Rousseau did initiate inquiries ten years later, they were completely unsuccessful.

What exactly was the Hôpital des Enfants-Trouvés? It had been founded under religious auspices in 1670, inspired by the charitable work of Saint Vincent de Paul, who was shocked by the number of infants being abandoned by their parents. It was not an orphanage but a hospice (one meaning of the word *hôpital*) for the temporary care of newborns whose parents were callously exposing them to the elements in public places. A quarter of all newborns back in Chambéry, and more than that in Paris, were thus abandoned. The most famous of these foundlings, abandoned by his aristocratic mother and recorded as having been discovered "in a wooden box on the steps of the church of Saint-Jean-le-Rond," from which he got his name, was the future scientist and writer Jean le Rond d'Alembert. D'Alembert's father managed to locate him and to place him in a suitable family, but such an outcome was exceedingly rare. Most of the foundlings were illegitimate, and Rousseau's comment about Thérèse's "honor" reflects the severity of the stigma, not just for unmarried mothers but for their children, who grew up despised and deprived of many ordinary rights. For this reason even well-to-do women often pretended to take a trip away from Paris during the final weeks of pregnancy, moving into houses like Mlle Gouin's. After delivering their babies, the midwife would handle arrangements at the foundling home. Reformers began to complain that an institution intended to succor unfortunates was actually creating them: "the tomb of maternal love," one writer called it.

During the time Rousseau and Thérèse were having children, approximately six thousand infants arrived each year at the Enfants-Trouvés. Nuns supervised wet nurses, who provided immediate nourishment, and as soon as possible the infants were consigned to permanent nurses in villages outside Paris. These women were paid a not very generous stipend and were expected to raise them for the next several years. In principle the children would then return to the city to learn useful skills, as Rousseau seems to have imagined his own offspring do-ing. Some did, while others remained in the country; but the great ma-jority simply died. The mortality rate was appalling. Infectious diseases were a constant threat for all children in those days, and foundlings were at far greater risk than others. They arrived malnourished and sickly, were crammed together in grossly unhygienic conditions, and were often badly cared for by their rural nurses if they lived long enough to get there. According to official records, in 1751, a year when one of Rousseau's infants was in all likelihood admitted, 70 percent of them died before they were one year old; still more died later. The re-cords show, incidentally, that on November 21, 1746, an infant named Joseph Catherine Rousseau was received, having been baptized the pre-vious day, and committed by a person identified as Marie Françoise Rousseau. It is suggestive that Thérèse's mother was Marie Françoise Levasseur, but it would have been normal to give a less obvious alias, and Rousseau was a very common name (d'Alembert's foster family were Rousseaus, unrelated to Jean-Jacques). At any rate, this baby's fate was a sad one. After being turned over to a rural nurse he died in Janu-ary, not quite two months old.

As early as 1751, Mme Levasseur betrayed the secret to Rousseau's patron Mme Dupin and her daughter-in-law Mme de Francueil, and he began trying to defend himself. In a letter to Mme de Francueil he gave not just one explanation but several, most of which he repeated later in the *Confessions,* in what a psychoanalyst would call a case of overdeter-mination. He claimed that since the children had been formally depos-ited, they were not really abandoned (*déposés,* not *trouvés*). Moreover, his hopes of doing important work would have been ruined by the need to provide for a family. Besides, he expected to die soon, and his illegiti-mate children would have ended up as boot cleaners or thieves. Even if he didn't die, he could hardly legitimate them by marrying Thérèse, since unjust laws would then condemn him to a lifetime commitment (by implication, to an unsuitable person). Clearly the foundling hospital was the best choice: it would raise the children to be sturdily self-suf-ficient, "not gentlemen but peasants or workers," using not the pen but "the plow, file, or plane, instruments that will allow them to lead a healthy, hard-working, and innocent life." Didn't Plato argue that chil-dren should be brought up by the state with no knowledge of their parents? This last rationalization was especially hollow, since Plato's plan was intended for all children in the ideal republic, not just for a minority of unfortunates. Rousseau's deep anxiety about the whole subject is indicated by the fact that his copy of the letter to Mme de Francueil was transcribed in code ("of a charming simplicity," Leigh comments, since the numeral 1 represented the letter A, 2 was B, and so on).

The one defense Rousseau never proposed was that the children weren't really his at all, although by the end of the eighteenth century it was widely suggested that he might have been impotent and Thérèse unfaithful. George Sand, long afterward, reported that her grandmother, the second wife of Rousseau's friend Francueil, responded when someone said that Rousseau had been an unnatural father, "Oh! as to that, we don't know anything about it, and neither did Rousseau himself. Was he even able to have children?" But if Rousseau did believe the children weren't his, he would surely have told his closest friends. Instead, he always declared that Thérèse had preserved "a spotless fidelity, about which she has never given me occasion for the slightest suspicion." So far as those years were concerned, he seems to have believed this completely, though there were some tensions later on.

Strangely, after supplying a good deal of circumstantial detail about the first baby, all Rousseau says in the *Confessions* about the other four is that they were taken to the Enfants-Trouvés as soon as they were born. It has even been doubted that they ever existed, especially since his sexual inhibitions and health anxieties — at some point during this period he developed a chronic urinary complaint that tormented him for the rest of his life — make it seem surprising that he sired five children in a space of six years, between 1746 and (at the latest) 1752. Virtually every testimony to their existence, including the story that Mme Levasseur is supposed to have told the Dupins, derives solely from Rousseau's own words or from contemporaries who heard about the children only from him. Even the exculpatory letter to Mme Francueil exists only in Rousseau's draft. The only real exception is the claim by a writer much later that he had lived across the street from Rousseau's lodgings and patronized a wigmaker there, who told him that he felt sorry for Thérèse "since the children she gave her master were barbarously sent to the Enfants-Trouvés." This may mean that she openly lamented her loss, and indeed it is hard to know how she managed to bear it. But the anecdote was recorded in 1791, at a time when the whole story had become public knowledge, and as thirdhand testimony it is not necessarily reliable. And one ambiguous bit of evidence suggests that Thérèse later remembered four children, not five, which makes the story murkier still.

Whatever the truth may have been, there is no doubt about Rousseau's later remorse, which helped to inspire the writing of *Émile*. Anyone who fails to bring up his own children, he wrote, "will weep long and bitterly for his error and will never be consoled." The abandonment of his children would also partly inspire the project of apologia that became the *Confessions*. Most writers at the time tried to keep their lives and their writings separate. Rousseau developed a uniquely new kind of personal image, as a sage who practiced what he preached, and he was driven to explain his behavior to himself as well as to the public. "Never for a single instant in his life," he declared in the *Confessions,* "could Jean-Jacques have been a man without feeling and pity, an unnatural father." But the guilt always remained, and it became a gnawing disturbance at the center of his existence. For Thérèse it was excruciating, and although no comments of hers have been recorded, it must have had a permanent effect on her relationship with him.

I I

A Writer's Apprenticeship

IN THESE EARLY YEARS in Paris, Rousseau was constantly oppressed by the problem of making a living. When Altuna departed in 1745, he was absolutely broke; he wrote to his friend Roguin to apologize for not repaying a loan and to ask whether the tradesman who supplied his fancy clothes for Venice might be willing to take some of them back. His idea for seeking his fortune at that point was to resume work on a "heroic ballet" or masque called *The Gallant Muses,* which he had begun two years earlier. "I have resolved to imprison myself in the Hôtel Saint-Quentin and not allow myself to go out until I've finished it." But he added bleakly that fame was no longer his goal. "I am so disgusted with society and dealings with men that nothing but a sense of honor keeps me here, and if I ever do attain the height of my desires, which is to owe nothing to anyone, I won't be seen in Paris twenty-four hours after that." Roguin replied that the debt was of no importance and that "if you are in trouble, I will share with you the little that I have, with pleasure and very sincerely." He signed his letter affectionately, "Adieu, my very dear friend," and indeed Roguin remained a friend for life.

After three months of labor *The Gallant Muses* was done. A combination of song, instrumental music, and dance, it was intended as a tribute to the power of love as interpreted by Tasso (whose style was to be elevated), Ovid (tender), and Anacreon (gay). The text was repetitive and obvious, and no doubt had to be, having no other purpose than to sustain the music and dancing. The score for the first act survives, described by a modern specialist as unremarkable except for occasional lively passages, and the libretto isn't even as good as that. Rousseau himself had no illusions about it. At some later time he inserted a disclaimer at the beginning of the manuscript: "This work is so mediocre in its kind, and the kind itself is so bad, that to understand how it could ever have pleased me, one must recognize the power of habit and prejudice." But in the *Confessions* he admitted that it pleased him because of the fantasy identification to which he was always prone. "I can say that my love for the princess of Ferrara (for I became Tasso for the time being), and my proud and noble sentiments toward her unjust brother, gave me a night that was a hundred times more delicious than I would have experienced in the arms of the princess herself."

The next step was to have *The Gallant Muses* produced, but that turned out to be impossible. Jean-Vincent de Gauffecourt, a Genevan whom Rousseau had known in Chambéry, gave him a valuable introduction to Alexandre-Jean-Joseph de Riche de la Pouplinière, a *fermier-général* of immense wealth. (Tax farming was a system established in the previous century when Louis XIV needed funds for his enormously expensive wars. Wealthy lenders advanced money — their own and deposits from investors — in return for the right to collect revenues and keep a handsome percentage for themselves.) La Pouplinière and his wife maintained a brilliant salon, even though their personal relations were frosty. Mme de la Pouplinière had originally been his mistress, and he expected to continue in that way, but powerful friends of hers persuaded his superiors that he had betrayed a young innocent and deserved to lose his official position unless he did the right thing. Once they were married, the couple treated each other with contempt; the philosophe Jean François Marmontel, who knew them well, said that at the dining table they could barely look at each other. Eventually La Pouplinière got his chance to dismiss his unwanted spouse when a cunningly hidden door was discovered that gave access to her lover, the duc de Richelieu (not the great Richelieu of Louis XIV's time), in an adjoining apartment. But meanwhile their salon attracted all the intellectuals and artists of Paris, in particular the celebrated composer Rameau. It was not necessarily auspicious for Rousseau that Rameau condescended to be Mme de la Pouplinière's music teacher and actually lived in her mansion, since it was he who had coldly exposed the weakness of Rousseau's scheme of musical notation when it was presented to the Académie des Sciences three years before.

When La Pouplinière agreed to assemble some first-rate singers and instrumentalists to give *The Gallant Muses* a private performance, Rousseau was sure that his career was launched at last. The outcome, however, was disappointing in the extreme. Although most of the listeners (Rousseau claims) were charmed with the piece, Rameau grumbled constantly and finally burst out, declaring that part of it was the work of a total incompetent and the rest must have been stolen. Rameau later repeated this judgment in print: "I was struck by finding in it some very beautiful airs for violin in an entirely Italian style, and at the same time everything that is worst in French music, whether vocal or instrumental . . . I asked the composer some questions to which he replied so badly that I easily saw, as I already suspected, that he had composed only the French music and had pillaged the Italian." That wasn't true, but Rameau undoubtedly believed it, and he did have reason to resent Rousseau. Quite apart from his invariable hostility to potential rivals, he cannot have appreciated that the title *Les Muses Galantes* mimicked his own much-admired *Les Indes Galantes*.

Rousseau never denied that his self-taught skills had produced uneven results and that his true passion for Italian music had not yet come into its own. "Nourished since childhood in French musical taste and in the kind of poetry that goes with it, I mistook noise for harmony, the marvelous for the interesting, and songs for an opera." But he was bitterly offended by the charge of plagiarism, as well he should have been, and by Rameau's brutality, for which the egotistical composer was well known. In one of Diderot's works Rameau's nephew is made to say of his uncle, "If he ever did any good to anybody, it was without realizing it . . . His wife and daughter can go ahead and die whenever they like, and as long as the parish bells that toll for them keep on sounding in intervals of a twelfth and a seventeenth, everything will be fine." In addition to being disagreeable, Rameau was avaricious to an almost fantastic degree. And he was so emaciated that one contemporary said he looked more like a ghost than a man; another compared him to an organ pipe without the bellows and added, "His whole mind and soul are in his harpsichord, and when that's closed up, there's no longer anyone at home."

The sequel was even more demoralizing. The duc de Richelieu, who was in charge of entertainments for the court, liked *The Gallant Muses* so much that he promised to have it performed at Versailles if Rousseau would replace the first act with a new version featuring Hesiod instead of Tasso. This he hastened to provide, summoning all of the clichés of routine amorous verse. "Lovely fire that consumes my soul," Hesiod sings, "Inspire my songs with your divine ardor; convey into my spirit that bright flame with which you're burning my heart." Rousseau alluded covertly to his own situation by suggesting that the muse had so inspired Hesiod that he could surpass better-trained musicians, with clear reference to himself and Rameau: "I am going to triumph over my jealous rivals." But Mme de la Pouplinière demanded that Richelieu respect Rameau's loathing for Rousseau, and the performance was dropped. "I have never seen such cabals and such animosity," Rousseau wrote to a friend. Yet to his surprise, he was also discovering a certain pleasure in defending himself against criticism. "I take courage in spite of that. The fury of my enemies has made me recognize my own strength, and without their jealousy I wouldn't have known that I was capable of fighting them." To be sure, Rousseau may not have been altogether guileless. A biographer of Rameau sees the situation as "an old musician's fear of losing his patron, and a young intriguer's ambition."

Since most of Rousseau's efforts to gain success as a musician came to nothing, they are often described as mere bids for recognition, but music meant far more to him than that. Inhibited in conversation, he found it possible to be vicariously eloquent when skilled performers interpreted his compositions. Melody, he later wrote, imitates emotion, "and not only does it imitate, it speaks, in a language that is inarticulate but lively, ardent, and passionate, with a hundred times more energy than speech itself." Rameau celebrated the mathematical rigor of harmony in a series of influential treatises, but for Rousseau even instrumental music had to sing.

Before 1745 was over, a new possibility materialized. In May the French army achieved a famous victory over the British and Austrians at the Battle of Fontenoy, and it was suggested that a revised version of

Voltaire's operatic ballet *The Princess of Navarre* might celebrate this triumph of arms. Voltaire had little inclination to bother with it, and Richelieu suggested that Rousseau could help out. This he gratefully did, meanwhile writing a fan letter to Voltaire, whom he had long admired, to explain what he was doing. "For fifteen years I have been striving to make myself worthy of your regard, and of the concern you show for young poets in whom you detect any talent; but having composed the music for an opera, I find myself somehow or other metamorphosed into a musician." He explained that Richelieu had commanded him to revise *The Princess of Navarre* as *The Fêtes of Ramire* and that the state of his finances obliged him to accept the assignment, with the understanding that any changes must be approved by Voltaire. The great man, no doubt intending to please Richelieu, whom he took to be Rousseau's patron, wrote back from his distant estate to say that it was extraordinary for a single person to be talented in both music and poetry and a shame that Rousseau should devote his talents to an inferior work. "I well know that the whole thing is paltry, and that it is beneath a thinking being to take such bagatelles seriously." Voltaire also admitted that he didn't actually remember the piece very well and gave Rousseau carte blanche to do what he liked with it.

The task was a thankless one nonetheless, since Rousseau was supposed to interpolate transitions and recitative that would conform to Rameau's existing score, along with occasional lines of verse consistent with Voltaire's libretto, without adding anything of his own. He labored for two months, impeded by constant interference from Rameau and Mme de la Pouplinière, and when the piece was staged at Versailles it was attributed only to Voltaire, with no mention of Rousseau. An apparent opportunity to collaborate with the greatest writer and the greatest composer of the age thus came to nothing. Still worse, Rousseau says, presumably accurately, that he never got paid, even though the official record of "gratuities accorded to the symphonists, actors, dancers, artists, composers, workers and others" has an entry naming "M. Rousseau, musician, 792 livres." As for the work itself, it was unremarkable. An expert who has studied the manuscript concludes, "Two months of labor for a result like this reflects either mediocre competence or a lot of time off."

For Rousseau the disappointment was stinging, and after an attempt to get the piece performed by the Opera, blocked once again by Mme de la Pouplinière, he "returned home with death in my heart; I fell ill, worn out by fatigue and devoured by grief, and for six weeks I was in no condition to go out." Starobinski calls this collapse a "symbolic death" in which Rousseau repudiated his allegiance to "the pair of great elders Rameau–Voltaire, objects of internalized love but henceforward objects of hatred." At this time also he abandoned — literally in mid-sentence — an essay that praised Rameau and asserted that French music was more moving than Italian. Before long he would achieve notoriety for saying exactly the opposite.

In the spring of 1746 Rousseau put his disappointments behind him and starting going once more to the salon of his old patron Mme Dupin, to whom he had written the ill-advised poem of homage and whose dreadful son he had attempted to tutor. He also began to study chemistry again with her stepson, his friend Dupin de Francueil, and he must have taken it seriously, for a letter to Rousseau survives from a young man calling himself a "disciple" who sought advice on the crystallization of salts. Some time later he moved to the rue Plâtrière to be as close as possible to the Dupins. He liked the street so well that he settled there again twenty-five years later; it forms part of the present-day rue J.-J. Rousseau. A notable benefit of this renewed association was the chance to stay for weeks at a time in the extraordinarily beautiful château of Chenonceaux in Touraine, which M. Dupin had recently purchased. Rousseau was not altogether comfortable with aristocratic pleasures, and it was probably there that he was reluctantly present at the death of a stag. He was shocked by the joyous baying of the hounds, who at least were obeying normal instinct, and still more shocked at the glee of the hunters. "In considering the desperate straits of that unhappy animal and its moving tears, I felt how much nature is a commoner, and I vowed never again to be seen at a fête like that one."

The Dupin family and their guests enjoyed putting on amateur theatricals, and Rousseau was inspired to write a verse drama for them called *L'Engagement Téméraire,* or *The Rash Vow.* Its characters love each other but are afraid to admit it, a congenial enough theme for him but by no means original; the models, which he followed slavishly, were the sprightly comedies of Marivaux, whose characters are regularly surprised by their own feelings and mistrustful of each other's sincerity. Although the plot is competent, there is no dramatic energy at all, just talk. Rousseau thought his play had "much gaiety," but it is hard to see why. At the Dupins' he himself probably played the role of the hero's valet, as he did soon afterward at La Chevrette, where a friend of Francueil's named Mme d'Épinay had a country house. Some years later Mme d'Épinay would become an important figure in Rousseau's life, but for the present she was just another hostess, and witness to his embarrassingly inept performance in spite of endless rehearsal. Francueil played the romantic lead, as was only appropriate, since he was not only a gifted actor but had recently become Mme d'Épinay's lover. In a roman à clef written years afterward, she gave her own description of Rousseau in those days: "He is full of compliments without being polished, or at least without seeming to be. He has no social graces, but it is easy to see that he has an infinite amount of intelligence. He has a very dark complexion, and flashing eyes that animate his features. When he's talking and you're looking at him, he seems handsome, but when you think about him afterward he always seems ugly."

Looking back, Rousseau regarded this whole period as an emotional blank. The years from 1746 to 1748 occupy barely a tenth of Book VII of the twelve-book *Confessions,* and apart from two letters to Mme de Warens, he apparently stopped keeping a record of his correspondence. Only the first of his five discarded children is specifically mentioned (if there really were five), and he makes only perfunctory mention of a major event of May 1747: "At about this time . . . I lost my virtuous father, who was roughly sixty years of age. I felt this loss less than I would have at another time, when the difficulties of my situation might have preoccupied me less." It is hard to understand how Rousseau could have mistaken his father's age as sixty rather than seventy-five, as was actually the case.

What Isaac Rousseau's death chiefly implied was that Rousseau, at the age of thirty-five, would finally get the rest of his mother's inheritance, amounting to some 3,000 livres. (The livre, or *livre tournois,* had not been a real coin for over a century. It was an artificial unit that could be translated into any kind of actual money.) In dire financial straits, he so longed for this windfall that he was anxious to confirm his own moral integrity. "Coming home one night, I found a letter that had to contain the news, and I seized it in order to open it with an impatient trembling that made me ashamed of myself. 'What!' I said scornfully to myself, 'can Jean-Jacques allow himself to be subjugated to this extent by self-interest and curiosity?'" He put the letter on the mantelpiece, managed to forget all about it, and opened it the next morning in a self-congratulatory frame of mind. "I felt many pleasures all at the same time, but I can swear that the liveliest of them was the pleasure of having conquered myself."

For years Rousseau had been vowing that if he ever did get any money, he would hasten to place it at the feet of Mme de Warens, in recognition of his undying love and of her financial support during ten years of his life. In fact he sent only a small amount, although she was in desperate circumstances and was appealing to everyone who might conceivably help out; M. Tavel, the seducer of her youth, actually did take pity and send some money. Rousseau's love turned out not to be undying, and he had well-founded doubts about emptying his own badly needed resources into the bottomless pit of her speculations, which had recently turned from making soap (she sent him some) to mining for copper and coal. "All of her letters reflected her distress. She used to send me heaps of recipes and secrets that were supposed to make my fortune and hers. Already a sense of her poverty was contracting her heart and narrowing her mind. The little that I sent her became the prey of the scoundrels who were besieging her, and she got no profit from it."

Still, it was a betrayal. None of Mme de Warens's letters from this time survive, but he did keep a copy of his defensive self-justification written a few months after receiving the inheritance, which she had always expected to share. "As for myself, I tell you nothing, and that's saying everything. In spite of the injustice you inwardly do me, it's up to me alone to change your perpetual mistrust into esteem and compassion. A few explanations would suffice, but your heart is too full of its own troubles to have room for anyone else's. I still hope that one day you will know me better and love me more." This bleak complaint, to the person who once knew him better than anyone on earth, ends with the mandatory obeisance to "the brother," Wintzenried.

Meanwhile, if Rousseau's inheritance was saved from the predators

around Mme de Warens, it was apparently only so that it could be devoured by the Levasseurs. "Time slipped away and the money with it.
There were two of us, even four, or to put it more accurately seven or
eight. For although Thérèse lacked self-interest to an exceptional extent, her mother didn't. As soon as her mother saw herself a bit better
off through my efforts, she summoned her entire family to share in the
spoils. Sisters, sons, daughters, and granddaughters, they all came."
Even worse, Thérèse herself was cynically abused by this gang of parasites. "It is remarkable that the youngest of Mme Levasseur's children,
and the only one who had no dowry, was the only one who supported
her father and mother; and that after having long been beaten by her
brothers, her sisters, and even her nieces, the poor girl was now being
robbed without being able to defend herself from their thefts any better
than she did from their blows." Without having a family, Rousseau had
somehow acquired a pack of grasping and dishonest dependents. And
perhaps Thérèse's experience of domestic abuse helps to account for her
apparent passivity in giving up her infants.

Fortunately, the Dupins had a job for Rousseau. Ten years earlier,
marking time in Chambéry, he had written to his father that his talent
for writing "might help me to find employment as a secretary to some
grand seigneur." Montaigu had been decidedly the wrong *seigneur,* and
the Dupins weren't noble at all, but self-made bourgeois who flaunted
their wealth. Francueil's granddaughter George Sand noted that "he
had in his employment a troupe of musicians, cooks, parasites, lackeys,
horses, and dogs." But the Dupins were friendly and intelligent, and
they needed a secretary. Francueil wanted help with a book on chemistry; he and Rousseau compiled a massive introduction to the subject
that never got beyond the manuscript stage. The senior Dupin intended
to write about politics and economics, and Mme Dupin had ambitions,
too. Rousseau became a sort of research assistant, and he did the work
energetically and well (at very moderate pay) over a period of five years,
from 1746 to 1751. M. Dupin was chiefly concerned to refute the great
Montesquieu, whose *Spirit of the Laws* came out in 1748 and among
other things was critical of tax farming. After much effort he produced
a three-volume set, *Observations on a Book Entitled Of the Spirit of the
Laws,* which went all but unnoticed. Several friends helped Dupin
compose this work, and Rousseau's part in it was extremely humble, but

it did require him to read widely in political writings, which laid a solid foundation for his own *Social Contract* later on.

Mme Dupin had a much livelier mind, and her project was more stimulating. She conceived the idea of a compendious book arguing for female equality, based on historical research into the status of women in various cultures and times. The 2,800 pages of notes that Rousseau produced have survived, and have been carefully studied by a scholar who concludes that his role was essentially "manual labor" and that his contribution is reflected mainly in grains of sand that he sprinkled to blot the ink, and occasional grains of coffee. However, in the course of compiling these notes, Rousseau read his way through countless books on politics, history, and foreign cultures, searching for anecdotes, legal codes, and anything else that might prove useful. Whenever Mme Dupin decided that he had amassed enough material on a given topic, she would take over, organizing and rewriting herself. She had no idea in the world that her assistant might be a thinker in his own right, and later on she admitted as much. Her daughter-in-law, Mme de Francueil, remarked in a similar vein, "But tell me, Monsieur Rousseau, who would have suspected it of you?"

The Dupins by no means engrossed all of Rousseau's time. His friendship with Diderot continued to deepen, and he was close also to the abbé de Condillac, whom he had known in Lyon. The three men were about the same age and full of ambitions that were not yet realized. Rousseau says in the *Confessions* that Condillac "was like myself a nothing in literature, but formed so as to become what he is today." Condillac quickly gained a reputation in 1746 with his *Essay on the Origin of Human Knowledge,* and he added to it with a series of works in the ensuing decade. Following the English philosopher Locke, he argued that all knowledge comes directly from sense perception, and in a thought experiment that became famous, he imagined a statue of a man acquiring each of the five senses one by one and becoming human in the process. Unremarkable as this approach may seem today, it was still a daring position to take in France, where all theologians and many philosophers believed that the mind enters the world furnished with innate intuitions of truth. Despite his theological training, Condillac was moving toward a radical materialism which held that everything that exists, including human thoughts and emotions, is nothing but matter in various combinations. Rousseau was never willing to go that far, but he found contact with advanced ideas invigorating, and he learned a great deal from Condillac's style of careful, reasonable persuasion.

Diderot, given to outrageous arguments on either or both sides of a question, was still more stimulating. Eventually he would make himself into a titan of literature, but in the 1740s he was as obscure as Condillac and Rousseau, and far more unpredictable. A policeman who kept a dossier on Parisian writers referred to him at the time as "a very clever boy but extremely dangerous." The epithet "boy," Robert Darnton comments, "implied marginality and served to place the unplaceable, the shadowy forerunners of the modern intellectual." Diderot always saw himself as a rigorous thinker and as a wise judge of his friends' behavior, but his imagination often ran away with him, and his tendency to admire his own conduct while moralizing about everyone else's would eventually prove fatal to his relationship with Rousseau. For the present, however, Rousseau was uncritically devoted to Diderot. An autobiographical fragment from this period celebrates "conversations with that virtuous philosopher whose friendship, already immortalized in his writings, has been the glory and happiness of my life — that astonishing and universal genius, unique perhaps, whose contemporaries do not understand his value, but of whom future ages will scarcely believe that he was nothing more than a man."

Still another major thinker among Rousseau's friends was the former foundling Jean le Rond d'Alembert, a bit younger than the others but already famous. His mother, the celebrated *salonnière* the marquise de Tencin, had adamantly refused ever to see him after discarding him at birth — curiously, she became the patron of his friend Condillac — but his father, an army officer named the chevalier Destouches, had provided for his education. D'Alembert, still living with the glazier's family in which he had been placed, had been recognized since his early twenties as a brilliant mathematician, at a time when mathematics still held the highest prestige. He divided his life between advanced theoretical work and playful salon conversation; he was small in stature, lively in manner, and a killingly accurate mimic. Condorcet, another philosophe, described "his gaiety, his cutting sallies, his talent for telling stories and even acting them out, the malice in his tone of voice together with the goodness in his character." Between them, Diderot and d'Alembert were everything Rousseau was not.

Soon after Rousseau introduced Diderot to Condillac, the three began meeting regularly at a tavern called the Panier Fleuri in the rue des Augustins. As Rousseau recalled, "These little weekly dinners must have pleased Diderot greatly, for although he hardly ever kept an appointment, he never missed a single one of those." After d'Alembert joined the group, it resolved into two pairs of close friends, Rousseau with Diderot and Condillac with d'Alembert, and for several years they cooperated closely on projects of various kinds. Some were relatively trivial, such as a scheme for a periodical, to be jointly authored by Diderot and Rousseau, which would be called *Le Persifleur,* the "banterer" or "mocker." Only one essay, drafted by Rousseau, ever got written, and it echoed Montaigne in declaring, "Nothing is more dissimilar to me than myself." In this piece Rousseau claimed to be a protean being, "subject to two main dispositions that change quite constantly from week to week; in one I find myself wisely mad, in the other madly wise." This was no doubt an artificial persona invented in the spirit of Diderot, who enjoyed being unpredictable, but at the same time it reflected Rousseau's quest to understand his own contradictions. To be like oneself, *semblable à soi-même,* is an idiom for consistency of character; in this essay Rousseau declares, "A Proteus, a chameleon, a woman are all beings less changeable than I." Diderot, like Montaigne, was a skeptic for whom the shifting weather of the self posed no threat, but Rousseau was writing out of character here; what he needed was to locate a deep self beneath the apparent contradictions. As it turned out, Diderot was overcommitted with other projects, and this one never saw the light of day.

No account of those weekly dinners at the Panier Fleuri was ever written down, but they were an indispensable stage in Rousseau's apprenticeship as a writer and thinker. When he came to write his treatise on education — influenced a good deal by Condillac, not to mention by his earlier experience as tutor to Condillac's exasperating nephews in Lyon — he acknowledged his debt unreservedly. "Few well-regarded books appear in Europe whose authors didn't form themselves in Paris. Those who think it's sufficient to read the books that are written there are mistaken. One learns much more from authors' conversation than from their books, and the authors themselves are not the source from which one learns the most. It is the spirit of social gatherings that develops a thinking head and pushes one's vision as far as it can go. If you have any spark of genius, go and spend a year in Paris. You will soon be all that you can be, or if not, you'll never be anything." At the time nothing could have seemed more commonplace: four ambitious young men, only one of whom had much reputation, getting together to argue about ideas. But in due course all four would turn out to be giants, and Rousseau, the least prepossessing of the diners at the Panier Fleuri, would become the greatest of them all.

As the friends continued to debate, an extraordinary project materialized. Diderot had translated a medical dictionary from English into French, and a publisher invited him to do a similar job with a more general dictionary called a *Cyclopedia.* As he considered the idea, his imagination was fired, and he enlisted d'Alembert to coedit a vastly ambitious compendium of all human knowledge, practical as well as theoretical, that would contain hundreds of plates illustrating up-to-date technology. This was the great *Encyclopedic Dictionary of the Arts and Sciences,* known for short as the *Encyclopédie.* When the first volume was published in 1751, it immediately became the centerpiece of the Enlightenment movement, attracting scores of contributors and alarming the authorities with covert hints of political and religious unorthodoxy. Casting about for writers when the project was being launched, Diderot asked Rousseau to supply the articles on music (after being turned down by Rameau), and Rousseau seized the opportunity gratefully. In the end he contributed nearly four hundred articles, mostly short ones, on politics as well as music. Diderot himself wrote many times that number and devoted twenty-five years of arduous labor to a project that he originally expected to finish in three. Unfortunately for the quality of Rousseau's work, he did it in great haste, meeting a three-month deadline and discovering only later that no one else had bothered to.

One other person joined the group and made himself indispensable, especially to Rousseau, whose love of music he shared. This was Frederick Melchior Grimm, son of a German pastor and graduate of the University of Leipzig, who came to Paris in 1748 and, with an insinuating personality and perfect command of French, made himself welcome in intellectual circles. Though not especially good-looking, he was inordinately vain and had a habit of wearing perfumed white face powder. In later years Grimm played an important role in the philosophic movement by disseminating its ideas to a select group of progressive European royalty in a closed-circulation newsletter called *Literary Correspondence,* but in these early days he was simply a companion of the Encyclopédistes, who teasingly called him Tiran lo Blanc, the White Tyrant of a medieval romance, in allusion to the face powder. Of all Rousseau's friends, Grimm was the one with whom he would eventually break most bitterly, but for the present they were inseparable. "He had a harpsichord, at which we used to get together, and where I spent every free moment with him, singing Italian airs and barcarolles without pause from morning until night, or rather from night until morning." Rousseau even convinced himself that Grimm and Diderot were prepared to spend a year touring Italy with him on foot, though neither of them had the slightest intention of ever doing so.

Through Grimm, Rousseau had a distressing experience. A German friend of theirs, a not very pious clergyman named Emmanuel-Christoffel Klüpfel, "was keeping a young woman in his apartment who was available to everybody, since he couldn't afford to support her by himself." Having drunk a good deal of wine one evening, Rousseau allowed himself to be dragged along to Klüpfel's place, where he and Grimm took turns with her. Thérèse was the fourth woman with whom Rousseau had ever had intercourse, the others being Maman (for a relatively brief time), Mme de Larnage (very briefly indeed), and the Venetian prostitute La Padoana (as briefly as possible). Once again, as with La Padoana and Zulietta, he described himself as lured by friends into a sexual encounter. In the *Confessions* he stresses his subsequent shame and abject confession to Thérèse; he may have resisted marriage, but he certainly meant to be faithful to her. No doubt alcohol and the encouragement of his companions had a lot to do with his transgression, as did the youth and timidity of "the poor girl, who didn't know whether to laugh or cry."

Rousseau always liked a glass or two of wine with meals, but drunkenness frightened him, and by the standards of the day he was abstemious. Diderot once coupled his name with Plato's in a way that stressed aversion to social pleasure: "Plato and Jean-Jacques Rousseau, who recommended good wine without drinking it, are two false companions of the gourd." (The irrepressible Diderot consumed food and alcohol on an epic scale and suffered constantly from indigestion.) Voltaire suggested in verse that the Garden of Eden was the worse for lacking wine: "Let him who will regret the good old days . . . The foam and sap of good cool wine never caressed the sad gullet of Eve." As for Rousseau, twenty years later he replayed in *Julie* his remorse over getting drunk, together with his lapse with Klüpfel's mistress. After Saint-Preux utters some improper language under the influence of alcohol, Julie sternly declares that if it ever happens again she will break with him forever. Saint-Preux calls wine a "mortal poison" that overpowered his will, and indeed what was at issue for Rousseau was the fear of losing control. Instead of encouraging truth to emerge, *in vino veritas,* wine liberated words that might be true but ought to be repressed.

At the same time, Rousseau yearned to be attractive to women, or at least to ladies. Looking back on this period years later, he wrote indignantly, "Pretty Frenchwomen used to offend me by treating me as an unimportant fellow, going so far as to dine with me tête-à-tête in the most insulting familiarity, and even embracing me scornfully in front of everybody, as if I were their nursemaid's grandfather." It must be remembered, however, that he was fond of exaggerating his social incompetence, and that plenty of women were strongly drawn to him. A visitor who saw him around 1750 noticed that despite his habitual reserve, Rousseau was very flirtatious, responding with special warmth to an attractive young woman who spoke with an Italian accent. "For two or three hours our philosopher deployed graces we didn't suspect he had, which would have been the envy of a gifted courtier accustomed to triumphing in this sort of gallant game."

What nobody could know, and what Rousseau himself didn't suspect, was that after forty years of disappointments and floundering, he was about to be launched as a major writer and celebrity. Like everything in his life, the opportunity came more or less by accident, but when it came he grasped its importance and suddenly knew that he had something important to say. The waiting and hoping were over at last.

12

The Beginnings of Fame

DIDEROT WAS IN THE HABIT of testing how far he could go with dangerous ideas, and in due course he went too far. In *The Promenade of a Skeptic* he argued for radical materialism, according to which nature is in constant flux and matter undergoes endless changes without purpose or meaning. This was bound to be unacceptable to orthodox religion, and so was *Letters on the Blind,* in which Diderot suggested that a person blind from birth would not perceive the signs of divine goodness that theologians took as self-evident and might even refuse to believe that God exists. By order of a *lettre de cachet,* a royal edict ordering imprisonment without trial or hearing (the *cachet* was the king's seal), he was conducted to the château of Vincennes near Paris and confined in a tiny cell. After a few weeks his confinement was relaxed, and he was permitted to move freely about the château and its pleasant grounds, while his friends in Paris worked to secure his release. It came after four months, mainly because his publishers stood to lose an enormous sum if the *Encyclopédie* didn't go forward. But the price of freedom was a promise never again to publish anything offensive to the government.

This condition Diderot faithfully obeyed, with the result that the works for which posterity has admired him most — *Rameau's Nephew, D'Alembert's Dream, Jacques the Fatalist* — appeared only in very limited editions or were never printed at all in his lifetime. Rousseau, on the other hand, never hesitated to publish controversial works and paid dearly for it. Both men thought of themselves in the role of Socrates, martyred for truth, and if Diderot had less justification than Rousseau for that flattering identification, he had good reason to be cautious. It was no mean feat to keep the great *Encyclopédie* alive, and he can hardly be blamed for not choosing martyrdom.

During the time of Diderot's imprisonment, Rousseau frequently went out to Vincennes to visit him, tramping for several miles along a dusty road. The first time he arrived, he found d'Alembert and a priest already with Diderot. When Rousseau burst into tears of joy on seeing him, Diderot offended him by turning calmly to the priest and remarking, "You see, Monsieur, how my friends love me." But whereas Rousseau saw tears as proof of sincerity, for Diderot they were manifestations that any actor could produce at will. No doubt, too, the visits meant more to Rousseau than they did to Diderot.

Rousseau continued to make the trek to Vincennes every couple of days. On one memorable occasion the summer heat exhausted him, and he stopped to rest while idly reading a copy of the *Mercure de France*. The physical experience of walking had helped, as it so often did, to liberate his imagination. Leafing through the journal, he noticed an announcement of a prize being offered by the Academy of Dijon for the best essay on the topic "Whether the restoration of the sciences and arts has contributed to purify morals." It was a trite enough question, practically taking for granted an answer in the affirmative, but when Rousseau suddenly saw a new way of arguing in the negative, "I beheld a different universe and became a different man." He was overcome by "dizziness like that of drunkenness," his heart pounded, and tears drenched his shirt. Sitting under a tree, he hastily scribbled down an imaginary speech of Fabricius, a champion of primitive Roman simplicity who returns from the past to denounce modern sophistication and cries out, "Madmen, what have you done?"

Something powerful clearly happened to Rousseau in what has become known as the illumination of Vincennes, and it turned out to be a breakthrough to a new way of understanding himself and society. But his descriptions of it date from long afterward, and they give a mythic flavor to the discovery of a vocation. Diligent scholarship has established that the event actually occurred in October 1749, not summer, and according to metereological records the temperature barely reached sixty degrees Fahrenheit. By remembering sweltering heat, he was perhaps attributing to the weather the physical symptoms that had overwhelmed him.

As many commentators have noticed, Saint Augustine also experienced deep agitation while seated beneath a tree, and also had his life transformed by encountering a text (in his case the Bible, a more authoritative source than the *Mercure de France*). From each of these conversion experiences, a book called *Confessions* eventually resulted. But Rousseau had a different reaction from Augustine, who realized that God was showing him his sinfulness. "I had placed myself behind my own back," Augustine wrote, "refusing to see myself. You were setting me before my own eyes so that I could see how sordid I was, how deformed and squalid, how tainted with ulcers and sores." Rousseau's illumination was exactly the reverse of Augustine's: man is naturally good, not wicked. Yet by the time he recorded his reminiscences of the incident, he had come to see irony in it as well. By competing for a prize, he was being co-opted by the very social pressures he intended to criticize. When Augustine cast off the sinful self, he put on the garment of righteousness; Rousseau too became a different man, but he later realized it was the wrong man.

The first thing to do was to tell Diderot about the revelation. Always competitive himself, Diderot was happy to encourage Rousseau to enter a contest, and he seems to have thought that the argument against progress was nothing more than a playful paradox. In later years, after he and Rousseau were no longer speaking to each other, Diderot freely told friends that the idea had actually been his own. Marmontel remembered him saying:

> "I was a prisoner at Vincennes; Rousseau used to come to see me. He had made me his Aristarchus, as he has said himself. One day, when we were taking a walk together, he told me that the Dijon Academy had just proposed an interesting question, and he wanted to take it up: Has the restoration of the sciences and arts contributed to purify morals? 'Which side will you take?' I asked. 'The affirmative,' he answered. 'That's the *pons asinorum*,' I said; 'all the mediocre talents

will take that route, and you'll find nothing but commonplaces there. The negative side, on the other hand, offers a new, rich and fertile field for philosophy and eloquence.' 'You're right,' he said after pondering a bit, 'and I'm going to follow your advice.'"

Marmontel retailed this anecdote to Voltaire, who was always glad to hear bad things about Rousseau, adding snidely, "From that very moment, his role and his mask were determined." Voltaire eagerly replied, "You don't surprise me; that man is artificial from head to foot, in mind and in soul."

On the face of it, Diderot's claim (which he never stated so baldly in writing) is highly improbable. As Rousseau described it, the illumination on the road was the logical result of a lifetime of disappointment and alienation. "I developed a contempt for my century and my contemporaries . . . and little by little I detached my heart from the society of men." Diderot, who loved to play with ideas — he said that he ran after them as rakes did after women — could not have truly understood the revolution in Rousseau's mind. Moreover, Diderot was the least systematic of writers, always improvising and inventing. It has been well said that "his thought is always in midstream; one never sees it except in the process of leaving one idea to look for another." He was like the fox in the Greek aphorism about the fox who knows many things while the hedgehog knows one big thing, and Rousseau was the hedgehog. Rousseau was slow in debate, easily flustered and confused, but the insight that human goodness had been corrupted by civilization became the foundation of his entire life's work. To feel alienated was to know the truth, and it was the socially well-adjusted people who were leading inauthentic lives.

Back in Paris, Rousseau set to work on his essay. Writing never came easily to him, to put it mildly. Sitting at a desk with pen in hand, he felt paralyzed. His preferred method was to compose paragraphs laboriously while walking or during long hours of insomnia. "I have turned and re-turned some of my sentences five or six nights in my head before they were in any condition to put on paper." By the beginning of 1750 Thérèse had at last moved in with him, on the fifth floor of an apartment house called the Hôtel de Languedoc in the rue Grenelle-Saint Honoré, the site of the present-day No. 27 rue Rousseau, and her parents lived in the garret above. Mme Levasseur came down every morning to help with housework, and, like Milton with his daughters, Rousseau would dictate to her while lying in bed before getting up. (Thérèse wasn't literate enough for the job.) "This practice, which I followed for a long time, saved me from forgetting a lot." Here again is a striking contrast with Diderot, who could dash off a brilliant page on any topic at a moment's notice. But when Rousseau finished the painful task of shaping a piece of writing, it had an oracular power that no other writer of his time even aspired to.

The essay was completed and sent off to Dijon, after which, Rousseau says, he forgot all about it. Half a year later, in July 1750, the announcement came that he had won the prize over a dozen other entrants. All but lost in the mists of time are a historian from Troyes who likewise argued the negative and took second place, and an ecclesiastic from Besançon who argued the affirmative and took third. The contest judges were careful to include a disclaimer — "In crowning the work of M. Rousseau, the academy does not claim to adopt his political maxims, which are not at all in keeping with our customs" — but they agreed that the sciences had produced more evil than good.

It is curious that this rather obscure body of lawyers, physicians, and churchmen should have launched a great career. Its members were a mediocre group who met to read humble cut-and-paste essays to each other. Their preferred topics were medical or scientific, and the annual prize usually went to friends of the directors. One of the directors was a hopeless alcoholic, and another, who had been a musketeer before becoming a magistrate, was fond of saying that an academy of horseback riding would have been a better idea. But they deplored the spread of secularism, and Rousseau's impassioned polemic appealed to them. They completely failed to grasp that his critique of civilization cut far deeper than their own grudges.

Little attention was normally paid in Paris to provincial competitions, but here too Rousseau was lucky. The Dijon committee members had connections with the *Mercure de France,* and its new editor was a friend of Rousseau's, Guillaume Raynal, who went out of his way to praise the essay and summarized it extensively. At the end of 1750 or early the next year it was published as a pamphlet, with a complicated title that is usually abbreviated as *Discourse on the Sciences and Arts* or simply as the *First Discourse,* and Rousseau became an instant celebrity.

It was a very brief piece — the rules required that it not take more than half an hour to read aloud — and readers today may well wonder what all the fuss was about. Attacks on modern corruption were boringly familiar, but Rousseau's approach was remarkable because he attacked the assumptions of the Enlightenment from within, in what has been called the autocritique of the Enlightenment. In his paradoxical but powerful argument, he agreed with the philosophes that civilization has brought much that is good, but he argued that at the same time it is destructive; its defects are not occasional exceptions to its virtues but a direct consequence of them. Measuring everything by the expectations and opinions of others, people conceal their true feelings even from themselves. "Suspicions, offenses, fears, coldness, reserve, hatred, and betrayal will constantly lurk beneath this uniform and treacherous veil of politeness, this vaunted urbanity that we owe to the enlightenment of our century." And the arts, just because of their charm, reinforce a bondage that is all the more insidious for being unperceived. "Even while government and laws give security and well-being to assemblages of men, the sciences, letters, and arts, which are less despotic but perhaps more powerful, spread garlands of flowers over the iron chains that bind them, stifle in them the sense of that original liberty for which they seemed to have been born, make them love their enslavement, and transform them into what are called civilized peoples."

Rousseau had been an outsider all his life; now he would show why marginality was a virtue. For a motto to the *First Discourse* he chose the Latin tag he had first adopted in Lyon, *Barbarus hic ego sum quia non intelligor illis.* As was usual at the time, no name appeared on the title page, but it carried the defiant identification "By a citizen of Geneva." It was a challenge to the cosmopolitan Enlightenment, whose propagandists deplored patriotism and called themselves citizens of the world. Perhaps, too, Rousseau was propitiating the shade of the citizen of Geneva who had taught him Roman ideals and had died too soon to see his success. "If only he had lived four more years," he wrote sentimentally in a notebook fragment, "to see his son's name spread throughout Europe! Alas, he would have died of joy!"

Clearly the *Discourse* struck a nerve. Multiple editions came out, and

PORTRAIT OF ROUSSEAU BY MAURICE QUENTIN DE LA TOUR

Painted shortly after Rousseau's sudden ascent to fame, after La Tour (whose mistress was starring in Rousseau's opera) met him at Fontainebleau, this pastel was exhibited in the Paris Salon of 1753 along with portraits of d'Alembert and other celebrities. La Tour did several versions of this portrait, the only one Rousseau ever cared for; the copy reproduced here remained in the artist's personal collection. In later years it cheered Rousseau to recall his ideal self-image, as he said when the painter sent him a new copy: "This admirable portrait, which in a way makes the original worthy of respect, will never leave me, Monsieur. It will be before my eyes every day of my life, and will speak ceaselessly to my heart." Diderot complained, however, that instead of showing the stern gaze of "the Cato and Brutus of our age," it gave nothing more than a pretty image of "the composer of *The Village Soothsayer,* well dressed, well combed, and well powdered."

a superb portrait of Rousseau by Maurice Quentin de La Tour was exhibited at the Salon of 1753. Not a few aristocrats, resenting the growing influence of *parvenu* wealth, appreciated Rousseau's critique. "This discourse is well written," the marquis d'Argenson said, "and notable above all for the nobility and elevation of its principles. This author is a good political thinker. I like his sentiments on equality and against riches and luxury." What d'Argenson had in mind was "those young financiers who throw money around with scandalous effrontery." Financiers like the Dupins, he could have added.

Numerous reviews and critiques were published — seventy-five within three years — and attempts at refutation came from all directions. One critic, whom Rousseau was careful to treat with respect, was his friend from Lyon Charles Bordes (also spelled Borde), a fervent believer in progress. Another, treated necessarily with even more respect, was a former monarch, Stanislas Leszczynski, a deposed king of Poland living in France as the duc de Lorraine. In responding to his critics, Rousseau showed a remarkable gift for lucid argument. Even more important, he realized that he needn't go on defending a work that was really the first stage in a much larger project. "My adversaries' example," he wrote later, "taught me how necessary it is to reflect and meditate before producing anything." While the critics flailed away at the *Discourse,* he was developing an altogether more powerful analysis of civilization and its discontents. "For two or three years I had the pleasure of watching them ceaselessly water the leaves of a tree that I had secretly cut off at the root."

Just as the *Encyclopédie* was about to appear, Rousseau was thus emerging as a potential traitor to the Enlightenment. In French the term for Enlightenment is *les lumières,* literally "lights," and Diderot wrote enthusiastically about philosophy advancing with giant strides while *lumières* spread all around. But Rousseau became convinced that what the light presaged was a destructive blaze. For the frontispiece of the *First Discourse* he chose an allegorical image to illustrate the point: "The satyr, says an ancient fable, wanted to kiss and embrace fire the first time he saw it, but Prometheus cried out to him, 'Satyr, you'll mourn for the beard on your chin, because it burns when you touch it.'"

For the time being, however, the philosophes assumed that he was merely exaggerating for effect, and they encouraged him to join them at the home of a new patron who was a progressive intellectual as well as extremely rich. Paul-Henri Thiry, baron d'Holbach, was a young German who had studied in Holland and would eventually contribute hundreds of scientific articles to the *Encyclopédie.* D'Holbach had an income of 60,000 livres per year, or about 59,000 more than Rousseau, and presided with great hospitality over a salon that convened every Thursday and Sunday and specialized in the free exchange of ideas. "There they esteem each other enough to contradict each other," Diderot said; "there the true cosmopolitan is found." Over the years almost every distinguished foreigner who visited Paris was a guest at the d'Holbach salon, and the regulars adored it. As Morellet recalled, there was "heavy but good food, excellent wine, excellent coffee, plenty of arguments but never quarrels, simplicity of manners . . . a gaiety that was real without being foolish, and, in short, truly captivating company."

Even here, however, Rousseau found himself a misfit. As Marmontel remembered him during this time, "One could see mistrust in his timid reserve. He kept his eyes lowered and watched everything with touchy attentiveness; he said little and never opened up." Rousseau's own opinion was that the free thought the philosophes prided themselves on was just another form of competition. A few years later he made a fictional spokesman say, "I found all of them proud, assertive, and dogmatic, even in what they claimed was their skepticism, ignorant of nothing, proving nothing, and each one mocking the others." For his own part, he never forgot that the root meaning of "philosophy" is love of wisdom. Grimm once complained that Rousseau merely put on "the livery of philosophy," a cruel sarcasm, since he had worn the actual livery of a footman in his youth and writhed because of it. But the remark was more accurate than Grimm knew. The philosophes wore a team uniform that allowed them, like bicycle racers, to profit from each other's slipstream. The uniform never fit Rousseau, and he knew what he was doing when he took it off. "Can one look for good faith in the leaders of a party?" he later asked.

Especially repugnant to Rousseau was the militant atheism of the d'Holbach circle, which would eventually cause public scandal in d'Holbach's *System of Nature*. Morellet said that although his own religious belief was treated courteously, d'Holbach and Diderot "dogmatically established an absolute atheism." Even the historian Edward Gibbon, no friend to religion, was disgusted by their arrogance. "They laughed at the skepticism of Hume, preached the tenets of atheism with the bigotry of dogmatists, and damned all believers with ridicule and contempt." Or, as an anonymous epigram had it,

Je suis bon Encyclopédiste,
Je connais le mal et le bien.
Je suis Diderot à la piste:
Je connais tout, je ne crois rien.

("I am a good Encyclopédiste, I know good and evil. I follow Diderot's track: I know everything, I believe nothing.")

Rattled by the atmosphere of cocky debunking, Rousseau made up his mind to think through his own position carefully and then stick to it. "Their philosophy is for others," he decided; "I need one for myself. Let me seek it with all my strength while there is still time, so as to have a fixed rule of conduct for the rest of my days." Conduct, not doctrine; but Rousseau did regard himself as a genuine believer. After a fashionable dinner at Mme d'Épinay's estate, when the servants had withdrawn and the guests could speak freely, several of them began making light of religious belief. Mme d'Épinay noticed that Rousseau grew indignant and muttered, "They're joking about it," under his breath. Then he spoke up: "If it's cowardly to speak ill of one's friend who is absent, it's a crime to speak ill of one's God, who is present. As for me, messieurs, I believe in God."

Of Rousseau's personal life during this time, not a great deal is known. A number of new friends did appear on the scene, notably the fellow Genevan Toussaint-Pierre Lenieps, a banker living in exile because of his radical politics. There were also the novelist Françoise de Graffigny, the marquise de Créqui, who kept a salon, and the historian Charles Duclos, but little has survived concerning Rousseau's relations with them. He and Thérèse continued to live in the Hôtel de Languedoc from 1750 to 1756, and if there really were five children, the last of them were still entering the world (and in all likelihood leaving it) during these years.

One incident left a documentary record. On Christmas Day of 1751, a burglar made off with some expensive linen from Rousseau's Venice wardrobe. Thanks to legal depositions by Mme Levasseur, Rousseau, and an investigating lawyer, the inventory of his wardrobe is as fully documented as anything in his entire life: twenty-two shirts, some of them embroidered, each marked with a blue *R* (this must have been for the laundresses in Venice), together with fourteen collars, nine nightcaps, and four handkerchiefs. The thief also broke a padlock on the Levasseurs' storeroom in the attic and took a few things from there. If Thérèse's ne'er-do-well brother was the culprit, as Rousseau suspected, he presumably added this second break-in to divert suspicion.

At about this time, Rousseau's urinary complaint set in as a permanent aspect of his life. As early as 1748 he had written to Mme de Warens to report "an attack of colic of the kidneys, with fever, burning pain, and retention of urine." When the symptoms kept recurring, he suspected a kidney stone and consulted a series of doctors, who could find nothing wrong. Eventually he decided that his urethra had somehow become partially blocked. One doctor, Jacques Daran, did give some relief with flexible catheters; Rousseau ordered a huge supply of these and continued to use them for the rest of his life. Whatever the cause of his condition, the constant probing — really a kind of daily torture — could not fail to provoke infections. His chief symptom was a continual need to urinate, which encouraged him to avoid social situations that could cause embarrassment. Many commentators have suspected a psychosomatic component; it certainly seems possible that anxieties about sex would have focused his attention on this particular kind of symptom. In a rather startling anecdote in *Émile,* he recounts a mother's answer when her little boy asks where babies come from. "'My son,' the mother replied without hesitation, 'women piss them out, with pains that sometimes cost them their lives.'" Even so had Jean-Jacques cost the life of Suzanne Rousseau.

Health worries continued to plague Rousseau from then on, as did financial ones, since he had still found no way to escape dependence on others. In 1749–1750 he wasted a whole year tutoring once again the wretched Dupin scion, Chenonceaux. The one consolation was that Chenonceaux had recently married a beautiful and intelligent bride who enjoyed talking with Rousseau; this time he had sense enough to attempt no advances, even though her ash-blonde hair "reminded me of my poor Maman's in her prime, and violently agitated my heart."

Around 1751 his friend Dupin de Francueil offered a new means of security that seemed very tempting, a cashier's position in his tax collection office. The work was easy and the pay good, but the responsibility of handling so much money was disturbing, and of course Rousseau could never bear to work in an office. He stuck with it for about a year, until Francueil went away on a trip and left him in sole charge of the money box, which so terrified him that he took to his bed in a fit of illness and resolved to resign. At about this time he involved himself in a further embarrassment with the ever tolerant Francueil, who had paid for Rousseau's ticket at the opera. When the two men got separated in the crowd, Rousseau seized his chance to return the ticket for cash. After the audience sat down, Francueil could easily see that Rousseau had disappeared. (Francueil himself, according to his granddaughter George Sand, "had no recollection of the incident at all, and even believed that Rousseau had made it up to demonstrate his sensitive conscience and to keep people from suspecting the faults that he didn't confess.")

If Rousseau had cast his lot permanently with the Dupins, as they would have liked, what would the future have held? A career as the loyal factotum of a rich family, tutoring as needed, and performing secretarial work for employers who had no idea how gifted he was. He had been offered similar prospects back in Turin by the comte de Gouvon, and a deep instinct had made him spurn them. It was time to spurn them again, and to symbolize his decision by a drastic change in lifestyle. "I applied all the strength of my soul to breaking the shackles of opinion." As his writings would consistently emphasize, those are the hardest of all shackles to break, and anyone who does break them is likely to face ostracism.

Ever since youth, Rousseau had fixed on the age of forty as the end point of any quest for success, and now that he was forty and had indeed achieved some success, he resolved "to pass the rest of my years living indeed from one day to the next, with no thought for the future." To symbolize worldly renunciation he began to dress more simply, stopped wearing a sword, and got rid of his watch, "saying to myself with incredible joy, 'Thanks be to heaven, I will no longer have any need to know what time it is.'" The portable watch was a relatively recent invention that was transforming the way people managed their lives. By discarding it he was refusing to let his life be structured by social demands, not to mention repudiating the very technology that had been his father's profession. From now on he resolved to make a modest living by copying music while refusing all other employment.

The result was successfully shocking. "We thus see," Marivaux was heard to say, "that one can become a singular person whenever one likes, for I've known Jean-Jacques for twenty years [actually it was ten] and he didn't use to be like that at all." In 1752 a visitor from Basel named Isaak Iselin dined at Grimm's and was shocked to discover how shabby Rousseau was. "As we went in, we saw a little man whose appearance was not at all good, dressed badly and in poor taste. I suspected at once who it might be, but Herr Albrecht assumed at first that it was Herr Grimm's tailor, until Herr Grimm said he was very pleased that he could give us a meal with Herr Rousseau." On a later visit Rousseau confided to Iselin that his chief maxim was "not to give orders to anyone or to take orders from anyone, no matter who." And he wrote to the marquise de Créqui that he had left the Dupins regardless of the likely consequences for his fortune. "I will earn my living and I will be a man. There is no fortune higher than that." At this point, incidentally, he had made no money at all from his publications, though that would later change.

Diderot, who arrived in Paris a decade before Rousseau, had made himself into the quintessential Parisian. Rousseau was beginning to understand that he would never be a Parisian, and he didn't want to be. Getting out of the city whenever he could, he accepted frequent invitations to the country retreat at Passy of a retired jeweler named François Mussard, and to a rectory in the village of Marcoussis where the priest was a friend of the Levasseurs. After one of his visits there, which included much convivial music making, Rousseau sent his host a verse letter that indicates clearly how he felt about the Dupins and their kind:

> No more of that rabble
> Who are called *grands seigneurs* . . .
> Proudly devouring our goods,
> Demanding everything, giving nothing,
> Whose false politeness,
> Endlessly deceptive and ingratiating,
> Is nothing but a clever snare to dupe
> The fool who lets himself be caught.

And his letter to Mme de Francueil about the disposal of his children included a new note of resentment: "The earth produces enough to feed everybody, but it's the station in life of the rich, it's your station, that steals my children's bread."

To his genuine love of rural life, Rousseau added a renewed taste for the kind of simple melody that his aunt Suzon used to sing. Quite suddenly the idea for a new kind of opera came to him, the very opposite of the rhetorical exaggeration still in vogue in Paris. "One sees the actresses almost in convulsions," he wrote in *Julie,* "wrenching shrieks violently from their lungs, hands pressed against their breasts, heads thrown back, faces inflamed, veins distended, stomachs quivering." During a week's stay with his friend Mussard at Passy, during which they shared their enthusiasm for Italian music, he sketched out two arias and a duet. Back in Paris, he went on composing at a furious rate, and within a couple of weeks had the complete manuscript of a one-act opera called *Le Devin du Village,* or *The Village Soothsayer.* At this time his new friend Lenieps wrote down a character sketch: "He has a very delicate constitution, tormented by a retention of urine and subject to frequent indigestion; he is small in size, with a slender torso, black and lively eyes, and leaden complexion; his humor is gay and lively; he is a great musician and still greater composer, playing the harpsichord with the score in front of him and singing with a weak voice, in Italian as often as in French."

Rousseau never received the technical training that would have allowed him to perfect his musical skills, and the failure of *The Gallant Muses* had laid him open to Rameau's sneers about plagiarism. In *The Village Soothsayer,* however, he made a virtue of his limitations. In this pastoral drama, the shepherdess Colette artlessly laments the loss of her rustic lover, Colin, to a fine lady, but the kindly soothsayer shows her how to revive his ardor by provoking his jealousy, and Colin and Colette reunite in a joyful duet. Duclos offered the work to the Paris Opéra (concealing Rousseau's authorship because the Rameau episode might have caused him to be blackballed), and it proved so appealing in rehearsal that a command performance was ordered for October at the royal court at Fontainebleau.

Even before the performance, Rousseau was haunted by a feeling that he was an impostor, and when a distinguished-looking officer at a café claimed to know the author, instead of confronting him Rousseau slunk away like a guilty criminal. When he entered the theater he felt even more out of place, having chosen to go unshaven and in shabby clothes, which would either demonstrate noble independence or else make him ridiculous. But once the performance began, he was able to relish the satisfaction an artist feels when complete strangers are moved by his work. In particular he observed that women who might well have ignored him in person were weeping uncontrollably under his influence. "I'm sure that at that moment the voluptuousness of sex entered into it more than the vanity of an author, and certainly if there had been only men there I would not have been consumed, as I constantly was, by the desire to catch with my lips the delicious tears I was causing to flow." King Louis XV adored the music, and so did his celebrated mistress, Mme de Pompadour, who was a generous patron of the arts. Rousseau's fortune seemed assured.

At this moment Rousseau made a decision that offended the court and baffled his friends. He received an invitation to meet with the king the next day, with a strong intimation that a pension would be forthcoming. Instead of complying, he returned to Paris early the next morning, giving no explanation. The opera's producer, Pierre Jelyotte, who sang the role of Colin, was horrified and wrote to him at once, "You were wrong, Monsieur, to leave in the midst of your triumph. You would have enjoyed the greatest success ever known in this country. The entire court is enchanted with your work. The king, who, as you know, doesn't care for music, is singing your airs all day long with the worst voice in his kingdom, and has commanded a second performance for next week." Diderot, also appalled, dragged Rousseau off the street into a cab and lectured him "with a warmth that I would not have expected from a philosopher on such a subject." The explanation Rousseau later gave was that his urinary troubles might have caused a disastrous embarrassment in the royal presence. He must also have feared that a kind of stage fright would cause him to make a fool of himself. Years later a friend described how unhinged he could become when he had to perform in even the most unthreatening circumstances: he was asked to sing for his friend's wife, "the least imposing of women, herself excessively timid," but when he sat down at his little spinet with trembling fingers and choked voice, he was unable to sing until he had calmed himself down.

Still more important, Rousseau had made up his mind to refuse patronage of any kind, though he could hardly insult the monarch by saying so directly. And it was surely this posture of independence that galled Diderot, since it implied tacit criticism of the way in which the philosophes were co-opted by the powers they claimed to criticize. Moreover, Diderot was genuinely concerned about Rousseau's unworldliness and had been secretly trying to help out. Knowing that Rousseau was sure to fly into a rage if he discovered their assistance, his friends used to divide up responsibilities, one taking charge of provisions and another of clothing, and employing the very willing Levasseurs as intermediaries. Someone who was familiar with their practice summed it up afterward: "Thus was our philosopher deceived from morning till night, and enabled to manage for a long time without detracting from his independence and his systematic poverty." D'Holbach once commented, "One cannot imagine a more painful contrast than the one between his Thérèse and his genius. Diderot, Grimm, and I formed a friendly conspiracy against that bizarre combination. He was wounded by our zeal and indignant at our disapproval." All too soon Rousseau did suspect a conspiracy, and not a friendly one.

As for *The Village Soothsayer,* it seems rather slight today. Even the most successful song, Colette's opening air, "J'ai perdu mon serviteur" ("I have lost my suitor"), is laboriously repetitive, which provoked a patron on the first night to call out, "Hurry up and find him again, Mademoiselle Colette, and stop tormenting us like this." But the public had an appetite for simple and melodious singing, and Rousseau was suddenly being hailed as a leading composer, even if a few ill-wishers still charged that his work must have been plagiarized from Italian sources. He never claimed that his opera was musically demanding; in fact, he was proud of it because it wasn't. "From a technical point of view, there's nothing in *The Village Soothsayer* that goes beyond the elementary principles of composition. Not only is there no music student who wouldn't be able to do as well after three months, but it's doubtful if any learned composer could resign himself to be so simple."

While basking in his triumph at Fontainebleau, Rousseau had the satisfaction of remembering his humiliation in Lausanne when he claimed to be Vaussore de Villeneuve. As it happens, a few years later the actual Venture de Villeneuve unexpectedly turned up, having learned that his former protégé was a celebrity. But Venture had lost all of his charm and was now boring as well as dissolute. "I saw him almost with indifference, and we parted coldly enough." Rousseau did shed some sentimental tears — seeing Venture brought back the poignant memory of picking cherries with the two girls at Thônes — but it was a reminder that he had made much more of himself than anyone in those early days would have believed possible.

The second performance at Fontainebleau went forward, the Paris Opéra mounted a new production in March 1753, and the reputation of *The Village Soothsayer* continued to grow. Even if Rousseau had thrown away the chance for a lifelong pension, he did realize more money from his opera than he had ever seen before. In all it brought him more than 5,000 livres — 2,400 from the king for the performances at Fontainebleau, another 1,200 from Mme de Pompadour for a performance at the Château de Bellevue, where she herself took the role of Colin (not Colette), 1,200 from the Opéra, and 500 from the publisher who printed it. Rousseau sent the publication proceeds to Mme de Warens, a substantial gesture toward paying his long-standing debt. During the course of the eighteenth century the opera was performed in Paris nearly four hundred more times, as well as in most of the major cities in Europe. In 1773 the great Christoph Gluck wrote, "*The Village Soothsayer* is a model that no composer has yet imitated." Five years earlier, the twelve-year-old Mozart had composed a pastoral *Singspiel* entitled *Bastien and Bastienne* that alluded to it affectionately. Another, less complimentary reaction must have delighted Rousseau if he ever heard of it. His old employer the comte de Montaigu noticed one day that *The Village Soothsayer* was on the schedule at the opera, and asked who wrote it. "You should know him well," was the reply. "It's Rousseau, your former secretary." "What? that imbecile?" Montaigu exclaimed in amazement.

More serious was the displeasure of the court, where it was unheard-of for patronage to be declined. Rousseau made matters even worse by declaring in the preface to the published version that its chief merit was to have pleased himself, neglecting to acknowledge that it had pleased the king. Louis XV was not amused. "People spoke in the king's presence of this impertinent advertisement," according to a confidential police report submitted to the inspector of publications, "and his majesty said, 'It might please me too to send Monsieur Rousseau to the Bicêtre prison'; to which the comte de Clermont added, 'and have him flogged there.'" This report was remarkably well informed: it recounted Rousseau's dismissal in Venice, his quarrel with Rameau, his urinary condition, and his refusal of the Dupins' patronage as well as that of the court. The informant also said that Rousseau's alleged indifference to money was the merest hypocrisy. "Since he is often ill, or acts like it, people who come to see him slip a gold louis furtively (so as not to wound our philosopher) under a candlestick or a box, or among some papers. Rousseau takes great care to recover these." It is not clear how this was known, but it is certainly possible that Mme Levasseur and Thérèse sometimes got their hands on such contributions while Rousseau looked the other way.

The Village Soothsayer was the last significant piece of music that Rousseau ever composed, but before 1753 was over, his commitment to lyrical simplicity established him at the center of a major cultural controversy. An Italian company had recently scored a big success with *La Serva Padrona,* an opera buffa by Pergolesi. A spirited debate soon arose concerning the respective merits of Italian and French music, with the king and his supporters letting it be known that they favored the French, while the queen and hers promoted the Italian. At issue was not just a difference in taste, but disagreement about the sources of pleasure in art. Rameau, in keeping with the Cartesian rationalism that still dominated French thought, had attempted to prove that mathematical relationships underlay all of music, as evidenced in harmony. The pro-Italians in the *querelle des bouffons* maintained that melody, not harmony, was the source of music's power, and that it appealed more to the emotions than to the mind.

The philosophes were all fond of music, and most of them contributed spirited pamphlets to the controversy. Rousseau was inspired to publish a brief satire, in the ironic mode favored at the time, entitled "Letter from a Symphonist in the Royal Academy of Music to His Colleagues in the Orchestra." The musician allegedly writing this piece confesses an inability to play Italian music properly — "At the end of a line or two I couldn't tell where I was, so I pretended to count out rests, or got out of the fix altogether by leaving to take a piss" — and proposes ways of "mangling this enchanting music" by insidiously distorting it. Half of the violins should play on key, for example, while a quarter would be sharp and another quarter flat — implying that the orchestra was already doing exactly that. As for the oboes, the speaker adds, there is no need to tell them what to do, since they're terrible no matter what.

On reflection, Rousseau saw an opportunity for something more significant than this pleasant but ephemeral squib. Toward the end of 1753 he brought out *A Letter on French Music,* a much longer and more serious work, and his highly critical analysis caused an immediate sensation. He couldn't claim to rival Rameau's excellence as a composer, but he could certainly compete with him as a thinker: "It's for poets to make poems and for musicians to make music, but it belongs to the philosopher alone to speak well about both." At the same time he began working on the *Essay on the Origin of Languages,* never completed but full of ideas that would bear fruit later on, in which he described speech as originating not in concepts but in emotional exclamations. Music and language were really two aspects of the same thing, and singing was the truest expression of music's purpose, "for it is not so much the ear that conveys pleasure to the heart, as the heart that conveys it to the ear." It is human feelings that we long to share. "As soon as vocal signs strike your ear, they announce a being like yourself. They are, so to speak, the organs of the soul . . . Birds whistle, man alone sings, and one cannot hear either a song or a symphony without saying to oneself at once, 'Another sensitive being is here.'"

All of this, Rousseau thought, the Italians understood, and *The Village Soothsayer* was intended to show that the simplest tunes could be the most compelling. Something much deeper than patriotism and xenophobia was thus at stake. Rousseau was rebelling against the assumption that music was a technical skill that only trained and indoctrinated experts could practice, and he was appealing to the experience of all cultures that music is a fundamental mode of expression, emotional and deeply human. At that time folk song was beginning to be taken seriously, and a response to familiar melodies was thought to be an especially Swiss trait, notably in the Alpine cowherds' song called the *ranz des vaches,* which was well known to arouse such painful homesickness that the French king forbade his Swiss troops to play it. In the *Dictionary of Music* that Rousseau began to compile at this time, he commented, "These effects, which do nothing for foreigners, derive only from habit, memories, and a thousand circumstances that this air retraces in its listeners, recalling for them their country, their former pleasures, their youth, and all their ways of living, awakening a bitter grief at having lost all of that." Germaine de Staël, herself a Swiss, said that some of the airs Rousseau composed "seem national to me; when listening to them, I have believed myself transported to the summit of our mountains, where the far-off sound of the shepherd's flute is slowly prolonged by the echoes that go on repeating it."

The sophisticated French, by contrast, were accused of having forgotten what melody was. Rousseau found their songs tuneless, and he later suggested that their attempts at lightness might be compared "to a cow that gallops, or a fat goose trying to fly." Another time he said of the French that even their dogs barked out of tune. And in the *Letter on French Music* he claimed provocatively that the language itself was unsuited to an art which, at that time, was still thought of as inseparable from vocal expression. Italian, he pointed out, has plenty of open vowels and few nasal ones, syllables in which vowels and consonants alternate flowingly, and a rhythm that gives shape to melody. French, on the other hand, is filled with awkward consonants and nasal vowels, and it is unaccented, so either the shape of the melody or the natural movement of speech is bound to be distorted. In Rousseau's opinion it was because French music lacked discernible rhythm that conductors were in the habit of banging out the tempo on the music stand with a big stick. At Mme de Warens's little concerts in Chambéry, "I had the honor of conducting, not forgetting the woodchopper's baton." This is the context of his deliberately outrageous statement at the end of the *Letter:* "I conclude that the French have no music and cannot have any; or if ever they do have it, it will be so much the worse for them."

Even if Rousseau didn't fully grasp Rameau's arguments about harmony, his writings on music were by no means amateurish. Twenty-five years later the pioneer musicologist Charles Burney wrote, "There was too much good sense, taste, and reason in this letter for it to be read with indifference; it was abused, but never answered." Answered or not, Rousseau was now persona non grata with the musical establishment. The Paris Opéra, which had granted him free admission after *The Village Soothsayer,* withdrew the privilege, and according to one report, when he showed up there he was ejected "with kicks on the rear end." He himself believed that a plot to assassinate him was being hatched, and it was certainly true that he was jostled by a hostile crowd and that the indignant orchestra hanged him in effigy.

More generally, Rousseau's image as a purveyor of paradoxes seemed to be confirmed. "As he constantly circles around the truth," a partisan of French music wrote, "he sometimes bumps into it, but he is not so constituted as to be able to show it to us. His torch produces more smoke than light." This kind of criticism was commonly joined to ad hominem attack, and the writer continued, "Born without fortune or looks, and delicate in health, he has had to suffer privations of many kinds . . . He believed that he was more unfortunate than others, he grew embittered, and this was the source of the acrid bile at the core of his philosophy." The stakes were not just aesthetic, since patronage of the arts had always carried with it an element of thought control. D'Alembert, a few years later, stated clearly the threat that custodians of established order perceived: "Freedom in music presupposes freedom of feeling, freedom of feeling brings with it freedom of thought, freedom of thought leads to freedom of action, and freedom of action is the ruin of states. Let us therefore preserve the opera the way it is, if we want to preserve the kingdom."

Rousseau's notoriety, however, did make it possible to retrieve his comedy *Narcissus, or, The Lover of Himself,* which had a long history of going nowhere. Conceived in Annecy, drafted in Chambéry, revised in Paris in 1742 following advice from Marivaux, and turned down by the Comédie Italienne a few years after that, it was finally performed by the Comédie Française in December 1752. A young fop named Valère, engaged to be married to Angélique, is so swollen with self-love that his sister decides to teach him a lesson by having his portrait retouched to look like a woman. Sure enough, he is hopelessly smitten, for as a saucy servant observes, "with his delicacy and the affectation of his adornment, Valère is a sort of woman hidden beneath male clothing, and this cross-dressing portrait seems not so much to disguise him as to show him in his natural state." For a while Valère's efforts are bent on locating the unknown beauty, but when the trick is revealed, he ruefully acknowledges his folly and embraces his relieved fiancée.

Modern concepts of narcissism were yet to be developed, but Rousseau certainly intended to expose the insidiousness of *amour-propre.*

Valère is not guilty of the crudest kind of self-love, since he is far too familiar with his true mirror image to be turned on by it; he says gloomily to his valet, "How do you find me this morning? I don't have any fire in my eyes, and my complexion looks as if I had been beaten up." What is involved is a deeper frustration in the experience of love or, rather, a pair of opposing frustrations. On the one hand, Rousseau yearned to find a true alter ego, a soul with whom his own could unite; on the other hand, he tended to fall for the unknown, responding to predictable stimuli in a depressingly automatic way. He never could reconcile these two kinds of desire, and he tended to distribute them between the sexes in a way that is embodied by the androgynous Valère. With male friends he sought a union of souls, meanwhile falling romantically for one woman after another in response to obvious charms, particularly ash-blonde hair and large breasts. From this point of view, the implications of *Narcissus* are quite moving. Valère learns to love Angélique as she is instead of pursuing a projection of his own fantasies. "When one loves well," he says in the last words of the play, "one no longer thinks of oneself." Narcissism can be overcome, or so the comedy implies. But in Rousseau's life it never worked out like that.

Narcissus was performed only twice, and Rousseau says in the *Confessions* that he left the theater before the end, went to the Café Procope (which still exists today), and was applauded there for declaring loudly that it was a terrible play. In a letter to Lenieps, who was in Lyon at the time, he said with calculated indifference, "I forgot to tell you that the Comédie Française put on a little piece of mine that failed, and well deserved to." However, he always liked to dramatize his failures, and it pleased him to know how far he had come from the obscure provincial who brought *Narcissus* to Paris ten years before. In fact, there is no reason to think that it failed. Since it was only a one-act play, the program had to be filled out with something else, and the managers, clearly wanting it to do well, paired it at each performance with a play that had already been successful (one was by Voltaire). *Narcissus* attracted almost eight hundred spectators the first night and over nine hundred the second, and it was apparently Rousseau's own decision not to attempt a third, which makes his editors suspect "a desire to fail." Certainly that was the opinion of Élie-Catherine Fréron: "M. Rousseau's passionate desire is not to be applauded, but to be hissed." But Fréron was notorious as an enemy of the philosophes; in a widely quoted epigram of Voltaire's, when a snake bit Fréron it was the snake that died.

When he published the text of the play, Rousseau made it clear that he was about to launch a new career in which conventional literary works would have no place. In his preface he said almost nothing about *Narcissus* itself, concentrating instead, as he would do again and again throughout his life, on correcting misunderstandings about his personal motives. "What is at stake here is not my play, but myself." Already it was being widely asserted that when he denounced modern civilization, he couldn't possibly believe it, since he went right on contributing to the fashionable arts. His answer was that although it was too late to reverse the damage done by centuries of so-called progress, and although he himself might be forgiven for reviving this work of his youth, he could promise that it would never happen again. He ended by issuing a challenge to his critics. "If ever they should perceive that I am beginning to covet popular approval, or that I am vain about writing pretty songs, or that I blush at having written bad plays, or that I try to damage the fame of my rivals, or that I affect to speak ill of the great men of the age in order to raise myself to their level by degrading them to mine, or that I aspire to a place in the academies, or that I pay court to the women who set the tone, or that I flatter the stupidity of the great . . . I promise that I will immediately throw my writings and books into the fire." He added, with an asperity that signaled his profound disaffection from the culture represented by Diderot and Voltaire, "It's true that people will be able to say one day, 'This avowed enemy of the sciences and arts nevertheless wrote and published plays'; and that comment, I admit, will be a very bitter satire, not on me, but on my century." A crucial threshold had been crossed. After years of painful anxiety over just these things, Rousseau was ready at last to assert himself with confident authority.

13

Rousseau's Originality

A DECADE EARLIER, in Lyon, Rousseau had told M. de Mably, "I carry a source of unhappiness in myself whose origin I don't know how to untangle." The masterpieces he was now beginning to write were sustained attempts to do just that, relating his personal experience of alienation to the deepest social and psychological causes. And indeed, it makes sense to see his books as the key to his imaginative life, the arena in which he forged a sense of mission and grappled with his deepest conflicts. In conversation he remained awkward and shy. In correspondence he had trouble expressing what he wanted to say — a typical letter of his, he said deprecatingly, was "a long and confused verbiage that can barely be understood when someone reads it" — and he was uneasy about revealing too much of himself. But in addressing the reading public, he could ponder and revise until he was sure he had gotten it right, and this sense of control and anonymity liberated him. "The course I have chosen, to write and to conceal myself, is precisely the one that has suited me."

Having achieved literary fame by winning a prize, Rousseau began to look about for other competitions, and in 1751 he set himself to answering a question proposed by the Academy of Corsica: "What is the virtue most necessary for a hero, and who are the heroes who have lacked it?" But after a few pages he put it aside, later adding the comment, "This piece is very bad, and I felt it so strongly after writing it that I didn't even bother to send it in . . . There can never be a good reply to frivolous questions. There is always a lesson to be learned from a bad piece of writing." Long afterward, when Rousseau's publisher asked permission to print this minor piece, he replied scathingly, "A *torche-cul* ["ass-wipe"] like that isn't worth the trouble."

An opportunity to compete for a prize came, once again, from the Academy of Dijon. Its question for 1754 was "What is the origin of inequality among men, and is it authorized by natural law?" The topic struck Rousseau as deeply thought-provoking, and he retreated with Thérèse to the forest of Saint-Germain to ponder the exploitation that seems inseparable from every human society. He had no real need any more of the Dijon imprimatur, and he ignored their length requirement — that the piece be short enough to read aloud in a half hour — so cavalierly that they rejected his submission without reading it (the winner was an abbé who explained inequality as a consequence of original sin). The result of this second illumination was a treatise of a hundred pages, finished in the summer of 1754 and published a year later, entitled *Discourse on the Origin and Foundations of Inequality among Men.* The *First Discourse* had made Rousseau a celebrity; this one revealed his greatness. Moreover, it showed that his thinking was developing a powerful unity, in what he had begun to think of as his *triste et grand système,* his "great and somber system."

Rousseau had been exposed to inequality as a fact of life. Descending in childhood from the patrician to the artisan class, he was further demoted to a servant in Turin, occupied low-level positions in the Savoie, and worked for years in Lyon and Paris as a tutor and secretary for the *haute bourgeoisie* and the aristocracy. Looking back on his career after his major works were finished, he was able to see that social marginality had given him an exceptional perspective on a culture that defined people by their *état,* or status. "Without having any *état* of my own, I've known and lived in them all from lowest to highest, excepting only the throne." At another time he said, in a letter to a prince, "The manner of life I chose, which was isolated and unpretentious and made me almost a nullity on earth, put me in a position to observe and compare all conditions from peasants to the great."

To justify inequality had been the goal of countless writers. By inviting inquiry into its causes, the Dijon Academy — probably inadvertently — opened up an entirely different way of thinking. And Rousseau cleared a new path still more boldly when he essentially dismissed their reference to natural law, which normally implied that the status quo was natural and therefore right. Montesquieu's *The Spirit of the Laws,* for example, published as recently as 1748, deduced general principles from the characteristics of republics, monarchies, and despotisms, and was widely admired as a centerpiece of the progressive Enlightenment. But from Rousseau's point of view it was fundamentally conservative — not surprisingly, since Montesquieu was both a nobleman and a lawyer. Rather than analyzing how existing societies worked, Rousseau wanted to understand the nature of society itself, and he offered a startling conclusion. In the *First Discourse* he had argued that progress led humanity astray from primitive simplicity; in the *Discourse on Inequality* he was prepared to argue that the very existence of society was a mistake.

The weakest point in the *First Discourse,* as its critics were quick to point out, had been a historical argument that made the arts and sciences responsible for everything bad in the world, wars and diseases included. But Rousseau came to understand that his theory was really not about history. In the *Second Discourse,* therefore, he launched a daring thought experiment. "Let us begin by setting all the facts aside, because they don't affect the question at all. One should not take our inquiry as a search for historical truths, but solely as hypothetical and conditional reasoning, more suited to illuminate the nature of things than to demonstrate their true origin." His goal now was to imagine what life might have been like before society ever existed, and to reconstruct the stages by which human beings became human. This line of thinking was so radically new that the great anthropologist Claude Lévi-Strauss once went so far as to claim — admittedly, at a conference celebrating the anniversary of Rousseau's birth — that he was the true founder of the modern "sciences of man."

The bleak moralists of the seventeenth century, living through scary wars and political crises, saw selfishness and cruelty as inseparable from human nature. "All men naturally hate each other," said the Catholic Pascal, and the secular writer La Rochefoucauld described selfishness as the mainspring of behavior: "*Amour-propre* is love of oneself, and of all things for oneself; it makes men idolaters of themselves and makes them tyrants over others if fortune gives them the means to be." Hobbes, appalled by civil war, concluded that even the most repressive government must be preferable to an anarchic state of nature in which there would be "no arts, no letters, no society, and which is worst of all, continual fear, and danger of violent death; and the life of man solitary, poor, nasty, brutish, and short."

By the middle of the eighteenth century, attitudes like these were widely dismissed as outmoded relics, and enlightened self-interest was promoted as the key to collective happiness. It became common to claim that benevolence, not selfishness, was instinctive in human beings, who were designed by nature to live in cooperative groups — the "herding impulse," as one writer approvingly called it. David Hume, soon to be a favorite in Paris salons as *le bon David,* condemned solitude and welcomed conviviality: "The blood flows with a new tide, the heart is elevated, and the whole man acquires a vigor which he cannot command in his solitary and calm moments."

Against this Enlightenment consensus, Rousseau took a completely unexpected turn. La Rochefoucauld and Hobbes had been perfectly right about selfishness, he decided, but where they went wrong was in assuming that it was inherent in human nature. On the contrary, it was society that made men selfish and wicked, whereas in a true state of nature they must have been good. Or, to put it more accurately, the very concepts of good and evil would have had no meaning, for our earliest ancestors were solitary hunter-gatherers wandering through the primal forests with no need at all of other people. Far from being the solution to our problems, society *was* the problem. Accordingly, Part I of the *Second Discourse* imagines natural man in the presocial state, which is really a prehuman state, and Part II mounts a trenchant critique of life as we know it from this radically new point of view. A few years later Rousseau commented, "I would rather be a man of paradoxes than a man of prejudices." Prejudices were received attitudes that made social norms seem normal; paradoxes were puzzles that exposed contradictions at the heart of experience.

Eighteenth-century science and philosophy were haunted by the mind-body problem, the gnawing feeling of dividedness in which, as Rousseau's character Julie says, we think as though we had no bodies and act as though we had no souls. For natural man, as Rousseau envisioned him, this problem could not exist. He would be perfectly at home with himself and with his world, living entirely in the present without remorse for the past or anxiety for the future. "His imagination paints nothing for him, his heart demands nothing of him . . . Nothing agitates his soul, which gives itself entirely to the feeling of its present existence." With no occasion to compete with other people, much less to exploit and abuse them, he would lack the corrosive *amour-propre* that measures itself against others. Instead, he would have only the *amour de soi* of a healthy animal, the simple instinct of self-preservation. To be sure, he would be incapable of truly knowing himself, but he wouldn't need to. He would simply *be* himself, whereas modern man, struggling to conform to society's demands, searches desperately and in vain for self-knowledge. Natural man would not even think. In a sentence that became notorious, Rousseau declared, "The state of reflection is a state contrary to nature, and the man who meditates is a depraved animal."

In short, natural man was natural because he was not yet man. He did possess an innate tendency to feel *pitié,* empathy with others if he saw them suffering, but this too was a simple instinctual response. As a Swiss admirer (writing in English) picturesquely put it, "Rousseau traced man to the nipple of nature, and found him wrapped up in instinct." And if the life of this proto-man — today we would call him a hominid — seems narrow and unsatisfying, that is only because we have tasted the poisoned fruit of progress and will never be able to turn back. Germaine de Staël observed that when the brilliant and sensitive Rousseau argued for a condition "close to brutishness," it was because he knew how bitterly one could be made to suffer for one's intelligence and sensitivity. Hobbes saw man's life in the state of nature as solitary, poor, nasty, brutish, and short. Rousseau's natural man was fortunate to be solitary, had no standard by which to define life as poor and nasty, and neither knew nor cared that it was brutish and short.

Natural man sometimes encountered other people, of course, and instinct impelled him to mate with natural woman, but for both it would be merely a chance encounter, and they wouldn't care if they ever saw each other again (who *was* that natural man?). Sex was a simple and adequate relief, like sneezing, free from the jealousy and possessiveness that undermine romantic love, which Rousseau explicitly called "an artificial sentiment, born of the usage of society." Likewise, mothers would nurse and care for their children, but here too the relationship would end as soon as the young ones could fend for themselves. It was usual in the eighteenth century to extol the family as the shaper of humanity and source of its consolations, but in Rousseau's experience these came at a steep price: patriarchal authority, coercive demands for affection, oedipal anxieties, and guilt. Even language would not have been necessary in the state of nature as he imagined it, for vocal sounds would have been direct expressions of emotion. Tormented constantly by being misunderstood, Rousseau imagined beings who had no need to communicate in words, relying instead on spontaneous cries, gestures, and blushes whose meaning was as unambiguous as the tongue-tied trembling with which he first responded to Mme de Warens.

So what went wrong? Rousseau speculated — much as modern anthropologists still do — that as population grew, people joined together to increase the food supply, and agriculture and metallurgy developed to meet the need. Once all of that happened, labor had to be organized and enforced, some people got richer than others, governments were established to protect their wealth, and the many became subordinate to the few. The moment of transition was crystallized when a man first enclosed a field and said *"Ceci est à moi,"* "This belongs to me." Pascal had said virtually the same thing a century earlier in the *Pensées:* "Mine, thine. *Ce chien est à moi,* 'This dog is mine,' these poor children say; 'that's my place in the sun.' There is the beginning and image of the usurpation of the whole earth." But for Pascal the tragic moralist, like the abbé who won the Dijon prize, ownership reflects the radical sinfulness of human nature. Rousseau, believing in the natural goodness of man, stood Pascal's idea on its head by defining the problem as social and political. In this altogether new perspective, human beings were victims of their own social behavior, not of primal sin. The loss of the state of nature was like a secular version of the fall described in the book of Genesis, from which a whole chain of misfortunes followed. "Equality disappeared, property was introduced, labor became necessary, and the vast forests changed to smiling fields that had to be watered with the sweat of men, where slavery and poverty were soon seen to germinate and grow along with the crops."

Long before Rousseau, the ancient author Tacitus gave a rather similar picture of the lost golden age. "Primitive man had no evil desires. Being blameless and innocent, his life was free of compulsions or penalties. He also needed no rewards, for he was naturally good." But the classical golden age was an imaginary society in which shepherds sang to win the hearts of innocent maidens, and the wisdom of elders was honored by the grateful young. Rousseau's insight was far more challenging. His thesis was that competition and inequality are intrinsic to every society, and that there could have been no golden age for beings who were anything like ourselves. The crucial point is that the things we most value carry the seeds of their own subversion. When communities were established, with the family at their center, "the habit of living together gave birth to the sweetest emotions known to man, conjugal and paternal love." But along with this charming development came inequality between the sexes, and some very undesirable emotions soon emerged.

> People grew accustomed to gathering in front of their huts or around a big tree. Singing and dancing, true offspring of love and leisure, became the amusement — or rather the occupation — of the idle gatherings of men and women. Each one began to look at the others and want to be looked at himself, and public esteem took on value. The one who sang or danced the best, the most handsome, the strongest, the most skillful or the most eloquent, became the most esteemed, and this was the first step toward inequality, and toward vice at the same time. From these initial preferences were born on the one hand vanity and contempt, on the other hand shame and envy, and the fermentation caused by this new leaven eventually produced compounds fatal to happiness and innocence.

In his own life, Rousseau smarted under the vanity and contempt of the great, and envy and shame were the sources of his deepest anguish. As for the sweetest emotions known to man, he had little personal experience of conjugal love, either in childhood or with Thérèse, whom he declared he didn't love; as for paternal love, Isaac Rousseau's was a mixed blessing, and he took care never to repeat it with children of his own. There were thus deeply personal feelings behind the *Second Discourse,* and critics would soon charge that it was merely an expression of envy and resentment. Voltaire wrote to thank Rousseau sarcastically for his "new book against the human race," adding that unfortunately he had given up the habit of walking on all fours. In a little pamphlet at about the same time, Voltaire imagined Rousseau exclaiming, "It is dreadful to live in cities where one can carry a golden means of measuring time in one's pocket, where silkworms are brought from China to cover one with their down, and where one can hear a hundred instruments in harmony that enchant the ears and soothe the soul in sweet repose. All of this is horrible, and it is clear that the Iroquois are the only good people; but they had better stay far away from Quebec, where I suspect the damnable sciences of Europe have been introduced."

Rousseau would not have denied that he shared the taste for beautiful music, if not for fine clothes and the obsession with telling time, but in his opinion the price for the benefits of civilization was exorbitant. Voltaire had no wish to understand that message. Still less, as a self-made *seigneur* who had amassed great wealth, did he want to hear Rousseau's claim that after the rich discovered the pleasure of dominating others they could never stop, "like those famished wolves that reject all other food after once tasting human flesh, and thenceforth want only to devour men." In the margin of his copy of the *Second Discourse,* Voltaire scribbled indignantly, "*Voilà* the philosophy of a beggar who would like to see the rich robbed by the poor." Voltaire could never imagine that Rousseau was turning his strange life story into a badge of honor, and that it was his experience as an apprentice and lackey that gave him the authority to analyze inequality as he did.

Even Diderot, who took a comradely interest in the composition of the *Discourse,* soon grew disgusted and wrote to a friend, "He who meditates may not be a depraved animal, but I'm sure he won't take long to become an unhealthy animal. Rousseau continues to meditate and to be unwell. Your humble servant continues to meditate, and isn't doing so well either. Too bad for you if you meditate, since you'll soon get sick too. In spite of that, I don't care for acorns and dens and hollow oaks. I require a carriage, a convenient apartment, fine linen, and a perfumed girl, and after that I would gladly accommodate myself to all the other curses of our civilized state. I go very well on my two hind feet." As for the view that it was not natural for man to think, Diderot took exactly the opposite view. A year later he wrote in the *Encyclopédie,* "Whoever does not want to reason is renouncing the status of being human, and should be treated as unnatural."

To stress the unattractiveness of primitive existence, as the critics all did, was to miss the point, however. Rousseau had read widely in accounts of exploration — Trousson says, "It would take a book to list the books read by this man who despised books" — and as was inevitable at the time, he did assume that "savage" peoples were closer to the state of nature than Europeans or Chinese. But he also understood very well that no human group still remained in the natural state. Every single one had language, government, wars, and all the rest of it. And he therefore meant what he said when he proposed the state of nature as an imaginary thought experiment, "a state that no longer exists, perhaps never has existed, and probably never will, of which one must nevertheless have an accurate idea in order to judge our present state properly." What the state of nature represented was a standpoint from which to think about what we might be like if our ideas, values, and even feelings had not been shaped by society for its own purposes. Henceforth the goal of Rousseau's life, as of his writings, would be to find an authentic self beneath the layers of role-playing and to conceive of educational and political programs that could help that authentic self to emerge.

Rousseau's critique was thus extraordinarily far-reaching. It was common to criticize specific inequities in society and to appeal for reform, but original to hold that inequality is both unacceptable and inevitable. It was common to acknowledge that labor could be harsh, but original to define it as a fundamental betrayal of our essential nature. It was common to say that we learn to see ourselves as others see us and become integrated with society, but original to describe that process as a betrayal of our true selves. In *Émile* Rousseau would make this point with memorable clarity: "As soon as you see through the eyes of others, you must will by their wills . . . You always say, 'We want,' and you always do what the others want." Natural man lived *en lui-même,* within himself, but modern man lives *hors de lui,* outside himself. Conflict and alienation are life as we know it. More disturbingly still, the logic of civilization is to make inequality ever more extreme. As Rousseau interpreted the course of history, "The status of rich and poor was authorized in the first epoch, that of powerful and weak in the second, and that of master and slave in the third, which is the final degree of inequality and the limit toward which all the others lead in the end."

With this radical reimagining of human experience, the *Discourse on*

Inequality was filled with latent possibilities. Starobinski says, "The immense echo of these words expanded in time and space far beyond what Rousseau could have foreseen." Since ancient times it had been commonplace to say that man is a social animal; Rousseau's challenge was to diagnose that fact as evidence of a disastrous wrong turning. What if every society ever created was a flawed attempt to repair the damage the human race inflicted on itself when it gave up its primal freedom? What if society, not ourselves, is ultimately responsible for suffering and crime? This idea has had enormous influence in the two and a half centuries since Rousseau advanced it. As Arthur Melzer shows, it underpins the great cultural move from an ethic of self-control to one of spontaneity, and it locates our problems in historical causes rather than in defects in human nature itself. Politically, oppression becomes a central concern, as it had not been for previous thinkers. "I hate servitude," Rousseau later wrote, "as the source of all the ills of human kind." And if his thinking was far-reachingly political, it was psychological as well. Freud was Rousseau's heir when he wrote, "The liberty of the individual is no gift of civilization. It was greatest before there was any civilization."

14

Lionized in Geneva,
Alienated in Paris

HAVING COMPLETED the *Discourse on Inequality,* Rousseau began to contemplate a major move. His fellow Genevan Gauffecourt was about to make a business trip home and invited him to come along. Suddenly it seemed to Rousseau that he might do much more than that. Although he had gained fame as the *citoyen de Genève,* he was really a *citoyen sans cité,* and he now resolved to embrace the religion of his fathers and recover the legal status he had lost when he converted to Catholicism a quarter of a century earlier. He was inclined to think of religion, on the whole, as a cultural institution, a means of affirming loyalty to one's group, and he had never been much interested in theology. Under the influence of the abbé Gaime and Mme de Warens, he had acquired an undogmatic faith that emphasized God's goodness and blurred the differences between Catholicism and Protestantism.

In returning to the Calvinism of his native city, therefore, Rousseau's focus was essentially political rather than religious. When he prepared the *Discourse* for the press, he dedicated it "to the Republic of Geneva" and declared that if he could somehow have chosen his place of birth, Geneva would have been his choice. This dedication used to be regarded as an idealized fantasy about a city he no longer knew, but the boy who grew up in the political hotbed of Saint-Gervais, and who saw his father exiled for quarreling with a patrician, had few illusions about the actual state of Genevan affairs. Rather, he was issuing an implied reproach to the leaders who had made a sham of democracy, and when he addressed the republic as a whole, he pointedly avoided flattering the governing council.

In June 1754 Rousseau and Thérèse set off by carriage with Gauffecourt. As was his habit, Rousseau often proceeded on foot (the carriage must have been very slow). Left alone with Thérèse, Gauffecourt saw his chance, and although "more than sixty years old, gouty, crippled, and worn out from pleasures and gratifications," tried earnestly to seduce her, even showing her a book of indecent pictures, which she virtuously flung from the window. Writing in the *Confessions* fifteen years later, Rousseau claimed that Gauffecourt's behavior shattered his belief in the purity of friendship, but perhaps he only wished it had. Certainly the two men remained on extremely cordial terms.

When they reached Lyon, Gauffecourt went on to Geneva while Rousseau and Thérèse made an important detour. He had not seen Mme de Warens for twelve years, and their occasional correspondence had been cool at best. In a letter dated in February 1754, just three months earlier, she had written to reproach him for some new failure to give financial help: "You can verify in me the chapter I've just read in *The Imitation of Christ,* that where we place our firmest hopes, there shall we be utterly disappointed. It's not the blow you dealt that wounds me, but the hand that dealt it." The meeting was bound to be painful, and whatever Rousseau was expecting, the reality was worse. "I saw her again — in what a state, my God! What degradation! What remained of her original virtues? Was this the same Mme de Warens, once so brilliant, to whom the curé Pontverre had sent me? How it broke my heart!"

Rousseau proposed that she come live with him and Thérèse in Paris, a plan that was highly unlikely to appeal to her, and the idea was allowed to drop. Shortly afterward she visited Geneva in order to avoid being in Chambéry while her belongings were auctioned off, and there was a touching scene in which she tried to put a ring on Thérèse's finger ("who instantly replaced it on hers, kissing that noble hand and wetting it with tears"), but that was all. Rousseau would later declare that his failure to remain with Mme de Warens caused agonizing remorse, but they both must have known that it was far too late for that. And indeed, the gulf between what they once were and what they had become was a major factor in inspiring the *Confessions,* in which Rousseau would make the lost past live again. Trousson evokes movingly what this last, melancholy reunion must have been like: "In this famous man did she recognize *petit,* the touching vagabond with the dark eyes? A young blonde woman once pursued an adolescent boy with bursts of laughter, smearing his face with her pretty fingers covered in syrup or preserves. Those were two different people, in another life."

Mme de Warens had eight more years to live, and as her friend Conzié later recalled, she sank steadily into hopeless poverty and illness. "I have always blamed Jean-Jacques," he observed bitterly, "whom she had honored with the name of her adopted son, for preferring the interests of Levasseur over those of a *maman* who was as deserving of his respect, in every sense, as his laundress Levasseur was not. He should have put aside his pride from time to time and labored to earn only the necessary minimum for himself, in order to repay at least in part what he had cost his generous benefactor." There is no record of the wealthy Conzié giving her financial help (he implies that she was too proud to accept it), and sadly enough Rousseau was not the only one to abandon her. A letter survives that was written to her just months later by Wintzenried, married by then and frantic to extricate himself from the doomed mining adventures, which had run out of borrowed funds. "Although I'm not fully informed as to your ideas and affairs," he wrote grimly, "the way of life you've followed until now has driven away all your friends. You want to entertain people at great expense, such as the most opulent lord wouldn't be able to manage . . . Having no other resources, as you know, and no employment, I await impatiently the fulfillment of your promises to me." Wintzenried waited in vain. All of the old relationships had broken down.

To be reinstated as a Protestant was not necessarily easy, as Rousseau well knew. The normal procedure entailed a series of public humiliations, interrogations before the Little Council and the religious Consistory, and three days in prison. The elders were eager, however, to welcome back a former apostate who had become a celebrated critic of modern civilization, so a committee of six well-disposed pastors asked some very vague questions, Rousseau stammered out even vaguer answers, and they then concluded that he had never really abjured Protestantism at all. Evidently the truth about his conversion in Turin was unknown, or at least covered up. The Consistory's decision was based on the supposition that he had somehow been "taken to France at an early age and raised there in the Roman religion" but had recognized his error and begun to attend Protestant services, after which he resolved "to come to his fatherland, make his abjuration, and return to the bosom of our church." He was excused from the public abasement and the prison stay on the grounds of poor health.

Thérèse's presence also had to be explained, since she was known not only to share his house but to sleep in the same room. A sentimental fiction was duly elaborated. According to the minister Jean-François Deluc, Thérèse claimed that her mother was skilled in medical arts and had taken Rousseau under her roof in Paris when he was gravely ill, so he was a patient as well as a boarder. And she explained that on a later occasion, when she received an accidental injury from some men who were fighting in the street, Rousseau came to her aid and "so generously paid back her mother's services that Mlle Levasseur vowed to serve him in gratitude until death." Just to be on the safe side, Rousseau himself added a note affirming that his urinary affliction made sexual relations impossible, as perhaps it did. How much of all this the ministers believed is hard to say. Regaining a philosophe for the Reformation was a considerable victory, and it was in their interest not to look closely into difficulties.

As for the sincerity of Rousseau's religious feeling, he always claimed that it was real. The pastor Jacob Vernes recalled being moved to tears during a moonlight walk by the lake when Rousseau "spoke of the divinity like a man inspired." Just as he had previously enjoyed the friendship of cultivated Catholic priests, he now formed friendships with a number of broad-minded Protestant pastors, with whom he would keep up regular correspondence for years. "What I am hungry for is a friend," he wrote to Vernes in 1758, and friendship at a distance was particularly agreeable. In letters he could assert unflagging affection without the uneasiness inspired by facial expressions or tones of voice, to which he was always hypersensitive. During his stay in Geneva he was particularly taken with Paul Moultou, who was twenty-three at the time and about to be admitted to the ministry. In the *Confessions* a decade later, Rousseau praised Moultou's "spirit filled with fire" and declared an intention of making him "the defender of my memory, and the avenger of his friend." This indeed came to pass, for when Moultou visited Paris at the very end of Rousseau's life, he was entrusted with a number of manuscripts, including the *Confessions*.

As a successful Paris intellectual and returning prodigal son, Rousseau was lionized in Geneva, and naturally he found that delicious. His enthusiasm is reflected in a letter written to Mme Dupin a couple of days before his readmission to the Protestant faith: "This city seems to me one of the most charming in the world, and its inhabitants the wisest and happiest that I know. Liberty is well established, the government is peaceful, and the citizens are enlightened, steady, and modest." He added that the temptation to settle there permanently was great but that he had promised the Levasseurs to stay in Paris, and that it would be hard to earn a living by copying music — the trade to which he claimed he was committed — in so small a city.

It does seem to have been a time of relative stability in Geneva. After the crisis that Rousseau had witnessed in 1737, when he saw men preparing to fight members of their own families, mediation by France the next year restored some rights to the full body of citizens, while real power was retained by the Little Council. Most of his acquaintances were satisfied with the political situation. In addition, just weeks before his arrival in 1754 a treaty was signed in which the Savoie at last renounced its claims to Geneva. Some of Rousseau's friends, including the exile Lenieps in Paris, were still committed to radical change in the city's government, and within a few years he would side with them passionately, but for the present the mood was tranquil. And as Cranston points out, the situation of workers in Geneva was very different from that in France. They were not oppressed by exorbitant taxes, food prices were kept moderate by government subsidies, and the upper class got its wealth from banking and investments rather than from the exploitation of laborers. All the same, Rousseau clearly hoped that his tribute in the *Discourse on Inequality* to the high ideals of Geneva might inspire meaningful reforms.

Rousseau was in Geneva for four months. It was noticed that he paid a visit to his old neighborhood in the rue de Coutance and had an affectionate chat with his nurse Jacqueline, nearly sixty now and the proprietor of a stall where she sold cheese, while bystanders crowded in to see the great man. A witness described the scene: "The people of the *rues basses* of Geneva are readers; they gathered to contemplate the philosopher in silence, proud that he was one of them, and even prouder perhaps that despite his long absence and his eloquence, he had kept their accent." A girl who was lifted up to see over the crowd recalled long afterward what she saw: "A cheap round wig, with no hat; gray jacket and pants; his right hand on his nurse's knee; round face, black eyes that were small, lively, and piercing, and a pleasant smile." But most of the time Rousseau mingled with members of the social class that his mother came from and his father resented. It was surely a sentimental rewriting of the visit when the son of one of the radical leaders later claimed, "He preferred the company of simple citizens to the wealthy, whose ostentatiousness and principles he detested. His attachment to the people, his relationship with the former deputy Deluc, his love of equality, and his sometimes extreme contempt for powerful men, made him hated by the aristocrats, who were the cause of all his troubles."

There was also a reunion with Rousseau's beloved aunt Suzon in Nyon; it seems to have been emotional, but no details of it survive. One thing he did not do was go out to Bossey, the scene of his childhood exile. And it struck some observers that however much he might play the *homme du peuple,* he betrayed a good deal of vanity "in wanting to be noticed for little things, above all by persons of distinction." It was perhaps in this mood that he went down to the lake every morning to throw bread to the fish, which learned to assemble expectantly at the appointed hour. This attracted the notice of the neighbors and, according to his host at the time, "added not a little to his reputation as a friend of humanity." ("Or rather, a friend of fishes," Leigh adds.) The most memorable aspect of the stay was a September expedition on Lac Léman, which included four companions as well as Thérèse. "We took seven days on the trip, in the most beautiful weather in the world. I have a vivid memory of the places that struck me at the far end of the lake, whose description I gave some years afterward in *The New Hélo-ïse*" (the alternative title of *Julie*). As usual it was the countryside that awakened Rousseau's imagination. And if he did still feel loyalty to his *patrie,* it was not to Geneva as it really was but to a Geneva of the mind.

So he and Thérèse returned to Paris, making brisk work of the journey in a mere five days, and as it turned out he would never see Geneva again.

It was time to prepare the *Discourse on Inequality* for publication, and Rousseau turned to one of the leading publishers of French books in Europe, Marc-Michel Rey. A Genevan himself, Rey had learned his trade in Lausanne and then settled in Amsterdam, where censorship was lenient. He had a network of intermediaries through whom he could smuggle books into France clandestinely if the authorities found them objectionable. A close relationship soon developed, conducted almost entirely through correspondence, that would last for years and would involve the publication of most of Rousseau's major works. He was an exceptionally difficult author to deal with, fussing endlessly about page design, paper quality, illustrations, and everything else. In addition, he quarreled repeatedly with Rey over property rights, since there was no copyright law, and once an author had sold a manuscript he had no legal claim to income from subsequent editions. But Rey and Rousseau genuinely respected each other and always apologized after their many spats. Rousseau became godfather to Rey's child, and he was stating the truth when he wrote to Rey in 1761, "I like to think that my writings and my name have contributed to making a name for you, and to the beginnings of your fortune."

Rather to Rousseau's surprise, official permission was granted to publish the *Second Discourse* in France. This was the decision of the *directeur de la librairie,* Chrétien-Guillaume Lamoignon de Malesherbes, a remarkable person who did everything he could to minimize the obstacles faced by the philosophes, and who became a valued friend to Rousseau. The entire process of censorship at the time was unbelievably convoluted. In principle all manuscripts, whatever the subject, had to be submitted to Malesherbes' office for review by its large staff of censors (at that time there were 130 of them). If they detected potentially dangerous views, they could reject a book outright or require revisions. If approval was secured, the publisher would be granted a *privilège d'édition,* which conferred an exclusive right to sell the book for a specified period of time. In effect a bargain was struck: the government policed what authors were allowed to say, and in return a favored group of publishers got a monopoly. Most works of current interest, however, ran a serious risk of rejection under this procedure, and it was common instead to grant a looser *permission tacite,* which looked the other way when a book was sold and made no guarantee to any individual publisher. Such books were usually printed abroad; if not, some foreign city was listed on the title page. In such cases, not only did the publisher stand to lose his profits when competitors brought out pirated editions, but the authorities might still decide to ban a book after all, confiscating whole crates of it before they could be sold.

The censors were relatively obscure people — a writer in 1789 lamented that the philosophes were "a flock of eagles submitted to the governance of turkeys" — but they were well educated and far from bigoted. The tone was set by Malesherbes, a cultivated aristocrat in his early thirties who was the son of the chancellor of France. However much Malesherbes might sympathize with the Enlightenment, he had no choice but to enforce the rules. When possible, he would suggest minor revisions to get rid of objectionable passages and allow at least a *permission tacite,* as he did for the *Discourse on Inequality.* But all too often he was forced to take actions that he regretted, and as he commented years later, "Because the law prohibits books the public cannot do without, the book trade has had to exist outside the law." Rousseau's career as a writer was continually compromised by these obstacles, and in 1762, when a savage government crackdown singled him out, not even Malesherbes could help him.

Meanwhile, if he was to remain in France, Rousseau had to decide how to live. Earlier in 1754 there had been an unpleasant scene at d'Holbach's salon when he exploded in fury at the self-satisfied philosophes. What made him unexpectedly snap was watching the group slyly deride a clergyman (appropriately named the abbé Petit) while he read aloud from a tragedy of his own composition that managed to make David and Bathsheba seem boring. D'Holbach told a friend long afterward that although it was always tempting to provoke Rousseau in order to hear what he would say, this particular outburst was utterly unforeseeable. The curé had read a preface to his tragedy in which he claimed that comic plots lead to marriage and tragic plots to murder — not a foolish idea, one might have thought — "and I admit that half laughing, half seriously, I teased the poor curé. Jean-Jacques hadn't said a word, smiled, or budged from his chair. All of a sudden he sprang up in a rage, and rushing up to the curé, he seized his manuscript, hurled it on the floor, and said to the alarmed author, 'Your play is worthless; your preface is crazy; all these gentlemen are mocking you; leave here and go back to being a vicar in your village.'" The reaction does seem excessive; perhaps Rousseau was projecting his own anxiety about derision and shame onto the unfortunate curé. Not surprisingly, his intervention was not appreciated, and the two had to be separated lest they come to blows. To d'Holbach's surprise, Rousseau refused from then on to be reconciled with him, though he did write a letter of heartfelt sympathy after the death of d'Holbach's wife, whom he had always liked.

By the time he returned from Geneva, Rousseau knew that he needed to extricate himself from the coterie milieu and to invent a new role for himself. Diderot and the rest of the philosophes were enthusiastically social, thriving on witty cut-and-thrust and critiquing society with ironic detachment. Rousseau's message was that society was not just imperfect, it was the root of all wickedness and misfortune. No one who remained inside it could hope to understand it properly, and it became his mission to secede from society altogether so that he would have a place to stand. But by continuing to address his contemporaries, he found himself maddeningly connected to society after all. Unlike hermits and saints, who become dead to the world, he kept on lecturing the world, writing with great eloquence in defense of silence.

Still more exasperatingly, hardly anyone seemed to understand what Rousseau was saying. There were few published responses to the *Second Discourse*, and the reviewers, far from hailing it as a groundbreaking work, dismissed it as an exercise in empty paradox. "He has written against society," a typical reviewer said, "in the same spirit in which he wrote against the sciences and arts, which is to say like a man who is not in the least convinced by what he has chosen to maintain." Grimm's comment a bit later was equally dismissive but more interesting: "No one else has the art to lead you as he does, by subtle and oblique reasonings, to a conclusion that is diametrically opposed to the place you started out from." What Grimm took for mere sophistry might better be called Socratic argument, encouraging readers to open their eyes to an altogether new angle of vision.

In short, Rousseau's isolation was also a form of exhibitionism. A perceptive writer commented after his death:

> Voltaire wanted to acquire esteem through riches, which is the common and ordinary method. Rousseau made himself worthy of respect through poverty, which is more philosophical. Voltaire had a gross self-love, a childish vanity that he could never conceal; he intoxicated himself with the vilest incense, relished the praise of the feeblest rhymer, and returned it with interest. Rousseau's pride was more refined. He seemed irritated by homage and indignant at his fame; he made himself invisible like an Asiatic despot, and treated his most zealous admirers with great harshness.

In Grimm's opinion, Rousseau was adopting a pretentious pose. "Up until then he had been a maker of compliments, gallant and sought after, to the point of being syrupy and tiresome with his turns of phrase. All at once he put on the cynic's robe, and since there was nothing natural in his character, he went to the opposite extreme." D'Alembert was more generous, commenting that Rousseau's genius could never have emerged without a willed transformation of his always awkward social persona. "One has to have known Rousseau, as I did, to see how the courage to defy everything made his spirit expand. Fifteen years ago I saw him circumspect, timid, and almost a flatterer, and what he wrote was mediocre. Anyone judging him at that time would have said plenty of foolish things. It shows we shouldn't be in a hurry to pass judgment on men before we're sure that they're in their right place."

Elisabeth Badinter, who recounts the month-by-month competition for prestige among the intellectuals during those years, suggests that Rousseau discovered the perfect way to beat them at their own game. By exalting moral virtue above all of the arts and sciences, and by promoting himself as virtue's embodiment, he didn't so much outplay them as overturn the chessboard entirely. But to pull this off, he had to make sure that his private life confirmed his public posture, and it didn't take his rivals and critics long to discover that he was vulnerable on that score. That is why Rousseau's major writings after 1762 were all defenses of his own integrity, and since he pursued self-analysis with extraordinary honesty, the totally unexpected result was an entirely new way of thinking about the self. It was the beginning, really, of a genuinely modern psychology. By the time he wrote the *Confessions,* he had come to see that his critics were partly right and that the role of virtuous philosopher had indeed been a role. In getting rid of wig, sword, and watch, he drew attention to himself by choosing to be different from everyone else, hoping that exterior changes would reflect real changes within. His avowed goal was "to be always myself," but how can one ever be sure of that? Diderot or Hume would have agreed with the modern sociologist Peter Berger: "Sincerity is the consciousness of the man who is taken in by his own act." Writing in his diary in 1755, the abbé Trublet diagnosed the situation with extraordinary insight: "Duclos says that Rousseau has an artificial character, but not a false one. He is not absolutely as he seems, but he believes that he is." Starobinski has emphasized the tension in Rousseau's thought between being and seeming, *être* and *paraître,* and this was a distinction that Trublet grasped very clearly: "The true hypocrite appears in order to appear; Rousseau appears in order to be."

But to cast the story in these terms is perhaps to let Rousseau's rivals define the debate. From another point of view, he was acknowledging the extent to which he, like everyone else, was a victim of social conditioning. As he came to see very clearly, the pose of righteous censor had indeed been a pose, however genuine it felt at the time. Playing that role was especially exhilarating because it freed him from social embarrassment, making artlessness into a virtue. "The scorn that my profound meditations had inspired for the mores, maxims, and prejudices of the age made me impervious to the banter of those who held them, and I used to crush their little *bons mots* with my pronouncements as I would have crushed an insect between my fingers." It was the inevitable consequence of his conversion experience on the road to Vincennes. As he preached the vanity of social forms, "the most noble pride grew up on the debris of my uprooted vanity," and the role of prophet in the wilderness became the most seductive role of all.

More immediately, however, the question was not of abstract ideals but of status, and Rousseau was well aware that the criticisms of his *Discourses* were really defenses of privilege. Of one critic he remarked, "The author is so preoccupied with his lands that he even speaks of mine. Land belonging to me! Jean-Jacques Rousseau's land! Really, I advise him to slander me more adroitly." And in his reply to his former friend Bordes, who had argued that luxury is beneficial because it indirectly feeds the poor, he expressed a fiercer resentment. "We must have gravy in our cooking, and that's why so many sick people lack broth. We must have liqueurs on our tables, and that's why the peasant drinks nothing but water. We must have powder for our wigs, and that's why so many poor people have no bread at all."

The awkwardness, bravado, and wounded pride in Rousseau's attitude are memorably embodied in an odd episode that took place just before Christmas of 1755. A basket containing a large pot of butter, intended for Mme Levasseur, was delivered by mistake to the kitchen of a comte de Lastic. When Thérèse went to retrieve it, the count and his wife sneered at her and ordered their servants to drive her away, after which Rousseau drafted a bitterly ironic letter to the count: "I have tried to console the distressed good woman by explaining the rules of high society and the upbringing of the great. I've proved to her that it wouldn't be worth the trouble of keeping servants if they weren't useful for chasing away poor people when they come to reclaim their property. By showing her that 'justice' and 'humanity' are commoners' words, I have finally made her understand that she should feel only too honored that a count ate her butter." He drafted a second letter to the count's sister-in-law, who had at least been fair enough to acknowledge that the parcel was misdelivered, asking her to learn from the misadventure: "How many injustices are hidden daily from those with rank and power, because the cries of the oppressed are too weak to make themselves heard!" Rousseau's friends implored him not to send these letters, and he wrote to one of them, "I must do as you wish, Madame. The letters will not be sent, and M. le comte de Lastic may steal butter from all the good women of Paris without my getting angry about it." But he kept copies, and he didn't forget. Years later the few people in the know were startled to find an otherwise incomprehensible footnote inserted in his novel. When Julie tells Saint-Preux that it is wrong to be wicked even in jest, the footnote comments, "The man with the butter! It seems to me that this warning would suit you rather well."

15

An Affair of the Heart

PERHAPS IT WAS NEVER REALLY likely that Rousseau would settle permanently in Geneva. He always found reasons not to do it;
for example, in 1757, when a friend there tried to get him a post as city
librarian, he objected that he had a weak memory, didn't know Greek,
and had no idea which editions of books were any good. But if Geneva's
appeal was beginning to fade, Rousseau was also sure that he didn't
belong in Paris. His disaffection from the philosophes continued to
deepen, although outsiders weren't yet aware of it, and in any case his
contributions to the *Encyclopédie* were relatively modest. For him the
return to Paris meant resuming a tedious chore that Mme Dupin had
persuaded him to undertake. For the next several years he toiled, off
and on, to extract a coherent argument from the seventeen printed volumes and five cartons of manuscripts that the aged abbé de Saint-Pierre
had left at his death in 1743.

The goal was to produce a readable abridgment of *A Project to
Achieve Perpetual Peace,* in which Saint-Pierre argued that wars of conquest always produced unintended results and that nations ought to negotiate instead. This was to be accomplished by establishing a sort of
league of nations to keep the member states in line. Rousseau had small
confidence in such a scheme; as Cranston observes, he regarded social
organization as the problem and not the solution. He drafted a short

piece of his own with the challenging title "That the State of War Is Born from the Social State" and a longer critique in which he identified the lust for power and fame as the fundamental motivation of princes. Neither of these was published. Rousseau's abridgment of the abbé's *Project* finally appeared in 1761, by which time he had left the whole business far behind; his own masterly *Social Contract* was by then in press. No doubt his labors on the Saint-Pierre papers were useful in stimulating his own thinking, but the job was a thankless one at best. In the words of a scholar who has read through all of the papers, "There was such a mania of ratiocination, such poverty of eloquence and shortness of breath, such absence of emotion and exhausting prolixity, so many inane little ideas made still more inane by immoderate repetition, that Rousseau must often have been exasperated."

While Rousseau was pondering what to do next, he received an unexpected and flattering invitation. Mme d'Épinay, whom he had seen occasionally at her country estate La Chevrette, ten miles north of Paris, was aware of his depressed state and decided to do something about it. On an earlier visit he had noticed a rundown little house known as the Hermitage at the edge of the forest of Montmorency, a mile or so from the château, and had playfully remarked that it would be just the place for him. Returning there in March 1756, he was astonished to find that Mme d'Épinay had had it completely renovated, with a pretty tiled roof and spacious windows, and was proposing that he move in along with Thérèse and her mother. Rousseau was overwhelmed. "I don't believe I've been more strongly and deliciously moved in my entire life, and I moistened with tears my friend's beneficent hand." He hesitated for a few days, she refused to take no for an answer, and on April 9, 1756, "I left the city, never to live there again." He did eventually live there again, but he would always remember the move as an exhilarating turning point, and for a while the Hermitage was indeed a refuge from care.

Rousseau's new patron was twelve years younger than he and well placed socially (though she was not a marquise, as is sometimes claimed). She was born in 1726 in northern France, the daughter of a military governor, and given one of those floridly elaborate names favored by the upper classes, Louise-Florence Pétronille de Tardieu d'Esclavelles. When she was ten her father died, and her mother and she moved in with an aunt at La Chevrette. There she encountered six

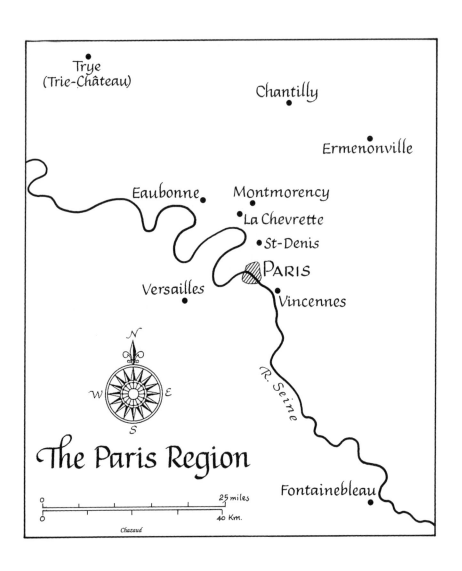

The Paris Region

MME D'ÉPINAY

The portrait was painted during Mme d'Épinay's stay in Geneva in the late 1750s, shortly after the breakdown of relations with Rousseau. She has chosen to be depicted with an inquiring expression as she looks up from her book; her biographer notes that her almost alarming thinness is not concealed, with a diaphanous gauze *fichu* "draped gracefully over the frail, slender shoulders."

cousins, two of whom later played important roles in her life. One was Sophie, with whom Rousseau would one day fall in love. The other was Denis-Joseph d'Épinay, who inherited his father's lucrative position as a tax farmer, and whom she married when she was nineteen (canon law allowed first cousins to marry). It was a love match at first, but her husband proved to be systematically unfaithful, openly keeping a series of mistresses and squandering fantastic sums on them. Still worse, he infected her with syphilis, and for the rest of her life she suffered from dreadful health, with fevers, migraine headaches, and agonizing gallstones, among other complaints. After a while she managed to secure a financial separation from her husband in order to protect herself and her children, but she never thought of herself as rich, although from Rousseau's perspective she unquestionably was.

Rousseau had first met Mme d'Épinay a decade earlier, when his friend Dupin de Francueil introduced him at La Chevrette and an amateur performance of his comedy *The Rash Vow* was staged there. At about that time Francueil became her acknowledged lover. For several years Mme d'Épinay was devoted to Francueil, but he too proved unfaithful and was even so crass as to share a mistress with her disagreeable husband. (After his wife's death in 1754, Francueil married again; weirdly enough, his second wife was a daughter of the mistress he had shared with d'Épinay. It was his son by that marriage who became the father of Aurore Dupin, better known to posterity as George Sand.)

Mme d'Épinay next settled down with a more reliable lover, none other than Rousseau's friend Grimm, with whom he had spent such happy musical evenings. Grimm was well connected in intellectual circles and was also, somewhat surprisingly, capable of ostentatiously romantic behavior. On one occasion he conceived a desperate passion for an actress and lay for days on his bed in an apparent trance, though when he suddenly sprang up and resumed normal life Rousseau suspected that it had all been an act. And shortly after becoming Mme d'Épinay's lover, Grimm actually fought a duel to defend her honor when she was accused of destroying papers that documented her husband's debts.

As Rousseau remembered it in the *Confessions,* the move from Paris to the Hermitage was altogether festive, with Mme d'Épinay coming to fetch them in her carriage, bringing a farmer along to take care of the baggage and making sure that everything was completed in a single day. Her own recollections, in a fictionalized account of her life that will be discussed shortly, were less enthusiastic. Mme Levasseur was over eighty, fat, and helpless, and when the carriage bogged down in mud the servants had to carry her the rest of the way in an improvised sedan chair. The old lady wept with gratitude, but Rousseau, according to Mme d'Épinay, "walked in silence with his head down, and without seeming to take the least part in what was going on." As for Thérèse's kindly but ineffectual father, he had been installed in a Paris hospice, where he soon expired, all but forgotten.

Once in the house (demolished, incidentally, in 1956), Rousseau retired for a nap, from which he was awakened by the song of a nightingale, which made him cry out joyously, "At last my wishes are fulfilled!" Or at least he remembered it that way; it is unlikely that a nightingale would have been heard in the north of France in early

THE HERMITAGE

A view of the little house — not so little, in fact — renovated by Mme d'Épinay for her "bear" Rousseau, seen from the ample gardens at the back. As a token alternative to rent, he paid the wages of the gardener, who clearly had a lot to do.

April. There was a parklike woods in which to take walks, springtime was at hand, and even the relationship with Thérèse promised to deepen. At any rate she became more confiding, revealing for the first time that her mother had appropriated numerous gifts from Mme Dupin that were intended for Rousseau, and had repeatedly colluded with Diderot and Grimm in their campaign to keep Rousseau from leaving Paris. Rousseau's term for Thérèse, *gouvernante,* is often translated "governess," but that is misleading. It should be translated "housekeeper"; one of its normal meanings in the eighteenth century was a woman who took care of a bachelor's household, and Rousseau was technically a bachelor. The sly Gauffecourt, to be sure, liked to call Thérèse and her mother *les gouverneuses,* which might indeed be translated "governesses."

Rousseau settled down at the Hermitage to enjoy "those fleeting but delicious days that I passed entirely alone with myself, with my good and simple housekeeper, my much-loved dog, my old cat, the birds of the countryside, and the deer of the forest, with the whole of nature and its inconceivable author." As he liked to remember it, he opened his heart to nature's author in a fervor that had nothing in common with the rationalism of the philosophes. "Losing myself in this immensity, I didn't think, I didn't reason, I didn't philosophize." Instead he cried out in ecstasy, "O great being! O great being!" Neither skeptical nor dogmatic, he was evolving a religious position of his own that would later provoke attacks from freethinkers and theologians alike. After being disappointed and wounded by human contact, he was seeking asylum in a spiritualized nature that stood in opposition to civilized life. Alone in the woods, he could enjoy a feeling of communion with the universe, and when he came home in the evening the support system was there to receive him, right down to the dog. "I used to return with short steps, my head a bit weary, but my heart contented . . . I found my dinner set out on my terrace. I dined with a fine appetite in my little home, and no sense of servitude or dependence disturbed the benevolence that united us all. My dog himself was my friend, not my slave; we always had the same desires even though he never obeyed me."

Occasionally other people turned up, for Rousseau's reputation was attracting admirers who came to pay homage. One such was François Coindet, a young Genevan who worked in a Paris bank and was eager to carry out errands of all kinds. Rousseau complained of his presumptuousness and shallowness but kept him around. A more important visitor was Alexandre Deleyre, another young man who had literary aspirations and who knew how to pay court to the often gloomy master. In a typical letter that summer, Deleyre sent Rousseau an article he had written, commenting solemnly, "I wouldn't know how not to say what I think; so much the worse for people who don't love truth. I know what sacrifices you have made for it, and your example emboldens me." This piece of flattery was followed by a teasing comment on Rousseau's way of life: "Amuse yourself, my dear hermit, with all that has driven you into solitude. And do laugh a little; constant grumbling wears us out."

The one person who never visited was Diderot, and Rousseau's feelings were hurt. True, Diderot was overwhelmed with editorial work for the *Encyclopédie,* but there did seem to be something high-handed in his behavior; he expected other people to come to him, and he was sending a signal that Rousseau belonged in Paris. By the end of winter the strain on their long-standing friendship would reach a breaking point. In addition, more immediate tensions began to invade the idyll, as Rousseau and his new patron negotiated their relationship. Mme d'Épinay undoubtedly expected that bringing a celebrated writer into her orbit would further her intellectual aspirations, for she was a serious thinker and writer, if diffident about publishing. She wrote extensively on education and the status of women, and has been called a feminist two centuries ahead of her time; Grimm made her a regular contributor to his *Correspondance Littéraire.* Rousseau, however, was unimpressed. "She had taken it into her head, willy-nilly, to write novels, letters, comedies, tales, and other trifles like that. But what she enjoyed most was not writing them but reading them, and if she ever managed to scribble two or three consecutive pages, she had to be sure of at least two or three well-disposed listeners at the end of this immense labor."

Rousseau had work of his own to do. In an atmosphere of quiet and leisure, he planned to devote himself to a pair of major books. One was to be called *Political Institutions,* a comprehensive analysis of forms of government and law; some elements of it eventually appeared in *The Social Contract.* The other was going to be *Sensitive Morality, or the Materialism of the Sage.* The idea was that although the atheistic materialism of d'Holbach and Diderot was repugnant, Rousseau could not deny that people respond to stimuli in what today would be called behaviorist ways. "Climates, seasons, sounds, colors, darkness, light, the elements, food, noise, silence, movement, repose, everything acts upon our bodies, and in consequence upon our souls." (The word *âme* is ambiguous; although it should generally be translated "soul," it is often closer to "mind." The ambiguity was a fertile one, allowing Rousseau to suggest spiritual value even when he was talking about mental processes.) The goal of *Sensitive Morality* was to create a way of life that would encourage good habits and minimize bad ones. In Paris Rousseau was at the mercy of other people; at the Hermitage he could be a hermit.

Mme d'Épinay had something different in mind. She promised to let Rousseau know whenever she was alone, in consideration of his dislike of company, but he soon grasped that this notification amounted to a summons. Though she spoke as if they were friends and equals, she assumed in effect a propriety right over him. In the years to come he would continue to accept lodging from wealthy admirers, regarding it as a relatively impersonal arrangement and always paying rent of some kind, but he was fanatical about refusing gifts. Even his music copying had to be strictly business. A Genevan who met him in 1754 related that when the duc de Richelieu sent him an enormous overpayment for some music notebooks (100 louis, the equivalent of 2,400 livres), he immediately returned 99 of them. "M. Rousseau believes that a gift is a trap set against our independence, and that most benefactors place such a high price on their presents that the sincerest gratitude cannot repay them."

It was to forestall any suspicion of dependence that Rousseau took a firm line — bordering on the churlish — from the very start. When Mme d'Épinay offered him a pension of 1,000 livres, he proclaimed that he could not be bought. "This proposition chills my soul. How badly you understand your own interest in wanting to turn a friend into a valet!" When this declaration drew an indignant reply from Mme d'Épinay, he explained that it was his custom to make words mean what he wanted them to mean. "Learn my dictionary better, my good friend, if you want us to understand each other. Know that my terms rarely have their ordinary sense and that it is always my heart that converses with you, and perhaps one day you will understand that it does not speak like any other." This was indeed a regular pattern with Rousseau: to believe that his pen expressed the true feelings of his heart and then to be offended if the recipient took it wrong. Apparently it never occurred to him that he was extremely demanding himself. Grimm warned Mme d'Épinay from the outset to be prepared for reproaches. "If you refuse one single time to be at his command, he will accuse you of having begged him to live near you and of preventing him from living in his native land."

In addition to temperamental differences between Rousseau and Mme d'Épinay, there was a profound class difference as well. She enjoyed her wealth and thought of patronage as an expression of affection, not of power. Moreover, she was unlikely to grasp that her motives might sometimes be mixed. According to a self-portrait that she wrote just at that time, "I am not pretty, but not ugly either. I am petite, thin, and very well formed. I have a youthful appearance, though without freshness; noble, sweet, lively, witty, and interesting." She considered her less visible qualities to be equally pleasing: she was truthful, trusting of friends, generous to those who injured her, and secure in her moral values; if she did have a fault, it was only that she was socially timid. Her relationship with Rousseau would require all of these virtues, while he in turn would conclude that her complacent self-image prevented her from recognizing how she actually treated her friends.

In the early days, however, Rousseau was a welcome addition to a group whom it amused Mme d'Épinay to call her "bears," as she said in a playful poem addressed to Grimm: "Myself, the queen of five bears, prescribing their laws to them." Rousseau probably didn't like being lumped into a very miscellaneous group (the others were Grimm, Gaufecourt, and a couple of very minor writers). And he, of course, was the most bearish of all, as Mme d'Épinay remarked to a friend. "The bear *par excellence* has had a tooth pulled; if only it had been the one he uses against the human race!"

Quite possibly Mme d'Épinay hoped that Rousseau would be taken with her charms, but he was not inclined that way. An apparent overture occurred when cold weather came on in the fall: she sent a little flannel petticoat and a charming note suggesting that he have it made into a waistcoat for himself. The prospect of wearing a woman's undergarment, suitably adapted, next to his body was so stimulating that "in my emotion, weeping, I kissed the note and the petticoat twenty times." Thérèse, who would have to make the alterations, thought he had lost his mind, but it never occurred to him that she might actually be jealous. Fortunately or unfortunately, Mme d'Épinay was simply not Rousseau's type. "I felt comfortable giving her little attentions and little fraternal kisses, which no more seemed sensual to me than they did to her, but that was all. She was very thin and very pale, and her bosom was as flat as my hand. This defect alone would have been enough to chill me. Neither my heart nor my senses have ever been able to regard someone as a woman if she had no breasts."

However demanding Mme d'Épinay may sometimes have been, Rousseau did have great tracts of time to himself, and he often felt lonely. Brooding about the past as he strolled in the woods, he found himself thinking a lot about love, or rather about the grand passion he had never experienced. The pastoral setting, evocative of the countryside of his youth, helped to conjure up vivid memories, and he understood very well that his fantasy life was compensating for the frustrations of middle age. "I meditated like this during the loveliest season of the year, in the month of June, beneath the cool boughs, to the song of the nightingale and the babbling of the streams . . . Soon I saw gathered around me all the objects that had filled me with emotion in my youth, Mlle Galley, Mlle de Graffenried, Mlle de Breil, Madame Basile, Madame de Larnage, my pretty pupils, and even the piquant Zulietta, whom my heart cannot forget." With the sole exception of Mme de Larnage, these were all women he had yearned for but never enjoyed; it is striking that he omits the name of Mme de Warens. But it was a truism that amorous old men were ridiculous, and this daydreaming was embarrassing. "My blood grew heated and effervescent, my head was turned in spite of its already graying hair, and *voilà* the grave citizen of Geneva, *voilà* the austere Jean-Jacques at almost forty-five, suddenly transformed again into an extravagant swain."

In the dominant psychology of the eighteenth century, imagination was deeply distrusted as escapism. Samuel Johnson wrote sternly at about the same time, "All power of fancy over reason is a degree of insanity . . . Fictions begin to operate as realities, false opinions fasten upon the mind, and life passes in dreams of rapture or of anguish." But that was exactly what Rousseau wanted (the rapture if not the anguish), and he sought it deliberately, just as in childhood he had escaped into courtly romance and ancient Rome. And since by now he was an accomplished writer, he began to create a romance by writing it himself.

At some point in the summer of 1756, Rousseau began a romantic tale called "The Amours of Claire and Marcellin," in which a pair of peasants fall in love in spite of the opposition of the young man's father, who wants him to marry for money. After a few pages the effort petered out, but it turned out to be a significant beginning, as did the even briefer "Little Savoyard." Rousseau was beginning to create characters whose rural obscurity gave them a greater integrity than city sophisticates had, and he was asserting the irrelevance of social class. "There are souls that belong in no rank, since they are superior to all . . . Nature does not make kings and laborers from different molds." There is a hint as well of the kind of self-portrait that he would go on developing for years to come: "The first and gravest of my misfortunes was to be mistaken in my vocation. Each step that I took in the world carried me farther away from innocence and true happiness."

Soon, and much to his own surprise, Rousseau found that he was writing not a short story but a novel, told in letters, as was fashionable at the time. He made its heroine Julie d'Étange, the teenage daughter of a minor Swiss nobleman, who falls in love with a tutor hardly older than herself and actually sleeps with him, a quite scandalous action in the literary code of the time. Julie, an ash-blonde like Mme de Warens, comes from the same village that she did, while the hero, Saint-Preux, is an idealized and youthful self-portrait of the author. Abetted by her cousin and alter ego Claire, Julie manages to keep the liaison secret, but when her father commands her to marry an older man whom she respects but does not desire, she bows to duty and commands her heartbroken lover to travel abroad. What would happen when he returned? Rousseau was making up the story as he went along and really didn't know, though he envisioned an ending in which the star-crossed lovers would drown, possibly on purpose, in Lac Léman.

During the long winter, confined to the house except for a couple of brief trips to Paris, Rousseau worked steadily at his novel, and by the spring of 1757 he had completed the first two books of what would eventually become six. He thought of it as *Julie,* and often referred to it by that name in later years, though when it was finally published, its title was *Letters of Two Lovers, Living in a Little Town at the Foot of the Alps.* It also acquired the subtitle by which it is widely known, *The New Héloïse,* alluding to the medieval story of Héloïse and her tutor, Abelard. The project pleased him so much that he copied the whole thing out on gilt paper (he had exceptionally elegant handwriting), drying the ink with azure and silver powder, and stitching the notebooks together with expensive blue ribbon. All he lacked was an audience. He liked to read aloud from the manuscript at the fireside, but although Thérèse sobbed sympathetically she had nothing to say, and her mother would only remark, "Monsieur, that is very fine." Both women desperately missed Paris, which they had no chance of visiting now that the roads were glutinous with mud, and listening to Rousseau read aloud was no compensation for what they had given up.

Suddenly Rousseau's emotional life went up in flames. During the winter Mme d'Épinay's cousin the comtesse d'Houdetot had made a vivid impression by turning up unexpectedly at the Hermitage in gales of laughter, wearing her coachman's boots because the carriage had bogged down in mud. She was renting a house at Eaubonne, a couple of miles away, and had come over to bring news of their mutual friend Gauffecourt, who was ill. In June she appeared again, this time on horseback and in men's riding clothes. "Although I don't much care for that sort of masquerade, I was taken with the romantic air of this one, and this time it was love." Rousseau had seen Mme d'Houdetot occasionally in the past, but now he was swept away. She was not exactly beautiful, with a face marked by smallpox as was all too common in those days, but her allure was completed by "a forest of thick black naturally curly hair that fell to her knees; she had a pretty figure, and in all of her movements she combined both gaucherie and grace." In accordance with his principles, Rousseau might have required a blonde, but for him blondes signified purity, whereas brunettes could be bad girls.

Rousseau's imagination had been scripting a role for a suitable candidate, and now the part was cast. "She came, I saw her; I was intoxicated with love without an object, this intoxication enchanted my eyes, and this object fixated on her. I saw my Julie in Mme d'Houdetot, and soon I saw only Mme d'Houdetot, but clothed in all the perfections with which I had been adorning the idol of my heart." Stendhal describes a process he calls crystallization, in which the lover projects an idealized image onto another person, on the analogy of a branch left in a salt mine on which jewellike crystals appear out of thin air, and that is what happened to Rousseau. With Mme de Larnage he had experienced (or so he later claimed) complete sexual gratification for the only time in his life. With Mme d'Houdetot he experienced romantic passion at long last; whatever his feelings for Mme de Warens had been, he never saw them in that light. Invoking the ambiguity of the verb *aimer,* which can mean anything from liking to adoring, he declares in the *Confessions* that this was the sole occasion when he was able "to love with love," *aimer d'amour.*

Élisabeth-Sophie-Françoise Lalive de Bellegarde — "Mimi" to her friends — had lived with her cousin Mme d'Épinay during their teens. In 1748 she married the comte d'Houdetot, with whom she had three children, and as a countess she outranked Mme d'Épinay socially. Since 1752 she had openly been the mistress of Jean-François de Saint-Lam-

THE COMTESSE
D'HOUDETOT
The tumbling black hair
that intoxicated Rousseau
is discreetly bound up;
the anonymous artist has
caught something of
Sophie's intensity, though
not the combination of
liveliness and sweetness
that her friends admired.

bert, with the complete approval of her husband, who had a mistress of his own; following the custom of their class, the spouses remained good friends while seeking romantic and sexual fulfillment elsewhere. Saint-Lambert was a marquis and had a reputation as a rake, having been for a time the lover of a former mistress of Voltaire, Mme de Châtelet. When Mme de Châtelet was forty-three he got her pregnant, a mishap that inspired a wit to comment, "The last person one would suspect is her husband. M. de Voltaire is equally guiltless. Everyone believes it is M. de Saint-Lambert who has committed this folly. However, she has been obliged, like an honest woman, to seek the company of her husband. On this, someone said, 'But what the devil has possessed Mme de Châtelet to sleep with her husband?' To which the reply was, 'It's a pregnant woman's craving.'" The affair ended tragically, with her death in childbirth. Saint-Lambert was a generous and sensible person, as well as a poet of some talent and interested in ideas, and he had become friendly with Rousseau. It was his idea, when he heard that Rousseau was living at the Hermitage, that Mme d'Houdetot should get to know him.

Saint-Lambert was a career army officer, and in 1756 he was stationed in Germany as a cavalry captain. Mme d'Houdetot's husband was in the army too, rising to the high rank of *maréchal* a few years later, and Grimm was a general's secretary. They were, in fact, engaged in the Seven Years War, the great struggle for empire that has been called the first true world war. Perhaps surprisingly, Rousseau scarcely mentions the war in his letters and other writings, and Diderot too paid hardly any attention to it. Unless one happened to live in a contested area, wars in those days could be all but ignored as nothing more than routine competition among nations. And like the other philosophes, Rousseau despised the colonial powers for "making a desert to assure themselves of an empire," burning down defenseless villages and transforming a quarter of the human race into beasts of burden.

Mme d'Houdetot had an artlessly ingenuous manner that men found charming, though Mme d'Épinay did not. A couple of years earlier she had written a description of Mme d'Houdetot, praising some good qualities but adding more sharply, "Since her mannerisms are totally opposed to my character, they seem intolerable to me. These are, for example, never to be ready at the agreed-upon hour, to wait until dessert to begin her own dinner, to take something from each dish in succession without eating any of it, to have a continual air of idleness, especially when her lover is away, to let everything drift, and to forget constantly where she is and what she needs to do." Diderot got to know her a few years later and wrote to his own mistress that she had "a hundred thousand enthusiasms of every color"; he was especially stimulated by a "Hymn to Breasts" that he believed she had written, "sparkling with fire, heat, and images of voluptuousness." In fact the piece was by somebody else, but Mme d'Houdetot definitely appreciated it. "Although she had courage enough to show it to me," Diderot admitted, "I didn't have enough to ask for a copy."

A friend who knew Mme d'Houdetot well commented that although she remained resolutely faithful to Saint-Lambert, "love was the motive force of her existence and the occupation of her whole life." Especially striking was a tendency, undoubtedly gratifying to Rousseau, to pick up the tone of the person with whom she was smitten. "She loved without transports, but with the most agreeable abandon. Like the ivy that takes the form of the tree to which it clings, her opinions, tastes, and inclinations all received the imprint of the person she loved." Moreover, she was young — she was twenty-six, Saint-Lambert forty, and Rousseau forty-five — and was still finding out who she was. Another friend left some interesting comments: "Married as one got married in those days, she held at first the same position in society that nearly all young women did. Between the ages of fifteen and twenty they resembled each other closely. Raised with the same habits, formed by the same education, in their youth they displayed more or less the same charms, but above all the qualities necessary for a girl who was about to be married. Consequently, they usually got married when no one — not even their relatives, not even themselves — knew the qualities or faults that were going to direct their conduct."

Once ignited, Rousseau's passion for Mme d'Houdetot burned fiercely. The two began taking long walks in the forest, and when Rousseau accused her of flirting just to make him look silly, "she changed her tone, her sympathetic sweetness was invincible, and she reproached me in a way that went right through me." He made a special point of feeling guilty for invading the rights of his friend Saint-Lambert, but actually the situation was exactly what he liked, a relationship *à trois* that protected him from the awkwardness and probable disappointment of consummation. "It would be wrong to call it a love that wasn't shared; mine was indeed shared, in a way. It was equal on both sides, even though it wasn't reciprocal. Both of us were intoxicated with love, she for her lover and I for her, so that our sighs and sweet tears mingled together."

The situation of deferred desire was familiar to Rousseau from the courtly romances on which his imagination had been formed, and of course he thought it confirmed his own virtue. It has been said that what he was really experiencing was *envie* rather than *désir:* not desire for what he would soon enjoy, but yearning for what he could never possess. Saint-Lambert was a soldier and a man of the world, while Rousseau offered himself as a very different romantic type, weak in health, unworldly by choice, but a master of language who specialized in sensitive emotions.

Even if the relationship was never consummated, that is not to say that it wasn't erotic. In a memorable set piece in the *Confessions,* Rousseau describes a moonlit night when he and Mme d'Houdetot (by then he was calling her Sophie, a familiarity he never attempted with Mme d'Épinay), sitting on a flowery bank beneath an acacia tree, exchanged a kiss that was all the more potent for being the only one of its kind. "What intoxicating tears I shed into her lap! How many tears I made her shed, in spite of herself! At last, in an involuntary transport, she cried out, 'Never was a man so lovable, and never did a lover love like you! But your friend Saint-Lambert hears us, and my heart could not love twice.' I fell silent, sighing. I kissed her, and what a kiss! but that was all." From allusions by Mme d'Épinay and others, it is possible to deduce that Rousseau not only spent a number of nights with Mme d'Houdetot in the park and at her house, but even slept in her bedroom, and that she allowed him a good many liberties. In short, he had his cake and didn't eat it, but was permitted to fondle it. And he also admits in the *Confessions* that as a precaution he customarily masturbated in the park while on the way to see her, or, as he puts it discreetly, "I don't believe that I ever managed to complete the journey with impunity. I would arrive at Eaubonne weak, exhausted, and spent, barely able to stand up."

This heady state of affairs lasted for little more than a month, and then jealousy and second thoughts intervened. The second thoughts came from Mme d'Houdetot, who was worried about what Saint-Lambert would think if he found out, and uneasy as well about how far she was permitting herself to go. Rousseau was in the habit of writing letters to her even though he was seeing her regularly; some he would secrete in a hollow tree while waiting for her to arrive, though as he wryly admitted, when she found one "all she could see in it was the truly deplorable state I was in when I wrote it." Not long afterward she demanded that he return her own letters, and their correspondence from that period seems to have been destroyed, despite his hope that "someone who has inspired such a passion will never have the courage to burn the proof of it."

Rousseau's copy of one letter (Leigh thinks it was never sent) does survive, in which he proclaims heroic self-control while hinting at a perverse pleasure in denial: "Do you remember reproaching me once for 'very refined cruelties'?" He also says plainly that the slightest encouragement from her would be irresistible. "No, Sophie, I may perish from my frenzy, but never will I make you vile. But if you are weak and

I perceive it, I will succumb on the instant . . . A hundred times I have willed the crime. If you too have willed it, then I will consummate it and become at once the most treacherous and the happiest of men; but I cannot corrupt the woman I idolize." In much the same way he had told Mme de Warens, "No, Maman, I love you too much to defile you; my possessing you is too precious to be shared." It is worth noting that in this letter he addresses Mme d'Houdetot as *vous*. In the *Confessions* he mentions that he had been using the familiar *tu* and that she was offended at his presumption but couldn't get him to stop.

Those were the second thoughts. The jealousy came from three directions, all of them predictable: Thérèse, Mme d'Épinay, and Saint-Lambert. Whether or not Mme d'Épinay had an erotic interest in Rousseau, she resented his infatuation with the cousin who was her social superior. As for Thérèse, who was expected to run back and forth carrying letters between Rousseau and both ladies, she surely resented being taken for granted, though it never occurred to Rousseau that she might. Mme d'Épinay began to confer secretly with Thérèse, demanding to be shown Mme d'Houdetot's letters and even to be given torn-up fragments so that she could piece them together. This volatile situation was bound to explode before long, and it left in its wake an impressive richness of documentation, in letters by Mme d'Épinay, Rousseau, Grimm, and Saint-Lambert. It is therefore possible to fill scores of pages (some biographers have) with the high-minded recriminations that were exchanged on all sides. But there is a fatal ambiguity about those letters. Many of the most important are known only from Mme d'Épinay's fictionalized version of the affair, and their authenticity is highly dubious.

In that same year, 1756, shortly after her association with Rousseau began, Mme d'Épinay began writing an epistolary novel inspired by *Julie*. It was eventually called *The History of Madame de Montbrillant*, with Émilie de Montbrillant as a thinly disguised version of herself, Mimi as Mme d'Houdetot, Volx as Grimm, and René as Rousseau. There is of course nothing reprehensible about writing a roman à clef, and she may have begun it, as a sympathetic scholar says, "for the good reason that she was cruelly lacking in imagination." And the bulk of the work, which eventually filled 1,500 pages, is concerned not with Rousseau but with her own personal affairs, including the struggle against a domineering mother and betrayals by her husband. In one chilling scene, he encourages a drunken friend to climb into her bed and make love to her, and she escapes only by shouting for the servants.

Unfortunately, when the book was finally published in 1818, thirty-five years after Mme d'Épinay's death, an enterprising editor entitled it *Memoirs* and substituted the real names for the fictional ones. Not only that, but he rewrote many passages to accommodate them to known dates and facts. For nearly a century the book was accepted as historical truth, much to the discredit of Rousseau, who cuts a very unattractive figure in it. Mme d'Épinay can hardly be blamed for that, but more disturbingly, it was discovered still later that she herself rewrote her original letters as well as Rousseau's, and that Grimm and Diderot assisted in further alterations to make Rousseau look bad. Mme d'Épinay has had defenders, but Diderot's biographers agree that probably there really was a conspiracy to blacken Rousseau's reputation, with the manuscript as "a kind of delayed bomb or booby trap waiting for someone to detonate it."

Rousseau believed at the time that Mme d'Épinay was jealous and had maliciously alerted Saint-Lambert to what was going on, either directly or through Grimm. Her own account in *Madame de Montbrillant* was totally different. As presented there, she behaved with unfailing generosity, even though Rousseau was proving to be "nothing more than a moral dwarf on stilts," and he was so overwhelmed by her kindness that he appeared at six in the morning to implore forgiveness: "Know, Madame, once and for all, that I am vicious and was born that way . . . Just to prove that what I'm saying is true, understand that I am incapable of not hating people who do good things for me." This improbable speech was very likely invented long afterward. Mme d'Épinay was careful also to exonerate herself from the charge of spying, claiming that when Thérèse tried to give her an incriminating letter, she virtuously refused to read it. "I said to the little woman, 'My child, when one finds letters, one must throw them into the fire without reading them, or else return them to the people they belong to.'"

Whatever Saint-Lambert was told or suspected, he could hardly help being concerned, and Rousseau tried rather awkwardly to patch things up. In mid-July he sent Mme d'Houdetot an extremely stilted letter, clearly intended to be shown to Saint-Lambert, in which he inquired politely after her health, regretted that the pleasant walks they used to take together had ceased, and expressed eagerness to see Saint-Lambert in Paris "if you could persuade him to drop by Diderot's place sometime tomorrow." As it happened, Saint-Lambert had been sent by the army on a brief mission to Paris, during which he found time to visit Mme d'Houdetot at Eaubonne and to dine with her and Rousseau at La Chevrette. Saint-Lambert behaved somewhat coldly, but Rousseau was relieved to find that they were still friends. At this stage Saint-Lambert still had no idea how involved his mistress was with Rousseau, though this may have been the time (the date is uncertain) when Rousseau read aloud from his writings and Saint-Lambert permitted himself to fall asleep and snore peacefully while Rousseau doggedly continued, too embarrassed to stop.

For whatever reason, Mme d'Houdetot began to grasp the full implications of what she was doing. Feeling guilty and constrained when she was with Saint-Lambert, she realized how deeply she loved him, and she began to avoid Rousseau. As he usually did in times of emotional distress, Rousseau fell ill, and his resentment turned toward Mme d'Épinay for supposedly betraying him to Saint-Lambert. The crisis arrived on what has become known as the day of the five letters (probably August 31), which volleyed back and forth between Rousseau and Mme d'Épinay. She began the exchange by writing that she hadn't heard from him for almost a week and feared that he must be ill. He replied, ambiguously but ominously, "I can't tell you anything yet; I'm waiting for better information, and sooner or later I'll have it. Meanwhile, be sure that outraged innocence will find a defender ardent enough to make the slanderers repent, whoever they may be." In *Madame de Montbrillant,* Mme d'Épinay claimed that she was "astonished by this letter, which appeared so unintelligible to me that I questioned the little woman [Thérèse, the mail carrier] on the state of René's health and head," and then sent a brief note asking for further information. That was the third of the five letters. In the text preserved by Rousseau, however — and he has never been suspected of altering documents — Mme d'Épinay's note was much longer and much more emotional: "Do you know that your letter frightens me? What does it mean? I've read it more than twenty-five times, and truly I understand nothing; I see only that you are upset and tormented . . . What has become of our friendship, our trust? And how have I lost it, what have I done? Is it against me or for me that you're angry?" Since Rousseau was convinced that she knew very well what he was talking about, this appeal to his feelings infuriated him, and he fired back what she regarded as "an impertinent reply," swearing that he would never harm either Mme d'Houdetot or Saint-Lambert, and accusing Mme d'Épinay of scheming against all three of them.

The versions of this fourth letter in the *Confessions* and in *Madame de Montbrillant* are in agreement, but that is far from the case with the fifth and last. In Mme d'Épinay's novel, her tone was haughty and stern: "You make me pity you, René. If I didn't believe that you're crazy, or on the point of it, I swear that I wouldn't give myself the trouble of replying, and I would never see you again for the rest of my life." But in the version that Rousseau preserved, she grew emotional again: "Although you make me pity you, I can't escape the bitterness with which your letter fills my soul. Me, using ruses and guile against you! Me, accused of the blackest of infamies! Farewell, I don't regret that you have — I don't know what I'm saying — farewell. I will be eager to forgive you." By suppressing this plea in *Madame de Montbrillant* (assuming she did suppress it), Mme d'Épinay rewrote the story to make herself less indecisive and vulnerable. The one thing that seems clear is that she really did have good intentions, was upset at the way Rousseau and her cousin were carrying on, and couldn't acknowledge that jealousy and rivalry on her part might be involved. The same cannot be said for her lover, Grimm, who went out of his way to stir up trouble with Saint-Lambert and was unquestionably something of a snake.

The state of affairs that followed is obscure, given the unreliability of *Madame de Montbrillant* as the main source of information, but everybody concerned was confused and depressed, apart from Grimm, who was enjoying the disaster thoroughly. According to Mme d'Épinay, Rousseau appeared unexpectedly at La Chevrette, pleaded with her to be friends again, and confessed that he was completely in the wrong, after which she promised to forgive him if he would behave himself in future. When she reported this encounter to Grimm, he was disgusted: "You should have listened to what he had to say, made him understand how shameful his conduct was, and then shown him the door and forbade him ever to return."

Rousseau himself seems not to have understood the extent of his disgrace. A few days later he wrote again to Mme d'Épinay to say that he was looking forward to seeing her as soon as he felt better, but that his condition was truly dreadful. "Everyone is unbearable to me, beginning with myself. I feel in my body all the pains that can possibly be felt, and in my soul the anguish of death." By now Mme d'Épinay was used to this kind of appeal, just as Mme de Warens had been, but she must have been relieved to hear that when Rousseau visited Mme d'Houdetot at Eaubonne, he found her disinclined to see him. As always, the account in *Madame de Montbrillant* is harsher. There is no mention of this letter, and instead a startling exchange is recorded in which Rousseau supposedly came again to La Chevrette, declared that if Mme d'Épinay refused to forgive him he would kill himself, and received the alarming reply, "You would be doing the right thing, if you don't have the courage to be virtuous."

Rousseau now decided that he had better write to Saint-Lambert, reaffirming friendship and mentioning that Mme d'Houdetot was avoiding him. Once again he asserted the perfect purity of his intentions. "No, no, Saint-Lambert, the breast of J. J. Rousseau does not enclose the heart of a traitor, and I would despise myself far more than you imagine if ever I had attempted to steal hers away from you." Having attained this altitude of righteousness, he couldn't resist a further jab: "Do not believe you have seduced me with your reasonings . . . I blame you for your liaison, which you could hardly approve of yourself, and so long as both of you remain dear to me, I will never give you an assurance of innocence in your present state." Incredibly, Rousseau was reproving Saint-Lambert for sleeping with a married woman who ought to have remained faithful to her husband, even while rationalizing his own equivocal relationship with her.

This letter took a month to reach Saint-Lambert, who was at Wolfenbüttel recovering from a stroke that had left him temporarily paralyzed on one side, but when his reply arrived it was generous. "Don't accuse our friend of fickleness or cooling off," he wrote; "she is incapable of either. She still loves, and anyone whom she has once loved, she loves more and more; it would not be toward such a friend as you that she would begin to be inconstant." If anyone was to blame, Saint-Lambert said, it was he, for having brought Rousseau and Mme d'Houdetot together and for suspecting them of betraying his trust. "Regard me and treat me as your friend, and be sure that this friendship will continue to be one of the greatest delights of my life." In fact they did remain on good terms, very much to Saint-Lambert's credit.

A couple of weeks earlier Mme d'Houdetot, who was in Paris at the time, had written to Rousseau with extraordinary awkwardness: "I dare to place myself in your heart among your friends. If the intensity of an emotion you're aware of, which unites me to a being from whom I am inseparable, takes something away in my heart from the perfection of friendship, the friendship that remains is sufficiently sweet and tender for you to give me some return for those feelings that I'm able to give to you, without reproaching me for the ones I'm not free to give." Rousseau began to draft one last bid for sympathy (though careful again to address her as *vous*) in a long letter that alternated between declarations of virtue and reminiscences intended to inflame: "I won't remind you of what happened in your park and in your bedroom . . . What — my burning lips would never again breathe my soul into your heart along with my kisses? . . . You used to take my arm when we went walking, you weren't so careful to conceal the sight of your charms from me, and when my mouth dared to press against yours, sometimes at least I felt a response." So it was not just a single kiss beneath the acacia! But Rousseau came to his senses in time, and didn't send the letter.

Meanwhile Mme d'Épinay was also working to smooth things over. She encouraged Rousseau to compose a motet for the ceremony dedicating a new chapel at La Chevrette; M. d'Épinay assembled a full orchestra and a famous Italian singer, and the piece was a great success. She also wrote a pantomime to be performed on her husband's birthday, for which Rousseau again composed the music (though it wounded him to see Mme d'Houdetot there dancing gaily with others). She took pains as well to assure him that Grimm was still his friend. If he sometimes seemed detached and indifferent, that was only because he had been "born melancholy" with a gloom that masked a truthful soul. Rousseau took this character sketch with plenty of grains of salt, but he agreed to come to La Chevrette for a reconciliation. On a previous occasion Grimm had ostentatiously avoided acknowledging that he was even there, sitting down to a dinner *à deux* with Mme d'Épinay while Rousseau wandered around the room waiting for another place to be set at the far end of the table. This time Grimm did address him, pompously and at length, reviewing his own virtues and Rousseau's faults. When that was finished, "he granted me the kiss of peace with a slight embrace that was like the accolade a king gives to new knights" or rather "the reprimand of a tutor who lets his pupil off from a whipping."

The last straw turned out to be a completely unexpected demand that Rousseau had to face shortly after M. d'Épinay's birthday fête in October 1757, just when the final reproaches in the d'Houdetot affair were being exchanged. Mme d'Épinay announced that she had decided to go to Geneva for a medical consultation with the celebrated Dr. Théodore Tronchin, and she asked Rousseau to accompany her. Since he was a Genevan and still talked about moving there, this might seem a reasonable request, and Diderot and Grimm were certain that it was. But Rousseau refused to go, partly because his health was bad but above all because it felt to him like a command from a patron, the very relationship he had been doing his best to avoid.

Now Rousseau found himself even more on the defensive, fending off pressure from all sides. He was conducting the entire quarrel by mail, and the documentary record is both fascinating and depressing. To Grimm he wrote an exceptionally long letter justifying his conduct, with a curious mixture of sensible arguments and injured pride. The sensible arguments were that his constant need to urinate would require the coach to stop repeatedly, that his own connections in Geneva would be less useful than the ones Mme d'Épinay could make herself, and that Thérèse and her mother needed him to stay. The injured pride derived from his feeling that Mme d'Épinay was behaving like a master and not a friend. True, she had given him a pleasant cottage to live in, but in return he had to be at her beck and call constantly, and his new friends were so tirelessly attentive that "they often made me weep with grief that I wasn't five hundred leagues away." In short, what Mme d'Épinay regarded as friendship was for Rousseau "two years of slavery," and her affection was no extenuation but rather the reverse, a kind of emotional blackmail. "But she loves me, it will be said, and she has need of her friend. Oh! how well I know all the meanings of the word 'friendship'! It's a fine name that often serves as wages for servitude, but the moment slavery begins, friendship ends."

Rousseau later admitted that these complaints were injudicious and ungrateful, but he also claimed that there was a more important reason, which he was not free to state. The unmentionable reason was a belief, based on gossip Thérèse had picked up from the servants at La Chevrette, that Mme d'Épinay was pregnant, was going to Geneva to have the baby in secrecy, and wanted to take Rousseau along to deflect suspicion from Grimm. The gossip about the pregnancy was probably mistaken, though that is unprovable. What she did definitely want was Tronchin's help with a stomach ulcer that was tormenting her, and with her venereal condition too.

Having taken his stand, Rousseau began to strike out in all directions, ensuring that he would be *non grata* henceforth at La Chevrette. He wrote to Saint-Lambert to lament, "One might say that there is a league among all of my friends to abuse my poverty and deliver me to the mercies of Mme d'Épinay . . . I won't be with her any longer as her friend but as her valet, and whatever happens, I don't want that." This was the first time Rousseau referred to a "league" or plot against him, an ominous term that would recur more and more frequently in the future. To the lady herself he wrote heatedly on the same day, "This zeal to make me go, without consideration for my own condition, has made me suspect a sort of league of which you are the prime mover," and he concluded insultingly, "When you no longer want me for a slave you will always have me as a friend."

Needless to say, these intemperate letters made matters worse. Mme d'Épinay did depart for Geneva, by herself except for the usual entourage of servants, and Grimm seized the occasion to deliver a crushing thunderbolt of his own. "You dare to talk to me of your slavery, when I have been the witness daily, for over two years, of all the tokens of the tenderest and most generous friendship that you have received from this woman . . . If I were able to forgive you, I would think myself unworthy to have a friend. I will never see you again as long as I live, and I will think myself happy if I succeed in erasing all memory of your actions from my mind. I beg you to forget me and never to disturb my spirit again." Grimm's letter ended with a naked threat: "If the justness of this demand fails to move you, remember that I have in my hands your letter that will justify the propriety of my conduct to all decent people." Before long he was indeed showing Rousseau's letter around Paris. Rousseau, goaded to fury, returned Grimm's letter the next day, along with an acidic note: "I withheld my true suspicions, and I have learned to know you too late. So here is the letter which you have given yourself the leisure to compose! I am sending it back to you; it is not for me. You may show mine to the whole world and hate me openly. That will be one less falsity on your part."

Mme d'Houdetot was more sympathetic, but she was seriously alarmed on her own account. Whatever she had been telling Saint-Lambert, it was clearly less than the whole truth. "So what are your grievances against your friends?" she wrote to Rousseau. "Pardon me, my friend, but I can't be so quick to condemn them as you are, especially when I know so little. Am I mixed up myself in all of this? And I gather that you suspect Mme d'Épinay of some strange misconduct; is there anything in that?" Mme d'Houdetot evidently feared that her cousin had betrayed more details of her affair with Rousseau than she wanted anyone to know. For some reason her letter didn't reach Rousseau for several days, and in his anxiety he grew panicky and composed yet another fervent defense of his own virtue, taking care to put it through several drafts. The next day, waiting nervously for a reply, he reached still greater heights of self-pity. "If I had any hope of swaying you, I would come, even if I couldn't reach you; I would wait at your door, prostrate myself before you, and be only too happy to be trampled by your horses' hooves and crushed by your carriage, so as to tear from you at least some regret for my death." Happily, a reassuring reply arrived from Mme d'Houdetot, which drew from him extravagant rhetoric of a happier kind: "Adieu, my dear and lovable friend, and my pen dares to write that word! My mouth and my heart dare to continue saying it! O joy! O pride!" In truth, he was writing like his own characters in *Julie,* and it was high time to extricate the still-unfinished novel from his life.

It was also time to leave the Hermitage, but since winter was coming on and Mme d'Épinay was far away, Rousseau hoped to remain there for a few months. Saint-Lambert, convalescing at Aix-la-Chapelle, wrote a thoughtful letter agreeing that Diderot and Grimm had behaved badly but urging Rousseau to remain on good terms with Mme d'Épinay. Mme d'Houdetot likewise urged him repeatedly not to leave the Hermitage; she was desperate to calm him down before he did something disastrous. But it was far too late for reconciliation with

Mme d'Épinay, who was now settled outside Geneva at Montbrillant — from which she took the title of her novel — and was more indignant than ever that Rousseau had refused her demands. (Grimm, incidentally, after being so peremptory with Rousseau, waited over a year to join her.)

Rousseau now wrote to Mme d'Épinay, with his usual rhetorical extravagance, "If one could die of grief, I would no longer be alive. But I have made up my mind at last. Friendship between us, Madame, is dead." He asked only that he be permitted to stay in the Hermitage until spring, "since my friends wish it." This request she treated with contempt, responding icily, "Since you wanted to leave the Hermitage and ought to do so, I'm surprised that your friends hold you back. For my own part, I never consult my friends about my duties, and I have nothing more to say to you about yours." Only a year and a half before, Rousseau had written enthusiastically, "You will be pleased, Madame, to hear that I find my dwelling more and more charming. Either you or I will change a great deal, or I will never leave it." Now he hastily arranged to rent a little house in Montmorency, a few miles away; by the middle of December, two weeks after Mme d'Épinay's ultimatum, he was living there.

In after years Mme d'Houdetot and Saint-Lambert kept their distance from Rousseau, and their own bond continued to be very deep, ending only at his death in 1803 at the age of eighty-seven. It was with justice that she then wrote, "He was a man whose principles were never contradicted by a single thought or action, even when living with those who did not share them or who did not apply them as he did." Undoubtedly she had Rousseau in mind. It is notable too that Saint-Lambert, in keeping with the ethic of his class and time, remained on good terms with Mme d'Houdetot's husband, who helped care for him in his final illness and to whom he left a medallion of "the wisest of the French philosophers who have occupied themselves with legislation, that is, the président de Montesquieu." To Mme d'Houdetot he left a bust of Voltaire, "bequeathed to me by M. d'Alembert, which makes it the more precious." There was no mention of Rousseau.

As for Mme d'Houdetot herself, when she was eighty, and flirtatious to the end, she told an acquaintance proudly that Rousseau had never succeeded in awakening her passions. "He was alarmingly ugly, and love didn't make him any more attractive, but he was touching. I treated him with gentleness and kindness; he was an interesting madman. He turned plenty of women's heads, but not mine — it was I who turned his. I kept trying to reconcile him with his friends, but it always had to be begun all over again." She enjoyed showing visitors the acacia tree, made famous by then in the *Confessions,* under which the kiss (or kisses?) had been exchanged. She died in 1813, ten years after Saint-Lambert. A few years before her death she visited Rousseau's tomb, prostrated herself before it, and shed some tears.

16

The Break with the Enlightenment

THE HOUSE ROUSSEAU had found was small and in bad shape, but it was adequate for him and Thérèse, and its modest size provided an excuse to get rid of Mme Levasseur, who was dispatched to relatives in Paris. The garden promised to be agreeable when winter was over, and in it was a little tower that Rousseau called his *donjon* and used as a study, despite its complete lack of heat. (*Donjons*, according to a foreign visitor at the time, were "what the French call little buildings that stand on a hill.") Today the house is a small Musée Rousseau.

Rousseau's new landlord was Jacques-Joseph Mathas, financial agent for a distinguished nobleman named the prince de Conti, who would later be very important to Rousseau. Mathas lived in the big house on the estate, known as Montlouis (Rousseau's was the Petit Montlouis), and dropped in for visits. For a self-proclaimed hermit, Rousseau was surprisingly sociable. As an admirer once remarked, "For him society was like a mistress to whom one keeps coming back a thousand times, saying in tears that one can no longer endure her." He spent time with his neighbors, a lawyer and two clergymen. He also saw Carrio (now known as the chevalier de Carrión), his old friend from Venice, who was now in the Spanish embassy at Versailles, and Jonville, who had been the French minister at Genoa in those days. Rousseau's Venetian colleague Le Blond lived nearby as well, but he kept putting off seeing

THE PETIT MONTLOUIS

The house in Montmorency as it appeared in Rousseau's time there (it was later altered and enlarged).

THE DONJON

The little garden house in which Rousseau liked to work. The windows (and a fireplace inside) were added when the main house was renovated.

him and never got around to it. He didn't mention whether he asked Carrio what became of the little girl they purchased together in Venice.

The Swiss trio of Roguin, Lenieps, and Coindet were regular guests who often stayed for meals, and then there were the Parisians, especially the brothers Condillac and Mably, and the Dupin family, with whom Rousseau had remained on good terms, including young Mme de Chenonceaux, who was renting a house nearby. But if this was a lot of socializing, it was not always satisfying. Many of the visitors were acquaintances, not real friends. In the *Confessions* Rousseau laments that he found himself caught up in a tedious way of life, "half for myself, and half for social circles that I wasn't made for at all." He was especially annoyed when well-intentioned admirers invited him to parties and sent a carriage to save him cab fare, claiming that the obligatory tips to their servants threatened to bankrupt him.

The one person Rousseau most wanted to see remained inaccessible. Mme d'Houdetot reluctantly agreed to let him keep writing to her, but she was apprehensive that he might wreck her relationship with Saint-Lambert and forbade him to visit. Unfortunately her attempts to be tactful only heated his resentment, and he wrote challengingly to contrast "my childish frankness, as you call it" with her sophisticated evasions. "I'll begin by telling you that the equivocal and ambiguous style of your latest letters has not escaped me . . . Frankness for you people of the *monde* means saying what you think with precautions and reserves, politely, and with *double entendres* and half-statements." Still worse, he interpreted her proposal to reimburse him for an elegant manuscript of the still-unfinished *Julie* as proof that her values were no better than Mme d'Épinay's. "I see clearly from your letters that what you value most in the world is money. The only benefits worthy of gratitude that you recognize are the ones of that kind, or at any rate, you don't put anything else in comparison with them."

Predictably, Mme d'Houdetot was wounded, and bade him a sad farewell, but she soon thought better of it and begged his pardon: "Reply, *mon cher,* to assure me that you've forgotten my sharpness as I have yours." Perhaps she feared that a decisive break would provoke further outrageous behavior, but if she was just humoring him he didn't suspect it. He replied joyously that her letter had given him "the purest and truest pleasure I have ever known in my life" and that he would carry their friendship to the tomb.

But the friendship was doomed, and by May she had had enough, reporting that Saint-Lambert had at last acquired a full understanding of their affair. "I owe it to my reputation to break off all contact with you. Any that I could preserve would be dangerous for it." This appeal to worldly reputation must have been particularly galling to Rousseau, who would have believed that it involved a cynical standard. It was acceptable for a lady to sleep with a man who was not her husband, but only with one at a time, and although Mme d'Houdetot had never slept with Rousseau at all, no suspicion must be allowed to arise. So the one grand passion of Rousseau's life was over, in his mid-forties. It is important, however, not to see that affair as dominating the story of these crucial years in the late 1750s, when he found ways to turn disappointment to imaginative advantage. He returned to his intellectual projects with renewed energy, and he resumed writing *Julie* from a sadder but wiser perspective.

Meanwhile another break had been developing, the most painful of all. Rousseau himself acknowledged that the affair with Mme d'Houdetot was essentially a projected fantasy in which he translated the novel he was writing into real life. His relationship with Diderot was very different. It was his most important friendship after the one with Mme de Warens, it launched his life as a writer and thinker, and it lasted fifteen years before collapsing in accusations and hurt feelings. And while it is true that Rousseau suspected Diderot of conspiring with Grimm and Mme d'Épinay, the rift had much deeper sources.

In part the problem was the difference in temperament, which had originally been a source of mutual attraction. It is true as well that whereas Diderot thought in terms of reciprocal favors, Rousseau believed that friendship dispensed with any such calculations. "Although ordinary company is odious to me, intimate friendship is precious, because with it there are no longer any obligations. One follows one's heart and all is done." It was Diderot's impression that the refusal to acknowledge obligations usually worked to Rousseau's advantage. The notion of following one's heart was unappealing to Diderot, too. In a fictional work he gives a materialist account of sensibility that could easily be a portrait of Rousseau: "What is a sensitive being? One who is abandoned to his diaphragm. When a touching word strikes his ear or something unusual strikes his eye, an inner tumult is stirred up; . . . tears flow, sighs choke him, his voice is halting; . . . no more calm, no more reason, no more judgment, no more instinct, no more resourcefulness."

For Rousseau, emotion was a better guide than reason, and he described his own behavior approvingly in terms that curiously mirror Diderot's: "The feelings to which he is most inclined are distinguished by physical signs. When he is even slightly moved, his eyes fill instantly with tears." In the growing cult of *sensibilité,* to which Rousseau himself was a major contributor, tears were proof of sincerity because they were regarded as involuntary and unstoppable, "the soul directly irrigating the countenance," as a modern historian says.

Words were more equivocal. In Rousseau's opinion a clever talker could simulate feelings without ever really experiencing them, and he may well have been thinking of Diderot when he wrote about people who always have words at their command and can produce an endless stream of clever repartee. "Even where feeling is concerned, they have a little prattle so well arranged that you would think they were moved to the very bottom of their hearts . . . Ideas ordinarily come to men of wit in ready-made phrases, but it's not like that with feelings. One must seek, combine, and choose language that can express what one feels, and what man of feeling will have the patience to suspend the flow of emotion and concern himself at every moment with this process of sorting?"

Rousseau knew that Grimm was a man of masks, and he was becoming convinced that Diderot was too. He was not altogether wrong. Not that Diderot was consciously duplicitous, but he did tend to reimagine the world in his own terms, even while congratulating himself on being a hardheaded realist. A friend wrote years later, "He is *un honnête homme* (an upright man), but wrongheaded, and so badly constituted that he doesn't see or hear anything as it really is. He is always like a man who is dreaming and believes everything he has dreamt." Certainly Diderot interpreted every aspect of the relationship with Rousseau in his own favor. He was even convinced that he had been assiduous in visiting the Hermitage — he told his daughter that he used to go there "two or three times a week, on foot" — although the documentary record shows that he scarcely went at all and often left Rousseau waiting all day at Saint-Denis, four miles away, for meetings that never happened.

Another illustration of the temperamental differences between the two men is furnished by their very different accounts of an annual birthday fête at La Chevrette, which they participated in four years apart. Rousseau's description recalls "the unhappy time when I was inserted among the rich and the men of letters, and was sometimes reduced to sharing their dreary pleasures." After a banquet in honor of M. d'Épinay's birthday in September 1756, the guests visited a fair where the local peasants were dancing. "The gentlemen condescended to dance with the peasant girls, but the ladies remained on their dignity." Soon the patricians got the idea of amusing themselves by throwing chunks of gingerbread into the crowd and watching everybody scramble for them. Rousseau was shocked by the ugliness of the scene. "What sort of pleasure could one take from watching herds of men, debased by poverty, who were piling together, suffocating and brutally crippling themselves, just to snatch hungrily at a few pieces of ginger-bread that were trampled underfoot and covered with mud?"

Diderot's account, written during the same fête four years later, is different in every way. He mentions the throng of people at the fair only casually, but lovingly describes the social scene inside the châ-teau. Grimm was there, striking a pose by the window while someone painted his portrait; Saint-Lambert lounged in a corner reading a pam-phlet; Diderot himself played chess with Mme d'Houdetot, while some-one else tried out a piece by Scarlatti on the harpsichord. Later there was an elegant dinner and then dancing, and the party went on until two in the morning. Occasions of that kind, which Diderot adored, filled Rousseau with panicky insecurity. He was a loner in the midst of any crowd, whereas Diderot was a delighted participant and was in-spired by the experience to tell his absent mistress, "If by some magic I could suddenly find you at my side . . . I would throw myself upon you, I would embrace you with all my might, and I would press my face against yours until my heart stopped pounding and I could regain the strength to pull back and look at you." Rousseau could write eloquently about the power of love, but he never wrote anything like that. For him passion needed to rise above mere sexual desire, whereas Diderot liked it to go the other way. "There's a bit of testicle at the bottom of our most sublime emotions and purest affections," he wrote to a friend at the same time.

Some years later, when Rousseau had left fashionable society behind, he gave a sympathetic nobleman a heartfelt account of the social agony he used to feel.

> I have to speak when I have nothing to say, stay in one place when I would rather walk, sit when I would rather stand, be shut up in a room when I'm longing for open air, go here when I would rather go there, eat when the others eat, walk at their pace, and respond to their compliments or sarcasms . . . I still shudder to think of myself in a circle of ladies, forced to wait while a fine talker finishes his fine phrases, not daring to go out lest they ask whether I'm leaving, and then on a well-lit staircase meeting other fine ladies who delay me, a courtyard full of carriages in constant motion that are ready to crush

me, chambermaids who stare at me, and lackeys who line the walls and mock me. I can't find any alley, archway, or miserable little corner to suit my purpose, and in a word I can't piss except in full view and onto some noble white-stockinged leg.

In addition to their temperamental differences, Rousseau was convinced that Diderot had begun to envy his growing celebrity, which was probably true. When they first met, it was Diderot who was the brilliant intellectual, initiating a disciple into the world of modern thought. Now Rousseau was the more famous of the two and was planning ambitious books that were likely to win still greater fame. And what would become of Diderot, who brooded constantly about his standing with posterity? His best works were not only improvised and unfinished — he has been aptly called "an uncompleting man" — but were full of subversive ideas that he could not afford to publish for fear of jeopardizing the great *Encyclopédie,* to which he had chained himself like a galley slave.

And even this explanation for the breakdown of the friendship is incomplete, if it stays at the level of personal rivalry. In truth, Rousseau's deepest values were at stake, and he knew it. When the crisis finally came, it centered not on the d'Houdetot affair, in which Diderot was only an outsider, but on Rousseau's choice to live at the Hermitage. Diderot decided to make a name in the theater, probably because writing plays was a credential for election to the Académie Française (he never got in, though d'Alembert, Condillac, Grimm, and Saint-Lambert all did) and in March 1757 he published a play called *The Natural Son, or Virtue Put to the Test,* together with extensive commentary. His intention was to promote a new kind of domestic drama that would embody everyday situations instead of exalted classical ones and would represent emotion in an affecting style known as *comédie larmoyante* or tearful drama. To his deep disappointment, the Comédie Française declined to produce the play, which didn't appear on stage until 1771. The printed version, however, attracted plenty of attention, partly for its high moral claims and critique of classicism, but mostly for its striking resemblance to a play by the Italian writer Carlo Goldoni, from which the plot seemed to have been lifted.

Rousseau didn't care about Goldoni and took no interest in the charges of plagiarism, but he cared very much about the moral claims, and one line stabbed him to the heart: *Il n'y a que le méchant qui soit seul,* "only the wicked man is alone." In the *Confessions* he misremembered this line as part of Diderot's commentary, but actually it is spoken by one of the characters, and the context is rich with significance for the breakdown of the friendship. A woman tells the man she loves, who is threatening to disappear into self-imposed exile, "You have been given the rarest talents, and you owe society an account of them . . . I appeal to you to question your heart. It will tell you that the good man lives in society, and only the wicked man is alone." This demand to turn one's talents to social use could indeed point at Rousseau, but perhaps the real offense lay in something else she says: "Your children will learn from you to think like you . . . On you alone it will depend that they have a conscience like your own." By abandoning his own children, Rousseau had thrown away any chance of doing that, and Diderot was one of the very few people who knew it.

With their relations increasingly strained, Rousseau and Diderot took turns making them worse. Diderot wrote to say that he was too ill to travel but expected Rousseau to come to Paris to discuss a business proposition, concluding sarcastically, "Adieu, Citizen! though it's a very singular kind of citizen who is a hermit." Rousseau later called this letter "very dry" and told Mme d'Épinay that "it pierced me to the soul." To Diderot he replied bluntly that he had resolved never to go to Paris again on any account. At this point Diderot got really angry — Trousson, in an engaging French expression, says he was feeling the mustard up his nose — and declared that he would make the trip to the Hermitage after all, at whatever cost to his health. He added cuttingly that Rousseau apparently enjoyed forcing his busy Parisian friends to visit him in the depth of winter even though they couldn't afford cab fare — "philosophers on foot, going out into the country with walking stick in hand, soaked to the bone and covered with mud up to their backs." This letter Rousseau characterized as "abominable," and he commanded Diderot not to come after all. "In our altercations," he declared, "you have always been the aggressor," and he concluded ominously, "If you have any respect for an old friendship, do not come and expose it to inevitable and irreversible rupture."

Matters were completely out of hand, and it was in vain that Mme d'Épinay (during the months before her own break with Rousseau) tried to intervene, assuring Rousseau that Diderot still loved him even if he didn't always show it. Rousseau responded coldly that whatever he and Diderot had once been to each other, they had become strangers. "Believe me, my good friend, Diderot is now a man of the fashionable *monde.* There was a time when the two of us were poor and unknown and were friends. I could say the same of Grimm. But they have both become important people, while I have continued to be what I was, and we suit each other no longer." When Mme d'Épinay wrote back to implore Rousseau to see the affair more objectively, he answered, "The Gospel commands anyone who has received a slap to turn the other cheek, but not to beg pardon . . . I will never in my life go to Paris again, and I bless heaven for making me a bear, and a hermit, and pigheaded, rather than a philosopher."

At this point Diderot, who regarded himself as saintly in his forbearance, decided he had had enough. "Oh, Rousseau!" he wrote accusingly, "you are becoming wicked, unjust, cruel, and ferocious, and I weep with grief." Rousseau's reply was calm but decisive: he had no use for friendship founded on services that needed to be repaid. As a reminder of what had been lost, he recalled the time eight years before, when Diderot was incarcerated at Vincennes. "Ingrate, I have never done you favors, but I loved you . . . Show this to your wife, who is more impartial than you are, and ask her whether, when my presence was soothing to your afflicted heart, I counted my steps or paid attention to the weather when I went to Vincennes to comfort my friend." The key to the whole depressing misunderstanding might be William Blake's saying: "Corporeal friends are spiritual enemies." Diderot saw himself as working selflessly to help his old friend, but Rousseau sensed a genuine coerciveness. One of Diderot's modern biographers notes that he enjoyed setting himself up as an informal director of conscience; another says that he could never admit that he was in the wrong or that his interference in people's affairs might reflect an appetite for power.

In July Rousseau and Diderot staged a reconciliation, but they both must have known how superficial it was. Diderot agreed to let Rousseau read aloud to him from *Julie,* but complained afterward that he droned on "pitilessly" from ten in the morning until eleven at night, allowing no interruptions even for meals, so that when he finished there was no time left to listen to anything by Diderot in return. All Rousseau says in the *Confessions* is that Diderot called the manuscript *feuillu,* "leafy," a term he apparently invented on the spot. (Rousseau understood it to mean "redundant" and admitted that it was accurate.) After that, contact largely ceased. In December Diderot did finally appear briefly at the Hermitage, after which he supposedly wrote to Grimm that Rousseau seemed deranged and scary, "as if I had a damned soul at my side," uttering tormented cries that pursued Diderot into the distance when he left. This letter, however, appears only in *Madame de Montbrillant* and looks like yet another attempt to revise the story in retrospect.

Rousseau had lost his most important friend, and his emotional pain very much resembled his feelings on losing Mme d'Houdetot. Still, there were compensations. From Rousseau's perspective, solitude allowed him to be himself, achieving to some extent the contentment he had imagined in natural man. He was coming to understand that what people condemned in him as laziness was something very different. When he truly believed in a project he could attack it with all his might. It was enforced tasks that he found intolerable, especially when they were undertaken to impress others. "What a spectacle for a Carib Indian," he wrote in the *Discourse on Inequality,* "would be the arduous and envied labors of a European cabinet minister! How many cruel deaths would not the indolent savage prefer to the horror of a life like that?" From this time forward he would be committed to *oisiveté* as constructive idleness, contrary to everything he had been taught in Calvinist Geneva. He was recovering the freedom of childhood, reacting against the remorseless structuring of civilized life and its tendency to deplore leisure as time stolen from work.

Rousseau's new life, then, was one of impressive intellectual labor sustained by long periods of meditative idleness, and it reflected his increasing disaffection from his workaholic colleagues on the *Encyclopédie.* His values were now very different from theirs, and a break with the movement was inevitable. The Enlightenment was other-directed and placed its highest value on social interaction; Rousseau was inner-directed and valued freedom from society's influence. The Enlightenment promoted competitive individualism as the foundation of the good life; Rousseau sought a collective spirit that would respect the individual but help each one to feel part of a communal whole. The Enlightenment specialized in information gathering and theoretical speculation; Rousseau, like the philosophers of old, sought wisdom. The Enlightenment championed technology as the basis of progress; Rousseau chose the simple life and declined the dubious gifts of progress. The Enlightenment was skeptical and even atheistic; Rousseau held firmly to belief in God and the soul. In addition, although the philosophes talked constantly about virtue, he was convinced that they were playing a double game, outwardly ethical but inwardly cynical, "this morality without roots or fruit . . . or rather, this cruel secret alternative morality, an esoteric doctrine for their initiates, for which the other one is merely a mask."

Rousseau's break with the Enlightenment was acted out not only toward Diderot but toward Voltaire as well. Voltaire was the godfather of the movement, a generation older than the editors of the *Encyclopédie,* a polymath who had begun as a poet and playwright and who wrote endlessly on philosophy, politics, and science. Born François-Marie Arouet, he broke with his family and gave himself a new identity, and after acquiring a fortune through shrewd investments he was free to devote himself to writing. To a sharp mind and brilliant prose style he added an extraordinary talent for publicity. His disciple Jean-François de La Harpe commented, "At a hundred leagues from the capital he exists only for it and in it. Once a week he sends a pamphlet to Paris and awaits its fate by the following post. Sixty years of fame have not reassured him sufficiently to permit a day of rest. It is not enough for him to be the hero of the century, he wants to be the news of the day, for he knows that the news of the day often makes people forget the hero of the century." This hunger for publicity was not merely vanity, since Voltaire was deeply and even heroically committed to exposing injustice, most memorably in the *affaire Calas* in the 1760s, when he rehabilitated the reputation of an innocent man who had been framed and executed by religious bigots. Rousseau hated injustice as much as Voltaire did, but he was never an organizer of opinion; he preferred to be a voice crying in the wilderness, and in praise of wilderness.

Voltaire came to believe that the *Encyclopédie,* to which he contributed only occasionally, was fatally compromised by the caution of its editors. He also thought that its massive, fact-laden articles were a poor weapon against oppression. He himself preferred to live on the move, out of reach of the French authorities who intimidated the Encyclopédistes, and to issue short, pungent polemics that could be counted on to stir things up. In 1755, after quarreling with Frederick the Great, in whose court he had been living in Berlin, he migrated to Switzerland and set himself up in Geneva on an estate called Les Délices. A few years later he moved to an even grander estate at Ferney, just outside the city, and became a patriarch, using his wealth and influence to develop the village, which began with half a dozen houses and by 1776 had over a thousand inhabitants well supported by thriving trades.

Rousseau and Voltaire probably never met, but Rousseau had admired the great man ever since he began reading his works at Annecy, while Voltaire knew that Rousseau had criticized progress in the *Discourse on the Sciences and Arts.* In that work Rousseau openly challenged Voltaire (using his real name rather than his nom de plume), complaining that his fame had been built on elegant plays and poems that were unworthy of his genius. "Tell us, celebrated Arouet, how many strong and masculine beauties you have sacrificed to our false delicacy, and how many great things the spirit of gallantry, so fertile in little things, has cost you!" But Rousseau still regarded himself as an admirer, and told a Geneva friend that he was pleased to hear that Voltaire might move there.

The turning point came in August 1756, when Rousseau read Voltaire's "Poem on the Lisbon Disaster" and was moved to reply. The previous November the Portuguese capital had been practically leveled by a violent earthquake that left tens of thousands dead; tremors were felt as far away as Chambéry, making the bells ring and toppling chimneys. Preachers seized the opportunity to proclaim that Lisbon was being punished for its sins; at the other extreme, most of the philosophes, Diderot included, saw nothing more than a random geological event with no meaning of any kind. But Voltaire was a deist who needed to believe that natural phenomena confirmed a benevolent deity, and he was seriously shaken. Why should Lisbon have been destroyed while people were dancing in Paris? Human beings were apparently nothing but "atoms tormented on this heap of mud, whom death swallows up."

Rousseau, just as much as Voltaire, needed to believe in a morally just universe, but in a long *Letter from J.-J. Rousseau to M. de Voltaire,* he argued that if people didn't foolishly pack themselves into cities, earthquakes would do little damage. In his opinion it was civilization that was at fault, not the universe, and he turned Voltaire's argument against him with brisk irony: "Should we say, then, that the order of the world must alter according to our caprices . . . and that to prevent an earthquake in a given place, we need only build a city there?"

What was at stake was the philosophy known as optimism, which Rousseau had already critiqued in a letter to Conzié when he was living in Lyon. He saw the fundamental issue clearly: "Instead of 'all is well,' it would be better perhaps to say 'the whole is good,' or 'all is good for the whole.'" Voltaire would soon satirize this philosophy mordantly in *Candide,* and it does seem a very pessimistic kind of "optimism" that found value in disaster, but the urgency of Rousseau's argument shows how far he had moved from the scientific materialism of the Enlightenment. What he was really asserting was religious faith: he needed to believe not just in an orderly universe but in a loving God who ensured personal immortality. With extraordinary eloquence he declared, "I have suffered too much in this life not to look forward to another. All the subtleties of metaphysics will never make me doubt for one moment the immortality of the soul and a beneficent providence. I feel it, I believe it, I want it, I hope for it, and I will defend it to my dying breath."

In addition, the social resentment that underlay the *Second Discourse* reappeared in the *Letter to Voltaire.* Though rich and famous, Voltaire couldn't stop complaining, Rousseau remarked, "while I, obscure, poor, and tormented by an incurable disease, meditate with pleasure in my retreat and find that all is well." Just as with Diderot, the opposition was temperamental as much as philosophical, though in this instance there was a curious reversal of postures that amused Grimm: "Heraclitus Rousseau defends the consolations of the best of worlds with a gloom that fills you with pain and despair, whereas Democritus Voltaire proves in his *Candide* that all is very bad in this world, while he makes you die laughing." Incidentally, Rousseau later made the bizarre claim that *Candide* was written specifically to answer his letter on providence.

Another provocation from Voltaire inspired a public manifesto that made Rousseau's position still clearer. D'Alembert, after paying an extended visit to Voltaire, wrote an article on Geneva for the *Encyclopédie* that shocked Rousseau deeply. It claimed approvingly that the ministers had abandoned their traditional faith for a tolerant and lukewarm belief known as Socinianism, and it recommended that Geneva continue its advance into modern sophistication by establishing a theater, which the Calvinist theocracy had always forbidden. Rousseau saw Voltaire's hand in both of these points, and he was struck by the inordinate length of the encyclopedia entry. He repaired to his *donjon* and in great excitement — "with no fire except the one in my heart" — composed the hundred-page *Letter to M. d'Alembert on the Theater,* which he finished in March 1758 after just three weeks' work. He wrote at once to his publisher that he had a potential bestseller for him, as indeed he did, though he added a characteristically gloomy prediction: "I am so sick, my dear Rey, that I won't be able to write you a long letter, and barring a miracle, I will not be writing to you much longer."

The two *Discourses* had established Rousseau as a powerful critic of modern civilization; the *Letter to d'Alembert* struck a new note as the personal testimony of a secular prophet. Whereas the philosophes normally protected themselves by publishing anonymously, Rousseau proudly identified himself on the title page as "J.-J. Rousseau, citizen of Geneva." And when he claimed "a disinterestedness for which few authors have given me an example," he was right in a sense: the book was not a career move, not a maneuver in the game of reputation, and not a bid for patronage. If anything it was likely to make powerful enemies, and it was certain to infuriate Voltaire. "Never have personal views," Rousseau continued, "sullied the desire to be useful to others that has placed the pen in my hand, and I have nearly always written against my own interest. *Vitam impendere vero* [devote life to truth], that is the motto I've chosen, and of which I feel myself worthy." The Latin phrase came from the satirist Juvenal, who like Rousseau was a fierce critic of the corruptions of his time.

In Geneva Rousseau saw a small city-state that was fortunate to be somewhat behind the times, and in France he saw an aggressive nation-state in which wealth and privilege were increasing unchecked, with disastrous results. Provocatively, he asserted that the simplicity of ancient Sparta was superior to the flashy amorality of Athens. In another essay on the subject he said more explicitly, "Among my contemporaries I see only unfeeling masters and groaning peoples, wars that concern nobody and leave everyone desolated . . . and subjects who are poorest when the state is richest." Even if it was true that the Genevan pastors were liberalizing their theology, d'Alembert was stirring up trouble for them by saying so in print. And even if it was true that the theater was relatively harmless in Paris, where Rousseau himself had been an enthusiastic playgoer, in Geneva it would be a Trojan horse for the worst kind of modernization. Far from learning moral truths, he asserted, audience members tended to admire clever rogues, laugh at virtuous people (including Molière's misanthrope, with whom Rousseau clearly identified), and applaud performers whose profession is fundamentally degrading.

In an eloquent denunciation that has much in common with the Calvinist values of his native city and also with Plato's rejection of the arts in the *Republic,* Rousseau rose to moral outrage.

> What is the talent of the actor? The art of counterfeiting himself, clothing himself with another character than his own, appearing different than he is, becoming passionate in cold blood, saying something other than what he thinks as naturally as if he really thought it, and at last forgetting his own place by taking someone else's. What is the profession of the actor? A trade by which he gives himself in performance for money, submits himself to the ignominy and affronts that people buy the right to give him, and puts his person publicly on sale.

This was not just reactionary moralism, but a reflection of Rousseau's fundamental insight that civilization rewards inauthenticity, and that its most successful members are role-playing actors in daily life.

In all likelihood Rousseau had often debated this subject with Diderot, who believed that role-playing is normal and would later argue in his *Paradox on the Actor* that the best actors are emotionally detached from their performances. In language that sounds like a direct echo of Rousseau, right down to the prostitution analogy (which was common even in ancient times), Diderot declared: "The actor weeps like an unbelieving priest who preaches the Passion; like a seducer on his knees before a woman whom he doesn't love but wants to deceive; like a beggar in the street or at a church door who abuses you when he gives up hope of moving you; or like a courtesan who feels nothing but swoons in your arms." If Rousseau's condemnation of acting seems excessively moralistic today, it reflects an anxiety that many of his contemporaries shared. In small, stable societies, everyone knows who you are; in the impersonal modern city you are whatever you can make people believe.

In addition to identifying with his native city, Rousseau harbored a very specific resentment. He thought that d'Alembert had naively allowed himself to be used as a tool by Voltaire, who was already putting on plays at his estate outside Geneva and was eager to sponsor a theater that would feature his own works. In condemning this project Rousseau was consciously speaking for the artisan class in which he had his roots. Increasingly the wealthy families of the Genevan upper town were building ostentatious mansions, adopting a lavish lifestyle, and looking to Paris for culture. The theater, under the aegis of the celebrated Voltaire, would be one more stage in their mutation into a subset of the French aristocracy. Instead of establishing a Parisian-style theater, Rousseau thought, Geneva should cherish its existing institutions: men's and women's social clubs, and public fêtes in which the people could be participants rather than passive spectators, like the one that spontaneously arose on that evening in his childhood when the militia danced after finishing their maneuvers and Isaac Rousseau cried out, "*Jean-Jacques, aime ton pays* (love your country)." Indeed, it was in the *Letter to d'Alembert,* in a long and deeply personal footnote, that Rousseau told that story. "Everything good that I have said," he wrote to a Genevan friend, "*je le tiens de mon pays* (I've gotten it from my country)."

In the contemporary politics of Geneva, with which Rousseau had been in close touch since his visit in 1754, two ideologies confronted each other around the issue of the theater. The patricians had several times invited French actors to visit and give performances in private homes, and in the lower town this was seen as one more sign of unwelcome rapprochement with France. Contrariwise, the popular festivals that Rousseau celebrated were perceived by the patricians as invitations to subversion. Throughout Europe, in fact, the ruling elites were committed to repressing such festivals. There can be no doubt that Rousseau wanted his *Letter to d'Alembert* to make a strong impression in Geneva. He had copies sent to some two dozen people there, and its implications were clearly understood. A couple of years later the popular party obtained permission to form a militia and perform elaborate exercises, after which they drank a toast in Rousseau's honor and deliberately re-staged the patriotic scene he had described. As a young pastor reported to him, they danced around the fountain in the Place Saint-Gervais, just as he had seen them do forty years before, "interrupting their joyous songs from time to time with cries of *Vive Rousseau!* that came from the bottom of their hearts." Another participant wrote to Rousseau in terms that anticipate the slogans of the French Revolution: "The finest pleasures of patriotism moved me and melted my heart: the pleasures of unity, equality, fraternity, and public trust . . . Ah, Monsieur Rousseau, what a day it would have been for you if you could have witnessed it!"

If the *Letter to d'Alembert* offended the patricians, it delighted the clergy, one of whom wrote to Rousseau that it was practically a commentary on the Sermon on the Mount, and that he deserved to be honored as a prophet. "Great Rousseau, you are by no means useless on this earth. There are still some mortals whose eyes are upon you in your desert, and whose courage swells when they see how you sustain the combat." The warmest admirers of the *Letter* regretted only that it was describing an idealized Geneva, not the actual one. "Oh, how you would change your tune," Tronchin wrote gloomily, "if you saw everything I see, and if the good pastors were to tell you, as every day they are telling me, that the morals of our people are withering before our eyes. Geneva is no more like Sparta than an athlete's gauntlets are like the white gloves of an opera girl."

D'Alembert himself wasn't annoyed at all. He wrote cheerfully to Malesherbes, "I have read M. Rousseau's work against me, and it gave me a good deal of pleasure." For Voltaire, however, the *Letter to d'Alembert* was absolutely the last straw. Up until then he had regarded Rousseau as an eccentric minor writer who deserved indulgence because he was connected with the *Encyclopédie.* Rousseau's letter on providence was nothing more than an irritation on a subject where Voltaire felt himself invulnerable, and anyway it wasn't published. But the *Letter to d'Alembert* was unforgivable. It was a frontal attack on the civilized values he held dear, and not only that, it might well mobilize opposition to his personal plans. From this moment forward Voltaire hated Rousseau, and he was a potent hater.

At a deeper level than personal resentment, moreover, Voltaire understood that Rousseau was subverting the Enlightenment from within. "The philosophes are disunited," he told d'Alembert; "the little flock are eating each other even as the wolves arrive to devour them. It's against your Jean-Jacques that I'm most furious. This arch-madman could have become something if he had allowed himself to be guided by you, but he has taken it into his head to go off on his own. He writes against the theater after having written a bad play, he writes against France which nourishes him, he has found four or five rotten staves from Diogenes' barrel and he gets inside to bark." Later that year Voltaire wrote yet again to d'Alembert, "The priests of Geneva have made a horrible faction against the drama. I'm going to shoot the first Socinian who steps on my territory. Jean-Jacques is a Jeanf . . . [*Jeanfoutre* or John-fuck] who writes every couple of weeks to those priests to stir them up against the theater. Deserters against their fatherland ought to be hanged." The ironies were multiple: calling the Calvinist pastors "priests"; emphasizing their Socinianism, for which d'Alembert had gotten into trouble with them; and implying that Rousseau's true *patrie* wasn't Geneva but the Enlightenment movement. D'Alembert wrote back charitably, "I admit that he's a deserter who fights against his fatherland, but he's a deserter who is no longer in any condition to fight or to do any harm; his bladder is making him suffer."

Rousseau, meanwhile, took it very personally, especially later on, when his letter to Voltaire on providence appeared in print (ostensibly from Berlin, though in fact from Geneva). He immediately suspected that Grimm must have made this happen, and when he wrote to tell Voltaire so, he could not resist adding an insult that Voltaire never forgave. "I do not like you at all, Monsieur . . . It is you who make it intolerable for me to live in my own country; it is you who will make me die in a foreign land, deprived of all the consolations of the dying, and with no more honor than to be thrown onto a dungheap . . . In short, I hate you, as you have wished."

Just to complete the wrecking job, the *Letter to d'Alembert* also contained an unmistakable attack on Diderot. When Mme d'Houdetot reported that Saint-Lambert had learned the truth about their affair and that she must never communicate with Rousseau again, he was certain that Diderot had betrayed him. For once he seems to have been right, since Diderot later admitted as much, with the lame defense that he assumed Saint-Lambert already knew all about it. At any rate, when Rousseau got his letter of rejection from Mme d'Houdetot in June, he happened to be correcting proofs for the *Letter to d'Alembert,* and he took the opportunity to add a comment explaining that he had no friend to help him improve the work. "I used to have an Aristarchus, stern and judicious. I no longer have him, I no longer want him, but I will regret losing him unceasingly, and my heart misses him far more than my writings do." (Aristarchus was a Greek grammarian and editor of Homer, and conceivably Rousseau's tribute was also a putdown.) While not explaining the falling-out with Diderot, this amounted to a public announcement of it, since his mentorship of Rousseau was well known, and in a footnote Rousseau added a shocking text from Ecclesiasticus. It was in Latin, but chapter and verse were cited, so readers could easily look it up, and its implications were brutal. "If thou hast opened thy mouth against thy friend, fear not, for there may be a reconciliation; except for upbraiding, or pride, or disclosing of secrets, or a treacherous wound. For these things every friend will depart."

Everyone who knew Rousseau was appalled. Even if Diderot deserved the rebuke, which they doubted, it was outrageous to injure him at the very moment when criticism of the *Encyclopédie* was mounting and the whole enterprise was threatened with collapse. Saint-Lambert, who had just assured Rousseau of his continued friendship ("I embrace you with all my heart") wrote again the next day to say that he had received the *Letter to d'Alembert* and regarded the Aristarchus passage as inexcusable. "Diderot may have done you wrongs, I don't know about that, but I do know that they don't give you the right to insult him publicly. You are not unaware of the persecution he is enduring, and you proceed to join the voice of an old friend to the cries of envy." The persecution was the struggle with censorship, and attendant threats of possible prosecution, that continually plagued the ongoing project of the *Encyclopédie.* Deleyre, who had been a regular member of Mme d'Épinay's social circle, told Rousseau frankly that he seemed determined to have no friends at all.

But Rousseau was unrepentant about his break with Diderot and his attack on the values of the *Encyclopédie.* "All my works have been successful," he wrote later in the *Confessions,* "but this one was still more favorable to me; it taught the public to distrust the insinuations of the d'Holbach coterie." And when a group of lawyers complained that some political reflections in the *Letter* contradicted the views of his comrades in the *Encyclopédie,* Rousseau declared in reply, "The opinion of any one Encyclopédiste is no rule for his colleagues. The common authority is that of reason. I recognize no other."

As for Diderot, he understood the Aristarchus passage to be a declaration of war, and whether or not he and Grimm had been deliberately conspiring against Rousseau before this, they certainly did so afterward. To ease his feelings, Diderot recorded his own version of what had happened in some notes known as "Tablettes," which detailed the *scélératesses* or "rascalities" of which Rousseau was guilty. These were locked away in his desk and probably not intended to go further, but he reread them regularly and they indicate the depth of his outrage. "This man is false, vain as Satan, ungrateful, cruel, hypocritical, and wicked . . . He sucked ideas from me, used them himself, and then affected to despise me. Truly this man is a monster."

Rousseau did try to make amends when Charles Palissot brought out a satirical play, *The Philosophes,* in which a character resembling him was shown eating lettuce and walking on all fours. Rousseau wrote to the publisher that the cruel treatment of Diderot offended him even more than his own portrayal: "I had the honor of being the friend of a worthy man who is blackened and calumniated disgracefully in this libel." Diderot was shown this letter, as Rousseau doubtless expected he would be, but he dismissed it a a hypocritical ploy.

With most of his important relationships compromised or at an end, Rousseau settled down once more to work. He tried his hand at a new strategy for reconnecting with Mme d'Houdetot, a series of didactic "Moral Letters" that discussed the nature of virtue from the perspective of temptation overcome. These were never sent. And he finally completed *Julie,* likewise from the perspective of temptation overcome, and was able to tell Rey in September 1758 that the novel was ready for the press. Half a year later, in April 1759, he had an unforeseen stroke of luck. One of the most eminent noblemen in the realm, the duc de Luxembourg, had been making a persistent effort to seek him out. Each time the duke and his wife visited their country estate at Montmorency, they sent a valet to give Rousseau their compliments and invite him to dine. Each time he failed to respond. Next they dispatched a more impressive emissary, the chevalier Lorenzy, a member of the court of the prince de Conti. Rousseau still held off. And finally, when he was least expecting it, the great duke himself appeared at his door with an entourage of half a dozen servants, and Rousseau was conquered. He visited the Luxembourgs at their hundred-room château, found himself repeatedly going back, and in May accepted temporary lodging there while the house he was renting was being renovated. They would become the most loyal supporters he had ever had, and with their encouragement he now pressed forward with two major works, *The Social Contract* and *Émile*. At last he had found patrons who were willing not to act patronizing, and his fame was about to ascend to unprecedented heights.

17

Peace at Last and the Triumph of *Julie*

INITIALLY, ROUSSEAU WAS UNEASY about getting involved with the Luxembourgs, whose social standing was exalted in the extreme. In England, under the system of primogeniture, there could be only one heir to each aristocratic title, and at the end of the eighteenth century the House of Lords had just two hundred members. In France, where every child of a nobleman inherited a title and where titles could also be freely purchased, there were perhaps as many as a quarter of a million nobles (the statistics are disputed), all of whom were exempt from any but the most token taxation. At the very top of this massive pyramid were the dukes, and as Stendhal wrote in the next century, "There is only one nobility, the title of duke. 'Marquis' is ridiculous, but you turn your head at the word 'duke.'" As befitted their status, the Luxembourgs were wealthy on an almost unimaginable scale. By way of comparison, d'Holbach was extremely rich with an income of 60,000 livres per year; the Luxembourgs' properties produced an annual yield of at least 500,000 livres, and at the time of the duke's death in 1764 their total value was assessed at well over 11 million livres.

Moreover, unlike the financiers Dupin and d'Épinay, Charles-François-Frédéric de Montmorency-Luxembourg had close contacts at court. He had distinguished himself in the War of the Austrian Succession and afterward became head of the royal guards, a position of great honor that required him to accompany the king in his travels during three months of each year. On top of that, he was the military governor of the sometimes turbulent province of Normandy, where he was charged with suppressing potential rebellion and also with remaining vigilant against any threat from England across the Channel. In 1757 he had been made a *maréchal de France,* the highest military rank.

The gulf in status between Rousseau and the Luxembourgs was thus enormous, but that, paradoxically, was the very reason they could become genuine friends. Eighteenth-century society was a complex web of interrelationships between patrons and dependents, superiors and inferiors, masters and servants, and Rousseau's goal was to escape the web as far as possible, to be no one's dependent and no one's master. At the outset of his new relationship he wrote to the duke, "I think that if both of us are as I like to believe, we may present a rare and perhaps unique spectacle, two men in a connection of esteem and friendship (you've dictated that word to me) even though their status is so different that they would seem to have no relationship at all. But for this, Monsieur, you must remain as you are, and leave me as I am." Remarkably enough, it turned out exactly that way. "I will honor and cherish the memory of that worthy lord as long as I live," Rousseau wrote after Luxembourg's death, and he told Malesherbes that to understand what the Luxembourgs meant to him, "you would have to know the state of neglect and abandonment by all my friends in which I found myself, and my profound mental suffering because of that, when M. and Mme de Luxembourg desired to get to know me . . . I was dying, and except for them I certainly would have died of sorrow."

So Rousseau and Thérèse moved into a lovely classical villa on the Luxembourgs' estate known as the Petit Château, designed originally by the famous painter Le Brun, with superb gardens by the equally famous Le Nôtre. They chose the simplest of its four apartments, neatly decorated in blue and white, and Rousseau was transported with joy. "I was in the earthly paradise there. I lived there with as much innocence, and I tasted the same happiness." He had been in paradise several times before — at Bossey, at Les Charmettes, at the Hermitage — and, like Adam, he had been expelled from each one. This time the happiness was more enduring, and when he did have to leave three years later, it was not because of any quarrel with his friends.

At the end of the summer, when the Montlouis house was ready for Rousseau's return, he agreed to keep the key to the Petit Château and continued to use it regularly. The Luxembourgs were in Paris most of the time when the duke was not traveling, and Rousseau occasionally stayed in their city mansion (leaving it only to get into the carriage, thus keeping his vow never to set foot on the streets of Paris). He now had several exceptionally agreeable lodgings, and whenever the Luxembourgs came to spend a few weeks in Montmorency, he was with them every day by his own choice. The usual routine was to attend Mme de Luxembourg in the morning and then to walk in the park with the duke, whose unaffected friendship was deeply satisfying. At long last Rousseau had found a father figure, albeit one who was only ten years older than himself.

Rousseau's former friends claimed to be disgusted by his new connections. Diderot wrote to Grimm (who had finally joined Mme d'Épinay in Geneva), "Rousseau has accepted lodgings with M. de Luxembourg, which makes people here say jokingly that he's gone to suckle at Mme de Luxembourg's breasts to correct the acidity of his blood." Since the duchess had had a quite scandalous reputation during a previous marriage, the quip was particularly pointed. As for Grimm, he attributed Rousseau's estrangement from the philosophes to simple envy of their abilities.

> He broke with all his old friends, among whom I used to share an intimacy along with the philosopher Diderot, and replaced us with persons of the highest rank. I won't determine whether he lost or gained by the change, but I believe he was as happy at Montmorency as a man with so much bile and vanity could expect to be. In the company of his former friends he had found friendship and esteem, but their reputation, and still more the superiority of talent he was forced to recognize in some of them, made the association painful to him. At Montmorency there was no rivalry, and he enjoyed the incense dispensed by the greatest and most distinguished in the kingdom, not to mention the throng of agreeable women who attended upon him.

Grimm was right enough about the people of distinction and the women. Rousseau took surprisingly keen pleasure in the stream of titled visitors, "Monsieur the duc de Villeroy, Monsieur the prince de

Tingry, Monsieur the marquis d'Armentières, Madame the duchesse de Montmorency, Madame the duchesse de Boufflers, Madame the comtesse de Valentinois, Madame the comtesse de Boufflers, and other persons of that rank who did not disdain to make, by a very tiring climb, the pilgrimage from the château to Montlouis." But as he explained in *Émile,* he was discovering that people of the highest status could exhibit a modesty and frankness that grasping social climbers never did. "The more they have, the more they are aware of what they lack . . . With the exclusive goods that they possess, they are too sensible to feel vain about a gift they didn't bestow on themselves." This was certainly a generous view of an aristocracy that was widely resented as parasitical. "It was during one of these transports of emotion that I said once to M. de Luxembourg as I was embracing him, 'Ah, Monsieur le Maréchal, I used to hate the great before I knew you, and now I hate them even more, since you make me feel how easy it would be for them to make themselves adored.'"

Rousseau was careful to make it clear that friendships with ordinary people, such as the local mason Pillieu, were just as satisfying as encounters with the great, and that after visiting the château he would return eagerly "to take my supper with the *bon homme* Pillieu and his family, sometimes at their place, sometimes at mine." A visitor to Montmorency after Rousseau was no longer there reported that the country people rushed up to ask for news of him and exclaimed, "He was a father to us all. He gave us wine when we needed it, there was no sort of good thing that he didn't do for us, we will never forget him." He seems in fact to have interceded for them with the stern Luxembourg, for one of them declared, "He was our protector with Monseigneur le Maréchal. In losing him we've lost everything, and we will miss him to our dying breath."

The Luxembourgs really did try to treat Rousseau as an equal, scrupulously avoiding the gifts and favors that Mme d'Épinay could never stop bestowing. Determined to be consistent, he refused gifts from all quarters, not just from the rich. When a Genevan friend sent some money, he wrote back to say that although people might try in that way to buy virtues they lacked, "noble souls like yours show their friendship through worthier attentions . . . Open your heart and shut your purse, that's the sort of friends I need." The Luxembourgs respected him all the more for his self-imposed code. "Is it possible," the duchess wrote from Paris, "that you could be so unjust as not to let me give Mlle Levasseur a cotton print dress? . . . Ah well, Monsieur, in spite of your threats I love you with all my heart, and I assure you I will never change." A few months later he wrote gratefully to her, "You haven't wanted to be my protectors or patrons, but my consolers and true friends. For my part, I have never sung your praises, but I have loved you tenderly." Mme de Luxembourg wrote back to thank him for sending "the most charming thing in the world," a handwritten copy of *Julie,* and added, "I am dying to see you; so long an absence is killing me. How can one love people one sees so seldom? Or rather, how can one so seldom see the people one loves? For I certainly do love you with all my heart." It was *Julie,* indeed, that attached her most strongly to Rousseau, and she encouraged him to read aloud from it whenever he visited her.

To have the great Mme de Luxembourg in his thrall was a remarkable development, and Diderot and Grimm had reason to be jealous. In her youth she was exceptionally beautiful and also exceptionally independent, with an ability to wither admirers with caustic epigrams. She and her first husband, the duc de Boufflers — himself a distinguished officer as well as a duke — had reputations for sexual freedom, or license, that aroused both envy and criticism. Voltaire favored her with a mildly blasphemous epigram, playing on the fact that she shared a name with Mary Magdalen (her given names were Madeleine-Angélique):

> Your patron saint, in the midst of the apostles,
> Kissed the feet of her divine spouse;
> Lovely Boufflers, he would have kissed yours,
> And St. John himself would have gotten jealous!

Whether or not the analogy with the penitent saint was apt, she did resolve to change her life when the duc de Boufflers died. After marrying the duc de Luxembourg in 1750 she adopted a style of serene stability and was genuinely devoted to him, while presiding over a brilliant salon.

After reviewing the many contemporary accounts of her personality,

MME DE LUXEMBOURG
This anonymous portrait of
the formidable maréchale
de Luxembourg catches her
ironic expression and
unsettling air of confidence,
but fails to do justice to her
widely celebrated beauty.

her biographer in the 1920s offered this admiring portrait: "She was not one of those timid, thin, and lachrymose women who slip modestly into a room like an unnoticed glimmer of light and discreetly hide the passion that is consuming them. She had an allure, an imposing stature, a magnificent figure, and a head full of majesty and also of ideas, and she advanced like a triumphant general." One of her closest friends, the marquise du Deffand, described her memorably: "She dominates wherever she finds herself, and always makes whatever impression she wishes to make. She uses her natural advantages almost in the manner of God, allowing us to believe we have free will even while she determines our fate and chooses the elect and reprobate from the height of her omnipotence. Those whom she punishes for not loving her could well say, 'You would have been loved if you had wanted to be.'" But to Rousseau's delight, she really did appreciate his straightforward simplicity and admire his mind. She and her husband were readers with wide tastes and possessed a remarkable library of many thousands of volumes, from which he was encouraged to borrow freely.

However much Rousseau's new life looked to his former friends like a social whirl, it also afforded the leisure he needed to think through his major projects and finish them. In the long run he hoped to realize enough money from his books to guarantee a comfortable retirement, but in the meantime he resolutely refused sources of income that would tie him down in any way, including a book-reviewing commitment that would have paid a handsome 800 livres a month for nominal labor. Instead he kept up his music copying, work that he continued to find congenial. It was structured and repetitive, requiring that conventional symbols be precisely duplicated, but it was by no means mindless. In a long article in his *Dictionary of Music* Rousseau discusses the many technical choices involved, emphasizes that beautifully executed notes may actually be hard to read if the relationships among them are not intelligently displayed, and concludes, "The most skillful copyist is the one whose music is most easily performed, without the musician himself suspecting why."

To be sure, there was an element of ostentatious humility in this unglamorous vocation. Morellet said that Rousseau liked visitors to find him busy copying, giving him a chance to explain that he was obliged to live by the work of his hands. And his refusal of patronage was not just a private ethical choice, it was essential to the public image Rousseau had created. Malesherbes saw this clearly: "If Rousseau had merely said, 'I despise nobility,' they would have answered, 'You are insolent, you despise it only because you can't attain it'; or rather, they would have said nothing, because there's not a clerk in Paris or Lyon who doesn't think and talk like that. But he said, 'I despise riches, and I scorn the means by which I could acquire them.' From then on public attention was fixed on him, because that was truly very singular."

Thérèse, a skilled seamstress who got work from Rousseau's wealthy admirers, also contributed a modest income. Her relationship to Rousseau, however, was increasingly puzzling to visitors. "We went into his kitchen," a young Genevan reported, "and sat down at the table with his servant and his dog, just as in the days of the patriarchs." Clearly Thérèse seemed a mere servant to this visitor, who also noted the shocking coarseness of the wine. Rousseau drained two glasses "as if it had been nectar," commenting cheerfully that an aristocratic guest had called it detestable. Another visitor had a similar reaction to Thérèse: "A girl, or woman, dined with us. She was, as I perceived, the servant, housekeeper, cook, etc. for M. Rousseau. She isn't beautiful, and

ROUSSEAU AT MONTMORENCY

A young artist named Jean Houel visited Rousseau at Montmorency, and when his host drifted off to sleep after dinner, Houel seized the occasion to sketch an informal portrait in pencil (reproduced here in a nineteenth-century lithograph). Wearing a cap and dressing gown against the cold, Rousseau is shown just waking up, with his cat, Doyenne, on his lap and his dog, Turc, at his feet.

from that point of view she wouldn't arouse suspicions in anyone."
(Leigh comments severely, "Thérèse was no longer Rousseau's mistress,
true enough, but the logic is far from impeccable"; and in fact there is
no way of knowing whether they were still sleeping together.) Casanova
recorded a story in which the prince de Conti spent an afternoon with
Rousseau but was surprised to find a third place set at the table when he
had expected they would be alone. He asked who it was for, and Rousseau responded, "The third person is another myself. It is someone who
is neither my wife nor my mistress nor my servant nor my mother nor
my daughter, and she is all of those." The prince, offended at having to
dine with an inferior, replied that he would depart and leave Rousseau
"with all those other selves." But however much Rousseau may have
valued Thérèse, there is no doubt that he condescended to her wound-
ingly. "I made a dictionary of her expressions to amuse Mme de Luxembourg, and her malapropisms became famous in the circles I lived in."

The one thing that would have threatened his contentment was bad
health, but just then Rousseau's condition finally began to improve. One
reason was that for the first time he received an expert opinion that he
was able to trust. During a particularly alarming bout of pain, the
Luxembourgs moved him into the château and summoned a distinguished surgeon, the frère Côme. The duke himself stood by sympathetically while Côme carried out a painful probing that lasted two
hours. At the end of the examination he announced that Rousseau had
an enlarged prostate but no sign of "the stone," that his organs were
formed normally, and that he might suffer a great deal but would live
for a long time. This oracular pronouncement was exactly what Rousseau needed. His malady had a physical cause but would not be fatal,
and in effect he was authorized to get well. Even before the examination, Rousseau had begun to grasp that his affliction was at least partly
psychosomatic. He wrote to one of his new admirers, "Ever since I
hardened my heart, no longer love any individual, and call everybody
my friend, I've been fattening like a pig. I know no better recipe for
good health than insensitivity."

At Montlouis and the Petit Château, Rousseau worked steadily on
the manuscripts that became *Émile* and *The Social Contract,* and proof
sheets of the already finished *Julie* passed back and forth between him
and his Amsterdam publisher, Rey. It turned out to be the most popular

of all his books, the best-selling novel of the entire eighteenth century, in fact. It is also the most revealing of his major works for his biography, and not just because it reflects the affair with Mme d'Houdetot. Indeed, *Julie* is far from being a simple roman à clef in the way that Mme d'Épinay's novel was. Once the affair was over, Rousseau strove to dramatize the insights he believed he had gained, which were social as well as psychological. Psychologically, he wanted to show that obsessive passion could be transformed into something healthier and more constructive; socially, he wanted to show that a communal mode of living was possible that would respect the freedom and individuality of its members.

Even from a biographical point of view, it is misleading to identify the heroine too closely with Mme d'Houdetot. The first two books of *Julie* were completed before the electrifying meeting ever happened. The next three were written under her influence, and the sixth and last at a time when Rousseau still planned to give her a present that was extravagantly laborious to produce, a handwritten copy of the entire work. (Indeed he did, in two thousand neatly handwritten pages; she declined to accept it in person and sent a servant for it.) But *Julie* could hardly have been the best-selling novel of the century if it had been merely a wish-fulfilling fantasy. A modern writer comments, "He never in his life met the woman he needed, and for good reason, since she never existed in this world." The whole point about Julie was her hard-earned wisdom; a deep impulse behind the novel was a desire to revisit past disappointments and make them come out differently.

In subtitling his novel *The New Héloïse,* Rousseau meant to recall the medieval story of the tutor who married his pupil and was brutally castrated by thugs working for her infuriated father. But the original Héloïse became a nun, tormented by hopeless desire for the emasculated Abelard. What is different about Julie is not just that she marries and has children but that she learns to relate to her former lover in an entirely new way. From another point of view, Rousseau's novel is an updated *Romeo and Juliet,* with the obstacle no longer family rivalry but social disparity; Julie's father, the baron d'Étange, clings to the hollow prestige of a Swiss aristocracy that has lost any real importance. But here there is no tragic mistake, no poison, no *Liebestod.* Although she and her former lover, Saint-Preux, still desire each other more than they want to admit, they stop believing that they would have been happier if only they could have married each other.

Even at the beginning of the story, passion is alarming. When the lovers permit themselves a first kiss, Julie faints dead away, and Saint-Preux writes the next day, "No, keep your kisses, I wouldn't be able to bear them — they're too acrid, too penetrating, they pierce, they burn to the marrow — they would drive me mad." Early in the relationship, Saint-Preux has too much to drink and ventures a glimpse into Julie's bodice, and in his next letter he wallows in shame but insists that he is innocent of crude lust: "If my ardent and fearful love has sometimes approached your charms with a timid hand, tell me if a brutal temerity has ever dared to profane them?" Nevertheless, he urges Julie to punish him severely, recapitulating the pattern in Rousseau's life that went all the way back to Mlle Lambercier and imperious little Goton. And when Saint-Preux gets the chance, he adores Julie's garments fetishistically, just as Rousseau passionately kissed the bed in which Mme de Warens had slept. "This slender corset that touches and embraces — what an enchanting shape — two slight curves in front — O voluptuous sight — the whalebone has yielded to the pressure — delicious imprints, I kiss you a thousand times!"

When they actually sleep together, it is Julie who makes it happen, and even then what they relish most is the communion of souls. "I imagined no other happiness," Saint-Preux says afterward, "than to feel your face against mine like that, your breath on my cheek, your arm around my neck. What a calm in all my senses!" In a heartfelt footnote Rousseau adds in his own voice, "O love! If I miss the time when you could be tasted, it is not for the hour of gratification, it's for the hour that follows it." Pleasure is intense but by its nature brief, and is often followed by suffering. Happiness is potentially a lasting state, but by its nature cannot be intense. Romantic love therefore has to be outgrown, lest it become, as Julie says, "the poison that corrupts my senses and my reason." Years later she tells Saint-Preux, "Love is accompanied by a continual uneasiness of jealousy or privation, ill suited to marriage, which is a state of enjoyment and peace." Saint-Preux, surrendering abjectly to Julie's power and adoring an idealized image of her, is a romantic swain with poor qualifications to be a spouse.

As Rousseau rather proudly acknowledged, *Julie* doesn't have much plot, but one decisive turning point is provoked by an upsetting event. Julie discovers that she is pregnant and briefly allows herself to hope that a child will legitimate her secret union. Unfortunately her mother discovers her correspondence with Saint-Preux, her father strikes her violently in his rage, and as a result she miscarries and her mother succumbs to a fatal illness. Saint-Preux is then obliged to leave. He joins the then-famous round-the-world voyage of the English admiral George Anson and doesn't see Julie again for six years. Long before his return she has married her father's candidate, Wolmar, and has become an exemplary wife and mother.

But when Saint-Preux returns from his sea change, the story springs its chief surprise. Instead of being jealous of his wife's former lover, Wolmar invites him to stay with them at their estate at Clarens near Lausanne. With an unemotional temperament that protects him from jealousy, Wolmar resembles the classical sages Rousseau admired, so different from his own volatile temperament. To become a tranquil observer of life was always deeply attractive to Rousseau, and he makes Wolmar say, "If I could change the nature of my being and become a living eye, I would gladly make the exchange." When he invites Saint-Preux to stay he knows he is taking a risk, but he believes it is the only way to cure Julie and Saint-Preux of a crippling passion. So he actually encourages them to kiss in the very bower where their first shattering kiss took place, and he then goes off on a trip so that their desire will no longer be inflamed by the obstacle of his presence.

It is a calculated process of deprogramming, and the cure is a success. "It's not Julie de Wolmar he's in love with," Wolmar says, "it's Julie d'Étange," which is to say, a Julie who no longer exists. "He loves her in time past, that's the true key to the enigma. Take away the memory and he'll no longer have the love." In a symbolically charged incident, Saint-Preux sails across the lake with Julie to a hamlet called Meillerie, from which he had once gazed at her distant home in an agony of desire. He shows her the rocks on which he carved her initials years before, which have become — as in the caption for the illustration Rousseau commissioned — "monuments of former loves." The poignant memories only prove to Saint-Preux that all is changed. "It's ended, I said to myself. Those times, those happy times are no more, they have vanished forever. Alas, they will never more return."

"MONUMENTS OF FORMER LOVES"

In one of the twelve illustrations that Rousseau commissioned for *Julie,* Saint-Preux, with tears in his eyes, asks Julie whether her heart tells her nothing as she looks at her initials carved into the cliff along with verses from Petrarch and Tasso; he had inscribed them ten years before while gazing longingly across the lake at her home. The actual cliffs at Meillerie are less craggy and oriental than the artist's conception, and the village of Vevey across the lake is much more remote than it appears here. The formality of eighteenth-century fashions is reflected by Rousseau's instruction to the engraver that although Julie should be elaborately clothed in other pictures, in this one she must be "without finery, and in her morning dress." However, he greatly disliked the result: "I get angry every time I see her — just look — doesn't she have the air of a Paris grisette?"

As this theme suggests, the true inspiration of *Julie* was not Mme d'Houdetot at all but Mme de Warens. Rousseau set the story in her native region, with details acquired during his lonely stay in Lausanne in 1730 and his happy tour of the lake in 1754, and he made the physical resemblance unmistakable. Julie is an ash-blonde like Maman (Mme d'Houdetot had black hair), with the same imperfectly concealed charms: "The avid and daring eye insinuates itself with impunity under the bouquet, it wanders beneath the chenille and gauze, and makes the hand sense the yielding resistance it wouldn't dare to touch." Most of all she resembles Mme de Warens in the charisma through which everyone around her comes under her benign influence, while those closest to her share a mutual bond like the one Jean-Jacques believed he shared with Claude Anet. "I felt from the way her husband clasped my hand that the same emotion overtook all three of us, and that the sweet influence of this expansive soul was acting upon all around her."

There are differences as well. Mme de Warens abandoned her country, religion, and husband; Julie is loyal to all three. Mme de Warens had a series of lovers and no children; Julie's first lover remains a soulmate, but she is steadily faithful to the husband whose children she has borne. In writing *Julie* Rousseau gave himself the role of Mme de Warens's original seducer, Tavel, but in the role of a faithful swain rather than a libertine rake, and he also erased the age difference between Mme de Warens and himself. She had been his teacher, and now he made himself hers. So if Saint-Preux was Rousseau, it was not in the literal sense that many readers supposed. When a friend asked, "Was it not your own story?" he replied, "It's not at all what I was, but what I would have liked to be." As for Wolmar, far from being a sexual rival, he serves as an oracle of paternal wisdom, so that Saint-Preux can exclaim gratefully, "O my benefactor! O my father!" This flawless patriarch is a great improvement on Isaac Rousseau, and perhaps he has some traits as well of the baron de Warens, whom Rousseau never met. It is as if Mme de Warens were being restored to her long-suffering husband rather than relinquished to the ignoble Wintzenried.

Since friendship, not romance, provides the basis for happiness, Julie's deepest and most sustained relationship is with her cousin Claire. Much has been made by modern scholars of the intensity of same-sex friendships in eighteenth-century culture, and Rousseau, who certainly experienced it himself, was keenly responsive to its presence among women. "What ecstasy," Saint-Preux exclaims with voyeuristic enthusiasm, "to see two such touching beauties tenderly embracing, the face of one resting on the other's breast . . . Nothing on earth can excite such voluptuous tenderness as your mutual caresses." The novel's editors warn sternly against suspecting lesbian tendencies, and indeed Rousseau suggests elsewhere that such behavior was staged mainly to arouse the male sex, "taking pride in stimulating lust with impunity by the image of those favors which they know how to make men desire." In any case, the erotic bond between Julie and Claire is safely sublimated, leaving them free to enjoy the perfect openness of soul Rousseau always longed for. "If I have imagined well the hearts of Julie and Claire," he told an admirer, "they were transparent to each other; it was impossible to hide themselves from each other." How different from the real-life cousins d'Houdetot and d'Épinay!

Rousseau was careful to provide Saint-Preux as well with a faithful friend, a high-minded English nobleman known as Milord Edward Bomston (the man who called himself Dudding during the coach journey to Montpellier had a gift for preposterous English names). Bomston too has known passionate love and has risen above it, for, strange though it may seem, he steadfastly refuses to sleep with either of two beautiful women who adore him. "Happier in the pleasures he denied himself than the voluptuary is in the ones he tastes, he loved longer, remained free, and enjoyed life better than those who use it up."

During these same years Rousseau was hard at work on his political and social writings, and in his account of the fictional Wolmar estate at Clarens he explored a question that preoccupied him deeply throughout his life. Since human beings have no choice but to live in society, how can society satisfy their needs instead of wounding and exploiting them? Rousseau was very much a modern individual, cut off from family and origins, self-defined, moving from place to place and from one set of relationships to another. In Clarens he created a fantasy of a stable mini-society, a sort of moral biosphere, in which everyone knows his place and likes it. With some justification Wolmar has been called "Big Brother in a powdered wig," and his regime "a gentle totalitarianism," but it is the brotherliness and gentleness that should be stressed. Unlike the absentee landlords of the time, Wolmar and Julie live as simply as possible and use any profits to make the estate still better.

A standard claim of eighteenth-century economic theory was that the luxuries of the rich provided work for the poor. Rousseau consistently argued the opposite. "Luxury nourishes a hundred poor people in our cities, and makes a hundred thousand perish in our countryside." The solution at Clarens is to drop out of the economic system altogether, creating a self-sufficient economy that escapes the enslavement of the countryside to the cities. (Rousseau always idealized rural labor, of which he had no personal experience beyond feeding the pigeons at Les Charmettes.) The farmers at Clarens sing at their work, "recalling all the charms of the golden age," and the grape harvest finds them "accumulating abundance and joy around them, and transforming the labor that enriches them into a continual fête."

There is no question, however, of true equality, which Rousseau considered unattainable in the modern world. Though Wolmar is enlightened, he is an enlightened despot, and even at the celebration that follows the harvest, "if anyone happens to forget himself, the festival isn't disturbed by reprimands, but he is fired without hope of appeal the next day." More surprisingly, household servants are segregated by sex and never escape the surveillance of their employers. In his own days as a resentful lackey, Rousseau spent a lot of time yearning for girls he couldn't get; at Clarens the servants are strictly forbidden to indulge in sexual relations, in what has been aptly called a "moral castration." In this paternalistic structure, Rousseau imagines one of the most painful errors of his life being redressed. When servants are accused of wrongdoing, Julie interviews them in private and "often she draws tears of sorrow and shame from them; it is not uncommon for her to be moved with pity at seeing their repentance." That was exactly what the comte de la Roque failed to do in Turin, when Jean-Jacques' accusation concerning the stolen ribbon ruined poor Marion's life. Under kindly questioning rather than public inquisition, he would have confessed to stealing the ribbon. If only Julie had been his employer and not the comte de la Roque!

As with every aspect of Rousseau's thought, the utopia at Clarens is filled with suggestive paradoxes. On the one hand, it presents a picture of rural life as the closest thing to healthy existence the modern world can offer. This vision was very appealing to Jeffersonian democracy, and it has resonated deeply in urbanized civilization. On the other hand, Rousseau always held that the true state of nature is unrecoverable and that human beings are incurably selfish and competitive because society makes them that way. Clarens is a simplified society that minimizes the damage, but damage can never be eliminated altogether. It follows that there always has to be some degree of artifice in the way relationships are managed, especially with employees. As Saint-Preux acknowledges, "Servitude is so unnatural to man that it could not exist without some discontent." The master therefore governs his domestics and farm workers by covert manipulation, "hiding control under a veil of pleasure or self-interest, so that they think they desire everything they're obliged to do." And this is where Julie's charisma is crucial. She acts as a loving mother to the entire community, making everyone feel appreciated as they carry out the duties expected of them. For women readers in the eighteenth century, this was a positive and empowering vision. To modern feminists it looks very different. But that is an issue to postpone for *Émile,* where Rousseau addresses it head on.

In addition to psychological and social concerns, Rousseau's novel had something else to offer: an inspiring vision of nature. In earlier times "nature" simply meant everything in the universe, cities included, since man is a social animal. During the eighteenth century, however, with Rousseau as an influential source, nature came to mean those aspects of the world least altered by human beings. Even Julie's garden, which she calls her Elysée, appears wild and uncultivated, although everything in it has been artfully placed — a fine metaphor for domesticated love. Nature in this sense is increasingly invested with spiritual value, as it was for Rousseau when he wandered in the forest of Montmorency and found himself exclaiming, "O great being! O great being!"

Lac Léman plays a major role in *Julie;* the erotic tension between the former lovers is resolved when one of Julie's children falls into the lake, and in saving him she contracts a fatal illness. The majestic Alps beyond are also important, though Rousseau liked cultivated foothills better than high peaks; it has been accurately observed that his gaze seldom

C L A R E N S

The hamlet at the eastern end of Lac Léman where Rousseau set Julie's home. The
original caption read, "This place is celebrated in the *Héloïse* of Rousseau."

extended above the tree line. In his youth he twice crossed the Alps
without remark, and a writer on alpine literature comments tartly that
his account of the Valais region in *Julie* is so lacking in color that "it
makes one think of the mountains of the moon." But accurate description was not the point. Rousseau wanted to evoke the psychological effect of a spiritualized nature, and in this he succeeded brilliantly. When
Saint-Preux makes a journey into the Valais he finds the air bracingly
pure — "one breathes more freely, one's body feels lighter, one's spirit is
more serene" — and he is overwhelmed by sublimity. "Sometimes immense crags hung in ruins above my head; sometimes high and roaring
waterfalls inundated me with their dense spray; sometimes a ceaseless
torrent opened an abyss before me whose depths my eyes dared not
sound." The Alps were well on the way to becoming a major attraction
for travelers, and as a scholar comments, soon everyone wanted to fill
his lungs with mountain air and his ears with the sound of cataracts. It
was the mood that counted. A Polish countess making a Rousseau pil-

grimage toward the end of the century noticed that his descriptions bore little resemblance to the actual scenes, but all the same she wept like a child. And readers for generations continued to make the world of *Julie* their own. As late as the 1950s, when a shabbily dressed fisherman on the banks of the Senegal River learned that a visitor came from Geneva, he pulled a well-worn copy of the novel from his pocket and exclaimed, "So, Monsieur, you can go to Meillerie as often as you like!"

As Rousseau proofread *Julie,* however, he was far from confident of success. In particular, he worried about how the public would respond to a stern moralist unexpectedly producing a romantic novel, a genre that was still widely regarded as trivial entertainment or worse, and especially a novel in which an unmarried girl voluntarily sleeps with her lover. (In his preface he solemnly suggests that unmarried girls should not be allowed to read it.) There was also the question of censorship, although unlike Rousseau's other works in those years, *Julie* had relatively little in it to cause concern. The main problem was that he made Wolmar an atheist, with the intention of showing that atheism was not necessarily immoral and could coexist amicably with faith. He rather naively hoped, as he told the Genevan pastor Vernes, to reconcile the warring intellectual camps of the day. "Julie the devout is a lesson for the philosophes, and Wolmar the atheist is a lesson for the intolerant." That sort of tolerance was totally unacceptable to the Church, and in order to ensure that the book could be openly distributed in France, Malesherbes took a personal interest and arranged to have Rey send the proof sheets to him for review before passing them on to Rousseau. (This had the added advantage of sparing Rousseau heavy postage costs, which in those days were paid by the recipient rather than the sender.) Even what may seem to us like trite generalizations could be politically explosive, and one such threat had to be defused after the book had been printed. "A coal merchant's wife is more respectable than the mistress of a prince," Julie says. Rousseau had already had second thoughts and substituted the word "prince" for the original "king," but Malesherbes went further and cut out this particular page from the copy that went to Mme de Pompadour, pasting in another that he had specially printed for the purpose.

By the time Rey's edition was ready for sale early in 1761, a competing French one was coming out, incorporating the cuts required by Malesherbes. Faced with competition, Rey was terrified, fearing that his investment would be lost, but he need not have worried. He was permitted an unofficial sale, and it turned out that the only difficulty for both publishers was to meet an insatiable demand. Rey told Rousseau a year later that he had made 10,000 livres by it. The success of *Julie,* in fact, was absolutely astounding. At least seventy editions had been published by the end of the eighteenth century (though it has to be said that new editions were not unusual in those days, when piracy of books was common and when it was cheaper to pay printers to reset a text from scratch than to keep expensive type tied up for a reprint that might never be needed). Towns everywhere had reading clubs, rental libraries, and bookshops where customers could read at their leisure for a modest fee without necessarily buying, and in all of these places the novel was eagerly devoured. *Julie*'s triumph was achieved in spite of obvious drawbacks: it was eight hundred pages long, with few incidents and with lengthy discourses on general topics. But it was soon obvious that it excited unprecedented emotional involvement. The passions in it were so fierce, one reviewer declared, that they burned the paper, and years later Germaine de Staël remarked that far from belying his reputation for virtue, Rousseau had managed "to make virtue into a passion" by giving it imaginative appeal.

Most novels were published anonymously, but Rousseau proudly put his name on the title page, "Jean-Jacques Rousseau spelled out in full," as he declares in his preface, and he was soon receiving voluminous mail from people who testified that *Julie* had changed their lives. As has been well said, he himself had been seduced by characters in search of an author, and readers gratefully participated in the seduction, falling in love with Julie and Saint-Preux as if they were real people. Rousseau did nothing to discourage them, writing later on, "Whoever does not idolize my Julie doesn't know what is worthy of love; whoever is not the friend of Saint-Preux could never be mine."

One reader who did not idolize Julie had already established himself as no friend of Rousseau. Grimm, in his limited-circulation newsletter, roundly condemned *Julie* as the worst book to appear in a long time, by "an author devoid of genius, imagination, judgment, and taste." The diatribe went on and on, with a resentment that would be inexplicable if one didn't know the story of Grimm's relations with Rousseau. More skillful was that other ex-friend, Diderot, who sought to point up the inferiority of *Julie* by publishing an extravagant encomium on one of its models, *Clarissa,* by the Englishman Samuel Richardson. "He carries the torch," Diderot declared, "into the depths of the cavern; it is he who teaches us to recognize the subtle and indecent motives that hide beneath decent ones . . . He breathes on the sublime phantom that presents itself at the entrance, and the hideous Moor that it masked then appears." Rousseau could have replied that his characters too are haunted by unacknowledged motives, but he would also have said that the sublime vision of moral integrity was not just a phantom. *Julie* does have elements in common with *Clarissa*. Both books exploit the epistolary mode, in which letters exchanged among the characters give the illusion of immediacy. And in both books a patriarchal father forces his daughter to marry someone she doesn't love. But there the resemblance ends. Clarissa is so tortured by shame after a heartless seducer drugs and rapes her that she wastes away and dies. Julie, after deliberately sleeping with the man she loves, accepts marriage with someone else and creates a good life for all. There are no villains in *Julie.*

Many of the letters Rousseau received were from women, providing him with regular doses of the pleasure he had experienced when the audience sobbed at *The Village Soothsayer.* He especially relished the story of a lady who started reading *Julie* after dinner while she was getting ready for a ball, at midnight gave orders for the horses to be hitched to her carriage, was still completely absorbed in the book when her servants came to remind her at two in the morning, and finally retired to bed at four, where she kept on reading. Another lady wrote to Rousseau, "I was beyond tears, a sharp pain overcame me, my heart tightened, the dying Julie was no longer an unknown being to me, I believed myself her sister, her friend, her Claire." She added that she greatly desired to see the portrait of Julie that Rousseau was believed to have, before which she would like to kneel in adoration. In the *Confessions* Rousseau boasts, rather startlingly, "Women above all were intoxicated with the book and its author, to such a point that there were few, even in the highest ranks, whom I could not have made a conquest of if I had tried."

Men, too, responded rapturously. For them *Julie* was a revelation of feelings that they didn't know how to express, or perhaps even to recognize. "If the great Rousseau did not exist," a country squire wrote from Provence, "I would have need of nothing. He does exist, and I feel that something is missing." An abbé in Lyon told him, "How much our hearts owe to you for causing feelings to grow that would have remained barren if you had not warmed them! Socrates was the midwife of ideas, and you are the midwife of virtues." The twenty-five-year-old Charles-Joseph Pancoucke, later to become a major publisher, wrote a modestly unsigned letter declaring that he had formerly been trapped in cynical skepticism, but that reading *Julie* converted him. "A god was needed, and a powerful one, to pull me back from the precipice, and you, Monsieur, are the god who has worked this miracle . . . Since this fortunate reading I have burned with the love of virtue, and my heart, which I thought extinguished, is hotter than ever." Not surprisingly, Rousseau hastened to make the acquaintance of this admirable man.

Pancoucke no doubt had the ulterior motive of hoping to publish future works by the author, but his rhetoric echoed what Rousseau was hearing from every side. A Parisian wrote to say that like Saint-Preux he had fallen in love with a young woman much richer than himself and that she was eager to read *Julie* but was frustrated by her parents' prohibition of novels. They had agreed therefore that the best thing would be for him to slip secretly into her bedroom so they could read it together. "She was sleeping, and I awakened her by throwing myself into her arms. You can well imagine that our first occupation wasn't reading. The thousand kisses she permitted me to take at her lips, the charms of her breasts which she surrendered to my discretion, set fire to my senses so much that in my intoxicated state, I was going to — but she halted my exertions, and spoke to me in terms that Julie and her lover would not have disapproved of." In short, she reminded him that he was a man of honor, and he proved equal to the challenge. "We continued to see each other almost every night. I slept in her bedroom, and very often with her. A hundred times I have seen her swoon in my arms. I have had the most violent desires, but I always overcame them . . . It is for you, Monsieur, to judge if I acted rashly, and if these multiple victories over myself are not worth more than the timid reserve of cooler souls." Combining erotic intensity with virtuous self-denial, letters like this suggest that the thrillingly painful scenes in Mme d'Houdetot's garden and bedroom were being reenacted all over Europe. But the writer's bid for a sympathetic reply failed. Rousseau wrote back sternly, "I don't know what you intend by these indecent details you've presumed to send me, but it's hard to read them without believing that you are either a liar or impotent." He added that if the lady swooned in her lover's arms, "you have achieved only the foolish pleasure of watching her swoon by herself." He didn't add that his own behavior with Mme d'Houdetot had been much the same.

In praising *Julie* for reconciling passion with virtue, Rousseau's readers were explaining its success in the moral terms then in vogue, but it would be equally possible to describe it sociologically. The theme of ideal yet impossible love, indulged but also overcome, was deeply appealing at a time when social constraints on marriage remained powerful. If Rousseau had exalted passion as the ultimate good he could never have been so successful. The secret of *Julie* is to cool down sexual love even while seeming to fan it, producing a mood that is more elegiac than inflammatory. The very first reader of *Julie* was Mme de Luxembourg, who never stopped praising it despite her reputation for acerbic wit. In all likelihood she saw in it a version of her own story: passionate in youth and blamed for it, wise and tranquil in later life. For readers like her, as her biographer says, it recreated "the infinite pleasure of letters, avowals, rendezvous, confidences, meetings, abandonment both desired and feared, and in short the entire poem of love."

Still more profound, and probably not entirely grasped by Rousseau himself, must have been his intuition that although Julie accepts her role at Clarens, it remains a role. Gazing into her eyes as she lies on her deathbed, Wolmar exclaims, "Julie, my dear Julie! you have wounded me to the heart . . . You are rejoicing to die, you are glad to be leaving me." He is right, for the letter she leaves to be read when she is gone discloses that her love for Saint-Preux remained strong and might still have impelled her to do something unforgivable. According to the mores that Rousseau shared with his readers, it would have been unacceptable for Julie to leave Wolmar for Saint-Preux, much less to conduct an adulterous affair. It would also have been unacceptable for her to choose to die. But by accepting death uncomplainingly when an accident occasions it — an accident, of course, created by Rousseau's plot — she escapes from the intolerable pressure of repressing her deepest feelings in order to be a good wife and mother. This pressure was all too familiar to many readers, and they must have been gratified when Saint-Preux refuses to fulfill Julie's dying wish that he marry Claire. He might have been happy with her in a way, but it would have been the wrong kind of happiness. So even if duty, family, and morality win out, romantic love does too, with all the poignancy of concealing its secret until death. As for Claire, she is frozen in her grief. "By myself I cannot weep, or speak, or make myself understood . . . I am all alone in the midst of everyone." *Julie* is about society and its demands, but Rousseau's deepest insights, here and always, are about aloneness.

Curiously, it was the intellectuals who waxed most moralistic, expressing outrage that a virtuous young woman could make advances to a man, and at the same time deploring the characters' tendency to philosophize. Rousseau's former friend Charles Bordes was typical, in a tongue-in-cheek prophecy attributed to an ancient manuscript: "The pupil will lose all shame and all modesty, and she will commit follies and maxims with her master. She will give him the first kiss on the mouth, and she will invite him to go to bed with her; she will become pregnant with metaphysics, and their love letters will be philosophical homilies." Voltaire's critique of *Julie* was similarly filled with sarcasms. He claimed to be shocked at the shamelessness of a girl giving herself to her tutor, particularly when the tutor is her social inferior, and he took it for granted that Saint-Preux was really Rousseau. "Milord [Bomston] proves conclusively that a watchmaker's boy who knows how to read and write is the perfect equal of Spanish grandees, English dukes and peers, princes of the Empire, and syndics of Geneva . . . Never has a trollop preached so much, and never has a girl-seducing valet been more of a philosopher." But Voltaire was swimming against the tide. His enemy Fréron was more typical in admiring the moralizing. "The author knows how to make virtue attractive and convincing, and in the end, one can't read him without becoming better, or at least wanting to be." But not everyone welcomed the moral influence of *Julie*. One reader complained that after four years of happiness his lover had read *Julie* and promptly banished him. "Condemned to pain, I swear eternal hatred to you. It means nothing to me that people admire Julie's virtue, she doesn't exist except in your letters, one never sees real examples like her."

In addition to the critics and the rapt admirers, some were surreptitiously irreverent, as in the anonymous verses that circulated in Paris:

> O Love, in the age in which we live,
> In spite of your laws of tenderness,
> We have to read through six volumes
> To find that they only fucked two times!
> If these foreign fashions
> Prevail over your teaching,
> That's so much the better for the booksellers
> But so much the worse for the cunts.

With the publication of *Julie,* Rousseau found himself occupying a new role that was just beginning to exist in the dawning age of mass publication. Readers felt that they were in direct communication with a noble soul, and he became a celebrity as much for his persona as for his writings. Countless strangers wrote to him for advice on life problems, and many sought personal encounters. To some extent this attention was invigorating, but it was also disturbing, for he had committed himself to an ideal of solitude, and as a historian of the phenomenon of fame says, he was now a recluse of a peculiarly modern kind, "the person who desires to be spiritually public and physically private, the shy star." Anxiety about his public image would haunt him obsessively in the years to come.

Meanwhile Rousseau had other projects to complete, and in short order he did complete them. In an amazingly brief span of sixteen months, three masterpieces issued from the press: *Julie* in January 1761, *Émile* in October 1761, and *The Social Contract* in April 1762, two months before he turned fifty. Remarkably enough, he was continuing his practice of writing a single book in each new genre and then moving on. He saw himself not as a professional author but as a man with a message, tracing its implications successively in personal relations, in education, and in political life. With this series of memorable publications, Rousseau's fame would reach unprecedented heights. And then it would all come crashing down, and he would flee into the wilderness as an exile and a pariah.

18

Rousseau the Controversialist:
Émile and *The Social Contract*

WITH *JULIE* out of the way, the next step was to resume work on a book on education, for which Rousseau had been accumulating notes ever since his days with Mme Dupin. It might seem odd for a middle-aged man who had never raised children to undertake a long book on the subject, but Rousseau found the project compelling for many reasons. In earlier days he had had a good deal of experience as a tutor, and by now he thought he understood why none of his methods ever worked. Whether he tried emotional appeals, reasoning, or anger, the result was always resistance, not cooperation. And he realized that his instruction had started too late: Chenonceaux was a sullen teenager, and even the young Mably boys were firmly set in their ways by the time he met them. In *Émile* he proposed a radically different course: a tutor would take charge at the very beginning and would work by subtle indirection to encourage a child to develop according to his own natural bent.

Beyond this immediate interest in education, Rousseau had begun reflecting on his own childhood — the premature introduction to adult reading, the combination of discipline and neglect — and was coming to understand how crucial early experiences are. Reaching middle age, moreover, brought a poignant awareness of what he had failed to become. "At the age of sixty," he wrote in *Émile,* "it is cruel indeed to die before having begun to live." He was only in his late forties at this point; for him it might not yet be too late. But in any case, he could not escape an awareness that although he felt sympathy for children, he was awkward and self-conscious around them. "Children sometimes flatter old men, but they never love them."

Most important of all was the memory of his own children consigned to the foundling home. "I still have an old sin to expiate in print," Rousseau told a correspondent, "after which the public will never hear of me again." And although his personal story was still a closely held secret, he referred to it indirectly in *Émile:* "Whoever cannot fulfill the duties of a father has no right to become one. Neither poverty nor labors nor other people's judgment can exempt him from nourishing his children and bringing them up himself. Readers, you can believe me. I predict that anyone who has a heart and neglects such sacred duties will weep long and bitterly for his error, and will never be consoled." To create an imaginary boy in *Émile,* and to show how a child ideally should be raised, would be a form of penance and expiation.

At first Rousseau envisioned the book as a conventional treatise, but it soon took on a novelistic flavor, with anecdotes and dialogues that enliven the argument. But if *Émile* resembles a novel in presentation, it is hardly a realistic one, since the child is effectively isolated from his family as soon as he enters the tutor's care. When someone complained that there seemed to be no role for Émile's father (the mother at least had nursed him in infancy), Rousseau replied cheerfully, "Oh, he hadn't any. He didn't exist." Real children, as he knew from his own experience, have a deep need for love, but his memories of childhood suggested as well that even the best-meaning parents inevitably distort development. Either they are too severe, in which case the children learn to resent tyranny, or they are too indulgent, in which case the children learn to be manipulative.

Few parents whom Rousseau knew took much interest in their offspring anyway. He was especially disgusted that middle- and upper-class mothers, in order to preserve their figures and please their husbands, routinely consigned their infants to wet nurses, who were often unhealthy as well as inattentive. And that was only the beginning of the problem. When the children returned home after being weaned, they were tended by paid servants, then sent to schools to acquire rote knowledge and precocious vices, and finally released into the world as slaves to conventional opinion. "All of our wisdom consists in servile prejudices, and all of our customs are only subjection, discomfort, and constraint. Civil man is born, lives, and dies in slavery: at birth they sew him into swaddling clothes, and at death they nail him into a coffin. So long as he retains human form he is enchained by our institutions." By escaping or at least postponing these pressures, Émile would have a chance to grow up as his own person.

Most of Rousseau's specific recommendations were conventional enough — more baths, less Latin, and so on — but what was truly original was his claim that each person has a unique temperament that needs freedom to flourish. His concern was not with methods of instruction but with its purpose. Plenty of writers had criticized the mindless memorization and brutal discipline of conventional teaching. The historian Gibbon, for example, wrote bitterly, "A school is the cavern of fear and sorrow. The mobility of the captive youths is chained to a book and a desk . . . They labor, like the soldiers of Persia, under the scourge." But the usual solution was only palliative, recommending reforms whose goal was still to produce docile members of society. John Locke in his influential *Thoughts Concerning Education* stressed the malleability of young minds, which resembled "white paper or wax, to be molded and fashioned as one pleases," and he placed heavy emphasis on discipline. "Those that intend ever to govern their children should begin it whilst they are very little, and look that they perfectly comply with the will of their parents. Would you have your son obedient to you when past a child? Be sure then to establish the authority of a father as soon as he is capable of submission, and can understand in whose power he is." Recommendations like these seemed self-evidently correct not just to conservatives but to progressive thinkers too, including Mme d'Épinay, who wrote a didactic treatise of her own called *Letters to My Son,* in which she argued for rigorous discipline.

In Rousseau's view it was a disastrous mistake to teach children to fear authority. He held that the only power they should face was brute necessity, the obstacles to freedom that are inherent in the very nature of things. They would then choose their actions because they understood what needed to be done, not to please adults or to escape punishment.

Locke recommended influencing children by alternating doses of "esteem and disgrace," but Rousseau wanted to protect his imaginary child from the pressure of other people's expectations. His intention was to show how a person might prepare for life in society without sacrificing integrity, "seeing with his own eyes, feeling with his own heart, and governed by no authority except his own reason." In another formulation, "He is a savage made to live in cities"; or again, "He is not the man of man but the man of nature."

As for the usual content of education, Rousseau held that it was worth having but was not an end in itself, and he challenged conventional pedagogy with insights that have been renewed and forgotten by every subsequent educational establishment. Like Socrates, he believed that true knowledge flowed from asking questions, not from memorizing answers. "I am teaching my pupil an art that is very long, very painful, and assuredly not what your pupils have, the art of being ignorant . . . You impart knowledge, well and good; I am concerned with the means of acquiring it." Underlying the entire work was the insight that had burst upon Rousseau on the road to Vincennes. As he ringingly declared at the beginning of *Émile* — all of his books are remarkable for memorable opening sentences — "Everything is good as it comes from the hands of the author of things; everything degenerates in the hands of man."

Years after *Émile* became a success, Rousseau restated his position more fully: "This book . . . is simply a treatise on the natural goodness of man, intended to show how vice and error are foreign to his constitution, invade it from outside, and imperceptibly alter it." Traditional religious teaching held that each person enters the world already infected by sin and needs to be forcibly shaped into a moral agent. Enlightenment theory held that each person enters the world a blank slate — Locke's famous tabula rasa — waiting to be written on by sensory experience and by parents and teachers. Rousseau believed that each person enters the world with a disposition that needs to grow according to its own nature. The child has much to learn, but only if he learns it in his own way, and most of what usually passes for education is counterproductive. "Dare I expound the greatest, most important, and most useful rule in all of education? It is not to gain time but to lose it."

Most compelling of all in *Émile* is the deep note of sadness over the waste in life and the insistence that education shouldn't make it worse. "How rapidly we pass our time on this earth!" Rousseau exclaims. "The first quarter of life flows away before we know what to do with it, and the last quarter after we have ceased to enjoy it. At first we don't know how to live, soon we're no longer able to, and in the space that separates these two useless extremes, three-quarters of our time is consumed by sleep, labor, pain, constraint, and distress of every kind. Life is short, not so much because it lasts such a short time as because we have almost none of that time to enjoy it." Close to half of the children born in the eighteenth century died before reaching adulthood, and their all too brief existence was being poisoned by needless constraint and beatings (a tutor in Fielding's *Tom Jones* is expressively named Thwackum). "Even if I were to suppose that this education had reasonable objectives, how can one see without indignation the poor unfortunates subjected to an intolerable yoke and condemned to continual labor like galley slaves, with no assurance that so much effort will ever do them any good? The age of gaiety goes by amidst tears, punishments, threats, and slavery."

To encourage Émile to think for himself, the tutor presents him with a series of covertly orchestrated challenges. When he figures out how to grow beans, he is in raptures over his achievement, but is thunderstruck afterward when the family gardener rudely wrecks his handiwork. Robert, the gardener, then explains that when Émile was digging he unknowingly ruined a crop of melons, and from this blunder he learns the value of private property. The point is that children need to grasp ethical principles through concrete experience, something very different from memorizing verbal formulas. "It is easy to put into their mouths words such as *kings, empires, wars, conquests, revolutions,* and *laws,* but when it becomes a question of attaching distinct ideas to these words, it will be a long distance from the conversation with Robert the gardener to all of these explanations."

On another occasion Émile is astounded when a conjurer gets a floating wax duck to follow a piece of bread in his hand. After he returns home, the tutor helps him make a duck of his own and explains the mystery by demonstrating what happens if a magnet is hidden inside. There must have been a magnet in the duck and a piece of metal in the bread. Swollen with pride at his own cleverness, Émile hurries back to the conjurer, whom he publicly embarrasses by duplicating the trick with some bread of his own that contains metal. "The boy cries out and shivers with pleasure. The clapping and acclamation of the crowd make him dizzy and he is beside himself." But the lesson is not over. The next time Émile shows up, the duck inexplicably recoils from his bread, but responds with alacrity to the conjurer's bare hand and even to the sound of his voice. The crowd jeers, and Émile returns home baffled and humiliated. Invited by the tutor, the conjurer drops by to explain how it was done: he had an accomplice hidden under the table with a powerful magnet of his own. The experience teaches Émile "how many mortifying consequences are attracted by the first movement of vanity," and he has thus learned two things at once, the principle of magnetism and the principle that pride goes before a fall.

When Émile learns to reason, then, it is in the context of immediate self-interest. Whereas writers on education normally thought of children as rational beings, Rousseau put emotions first, suggesting that the age of nature lasted until the age of twelve and that the age of reason did not begin until then. Since children are necessarily self-centered, they keep on pushing until they get what they want, and they need to learn that limits are imposed by existence itself, not just by the arbitrary decrees of adults. Rousseau describes another boy, more willful than Émile, who would insist on going for walks whenever it was most inconvenient for his tutor. The solution was to let him go off by himself, whereupon he got lost, was jeered at by passersby, and became seriously scared. An accomplice of the tutor's, following to make sure the boy came to no harm, then brought him home chastened and repentant. Such a scenario is obviously manipulative, especially when Rousseau adds that the neighbors had all been coached to play their parts. At times the tutor's satisfaction at his power almost deserves to be called sadism; Starobinski does call it that. But manipulativeness is the point. Growing up in society, no one can possibly live as a natural man, and the tutor's role is to create artificial situations in which Émile will develop properly without realizing it, just as the servants at Clarens believe they are following their own wishes when they carry out Wolmar's.

No doubt it is true as well that Rousseau identified with the all-seeing mentor. In *Julie* Rousseau transforms himself into a youthful tutor who wins an ideal intellectual and sexual partner — something that never happened when he fell in love with his music students — and then gets to experience the nobility of renunciation. In *Émile* he becomes an older and wiser guide who exerts total control over the son he never had, or didn't keep, and instead of being resented for his power is unstintingly adored. Or perhaps in *Émile* he has actually split himself into two, the openhearted young Jean-Jacques and a surrogate father who selflessly devotes his life to the child.

But such motivations lie deep, not at the surface, and *Émile* is impressive most of all for its unsentimental realism. "None of us is philosopher enough to know how to put himself in a child's place," Rousseau says, but in fact he does it extraordinarily well. In a fine piece of dialogue, he demonstrates the vicious circle that didactic lessons produce:

> MASTER: One must not do that.
> CHILD: And why mustn't one do it?
> MASTER: Because it's bad to do.
> CHILD: Bad to do! What is bad to do?
> MASTER: What you are forbidden to do.
> CHILD: What's bad about doing what I'm forbidden to do?
> MASTER: You'll get punished for having disobeyed.
> CHILD: I'll do it in such a way that no one will know.
> MASTER: You'll be spied on.
> CHILD: I'll hide.
> MASTER: You'll be questioned.
> CHILD: I'll lie.
> MASTER: One must not lie.
> CHILD: Why mustn't one lie?
> MASTER: Because it's bad to do, etc.

Not only was Rousseau critical of overt moralizing, he was unimpressed as well by the claim that literary texts, such as the fables of La Fontaine, which enjoyed universal esteem, could smuggle in instruction along with entertainment. To make the point, he goes line by line through the fable of the fox and the crow, in which the fox praises the crow's voice so seductively that he tries to sing and drops his piece of cheese. Far from teaching children to despise flattery, Rousseau argues, the story only encourages them to find stupid victims. "No one likes to be humiliated. They will always take the attractive role, it's the choice of *amour-propre,* and a very natural choice too."

Reading of any kind, in fact, is actively discouraged by the tutor, since it stimulates escapist fantasies. The only approved book is *Robinson Crusoe,* with its efficient hero who pragmatically masters his island. So Émile is to be nothing like the young Jean-Jacques, who lost his heart to romantic heroines and to ancient Romans, and who learned very early to wish he was someone else, living somewhere else. Puberty will bring new complications, but until then, Rousseau says, "I see [Émile] ardent, lively, and animated, without gnawing cares or long and painful foresight, completely whole in his present being and enjoying the fullness of life." This is the pure sensation of living, the *sentiment de l'existence,* that Rousseau always yearned for and seldom achieved. However, while precocious reading was to be avoided, he had no objection to training gifted children to perform elaborate music, on the grounds that they were not aping adult skills but fully mastering them. He gave several examples, and added in a note in a later edition, "Since that time, a little boy of seven has done even more astonishing things." The boy was Mozart.

Natural man, as Rousseau imagined him, was entirely contented with a solitary life, but Émile lives in the modern world and must eventually become a member of society. Moreover, since the public world is full of jealousy and competition, he will need an emotional relationship that can provide a secure haven. "I know that an absolute solitude," Rousseau once wrote, "is a gloomy state, and contrary to nature. Affectionate feelings nourish the soul, and communication of ideas enlivens the mind. Our sweetest existence is relative and collective, and our true 'me' is not entirely within ourselves." So Émile needs a wife, and the challenge is to find the right one, forestalling the tendency of erotic passion to fix on inappropriate objects. "Rather than destine a spouse for my Émile from childhood," the tutor says, "I have waited to know the one who will be suited to him . . . My task is to discover the choice that nature has made."

To prepare Émile while he waits for this person to appear, the tutor encourages him to imagine an ideal woman who will be modestly feminine, adequately intelligent (he isn't brilliant himself), and well trained in domestic skills. As Yves Vargas observes, it is intended to be a fantasy ideal so compelling that Émile will avoid shallow entanglements and wait to bond permanently with the real person once he finds her. "We love the image we form for ourselves," Rousseau says, "far more than the object to which we apply it. If we saw what we love exactly as it is, there would be no more love in the world." The goal is to channel Émile's desires in a positive direction without attaching them prematurely to actual women. "Let us call your future mistress Sophie," the tutor says, "it's a name that augurs well." True enough, since the name derives from the Greek word for wisdom, and Rousseau must have remembered what he said to Mme d'Houdetot: "Sophie, my dear Sophie, permit me sometimes to give you a name that augurs so well."

After becoming disillusioned with sophisticated city girls, Émile and his tutor travel to a remote mountain valley, where they are received by a hospitable family, well born but not rich, whose daughter by happy coincidence is named Sophie. She herself has been yearning for an ideal mate, having fixated on the hero of one of Rousseau's favorite books, the *Telemachus* of Fénelon. In that work the virtuous prince shows himself susceptible to passion but is able to repress it under the guidance of his wise mentor, who is literally named Mentor, though in reality it is the goddess Athena in disguise. Rousseau may well have been interested in Athena as the avatar of reason with no sex life of her own.

The moment he sees this real-life Sophie, Émile is keenly interested, as he was programmed to be. Rousseau was well aware that he himself was smitten with certain female types in a very predictable way, and he regarded romantic love as a social creation, not a natural tendency in human nature. So that he won't be a victim of his passions, Émile has been carefully prepared to feel just the right amount of passion for just the right young woman.

He likes her looks, and when she speaks, her sweetness utterly demolishes him, as Mme de Warens had demolished Jean-Jacques long before. "At the first sound of this voice, Émile surrenders. This is Sophie, he doubts it no longer." But if love is sweet, it is also an infection, as the classical moralists always said. Sophie's charms pour like a torrent into the heart of the tongue-tied Émile, "and he gulps down the poison with which she is intoxicating him."

A discreet courtship follows, chaperoned by the tutor, who knows that postponement sharpens desire; at last, when Émile has proved himself a true Telemachus by showing generosity to some unfortunates instead of keeping an appointment with Sophie, she too is ready to surrender. She puts an arm (not both arms) around his neck, kisses him (on the cheek), and declares, "Émile, take this hand, it is yours. Be, when you wish, my spouse and my master; I will try to deserve that honor." Her father applauds and exclaims, "Again, again," at which she kisses Émile's other cheek and then hides blushing in her mother's arms. This little scene contains everything Rousseau wished for in love. Émile has had to do nothing overt to win Sophie, she yields of her own volition, and he will become her master while remaining her lover and friend.

What is startling in Rousseau's presentation of Sophie, not just to modern readers but to many of Rousseau's contemporaries, is the drastic difference between her upbringing and Émile's. He has been protected from socialization for as long as possible. She, on the other hand, has been socialized from the very beginning, with the customary female accomplishments of cooking, sewing, music, and so on. Rousseau actually declares that nature intends a girl to be preoccupied with clothes and adornment. "She is entirely in her doll, she puts all her coquetry into it, and she won't leave it like that; she's waiting for the moment when she can be her own doll." A submissive role for a wife is said to be obligatory, whether she finds it painful or not. "Made to obey so imperfect a being as man, who is often full of vices and always full of faults, she must learn early to endure injustice and to bear a husband's wrongs without complaint."

Published criticism of Rousseau's position did not appear until the end of the century, when Mary Wollstonecraft trenchantly exposed some of the assumptions in *Émile*. But plenty of women were already committed to feminist thinking, and most of the male philosophes, including Voltaire, d'Alembert, and Diderot, held views that were much more progressive than Rousseau's. His insecurity around women was certainly at the bottom of the superior attitude he affected, but Sophie's role in *Émile* was also part of a theoretical argument. Émile has been carefully raised in isolation from social conventions, and if he is to take his place in society, he needs a partner who already knows the rules by heart. Moreover, Rousseau was doing something quite new in proposing that women, presiding over the home, should be the emotional and moral center of the family. In the state of nature they would have enjoyed de facto equality, living independently, but in social life their physical weakness makes them vulnerable to male power unless they counteract it with a subtler power of their own. "A woman should reign in the family as a minister does in the state, getting herself commanded to do what she wants to do. In this sense, the best households are always the ones in which the woman has the most authority." By postulating a true partnership of husband and wife, each important in complementary roles, Rousseau was recommending what has been called the modern sentimental family, based on affective relationships and not just on hierarchical authority. In the context of eighteenth-century culture, a historian says, "Rousseau was influential because he offered women the better deal."

In a striking passage in *Émile,* Rousseau describes a dinner party at which the host carefully serves each guest in turn, hospitably enough, but with no awareness of their individuality. "But his wife divines what you are looking at with pleasure and offers it to you. While talking with her neighbor she has her eye on the far end of the table; she distinguishes between the person who is not eating because he isn't hungry, and the one who doesn't dare to help himself or to ask because he is awkward or timid. When they leave the table each one believes she has been thinking of him alone." Something very much like this happens during the famous dinner party in Virginia Woolf's *To the Lighthouse,* where it is Mrs. Ramsay's skill but also her burden to intuit the feelings of each guest. The timid and awkward Rousseau often had occasion to be grateful to such women.

What contemporary readers most remembered, in any case, was something more specific. Rousseau made a point of insisting that mothers should breastfeed their children instead of consigning them to wet nurses, and mothers listened. "We all said it," the great naturalist Buffon remarked, "but M. Rousseau alone commanded it and made himself obeyed." Long after his death, women still held him in high esteem on this score. Marmontel described a near-disaster his infant son suffered when given to a wet nurse who almost starved him, and said that his wife could never accept his constant denigration of Rousseau. "She had a weakness for Rousseau; she felt infinite gratitude for his persuading women to nurse their infants, and for taking care to make the first stage of life happy. 'One must forgive something,' she said, 'in one who has taught us to be mothers.'"

If the treatment of women in *Émile* did not elicit objections in Rousseau's lifetime, it was altogether different with his treatment of religion. Women, to be sure, were to receive religious instruction in the most conventional way. "Inasmuch as a woman's conduct is subservient to public opinion, her belief is subservient to authority. Every girl should have her mother's religion, and every wife her husband's." But Émile is completely shielded from religious questions until he is old enough to address them rationally, and when the time finally comes, much of orthodox belief turns out to be expendable for males. Rousseau's own beliefs rested on the inner intuition of conscience, and conscience did not require him to accept anything that didn't make sense. He later wrote, after his views had come under widespread attack, "I do not think one has to suppress objections that one can't resolve. That surreptitious cleverness has an air of bad faith that revolts me, and it makes me fear that at bottom there are all too few genuine believers." To his friend Moultou, who feared he was losing his faith, Rousseau said still more succinctly, "What I ask of you is not faith, but good faith."

The heart of Rousseau's thinking on religion is contained in the most controversial thing he ever wrote, a lengthy section of *Émile* entitled "The Profession of Faith of the Savoyard Vicar." The adolescent Émile needs a guide who can do for his soul what the tutor did for his mind. The abbé Gaime of Turin served as the principal model for this guide, together with the abbé Gâtier, with whom Rousseau studied briefly in Annecy. Both men had impressed him as deeply spiritual individuals who were misunderstood and persecuted by narrow-minded superiors. The Savoyard vicar of *Émile* gets into trouble, as Rousseau believed Gaime had, for falling in love with an unmarried girl instead of sleeping with married women, as priests were expected to do. Even his humble status is a challenge to contemporary values. Rousseau's friend Bernardin noted that it was highly unusual to idealize an obscure *curé*.

What does not interest the vicar is theological doctrine, and Rousseau saw this undogmatic attitude as crucial to restoring respect for religion in a skeptical age. The faith he settled on was his personal version of what was known as natural religion, a belief that the Bible and church authority were not the sole source of knowledge about God, whose goodness could be amply deduced from the visible universe. Another name for this belief was deism, affirming that a being of some kind must have made the world, but not necessarily a personal God who cares about individual humans and rewards or punishes their actions. Where Rousseau's deism differed from the usual kind was in its intense emotionality. Voltaire's was more typical, a theoretical construct more than a faith. As Voltaire's anxiety about the Lisbon earthquake suggests, his deity was philosophically indispensable — it wasn't just a quip when he said that if God didn't exist, it would be necessary to invent him — but he saw nature as an intricate clockwork, not a revelation of divine tenderness. Rousseau, very differently, needed faith as a bulwark against despair. "In any other system I would live without resources and die without hope, and be the most unfortunate of creatures. Let me hold, then, to the only system that can make me happy in spite of fortune and other men."

From Rousseau's point of view, the most important aspect of the vicar's teaching was an insistence on the immortality of the soul. In opposition to the materialist philosophy of the Encyclopédistes, he accepted a traditional dualism, in which soul and body were utterly distinct. He was scandalized by Diderot's willingness to reduce everything, the human mind included, to physical causes. Indeed, Rousseau was never really at home in his body, and preferred to think of it as a detachable encumbrance. "I look forward to the time," the vicar exclaims, "when delivered from the shackles of the body I will be *me* without contradiction or dividedness."

Benign though the vicar's faith may appear today, it would soon get Rousseau into deep trouble, and the attack would come from his right flank, not his left. The atheists and agnostics of the Enlightenment were careful to be covert. They cared little about theology, were concerned mainly to oppose the worldly power of the churches, and didn't mind what ordinary people believed as long as it kept them happy. "The various modes of worship which prevailed in the Roman world," Gibbon wrote, "were all considered by the people as equally true, by the philosopher as equally false, and by the magistrate as equally useful." Rousseau did care about belief, and there is some truth to Germaine de Staël's comment that he was "the only man of genius of his time who respected pious thinking," but he never for a moment considered being covert and was outspokenly dismissive of orthodoxy. As early as the 1740s he described some theological concepts with an almost Voltairean irony: "They speak of a God in three persons, no one of whom is the others, and each of whom is nevertheless the same God; of the mystery of the Eucharist in which a span of five feet is contained in a span of two inches; of original sin by which we are very justly punished for faults we didn't commit; and of the efficacy of sacraments that bring about spiritual effects through a purely corporeal application." In *Émile* the irony is gone but the distrust of dogma remains, and the whole argument is put provocatively into the mouth of a priest. Even the appeal to conscience looks suspect since, as Starobinski observes, the point about conscience was supposed to be that it transmitted divine warnings and reproofs. Rousseau's conscience could be relied on to approve almost everything he did.

As he put the finishing touches to *Émile,* Rousseau was oblivious to the distant thunder. Mainly he was concerned with the difficulty of adapting his hero to live in society, and he never felt satisfied that the story was finished. For years he tinkered with a strange, sad sequel entitled *Émile and Sophie, or, The Solitaries.* The premise all along had been that the intoxication of courtship would give way to something milder but more lasting. To defer that anticlimax and to shore up Émile's self-control, the tutor orders him to travel abroad for two years before getting married. "You have enjoyed more in anticipation," he explains, "than ever you will in reality. Imagination adorns what we desire and abandons it once it's possessed." Sure enough, in *The Solitaries,* after Émile and Sophie have been married for some years, things begin to unravel. Their child dies and they move to Paris, where they grow distant from each other and begin to have desultory affairs, which in Sophie's case leads to a shameful pregnancy. When Émile leaves her, she disappears. To support himself with a trade, he takes up cabinetmaking (in which the tutor has had him trained so he will always have a skill to fall back on). Some time later he takes ship at Marseille and is captured by pirates, who sell him into slavery in Algiers, in a story that almost begins to resemble *Candide.*

The manuscript breaks off there, although Rousseau often talked about how it might continue, and its significance is hard to determine.

Two points seem clear: even an ideal education cannot prevent society from ruining people's lives, and Émile's best hope lies not in relationships but in an inner tranquility like that of the ancient Stoics. What he needs above all is simply to live in the present moment, as natural man once did and as he himself did as a boy. In the most eloquent passage in the work, Émile says, "Delivered from the anxiety of hope, certain of gradually losing the anxiety of desire, and seeing that the past was nothing to me anymore, I tried to put myself entirely in the condition of a man who is beginning to live. I said to myself that in reality we never do anything but begin, and that there is no other connection in our existence than a succession of present moments, the first of which is always the one that is just happening. We die and we are born each instant of our lives." Remarkably enough, as time went on, Rousseau himself succeeded increasingly in living according to this ideal. There would still be years of suffering, but when they were over he would enter a final period of relative peace.

Émile had quite a vogue in the decades following its publication, and numerous attempts were made to raise children (usually boys) *à la Jean-Jacques.* A certain number of notable figures did emerge from this progressive experiment, for instance the physicist Ampère, who gave his name to the ampere, and the liberator Bolívar, who gave his name to Bolivia. More remarkably, Rousseau's advice to teach a boy a craft in case he ever fell from high status was so widely heeded that no less a person than the dauphin had his son trained as a locksmith. His ability to support himself in this way was never tested, since he lost his head at the guillotine (many of whose sponsors regarded themselves as disciples of Rousseau). And in truth, the implications of *Émile* were more radical than was recognized at first. Even though everyone agreed that Rousseau's educational program was ideal rather than practical, a writer just before the French Revolution saw perceptively that practicality was not the most important consideration. "A perfect Émile, such as is formed in this book, is doubtless not possible in the present state of society; but at least the old idol has been shattered."

Rousseau's other great work of this period, shorter and more technical but in the long run even more influential, was *The Social Contract.* For many years he read widely on politics and society, intending to produce a comprehensive survey of governments and institutions, and *The*

Social Contract was the residue of the big book that never got written. Social contract theories had been around since ancient times, but previous versions imagined a binding agreement between rulers and ruled. In older theories, the contract was between a people and a king to whom they swore allegiance. In more recent theories, the contract was an agreement among the citizens themselves, but they still undertook to obey a government empowered to make laws and enforce them. Their government might treat them badly, but they had agreed to the contract and had no right to complain. The philosophes' enthusiasm for enlightened despotism was grounded in this view. Theirs was a liberalizing program, working within existing institutions to improve them. But Rousseau didn't want to liberalize, he wanted to rethink political life at its very heart, and he couldn't help noticing that theorists always managed to justify the status quo. "The truth doesn't lead to fortune," he said sardonically, "and the people don't bestow ambassadorships, professorships, and pensions."

The challenge of *The Social Contract* is announced at the very beginning, in the most memorable of Rousseau's brilliant opening sentences. "Man is born free, and everywhere he is in chains." This sounds almost like the Marxist "Workers of the world, unite; you have nothing to lose but your chains," and Maurice Cranston (a distinguished political scientist as well as Rousseau scholar) states flatly that "the argument of the book is that men need not be in chains." But to put it like that oversimplifies Rousseau's subtlety and ignores his pessimism, for the sentences immediately following strike a very different note. "Each one believes he is the master of the others," Rousseau continues, "and yet he is a greater slave than they. How did this change come about? I do not know. What could render it legitimate? I believe I can answer that question." As the *Discourse on Inequality* makes clear, in society of any kind there will always be inequality and exploitation; these are facts of life, not mistakes that can be corrected. So the goal cannot be to throw off the chains, which is impossible, but to find a way to make them freely accepted rather than imposed.

In proposing a solution to this problem, Rousseau made two moves that were remarkably original. He invented a whole new way of thinking about the social contract and about the sovereign. Whereas previous writers thought of the contract as a historical event, Rousseau's innovation was to see it as unconnected with history. He understood it to mean an implicit understanding that exists continuously, here and now, as the shared commitment without which no system of any kind can be legitimate. And whereas previous writers referred to the king as the sovereign, a ruler whose subjects were literally "subjected" to him, Rousseau insisted that the people as a whole were the sovereign. This meant that whatever ruler they might have was simply a civil servant, and that there was no conceptual difference between monarchies and republics. The royal absolutism of France, the constitutional monarchy of England, and the republic of Geneva all had executives responsible for carrying out the will of a sovereign people. If today we hold this truth to be self-evident, it is in large part because we are heirs of Rousseau.

Government is still necessary, and although the people are the sovereign, they cannot make day-to-day decisions. But it is essential that no decisions be made without their understanding and approval, and for this reason Rousseau believed that a true social contract could exist only in small city-states like those of ancient Greece. A large nation like France was, by implication, simply illegitimate, and not just because it was a monarchy; Rousseau was equally critical of representative government. "The English people think they are free, but they are greatly mistaken. They are free only at the moment when they elect members of Parliament, and once those are elected, the people are slaves, they are nothing." And since even in a city-state total participation by the people is impracticable, the social contract remains an ideal against which existing compromises should be measured. "Taking the term rigorously, a true democracy has never existed, and never will."

Underlying Rousseau's theory was another radically new principle, that each individual is legally and morally the equal of every other. Geneva, small enough to qualify as a city-state, was nominally controlled by the General Council of all citizens, but the majority of residents did not possess citizenship, and in any case actual power was delegated to the Council of Two Hundred and by it to the aristocratic Little Council. As for France, which was huge, the largest country in Europe, it didn't even pay lip service to equality. The law there was a bewildering medley of some three hundred legal systems, and the population was divided into three distinct estates with different privileges, the nobles who governed and fought, the clergy who prayed and taught, and everybody else. Of course the category of everybody else was extraordinarily complex, ranging from merchants and bureaucrats, who had more real power than most nobles, down to the vast underclass of workers, who could barely earn a subsistence and were lumped together as "the poor."

The philosophes were far from sympathetic to the underclass. Critiquing Rousseau's political writings, Grimm expressed a typical view: "The generality of men aren't made for liberty any more than for truth, although they have those words constantly on their lips. These inestimable goods belong to the elite of the human race, on the express condition that they enjoy them without boasting too much. The rest are born to servitude and error. Their nature places them there and keeps them invincibly fettered. Read history and you'll be convinced of this." It is interesting that Palissot, a consistent enemy of the philosophes, had a much more generous opinion of Rousseau. "He is Demosthenes thundering from his rostrum. His moral doctrine is, from many points of view, true, sublime, sympathetic to the oppressed, and inexorable toward oppressors."

Grimm thought fetters were both natural and inevitable; Rousseau thought they were inevitable but very far from natural. It was common for progressives to call for governments of laws rather than men, but in Rousseau's opinion that was an inadequate solution, since as he says in *The Social Contract,* "The laws are always useful to those with possessions and harmful to those who have nothing." In an article in the *Encyclopédie,* he was still more explicit: "When a man of importance robs his creditors or gets up to other mischief, isn't he always sure of doing it with impunity? . . . When that man gets robbed, the police go into action right away, and woe to the innocents whom he suspects."

The heart of Rousseau's thinking, as Arthur Melzer and others have shown, is to honor modern individualism but at the same time to subject it to a devastating critique. Progressive writers in the eighteenth century thought that the good of the whole was served by competition among individuals, who would find that it was in their own interest to cooperate as well as compete, and Adam Smith extolled the virtues of sociability even as he called for a free market. Rousseau took a more pessimistic view of self-interest, much like seventeenth-century moralists such as Pascal, who said grimly, "Each *me* is the enemy of all the others, and would like to be their tyrant." But whereas Pascal ascribed selfishness to original sin, Rousseau ascribed it to society. Natural man experienced neither competition nor tyranny, but those days are gone forever, and the solution now is to counteract selfishness by creating a *volonté générale,* a general will that can transcend individual self-interest. In Rousseau's deliberately paradoxical formulation, "Each one, uniting himself to the rest, still obeys only himself and remains as free as before." Even more paradoxically, the group becomes a *moi commun,* a "common me."

Often enough, an individual's personal wishes run counter to the will of the whole. That is inevitable. What matters is that it *is* a will and that he accepts it. Rousseau has sometimes been blamed for contributing to modern totalitarianism, but nothing would have horrified him more. In his own time critics saw his thought as tending in the opposite direction, toward anarchy, or at best (as a Geneva conservative put it), toward "a monstrous democracy." This writer accurately recognized the key ideas in *The Social Contract* that would soon inspire a generation of revolutionaries: "that the people are the sovereign in every state, and that their rights are inalienable." A decade and a half later Thomas Jefferson would write, "We hold these truths to be self-evident, that all men are created equal, that they are endowed by their creator with certain unalienable rights."

In any case the concept of totalitarianism is anachronistic, since what Rousseau had in mind was altogether different from the surveillance and thought control of a modern police state. Instead, he was imagining voluntary commitment to the good of the community. The idea was to give people a reason to overcome their own selfishness by sublimating their separate egos in a kind of collective ego. In Rousseau's rather odd mathematical analogy, the city is the denominator and each citizen a numerator. No one can be a whole integer in himself, as natural man once was, but at least he can be a fractional part of a single whole, whereas in the modern world, as Christopher Kelly says, "human beings are numerators with no known denominator."

Rousseau never supposes that unity will be easily achieved, and in the most notorious pronouncement in *The Social Contract* he says, "In order that the social compact should not be an empty formula, it tacitly includes this commitment which alone can give force to the others, that whoever refuses to obey the general will must be compelled to do so by the whole body. This means nothing else than that they will force him to be free." (In French the expression is conveniently impersonal, *on le forcera d'être libre.*) That does sound totalitarian, but what it means is that in modern society people no longer know how to be genuinely free. Much of the time they are really injuring themselves as well as their fellows, like drug addicts who stop at nothing to get more drugs; there is nothing free about compulsively repeating destructive behavior. Nevertheless, "they will force him to be free" remains a disturbing indication of the limits of individualism. One can easily imagine, as one writer comments, that a young man in Rousseau's ideal city might get locked out at curfew and take to the road in search of a different kind of freedom. Indeed, the heart of his argument is that the freedom once enjoyed by natural man is utterly incompatible with social existence. The best that social man can hope for is the limited freedom appropriate to a citizen. Merging with the *moi commun,* he surrenders the autonomy of his personal *moi.*

Emotions are more powerful than reason, and the citizens of Rousseau's republic need to have an emotional belief in their system regardless of its faults. To create this, he imagined a lawgiver like Lycurgus, who was supposed to have bestowed a constitution on Sparta. That the modern world would heed such a person was, of course, improbable in the extreme, but that was precisely the point. At this point in the argument, religion again appears, in a way that could hardly fail to create trouble for Rousseau. He suggests that in order to reinforce belief in the system he has devised, the lawgiver should fabricate a "civil religion" while making people believe he has received it from on high. This new belief might take many different forms, but one form it should definitely not take is Christianity. In a startling analysis Rousseau argues that since Christianity regards another world as superior to this one, "I know of nothing more contrary to the social spirit." Moreover, since it preaches humility and submission, "its spirit is too favorable to tyranny for tyranny not to take advantage of it. True Christians are made to be slaves." That kind of claim would still be scandalous when Nietzsche made it a century later, and in the 1760s it was absolutely shocking. The point was not just that tyrants misuse religion for their own purposes; any preacher could have said that. The deeper implication was that the Christian view of life is simply wrong in blaming human nature for aggressive impulses that are actually the creation of society, and in counseling believers to submit to worldly authority while they await deliverance from this vale of tears. For obvious reasons, the section on civil religion in *The Social Contract* was condemned by established authorities everywhere. They were not pleased, either, that the atheist Wolmar in *Julie* approves of his wife's piety in terms that virtually anticipate Marx, as an "opium for the soul."

As for the political message of *The Social Contract,* it was a long time before it was clearly heard. As late as 1785 a writer surveying Rousseau's career said with contempt, "Most of it is a bad novel. It's quite incredible that a man who claims to be a philosopher and a friend of humanity should have published, in a monarchy, the claim that the only legitimate government is republican, that kings merely have a 'commission' and 'employment' in which they are 'simple officers of the people who execute in their name the power that the people has placed in them,' and that 'the people have the inalienable right to limit, modify, and take back this power when they please.'" Today these are the veriest commonplaces; in the eighteenth century they were bombs waiting to explode, and in 1789 they did. Two years later Louis-Sébastien Mercier published a book with the title *Rousseau Considered as One of the First Authors of the Revolution,* and soon the revolutionary leaders were hailing him as their prophet.

By then Rousseau had become a symbolic figure. There were so many sides to his thought that almost any group, from left wing to right, could claim him for its own. And the way he was viewed kept changing, of course. In 1791 a soldier of twenty-two entered (but didn't win) the Lyon Academy competition on the topic "What truths and sentiments are most important to inculcate in men for their happiness?" Remembering that a prize competition had launched Rousseau's career forty years before, the entrant paid tribute to *The Village Soothsayer,* "that masterpiece of music, or rather of natural feeling. Fear not that your soul will be softened by the tears you will shed. Oh no! It is the accent of virtue that makes them flow." A few years earlier, as a young cadet brooding on an unpromising future, he had written, in highly Rousseauian language, "Always alone in the midst of men, I return within myself to dream and to give myself up to the keenness of melancholy." The mood didn't last, and neither did the passion for Rousseau, for this was Napoleon Bonaparte, who soon decided that *The Social Contract* was no guide at all for gaining and administering an empire. But he did leave one memorable further comment when he visited Rousseau's grave. "It would have been better for the peace of France if this man had never existed. It is he who prepared the way for the French Revolution." His host responded in surprise, "I would have thought, Citizen Consul, that it was not for you to lament the Revolution." "Ah well!" Napoleon replied, "the future will show whether it might not have been best for the peace of the world if neither Rousseau nor I had ever existed."

As the final proofs of *Émile* and *The Social Contract* were being corrected and returned to the printers, Rousseau felt sure that his career as a writer was over, and not a bit too soon. A year earlier he had written to a friend, "Seeing men of letters tearing each other like wolves, and feeling the warmth die out that made me take up the pen when I was nearly forty, I have laid it down once more before the age of fifty, never to take it up again." His days as a theorist were over, that much was true. But a very different kind of writing lay before him, and plenty of it. His books had always been controversial, and soon he would find himself the target of vituperative personal attack. The defense of his character and values would become his obsession, and in due course — as no one could have predicted — he would invent modern autobiography.

The first prompting seems to have come from Rey, who had nothing more in mind than to add something new to the projected edition of Rousseau's works and thereby increase its value. He wrote at the end of 1761, "I venture to ask you something that I've been thinking about for a long time, and that would greatly please me and the public. This would be your life, which I would place at the head of your works." Rey also won Rousseau's gratitude at this time by conferring a pension of 300 livres a year upon Thérèse, to assure her subsistence in the event of his death. Rousseau's letter of heartfelt thanks has the additional interest of revealing the state of Thérèse's literacy: "She ought to write herself to thank you, and she wants to, but her pen has been so much neglected that she must apply herself all over again before you'll be able to read her writing. She'll begin, since your gift obliges her to, by learning to sign her name." Thérèse was not illiterate, but her letters (some of which survive) were so weirdly spelled that they were almost impossible to read.

More immediately, an occasion for autobiographical writing came from the official censor Malesherbes, who was genuinely concerned about Rousseau's emotional state and still more about his physical state. In November one of his catheters had broken off and could not be extracted, and Rousseau was sure that it would cause a fatal obstruction or at the very least promote bladder stones. During this time of high anxiety, he became alarmed when there were delays in getting back the proof sheets of *Émile* and conjured up a nonexistent plot by the Jesuits to prevent publication until his presumably imminent death, after which they would issue a spurious version of their own to defame him. Malesherbes succeeded in disabusing him of this fantasy, and wrote sympathetically to say that Rousseau's malady seemed to be mental as well as physical, and that his solitary way of life encouraged delusional thinking.

This well-intentioned hint inspired a series of four lengthy replies from Rousseau, published long afterward as *Letters to Malesherbes,* in which he insisted that solitude was his true vocation and that he had never been happier than at Montmorency. He rose at dawn, gave the morning to domestic tasks, hurried through lunch for fear that visitors would interrupt him, and spent the afternoon walking in the woods with his dog, Turc, as his sole companion. (The dog was originally called Duc, but Rousseau changed its name to avoid embarrassing the duc de Luxembourg.) By the time the *Letters* were written, incidentally, the faithful Turc had fallen ill and had had to be put down, much to Rousseau's grief.

Although the *Letters to Malesherbes* try to make a virtue of isolation, they betray a wounded spirit as well. "I have a very loving heart," Rousseau says, "but one that's able to suffice for itself. I love men too much to have to choose among them. I love them all, and it's because I love them that I hate injustice." To put it the other way around, "It is because I love them that I flee from them; I suffer their ills less when I don't see them." Even close friends almost always ended up disappointing Rousseau, and he lamented a few years later, "There is no place in my heart that has not been torn by some attachment." In truth, the vocation of

heroic solitude was a defensive retreat, and he knew it. He told Malesherbes, "Embittered by the injustices I've experienced and witnessed,
afflicted often by the disorder into which I was dragged by the example
of others and by the force of things, I began to scorn my era and my contemporaries, and feeling that I would never find a situation among
them that could satisfy my heart, I detached myself gradually from the
society of men and made another one for myself in imagination."

From the point of view of the philosophes with whom Malesherbes
was allied, this kind of withdrawal was unhealthy and self-destructive,
but in Rousseau's case, at least, it bore fruit. According to Freud, it is
precisely because the artist cannot bear the constraints of reality that he
transposes his desires into a fantasy realm and gains the mastery he
wants by creating a new reality of his own, the work of art. All of Rousseau's writings, from the very beginning, were works of art in that
sense, seeking to resolve his own deepest anxieties and yearnings. He
was acknowledging this when he described for Malesherbes the conversion experience on the road to Vincennes. "When I was least thinking of
it, I became an author almost in spite of myself . . . If I had written only
in order to write, I'm certain that no one would ever have read me."
Malesherbes understood very well that Rousseau's troubled spirit had
everything to do with his genius, and told Mme de Luxembourg that
his turbulent emotions were "the torment of his life, but the source of
his works."

Rey began to ship the *Social Contract* from Amsterdam in April
1762, and in Paris Duchesne had *Émile* ready a month later. (Mme de
Luxembourg had negotiated the exceptionally high price of 6,000 livres
to be paid to Rousseau for *Émile*.) And now the storm broke. Rousseau
was well aware that the "Profession of Faith" was provocative, and he
wanted it to be separately published outside France, but Duchesne refused. He did take the conventional precaution of claiming on the title
page that the book was published at the Hague by Jean Néaulme, who
had the rights to a Dutch edition, but nobody was fooled by that. *The
Social Contract* was still more objectionable, and there was never any
possibility of official approval for it. Grimm remarked that the only way
to get a copy was to go to Holland and bring it back in one's pocket. Despite the efforts of the authorities, however, clandestine copies soon began to spread; France was an absolute monarchy in principle but very

far from a police state in practice. As Leigh points out, this makes nonsense of the view long accepted by scholars, that the absence of the *Social Contract* from sale catalogues proves that it was little known. In fact very large numbers circulated illegally; Leigh estimates that within two years close to 20,000 copies were in print. As for *Émile,* it had already received permission to be printed in France, and although the censor Malesherbes now felt obliged to order that all copies be seized, he waited until Duchesne had had time to conceal them.

What Rousseau seems never to have understood, even in retrospect, was the ulterior motive of Luxembourg and Malesherbes in encouraging him to publish these inflammatory works. The meaning of Louis XIV's famous *"L'état, c'est moi"* was that power centered in the royal bureaucracy rather than in the patchwork of feudal dominions inherited from the Middle Ages. But when his five-year-old son succeeded him in 1715, a regent governed France and was forced to grant concessions to the aristocracy. As the decades went by (Louis XV reigned, fecklessly, until 1774), the nobles increasingly made gains against the crown. Many regarded themselves as progressives inspired by the Enlightenment, seeking not to bring back the Middle Ages but to confirm the separation of powers that Montesquieu had promoted in *The Spirit of the Laws,* and that would soon be invoked in the American constitution.

It was in this context that two noblemen of the very highest rank, the duc de Luxembourg and the prince de Conti, had taken an interest in Rousseau's political writings. Without question they liked him personally. But without question they also had an agenda of their own. Conti — a prince of the Bourbon blood and close adviser to the king on foreign affairs until Mme de Pompadour had him exiled from court in 1756 — and Luxembourg were among a growing number of aristocrats who were alarmed at the isolation of the monarchy and wanted the king to take advice from his nobles instead of hiding behind his professional bureaucracy. Malesherbes was very much in sympathy with this goal, which was why he tried so hard to get Rousseau's books published in France. His whole life was spent, he wrote later, "in what would be called in other countries the opposition party." Even with respect to Rousseau's "Profession of Faith," the implications were not just theological. The reactionary wing of the Church loyally supported royal absolutism, and the progressive aristocrats were eager to see its influence diminish.

In trying to make use of Rousseau, however, these grandees were terribly shortsighted. In the short run, they were pushing him out in front for a punitive response that was bound to come. And in the long run, as Pierre Serna observes, the *Social Contract* reflected a major shift in political thinking; later reformers would promote a concept of society in which birth was simply irrelevant. Looking back ruefully after the Revolution, the comte de Ségur thought that the nobles had been far too complacent in their indulgence of radical ideas. "Those were mere battles of pens and words that seemed incapable of doing the slightest damage to the superiority we enjoyed . . . Lacking foresight, we tasted, at one and the same time, patrician privileges and the pleasures of plebeian philosophy."

In addition to trusting his powerful friends, Rousseau had another reason for thinking himself safe: he confined his books to general principles and avoided involvement in French politics. Only a few months earlier, he had refused just such an opportunity, when a Protestant pastor named Rochette and some associates were imprisoned in the south of France for conducting clandestine services. (Protestants at this time comprised no more than 2 percent of the population and were often subject to official harassment.) Their supporters implored Rousseau to lend his eloquence to the cause, and he politely declined. He did not deny that the victims had received harsh treatment, but he showed no enthusiasm at all for defying authority. "To forbid assembly is unquestionably within the right of princes, and after all, those assemblies are not essential to Christianity, and one may abstain from them without renouncing one's faith." A year later Voltaire would take a very different line in the celebrated Calas affair, conducting a brilliant propaganda campaign to show how a Protestant had been framed, arrested, tortured, and executed as a result of religious bigotry. Of course there was less risk in rehabilitating the reputation of a dead man than in trying to get live ones out of jail. "The attempt to liberate a man from the hands of justice or its ministers," Rousseau went on to say, "even if he has been wrongly detained, is still a rebellion that cannot be justified, and those in power always have the right to punish it." A few weeks later the unfortunate Rochette was hanged.

Also, Rousseau had not forgotten that he had recently made his sole public comment on French politics and quickly regretted it. Étienne de Silhouette was driven from office as *contrôleur général* after an abortive attempt to limit the power of tax farmers and to find new ways of taxing the nobility. (It was in mockery of his paring down of expenses that comic portraits *à la silhouette* began to circulate, lending his name to a minor art form.) In an open letter to Silhouette that quickly became notorious throughout Paris, Rousseau solemnly wrote, "Deign, Monsieur, to accept the homage of a solitary who is not known to you, but who esteems you for your talents, respects you for your administration, and has done you the honor of believing that it would not be yours for long. Unable to save the state except at the expense of the capital city that has ruined it, you have braved the outcry of the moneymakers . . . The maledictions of rascals are the just man's glory."

There was no official reprisal, but as Rousseau admits in the *Confessions,* to circulate such a letter was extremely unwise. Many of his own personal relationships were with tax farmers, and still worse, he gave Mme de Luxembourg a copy of the letter before he discovered that she was one of those very "moneymakers" who had been involved in Silhouette's expulsion. Her only comment was to say dryly, "I find the letter to M. Silhouette very fine, but I fear he doesn't deserve it." To be sure, she concluded her letter reassuringly, "Adieu, Monsieur, no one in the world loves you more tenderly than I do," but Rousseau suspected that his faux pas had offended her deeply, and he resolved to leave French affairs strictly alone.

As soon as *Émile* and *The Social Contract* were in circulation, the authorities acted decisively, and for tactical reasons they pressed the religious case rather than the political one. By now the warning signs were unmistakable even to Rousseau, and he wrote to Moultou in Geneva, "They say that the parlement of Paris, to justify their zeal against the Jesuits, intends to persecute likewise anyone who doesn't think as they do, and the one man in France who believes in God must be the victim of the defenders of Christianity." The parlement (not to be confused with a parliament in the British sense) was one of a dozen such bodies throughout the country, a court of appeals controlled by powerful nobles. The one in Paris was sympathetic to the Jansenist wing of the Catholic Church and a center of opposition to papal interference. The

Jesuits, conversely, were much resented for their "ultramontanism," loyalty to the pontiff beyond the Alps. Having taken on the Jesuits in open battle — two years later they would be outlawed in France, and remain so until 1814 — the parlement needed to show that it still remained faithful to religion. Already, in 1759, it had succeeded in getting the *Encyclopédie* temporarily banned, and in Rousseau it found a convenient victim to continue its attack on liberal thought.

When Rousseau included the "Profession of Faith" in *Émile,* he thought he was defending religion against Enlightenment skepticism, and Diderot thought so too. As he wrote to his mistress, "He has the *dévots* on his side, and the interest they take in him is due to the bad things he says about the philosophes. Since they hate us a thousand times more than they love their God, they don't care that he has dragged their Christ in the mud, so long as he's not one of us." But they did care, and they were quick to strike. The Jansenists of the Sorbonne, who had great influence with the parlement of Paris, began issuing denunciations that were almost hysterical in tone. According to them *Émile* was filled with the poison of religion's enemies, who "think only of pillaging, massacring, burning, and ravaging." Rousseau became convinced that a pair of men who took up lodging next door in Montmorency — Thérèse called them contemptuously *commères,* female gossips — were Jansenist spies who climbed over a wall to look at his papers and even drafted a warrant for his arrest. A scholar who has explored the question thinks he was right.

On June 9 the parlement published a formal *arrêt,* or judgment, that enumerated the impieties of *Émile* and deplored Rousseau's brazenness in signing his name instead of observing the customary anonymity. "The author of this book having no fear of identifying himself, he cannot be too promptly hunted down, for it is important, inasmuch as he has made himself known, that justice make an example of this author and of those who may be shown to be involved in printing and distributing the book." Copies of *Émile* were to be "lacerated and burned at the foot of the great staircase in the courtyard of the Palais de Justice," and a warrant was indeed issued for Rousseau's arrest. Malesherbes had the power to approve a book for publication but not to prevent legal action against it, and from now on he kept completely out of sight.

The one consolation was that Rousseau had time to get away. His protectors had been forewarned, since the authorities were not eager to create a martyr and had small appetite for confronting a powerful duke and prince. Rousseau himself remained complacent almost to the end, brushing off increasingly urgent warnings. Just two days before the *arrêt* he wrote to an admirer, the marquise de Créqui, "Jean-Jacques Rousseau does not know how to hide. Besides, I assure you that it's impossible for me to conceive that a citizen of Geneva, printing a book in Holland, and with the approval of the Dutch Estates General, can be answerable for it to the Parlement of Paris." Mme de Créqui replied that his health would never stand up to imprisonment and that he had no choice but to flee.

The Luxembourgs were still more insistent, well aware that their complicity in publishing *Émile* would become known if Rousseau went to jail. Shortly after midnight on June 9, just hours before the *arrêt* was to be formally issued, Mme de Luxembourg sent her trusted steward La Roche to wake Rousseau at Montlouis with a note that read, "In the name of God come here. It's the greatest mark of friendship you could give me. La Roche will tell you my reasons for sending for you at night." She enclosed a letter from the prince de Conti reporting that bailiffs would appear that very day at Montmorency to arrest Rousseau, and that the best he could do was to secure a promise that if Rousseau had already left, he would not be pursued. Rousseau hurried to the château as requested and found the duchess greatly agitated, something he had never seen before. She and the duke pressed him more strongly than ever to leave France without delay, and so did Conti's mistress, the comtesse de Boufflers, who was also present.

Where to go was the question. Geneva might seem obvious, but Rousseau knew that the religious establishment there was deeply offended by *Émile,* and indeed both it and *The Social Contract* were publicly burned in Geneva a few days later. Mme de Boufflers urged England, since she was close friends with David Hume and could make arrangements through him, but Rousseau knew no English, and despite having invented the admirable Lord Bomston he had a low opinion of the country. An alternative in Switzerland quickly occurred to him. He had recently been corresponding with his old friend Daniel Roguin,

ROUSSEAU ABOUT TO ESCAPE FROM FRANCE

An artist's rendering of the emotional scene in the afternoon of June 9, 1762. At the left, the duc de Luxembourg anxiously pulls Rousseau, already equipped with overcoat and walking stick, toward the door, while he exchanges a last look and handclasp with the duchess. In the *Confessions* he says, "She embraced me several times with a sad enough expression, but I didn't feel in those embraces the firmness of the ones she used to lavish on me two or three years before." Two of the other ladies are the comtesse de Boufflers, mistress of the prince de Conti, who helped to negotiate Rousseau's escape, and Mme de Mirepoix, who surprised him by showing uncharacteristically warm emotion. The identity of the fourth woman in the picture is not clear; it is certainly not Thérèse, who was not present and would not have been elegantly dressed. The artist may have meant the dog to be the adored Turc, who in actuality had recently died, much to Rousseau's grief.

who had retired from banking in Paris, about paying him a visit at Yverdon, a pleasant town at the western end of the Lac de Neuchâtel. With no time to waste, that became his choice.

Back at Montlouis, Thérèse was terrified, believing that Rousseau had already been spirited away. La Roche brought her to the château, and when she saw Rousseau, "she pierced the air with her cries and threw herself into my arms." The scene was so moving, Rousseau says, that the duke himself shed tears. After reassuring Thérèse as best he could, Rousseau directed her to stay behind, since otherwise their property was likely to be confiscated; he promised to send for her as soon as he had a safe place of refuge. He didn't mention Yverdon so that she could truthfully say she didn't know where he was. He and the duke then busied themselves sorting through papers and burning any that seemed compromising. By late afternoon he was in the duke's cabriolet, traveling alone. On the road he passed the officers of the court on their way to the château. They saluted courteously but made no move to stop him, and his new life of exile had begun.

19

Exile in the Mountains

TRAVELING BY COACH, Rousseau made good time, and had only one real scare. At Dijon, the city that had launched his career as a writer by honoring the *First Discourse,* he was ordered to sign his name. He thought of giving as an alias his mother's maiden name, Bernard, but "my hand shook so much that I had to put down the pen twice, and finally Rousseau was the only name I could write." The anxiety was terrible. "The whole time I thought I could hear the police hot on my heels, and when a courier passed under my window that night, I believed at first he was coming to arrest me. What must the torments of crime be like, if persecuted innocence suffers like this?" The rest of the journey passed without incident, however, and he soon left France behind. "On reaching the territory of Berne I made the coach stop, got out, lay down, and hugged and kissed the earth. 'Heaven, protector of virtue,' I cried out in rapture, 'I praise you, I've reached a land of freedom.'" The postilion thought he was crazy.

The journey had one other interesting aspect. To distract himself from his sorrows and fears, Rousseau composed a short prose poem that elaborated on the biblical text he had been reading during his last night in Montmorency. He called it "The Levite of Ephraïm," and he said some years later, "If it's not the best of my works, it will always be the one I love the best." What it lacks in literary merit, which is pretty much everything, it makes up for in psychological interest. In the story Rousseau chose, from the end of the book of Judges, a Levite traveling with his concubine finds lodging with a kindly member of the tribe of Benjamin. But a gang of louts starts banging on the door — Milton, recalling the same story, called them "sons of Belial, flown with insolence and wine" — and they demand to be given the stranger so they can rape him. To avert this abomination, the host offers them his own virgin daughter, and then the Levite intervenes by surrendering his concubine. They abuse her so violently that she dies, after which the heartbroken Levite cuts her body into twelve pieces and sends one to each of the twelve tribes of Israel as a sign of the outrage. The Israelites muster an army, tens of thousands die on both sides, and the tribe of Benjamin is all but exterminated.

Rousseau seems to have believed that in retelling this appalling tale, he was counteracting the malice of his enemies by transforming sadism into the pastoral love story of the Levite and his concubine. He also added an ending in which the Levite and several invented characters reestablish harmony out of anarchy. But as critics have observed, deep anxieties were certainly involved. He might well have seen himself as a sacrificial victim, he had abandoned his own concubine to an uncertain fate, and the traumatic experience at the hands of the dirty "Moor" in Turin had left him deeply disturbed by the idea of homosexual rape. It may be relevant, too, that he emphasizes guilt for matricide. "Benjamin, sad child of pain, who gave death to your mother, from your own breast came the crime that destroyed you." It was common to refer to the youngest child in a family as the benjamin, and Rousseau was a benjamin who had caused his mother's death.

At Yverdon, twenty miles beyond the French border, Rousseau's old friend Daniel Roguin was eagerly waiting, and soon made him feel at home amid an entourage of charming nieces — his *roguinerie,* as he playfully called them. Unfortunately, the Swiss canton of Berne to which Yverdon belonged shared Geneva's aggressive Calvinism, and Rousseau was soon informed that he would have to leave. The neighboring principality of Neuchâtel (not part of the Swiss confederation until 1815) was somewhat more liberal. Like many another small state, it had changed hands often through the centuries, and since 1707 it had belonged to far-off Prussia, an allegiance preferred by its leaders to alternatives that might have led to annexation by France.

Frederick II of Prussia, who liked to be known as the Great, had been aggressively conducting the Seven Years War, but he saw himself as an artist and thinker and appreciated the chance to patronize a writer who was being persecuted by France. Rousseau, of course, was determined not to grovel. "I have said a good deal that is bad about you," he told the king (though it's not clear that the letter was actually sent), "and perhaps I will again. However, I have been driven from France, from Geneva, and from the canton of Berne, and I come seeking asylum in your territories." It appears that Frederick had not yet actually read anything by Rousseau, and when he did get around to *Émile* he was not pleased. "There are few solid arguments and much impudence, and this boldness that derives from effrontery is so irritating that the book becomes intolerable and the reader throws it aside in disgust."

But in the governor of Neuchâtel, through whom the royal approval was transmitted, Rousseau unexpectedly found a new patron and friend to take the duc de Luxembourg's place. George Keith — Rousseau pronounced it "Keet" and always addressed him as Milord — was quite a romantic figure. Now in his mid-seventies, he was the tenth (and, with no heir, the last) Earl Marischal of Scotland. As a young man he had fought under the great duke of Marlborough against Louis XIV. When George I became king, he joined the Jacobite rebellion of 1715, which sought to restore the Stuart pretender to the throne but ended in disaster. Condemned to be beheaded for high treason, Keith managed to escape to France, but his estates and wealth were confiscated. In 1719 he returned to Scotland, leading a force of soldiers in a small-scale rebellion that likewise ended in disaster. It does not appear that he distinguished himself; one of his colleagues wrote bitterly, "All we could make of my lord Marischal's ill-concerted expedition is to be shamefully dispersed at last." After hiding out for weeks in the Highlands he managed to reach France again, and a few years after that he was in Spain, taking part in an assault on the English garrison at Gibraltar. It was a disaster. "All we had gained," his brother James wrote, "was the knowledge that the place was impregnable by land."

By then George Keith was in his forties, described by an Englishman

GEORGE KEITH, MILORD MARÉCHAL
Notwithstanding his strong preference for informal simplicity, Keith is portrayed here with a majestic wig and a prominently displayed emblem of the highest British honor, the eight-pointed star of the Order of the Garter, with the cross of Saint George in the center and the motto *Honi soit qui mal y pense* surrounding it. To be named one of the twenty-five Knights Companion of the Garter was a signal confirmation of Keith's return to favor in his native land after a half-century of proscription and exile.

who knew him as "wild, inconstant, passionate; does everything by fits and starts; hath abundance of flashing wit; a thorough libertine, a hard drinker, a thin body, a middle stature, ambitious of popularity." He and his brother James continued on as soldiers of fortune for various continental powers, and James eventually became a field marshal under Frederick the Great. (The Scottish title "Marischal," incidentally, originally meant the same thing, but it had become a hereditary title rather than a military rank.) George joined James in Berlin, formed a close and lasting friendship with the king, and spent several years as Prussia's ambassador to France. Since 1754 he had been in semiretirement as governor of Neuchâtel, where he found the politics exasperating and the winters intolerable. He never married, though he adopted as his daughter a pretty Muslim Turkish girl named Emetulla who had been given him as a present after a battle. (Presumably she was intended for a concubine, but Voltaire — hinting that Keith's sexual tastes were either irregular or nonexistent — commented slyly, "It seems he doesn't have much use for her.")

Keith was a reader, and he admired Rousseau's *Discourse on Inequality* when it first came out. He was delighted to meet the author, and Rousseau was equally delighted when "I saw in Milord's keen eye a *je ne sais quoi* so affectionate that I immediately felt at my ease, and unaffectedly went to share his sofa and sit at his side." Before long Rousseau was describing him as "my friend, my protector, my father," and he wrote to Keith, "Milord, I have a heart constantly full of you; think sometimes of your youngest son." He declined an invitation, however, to take up lodgings in Keith's château near Neuchâtel, and made inquiries for a quiet refuge somewhere deep in the countryside. The solution came from Roguin's niece Julianne, a banker's widow from Lyon known as Mme Boy de La Tour, who was visiting Yverdon at the time. She happened to own an unoccupied house in a mountain valley, and it was agreed that Rousseau would settle there.

In early July, less than a month after arriving at Yverdon, Rousseau set out on foot for Môtiers in the Val de Travers in the foothills of the Jura Mountains. Traveling by road would have required a long detour, and as he nonchalantly remarked, "I had only to cross one mountain to get there." The steep and winding trail he took was at least twenty miles long, a reminder that despite constant complaints of ill health, he showed extraordinary stamina throughout his life.

Ten days later Thérèse arrived, to Rousseau's immense relief. He had written earnestly from Yverdon to say that she might feel a life of isolation and persecution was too much to endure. She replied in a very affecting letter, "My heart has always been yours and will never change, so long as God gives you life and me as well . . . I would go to join you

THE VAL DE TRAVERS

A view looking eastward some miles below Môtiers, where the narrow valley opens out toward Neuchâtel.

even if I had to cross oceans and precipices . . . It's my heart that speaks to you, not my lips." As always, her spelling was astoundingly phonetic, but the feeling was clear: *Monquer atous gour êtes pour vous e quies ne changeraes ga mes tan que dieu vous doneuraes des gour eamoiosies* ["mon coeur a toujours été pour vous et qui ne changera jamais tant que Dieu vous donnera des jours et moi aussi"]. Traveling alone, Thérèse had to fend off advances from some young men and was reduced to tears, but a kindly priest persuaded an official to warn that the men would be thrown off the coach if they misbehaved again. Rousseau later wrote him a letter of appreciation. When she reached Môtiers, "What emotions overcame us as we embraced! O how sweet are the tears of tenderness and joy!"

The environs of Môtiers were picturesque, described two years later by James Boswell as "a beautiful wild valley surrounded by immense mountains, some covered with frowning rocks, others with clustering pines, and others with glittering snow." But Boswell was an admirer of the Scottish Highlands, and Rousseau preferred more domesticated landscapes. "Grand though the spectacle is," he wrote to the duc de Luxembourg, "it seems rather bare. One sees very few trees in the valley, they grow badly, and they bear hardly any fruit. The mountains slope steeply and show gray crags in many places, and the darkness of firs breaks the gray with a cheerless tone." In the *Letter to d'Alembert* four years before, he had recalled wandering in these same mountains during his early stay in Neuchâtel and admiring the self-sufficiency of the farmers. "Today," he exclaimed in the *Letter,* "when I would bring different eyes to it, must I never see again that happy land?" Now he was indeed seeing it with different eyes. "I believed I would find again that which charmed me in my youth. All is changed. It's another countryside, another air, another heaven, and other men, and now that I no longer see my mountaineers with the eyes of a twenty-year-old, I find them greatly aged."

Môtiers itself was a rather unremarkable village of 400 people (Neuchâtel, the largest town in the region, had only 3,500). Most of the inhabitants were farmers, though a contemporary guidebook mentions some artisans, including several watchmakers, a jeweler, and a craftsman who made fire extinguishers. But by now Rousseau had little use for the kind of *métier* in which his forebears had earned their living. "The abundance of money and the scarcity of commodities," he complained, "make prices go up every day. Soon, if we want to live, we'll have to eat watches and textiles, since agriculture is absolutely abandoned for more lucrative arts."

Mme Boy's house was one of the oldest and most modest in Môtiers. A visitor sixty years later noticed that it was still roofed with planks rather than tiles, and the staircase was so awkward that one had to climb it on all fours. Rousseau and Thérèse climbed it every day, for someone else occupied the ground floor. Their quarters included a bedroom for each, a living room, a kitchen, and a wooden balcony (still there today), from which a waterfall could be seen and heard. According to an inventory after their departure, in the bedrooms were a curtained bed for Rousseau and a humbler one for Thérèse, a fir wardrobe, a few bookcases, a tall desk at which Rousseau wrote standing up, some straw-bottomed chairs, and a pair of chamber pots. The kitchen was well equipped, with a stove, a double oven with iron doors, and a roasting spit, and there were thirteen faience plates, two iron pots, an iron

THE VILLAGE OF MÔTIERS

Rousseau and Thérèse lived in the house at the right, which still stands, complete with their balcony on the second floor. It is accurately represented in this engraving from the 1780s, but artists who visited Môtiers after Rousseau made it famous could not resist romanticizing the landscape to suit his descriptions. The waterfall as shown here is grander than it really was.

broiler, a copper kettle, and a brass casserole, along with chairs, two tables, and "a bad footstool with no decoration." In the living room, in addition to the usual furniture, there was a spinet belonging to Mme Boy, evidently the miniature type that was just a keyboard, since it rested "on the arms of the armchair."

The most important room was the kitchen, for they took their meals seriously and Thérèse was a remarkably good cook. The local provisions were on the whole disappointing, though the wine was not. "In order to have bread that's edible one must make it at home, and that's the course I've taken with the help of Mlle Levasseur. The meat is bad . . . The wine comes from Neuchâtel and is very good, above all the red; for myself I stick to the white as much less harsh, cheaper, and in my opinion far healthier. No fowls at all, not much game, and no fruit, not even apples, only strawberries that are fragrant, abundant, and long-lasting." But much was achieved with these scanty materials. "It is

ROUSSEAU'S BALCONY
The balcony as it appears
today. The house is
now a small Rousseau
museum and bears a
plaque that reads: HERE
LIVED J.-J. ROUSSEAU,
FROM 10 JULY 1762 TO
8 SEPTEMBER 1765.

not possible," an appreciative visitor declared, "to do better than Mlle Levasseur. There were succulent vegetables and *gigots* of mutton raised in the valley on wild thyme, giving off a wonderful fragrance and roasted to perfection." When Boswell visited he was warned to expect a very ordinary meal but was gratified to be served a good soup, vegetables, a *boulli* of beef and veal, cold pork, pickled trout, chestnuts, and pears, along with red and white wine. Rousseau had a great fondness for coffee, too. It cleared his head and gave him energy, and he often got up to make it at two in the morning. His acquaintances were aware that good coffee was a very acceptable present; a gentleman in Provence sent some in a red silk bag, itself in a sheath closed with sealing wax, "and the whole thing wrapped in oilcloth for greater security."

Interesting visitors were one thing; the neighbors were another. In Montmorency Rousseau had made friends with many local people, but in Môtiers he mingled almost entirely with the *bourgeois* from Neuchâtel who had country places there, especially a charming woman in her twenties named Isabelle d'Ivernois. "She called me her papa, and I called her my daughter." Most of the villagers regarded him with suspicion as an interloper who enjoyed the protection of a foreign king and his widely distrusted administrators. Nor was fame any recommendation. A resident recalled long afterward that he was despised "because it was said that he wrote books."

Rousseau didn't make acceptance any easier when he adopted an exotic mode of dress that he had experimented with in Montmorency, where an Armenian tailor gave him the idea for a full-length robe, which would be convenient for his chronic urinary condition. He decided to have one made, and his letters to friends who were helping him complete the costume show a surprising interest in elegant adornment. When Mme Boy sent some fabric samples from Lyon, he replied, "It seems to me that the sample I marked was brown, whereas the background of this one is lilac, but that doesn't matter. In a fine lilac-colored caftan I'll look like a pleasant little fellow from Teflis or Erevan, which I believe will suit me very well." After much negotiation the outfit was ready, and Rousseau described it in loving detail to his Paris publisher, who wanted to have a new portrait engraved. "In all seasons I wear a cap with a border of fur four or five inches high, sometimes sable, sometimes gray squirrel or Tartar lamb's wool, etc. As for the garment, the dolman or under robe is always plain colored; the caftan or top robe is likewise plain in summer, but for winter I have a double one bordered with Siberian fox, and a cap with fur of the same kind." It may well be, as Frédéric Eigeldinger suggests, that the costume attracted disapproval not just for its strangeness, but also for the kind of ostentation that was regularly condemned by Calvinist preachers. In any case it was an overt symbol of differentness. Blake once wrote about himself, in lines that are highly appropriate to Rousseau as well,

> O why was I born with a different face
> Why was I not born like the rest of my race
> When I look each one starts! when I speak I offend
> Then I'm silent and passive and lose every friend.

Rousseau's solution was to emphasize his differentness and proclaim it a virtue.

From Mme Boy Rousseau also obtained a supply of silk in many colors and began weaving the laces that cinched up women's bodices. "They are intended for young women of my acquaintance who get married, on condition that they nurse their first child. Without that, no laces." The laces, of course, would be loosened interestingly when the nursing began. Isabelle's sister was one of the favored recipients and received a letter that became widely known: "Wear under happy auspices this emblem of the ties of sweetness and love with which you will hold your fortunate husband enlaced, and reflect that to wear laces fashioned by the hand that traced the duties of mothers is to commit yourself to fulfilling them."

The lace-making attracted even more attention than the robe, and Rousseau commented explicitly on his newly feminized dress and avocations. "I am trying to lose all memory of the past. I have adopted a long robe, and I'm making laces: there you see me more than half a woman, and if only I had always been one!" In a quip that was much quoted at the time, he observed, "I thought as a man, I wrote as a man, and they disapproved; I'm going to turn myself into a woman."

Perhaps also these new practices were intended to divert attention from the fact that Rousseau was living with an unmarried woman — no great problem in Paris but a potential source of scandal in the conservative Swiss countryside. The story he apparently encouraged was that Thérèse was the daughter of an impoverished man of letters who had committed her to his protection at his death, but this fooled no one. Within a year the villagers thought she was pregnant (probably she was putting on weight), and they openly expressed contempt. "Their curious glances, their brutal double-entendres, and their stupid whispers soon made me guess what was going on." Rousseau complained to Mme Boy of "poisonous tongues that distill more venom than all the serpents of Africa," and he concluded grimly, "With the exception of a very small number of people, I regard Môtiers as the vilest and most venomous place that one could inhabit." He began to make inquiries about other places to live, but none of them seemed to work out.

There was one resident of Môtiers who had to be propitiated right away, and fortunately he was eager to be. It was crucial that the author of *Émile* be accepted by the local minister as a member of his congregation. Frédéric-Guillaume Montmollin was more than ready to have a celebrity under his pastoral care and to win praise for arguing him back to orthodoxy. Montmollin had intellectual pretensions and liked to be called "the professor," on the strength of a chair he hoped to occupy in an as yet nonexistent university of Neuchâtel. Eager to be accommodating, he accepted at face value Rousseau's claim that the religious criticisms in *Émile* had been aimed entirely at Catholics and atheists, and got him to declare in writing, "I am attached in good faith to this true and holy religion, and will continue to be to my dying day." Rousseau was then permitted to take communion, and the congregation saw him in tears as he came away from the holy table. So far so good. Montmollin even lent Thérèse his own carriage so she could attend mass at the nearest Catholic church, just across the French border. He was immediately under scrutiny, however, from his colleagues in the ministry, and he began pressing Rousseau for a second letter that would go into theological detail. This Rousseau firmly refused to provide.

The stage was set for trouble, and before long there came a blow, but of a different kind. Fed up with the pettiness of Neuchâtel affairs, Keith left. His plan was to settle in Scotland, having recently made his peace with the British throne and secured the right to return. Rousseau had known him for less than a year, but they had become close friends. Like the duc de Luxembourg, Keith appreciated being treated simply as a human being by a person of integrity (Frederick's brother said, "Rousseau, and Rousseau alone, says only what he thinks"). Every couple of weeks Rousseau made the fifteen-mile journey on foot to Keith's lakeside château, where he enjoyed the company of a rather exotic ménage; in addition to the Turkish daughter, the servants included another Turk, a Negro, and a Kalmuk. Keith affectionately called Rousseau *mon fils le sauvage,* and they began to take seriously a notion of settling down with Hume at Keith Hall in Scotland, growing their own vegetables, and eating trout and salmon from the river ("David will pay for the sirloins because he's the one who eats them").

However much Rousseau may have respected Keith's decision to leave, he had to feel that yet another father figure was deserting him. More immediately, his security in the territory of Neuchâtel had depended greatly on the presence of its now absentee governor. Once Keith was gone, his subordinates were in a weak position to protect Rousseau. Moreover, Rousseau rejected a chance to improve his position by accepting largesse from Frederick, to whom he wrote pointedly,

"You want to give me bread; aren't there any of your subjects who lack it?" He also suggested rather daringly that it was time for the king to put away the sword, and to Keith he expressed this more sharply: "Let him make a glorious peace, reestablish his finances, and revive his exhausted territories. If I'm still alive, and if he has the same good intentions toward me, then you'll see whether I'm afraid of his benefactions." Keith replied dryly that he didn't expect to be alive himself when all of that came to pass, but he duly forwarded Rousseau's letter to the king, and it remains to this day in the German national archives. Frederick told Keith with grudging admiration, "One must admit that disinterestedness could not be pushed further than he has done, which is a long way toward virtue, if not virtue itself." At this point Rousseau did accept a small annuity from Keith but refused to be remembered in his will, to ensure that he could have nothing to gain by his death.

Rousseau repeatedly claimed that his days as a writer were over, and one condition of Frederick's approval of his residence there was a tacit understanding that he was through with controversy. The impulse to defend himself, however, was irresistible. In March 1763 Rey brought out a work that Rousseau had composed in great secrecy, a *Letter to Christophe de Beaumont,* responding to the pastoral letter in which the archbishop of Paris had prohibited the reading of *Émile* on the grounds that it contained "a very great number of propositions that are false, scandalous, full of hatred against the Church and its ministers, derogating from the respect due to Holy Scripture and Church tradition, erroneous, impious, blasphemous, and heretical." In his reply Rousseau defiantly reiterated the very points that had caused *Émile* to be condemned: man was naturally good, Christianity didn't need the support of miracles, and children shouldn't parrot doctrines they can't understand. To publish again on this subject was asking for trouble, but as one eighteenth-century commentator observed, "A genuinely apostolic quality of Jean-Jacques was his love of persecution." In the *Letter to Beaumont* Rousseau said darkly, "I have been surrounded by spies and ill-wishers, and the world is full of people who hate me on account of the evil they themselves have done me." It was a note that he would sound increasingly in the years to come.

Pointedly addressing the prelate by his long string of pompous titles, Rousseau demanded, "What common language can we speak? How can we understand each other?" And after comprehensively reviewing his religious position and the injustice of the treatment he had received, he concluded, "Monseigneur, you have insulted me publicly, and I have just proved that you have slandered me as well. If you were a private individual like me, I could have you cited before an impartial court . . . but you hold a rank that dispenses you from being just, and I am nothing." This was strong talk, and it created a sensation in Paris. "Whatever they may say," d'Alembert commented, "it's no bad thing that a poor devil, retired to Môtiers-Travers, should speak some truths to these men who think their status gives them the right to say and do everything." Even Grimm put sarcasm aside. "In this piece there are passages of great eloquence and reasonings of great power, and what is more singular, a lightness of wit that doesn't belong to the Citizen of Geneva, for he has always been ponderous when he wanted to be witty." As for Rousseau's religious position, Grimm, who had none himself, was severe but accurate. "What is no less singular, but more in keeping with the author's character, is that he declares in the face of heaven and earth that he is a Christian to the bottom of his soul, in a piece of writing in which he exposes the most dreadful difficulties for Christianity and revelation."

Meanwhile, Rousseau's Genevan friends were laboring to have him reinstated there, as part of their campaign to curtail the power of the governing oligarchy. A long and tortuous struggle developed between a party known as the *représentants,* spokesmen for the middle class who were presenting remonstrances to the Little Council, and the *négatifs,* members of the council who denied or "negated" the public's right to submit complaints. Among the most active of the *représentants* were Guillaume-Antoine Deluc, a passionate supporter of the cause who constantly exhorted Rousseau to fight the good fight, and his old friend Moultou, who hailed the *Letter to Beaumont* rapturously. "O my dear, my very dear fellow citizen, what a book! What soul! What candor! What sublimity!" But the Geneva authorities immediately banned it, on the grounds that it cast doubt on articles of faith and besides was insulting to a distinguished archbishop. (Another friend of Rousseau's commented disgustedly that they were so anxious to observe good manners that instead of saying with Christ "Get thee behind me, Satan," they would probably say "Monsieur Satan.")

This new rejection so infuriated Rousseau that in May 1763 he formally renounced the Geneva citizenship that he had won back in 1754, shocking his supporters, who would now find it much harder to use him against the Little Council. His action, one of them told him grimly, "struck me like a thunderbolt, and I don't understand it at all." Still, they had to recognize a nobility in his giving up the status that was fundamental to his self-image. His enemies, meanwhile, simply gloated. "Rousseau is no longer a fellow citizen," crowed Théodore Tronchin, the doctor who had treated Mme d'Épinay; "his abdication has been the last gasp of his pride, or at least takes it to the limit."

Rousseau's involvement in Genevan affairs was not entirely over, but it receded from the center of his life. He was making new friends whose focus was in Neuchâtel, including Abram Pury, a retired colonel who had a country retreat — he called it his *vacherie* or cowshed — at nearby Monlési. At Pury's house a still more important connection was formed, with Pierre-Alexandre Du Peyrou, who would remain a steadfast friend and the most reliable of Rousseau's literary executors. Du Peyrou had had an exotic early life. His French Protestant family had emigrated to Holland and then to South America, where they became fabulously rich. He himself was born at Paramaribo in Surinam in 1729. At the age of six he was sent to study in Holland, and when his father died and his mother remarried, she moved to Neuchâtel, her new husband's hometown. Du Peyrou was only nineteen when he settled there for life, but he was never really accepted by the locals, both because he spent outrageously (some 20,000 livres per year, and his palace cost a million livres and took years to build) and because he was a freethinker with illegitimate children here and there. Someone who knew him later on said that he remained a stranger to the mores of Neuchâtel, "disposed to believe himself superior through the splendor of his fortune and his philosophical enlightenment." Despite his many advantages, Du Peyrou was awkward and diffident, in part because he was hard of hearing, and he was easily dominated by the forceful Pury, whose young daughter he eventually married.

Rousseau had many other visitors, a steady stream of them, which caused a good deal of annoyance in little Môtiers. Often they annoyed Rousseau as well, but occasionally someone turned up who genuinely appreciated his writings. One such was a pastor named Jacob Wegelin,

PIERRE-ALEXANDRE DU PEYROU

This portrait of Du Peyrou was painted not long after Rousseau's time in Môtiers. Although fabulously wealthy, Du Peyrou has had himself depicted in simple costume, with an expression that perhaps suggests his social awkwardness (due in part to deafness). Eventually, through no fault of his own, his relations with Rousseau became badly strained, but he remained loyal to the end and was the most faithful of Rousseau's literary executors.

who was impressed by the unforced originality of Rousseau's conversation and by his independence of mind on every topic that came up. "All of it flowed from a full spring, and all of it was felt and thought for himself, not embellished with borrowed blossoms or washed with commonplaces. His own spirit was woven completely into his learning and experience." But Rousseau commented sadly that it was his very differentness that had created enemies. "I didn't intend to teach, I only wanted to express my opinion, but people can't tolerate that. They believe their understanding is being slandered if someone thinks differently from them, and they avenge themselves on him with hatred and injustice."

Other visitors were youthful enthusiasts who hoped for a life-changing experience. When a young minister from Geneva named Pierre Mouchon turned up unannounced with a couple of companions, Rousseau cut short a visit with Keith to hurry home and entertain them, and he was far different from the misanthrope they expected to meet. "To a mild countenance he joins a gaze full of fire, with eyes of an unequaled vivacity, and when a subject that interests him comes up, his eyes, his mouth, his muscles, and his hands all speak for him. It would be very wrong to imagine him a troublemaker or perpetual censor; far from it! He laughs with those who laugh, he banters, he chats with children, and he jokes with his housekeeper, Mlle Levasseur." Back home, Mouchon wrote to assure Rousseau that he was "the father of my soul" and had effected "an epoch in my life." (To some extent, of course, emotions like these were self-induced. The young intellectual Suzanne Curchod commented that when Moultou and another friend rhapsodized about Rousseau, "they make me die laughing. I beg Rousseau's pardon, but I think I'm watching a pair of drunks sobbing with joy as they embrace each other.") When Rousseau sent Mouchon a friendly reply, the young man was utterly overcome, expressing the adoration that admirers of both sexes often felt. "I think only of you, I take pleasure only among your friends, I read only your pages, I converse only about you. I wish souls had the ability to interpenetrate like two fluids that merge and are confounded in each other."

Rousseau wished the same thing, though not with respect to Mouchon. In the spring of 1763 an interestingly mysterious young man took up residence in the local inn, with the avowed intention of getting to know Rousseau. He called himself the baron de Sauttern and explained that he was a Hungarian officer fleeing religious persecution on account of his Protestant faith. "He was tall and well formed, with attractive features and gentle and sociable manners . . . great personal cleanliness, extreme modesty in speech, and in short all the marks of a well-born man." Rousseau fell for him heavily. "My heart cannot give itself halfway. Soon he had my complete friendship and confidence, and we became inseparable." They took long walks and had long conversations, which had to be in Latin, since the newcomer knew no French.

Almost immediately Rousseau began to receive warnings that this new friend might be a spy of some kind, and he made efforts to confirm his identity, but nothing would shake his trust. One thing he was always vain about was his ability to read a person's character. But while it was true that Sauttern wasn't a spy, he wasn't Sauttern either. He was Jean-Ignace Sauttermeister von Sauttersheim, a clerk rather than an officer, fleeing Hungary only to escape enormous debts.

It was quite some time before Rousseau found out any of this, and meanwhile he was enchanted with his disciple. "He told everyone, and made me understand too, that he came to Neuchâtel only on my account, to shape his youth toward virtue by associating with me." A scholar who has pondered this curious relationship comments that Sauttersheim presented himself as an Émile seeking a mentor. Far from perceiving the relationship as homoerotic, Rousseau thought of it as altogether different from the wounding passion of love, much as he made Bomston say to Saint-Preux, "The reign of love is past, let the reign of friendship begin!"

Sauttersheim left abruptly after a few months, and an unpleasant revelation soon followed. While staying at the inn, he had gotten a servant pregnant — thus his sudden departure. Rousseau's first reaction was to deny categorically that Sauttersheim could have done such a thing, since he was gentlemanly and clean, while the woman was a *vilaine salope,* a nasty slut. He told Roguin that his friend had "morals of the purest," and it was inconceivable that he could have gotten involved with "the foulest stinking bitch, the most hideous monster that Switzerland ever produced." This extreme reaction is strange, to say the least, and although nothing is known of the woman's previous life (her name was Marie Lambert), when she was interrogated in the very midst of her labor pains, she swore that she had slept with no one but Sauttersheim, and he then wrote to admit his guilt.

The whole business was extremely damaging to Rousseau's reputation in Môtiers, both because his friend had flouted the puritanical mores of the region and because he had taken it for granted that the unknown foreigner was telling the truth and the local woman was lying. He was profoundly embarrassed, and seems to have helped Marie Lambert financially, though it isn't clear whether she was being sarcastic or grateful when she named her baby Jean-Jacques. As for Sauttersheim, who wrote imploring forgiveness, Rousseau told him coldly that he had no intention of resuming the friendship.

And then there was James Boswell, future author of the *Life of Johnson,* aged twenty-four, charming, willful, and self-satisfied in an insecure sort of way. He paused only briefly in Môtiers during a tour of Europe in December 1764, but he had a history of spaniel-like devotion to admired elders, and he would certainly have stayed on as another Sauttersheim if circumstances had permitted. Though a casual if not superficial reader, he admired Rousseau's books and prepared himself for weeks in advance as if for a confessor. "I swore solemnly neither to talk as an infidel nor to enjoy a woman before seeing Rousseau." Access to the great man should have been easy, since Boswell had a letter of introduction from Keith, with whom he had traveled from Scotland to Potsdam, where Keith had decided to live after all. But since Boswell's anxious narcissism required repeated proofs of his innate appeal, he preferred to invade Rousseau's privacy on his own terms. At the Môtiers inn he drafted and redrafted a letter in which he declared, in clumsy but serviceable French, that he was a Scottish gentleman from an ancient family with "a feeling heart and a lively but melancholy spirit." This was language calculated to appeal to Rousseau, as was the testimony that he had won yet another disciple. "If all that I have suffered does not give me singular merit in the eyes of Monsieur Rousseau, why was I made as I am? Why did he write as he has written?"

Rousseau took the bait, sending back a note to say that he was unwell but could permit a brief visit. Noting as he entered that Thérèse was "a little, lively, neat French girl," Boswell immediately became familiar with his host. "I had a free air and spoke well, and when Monsieur Rousseau said what touched me more than ordinary, I seized his hand, I thumped him on the shoulder. I was without restraint." Boswell was behaving, in fact, like a young Diderot. The conversations that followed were not especially remarkable — Boswell's French wasn't fluent enough — and Rousseau kept trying irritably to get rid of him. But he did elicit one memorable remark: "I have no liking for the world. I live here in a world of fantasies (*chimères*), and I cannot tolerate the world as it is." Rousseau was remembering *Julie,* in which his heroine tells Saint-Preux that the land of chimeras is the only one worth living in.

During the long winters Rousseau was often unwell, though the nature of his condition is unclear. Perhaps it was partly psychosomatic, as had been the case in Chambéry. He told Moultou, "Day and night I never have a single instant without suffering, which is driving me completely out of my mind." When he could, he would deliberately work up a sweat by splitting firewood, but often he felt too weak for that. On one occasion he drew up a will, expecting to die at any moment. And indeed the cold was awful. The winter of 1762–63 was one of the most brutal of the entire century throughout Europe (the Thames and the Seine both froze). On the last day of April Rousseau complained that it was still snowing "and I feel in every way that there is no more springtime for me." On the same date in 1764 he was similarly confined by snow, and 1765 was no better. In late February he complained that he had been imprisoned by biting cold for four months "without setting foot in the street."

Once warm weather returned, Rousseau's spirits rose, as they always did, and he resumed his wanderings in the hills. It happened that Du Peyrou was an enthusiastic amateur botanist, and under his influence Rousseau began to take a serious interest in an avocation that had bored him back in Chambéry. Botany was the favorite pastime of a surprising number of people in the eighteenth century. It was a branch of science that required no technical training, gave pleasure to gardeners, and provided an agreeable hobby in which specimens of plants and flowers could be collected, dried, and pressed into albums. Rousseau sent for books and equipment and took instruction from a skilled botanist named Jean Antoine d'Ivernois, Isabelle's uncle. He began corresponding on the subject with Malesherbes, who, having lost his position as censor when his father the chancellor fell into political disfavor, was living on his rural estate. (It is interesting, incidentally, that Duchesne and his associate Guy went right on selling *Émile,* taking care merely to include a false title page. As Leigh says, this lends credence to the suspicion that the 1762 prosecution was mainly intended to scare Rousseau out of the country.) Memorizing the names and attributes of hundreds of plants became Rousseau's new passion, enjoyable on multiple counts: it was knowledge for its own sake, an occasion to be outdoors, and a refuge from controversy. He told Malesherbes, "I never get a virtuous or useful idea without seeing the gallows or the scaffold before me. With a Linnaeus in my pocket and hay in my head, I hope not to be hanged."

A particularly enjoyable excursion had as its goal a mile-high moun-

VIEW FROM LE CHASSERON

The view to the north from the summit of Le Chasseron (elevation 5,300 feet). Though he complained constantly of ill health, Rousseau had no trouble ascending this imposing peak "like a goat."

tain called Le Chasseron. A young friend named François-Louis d'Escherny left a lengthy account of the trip. A group of five set out with a mule laden with bedding and provisions, including pâtés and roast fowl. Rousseau, as eldest, was the captain, charged with maintaining good discipline. A doctor and justice of the peace named Clerc took care of the supplies, Colonel Pury handled the compass, Du Peyrou carried the *herbiers* in which plants would be preserved (some of Rousseau's survive to this day, beautiful books of pressed specimens), and d'Escherny made fires and prepared coffee. At the summit, which Rousseau reached nimbly while the others struggled behind, they ate lunch while admiring the expansive view, and it struck d'Escherny that despite Rousseau's complaints of poor health he seemed exceptionally vigorous and cheerful. In the evening they found a chalet belonging to some makers of Gruyère cheese, from whom they got a wooden pot of cream that sent Rousseau into ecstasies of appreciation (when he put it in his coffee he added a huge helping of sugar). They spent the night in

THE PERIWINKLE
A page from an opulent
edition of Rousseau's
introduction to botany
that was published in the
early nineteenth century.
From bottom to top, it
shows two examples of
hemp, a castor oil plant,
and a periwinkle, the sight
of which provoked a
reminiscence of Chambéry
when Rousseau was bot-
anizing with Du Peyrou.

a barn on an immense heap of hay, and when Rousseau claimed the next morning that he hadn't slept a wink, the colonel retorted indignantly, "My God, Monsieur Rousseau, you amaze me! I heard you snoring all night long. It was I who never closed my eyes."

On one of his rural walks, Rousseau had a memorable flashback of the kind that would nowadays be called Proustian. He bewildered Du Peyrou by exclaiming joyously, "Oh look! There's some periwinkle!" He had suddenly remembered Mme de Warens pointing out periwinkles on their very first day at Les Charmettes, and he was plunged nearly thirty years into the past. The experience was all the more poignant since he had recently learned that she had died, in Conzié's words "overwhelmed with maladies and poverty, and abandoned by unjust mankind." Rousseau wrote back to assure Conzié that he was eager to revisit Chambéry "to cover with flowers the tomb of that incomparable woman whose eyes you closed." Eventually he did make the trip, but his feelings at that time are not recorded.

A more painful loss, at this stage in Rousseau's life, was that of the duc de Luxembourg, whose worsening state of health he had been following with alarm. "I made one friend among the great," he told Deleyre; "it was he who stood the test, and death has just taken him from me . . . I have lived too long." To Mme de Luxembourg he sent strangely inept condolences, ending with amazing tactlessness, "How much more have I to lament than you!" In a letter to her steward La Roche he explained the logic, such as it was. "I feel Mme la Maréchale's grief by my own, but she does not lack for consolations, whereas I am abandoned by everyone and remain alone on the earth, overwhelmed by woes, without friends, resources, or consolations." This was at a time when Thérèse continued to minister to his needs and when Roguin, Moultou, Du Peyrou, and (from afar) Keith were only the most prominent among a host of friends and admirers. Rousseau could not help feeling ashamed when the duchess wrote back, "In God's name, in my terrible misfortune don't burden me with your indifference! Be sure that I will always love you most tenderly."

More than ever, Rousseau threw himself into correspondence. In addition to keeping up with numerous friends and acquaintances, he had to deal with an endless succession of complete strangers who wrote to ask his advice, a consequence of fame that had been gratifying in Montmorency but by now was exasperating. It has been calculated that he received communications from over two hundred people during the two and a half years at Môtiers, and no fewer than 850 letters by Rousseau himself have survived, an average of five per week.

Rarely, a stranger would arouse genuine concern. An unusually thoughtful letter came from a woman in Paris who identified herself only as "Henriette." Her identity has never been traced, though her correspondence ended up in the great Rousseau collection at Neuchâtel. She was subject to what today would be called depression, which she described in harrowing detail. "The moment of waking up is the most dreadful of my existence. I feel a sharp pang in my heart that wrenches me from sleep, a piercing shaft of pain shatters the numbness of my senses, and the fear and terror of awakening completes it . . . A thousand gloomy and confused ideas gather in a thick cloud that seems to envelop me. I try to push them away, I struggle, I look around, I ponder everything near me, and I see nothing to console me." Rousseau replied sympathetically but declared that he found her case puzzling, since it was so remote from his own experience, and his reaction makes one realize that despite all his complaining, he never suffered from true depression. "You are a distressing and humiliating enigma to me. I believed I knew the human heart, and I know nothing of yours. You're suffering and I'm unable to relieve you." When Henriette wrote back, he neglected to answer.

With one other person the exchange of letters was so extensive that it could fill a book, and in fact it has, three hundred pages long. When Rousseau was still at Montmorency, a pair of Parisian ladies wrote to him, coyly calling themselves Julie and Claire. Claire soon dropped out, but Julie, who eventually revealed herself to be Marianne Alissan de La Tour, kept up a correspondence with him for many years. She was fifteen years younger than Rousseau, childless and separated from a dissolute husband; she seems never to have taken lovers, and the editor of the correspondence suggests that this may have been her one great affair. It was always she who took the lead, demanding attention, insisting on using first names, rebuking Rousseau if he seemed indifferent, and behaving altogether like a grown-up version of imperious little Goton. Of course the whole thing was a game. "To write to you more often," he said after one spat, "would no doubt be a very pleasant occupation for me, but then I would lose the pleasure of seeing the prodigious variety of elegant expressions with which you reproach me for the rarity of my letters." All the same, when things started to go badly in Môtiers, he found he was grateful for her attention. "You have a very unhappy friend," he told her, "but you will have him forever."

And what of Rousseau's publications? He had vowed not to attempt any new ones, but he still had some unfinished projects. One was a long-planned edition of his complete works, to be brought out either by Rey or by Du Peyrou, who believed for a while that he could get permission to print it in Neuchâtel. The motive was mainly financial, to secure an adequate income for old age. In time Duchesne did publish an edition of the works in Paris; it was not the impressive standard edition

Rousseau was hoping to create, but it did augment his savings. He was also making notes for the memoir that would introduce the projected collection, and he labored on the *Dictionary of Music,* which was sent off to Duchesne in 1764 and eventually came out in 1767. He always spoke disparagingly of this work, but it was actually an impressive achievement. Far from simply reprinting his *Encyclopédie* articles, he rewrote them and added five hundred entirely new ones. And his thinking on music had deepened since the days of Paris polemic. In particular, he was no longer wedded to the idea that music needed language to be expressive. "It is one of the great advantages of the musician," he now wrote, "to be able to paint things that cannot be heard, whereas it is impossible for the painter to paint what cannot be seen . . . Sleep, the calm of night, solitude, and even silence enter into the tableaux of music." When the *Dictionary* was published, one reviewer said, "Several articles are treated with a profundity that is beyond the reach of ordinary composers, and astonishing to the most skillful. One cannot imagine how a man who has felt and thought so much could have acquired to this degree an art that is as arid and forbidding in its principles as it is agreeable in its effects."

There were also two unpublished projects in these years. One was a prose poem called *Pygmalion,* reflecting the experience of *Julie.* Having finished his statue, the artist shrinks from the realization that he might lose himself in his creation — "If I were she, I wouldn't see her anymore, I wouldn't be the one who loves" — but when the statue comes to life his final words are "I've given you my entire being, and I will live only through you." In a way it was Rousseau's farewell to his art.

Another project was a direct outgrowth of his fame as a political theorist. In *The Social Contract* he had remarked that one place in Europe was still capable of becoming a true republic: the remote island of Corsica, which had been governed for centuries by Genoa and was struggling to win independence. "These brave people have recovered and defended their liberty with such valor and constancy that they deserve to have some wise man teach them how to preserve it. I have a premonition that one day this little island will astonish Europe." Out of the blue, a Corsican officer in the French army named Matthieu Buttafoco wrote to Rousseau, claiming to speak for the Corsican leader Pasquale Paoli, and inviting him to be that wise man. The idea excited

Rousseau. As Trousson says, what superb revenge for being dismissed as a utopian dreamer or as a subversive! He warned Buttafoco that his health would not permit him to visit the island, but books and documents were sent to him and he drafted some dozens of pages, including an oath of allegiance that would bond each citizen to the Corsican general will: "In the name of all-powerful God and of the holy evangelists, by a sacred and irrevocable oath, I unite myself to the Corsican nation with body, possessions, will, and all my strength, so that I may belong to it completely, myself and all that depends on me. I swear to live and die for it."

Rousseau's larger argument was that Corsica should resist modernization at all costs in order to preserve its primitive simplicity. That was hardly what Buttafoco and Paoli wanted, and they probably had no intention anyway of adopting anything drawn up by Rousseau, meaning only to borrow his prestige. Moreover, it became obvious that the whole thing was a waste of time, since a French army soon occupied the island and Rousseau correctly foresaw that they would never leave. When Corsica did astonish Europe it would not be for primitivist liberty but for producing Napoleon Bonaparte. And when Rousseau did get involved in political affairs, it would be much closer to home, and with disastrous results.

20

Another Expulsion

Rousseau had hoped to disengage himself from Genevan politics, but by now he had too many ties and obligations to do that. Letters (with names in code, since it was apparent that his mail was being opened) flew back and forth between Geneva and Môtiers, and he even made a trip to Thonon, on the southern shore of Lac Léman, to take part with Deluc and others in an abortive conference of conspirators. He also brooded about a pamphlet called *Letters Written from the Country* that was published in 1763 by Jean-Robert Tronchin. Tronchin (Théodore's cousin) was the public prosecutor in Geneva, and his carefully argued defense of the Little Council's actions made a strong impression on the public. In December 1764, working as before in total secrecy, Rousseau unexpectedly brought out a publication that precipitated his worst disaster yet. It was called *Letters Written from the Mountain,* and it was a highly polemical rejoinder to the *Letters Written from the Country,* filling 550 pages in Rey's octavo format (nearly 200 in a modern edition).

Rousseau's argument was that the ideals of Geneva were being betrayed by the Little Council, which acknowledged no constraints except its own good will. It was a powerful piece of writing, full of close detail. The citizens of a supposedly free republic, he proclaimed, had become "slaves of an arbitrary power; they have delivered themselves defenseless to the mercies of twenty-five despots." And he told the Genevans — no longer his fellow citizens — that it was their own fault. Far from being Spartans or even Athenians, "you are merchants, artisans, bourgeois, occupied always with your private interest, your work, your commerce, your gain."

Aristocrats and administrators everywhere were filled with alarm, and the book was soon burned at the Hague and in Paris. *The Social Contract* had concentrated on general principles, but now it could be claimed that Rousseau wanted to overthrow an established government. Moreover, it was soon apparent that only a radical minority in Geneva felt comfortable with his views. "Our people are saying openly," an admirer told him, "that your book is the gospel we must follow, others say it's the torch of liberty, and still others call it a flaming grenade in a gunpowder magazine." For this very reason the moderates feared that France, which had the right to mediate in Genevan affairs, would seize the opportunity to take over. So they made peace with the Little Council, and Rousseau was abandoned by the middle-class citizens he thought he was helping. He decided to give up the fight, telling Lenieps sardonically, "I'm going to behave as children or drunks do when they let themselves fall freely if someone pushes them, and avoid getting hurt that way."

Throughout all of these troubles, the most famous writer in all of Europe, living just outside Geneva in his estate at Ferney, was working insidiously against Rousseau. Voltaire had never believed that Rousseau was a significant writer. Far from seeing him as a rival, he despised him as a minor disciple who had become a nuisance. He mocked the *Discourse on Inequality*, he mocked *Julie*, and he mocked *Émile*, always with dismissive putdowns ("The author of *Émile* is like a child who thinks he has done something impressive when he blows soap bubbles or makes ripples by spitting into a well"). When Rousseau attacked Voltaire's plans for a theater in Geneva in the *Letter to d'Alembert*, he not only resented the interference but thought it was a ploy "to prepare for a triumphant return in his *rues basses*," the plebeian streets of the lower town. During the course of various behind-the-scenes maneuvers, Voltaire indulged in class contempt by misquoting letters of Rousseau's —

which had somehow come into his possession — to suggest that he had not been a secretary in Venice at all, but a mere valet. The lie rankled deeply, given Rousseau's bitter memories of serving as a valet in his teens.

Rousseau's political masterpiece, according to Voltaire, was nothing more than "a little book entitled *The Social Contract,* or *Unsocial Contract,* by the not very sociable Jean-Jacques Rousseau." As Voltaire's biographer acknowledges, "It would never have occurred to Voltaire to take Rousseau seriously as a writer on such a subject as government." When the *Letters Written from the Mountain* appeared, Voltaire sided wholeheartedly with the oligarchy, telling a member of the Tronchin clan that this time merely burning the book wouldn't be enough. "Let the Council punish him with the full severity of the laws . . . as a blasphemous subversive who blasphemes Jesus Christ while calling himself a Christian, and who wants to overturn his country while calling himself a citizen." (Privately, Voltaire could smile at Rousseau's suggestion that if communion bread was literally the body of Christ, Jesus must have put his own head in his mouth at the Last Supper. But he preserved the conventional decencies, and it has been said that he died a Catholic though he wasn't a Christian.)

At just this time a little eight-page pamphlet was published that staggered Rousseau as nothing had ever done before. Called *The Sentiment of the Citizens,* it pretended to be the work of an earnest Geneva preacher. In the course of critiquing his *Letters Written from the Mountain* it dropped a bomb: "We avow with grief and shame that he is a man who still bears the deadly traces of his debauches, and dressed as a mountebank drags with him from village to village and from mountain to mountain the unfortunate woman whose mother he killed, and whose infants he exposed at the door of an orphanage." Most of it was untrue, but it insidiously resembled the truth. The "deadly traces" made his urinary condition sound like venereal disease, which he never suffered from. His Armenian robe was not the costume of a mountebank, but it was certainly peculiar. Thérèse was not being dragged, but she did accompany him from one place of exile to another. Her mother was in fact still alive, but Diderot and Grimm had long accused Rousseau of behavior that would shorten her life. And one part was all too true. He really had given away the children, even if when publishing a rejoinder he fell back on a pitiful equivocation: "I have never exposed, or caused to be exposed, any infant at the door of any orphanage, or elsewhere." That was correct only in that they had been taken inside.

Rousseau unwisely prided himself on having an unerring ear for style, and he was sure he knew who was responsible. He was convinced that the culprit was the pastor Jacob Vernes, once a friend and now a strong voice in the conservative camp, who had recently published a careful critique called *Letters on the Christianity of M. Rousseau.* When Rousseau said so in print, Vernes, who was entirely innocent, was appalled and wrote a series of increasingly angry letters, which Rousseau shrugged off. It is strange, in fact inexplicable, that Rousseau never considered Voltaire, who had an obvious motive for revenge. More than once Rousseau had referred to Voltaire by name as the author of disreputable works that he had indeed written, when the custom was to respect anonymity. Still worse, in 1764 Duchesne published a brief open letter from Rousseau denying (rightly) that he had written an anti-Jesuit pamphlet that had his name on the title page, and mentioning quite casually that the anonymous author evidently admired Voltaire, "the most ardent and adroit of my persecutors." Voltaire was proud of his reputation as the enemy of persecution, and this public accusation infuriated him. From then on he waited for a suitable occasion to strike back, and *Letters Written from the Mountain* provided it.

When *The Sentiment of the Citizens* came out, Voltaire assured everyone that it was a despicable libel utterly inconsistent with his own feelings. For years he had been declaring that he loved Rousseau and tried to help him in time of need, while at the same time colluding tirelessly against him behind the scenes. And now he deployed the weapon he had been holding in reserve, the foundling home story that had been kept secret from all but a very few. It was probably Mme d'Épinay and Théodore Tronchin who told him about it. Voltaire covered his tracks so efficiently that to this day some scholars have refused to believe he wrote *The Sentiment of the Citizens.* But apart from plenty of circumstantial evidence, a decisive document was eventually obtained by Vernes in order to clear his own name. He got it after Voltaire's death from his private secretary: "I the undersigned declare that the late M.

Voltaire, justly angered by the insults against him by M. Rousseau in his *Letters Written from the Mountain* and by other outrages, took revenge in the little pamphlet entitled *Sentiment of the Citizens*."

For Rousseau, it hardly mattered who wrote the wretched libel. The thing he most feared was a public perception that he practiced the opposite of what he preached. Parents all over Europe regarded him as their guide. As Deleyre said, "You have shown us the duties of a husband and a father without being either one." But now it was coming out that he had indeed been a father and had gotten rid of the children in an absolutely shocking way. Many people were inclined at first to think the story must be false, but Rousseau knew it wasn't, and to establish his integrity even while admitting his faults was now the motivating principle behind the autobiography he was planning to write. "I will depict myself," he told Duclos, "such as I was, and such as I am. The bad will sometimes obscure the good, and in spite of that, I can hardly believe that any of my readers will dare to say 'I was better than that man.'" Almost the same words appear on the first page of the *Confessions*.

While Rousseau's eyes were focused on his native city, he was inattentive to danger closer at hand. When he told the Môtiers pastor Montmollin, apparently expecting support, that *Letters Written from the Mountain* was his first act of hostility in a war started by the Geneva ministers, a friend of Montmollin's said, "Either Monsieur Rousseau has lost his mind, or he believes you have lost yours." Montmollin was under increasing pressure to do something about the renegade he had unwisely admitted to communion, and he decided to go on the attack. The Protestants had no formal hierarchy, but they had plenty of discipline all the same, an association of ministers and elders known as the Vénérable Classe. The 1707 act of union with Prussia had expressly guaranteed the Neuchâtel ministers' right to conduct their affairs as they saw fit, and only a few years before they had successfully expelled one of their number named Petitpierre for the crime of doubting that God punishes sinners for all eternity. All too familiar with the trouble they could cause, Keith wrote from Potsdam to warn that since the ministers were "catching fire like straw," Rousseau had better think of taking flight.

In March 1765 the Vénérable Classe made its move. Rousseau was directed to appear before a special consistory to be convened in Môtiers and was told that he would be excommunicated unless he recanted his writings and swore "that he believes in Jesus Christ who died for our sins and was resurrected for our justification." Rousseau's understanding of faith entailed freedom of conscience, and he was totally opposed to the rigorous theology of the ministers. As his friend Deleyre said, "he deleted from the divinity anything that wasn't human, fatherly, and merciful." Nevertheless, he had no choice but to comply. Afraid to risk direct interrogation, he insisted on submitting his views in writing, and the consistory convened in his absence. Along with Montmollin, there were six lay elders, a deacon, and the local *châtelain* or administrator, Jacques-Frédéric Martinet, whose office entitled him to attend. When the vote was taken, Montmollin was thunderstruck to find himself in the minority, at which point he declared that the deacon had no right to vote. This meant that the votes were now evenly divided, and Montmollin announced that he would personally break the tie. Since he had already cast a vote, he was now giving himself two votes, which anyone could see was improper, and the Council of State in Neuchâtel accordingly struck down the decision against Rousseau.

Rousseau's supporters exulted in their victory, but the ministers were not so weak as all that, and Rousseau's allies were less powerful than they supposed. The pattern of Montmorency, in fact, was being repeated: he was being used by friends with agendas of their own. Pury's covert goal was to work toward an independent republic of Neuchâtel, and Pury and Du Peyrou were both freemasons, members of a secret society of freethinkers that was widely perceived as dangerously subversive. By no means were they deliberately misleading Rousseau. Pury regarded him as a dear friend, and Du Peyrou would remain unswervingly loyal even when Rousseau cooled toward him later on. But they were not helping him by encouraging active resistance, and he would have done better to follow Keith's advice and move away. He did, in fact, spend a good deal of time considering possible places to go — Venice perhaps, or Berlin — but he believed he was too ill too travel and, as before, no concrete plans were made.

The Council of State in Neuchâtel would have been glad to see the matter closed, since Frederick had sent an angry message demanding that they honor his protection of Rousseau, and Rousseau did promise never again to write on controversial topics. This time he probably meant it. But the ministers were far from ready to accept defeat, and

Montmollin was especially bitter, since he had been caught in the middle and made to look like a fool. He was self-important and conventional but no fool, and he understood the power that a pastor could wield among his parishioners. He started preaching sermons that were clearly intended to stir up hostility to Rousseau, which wasn't hard, since the villagers had little sympathy with a foreigner who consorted with the privileged class, attracted annoying visitors, took sides against a local woman in a morals case, and was known to be under an arrest warrant for impious writings. Moreover, as numerous testimonies make clear, Thérèse made herself thoroughly objectionable by gossiping and putting on airs. A visiting minister wrote to Moultou (whom Rousseau had dropped by then because of his growing friendship with Voltaire), "Mlle Levasseur, whom I am starting to despise with all my heart, is contributing not a little to embroil him with everyone, by her malice as much as her imprudence." D'Escherny remembered hearing numerous complaints of "her extreme intemperance of tongue," Du Peyrou said much the same thing, and so did the Genevan pastor Sarasin (unfriendly to Rousseau, but an honorable man): "They say it was less against Rousseau than his housekeeper that people were ill disposed. She never made anyone like her, far from it."

Thérèse made a practice of grilling visitors and, if she felt like it, turning them away. Socially inferior persons stood no chance at all; she seems to have acquired a good measure of snobbery during her time at Montmorency. A textile designer from Verrières, the French town where Thérèse used to go to mass, wrote indignantly to Rousseau that after noticing his dusty shoes — he had walked all the way to Môtiers — Thérèse told him coldly that Rousseau was ill and couldn't see him, although he had just been seen strolling cheerfully home from church. This writer added that rich visitors were well known to bribe her to get in. "If you reply," he told Rousseau, "I will be overcome with joy; if you don't, you are a philosopher à la mode, and I'll have lost nothing since there are plenty of those in the world." Rousseau didn't reply.

In September the storm broke. It was triggered by a particularly inflammatory sermon on September 1, in which Montmollin chose as his text Proverbs 15: 8, "The sacrifice of the wicked is an abomination to the Lord, but the prayer of the upright is his delight." Everyone knew he meant that Rousseau's taking communion was an abomination to the

Lord, and it was reported further that Montmollin "spoke with foaming rage about the scandal of neutral people." Clearly he was exhorting the townspeople not to be neutral, and the *chatelaine,* Martinet, wrote sternly to tell him to stop being provocative. Montmollin blandly replied that it was his sacred duty to edify his flock and that he had no individual in mind. "I have other business more useful and interesting than M. Rousseau's, which I neither want nor am able to waste time thinking about."

It happened that just then Mme de Verdelin, who had been staying at a health spa not far away in France, finally made a long-postponed visit to Môtiers. Rousseau was delighted to see his old friend from Montmorency — they habitually addressed each other as "neighbor," *voisin* and *voisine* — but that very night stones were thrown at the house, someone tried to force the door, and a big rock balanced on a pair of harrows was set up as a booby trap. After the harassment was repeated the next two nights, Mme de Verdelin abruptly departed at four in the morning on September 3, and later that day people jeered at Rousseau while he took his walk and even called out for a gun to shoot him.

Friday the sixth was the day of the monthly fair at Môtiers, at which misbehavior of various kinds was customary, and at ten that night the worst assault of all occurred. More stones than ever were thrown, and one of them broke a window. By the time Martinet hurried to the scene, a particularly heavy stone was found at the door of Rousseau's bedroom, and so many were piled on the balcony that Martinet exclaimed, "My God, it's a quarry!" Rousseau could delay no longer, and two days later he left for Neuchâtel. Thérèse remained behind under armed guard to take care of their belongings.

Despite numerous eyewitness accounts, it is not easy to be sure what was going on. The event was quickly mythicized as *la lapidation de Môtiers,* with connotations of the stonings in the Bible. Those implications were not lost on Voltaire, who published a facetious homily that recalled Jehovah raining stones on the Amorites, David slaying Goliath with a stone, and children throwing stones at Diogenes (the name he had been giving Rousseau for years). Quite a few people thought the whole thing was absurdly exaggerated. Grimm believed that a few drunks had pelted the house at random, but "with a heated imagination, it's easy to transform little pebbles into a hail of big stones, and two or three inebriates into a gang of assassins." One girl who was fourteen at the time even claimed, long afterward, that the village adolescents who used to amuse themselves by teasing the eccentric Rousseau were responsible for the stones.

There were certainly elements of the traditional *charivari,* in which an unpopular person was mocked and humiliated, and a week after Rousseau's departure an effigy representing him was found in the market fountain. It bore a satirical document recalling rumors that Thérèse had experienced some sort of disgrace in Montmorency, and deriding the "Bavarian castrato" who wanted to enforce his rule (Frederick's homosexuality was well known). Martinet, who was mentioned as an "old baboon" whose inquiries were causing needless trouble, kept the document as evidence but had the effigy dismembered and flung into the river.

The villagers immediately banded together against the officials, who attempted, not very energetically, to establish the truth. When the preliminary insults were investigated, witnesses testified that if someone had been heard to say "Bring me a gun to shoot that dog" when Rousseau was taking his walk, the reference was merely to a big gray dog that had been running loose, and that if people spoke about a false prophet, they meant nothing more than a mistaken prediction of rain. Three witnesses concurred in this story, and others were even less forthcoming. "Abram Clerc Guet, David Yersin, Philibert Lassieu, Jacques Lassieu, and David Bugnon all deposed that they didn't know anything." As for the lapidation, witnesses swore that the stone inside the house was too large to have gone through the hole in the window, so Thérèse herself must have put it there to provoke Rousseau into leaving Môtiers. The stones on the balcony were said to be her work as well. It is notoriously difficult for a legal inquiry to extract the truth from a village determined to stick to its story, and the matter had to be dropped. One of Keith's subordinates said he was sure they were covering up for more highly placed people who had instigated the affair.

So the lapidation passed into legend, while Rousseau's supporters talked darkly of Montmollin's auto-da-fé, referring not just to the Inquisition but to an incident years before when he had preached at the execution of two Môtiers men who were burned at the stake for "magic and sorcery." In Keith's opinion he was "much like the Old Man of the Mountains in the time of the Crusades: he made his followers believe that by carrying out an assassination at his orders, they would gain paradise." Montmollin himself remained convinced that he was the injured party, and years later was still telling visitors that Rousseau had repaid his kindness with the blackest ingratitude. For Rousseau it was a relief to leave. He didn't know, however, that a new stage of persecution and exile was about to begin.

Just east of the lac de Neuchâtel is the smaller Lac de Bienne (modern maps use its German name, the Bielersee). Near its western end is the little Île de Saint-Pierre, half a mile across in its longest dimension and divided equally in those days among fields, vineyards, and woods. The island was owned by a hospital in Berne that got income from farming it. There was a large house (adapted from a pre-Reformation monastery) inhabited by the steward, Engel, and his wife, Salomé, and it was administered by Karl Emmanuel von Graffenried, prefect of Nidau, at the end of the lake. Earlier that summer Rousseau had spent a very enjoyable ten days there, and Graffenried had been urging him to return. To be sure, the Bernese prohibition against Rousseau remained in force, but three years had passed and perhaps the authorities would be willing to look the other way. On September 8, two days after the stoning, Rousseau left Môtiers forever, and the next day he arrived at the Île de Saint-Pierre. A week later Thérèse joined him with their belongings.

The idea of an island had always appealed to Rousseau, and this one was "singularly situated for the happiness of a man who loves to circumscribe himself." *Robinson Crusoe* was to be Émile's only book, and Deleyre, writing from Italy when he heard of Rousseau's new refuge, got the point: "You recall Robinson to me; why can't I be Friday?" It was of course Thérèse who served as the faithful Friday, and quite a few other people were present, in addition to Engel and his wife. Autumn was harvest time, which attracted a large influx of workers. Rousseau proudly mentions visitors finding him up a tree with a sackful of apples hanging from his waist. He especially enjoyed the *vendanges* or grape harvest, a communal effort that he had already idealized in *Julie*. The island was in fact much more like the Wolmars' estate than like Crusoe's desert island, and it provided exactly what Rousseau liked, the sensation of solitude together with the conveniences of civilization,

THE HOUSE ON THE ÎLE DE SAINT-PIERRE

The keeper's house as Rousseau would have seen it (another wing, not shown here, was later added at the back). Rousseau and Thérèse had a corner room on the second floor, hidden here by trees. Not much farming is done there today, but a vineyard can still be seen at the right.

where he could comfortably exclaim, "O nature, O my mother, here I am under your protection alone."

Rousseau threw himself into botany, mapping out sections of the island to be studied exhaustively, and dreaming of a *Flora Petrinsularis* that would catalogue every plant. At other times he sought a kind of purposeless free-associating vacancy. The stay on the island so affected him in this way that he later made it the centerpiece of his final book, *The Reveries of the Solitary Walker,* in which he describes how he would lie down in a little boat while it drifted on the lake and gaze into the sky for hours on end. When it was too windy for boating he would sit by the shore and give himself up to the sensations of the moment. "The sound of the waves and agitation of the water caught hold of my senses and drove all other agitation from my soul, plunging it into a delicious reverie in which nightfall often surprised me. The ebb and flow of the water, with its continuous but varying sound, ceaselessly struck my eyes and ears." In this state of near-hypnosis Rousseau was able at last to "feel my existence with pleasure, without any effort to think," and ideas of every kind were dispelled by "the uniformity of the continuous motion that lulled me." The word for "lulled" is *berçait,* rocked like an infant in a *berceau* or cradle.

These moments could only be occasional, and Rousseau enjoyed evening social gatherings at a pavilion that had been set up for the purpose. "We relaxed in the pavilion, laughed, chatted, sang some old song worth far more than modern showiness, and went to bed well contented with the day, wishing only that the next one would be just like it." If anything, the place was a hive of activity, not solitude. Keith said he had been told that "so much is going on there, one might think the island would sink under it." In Môtiers Rousseau had acquired a new dog, Sultan, to fill the place of the lamented Turc, and on one occasion Sultan accompanied his master on an expedition to establish a new rabbit colony on a tiny island a few hundred yards from the larger one. As with the miniature aqueduct at Bossey, it was a chance to be a mythic hero in fantasy. "The founding of this little colony was a day of *fête,* and the pilot of the Argonauts was no prouder than I." After the *Confessions* and *Reveries* were published, the Île de Saint-Pierre became a place of pilgrimage, and eighteenth-century atlases began to identify the hitherto nameless little outcrop as *l'Île des Lapins,* Rabbit Island.

TRANSPORTING THE RABBIT COLONY

Rousseau, Thérèse, and the wife and sister of the island's steward are conveying the rabbits to the tiny island that Rousseau named the *Île des Lapins*. The artist took pains to make the bunnies, alarmed by the barking of the dog (Turc's successor, Sultan), as appealing as possible, and he placed conventionally "Swiss" crags in the background, where in actuality there are rolling hills. In successive editions of the *Confessions* illustrators concentrated on the more charming scenes, such as the episode of the cherries with the two girls near Annecy or the abbé Gros tightening the laces of Mme de Warens's bodice.

What Rousseau could never endure were celebrity seekers who came with the sole purpose of meeting him. A trapdoor in his room gave access to a space beneath, and he sometimes took advantage of it to escape. At other times he would try to conceal himself in the woods, and there were stories of his turning a cold shoulder to admirers who did manage to accost him. "Monsieur Jean-Jacques Rousseau, I salute you," one stranger called out, to which Rousseau replied, "If I knew your first and last names as well as you know mine, I would do the same." He then disappeared into the trees. When another visitor said politely,

ROUSSEAU'S ROOM IN THE ÎLE DE SAINT-PIERRE HOUSE

Thérèse is receiving a pair of uninvited visitors eager to see the great man, while Rousseau takes advantage of a trapdoor (which may still be seen today) to escape into the room below.

"Monsieur, I have the honor of being your most humble and obedient servant," Rousseau retorted, "But I, Monsieur, am not yours."

By mid-October the harvest was finished and the island settled in to sleepy isolation, which Rousseau felt prepared to enjoy. Declining an invitation from his "cher papa" Roguin to spend the winter in Yverdon, he explained, "I'm counting on finding this winter, amid the wind and ice, the peace and quiet I so badly need." It was not to be. A few members of the governing body in Berne had assured Rousseau that he could stay, but it turned out that the majority of their colleagues disagreed. The prefect Graffenried, "with the greatest regret and the most painful bitterness," had to order Rousseau to leave at once. He added, sympathetically but not very helpfully, "The entire universe is the fatherland of an upright man."

The decision was not hard to understand; Berne was under pressure from Geneva to keep radical protests from spreading throughout Switzerland. Rousseau saw it coming, remarking gloomily that while governments might sometimes revoke the good things they did, they never revoked the bad ones. In a way the ejection must have seemed inevitable. As Starobinski says, Rousseau's whole life had been a series of temporary paradises — Bossey, Les Charmettes, the Hermitage, Montlouis — from which he was unjustly expelled.

Facing a winter journey into the unknown, Rousseau made a desperate proposal that he be allowed to stay on if he would promise to give up paper, ink, and communication with the outside. This of course was rejected. The last thing the authorities wanted was to create a martyr; their only wish was to make him go away. So he prepared to leave, with the initial idea of going to Potsdam, where Keith was eagerly awaiting him. The people of the island remembered his last night there as a sad one, during which he took a lute and sang some farewell verses that he had composed. On October 26 he departed.

The island itself underwent a curious transformation a century later. In the 1870s the water level was lowered by more than two meters as part of a regional public works project known by the sonorous name Juragewässerkorrektion. As a result, the Île de Saint-Pierre is now joined to the mainland, so while Rousseau is remembered in Geneva by an Île Rousseau that didn't yet exist in his day, he is remembered at the Lac de Bienne by an island that isn't one any longer. As for the rabbit island, it has merged completely with the larger one, surviving as nothing more than a hillock in the woods. The rabbits are still there, though.

21

In a Strange Land

ROUSSEAU'S FIRST STOP in his wanderings was Bienne, at the head of the lake, where he was lodged in a disagreeable back room of an inn and oppressed by the stench from drying chamois skins. He was ordered to leave at once. Next he went to Basel, where he was equally unwelcome. He wrote gloomily to Thérèse, who agreed to remain on the island until a permanent destination could be decided: "I arrived in this town today without any great accident, but with a sore throat, fever, and death in my heart." The one comfort was Sultan, "lying at present on my coat under the table where I'm writing," who had cheerfully scampered for miles ahead of the coach. Leaving a glum note on a table in the inn — "J. J. Rousseau, proscribed, wandering, and sick" — he took a coach for Strasbourg, in Alsace. Though a territory of France, Alsace was outside the jurisdiction of the parlement of Paris, and he would not be in any danger of arrest.

Rousseau would never see Switzerland again, and plenty of people there were glad to see him go. Théodore Tronchin was as unforgiving as ever: "That man has made himself truly unhappy, and doesn't know where to lay his head. How true it is that pride goeth before a fall!" Montmollin was especially disgusted at being forced to send a groveling letter to Frederick, avowing insincerely that he had always been devoted to "the gracious and glorious sovereign who governs us with such wisdom and goodness." As for Rousseau's Neuchâtel supporters, they were seriously discomfited. His departure, a historian of the city later said, marked "the end of the troubles that he alone had occasioned."

The trip to Strasbourg, with the autumn rains coming on, was particularly nasty — Rousseau told Thérèse that it was the most disagreeable of his life — but at least he was no longer on the run. Rather unexpectedly, he found himself lionized in Strasbourg, and he ended up staying for five weeks at the La Fleur inn. A successful production of *The Village Soothsayer* was mounted, for which he was invited to conduct rehearsals, and as he told Du Peyrou, the social demands soon became so onerous "that I had to break it all off and become a bear again."

Though he would have liked to join Keith in Potsdam, Rousseau had been warned that the winters there were dreadful, and perhaps he suspected that he would find it hard to pay court to the king. Rey had been urging him for a long time to go to Amsterdam, but there too the winters were severe, and the best route was by the Rhine, which might be blocked by ice. Rousseau would have preferred France if he could be safe from arrest; Mme d'Houdetot and Saint-Lambert both offered him country houses, which he found especially touching coming from them, but he didn't dare accept. "Having weighed everything well," he told Du Peyrou at the end of November, "I've decided to go to England." Mme de Verdelin and Mme de Boufflers had been pressing him all along to do so, and they persuaded Choiseul, the first minister, to grant a passport ensuring his safe passage through Paris on the way. In addition, they had been conferring with David Hume, who was serving as chargé d'affaires at the British embassy in Paris, and who had already assured Rousseau that he would help him get settled in a country where "you would find an absolute security against all persecution, not only from the tolerating spirit of our laws, but from the respect which everyone there bears to your character." Rousseau replied gratefully that he accepted Hume's offer and would soon set forth "to throw myself into your arms." For all he knew, he might remain in England for the rest of his life.

Engaging a post chaise, in which he traveled alone, Rousseau left Strasbourg on December 9 and reached Paris a week later after a leisurely journey. He was expecting to stay with his publisher, Guy, looking over proofs for his *Dictionary of Music* "and seeing absolutely no one," but his powerful friends had other ideas. The prince de Conti offered him quarters in his palace at the Temple, which belonged to him as grand prior of the Knights of Malta; its extraterritorial status made it untouchable by the parlement of Paris. Rousseau could hardly refuse. Conti's motives were not entirely disinterested; he feared that Rousseau would get arrested or even turn himself in, with damaging consequences for himself as an early promoter of *Émile,* and at the Temple he could keep Rousseau under his control.

Once settled there, Rousseau was immediately overwhelmed with visitors. He met Hume, of course, and he saw a number of old friends, including the officious Coindet and the abject Sauttersheim, who visited him several times. But mostly there was a stream of distinguished well-wishers, encouraged by the prince and his mistress, Mme de Boufflers (often referred to by her friends as the Idol of the Temple), who were enjoying their role as patrons. For Rousseau, it was much worse than Strasbourg. "I have people of all sorts," he wrote to Du Peyrou, "from the moment I get up till the moment I go to bed, and I'm forced to dress myself for the public. I've never suffered so much, but happily it's going to end."

Throughout his life Rousseau complained of social activity, but to many people it seemed that he courted it all the same, denouncing fame but loving it. The Genevan representative in Paris, who was keeping a close eye on him, reported indignantly to his superiors that the passport had been granted under false pretenses, since Rousseau was far from being an invalid on his last legs. "Rather than remaining incognito, he has gone for a stroll in the Luxembourg Gardens in his Armenian costume, he has been seen with ladies in a carriage on the ramparts, and he receives those who come to see him in a magnificent room where he grants audiences from nine until noon and from six until nine . . . In the midst of this triumph, Rousseau appears to enjoy the best of health, and coldly refuses to see certain persons while admitting the elect with all possible grace." Hume, however, was convinced that Rousseau did all this under duress. "I know that two very agreeable ladies breaking in upon him discomposed him so much that he was not able to eat his dinner afterward . . . If he heard the door open, the greatest agony appeared on his countenance, from the apprehension of a visit, and his distress did not leave him unless the person was a particular friend."

Three other visits deserve mention, one because it finally occurred and two because they didn't. Rousseau's longtime correspondent Mme Alissan launched yet another complaint when she learned that he was in Paris and hadn't contacted her, but she concluded theatrically, "I have loved you, I love you, and I will love you." After Rousseau replied tartly that he was accustomed to her reproaches but determined to see no one, a white lie at best, she turned up at his door and sent in a note begging to see him if he was alone. He replied, also in writing, "I am not alone, Madame, but that won't prevent me from receiving you with the greatest of pleasure if you judge it appropriate to come in." There is no record of what was said when they met, but he wrote to her shortly afterward, "After seeing you I have a new interest in not being forgotten by you," and offered to stay in touch.

One would-be visitor was the desperately unhappy Henriette, who wrote again after the lapse of a year to implore Rousseau's counsel. "Since it's necessary that I live, teach me to live. If you can't do it, who can? . . . What an obligation I will owe to you if you can make me endurable to myself!" Rousseau seems not to have responded, and when she wrote to him one more time, five years later, he had to admit that he didn't even remember who she was. The other and more fateful nonevent was a meeting with Diderot, who entertained thoughts of reconciliation but was unwilling to make the first move. Needless to say, so was Rousseau. When it became clear that they would never see each other again, Diderot wrote to his mistress, "I do well not to give him easy access to my heart. Once someone has entered there, he doesn't get out without tearing it, and that's a wound that never heals."

On January 4, 1766, Rousseau left Paris with an old friend and a new one. The new one was Hume, whom he still barely knew. The old one was Jean-Jacques de Luze, a merchant with relatives in Yverdon, whom Rousseau described as having a cold manner but a warm heart. Hume and De Luze each had a small carriage, and Rousseau alternated between them during the four days they spent on the road to Calais. After two nights there they boarded a ship for Dover, and Rousseau left the Continent for the only time in his life.

It was a rough twelve-hour crossing, and Hume, tormented by seasickness, spent the voyage holed up in his bunk. Rousseau preferred to stay on deck, and astonished Hume with his stamina. "He imagines

DAVID HUME
Louis de Carmontelle's portrait, made just a year before Rousseau went to England with Hume, shows the relaxed urbanity of a man of the world, comfortable in wig and lace while relaxing at an elegant escritoire. It also hints at the substantial girth of someone who was always, as a friend commented, "a great eater."

himself very infirm. He is one of the most robust men I have ever known. He passed ten hours in the night time above deck during the most severe weather, when all the seamen were almost frozen to death, and he caught no harm." The moment they set foot on English soil, Rousseau startled Hume with one of his emotional performances: "I threw myself on his neck and embraced him tightly without saying anything, but covering his face with kisses and tears that spoke for themselves."

Hume spoke French but not the language of tears and kisses, and the temperamental gulf between the two men was bound to reveal itself before long. In 1766 Hume was fifty-five, one year older than Rousseau, a large, humorous, and comfortable man, and a leading light of the Scottish Enlightenment, British but emphatically not English. Whereas

Boswell took elocution lessons to get rid of his accent, Hume's remained so thick that he called it "totally desperate and irreclaimable." (His French accent too was said to be awful.) Hume is recognized today as one of the world's great philosophers, but in his own day he was known mainly as an essayist and historian, and his *History of England,* in French translation, was the only work of his that Rousseau had read. On the strength of that, together with Keith's warm recommendation, Rousseau had written from Môtiers with fulsome praise: "Your broad perspective, astonishing impartiality, and genius would elevate you too far above men, if your good heart didn't draw you closer to them."

Hume's intellectual skepticism went along with political conservatism, asserting that human beings are taught by nature to accept the assumptions of their tribe, whereas Rousseau opposed social assumptions and espoused ideas that were potentially subversive of established order. Still, the deeper gulf was that of temperament. Hume was gregarious and charming, *le bon David* as people called him, and women were especially attracted to him. Rousseau was awkward and shy, drawn to charming people but suspicious of them, and within a few months he would become more than suspicious of Hume. "Company is naturally so rejoicing," Hume once wrote, "as presenting the liveliest of all objects, *viz.* a rational and thinking being like ourselves, who communicates to us all the actions of his mind, and makes us privy to his inmost sentiments and affections." That mutual openness was just what Rousseau craved but could never find, and he would soon become convinced that Hume's genial manner was really a cynical mask. Hume, in turn, formed an all too accurate opinion that Rousseau was "like a man who was stripped not only of his clothes but of his skin, and turned out in that situation to combat with the rude and boisterous elements."

For the time being, however, all was well, and Hume relished his own generosity toward "the celebrated Rousseau, who has rejected invitations from half of the kings and princes of Europe in order to put himself under my protection." Lodging with an acquaintance of Hume's in London, Rousseau was once again subjected to a host of visitors — an English friend later spoke disparagingly of the time when Hume "was making a raree show of him in London" — and he also got out and about a good deal. Hume took him to the Drury Lane Theater to see David Garrick, the greatest English actor of the century, in a tragedy by Voltaire and a comedy by Garrick himself. Rousseau got so excited that he leaned out of the box and had to be held back from falling, and he assured Garrick afterward that the performance made him weep during the tragedy and laugh during the comedy, even though he understood almost none of the dialogue. But it seems that Rousseau himself was the chief attraction that evening. Hume noticed that the king and queen, seated in the opposite box, looked at Rousseau more than at the stage. So many people struggled to get into the theater that night that many ladies lost their bonnets, and gentlemen their wigs.

Back in Paris it was taken for granted that Rousseau enjoyed being a celebrity, and a bon mot by Saint-Lambert made the rounds: "It's not as bad as you make it out to be: he's traveling with his mistress, his reputation." In reality, though, he was dreadfully out of his element. Apart from a cousin, Jean Rousseau, with whom he was on friendly terms, he knew almost no one in London. For affection he clung to Sultan, whom Hume dismissed as "no better than a collie," and whom he deplored as a ridiculous surrogate for Thérèse: "M. de Luze, our companion, says that she passes for wicked and quarrelsome and tattling, and is thought to be the chief cause of his quitting Neuchâtel . . . yet she governs him as absolutely as a nurse does a child. In her absence his dog has acquired that ascendant. His affection for that creature is beyond all expression or conception." Hume himself was becoming disenchanted with his high-strung charge, and began referring to him condescendingly. An acquaintance noted, "He is confoundedly weary of his pupil, as he calls him; he is full of oddities and even absurdities."

After a separation of three months, it was high time for Thérèse to rejoin Rousseau, and she was indeed on her way. Having waited on the Île de Saint-Pierre until word arrived that Rousseau was going to England, she immediately set out, leaving Neuchâtel the same day that Rousseau left Paris. Delayed by heavy snows, she reached Paris two weeks later, by which time Rousseau had moved to temporary lodgings in Chiswick, just outside London, and was making inquiries about a permanent refuge in some remote country place. While there he saw a few people, including a naturalist, Daniel Malthus (father of the future economist), who had visited him in Môtiers, but essentially he was just marking time.

A traveling companion for Thérèse unexpectedly offered himself.

James Boswell turned up in Paris at the end of his grand tour, which had included an extended stay in Corsica inspired by Rousseau; he would presently publish a widely noticed *Account of Corsica* based on that trip. Boswell had been favorably impressed with Thérèse in Môtiers, going so far as to send her a garnet necklace afterward and writing rather provocatively to Rousseau, "You won't be annoyed if I write sometimes to Mlle Levasseur? I swear that I have no intention of carrying off your *gouvernante*. I sometimes make romantic plans, but never impossible ones." Hume suspected what was coming. "He has such a rage for literature," he wrote to Mme de Boufflers, "that I dread some event fatal to our friend's honor," and he mentioned the story of the Roman nobleman who married the former wife of Cicero and Sallust in the belief that "she must possess some secret which would convey to him eloquence and genius." Keith, who knew Boswell less well, wrote more optimistically to Rousseau, "He is a true man of honor, a *preux chevalier.*"

Whether or not Thérèse possessed the secret of wisdom, she had a lot to teach the brash young Boswell, and she was old enough, as Cranston severely observes, to be his mother. They were together for more than a week, owing to a delay while waiting for a boat, and a note in Boswell's diary after they reached Dover indicates unambiguously what happened. "Yesterday morning had gone to bed very early, and had done it once: thirteen in all." Unfortunately Boswell's full account of the liaison, which was undoubtedly richly detailed, was torn out and destroyed by his embarrassed heirs when they sold the journal to a collector in the 1920s. According to the collector, who claimed to have read the missing pages in the nick of time, Boswell boasted of his prowess in bed but required a bottle of wine to inflame his courage, and was then humiliated when Thérèse told him he lacked skills and needed to learn to use his hands. She thereupon undertook to instruct him in the art of love, rather boisterously in his opinion (riding him "agitated, like a bad rider galloping downhill"), and wounded him further by saying, "Don't imagine you are a better lover than Rousseau." If all of this really happened, it would throw a very interesting light on Thérèse's relationship with Rousseau, but no further evidence is likely to emerge. What does seem clear is that she told Rousseau about it afterward, most probably casting the story as her own virtuous resistance to seduction, just as she had done with Gauffecourt in a stagecoach long before. For his part, Boswell promised never to mention their brief affair to anyone, and he kept his promise.

Boswell had been counting on forming a close connection with Rousseau in Britain, and he had an item inserted in the newspapers announcing the arrival of James Boswell, "a friend of the celebrated John James Rousseau, who is an enthusiast for the Corsicans, and has been honored with the title of their legislator." But when he wrote after a while to inquire after Rousseau's health, he got the most dismissive of replies, ending with the pointed advice, "Permit me in turn to recommend the care of your health, and especially to have yourself bled from time to time. I believe this would do you good." In any case, Boswell's hero, Samuel Johnson, would have opposed a friendship with Rousseau. Johnson declared roundly, "I think him one of the worst of men, a rascal who ought to be hunted out of society, as he has been. Three or four nations have expelled him, and it is a shame that he is protected in this country."

Seeking advice on where to live, Rousseau received numerous suggestions, but they kept falling through. The first thought was to find a village somewhere near London, which proved unexpectedly difficult. Since Rousseau and Thérèse could speak no English, they were loath to set up housekeeping on their own, preferring to board with a landlord who would take care of domestic arrangements. But they were not married, and people who were approached by Rousseau's intermediaries took umbrage at accepting a social relationship under the circumstances. Voltaire's revelations in *The Sentiment of the Citizens* made it impossible to invoke the cover stories that had seemed acceptable in Môtiers. At one point Rousseau thought he had definitely fixed on a remote dwelling in Wales, but in late February a new possibility turned up. Richard Davenport, a wealthy widower in his seventies who spoke French reasonably well, proposed that Rousseau and Thérèse move to Wootton Hall, a mansion of his in the Midlands that he visited only occasionally. There were servants to look after the housekeeping, there were woods and hills for pursuing the study of botany, and there would be all the solitude anyone could wish. Rousseau gratefully accepted Davenport's offer on condition that he pay a modest rent, and in mid-March he and Thérèse began the 150-mile journey to their new home.

WOOTTON HALL

Wootton Hall in a nineteenth-century engraving; it was later torn down and its stones used for other buildings. "The house, although small," Rousseau wrote, "is very habitable and well arranged." It is hard to imagine on what basis he regarded it as small. His quarters, on the second floor (around the corner to the left in this view), were commodious, with a fine view of the grounds and valley below.

Settling in at Wootton Hall, Rousseau was at first ecstatic. "It's been frozen ever since I've been here," he wrote to Hume at the end of March, "it has snowed every day, and the wind cuts your face. Despite all that, I would rather live in the hole of one of the rabbits in this warren than in the finest apartment in London." Writing on the same day to Coindet, his longtime intermediary with publishers, he put it more positively: "Here I am as if born again through a new baptism, washed in my passage over the sea. I have cast off the old man, and apart from some friends, among whom I include yourself, I've forgotten everything that has to do with that foreign land called the Continent. Authors, arrest warrants, books, the acrid vapor of fame that makes one weep, all of those are follies of the other world that I take no part in and am hastening to forget."

Wootton ("woot" rhymes with "foot") lies at the southern end of the Peak District, thirty miles north of Birmingham. On modern maps it is in Staffordshire, but when Rousseau was there it seems to have belonged to Derbyshire. The village itself was barely a hamlet, a few houses at the foot of the rolling Weaver Hills, and its residents were well aware of its remoteness, "Wootton under Weaver, where God came never." A London wit invoked the nickname of a local landmark:

> Rousseau in Derbyshire! no farce
> Was ever sure so odd,
> That he should seek the Devil's Arse
> Who turned his arse on God.

But in fact one issue that finally disappeared in England was the religious one, which had been at the center of the Môtiers storm. If Rousseau ever went to church at all, there is no record of it, and the nearest one was a good distance down the hill in Ellastone, where George Eliot's father would one day be buried. Its vicar sometimes came to call but unfortunately couldn't speak much French.

The environs satisfied the requirement that Hume mentioned when he was negotiating for Rousseau's stay: "Is there wood and hills about Mr. Davenport's house?" There were indeed, but the climate was depressing. A couple of months after his arrival Rousseau told a Neuchâtel friend that springtime was "belated and cold, and the country beautiful but gloomy; nature here is numbed and sluggish." Even in mid-May "the trees are still leafless, and nightingales are never heard." Behind the house was a park with large trees, and rising above it the hills; a little farther off was one of the lead mines that abounded in the area. To post-Romantic taste — Wordsworth and Coleridge would later celebrate nearby Dovedale — the region is beautiful, but it could also be seen as rather barren. Charles Cotton, who lived not far away in the seventeenth century, acknowledged as much in his continuation of *The Compleat Angler.* Piscator says, "These hills, though high, bleak, and craggy, breed and feed good beef and mutton above ground, and afford good store of lead within." To this his guest Viator rather sourly replies, "They had need of all those commodities to make amends for the ill landscape."

WOOTTON FROM THE WEAVER HILLS

The Weaver Hills were an easy ascent for someone used to scrambling over the mountains in the Val de Travers. Looking south, a modern house on the site of Wootton Hall is slightly to the left of center, with the village of Wootton to the right. It is a classic English landscape: fields divided by hedgerows in the plain below, and broad grazing land on the limestone hills.

When warm weather finally came, Rousseau wandered in the hills collecting plants, but he was discouraged to find that even after he obtained some books, he had trouble learning anything. "My faculties are weakening, I have neither eyes nor memory any more, and far from aspiring to understand botany someday, I can barely hope to botanize as well as the sheep that pass beneath my window." Anyway, he could hardly fill up all of his time with botany. The huge difficulty was the language barrier, and although Du Peyrou suggested encouragingly, "You'll hold conversations with the plants," he had to admit that Thérèse wouldn't have that consolation. No one at Wootton Hall knew any French; when it was necessary to deal with Davenport's servants, who were clearly unenthusiastic about these demanding foreigners, "Mlle Levasseur acts as my interpreter, and her fingers speak better than my tongue." In their letters Rousseau's friends regularly inquired whether

Thérèse was happy and whether she was learning English. They were well aware that she tended to be dissatisfied and that her feelings influenced Rousseau. "She hasn't learned a single word of English," Rousseau reported after they had been in England for half a year. "I learned thirty or so in London but I've forgotten all of them here, because the dreadful jabbering is unintelligible to my ear."

Of course Rousseau exaggerated his ignorance. His vocabulary lists still exist, concentrating on kitchen needs:

> currans & raisins of the sun
> pouder sugar
> flower a quart
> butter fresh charned
> cheese when wanted right good

He did make regular visits to the village to purchase supplies, and to bestow a shilling here and there on the farmers and mine workers. But if the villagers treated him with respect, they remembered him afterward only as an amiable eccentric. A nineteenth-century visitor was told of a strange Frenchman known as "owd Ross Hall" (some ran the sounds together as Dross Hall), who had with him a woman known as "Madame Zell," which was how they heard "mademoiselle." Rousseau's interest in botany was especially remembered. "He war mighty curious in yarbs [herbs]," an old man told a visitor, "and ah've heered see, war skilled to cure welly ony disease wi' em." The Armenian costume was also notable, "his comical cap and ploddy gown" (they thought of stripes as plaid). No one could converse with Rousseau, however, for "he could na speak no English, nubbut a wod or two," and children tended to take alarm when they saw him. The visitor gathered that "his long gown and belt, and his black velvet cap with its gold tassels and pendent top, made him a most awful figure to them, especially as they used to see him poring on the park wall for moss, or groping in some lonely nook after plants. As he could not address them in English to dissipate their fears, they used to run off, if possible, at the very first glimpse of the terrible outlandish man." Thérèse, dealing with servants and shopkeepers, did eventually pick up a smattering of English. One man remembered a story that when the Wootton Hall housekeeper was being beaten by her husband, "Madame Zell" exclaimed to some young women who were there, "Never marry! Never marry! You see! You see!"

However much Rousseau may have hoped to live in pastoral simplicity, everything was somehow wrong. "Just a few things would satisfy my wishes," he wrote during the second winter at Wootton, "fewer bodily pains, a milder climate, a purer sky, a more serene atmosphere, and above all hearts that are more open, so that when my own heart needs to pour itself out, it can feel itself entering another." Starobinski comments sardonically that he asks only that the air be always clear and the obstacles between human hearts abolished.

Rousseau may have thought of Wootton Hall's proprietor, Davenport (whose name he sometimes wrote as "d'Avenport"), as a promising companion, since he was a Cambridge graduate inclined toward deism and a progressive country squire interested in agriculture. But he stayed at Wootton Hall only twice a year for a couple of weeks each time, preferring the less isolated setting of another of his houses, Davenport Hall, in Cheshire, thirty miles to the northwest, and the winter months he spent in London. And although he was unfailingly generous and kind, he tended to be phlegmatic in what Rousseau regarded as a typically English way. "M. Davenport does favors for me with much affection and zeal," he told the ever faithful Du Peyrou, "but he never says anything or responds to my outpourings. Never in my life have I seen a man who is so reserved, so profoundly mysterious." That is not to say that their relations weren't amicable, however, and Rousseau grew especially fond of Davenport's grandchildren. Perhaps, also, Davenport was inhibited by awkwardness in speaking French, and was more relaxed in his own language. After a visit to Wootton one of his friends reported, "His vivacity and the singularity of his character and of his ideas kept me in an almost constant laugh."

The only reliable new friend was Bernard Granville, who had recently purchased Calwich Abbey, a mile and a half away, with impressive gardens and a lake formed by widening the little river Dove. Granville loved music (he had been friendly with Handel) and was fluent in French, as was his charming twenty-year-old niece Mary Dewes, with whom Rousseau was soon smitten. They had musical evenings during which Rousseau sang his own airs and accompanied himself on the harpsichord. Soon he was sending Mary flirtatious little notes, for instance when she made a collar for his dog and he appropriated it for his own fetishistic purposes: "My lovely neighbor, you are making me unjust and jealous for the first time in my life. I can't see without envy the chains with which you've honored my Sultan, and I have deprived him of the privilege of being the first to wear them." She wrote back courteously, "You say more about the little collar than it deserves. I'm not so vain as to believe myself able to make something that would be worthy of your acceptance, and that's why I intended it for Sultan." Granville also introduced Rousseau to the duchess of Portland, an accomplished student of botany who even roamed the hills with him. Though only three years younger than he, she would "climb over rocks where I had difficulty following her, to find *Chamaedrys frutescens* and *Saxifraga alpina*."

But as the winter drew on, visitors came less frequently, and Rousseau wrote in January 1767, "Never in my life have I felt such biting cold." Granville confirmed, "The snow here is incredibly deep," keeping him housebound, and a month later he was taking the waters at Bath, leaving Rousseau to lament the season "that has kept Calwich deserted for so long." The only other suitable neighbor, five miles off at Ashbourne, was an intelligent young aristocrat named Brooke Boothby, to whom Rousseau would one day entrust an important manuscript. "I was well received and went frequently," Boothby later wrote, but unfortunately he recorded nothing about their encounters except that Rousseau "passed his time chiefly in botanizing upon the hill in his Armenian dress." Twenty miles away, an intellectually active circle at Litchfield (the birthplace of Samuel Johnson) centered on the botanical studies of Erasmus Darwin, a well-known naturalist and grandfather of the great Charles Darwin. Daniel Malthus, with whom Rousseau had stayed in touch after their meeting in London, was a member of the group, but there is little evidence that Rousseau had contact with the others. There was a story that Erasmus Darwin placed himself surreptitiously where Rousseau would encounter him gazing at plants. "Are you a botanist, sir?" Rousseau inquired in French, after which they walked on companionably together, but when Rousseau learned his companion's name he suspected that he was being stalked or spied on. He supposedly cried out, "Ha! a concerted plan!" and refused to see Darwin again.

Even at its best, then, life at Wootton was only intermittently agreeable, and meanwhile Rousseau's thoughts darkened in a different way. Cut off from friends and even from French-speaking acquaintances, cold and lonely, he was overtaken by paranoid obsessions. His fear of persecution was not in itself irrational. Rousseau was the only important writer in Europe who had been systematically expelled from one country after another and denounced by former friends and associates as well as by governments and churches. After visiting Rousseau in Môtiers, an eminent doctor said, "This worthy man is being persecuted in the cruelest way in the world; there is nothing his enemies don't imagine and do to afflict him and ruin him." And that was before the lapidation and the expulsion from the Île de Saint-Pierre.

Moreover, as Mély comments, Rousseau had been rejected as a pariah not just by France and Switzerland but by the republic of letters as well. With the conservative establishment actively hounding him, the Encyclopédistes could demonstrate how much less dangerous they were by joining in. And the opposition was disquietingly mysterious. "I have powerful and illustrious friends everywhere," Rousseau told Du Peyrou during the last winter in Môtiers, "and I'm certain that they love me with all their heart, but they are upright, good, gentle, and peaceful people who despise indirect methods. By contrast my enemies are ardent, skillful, intriguing, crafty, and tireless to destroy, and they maneuver underground like moles." And now, in a strange land where he was helpless to defend himself, Rousseau suspected that the plots were starting up all over again. Unfortunately, the person his suspicions fixed on was David Hume. It had been unjust and embarrassing to insist that Jacob Vernes had written *The Sentiment of the Citizens;* it was absolutely disastrous to insist that his greatest enemy was Hume.

The crisis came on in stages, and at first was not public. It amounted to circumstantial evidence that Rousseau became convinced was decisive proof, though in every instance he misunderstood, or at least exaggerated, the implications of Hume's behavior. One theme was interference with his mail, which had happened in Môtiers and was happening again. The wax seals on his correspondence often seemed to have been damaged and ineptly repaired, and on at least one occasion in London Hume seemed eager to lend Rousseau his own seal, which would have made it easy for him to reseal the letter after sneaking a look at it.

Hume's biographer calls this an "absurd charge," but actually it was well founded. Théodore Tronchin's son Louis-François, who happened to live in the same London building as Hume, learned to his amazement that to save Rousseau expense, Hume was in the habit of opening all letters addressed to him and returning to the sender any that he judged unimportant. As Hume sheepishly admitted in a letter to d'Alembert, "What could I do more friendly than to save, at my own expense, his letters from the curiosity and indiscretion of the clerks at the post office? I am indeed ashamed to find myself obliged to discover [that is, to disclose] such petty circumstances." Rousseau was bound to take alarm. He told most of his correspondents to stop writing to him altogether, and with others he resumed using a code, as he had in Môtiers. "The man I mentioned in my previous letter, O, has placed his son F with B who is on his way to C . . . I have warned D of this." This not very mysterious message indicates that Théodore Tronchin had placed his son Louis-François (whom Rousseau unfairly distrusted) with the British ambassador to Prussia, and that Keith had been duly alerted.

Another source of suspicion was Hume's snooping into Rousseau's financial and personal affairs. Here again his motives were probably generous; he intended to do what he could to ensure financial security for the stateless exile, but he needed to know first whether Rousseau's claims of poverty were exaggerated. In point of fact they were, since he had a guaranteed annual income of 600 livres from Keith, 300 each from Rey and Guy, and potentially a large sum from Du Peyrou as an advance on a Neuchâtel edition of his works (he eventually accepted 2,400 livres before calling a halt when it became clear that the edition wouldn't be published). On the other hand, it was also true that Rousseau never asked for money and ostentatiously refused patronage, and that he had every right to think that his finances were none of Hume's business. He was especially offended when he discovered that Hume had colluded with Davenport to make him believe, when they hired a carriage to take him to Wootton, that there would be no charge since it was returning there anyway. "Liberality is doubtless a very fine thing," he wrote sternly to Davenport, "but I believe candor is even more valuable."

Hume's plan for helping Rousseau financially led to misunderstanding on a much more serious scale. His idea was that George III, in his capacity as an enlightened monarch, should bestow a pension of £100 a year on Rousseau, the equivalent of 2,000 French livres. This was a generous sum but not extravagant; Samuel Johnson had a pension of £300. The case of Johnson is interesting in another way, however. Accepting his pension caused him considerable embarrassment, because a few years earlier, in his famous dictionary, he had defined "pension" in satirical terms that brought out its relation to the very kind of patronage that Rousseau always avoided: "An allowance made without an equivalent. In England, it is generally understood to mean any payment given to a state hireling for treason to his country."

Hume took it for granted that the king would want his generosity kept secret to avoid seeming to approve of Rousseau's political and religious views. Rousseau, in turn, felt awkward about accepting a pension of any kind from the king of England, in whose realm he was only a visitor, after he had refused one from the king of Prussia, whose protection he had gratefully enjoyed. What he especially didn't want was a secret pension that might later become publicly known, thereby damaging his reputation for probity. So he asked Hume to find out whether it could be revealed from the start. This Hume reluctantly did, but the new complications stalled negotiations for a considerable time.

In each of these matters, Rousseau had reason to be concerned, but other suspicions were clearly groundless. One concerned a frivolous parodic letter, ostensibly by Frederick the Great and addressed to Rousseau, that Horace Walpole had written in Paris to amuse his society friends. Walpole was the son of the great prime minister Robert Walpole, but unlike his father he was a dilettante, best known today for his gossipy letters, a Gothic novel called *The Castle of Otranto,* and the invention of the word "serendipity." This letter, which was widely copied and soon made its way into print, took exactly the line on Rousseau's sufferings that he most resented. "If you persist in racking your brains to find new misfortunes," Walpole made Frederick say to Rousseau, "choose any that you like; I am a king and can procure them according to your wishes. And as will never happen with your enemies, I will stop persecuting you when you stop glorying in persecution." Actually Walpole rather admired Rousseau and was just trying to be funny, in the spirit of his own aphorism that life is a comedy to those who think and a tragedy to those who feel.

Thunderstruck, and not believing that Walpole could write French so well (in fact his friends had corrected the letter for him), Rousseau decided that it could have been written only by d'Alembert, of all people. This not only had the effect of alienating one of the few philosophes who had defended him until then, but it turned out to be the first falling rock in a gathering avalanche. Hume assured Rousseau that Walpole was the true author, which the rather ashamed Walpole admitted. But instead of believing them, Rousseau concluded that Walpole, d'Alembert, and Hume were all complicit in an insidious plot to undermine him. Soon he was calling them a fearsome "triumvirate" and declaring that they had an evil plan, though he had not yet succeeded in penetrating it. When unkind references to Rousseau occasionally appeared in the London papers (though it's not clear how well he was able to understand what he read), these too he ascribed to their malevolent scheming. And why did Hume lodge near young Tronchin, anyway? Might not the elder Tronchin and Voltaire be in on the plot?

In short, Rousseau was succumbing to paranoia, more deeply than he had in Montmorency, when he briefly believed the Jesuits were trying to destroy *Émile,* and this time there were no trusted friends to rescue him from delusion. In this frame of mind he began to reconsider not just what Hume might have done but also what kind of person he was. Years before, when he knew Hume only through his writing, he had said that Hume "measured and calculated the errors of men like a being who is above their weaknesses." Unfortunately Hume had a tendency to gaze fixedly at his companions in a manner that could seem judgmental in just that way, though he insisted he meant nothing by it. And whereas Rousseau was uncommonly expressive and keenly responsive to other people's feelings, Hume's demeanor was so unrevealing that a friend of his referred to "his broad unmeaning face."

While Rousseau was still in London, this temperamental dissonance produced a moment of genuine terror. "After supper," Rousseau recalled, "the two of us were silent beside the fire when I noticed that he was staring at me, as he often did, in a way that is hard to describe. This time his dry, burning, mocking, and prolonged gaze became more than disturbing. To free myself from it I tried to stare back, but when my eyes met his I felt an inexplicable shudder, and I was soon forced to lower them. The countenance and manner of *le bon David* are those of a good man, but my God, where did this good man get the eyes with which he transfixes his friends?" Hume, who was unaware of Rousseau's feelings and was only gazing blankly as he often did, was astonished by what came next. Both of them later reported the episode in terms that show they remembered it accurately but interpreted it altogether differently. In Rousseau's account, he felt a sudden revulsion against his own mistrust. "I threw myself on his neck and embraced him tightly, and, suffocated with sobs and streaming with tears, I cried brokenly, 'No! No! David Hume is no traitor! If he is not the best of men, he would have to be the worst.' Hume returned my embrace politely, and, patting me on the back with little taps, repeated several times in a tranquil tone, *Quoi, mon cher monsieur? Eh, mon cher monsieur! Quoi donc, mon cher monsieur?*"

In Hume's opinion, however, he showed much more emotion than was usual with him. In fact he was rather embarrassed, but he appreciated Rousseau's need for an expression of emotion. "I hope, dear Madam," he wrote (in English) to Mme de Boufflers, "that you have not so bad an opinion of me as not to think I was extremely affected with this scene. I confess that my tears flowed as plentifully as his, and that I embraced him with no less cordiality." Hume was so conscious of having behaved atypically that he asked Mme de Boufflers to show his letter only to women; "I scarce know a male who would not think it childish." To his Scottish friend Hugh Blair, Hume put it even more strongly: "I hope you have not so bad an opinion of me as to think I was not melted on this occasion. I assure you I kissed him and embraced him twenty times, with a plentiful effusion of tears. I think no scene of my life was ever more affecting."

But the tears were not plentiful enough for Rousseau, whose criterion for friendship was spontaneous and overwhelming emotion, and he made no allowance for Hume's cautious temperament. His perception was that Hume behaved much as Diderot had done when Rousseau wept at Vincennes. "Instead of melting along with me, or getting angry and demanding explanations, he remained calm and responded to my transports with cold caresses." And the embarrassed "How now,

PORTRAIT OF ROUSSEAU BY RICHARD PURCELL, AFTER RAMSAY

In London, Hume arranged to have Rousseau's portrait painted by the distinguished Scottish artist Allan Ramsay, showing him in Armenian robe and fur hat. Engravings based on it, including this one by Richard Purcell, were widely distributed. Rousseau detested them and believed that a "Cyclops face" was deliberately intended to damage his public image. "Skillfully darkening that frightful coloring, little by little they made the formidable and vigorous man of the original into a deceitful little fellow, a petty liar, a petty swindler, a frequenter of taverns and low places." Ramsay has caught the expression of caution that Rousseau undoubtedly had at the time, but it is hard to see the portrait as unflattering, deliberately or otherwise. Rousseau's friend Bernardin said flatly that of all the available engravings of Rousseau, this was the only good likeness.

my dear sir" was very far from adequate. Deleyre told Boswell with shrewd insight that Rousseau treated friendship the way most people treat a first love, and was expressing the reproaches of a disappointed lover.

Brooding about all of this in the frigid isolation of Wootton, Rousseau began to think of Hume as an insidious enemy, and then a buried memory burst upon him. On the trip from Paris to Calais, he and Hume had shared a room at Senlis, and he suddenly recalled, or thought he recalled, another moment of high anxiety. "Several times during the night I heard him cry out in French, with extreme vehemence, *Je tiens J. J. Rousseau.* I don't know if he was awake or asleep." What would it mean to say "I've got J. J. Rousseau?" Rousseau told Mme de Verdelin that he tried at first to interpret this mysterious remark favorably, "but there was something alarming and sinister in his tone that I will never forget." For Rousseau this was the decisive piece of evidence, but when Hume heard about it he was altogether baffled and suggested, reasonably enough, "I cannot answer for everything I may say in my sleep, and much less am I conscious whether or not I dream in French. But pray, as M. Rousseau did not know whether I was asleep or awake when I pronounced those terrible words with such a terrible voice, how is he certain that he himself was awake when he heard them?"

Since Hume unquestionably had good intentions and since Rousseau imagined treachery that didn't exist, it has been usual to regard Hume as an entirely innocent victim. But without calling his good faith into question, it is still possible to accept Mély's suggestion that Rousseau's suspicions could have had some basis. Hume was, after all, a diplomat with a career to protect (in 1767 he became undersecretary of state for northern affairs), and the British government was certainly alarmed by the inflammatory politics of *Letters Written from the Mountain.* The French authorities too may have expected Hume to keep Rousseau under informal surveillance. In this light, the proposed pension from the English king could be seen as a further means of keeping him quiet. After indicating at first that he would accept it gratefully, Rousseau grew alarmed when he realized that it would be a secret arrangement to be paid through Hume; this might well have seemed a plan to control him. And when Hume agreed to negotiate for an openly disclosed pension, Rousseau still held back, convinced by then that he was somehow being used. Hume wrote indignantly to Davenport, "You will be astonished, as I was, at the monstrous ingratitude, ferocity, and frenzy of the man." But if Rousseau misjudged Hume's good intentions, Hume in turn exaggerated them, not admitting the personal considerations that surely influenced his actions.

This is not to say, however, that Hume was knowingly in the wrong. As has often been remarked, a paranoid is blind to his own unconscious hostility but hypersensitive to the hostility of others. Rousseau was a difficult character, and it would not be surprising if Hume did feel more hostility than he wanted to admit, bullying Rousseau genially while telling himself that he was acting selflessly. For Rousseau, it had all happened before, with Diderot, and it is with justice that a psychoanalyst observes in Rousseau a repetition compulsion, condemning himself repeatedly to exile, provoking quarrels with friends as well as enemies, putting himself in a position to endure humiliations, and convincing himself meanwhile of his innocent victimhood. There may even be something to Clément's theory that Rousseau projected his feelings of guilt onto a succession of "bad brothers" who occupied the role of the long-lost François Rousseau.

Hume's unwavering gaze must have been peculiarly disturbing, since although Rousseau aspired to be open to others, his tendency was always to throw up defenses. He may well have feared that Hume, the analyst of behavior who measured human errors as if he were above them, could pluck out the heart of his mystery and thereby control him. *Je tiens J. J. Rousseau.* In a comment made when he was obsessing about the alleged plot, Rousseau seems even to have hinted (though he was writing in very general terms) that the roles might have been reversed: "The vices of men are in large part the result of their situation. Injustice goes along with power, and we who are persecuted victims, if we were in our pursuers' place, might perhaps be tyrants and persecutors like them." In a draft of the *Confessions* Rousseau said even more startlingly, "David Hume is only doing today what I once did to poor Marion."

It needs to be remembered also that Rousseau's health and spirits always declined in the winter, even when he was among people he liked and trusted, and inveterate insomnia was bound to encourage dark thoughts. "My nights are cruel," he wrote to Malesherbes, "my body suffers even more than my heart, and total loss of sleep delivers me to the gloomiest ideas. The air of the country joins a dismal influence to all this, and often I begin to feel that I've lived too long."

Davenport was deeply upset when he realized what was happening, and implored Rousseau to clear the air by speaking openly to Hume, who had already been staggered by a brief accusatory letter from Rousseau. Thus prompted, Rousseau took the next step in the growing catastrophe. He composed a long letter to Hume reviewing the whole series of *soufflets,* or slaps in the face, that he believed he had received, and declared that Hume must have lured him to England in order to destroy him. On July 10 he sent it off, and Hume was astounded. The letter seemed to him a "perfect frenzy," as he told Davenport, and now it was his turn to feel scared. His reputation was everything to him, and he had in his hands an eloquently written denunciation that seemed all too probably intended for publication. Even if it was not, Rousseau was known to be writing his memoirs, and many people had reason to fear how they might be portrayed there. The first thing Hume did was to send accounts of what was going on to his friends in Paris, in terms that were apparently so intemperate that d'Holbach and d'Alembert both took care to destroy his letters. D'Holbach could not have been surprised, for according to his friend Morellet, he told Hume before he sailed for England, "It won't be long before you'll be sadly undeceived. You don't know the man. I tell you frankly, you'll be nursing a viper in your bosom." In the version recalled by Marmontel, another member of the circle, he added, "I'm warning you, you will feel his bite."

The d'Holbach coterie eagerly publicized the affair and then, having made sure it was widely known, told Hume that he had no choice but to publish a defense of his compromised reputation. This Hume promptly did, in a pamphlet of 130 pages that reprinted all of the letters between Rousseau and himself, some of which represented his own explanation of the affair. It was published first in French (translated by Jean-Baptiste Suard, one of the *Encyclopédie* coterie) as *Exposé Succinct de la Contestation qui s'est Élevée entre M. Hume et M. Rousseau,* and shortly afterward in English as *A Concise and Genuine Account of the Dispute between Mr. Hume and Mr. Rousseau.*

Some of Hume's friends did urge him to keep quiet, including his fellow Scot Adam Smith, who realized that the affair could easily become a political weapon. "The church, the Whigs, the Jacobites, the whole wise English nation will love to mortify a Scotchman, and to applaud a man who has refused a pension from the king." Mme de Boufflers acknowledged that Rousseau was behaving insanely, but she could not believe his motives were wicked, and she warned that Hume would damage only himself by attacking him. But she concluded gloomily, "You are too confirmed in your opinion, too *engagé,* too persistent in your anger to listen to me." Walpole, who understood that the Holbachians were pushing Hume into publication "to gratify some spleen against Rousseau," gave the same unheeded advice. After the pamphlet was in print Walpole told Hume, "All Europe laughs at being dragged every day into these idle quarrels, with which Europe only wipes its backside."

Grimm, too, understood the self-defeating consequences of Hume's action and said that in Hume's place he would have rubbed his eyes in amazement at Rousseau's denunciation, bade him farewell, and never given him another thought. And he concluded generously enough, "I don't think anyone can read these strange proceedings without deep pity for the unhappy Jean-Jacques, for if he ends up offending his friends, one must admit that he punishes himself most cruelly for it." Diderot too took a charitable view, telling a visitor, "I knew these two philosophers well. I could write a play about them that would make you weep, and it would excuse them both."

Others were less charitable. Voltaire was exultant, and intensified his unrelenting campaign, dispatching letters in all directions to emphasize Rousseau's viciousness while protesting that he himself had nothing to do with the attacks on him. Voltaire had in fact published a *Letter to Dr. Pansophe* that reviewed Rousseau's follies in detail, though he told everyone a certain abbé Coyer must have written it. Later he wrote to Charles Bordes, "The abbé Coyer swears to me that he's not the author of the *Letter to Pansophe,* so is it you? You say it's not, and that it has to be the abbé Coyer. Certainly there's no one but the two of you who could have written it. No third person exists."

More painful was the reaction of Rousseau's dwindling number of allies in France. This time he had really succeeded in driving himself into the wilderness. D'Alembert and Duclos both gave up on him, and even the great ladies who had stuck with him through thick and thin — Mmes. de Luxembourg, de Boufflers, and de Verdelin — began to turn away. Rousseau seems never to have grasped that they all knew Hume so well that they simply could not believe in his guilt, especially after Rousseau wrote coldly to Mme de Boufflers that she was prejudiced in Hume's favor "but prejudices are as nothing against facts." There really didn't seem to be any facts, for as a London satirist observed, the evidence apparently amounted to Hume's staring at Rousseau and then saying "My dear sir" while patting him on the back. Mme de Verdelin told Coindet that the troubles were ultimately Thérèse's fault, and there may have been some truth to that. "Be sure that they're not due to our friend's mind, it's his unfortunate tendency to believe that imbecile female he has with him." Shortly afterward Mme de Verdelin stopped writing to Rousseau altogether, as did his other Paris friends, and the last of his connections with the cherished Montmorency period were gone. With relish Théodore Tronchin described the situation: "My good friends mesdames de Luxembourg, de Beauveau, and de Boufflers have abandoned him. They no longer speak of him except as a wicked rascal, there's but one voice on that. Never has a man fallen more rapidly into the depths."

Most tragically of all, it was the end of the relationship with the person Rousseau most trusted and depended on, the Maréchal Keith. Hume was one of Keith's closest friends, as Rousseau knew perfectly well, and for years Keith had entertained the dream of settling down for good with him and Rousseau. When Rousseau was preparing to go to England, Keith wrote to say, "You are not fleeing mankind, but avoiding — and with good reason — the yahoos. David isn't one of those, he is a man . . . He is the houyhnhnm who will protect you from the yahoos." The yahoos are the foul humanoid apes in *Gulliver's Travels,* and the houyhnhnms are the benign rational horses who are incapable of lying, "saying the thing that is not." But now Rousseau was declaring that Hume was a diabolical liar, and Keith was appalled. He stopped answering Rousseau's letters, much to his alarm. "What, Mylord, not a single word from you, what silence! and how cruel it is! . . . I prostrate myself at your feet to beg just one word . . . The pen drops from my hand." It was too late. Rousseau had already received a sad farewell from the one friend he thought he would never lose. "I am old, infirm, and weak in memory," Keith wrote. "Perhaps I have committed some follies, but to avoid them in the future, don't take it wrong if I cut short my correspondence, as I have already done with nearly everyone, even my closest relatives and friends, in order to end my days in tranquility. *Bonsoir.*" The letter was unsigned.

Two years later, when it was clear that the breach was permanent, Rousseau did get a further message, but judging from his mention of it to Du Peyrou and his failure to keep the letter, it cannot have been very gratifying: "I don't know how I forgot to tell you that I've at last had the consolation of receiving a letter from Mylord Maréchal." So far as is known, there was no further communication between them, although Keith lived to the age of ninety-eight and died in 1778, the same year as Rousseau. In his will he left Rousseau the watch he always carried, and it was duly sent to Thérèse.

Rousseau was entering his second winter at Wootton. The royal pension finally came through, promoted honorably behind the scenes by Hume and Walpole; very possibly they were both feeling remorse, though in Walpole's case the spurious Frederick letter was a minor piece of folly. Rousseau, in his turn, may have begun to suspect that he had behaved badly, but since the affair was public knowledge he couldn't turn back. His long letter to Hume, now in print, had ended with the declaration, "I am the most unfortunate of mortals if you are guilty, and I would be the most vile if you are innocent." With a deep conviction of innate innocence, it was inconceivable that Rousseau would ever avow that he was the vilest of mortals.

At Wootton, meanwhile, Thérèse stepped up her own campaign. No one had a good word to say about her. She struck Boothby as "a vulgar old kitchen maid," and Hume reported, "I find that Mr. Davenport had entertained no very advantageous idea of her character or conduct . . . It is suspected that she has nourished all Rousseau's chimeras in order to chase him out of a country where having no person to speak to, she tired most desperately." Mme de Verdelin, who was well aware of the bad name Thérèse had left behind at both Montmorency and Môtiers, heard from English friends that according to Davenport, "her venomous tale-telling caused all of her master's suspicions." It may well be, however, that Rousseau's fears stimulated hers and that the anxiety was mutual. Meanwhile, news arrived in the autumn of 1766 that her aged mother had died, and that must have made her feel still more cut off.

In the end it was Davenport's servants who drove Rousseau out. There were half a dozen of them, including a well-intentioned steward who looked after the house, an aged former nurse of Davenport's with whom Thérèse constantly quarreled, and a housekeeper who likewise had a chip on her shoulder. As early as December 1766, Rousseau surprised Davenport with a letter saying that he felt unwelcome at Wootton and should probably leave. And although Davenport reassured him at the time, by the following April Rousseau had had enough. "The master of a house, Monsieur," he wrote angrily in a letter that he left on a table for Davenport to find, "is obliged to know what goes on in it, especially with respect to strangers whom he has received there. If you are unaware of what has been happening to me since Christmas, you are in the wrong. If you do know about it and permit it, you are even more in the wrong . . . Tomorrow, Monsieur, I am leaving your house . . . It is easy to oppress me, but hard to debase me." At this very moment, as it happens, Hume was writing to tell Davenport that the king had approved Rousseau's pension, adding "I hope he will enjoy this mark of his majesty's bounty with tranquility and peace of mind." And whatever Hume had feared, his own reputation seems not to have suffered from the affair.

By now Rousseau was prey to overwhelming delusions, convinced that even his affectionate cousin Jean Rousseau had been brought into Hume's plot. "I am surrounded by snares on all sides," he wrote to Du Peyrou in a letter that he arranged to send by an indirect route, dispatching a different version by regular post for his enemies to intercept. For the rest of April he waited anxiously for Davenport's arrival, which was unfortunately delayed by an attack of gout. Not knowing the reason for the delay, Rousseau panicked, and on the first of May he and Thérèse disappeared for parts unknown. With Davenport's help he had already sold his large collection of books and prints, so he did not leave much behind, just three trunks containing clothing, papers, and music.

When Davenport arrived shortly afterward and discovered the letter, he was astounded, though he soon confirmed that Rousseau had some grounds for complaint. He told Granville that the housekeeper "behaved in such a brutish manner toward him and Mlle Levasseur" that they were driven to leave, and added in a letter to Hume, "His *governante* has an absolute power over him, and without doubt more or less influences all his actions." A friend of Davenport's helped him piece together what had happened: "I had some conversation with the old passionate woman of ninety who threw ashes into Rousseau's soup, which hastened though it did not cause his departure. She mentioned him with the highest respect, but did not spare her abuse on Mlle Levasseur, whom she called a base woman and a liar, in which I suspect she judged not amiss. The old grayheaded steward seemed quite to adore him, and could not mention his name without tears; he keeps one of his Armenian dresses as a relic, and will keep it he says till his dying day. The histories he gave me of Jean-Jacques' charity and benevolence to the country people and to the poor in the neighborhood made me almost cry also."

For several days no one had any idea where Rousseau had gone, and then on May 5 he turned up inexplicably at the White Hart Inn at Spalding, a rather nondescript town — "one of the most cursed disagreeable places in England," Davenport said — in the flat fenland of Lincolnshire, a hundred miles to the east. The best guess is that he wanted to reach a Swiss man named Jean-François-Maximilien de Cerjat, who had married an Englishwoman and settled in another part of Lincolnshire. Rousseau had never met Cerjat, but Du Peyrou had recommended him as a reliable ally in case of need, and they had already corresponded on that basis. Apparently Rousseau intended to entrust him with the manuscript of the unfinished *Confessions,* which he expected his enemies to destroy if it ever got into their hands. Whether or not he managed to make contact with Cerjat is unknown, but at any rate he ended up in Spalding, not far from the coast, perhaps imagining that he could get passage to the Continent there. It is just as well that he never knew of Hume's comment to Davenport when he heard where Rousseau was: "It seems he wrote to a gentleman in Lincolnshire, whose name I have forgot, and offered to come and live with him — an honor which the gentleman declined." It is hard to avoid the conclusion that Rousseau's surreptitious letters to Cerjat had been intercepted and read by Hume!

Rousseau proceeded to loiter rather aimlessly in Spalding, even allowing himself to be courted by the members of a book club (though he said he was no longer a writer and reproved them for addressing him in Latin). He did take the precaution of wearing ordinary clothes rather than the all too recognizable Armenian robe. His plan now was to go to Dover, where it would be easy to find a ship bound for France, but he was held back by the conviction that he would be arrested on the way. At this point he wrote, incredibly enough, to the lord chancellor of England, imploring him to send a guard who could conduct him to Dover past the perils along the road. The response, understandably, was that ordinary postilions would be more than adequate, but now at least Rousseau's whereabouts were known. Hume informed Davenport, commenting, "He is plainly mad, after having long been maddish," and Davenport attempted to reach Rousseau to encourage him to return to Wootton. Suddenly, however, he was on the move again. On May 14 he left Spalding, and only two days later he was at Dover, after a journey of two hundred miles. Along the way he ran out of money (Davenport owed him a hundred pounds for the sale of the books but was unable to make contact to give it to him), and he paid his way by selling off items of silverware.

After grasping that he had actually reached Dover unimpeded, Rousseau finally began to suspect that he was behaving irrationally, and even thought of returning to Wootton. But another alarm occurred when he happened to read a hostile newspaper account of his flight that he wrongly attributed to Davenport. He still expected to be forced to remain in England, and from Dover he wrote to Hume's superior, General Conway, the secretary of state, whom for some reason he trusted. In this long, desperate letter he admitted that the reason he had been brought to England remained hidden from him, although "I have tormented myself in vain to penetrate it." He was right enough about the torment, though not about the secret plan, let alone about the "captivity" in which he claimed to languish. In this letter he gave Conway a solemn promise that if only he could be permitted to leave the country, he would surrender the manuscript of the *Confessions* and never say or write a single word about what had happened to him. And he ended with a declaration whose nobility of rhetoric was matched only by its absurdity: "I see my final hour approaching. I am resolved if necessary to go and seek it, and to die or else be free. There is no longer any middle way."

Long afterward Rousseau admitted that at the time he really had been subject to "an attack of madness." He remembered thinking, when he was told that the winds were unfavorable for sailing to France, that this too was a deception being practiced by his enemies, and he rushed out of a dinner party given by a kindly stranger to run on board a ship and harangue the bewildered bystanders in French. He even began to suspect Thérèse of complicity in the plot when she intervened; according to a witness, "Vexed at the obstinacy of John James, she began to menace and abuse him most unmercifully," until he meekly returned to the dinner "and conversed sociably with that gentleman and his family till late in the evening." As always, Rousseau was able to set aside his fears temporarily, a tendency that misled Hume, who had heard from Davenport that Rousseau was cheerful at Wootton at the very time that he claimed to be miserable, and also that he comported himself very agreeably at Spalding. But the fears were all too real; it was just that Rousseau was able to compartmentalize them. (After reading the letter to Conway, Hume admitted that it was "seemingly rational, and so probably will his memoirs be, and perhaps as full of genius as any others of his writings.") At last Rousseau and Thérèse set sail, and on May 22 they landed at Calais. "I would give half my life," he had told Du Peyrou a few weeks before, "to be on terra firma again," which was a common term for the Continent but still carried the implication that England wasn't solid ground. At last he was there, but with a far from clear understanding of his situation. In England he had felt under constant threat but was actually in no danger at all. In France he apparently intended to move about openly, but the warrant for his arrest was still outstanding, and the danger was very real.

22

The Past Relived

IN THE FINAL FLIGHT from Wootton to Spalding and Dover, Rousseau behaved like a lunatic. Even Du Peyrou, who stood by him loyally throughout, recognized that he was delusional and deplored "this infernal affair." Yet Rousseau eventually achieved a remarkable degree of tranquility, and even during the dark days at Wootton, he was completing the first half of the *Confessions*. At the very time that he struck observers as sadly lacking in self-knowledge, he was achieving a profoundly original self-analysis whose influence has been enormous. The *Confessions* are at once the record of a life, a recreation of its meaning, and an imaginative space in which the author found relief by recovering what it felt like to be his earlier self. "It's the past," he wrote at Wootton, "that makes the present bearable."

During the years in Môtiers, Rousseau had become aware that others were discussing details of his life. He received a long anonymous letter from Geneva that referred to his father's stay in Constantinople and exile after a street quarrel, his own time at Bossey with the Lamberciers, his apprenticeship to "a brutal, barbarous master," his flight from Geneva and refuge with *la folle de Varrens* in Annecy, and his ostentatious display of feeding "numerous schools of fishes" during his visit in 1754. Later *The Sentiment of the Citizens* gave its viciously slanted account of Rousseau's recent life. He assumed that the information in it came from

Mme d'Épinay (some of it undoubtedly did), and he vowed to clear his name as well as to exact revenge by giving his own recollections of her and other ex-friends. Like Augustine, from whom he borrowed his title (though he never mentions the earlier *Confessions*), he would acknowledge his sins, but unlike Augustine he would also prove his essential goodness.

The influence of the *Confessions* has been so pervasive that it is hard today to appreciate how original the book really was. To trace formative experiences, and in particular to take childhood experience seriously, was virtually unheard-of in Rousseau's day. A few earlier writers had recounted occasional anecdotes of childhood, but compared with the *Confessions* these were thin and unrevealing. When Voltaire drafted an autobiographical sketch at the end of his long life, he dismissed his early years with the comment, "Nothing is more insipid than the details of infancy and the time spent at school." As for Diderot, his biographer says that he was "almost intentionally inscrutable" about his first thirty years and that he pitied the state of childhood for its helplessness and ignorance. When he did mention his early days, it was to congratulate himself on precocious brilliance, not to disclose errors and humiliations. "One of the sweetest moments of my life — it happened more than thirty years ago and I remember it as though it were yesterday — was when my father saw me coming home from school with my arms full of prizes I had won and my shoulders loaded with crowns they had given me that were too big for my brow and had slipped down over my head . . . From the farthest distance that he saw me, he dropped his work, came to the door, and burst into tears."

Rousseau was well aware that the story of a working-class boy struggling to find himself was in itself unusual. "Many readers will be prevented from continuing by this sole idea. They can't conceive that a man who needs bread could be worthy of their acquaintance." But that was the whole point: it was his unusual history that had allowed him to develop into a challenging and original thinker. However, his outsider role also explained why people found it so hard to understand him, even after he acquired fame. He had always had a sense of being misunderstood, even as a child, and becoming a writer was at first a way of compensating for it. "The course I have chosen," he acknowledged in the *Confessions*, "to write and to conceal myself, is precisely the one that has suited me." But the concealment was all too successful, and he was discovering just how deeply his self-image was threatened by other people's perceptions. George Eliot asks, "Who can know how much of his most inward life is made up of the thoughts he believes other men to have about him, until that fabric of opinion is threatened by ruin?" Rousseau's English disaster was a classic illustration of that. So now he proposed to reveal everything. "I must keep myself constantly before the reader's eyes, so that he can follow me in all the aberrations of my heart and all the recesses of my life."

By addressing the reading public rather than the deity, as Augustine had done, Rousseau was inaugurating a modern confessional mode in which private secrets are exposed to the largest possible audience. At the very beginning of the *Confessions,* indeed, he exclaims with ringing eloquence that he is certain God will forgive him:

> Let the trumpet of the Last Judgment sound when it likes; I will present myself with this book in hand before the sovereign judge . . . Eternal Being, assemble around me the numberless throng of my *semblables;* let them hear my confessions, let them groan at my disgraceful actions, let them blush at my wretchedness. But let each of them reveal his heart with the same sincerity at the foot of your throne, and then let a single one say, if he dares, "I was better than that man."

The throng are the readers who had bought Rousseau's books and presumed to stand in judgment, and he demands that they follow his example in telling the truth about their own faults.

It might well seem that such a procedure was no confession at all. Grimm rather snidely remarked, "If Monsieur Rousseau were ever to become pope, he would delete penitence from the list of the seven sacraments," and another writer saw even the most shaming revelations as self-serving: "He seems to have formed the plan of depicting himself in the mire in order to show that he escaped from it. There is a kind of vanity in saying, 'I was nothing and I became famous; I was a liar and I chose the motto *vitam impendere vero.'*" As Blake trenchantly put it long afterward, "The book written by Rousseau called his *Confessions* is an apology and cloak for his sin and not a confession." But even if Rousseau denied other people's right to judge him, he never stopped judging himself. Unappeasable guilt for actions long past — the abandoned children, the stolen ribbon — lay at the heart of the *Confessions.* Rousseau got rid of original sin and held that man is naturally good, but much of his own behavior remained bafflingly bad, and when he set out to penetrate the inner darkness he invented modern autobiography. He probably believed at first that by reviewing his life he could explain clearly who he was and why. But the more he probed his recollections, the more he was brought to a halt by incidents that made no sense and yet seemed profoundly significant. And although he was convinced that he possessed an essential integrity to which he must be true, he was forced to acknowledge, as he says when narrating his encounter with Mme de Larnage during the journey to Montpellier, "There are times when I seem so little like myself that one would take me for another man of completely opposite character."

Montaigne, Rousseau's great predecessor in self-analysis, pursued an intellectual quest, with a genial skepticism and the motto *Que sais-je,* "What do I know?" Rousseau's quest was more visceral, as Trousson says: "the anguished and contradictory 'Who am I?' of modern consciousness." Pondering the strange vicissitudes of his life, Rousseau came to believe that he was most himself when he was acting most unpredictably. He repeatedly tells of moments that he describes with words like "caprice," "intoxication," "extravagance," "delirium," and "madness," moments that are pressure points in what Marcel Raymond calls "a psychology of rupture and discontinuity." Instead of singling out typical episodes, he focuses on atypical ones, strange and unsettling occasions when he seemed to act totally out of character and yet was profoundly himself. It is as if his true and deepest self is released by these ruptures, like volcanic vents.

There is a double perspective throughout the *Confessions,* and the tension between the two angles of vision gives it a kind of stereoscopic depth. On the one hand, Rousseau never abandoned his conviction of a fundamental core of self. But on the other hand, he understood that the self is profoundly shaped by life experiences. To probe the ones that seemed most hauntingly peculiar became his method for finding out who he was, and in seeking to detect hidden patterns in them, he was starting out on a path that would lead eventually to psychoanalysis. Freud wrote as Rousseau's heir when he proclaimed, "Turn your eyes inward, look into your own depths, learn first to know yourself! Then you will understand why you were bound to fall ill, and perhaps you will avoid falling ill in future."

What Rousseau does, really, is not to lay his guilt to rest but to make it ambiguous. In traditional morality, either you have sinned or you haven't. In the stories Rousseau tells, the complicating factors are endless. Was he guilty of ruining Marion's life? Yes and no. He was guilty of stealing the ribbon, certainly, but in another sense he was innocent, for the theft had multiple causes: the humiliating apprenticeship that conditioned him to be a thief, the hopeless yearning for girls he couldn't have, the crisis of public interrogation that he couldn't face, and so on. And is "theft" only a single category, anyway? Was he a thief in the same way on those different occasions when he pilfered apples from Ducommun, wine from M. de Mably, the ribbon from the Vercellis household, and the price of a theater ticket from Francueil? No, not in the same way. To make such distinctions is a recognition of the complexity of human motivation, and this too is an essential element of Rousseau's originality. When one of his most confident modern interpreters says, "What Rousseau *really* wanted is neither the ribbon nor Marion, but the public scene of exposure which he actually gets," that is just too simple. There was no one thing that he "really" wanted, and in brooding on memories that wouldn't go away, he brought the past to life in all its fullness.

Yet it is misleading to take the stories in the *Confessions* simply at face value. So far as factual veracity goes, Rousseau did his best to be accurate, with remarkable success. Of some six hundred persons whom he mentions by name, all but half a dozen have been confirmed to exist by later research. Of course he didn't always keep the chronology straight, and he was aware that he filled in some gaps by imaginative guesswork. Recent research on memory suggests that everyone creates a sense of personal history by combining specific recollections with a more generalized sense of self. Certain incidents stand out from the rest and are felt to be especially significant, and as Rousseau says, "These moments would still be present to me if I were to live a hundred thousand years." But separating them are broad, featureless tracts of time that have to be bridged by a generic sense of how one tends to behave, and this generalized self-image in turn influences the way one makes sense of particular incidents. Rousseau was quite right to conclude later on that the truth he aimed at in the *Confessions* was psychological rather than factual. "I loved to expand on the happy periods of my life, and at times I embellished them with such ornaments as my tender regrets provided. I described things I had forgotten as it seemed to me they must have been, and as they may indeed have been, but never in contradiction to the way I remembered them."

For the *Confessions* were not just an apologia, they were a means of living the most meaningful experiences all over again. "It's not a present that speaks *of* the past," Lejeune says, "but a past that speaks *in* the present." In his late *Reveries* Rousseau found a perfect metaphor for what he was doing: "Wanting to recall so many sweet reveries, instead of describing them *j'y retombais*" ("I fell back into them"). He was at Wootton when he wrote the unforgettable account of the charming young women who picked cherries with him near Annecy, and the poignant contrast gave life to his pen. "All the birds in concert were bidding farewell to spring and singing the birth of a fine summer's day, one of those fine days that are never more seen at my age, and have never been seen at all in the gloomy land where I'm now living."

Rousseau was well aware of the originality of what he was trying to do — "I am undertaking an enterprise for which there is no example" — and he wrote in his notebook, "It's necessary to invent a language as new as my project; for what tone or style should I adopt to unravel that immense chaos of feelings, so diverse, so contradictory, often so vile and sometimes so sublime, by which I was ceaselessly agitated?" At times an amused irony allows him to expose his youthful follies or to present a memorable individual in the manner of a picaresque novel. (Thus he depicts the Annecy judge Jean-Baptiste Simon as a witty and intelligent dwarf with a magnificent head and tiny body who preferred to receive visitors in bed, "for when one saw a fine head on the pillow, no one would imagine that that was all there was," and who was mistaken for a woman when his deep voice gave way to a piping squeak.) At other times elegiac nostalgia takes over, and then the lost happiness casts an implied reproach on later worldliness. Or the alternation can happen the other way round: first a painful scene and then a seriocomic alternative. The fateful spanking by Mlle Lambercier is followed by the inadvertent display of her posterior to the king of Sardinia; the punishment for the broken comb is followed by the mock heroic aqueduct. The hero of a picaresque novel might steal a ribbon for a girl or assume an alias on the road, but Rousseau wants to know why he did those things and how they can be consistent with his image of himself. And his analysis is sociological too. A picaro would keep changing jobs just to stay one jump ahead of the law, but Rousseau wants to understand why work itself is oppressive and the law so often unjust.

Since Rousseau left such a rich account of his psychic experience, every school of interpretation has had grist for its mill. In the nineteenth century various diagnoses were proposed that now seem quaint: "dromomania" for example, a morbid impulse to wander or run. Rousseau did enjoy traveling, but he got so much pleasure from it that it's hard to see it as morbid. In the twentieth century psychoanalysis took over, producing myriad attempts to identify causes for masochism, exhibitionism, and paranoia. Most interpreters agree that Rousseau became paranoid, but that is all they can agree on. How unbalanced he actually was, and how much of the time, and for what reasons, and with what consequences, are questions that each analyst answers in terms of a preferred theory. In every instance the evidence exists only because Rousseau himself considered it important and tried to explain it. And although it has been easy to reduce him to a "case," he never experienced incapacitating mental illness. On the contrary, over time his self-knowledge deepened, his ability to take pleasure in life expanded, and his writings lost nothing of their clarity and force. To open any of his books, including those written at the very of his life, is to be reminded that a genius can turn misfortune and neurosis to advantage.

The most valuable contribution of psychoanalysis is not any particular diagnosis, which might be debatable even for a living patient and can only be hypothetical for a person who died two centuries ago. More helpful is the general recognition that someone who complains constantly about ill health may unconsciously want it. Freud describes people who cannot relinquish neurotic symptoms because their feelings of guilt require punishment. Another analyst, interestingly, speaks of diseases whose tending takes the place of religious faith, "the malady substituted for God." And here, as always, it would be condescending to imagine that we see what Rousseau could not. He was the first to admit that being persecuted was inseparable from his sense of self, and that in some sense he needed it. "Persecution has elevated my soul. The love of truth has become dear to me because it has cost me so much. Perhaps at first truth was merely a system, but now it has become my dominant passion." To be persecuted, indeed, might seem an authentication of virtue in a hostile world, as in the metrical psalms that he often heard sung when he was a boy in Geneva:

> Rends confus mes accusateurs,
> Et poursuis mes persécuteurs,

"Send confusion to my accusers, and pursue my persecutors." Starobinski puts it very neatly: "He needs the dark mirror of persecution in order to see his face of shining innocence."

Another way of describing Rousseau's originality is to recall that the normal goal in his day was to present a coherent character to the world, with rough edges smoothed down or eliminated. One way of accomplishing this was to see human beings as generic types, and another was to stand apart from one's own experience with ironic objectivity. Gibbon, in multiple drafts of an autobiography he could never bring to completion, did both. In the *Confessions* Rousseau sees his erotic relationships, including the failed ones, as providing an essential key to understanding, but when Gibbon describes his (rather lukewarm) amorous feelings he says that "the grosser appetite" is not worth mentioning, for "it less properly belongs to the memoirs of an individual than to the natural history of the species." And irony is his preferred means of detachment from himself. He served for a couple of years in a militia that was preparing to repel a possible French invasion, about which he says deprecatingly, "The captain of the Hampshire Grenadiers (the reader may smile) has not been useless to the historian of the Roman Empire."

Still more telling is the brief narrative entitled "My Own Life," which Hume wrote when he knew he was dying of cancer. Describing himself in the past tense, he declares that he never failed to live up to his own character ideal.

> To conclude historically with my own character, I am, or rather was (for that is the style I must now use in speaking of myself, which

emboldens me the more to speak my sentiments); I was, I say, a man of mild dispositions, of command of temper, of an open, social, and cheerful humor, capable of attachment, but little susceptible of enmity, and of great moderation in all my passions . . . In a word, though most men anywise eminent have had reason to complain of calumny, I never was touched or even attacked by her baleful tooth . . . I cannot say there is no vanity in making this funeral oration of myself, but I hope it is not a misplaced one; and this is a matter of fact which is easily cleared and ascertained.

The emotional moderation was real enough, but Hume can hardly have believed that he was never calumniated; it is as if the whole dreadful quarrel with Rousseau had never happened. As for how he felt in moments of doubt and distress, such as the nervous breakdown that he is known to have suffered in his teens, he gives no hint at all. Hume depicts himself in the most advantageous light and asserts an objectivity that makes his entire being "a matter of fact which is easily cleared and ascertained."

However much Rousseau may sometimes excuse his own failings, his quest for self-understanding takes place at an imaginative level that Hume never sought and perhaps would have been unable to recognize. They might as well have come from different planets, and the nature of Rousseau's achievement was literally a closed book to Hume, just as Hume's kind of philosophy was of no interest to Rousseau. When Rousseau first arrived in London, Hume told a friend, "He has read very little during the course of his life, and has now totally renounced all reading. He has seen very little, and has no manner of curiosity to see or remark; he has reflected, properly speaking, and studied very little, and has not indeed much knowledge. He has only felt, during the whole course of his life." Given Hume's notions of what reading, studying, and thinking should be, one can see how he might form such an opinion, but all the same the condescension is staggering. Still less would he have been able to credit Rousseau's claim that the *Confessions* would become "an invaluable book for philosophers." Empiricist philosophers insisted that nothing exists except individual particulars, yet when they talked about psychology they didn't mind generalizing in the grandest terms. It was Rousseau who took individuality seriously and resisted the seductions of generality. Writing to a stranger who had sent him a philosophical treatise, he said firmly, "Our senses show us individuals only. Reflection is able to separate them, and judgment can compare them with each other, but that's all. To hope to reunite them exceeds the power of our understanding; it's wanting to push the boat one is in without touching anything outside it." Hume was a great philosopher whose thinking contributed to the course of later philosophy. Rousseau was a great creator whose writing helped to shape the imaginative world we still inhabit.

But history isn't monolithic, and if Rousseau is the prophet of introspective analysis, we have other models too. Perhaps the most interesting contrast of all is with Benjamin Franklin, whom Rousseau admired by reputation but didn't know personally. The book known as Franklin's *Autobiography* (begun in the 1770s, but not published until the nineteenth century, which is when the word "autobiography" was invented) had a major influence for generations in America, if not elsewhere, because it showed how a self-made man did the making. We remember Franklin as he wanted to be remembered, a tireless inventor and organizer in a world of projects and public works, founding fire departments and post offices and public libraries and universities, inventing the lightning rod and bifocal glasses and the Franklin stove. His inner life is another matter, obscure to the point of opacity, and a scholar who has studied every word he wrote concludes, "Who can do more than guess about this man?" But if Franklin wore a mask, it was one that fitted his face comfortably, and he liked best to merge himself in a group identity. He was committed to politics not as high theory (as in the Rousseauian "inalienable rights") but as compromise among interest groups, the very thing Rousseau's general will was intended to prevent. Rousseau was a prophet; Franklin was a facilitator.

Psychologically, Franklin embodied the ideal of being well adjusted, and in the life story he tells he turns every setback around. He was born just one year after Rousseau, and at the outset had surprisingly similar experiences, with a limited formal education and a hated apprenticeship. He even devoured Plutarch's *Lives,* but whereas Rousseau learned from Plutarch that the days of greatness were past, Franklin saw no reason not to become a national hero himself. Again like Rousseau, Franklin developed a lifelong resentment of maltreatment by employers, and he says that his first master's harsh treatment encouraged "that aversion to arbitrary power that has stuck to me through my whole life." But Franklin was not interested, as Rousseau was, in the ways in which servitude could socialize a youth into profoundly inauthentic behavior. Rousseau became an idler and petty thief, ran away from Geneva with no idea what to do next, and drifted aimlessly for the next ten years. Franklin ran away from Boston with plenty of self-discipline and skills, promptly set himself up as a printer in Philadelphia, and almost immediately became a watchword for industriousness and honesty.

To build up the kind of stable character that eighteenth-century society admired, the best means was to condition oneself to act in the desired ways. Franklin figured this out very early, and at the age of nineteen he drew up a "Plan of Conduct" to accomplish it. He realized that he had begun to strike people as an assertive freethinker and that he was given to outbursts of anger that alienated them. So he set out to delete the undesirable tendencies and acquire the correct ones, making a chart of thirteen virtues and attacking them systematically, one virtue per week, four cycles per year. This was a behaviorist experiment with himself as subject, and the contrast with Rousseau could not be more marked. Rousseau wanted to recover his true self by getting rid of the habits that social life called for, whereas those habits were exactly what Franklin wanted to acquire. Franklin showed that he was able to learn from mistakes and correct them (he called them "errata"), while Rousseau showed that mistakes form a pattern and reveal deep aspects of the self.

It is no exaggeration to say that Franklin and Rousseau stand at opposite poles of the legacy we have inherited from the eighteenth century. Contemporary American culture talks the Rousseau line but lives the Franklin life. When we talk about getting in touch with our true selves or about being what we were meant to be, we're talking like Jean-Jacques Rousseau. When we commit ourselves to careers or strive to be "team players," we are living like Benjamin Franklin. To say it another way, Franklin's *Autobiography* encourages readers to construct a public life, while Rousseau's *Confessions* challenges them to make a journey into the self. These are fundamental tensions in modern life, and their first great analyst was Jean-Jacques Rousseau.

But it is only with centuries of hindsight that we can recognize these implications. Franklin's virtues and achievement were widely appreciated during his lifetime, but Rousseau's were only dimly grasped at first. The *Discourse on Inequality, The Social Contract,* and *Émile* were widely dismissed as provocative but absurd, describing a state of nature that never existed, a political system that never could exist, and an educational scheme that never should exist. Gradually, however, thoughtful people began to understand the radical implications of Rousseau's analysis of social inequality, and of governments that failed to embody the will of the people. Not a few tried to raise their children on Rousseau's principles, and educational reformers increasingly invoked them. When the *Confessions* finally appeared, four years after Rousseau's death, that book too aroused very mixed feelings. Readers had been expecting a high-minded review of a celebrated intellectual career, mingled with juicy anecdotes about famous people. Instead, Rousseau wrote mostly about people no one had ever heard of, and much of what he described seemed trivial. "What will it matter to posterity," a reviewer demanded, "to know that Jean-Jacques was once with a M. Grapignan, then apprenticed to an engraver, then to a sort of charlatan, and then to a mendicant archimandrite, or that he stole asparagus, apples, and bottles of wine?"

Even more inexplicable were the sexual revelations, both because they seemed embarrassingly perverse and because readers were not accustomed to thinking such information relevant to understanding a person's life. Rousseau enjoying a childhood spanking by Mlle Lambercier, exposing himself in Turin, and sleeping with the woman he called Maman, all gave offense, but it was the spanking that was most often singled out for derision. Rousseau calls it "the first and most painful step in the obscure and miry labyrinth of my confessions," but a reviewer's reaction was typical: "If the over-sincere Jean-Jacques had no respect for modesty and was not afraid to wound his readers' delicacy with such strange ideas, he should at least have dreaded the shame and contempt that the world attaches to bizarre tastes that reveal a vicious temperament. This admission of an involuntary but outrageous weakness, made public unnecessarily and pointlessly, will astonish some, make others blush, provide the greatest number with an inexhaustible source of bad jokes, and stamp Rousseau's memory with something indelibly ridiculous."

Surprisingly, it was Rousseau's old enemy Grimm who saw the point of such revelations: they show that "a man like Rousseau is aware of his most secret feelings . . . and offers valuable instruction in the art of observing ourselves, penetrating to the most hidden motives of our conduct and actions." Two centuries later, that kind of understanding had become altogether familiar. "Autobiography is only to be trusted," George Orwell once said, "when it reveals something disgraceful. A man who gives a good account of himself is probably lying, since any life when viewed from the inside is simply a series of defeats." Gibbon and Hume and Franklin were not liars, but they highlighted their achievements, minimized their defeats, and presented idealized self-images. Rousseau confronted his defeats with unflinching honesty.

Above all, Rousseau showed how a mosaic of remembered details, some inconsequential, some haunting and thought-provoking, could build up an understanding of a unique individual. "I am made like no one I have seen," he declares at the beginning of the *Confessions,* "and I dare to believe that I am made like no one who exists. If I am not worth more, at least I am different." And he follows this assertion of individuality with a challenge that is both a defiance and an invitation: "Whether nature did well or badly in breaking the mold in which I was cast, that is what no one can judge until after they have read me." Another writer would probably have said "until after they have read my books"; Rousseau insists that he himself must be read. At first, this struck many readers as blatant egoism, but for Rousseau a subjective vision is the only true one. Even *The Social Contract,* the most abstract of his works, begins with the word *je* and ends with the word *moi.* And one of his greatest achievements is to show how subjectivity, far from compromising a writer's ideas, gives them authority and depth. As Lionel Trilling has said, "The author of the *Discourses* has the more power over us because he is the subject of the *Confessions.* He is the man; he suffered; he was there."

23

<hr/>

Into the Self-Made Labyrinth

WITH THE *CONFESSIONS* half finished, and exulting at his escape from nonexistent danger, Rousseau was back in France, where the danger was real. The parlement of Paris had jurisdiction over a large area of northern France; its arrest warrant for Rousseau was still very much in force, and any prosecutor could initiate a process that would be impossible to halt. Jean Guéhenno, writing his biography of Rousseau during the Nazi occupation, aptly invokes that dark era of informers and of detention without trial. At the very moment that Rousseau returned to France, two of his friends were in the Bastille, Guy for importing prohibited books, including *The Social Contract,* and Lenieps for radical opinions that were revealed when his private papers were seized.

At first Rousseau somehow allowed himself to ignore the threat. He went to Amiens, where he appeared in public and enjoyed a banquet in his honor. But this respite soon ended, and the next three years, from mid-1767 to mid-1770, would be the worst of his life. By a kind of tragic irony, his deepest troubles would flow from a patron who regarded himself as acting in Rousseau's best interest as well as his own. The prince de Conti, a regular visitor at Montmorency, had strongly encouraged him to publish *The Social Contract* and *Émile.* Together with his ally, the late duc de Luxembourg, Conti had hoped that those books would contribute to a campaign to liberalize the royal government. But after the firestorm of reprisal burst over Rousseau, it was crucial that Conti keep his own involvement secret, and if Rousseau was interrogated he would surely expose it. So it became the business of Conti and his mistress, Mme de Boufflers, to keep him out of circulation while convincing him that they were acting for his own good. Perhaps they did believe that, but the result was that Rousseau's paranoid fantasies deepened until he became frantic with terror.

After leaving Amiens, he stayed with an aristocratic admirer near Paris, calling himself "Monsieur Jacques" but still appearing openly, and Conti caught up with him there. Conti owned a château at Trye (modern Trie-Château) in the Oise district, forty miles northwest of Paris, and he decided to sequester Rousseau there. Trye was an out-of-the-way place, a small village near the town of Gisors, and although it fell within the jurisdiction of the parlement of Paris, the Normandy border was close by, and a retreat could be easily managed if necessary. With his influence at court, Conti had obtained assurances that Rousseau would be safe so long as he behaved with total circumspection. "If you change your name completely (I say completely, because the name of Jacques that you've taken isn't enough of a change) and if you are willing to stay there without writing anything, peaceful and unknown, you will not be disturbed." Rousseau now adopted the name Jean-Joseph Renou — Renou was the maiden name of old Mme Levasseur, who had died while they were in England — and Thérèse became his sister.

The château at Trye dated in part from the thirteenth century, with a picturesque stone tower in which Rousseau and Thérèse would live. Rousseau no doubt hoped that Conti, with whom he had stayed in Paris during the journey from Switzerland to England, would visit often and develop the kind of relationship he had had with the duc de Luxembourg, but that was not to be. Unlike Luxembourg, Conti was very much a *grand seigneur,* and although he approved of Rousseau's political views he had no intention of becoming an intimate friend. In the Montmorency days Conti had refused to dine with him when he realized that Thérèse would be at the table, and he and Mme de Boufflers were seriously offended when Rousseau refused a gift of game that the prince himself had shot.

THE CHÂTEAU AT TRYE
The tower is unchanged from Rousseau's time; then as now it overlooked the main road through town. Rousseau and Thérèse are believed to have lived on the top floor, inhabited today only by pigeons. The rest of the building houses municipal offices.

It is likely, too, that Conti had not appreciated being beaten soundly at chess in those days. His entourage used to make urgent signals to Rousseau to start losing, but he went right on winning and said grandly afterward, "My lord, I honor your serene highness too much not to beat you always at chess." When someone suggested later on that he could at least have let Conti win occasionally, he answered in surprise, "What! I did give him a rook!" If the prince couldn't win with an advantage like that, he deserved to lose. But they were playing a different game now, in which Rousseau's vulnerability was the essential fact of their relationship, and Conti never let Rousseau forget it. He gave vague assurances that he would visit Trye sometime, but months went by and he never did.

At first Rousseau was prepared to accept this new life, and he felt less cut off than at Wootton. He renewed his friendship with Coindet, who was working for the Necker banking family in Paris; in the Montmorency days young Coindet had been eager to run errands for Rousseau, and he was happy to resume that role. He procured clothing (it was months before Rousseau's belongings arrived from England), tableware, and books, and he not only retrieved Sultan from a veterinarian in Amiens but had the foresight to engrave the château's name on his collar, which proved invaluable when the coachman lost him along the way. Rousseau had written in despair, "Such has been the fate of the unfortunate Sultan, and such is mine"; then, when Sultan was recovered, he exclaimed joyously, "I thank you for everything, and embrace you with all my heart." Best of all, Du Peyrou, who was in Amsterdam on business, promised to visit on his way back to Switzerland.

Things soon went wrong, however. At Wootton there had been a grumpy housekeeper and cook; at Trye the whole staff was snobbish and insolent. A haughty individual named Manoury, who held the most important position at the château as master of the hunt, was openly contemptuous of Rousseau's manners and clothes, "rather lower than bourgeois," as Rousseau acknowledged. It didn't help that Rousseau never wanted to go hunting. Worst of all was the gatekeeper, a sour fellow named Deschamps, who made indecent remarks about Mme de Boufflers and amused himself by locking Rousseau inside the château when he wanted to go out and locking him out when he wanted to come in. Even getting into the woods and fields was difficult. Sometimes Rousseau was told that dangerous brigands were about and that he would have to be accompanied by a man with a gun; at other times the villagers jeered at him, stirred up by the local priest against a stranger who never went to mass. In short, this new way of life amounted to house arrest.

Conti eventually did come to Trye; he dined formally with Rousseau to demonstrate his esteem and threatened to punish the servants if they misbehaved. This was no consolation for Rousseau, who thought the servants had merely managed to hoodwink their master. He told Coindet darkly, "The root of the evil that snakes along underground has not been cut off." All of his hopes were now placed on the arrival of Du Peyrou. "I have no one but you," he wrote to him in September. "From now on you will be the entire human race for me."

Unfortunately, Du Peyrou, who was still in his thirties but had long suffered from gout, came down with a crippling attack in Paris and was laid up there for two months. It is worth remarking that serious illness was normal in the eighteenth century on a scale that would seem appalling today. In the fall of 1767 alone, Du Peyrou and Davenport were both bedridden with gout, Coindet had a dangerous fever, Granville had arthritis so severe that he couldn't write, and Mme de Verdelin, in addition to suffering illnesses of her own, was nursing a beloved daughter in irreversible decline with some kind of wasting disease. At the same time, Rousseau had a stomach complaint and a terrible toothache, which he cured by extracting the offending molar himself.

Du Peyrou was finally well enough in November to get to Trye, but after a joyous first week, he succumbed to another attack of gout so violent that it provoked one of the strangest episodes of Rousseau's life. As Rousseau afterward described the crisis, Du Peyrou was alarmed by a worsening of his long-standing deafness as well as by excruciating gout, and he dosed himself with various drugs that Rousseau thought ill advised. One day when Du Peyrou woke up, he found that a hand and a foot were swollen, which was not unusual, but also that his head, throat, and stomach ached painfully, and he was so weak that he could hardly stand. Rousseau, who was nursing him, suddenly panicked. "He spoke ceaselessly of having a bad fermentation in his stomach. His looks, his manner, and his stifled words had something so strange about them that I finally got thoroughly alarmed, and resolved to penetrate the mystery . . . At last I grasped that he believed he had been poisoned, and by whom? My God!" It was Rousseau whom Du Peyrou suspected, or so Rousseau believed, and this was therefore to be "a fatal night, the most dreadful of my life."

The doctor who was called in confirmed that the patient had nothing wrong except gout, and he prescribed a cordial that Du Peyrou was reluctant to take. Unfortunately, when he did drink it, a powdery residue remained at the bottom of the cup, and Rousseau felt certain that he imagined it was poison. In reality it seems clear that Du Peyrou had no such notion, but when Rousseau threw himself upon his friend in a flood of tears, Du Peyrou failed to respond with sufficient animation. "The barbarous man dared to reproach me for choosing the moment of his greatest weakness to give him a shock that could finish him off." Always self-regarding, Rousseau made no allowance for Du Peyrou's shattered condition and fear of dying. "At that moment I felt all my esteem, affection, and tenderness for him extinguished to the last spark."

Du Peyrou recovered rapidly, but relations between the friends were irrevocably damaged. He told Rousseau (in writing, though they were living under the same roof) that he felt deeply hurt by the accusation that he had suspected poison at a time when he had been totally delirious. Rousseau replied coldly that although some intemperate words might have escaped him, Du Peyrou's behavior was still inexcusable. "You say you were delirious because of fever. That's true, but if you had stabbed me in your delirium, would you have had no regret afterward? And you've done worse than stab me." At the best of times, Rousseau tended to suspect that his feelings for others weren't reciprocated, and in this period of high anxiety his own sufferings made it impossible to understand his friend's.

In the past their relationship had been largely epistolary, with only intermittent visits between Môtiers and Neuchâtel. Now that they were together for weeks on end, their temperamental differences would have become obvious even without the poisoning scare, and by the end of December Rousseau admitted to Coindet that he and Du Peyrou had simply tired of each other. On January 3, after a stay of two months, Du Peyrou finally departed, still in such shaky health that Rousseau sent for their old friend Colonel Pury to come from Switzerland and escort him home. Once they were writing from a distance, more or less amicable relations resumed, Rousseau using his customary salutation *mon cher hôte* and Du Peyrou replying *mon cher citoyen,* but at a deeper level the estrangement was permanent.

Far from being victimized by friends, Rousseau was exceptionally fortunate in them, but he could never really believe it. Abandoned by his father, rejected by Mme de Warens, and let down if not betrayed by Grimm and Diderot, he could seldom trust anyone for long. "Solitude used to be your mistress," one correspondent said shrewdly, "and you have taken it to wife." Rousseau's obsessions had become all too necessary to him, and he went on alienating the few friends he still had. When Conti kept finding reasons not to visit Trye again, Rousseau wrote to Mme de Boufflers to complain rather petulantly; her reply was so chilly that he promised, "I will never importune you again with my complaints." So far as is known, he never heard from her again, and he decided to stop writing even to Coindet and Du Peyrou.

Living in a state of generalized dread, Rousseau soon experienced another crisis. The idea of poison was now firmly lodged in his imagination, awaiting some new ambiguous situation. Deschamps, the gatekeeper who had been hostile all along, fell seriously ill with the kind of heart condition that used to be called dropsy. Out of kindness Rousseau gave him some preserves, a bit of nicely cooked fish, and a bottle of Burgundy. Other people shared these delicacies with no ill effects, but when Deschamps continued to worsen and then died, Rousseau became convinced that the château staff was going to accuse him of murder. His books had been accused of poisoning people's minds, and now in his mind the poisoning became literal. Working himself up into a state of terror, he insisted that an autopsy be performed to rule out the possibility of poison. Also, concluding that there was no use hiding any longer, he decided to go to Paris and force the authorities to resolve his legal situation once and for all. In the meantime he proposed to commit himself to the local jail, apparently to put himself out of reach of his enemies, real or imagined.

If Rousseau went to Paris and provoked legal proceedings, Conti's complicity would certainly be dragged into the open, and the prince was horrified at the prospect. His only recourse was to try to calm Rousseau down and then remove him as far from Paris as possible. "I ask you in your friendship," he wrote to Rousseau, "and in recognition of mine, to wait until I get there without saying or doing anything . . . For God's sake wait for me. I'll be with you on Sunday. Stay calm until then." Hastening to Trye, Conti found nothing to confirm Rousseau's fears but agreed to let him travel to Lyon, which Rousseau regarded as a hopeful destination. He had slept by the river there as a youth, he had lived there later on with the Mably family, and it was one of the few places where he still had trusted friends: "Papa" Roguin's charming niece, Mme Boy de la Tour, and her charming daughter Madeleine-Cathérine Delessert. One thing the Roguin clan had done right was not to see Rousseau for years, unlike poor Coindet and Du Peyrou. Just at this time, in fact, Du Peyrou wrote a moving letter to Coindet, sympathizing with his bitterness at being rejected. "M. Rousseau's disposition is never to be happy. His mistrust is now total, I believe, or nearly so . . . Let us pity him, Monsieur, but don't let's stop loving him . . . He's a spoiled child, true enough, but he was made like that."

Rousseau spent some happy weeks in Lyon, but it too was within the jurisdiction of the parlement of Paris, so he moved on to Grenoble, in the eastern province known as the Dauphiné, where he would be safe. Now, however, he was entirely among strangers, and his fears began to

ROUSSEAU MEMORIAL AT TRYE

Rousseau is remembered at Trye, where he suffered so much, with this charming monument (by H. Gréber). Its inscription reads: J. J. ROUSSEAU WRITING UNDER THE INSPIRATION OF TRUTH AND OF NATURE. Nature has eroded quite a bit since the monument was erected in 1911, but she is still very much Rousseau's type.

blossom once again, provoked in part by a warning from Conti that the Grenoble police had him under surveillance. When he made a brief excursion to Chambéry in the Savoie — the last time he was ever outside of France — he hastily returned, convinced that his old friend Conzié was part of a plot, "as deep as it is shadowy," that was spreading across the face of Europe.

Grenoble didn't work out well. A half-crazy individual turned up who claimed that Rousseau had borrowed a small sum of money from him when he was in Môtiers years before and had failed to pay it back. Although the charge was demonstrably absurd, Rousseau suspected that the man had been coached to alarm him. In addition, some local admirers, who knew perfectly well that "Renou" was really Rousseau, gave offense by hosting a dinner at which he was insulted by a drunken schoolteacher who made sarcastic remarks about the philosophes and proposed a public debate. Rousseau instantly surmised that this person too had been coached to provoke him, and he was understandably outraged that his true identity was widely known. It got about so quickly, in fact, that crowds applauded him on the road and choruses sang airs from *The Village Soothsayer* under his window. "Receive my adieux, Monsieur," Rousseau wrote to his host. "Do not think I retain the foolish hope of finding a peaceful refuge where I can be shielded from hidden snares, insults, and affronts."

To the astonishment of his new acquaintances, Rousseau then abruptly left town, forgetting his dressing gown and carrying off his apartment keys in his haste. They assumed his departure had to do somehow with the schoolteacher's behavior, but there was a more pressing reason that they didn't suspect. Thérèse, who had waited at Trye until a safe place of refuge was secured, was now on the road, and Rousseau was anxious to keep her away, for he knew that this time he could not pass her off as his sister. Everyone in Grenoble knew who Rousseau was, and *The Sentiment of the Citizens* had exposed the truth about Thérèse and the abandoned children. Suddenly finding himself in a corner, Rousseau rashly announced that Thérèse was his wife, and now it was time for damage control.

He still had plenty of reasons not to marry Thérèse. Unions between Catholics and Protestants were legally void in France. Furthermore, marrying under assumed names was prohibited, but if Rousseau were to reclaim his real name he would be disobeying the explicit order of the prince de Conti. On top of all this, he had told Thérèse from the very outset that he would never marry her, he had treated her increasingly as a servant, and he had already made provision for her financial support in case of his death. But he now felt that his reputation depended on being properly married, or at least on seeming to be.

Where to live, however, was the immediate problem. On August 12 Rousseau headed back toward Lyon, halting at the last sizable town within the Dauphiné. This was Bourgoin, an unremarkable place in a disagreeable marshland setting, but it would have to do. He took a room at the Fontaine d'Or, and Thérèse finally arrived. Three days later he invited the local mayor and a friend to dinner and unexpectedly asked them to witness what he described to the mayor as "the most important action of his life." After delivering a moving speech on the duties of marriage, which drew tears from his guests, he exchanged impromptu vows with Thérèse. They then sat down to a wedding dinner at which he sang gaily and declared an intention to remain in Bourgoin for the rest of his days. The marriage had no legal standing whatsoever, both because a Catholic priest had not officiated and because no document was signed or preserved.

To friends who needed to be told what he had done, Rousseau stressed the moral aspects of the event rather than the prudential ones. He wrote to Moultou, "My housekeeper, my friend, my sister, and my everything has at last become my wife. Since she has been willing to follow my fate and share all the misfortunes of my life, I must at least make sure that it has been done with honor. Twenty-five years of the union of hearts has ended by producing a union of persons." He assured another correspondent that "the tender and pure fraternity in which we have lived for thirty years has not changed its nature through the conjugal knot; she is and will remain until death my wife by the strength of our ties, and my sister by their purity."

Rousseau expected the stay in Bourgoin to be brief, which is why he took up residence at an inn, but he and Thérèse lived there for five dismal months. He was constantly casting about for somewhere to go. He had ideas of Italy, or maybe Cyprus or Minorca, or even Wootton, for both Davenport and Granville had invited him to return there. But most of the imagined destinations were too remote, and he abandoned any thought of Wootton when he discovered that the English ambassador in Paris, from whom he would need to obtain a passport, had a secretary named Walpole. In fact it wasn't the hated Horace Walpole at all but a cousin of his; still, it didn't take much to knock Rousseau off balance.

Du Peyrou kept urging Rousseau to live with him in his newly completed palace in Neuchâtel, but Rousseau would not consider it. He explained to Mme Delessert in Lyon that the mysterious "they" had gained sinister control of his former friend. "Not only have they succeeded in taking Du Peyrou from me, in whom I had placed all my hopes, to whom I had confided all my papers, projects, and secrets, from whom alone I expected my deliverance, for whom I left England, and with whom my last and sweetest hope was to live and die; they have taken him from me, as I say, but in such an incredible, sudden, and completely inconceivable way that never has there been so strong and monstrous an alienation as I've found in him." Rousseau could not bring himself to understand that if it seemed incredible and inconceivable, it was because it wasn't true. Du Peyrou remained the most faithful of his friends to the end of his life.

As autumn turned to winter, Rousseau's health worsened dramatically. His stomach became grossly distended and was so painful that he couldn't even bend over to put on his shoes. He blamed the bad air of Bourgoin and, more plausibly by modern standards, the bad water. As always, it is impossible to know how much of the trouble was physical and how much was emotional, but the description he sent to a Swiss doctor is strikingly reminiscent of his psychosomatic breakdown long before in Chambéry. In addition to the swollen stomach, he mentioned fever, headaches, heart palpitations, a feeling of suffocation, ringing in the ears, and insomnia. The doctor's opinion has not been preserved, but judging from Rousseau's reply, he diagnosed a diseased liver and confirmed Rousseau's belief that he had only a short time to live.

The immediate concern was to get out of Bourgoin. Rousseau left behind a remarkable summary of his plight, written in pencil on the door of his bedroom at the inn, and he liked it so well that he sent copies to several friends. It is especially striking that he still believed that the higher aristocrats were well disposed toward him and that he was being victimized by an alliance between intellectual rivals and a gullible public.

> Kings and the great don't say what they think, but they will
> always treat me with magnanimity.
> The true nobility, who love glory and know that I understand it,
> honor me and keep silent . . .
> The philosophes, whom I have unmasked, want to destroy me,
> and they will succeed . . .
> The people, whom I idolized, see nothing more in me than an
> unkempt wig and a man under warrant for arrest.
> Women, duped by two wet blankets [*pisse-froid,* literally "cold
> pissers"] who despise them, betray the man who deserved the
> best from them.

The wet blankets were Diderot and d'Alembert (or possibly Grimm), much sought after by society women but in Rousseau's opinion privately contemptuous of them. The piece ends with a shrewd hit at Voltaire, whose letters had been filled for years with labored sarcasms about walking on all fours and Diogenes' dog. "Voltaire, whom I prevent from sleeping, will parody these lines. His gross insults are the homage he is forced to pay me in spite of himself."

At this juncture a certain marquis de Césarges and his wife offered an attractive place to stay, a farmhouse near the little village of Maubec, a couple of miles outside Bourgoin. Known as Monquin, the farm had once been a *maison forte* or fortified manor, but was now in disrepair and uninhabited in winter. It lay on a plateau well above the damp valley, with a vista of broad fields and, on a clear day, a distant view of the great massif of Mont Blanc. (To be sure, there was a saying in Lyon, "If you can see Mont Blanc, tomorrow it will rain.") So in February 1769 Rousseau settled there quite optimistically; Thérèse was less happy, since she still yearned for Paris and hated living where she had nobody to talk to. Unfortunately, winter on the exposed heights was awful. Thanking Mme Boy for sending some wine, Rousseau remarked that it helped him to endure "a veritable ice-house, where even the fiercest fire just roasts me on one side while I'm freezing on the other." He got Mme

THE FARM OF MONQUIN

This impressive gate, all that survives from the structure as Rousseau knew it, was a relic of the farm's earlier days as a manor. It is still a farm today.

Boy to rent a spinet for him, which was carried in on a man's back and was an invaluable diversion when he was warm enough to play it.

When spring finally arrived, Rousseau resumed his rambling walks, and when he set out on a longer expedition, he left a remarkable letter for Thérèse. She was apparently considering a permanent separation, and he addressed the grievance that lay at the bottom of it. "When we united in marriage I made my conditions, you agreed to them, and I have fulfilled them. It was only a tender attachment on your part that could make me dismiss them and listen only to our love at the risk of my life and health." He had always feared that sexual relations were physically dangerous for him, and he now claimed that Thérèse's affections had diminished so much that he could no longer endure them. "Your cooling toward me has held me back, and provocativeness isn't enough to attract me when the heart repulses me." Rousseau enjoyed playing at seduction with sophisticated ladies, but overt advances by Thérèse were unacceptable. In pleading for her to come back, however, he promised "to have only one bed from now on, since we will share a single soul." Evidently she had expected that marriage would put an end to separate bedrooms and was indignant when it didn't. Also, it is easy to imagine — though no documentary evidence survives — that she was still bitter over the loss of her children. There seems to be a possibility, as well, that she had formed an improper relationship with a monk. Rousseau said darkly that if she did decide to leave, "let no monk get involved with you or your affairs in any way whatsoever," and Grimm later reported a rumor that Rousseau had actually surprised her *in flagrante* with the monk.

During these gloomy months Rousseau was hard at work on the continuation of the *Confessions,* and although it contains many memorable stories — the Venetian period, the illumination of Vincennes, the affair with Mme d'Houdetot, the friendship with the Luxembourgs, the idyll on the Île de Saint-Pierre — the narrative is congested with detail, and the tone increasingly paranoid. "The ceiling above me has eyes," he wrote when he resumed the book, "the walls around me have ears. Surrounded by spies and by malevolent, vigilant watchers, anxious and distracted, I write down in haste a few disjointed words that I barely have time to reread, let alone to revise."

Rousseau's anxiety came to a head on the night of November 8, 1769. Sorting through his papers, he noticed a striking gap. Not one letter survived from a six-month period in 1756–57 when he had been living in Montmorency. What had happened? The letters must have been stolen, but why? The real explanation was that Rousseau himself had misfiled the letters, which eventually turned up, but on this fateful night he suddenly saw all the pieces coming together. To ensure that some record of his ordeal would survive even if the manuscript of the *Confessions* was seized, he composed an account known as the "Letter to Saint-Germain," addressed to a local gentleman whom he barely knew but who had a reputation for uprightness. This document is at once lucidly written and, as Leigh says, "painful in its tragic absurdity." Rousseau convinced himself that the plot against him was being masterminded by Choiseul, the powerful prime minister whom he had once offended by an inept compliment, and that Choiseul was working through a vast network of agents to frighten and eventually destroy him.

Now the whole sequence of events became clear to him. Grimm and Diderot had originally intended to coach Rousseau to write wicked books in order to blacken his reputation, but he had escaped from their clutches (and Mme d'Épinay's) and was taken up by the duke and duchess of Luxembourg. His enemies' countermove, working through Choiseul, was to engineer the denunciation of *Émile* by the parlement of Paris. With the Luxembourgs' help he had escaped yet again and found a new protector in Maréchal Keith. This time, working through Voltaire, his enemies had him expelled from Switzerland and isolated in England under the supervision of Hume. Yet again he managed to get away, and the prince de Conti concealed him at Trye, but there too they were able to scare him into leaving. Most diabolically of all, they had formed a plan to associate him with the would-be assassin Damiens, whose notorious attempt on the king's life had occurred at the very time of the missing letters. The implication was plain: Rousseau's letters from that period had been stolen so that they could be replaced with documents that would implicate him in the assassination attempt, and these would be released to the public when the moment was ripe for his destruction. The fantasy of a *complot* or conspiracy had thus developed into something like a literary plot, elaborated by Rousseau's novelistic imagination and projected onto the world around him. Only the dénouement remained unknown.

So now Rousseau was in terrified seclusion in the Dauphiné, writing with freezing fingers during the interminable winter, and demanding in Kafkaesque terms that his accusers declare themselves. "Let me know, at all costs, what I am guilty of!" There could no longer be any question of fleeing France. Instead of trying to escape from his enemies, whose allies were in place all over Europe, he must confront them directly in their Paris stronghold. The result might be fatal, but death would be better than ceaseless uncertainty. He knew, of course, that he would be told that no one was attacking him, but in the circular reasoning to which he was now committed, that merely proved his point. If his enemies refused to accuse him openly, that would confirm that they were doing it secretly; the shadowy obscurity of their plot was the strongest evidence for its satanic cleverness. For the rest of his life, and he had eight more years to live, he held to this bizarre story with unshakable conviction. Evidently he needed to believe it. It explained his feeling of undeserved and perpetual isolation, and it gave him a way to project his gnawing sense of guilt onto agents outside himself, with a Lear-like sense of loss, grief, and undeserved suffering.

Eventually Rousseau managed to secure an interview with Conti, who was visiting a spa nearby, and although there is no record of what was said, it looks as if a grudging permission to emerge from hiding was finally granted. As soon as the weather relented at the beginning of April, Rousseau and Thérèse went straight to Lyon, where the parlement of Paris had the power to unleash its wrath if it so chose. It did not. In fact, the next two months turned out to be an exceptionally agreeable interlude. A particularly happy friendship developed with a young man named Horace Coignet, a designer of fabrics (the chief industry of Lyon) who was an enthusiastic amateur musician. According to Coignet's account, he met Rousseau at a concert and was invited for a visit that was supposed to end after a quarter of an hour but lasted for five. Coignet sang a composition of his own, Rousseau sang some of his in return, and they sat down to a cheerful dinner with Thérèse. "We drank," Coignet recalled, "and we were on our second bottle, when I told him I was afraid of getting intoxicated. He replied laughing that he would get to know me better that way, since the wine would bring out my character."

Soon Rousseau was proposing that Coignet compose musical interludes for the little prose poem *Pygmalion* that he had completed in Môtiers years before. It was performed publicly to great acclaim, together with *The Village Soothsayer,* and from then on during Rousseau's stay in Lyon, Coignet never went more than a day without seeing him. They especially enjoyed rambling near a country house that belonged to Mme Boy. "When we went for a walk there one morning, the Boy de la Tour girls, young and full of graces, came along and nimbly climbed the hill. Rousseau botanized while admiring the beauty of nature, and I sang his romance from *The Village Soothsayer* to him, accompanying myself on the violin. He exclaimed, in a moment of enthusiasm, that everything he saw and heard was romantic, and that it was one of the happy days of his life."

If only Rousseau had been content to stay in Lyon, where he was admired by the public, loved by friends, and genuinely secure! But his obsession was far too deeply rooted for that. Paris was the citadel of enemies who apparently wanted to let him agonize in suspense, and he had no choice but to carry the fight to their lair. On June 8 he and Thérèse took to the road once again, and two weeks later they were installed in an apartment in their old Paris street, the rue Plâtrière. Let the authorities throw him in jail if they liked; he felt ready for the ultimate showdown. But in actuality Conti had grossly exaggerated their hostility. It turned out that so long as Rousseau kept quiet, the government had no wish to disturb him. His paranoia was by now in full flower, too deeply rooted to relinquish, yet Rousseau's final years would be a time of remarkable tranquility.

24

The Final Years in Paris

"ADIEU THEN, PARIS," Rousseau had written in *Émile* a decade earlier, "celebrated city of noise, smoke, and mud, where the women no longer believe in honor or the men in virtue. Adieu, Paris; we seek love, happiness, and innocence, and we will never be far enough away from you." A few years later, describing the move to the Hermitage, he said decisively, "It was on the ninth of April, 1756, that I left the city never to inhabit it again." But now, in 1770, he was glad to be back. Thérèse, of course, was even more delighted; for her, Paris was home.

It almost seemed as if the last decade had never happened. Waiting for the arrest that never came, Rousseau was often seen strolling in the Luxembourg Gardens, going to the theater, or playing chess. A newsletter gave a friendly account of his reappearance: "Some days ago he presented himself at the Café de la Régence, where he soon attracted a considerable crowd. Our cynic philosopher sustained this little triumph with great modesty. He didn't seem alarmed by the multitude of spectators, and conversed with great affability, contrary to his custom. He is no longer dressed as an Armenian, but like everyone else, neatly and simply." Grimm, admitting that Rousseau attracted crowds, suggested however that this wave of attention should not be mistaken for admiration. "When half of those people were asked what they were doing there, they said it was to see Jean-Jacques. When they were asked who this Jean-Jacques was, they said they had no idea."

Rousseau paid numerous calls on friends, though he made sure never to encounter those with whom he had become disillusioned, including of course Grimm, Diderot, and d'Alembert, but also Coindet, the duchesse de Luxembourg, the comtesse de Boufflers, and the prince de Conti. Nothing is known about Conti's attitude at this time; he may have been surprised that Rousseau was left unmolested, or he may have expected it and simply regretted that Rousseau had escaped from his supervision. In a note in the *Confessions* manuscript, Rousseau commented ruefully that it had taken him incredibly long to get over his "blind and stupid confidence" in the imperious prince. But there were many people he still enjoyed seeing, including Malesherbes, with whom he resumed a shared interest in botany. He wrote to Saint-Germain in Bourgoin, "I've returned to my old dwelling, I see old acquaintances again, and I follow my old way of life. I'm pursuing my old trade of copyist, and thus far I find myself in almost the same situation that I was in before I left." He stopped using an ominous quatrain about unmasking impostors that had introduced his letters for the past year, and when he wrote to Du Peyrou to say that their friendship might be revived, his letter was headed with the Reformation motto of Geneva, *post tenebras lux,* "light after darkness." Du Peyrou eventually did pay a visit, about which nothing is known except that they talked affectionately about Keith.

When Rousseau and Thérèse settled in the rue Plâtrière, a few blocks north of the Louvre, they were in familiar territory indeed. He had frequented the Dupin mansion there in the early 1740s (it still stands at No. 68), and from 1747 to 1750 he had lived close by in the Hôtel du Saint-Esprit, on the site now occupied by No. 56. Now they returned to the Hôtel du Saint-Esprit while looking for permanent quarters, and in December they moved into No. 60, also still standing today. In 1791 the rue Plâtrière was merged with the rue de Grenelle-Saint-Honoré and renamed the rue Jean-Jacques Rousseau. To a visitor who expressed surprise that he lived in a noisy street rather than in rural tranquility, Rousseau explained that he loved good fruit, vegetables, and fowl, and could get them cheaply in an unfashionable neighborhood. Moreover, in those days the woods and fields were close enough

ROUSSEAU'S PARIS LODGINGS

Rousseau and Thérèse lived on the sixth floor of this apartment house on the rue Plâtrière in the 1770s. The print was made after the café on the ground floor had named itself in his honor.

to be reached easily on foot, and he enjoyed regular *herborisations* conducted by the royal gardener at the Jardin des Plantes.

At this point also, Rousseau's health improved, and he acknowledged that the mysterious urinary complaint had greatly abated after he stopped listening to doctors. "I am living proof of the vanity of their art and the uselessness of their treatment." It was undoubtedly true that the medical procedures of the time tended to make things worse and that it was often better to let nature take its course. As Rousseau said at this time, "Doctors sometimes effect cures, I don't doubt it, but they often kill and they always torment. It's a fool's lottery, and I'm not going to gamble my life on it." And if his malady did have a psychosomatic component, perhaps it had served its purpose as a reaction to fame. Writing of himself in the third person, he commented, "He no longer has that chronic suffering, that leanness, that pale complexion, that appearance of a dying man that he bore constantly for ten years of his life: that is to say, during the whole time he involved himself with writing, a trade that was as damaging to his constitution as contrary to his taste, and that would have ended by sending him to the grave if he had continued it any longer." A visitor commented that although Rousseau was nearly sixty, "I would never have thought he was that old if he hadn't assured me himself. He seemed far younger to me." People noticed also that he still spoke with a Genevan accent, and that he wore rings engraved with his parents' names in Persian characters, which had been brought back by Isaac Rousseau from Constantinople. A friend from this time recalled that "he never spoke to me of his father without tenderness."

Although it became clear that Rousseau could move about Paris with impunity, he grew weary of public attention and resumed a life of seclusion. Thérèse protected him from visitors so efficiently that he called her (rather unflatteringly) his Cerberus. When Manon Philipon, later to become the celebrated Madame Roland of the Revolution, approached his door with feelings of veneration, Thérèse calmly repelled her attempts to ingratiate herself:

> "Madame, does M. Rousseau live here?"
> "Yes, Mademoiselle."
> "Might I speak with him?"
> "What do you want?"

"I want to get his response to a letter I wrote him some days ago."

"Mademoiselle, he doesn't speak with people . . . My husband has renounced everything, he has given it all up. He would like nothing more than to help you, but at his age he needs to rest."

Many visitors noted that Thérèse pointedly referred to Rousseau as her husband. She was determined not to be mistaken for a servant.

The apartment was far from convenient, on the fifth floor in French reckoning (the sixth floor in modern American), and reached by dark and dangerous stairs. When Rousseau accompanied one guest down to the street he remarked, "It's not to show you the way, but to keep you from breaking your neck." For many visitors, the proletarian lifestyle was a source of wonder and pity. "My heart was wrenched," the playwright Goldoni wrote, "to see the man of letters turned into a copyist and his wife acting as a servant. It was a distressing sight, and I was unable to hide my astonishment and grief." An aristocratic admirer who managed to reach the garret — "abode of rats but sanctuary of genius" — was enchanted by Rousseau's conversation but contemptuous of Thérèse. "His ugly wife or servant interrupted us from time to time with ridiculous questions about the laundry or the soup. He answered her gently, and he would have ennobled a piece of cheese if he had spoken of it." Their life was in fact simple but not ascetic, as Rousseau's account of wine drinking confirms. "At one time my wife and I drank a quarter of a bottle of wine at supper; later it became a half bottle, and at present we drink the whole bottle. It warms us up." But wine created problems of its own. A visitor asked why he struggled painfully down to the cellar to fetch up the wine, despite his age, when Thérèse could easily have gone. "What would you have me do?" he replied. "When she goes down there, she stays there."

As Rousseau saw it, this lifestyle was entirely appropriate to the *métier* of copying music (it was often easier in those days to have sheet music copied by hand than to obtain published versions). "For me," he said, "it's a labor and a pleasure at the same time. I am neither raised above nor sunk below the condition in which fortune placed me at my birth; I'm the son of a worker, and I am one myself. I'm doing what I've done ever since I was fourteen." He enjoyed keeping track of the number of pages he copied, and by 1777 these came to more than 11,000, an average of over 1,500 a year. He carried out the work faithfully and with high standards, but as a friend commented, he could never really be a simple journeyman. "He copied with an exactitude that is rare among those who ordinarily live by this work; he was paid at a higher rate, and no doubt curiosity attracted to him, on this pretext, a large number of people who provided for him this daily and very assiduous labor." Still, by doing small jobs for modest sums, he escaped dependence on patrons who would assume the right to advise, criticize, and manipulate him. "I am poor, in all truth," he said, "but I don't have a *cou pelé,*" a neck rubbed bare by a dog collar.

Rousseau began to make new friends in these years, especially some younger people who were engaging companions, such as a financier and music lover named Guillaume-Olivier de Corancez. The most important of these friendships was with Jacques-Henri Bernardin de Saint-Pierre, a world traveler and passionate amateur naturalist. Bernardin had first gone to sea as a ship's boy at the age of twelve, to Martinique in the West Indies; he then trained as a military engineer and served as a soldier of fortune for several monarchs; and for the past three years he had lived on the island of Mauritius in the Indian Ocean. Eventually Bernardin would achieve literary fame with his tropical romance *Paul and Virginia,* but when Rousseau knew him he was a restive young man who shared his rambles in the countryside and plied him with flattering questions. They saw each other often, and Bernardin's notes for a never-completed book on Rousseau preserve more anecdotes of his conversation than were recorded by anyone else. Many of these have already been quoted in the present volume.

On Bernardin's first visit to the Rousseaus' apartment, he passed through a little antechamber where domestic utensils were neatly arranged and entered the room where Rousseau was copying music. The furniture was very simple: two small beds, covered with blue-and-white-striped cotton, curtains of the same pattern, a chest of drawers, a few chairs, and a small spinet. A canary was singing in a cage that hung from the ceiling, and sparrows came to take bread from the open windows. Bernardin carefully described his first impression of Rousseau's appearance at the age of sixty. "He had a dark complexion, with some coloring on the cheeks, a handsome mouth, well-shaped nose, high rounded forehead, and eyes full of fire. The slanting lines that descend from the nostrils to the corners of the mouth, and that characterize a physiognomy, expressed in his case great sensitivity and even some suffering. One could see in his face several characteristics of melancholy: recessed eyes and sagging eyebrows, a deep sadness in the creases of the forehead, and a very lively and even somewhat caustic gaiety in the thousand tiny folds at the edges of the eyes, whose orbits disappeared when he laughed."

On the next visit, a casual mention of Rousseau's tastes led to a characteristically prickly exchange. While they were taking a walk, Bernardin happened to remark on the smell of coffee. Rousseau replied, "I love that perfume. When they roast it in my entryway, some of my neighbors close their doors, but I open mine." Bernardin then sent him a packet of coffee from his travels and received this answer: "We have scarcely made each other's acquaintance, and you begin with gifts. This makes our association too unequal; my fortune does not permit me to do the same. Choose either to take your coffee back or never to see each other again." In the end Bernardin persuaded Rousseau to keep the coffee, accepting in return a ginseng root and a book on ichthyology.

Pondering Rousseau's temperamental oscillations, Bernardin made two lists of adjectives. One described a manner that all too often prevailed: "mistrustful, timid, solitary, gloomy, caustic, proud." But a second list defined his "natural character": "gay, humane, compassionate, sensitive, frank, friendly and confiding, religious, simple." Rousseau himself told him, "I have a daring nature and a timid character," meaning that social life had replaced his natural confidence with bashfulness and hypersensitivity. Bernardin recalled an episode when he dropped in for a visit and Rousseau barely looked up, but went on copying music. When Bernardin politely began to read a book, however, Rousseau exclaimed in a troubled voice, "Monsieur likes reading." Bernardin then got up to leave, whereupon Rousseau insisted on accompanying him to the door with the comment, "One has to behave like this toward people whom one doesn't know very well." Bernardin was deeply hurt and stayed away for two months. When he came again Rousseau explained, "There are days when I want to be alone. I was annoyed at seeing you too often, but I would be even more annoyed not to see you at all." Then he added, in an emotional tone, "I dread intimacy; I have closed my heart — but I have a leaden one."

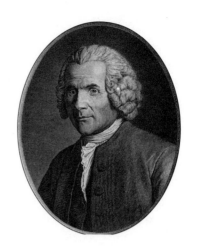

ROUSSEAU IN LATER LIFE

A portrait engraved for a posthumous edition of Rousseau's works, after an original by Angélique Briceau. The artist has caught the marks of lifelong physical pain, and the penetrating gaze that he retained right up to the end.

As he pondered the paradoxes of Rousseau's temperament, Bernardin concluded that he had paid a high price for his lifelong struggle to embody virtue and truth. "Young men, these are the arrows of Hercules! If you dare to handle his bow, beware the sufferings of Philoctetes, the cries of pain, the solitude, the rejection." A less heroic way of putting it would be to say that Rousseau had been hurt so often that he was no longer willing to expose himself emotionally. Companionship could still be agreeable, but not if it entailed the potential pain of friendship. Bernardin remembered that on another occasion Rousseau saw him coming and called down the stairs, "Monsieur, go no further, I can't receive you, you've become too dangerous for me! If you don't mind, I will remain the sole master of myself." But unlike other would-be disciples, Bernardin always returned.

Botany was one pursuit that never failed, and Rousseau resumed the pleasantly endless task of identifying plants. To a Swedish visitor he exclaimed, "So you know my master, my teacher, the great Linnaeus! Tell him that I know of no man on earth who is greater than he. Tell him that I owe him my health and my life." Rousseau continued to relish daylong excursions in the country, and as Bernardin commented, "His health regime kept him fresh, vigorous, and cheerful up until the end of his life." He enjoyed displaying his knowledge, and when a shepherd showed him a plant he didn't recognize, he commented wryly, "There is always something to wound the master's pride. Of the fifteen hundred plants in the Paris environs, there is not a single one I don't know except for that one." The walks were occasions for sensual pleasure, not just taxonomy. "He never gathered plants without smelling them," Bernardin recalled, "and I believe he could have made a botany of odors if there were enough proper names to characterize them as there are odors in nature. He taught me to recognize them by their scents alone." Rousseau's nearsightedness, so inconvenient in other ways, was an advantage here. "Close up he could distinguish parts within the calyx of the tiniest flowers that I could barely see with a strong magnifying glass." In addition to plants, he especially loved the song of birds and would always pause to listen to a nightingale. "'Our musicians,' he would say, 'have all imitated its high and low notes, its runs and capriccios, but what characterizes it — its prolonged piping, its sobs, the sighing sounds that go to the soul and pervade its song — that's what no one has been able to capture.'"

At home after these excursions, Rousseau continued his custom of pressing leaves and flowers in beautifully arranged *herbiers*. He wrote a series of letters to Mme Delessert in Lyon for her daughters to use in studying botany, avoiding the usual bewildering Latin names and trying to make the subject accessible to beginners. The girls' tutor, who later became a distinguished scientist, greatly admired the results: "Never has a botanist carried so far the delicacy and correctness with which he arranged the plants on paper . . . His book of mosses, in duodecimo format, was a little masterpiece of elegance." It was important to Rousseau that these botanical writings remain unpublished. "When one studies botany for itself," he told Bernardin, "it sweetens the character, but when one studies it in order to teach others, one generally becomes envious, jealous, and intolerant. It's our self-interest that spoils everything." When the letters on botany were eventually published after Rousseau's death, they were widely admired. "It's a true pedagogical model," Goethe said, "and it complements *Émile*."

In addition to botany, Rousseau had of course another and even longer-standing interest, his love of music. *The Village Soothsayer* was performed at Fontainebleau in 1770 at the marriage of the future Louis XVI and Marie Antoinette. Rousseau took no part in the production, but he appreciated the recognition; there were further revivals throughout the decade. He began work on a *Daphnis and Chloe,* which was never finished, and gave permission for a production of his *Pygmalion* at the Comédie Française in 1775. Reviewers acknowledged that the work was more philosophical than dramatic, but they found it moving all the same, especially when the statue came to life, reached out to her lover, and cried "It's me, it's still me." It didn't hurt, one reviewer commented, that the role gave the actress "an opportunity to display all the advantages that nature had given her," though another said maliciously that when she stood motionless it was the best performance of her career.

Music also brought Rousseau a distinguished acquaintance, the composer Christoph Willibald Gluck, who honored him as a pioneer of the expressive natural style. Rousseau attended rehearsals of Gluck's *Iphigenia* and wrote to say "I'm enchanted with it! You've accomplished what I believed impossible until now." He soon broke off the connection, however. Gluck was only two years younger, and a far greater musician; probably the disparity became too painful at a time when he preferred youthful admirers who represented no challenge.

Rousseau amused himself also with less ambitious musical projects. He wrote an arrangement of Vivaldi's *Spring* for solo flute, and composed nearly a hundred melodies to accompany his own songs (of slight interest in themselves) together with songs by other writers, including classic French and Italian poets. His modest working title was *Collection of Airs, Romances, and Duos,* but the publisher who subsequently acquired the manuscript from Thérèse published it in 1781 as *Consolations for the Sorrows of My Life,* with the profits to go to the foundling hospital in posthumous expiation. Benjamin Franklin was one of the subscribers. Rousseau's own abilities as a performer, never notable, had not improved with time. When a visitor persuaded him to sit down at his spinet, "he sang a mediocre cantilena in a trembling voice; the harpsichord, horribly out of tune, made the accompaniment a torture."

Years later a musician who went to the rue Plâtrière met a number of women who remembered Rousseau with affection but still had no idea who he was. When one of them was young, Rousseau had heard her singing, and they began to talk. "He told me he would give me advice about my talent. I looked at him, laughing, and said, 'So you sing, do you?' 'Yes,' he answered, 'and sometimes I compose music.'" Eagerly, the visiting musician asked her what further conversation ensued. "He looked at me a lot and said almost nothing. I did my housework, I sang, and I left him in his corner." She did recall one charming episode,

though. When Rousseau complained that she shouldn't put on rouge —
"At your age there's no need for artifice; I can hardly recognize you" —
she retorted impishly that a pale complexion required rouge at any age,
jumped on his lap, and started applying it to his face. "He ran away,
wiping it off, and I thought he would choke with laughter on the
stairs."

In these ways Rousseau made an agreeable life for himself, and on
the whole he enjoyed more contentment than he had known for many
years. But one major source of distress remained. His principal motive
for returning to Paris had been to confront his enemies, and they continued to be as elusive as ever. The first step in his defense was to use the
Confessions to reveal his true nature to the world. Books seven through
twelve had been completed by the time he left Bourgoin, and he now
retrieved the first six books from an abbess near Trye with whom he
had left them for safekeeping. He would not publish the work, true to
his resolve not to publicize embarrassing stories about people who were
still living, but he would give private readings to influential Parisians.
Accordingly, between December 1770 and the following May he read to
groups on at least four occasions. The man who had preferred to remain hidden while writing was at last speaking his words with his own
voice, and as Lejeune remarks, "What wouldn't one give for a recording of those readings!" Some of the listeners, at least, were impressed.
One sat down at three in the morning to write to his mistress: "I expected a session of seven or eight hours; it lasted fourteen or fifteen . . .
Rousseau drew tears from us by the moving and truthful picture of his
misfortunes, his weaknesses, his trust repaid by ingratitude, and all the
tempests of his sensitive heart . . . The writing is truly a phenomenon of
genius, of simplicity, candor, and courage. How many giants reduced to
dwarves! How many obscure but virtuous men restored to their rights
and avenged against the wicked by the sole testimony of an honest
man!"

On another occasion a friend was present at a session at which Rousseau read for a full seventeen hours with only two brief pauses for re-
freshment. When he came to the subject of the abandoned children, he
stared at his audience challengingly, and no one made any response; at
the end they kissed his hands and tried to console him. "He wept, and
all of us wept hot tears." Later on, however, Rousseau pumped his

friend to find out what the reaction had really been, "like those jealous lovers who are burning to know that which will make them still more unhappy." Undoubtedly many listeners were bewildered and disappointed, as the reviewers of the *Confessions* would later be. Condorcet was shocked to discover what a "little good-for-nothing" Rousseau had been, and was contemptuous that he apologized to the memory of Mme de Warens for revealing her sexual lapses and to the girls of the cherry-picking episode "for having sat behind a young lady on horseback without thinking to take hold of her breasts." What most struck Condorcet was that such a person could ever have developed into the brilliant writer he knew. "It really is extraordinary that he should have become what he did. His mind at forty is a phenomenon." To modern eyes, the greatness of the *Confessions* lies precisely in showing how the young good-for-nothing became the author of the *Discourse on Inequality* and *Émile,* but few people then could see it that way.

Most listeners were too shocked or embarrassed to say anything at all. On the last page of the manuscript Rousseau added a note describing the final reading in May 1771, at the château of the comtesse d'Egmont. "I finished my reading and everyone was silent. Mme d'Egmont was the only one who seemed to be moved, and she trembled visibly, but she quickly recovered herself and kept silent along with the rest of the company. Such was the fruit that I took from this reading and from my declaration." The declaration they had just heard was indeed likely to stun them into silence: "I declare openly and without fear that whoever, even without reading my writings, will examine with his own eyes my natural disposition, my character, morals, inclinations, pleasures, and habits, and can still believe me to be a dishonorable man, is himself a man who ought to be choked."

In any event there could be no more readings, for Mme d'Épinay, who had not seen Rousseau again and never would, took alarm at the possibility that the *Confessions* might contain still more damaging material than had yet come out. She wrote accordingly to the chief of police, Antoine Sartine, who happened to be a friend of hers, and implored him to order Rousseau to stop. "I think you must speak to him with such kindness that he can have no complaint, but with such firmness that he will never do it again. If you make him give his word, I believe he will keep it. Forgive me, but it concerns my peace of mind." Sartine did call in Rousseau, who did promise, and the *Confessions* vanished from view until they were finally published in 1782, four years after Rousseau's death. Bernardin could hardly ever get him to talk about his past. "He would say to me, 'Let's not speak of men, let's speak of nature.'" Mme d'Épinay, meanwhile, set to work with Diderot and Grimm to poison Rousseau's posthumous reputation with the forged letters in *The History of Mme de Montbrillant.*

Rousseau was thus thwarted in his attempt to repair his reputation in the way he had intended, and he felt more remote than ever from the books that had taken Europe by storm a decade before. In 1770 he noticed a row of them on an admirer's shelf and exclaimed, "Ah, there they are! I meet them everywhere, it seems as if they're following me. How much pain those fellows have given me — and how much pleasure!" He began striking and caressing them by turns. *Émile,* he said, had cost too much labor and aroused too much enmity; *Julie* had given him some happy moments; but the *Letter to d'Alembert* remained his favorite. "It's the one I produced without effort, at the first blow, and at the most lucid time of my life." As for *The Social Contract,* "Those who boast that they fully understand it are brighter than I am. It's a book to be done over again, but I no longer have the strength or the time." (He did spend some time trying to compose a plan for a projected new government in Poland, just as he had once done for Corsica, but he soon dropped the project as unworkable.) In the past he had sometimes called *Émile* his best book, but by now he had lost all enthusiasm for it. "I don't know when I'll set myself to reading it," he told his publisher, Rey, a couple of years later; "that would be a dreadful chore, and practically useless, since I have only a confused recollection of its contents. There's only one of my writings that I would still reread with pleasure, and that's *Héloïse.*"

But if Rousseau was no longer an author, he was still a writer and always would be. And it was in writing that he found a new way to deal with his perception of the insidious plot: a self-analysis in dialogue form. The result was the strangest and, except for intermittent moments of eloquence, the most unreadable of his works, generally known as the *Dialogues* but entitled by him *Rousseau Judge of Jean-Jacques.* At bottom, what tormented him was the experience of becoming a celebrity, of which he was one of the first modern examples. Famous not just for his writings but for his character — a distinction he himself earnestly promoted — he was baffled and alarmed at being turned into a legend. Not only were there detractors and ill-wishers, but praise itself was painful if aimed at an unreal image of himself. As Leigh says, incense can be an irritant instead of a balm. The split between the public image and the sense of a true self was something quite new in the eighteenth century, when a rapidly growing reading public began to assume a personal relationship with authors they had never met. In later years this aspect of celebrity would become commonplace, but to Rousseau it felt like a uniquely personal injustice. And he was a collector of injustices.

It is easy enough to dismiss Rousseau's ongoing paranoia as absurd. Plenty of people did so in his own time, including some who knew him well, and later interpreters have been concerned mainly to promote one or another kind of clinical diagnosis. But given the rooted existence of his paranoia in his mental and emotional life, it is perhaps more interesting to focus on how he himself perceived it. Once he became convinced that the walls had ears and that insidious schemers were laying traps in the most innocent encounters, he lived under what felt like a continuous state of siege. It was slow torture with no hope of release. "Picture to yourself," he wrote in the *Dialogues,* "people who begin by each putting on a closely fitting mask, arming themselves to the teeth, and who then take their enemy by surprise, seizing him from behind. They strip him naked, and they tie up his body, arms, hands, feet, and head so that he can no longer move. They put a gag in his mouth, they blind his eyes, they lay him out on the ground, and in short they spend their noble lives murdering him gently, for fear that if he dies of his wounds he will stop feeling them too soon."

The *Dialogues* were thus a desperate attempt to remake Rousseau's public image in line with his own sense of reality, and to accomplish it he invented a most peculiar format, a discussion between a character called "the Frenchman" and a character called "Rousseau," who argue about an author they refer to as "Jean-Jacques." The Frenchman has never read Jean-Jacques' books — Rousseau was widely referred to by his first names — because he has heard that they were written by a hypocritical monster. "Rousseau," on the other hand, has read the books but knows nothing of their author, and refuses to believe that anyone who could write like that could be wicked. In effect he is the actual Rousseau detached from his own life's work, attempting to see himself as others see him. "It was necessary for me to say with what viewpoint, if I were someone else —*si j'étais un autre* — I would regard a man such as myself." The upshot, after three hundred tortuous pages, is that the Frenchman does read the books and finds them virtuous, while "Rousseau" visits "Jean-Jacques" — me, myself, and I! — and finds him virtuous too. He mentions that he found Jean-Jacques writing a dialogue about himself, which effectively catches the hall-of-mirrors quality of the book, a dialogue about a dialogue about a dialogue, all to prove the fundamental unity of Jean-Jacques Rousseau.

For anyone who cares about Rousseau, the result makes heartbreaking reading. He tries doggedly to understand why his life is so painful, weighing apparent evidence, inventing explanations in order to refute them, never able to stop. But it is important to note that he found the writing so unpleasant that he could give it only a few minutes a day, over a space of nearly four years. "What I had to say was so clear and so deeply felt that I can't marvel enough at the longueurs, repetitions, verbiage and disorder of this work . . . Unable to bear such a painful occupation continuously, I gave myself over to it for very brief periods only, writing down each thought as it came to me and stopping there, writing the same thing ten times if it came to me ten times, and never recollecting what I had already written." Far from being a coherent defense of his character, the *Dialogues* became an improvised form of therapy, a receptacle into which Rousseau could pour his anxieties in order to set them aside. People who knew him in those years were well aware of flareups of distrust — Malesherbes and Mme de Créqui were two of the many he broke with when he suspected disloyalty — but most of the time he struck his friends as energetic and even optimistic.

The old anxiety at being looked at in public, which went all the way back to Rousseau's childhood, was now a constant burden. He suspected that almost everyone who glanced at him in the street had been coached to hate him. Someone who knew him in those years gave a clear description of what today would be called projection: "His suspicious gaze closely watched people's eyes for what they were thinking about him, and he was pierced to the depths of his soul by the slightest gesture or smile that didn't accord with his thinking. He experienced mortal anguish unknown to other men. We have seen him pass all at once from joy to the deepest distress, and be happy and unhappy in the space of three minutes, without anything having changed around him. His frightened imagination did it all." In the *Dialogues* he described himself as "buried alive among the living," leading a sort of posthumous existence, a ghost unable to stop haunting a world that saw him only with fear.

In all likelihood most Parisians, once the initial excitement of his return had died down, paid no attention to Rousseau at all. In 1775 La Harpe remarked that although his books were read with as much pleasure as ever, "he could pass today along the grand avenue of the Tuileries, or along the boulevards at the hour of promenade, and no one would notice him." Corancez believed that his delusion was hereditary, instancing a cousin of Rousseau's whose features resembled his to a startling degree and who inexplicably charged a blameless coachman with taking an unfamiliar road in order to deliver him to criminal accomplices. At any rate Rousseau's narcissism, as Françoise Barguillet suggests, disastrously reversed direction during the course of his life. In earlier days it gave energy to his creative thinking, when he was proud to distinguish himself from the common herd, me against them. Now the direction of force was reversed, them against me.

One curious fragment of evidence, if evidence it is, survives from Rousseau's final years and suggests that his masochism may have found a new, if conventional, outlet. A writer in 1783 claimed that toward the end of his life "Rousseau used to go to the rues du Pélican and de Maubuée to have himself whipped *pour son petit écu,*" for a small fee. The *Confessions* had been published the previous year, and this writer may only have been elaborating on the hints there. But it is at least interesting that such rumors were circulating not long after Rousseau's death. In the *Confessions,* to be sure, he solemnly declares that shame prevented him from ever asking a woman to give him what he wanted, which implies a lifetime of frustration. But perhaps what he meant was that he could never ask a lady.

When Rousseau decided at last that he had nothing more to add to the *Dialogues,* he made yet another quixotic gesture. After repeated visits to the cathedral of Notre-Dame to reconnoiter, he concluded that the choir was always deserted on Saturday afternoons, and on February 24,

1776, he brought the manuscript there with the intention of placing it surreptitiously on the high altar. On the outside of the parcel he had written "A deposit committed to providence," with the further inscription, "Protector of the oppressed, God of justice and truth, receive this deposit that is placed upon your altar and entrusted to your providence by a foreigner who is alone, without support, and without any defender on earth, insulted, mocked, defamed, and betrayed by an entire generation . . . Deign to take my deposit into your care, and cause it to fall into young and faithful hands that may transmit it free from fraud to a better generation." Rousseau apparently thought of the young hands as those of the recently crowned king. But to his great surprise, the grill enclosing the choir was closed and locked, something he had never seen before. This he took to be a dire sign. Heaven was rejecting his appeal. He wandered for hours like a sleepwalker until he gradually came to his senses. Not only would it have been highly unlikely for the king to read such a long document, but more probably Rousseau's enemies would have gotten hold of it first. Far from rejecting him, heaven had actually preserved him from a disastrous blunder.

At this point Rousseau sought out his old friend Condillac, one of the few writers he still trusted, and gave the manuscript to him. Two months later he also gave a copy of the first of the three dialogues, all that he had time to transcribe in haste, to Brooke Boothby, of all people. The young Englishman whom he had known at Wootton happened to be passing through Paris, and Rousseau imagined that getting the manuscript out of the country might be a means of preserving it. The first publication came in 1780, when Boothby had a scrupulously accurate edition of the first dialogue printed at Lichfield.

One final, futile effort remained. Rousseau wrote out multiple copies of an open letter "to all Frenchmen who still love justice and truth" and began silently handing them to strangers in the streets and including them in letters to his remaining correspondents. In this strange document he sounded more than ever like a Kafka character. "The least that is due to me . . . is to tell me at last what my crimes are, how and by whom I have been judged!" The result was inevitable. Some people refused to take the letter, some laughed, and those who did read it "told me, with an ingenuousness that made me laugh in the midst of my grief, that it wasn't addressed to them." He laughed because they seemed to be acknowledging that they no longer loved justice and truth.

This pathetic story might suggest that by now Rousseau was entirely unhinged, but that was far from the case. Only a few months later he began writing an altogether new kind of book, a superb series of essays with the title *Rêveries du Promeneur Solitaire* (*Reveries of the Solitary Walker*). To be sure, the first essay starts with an assertion of complete isolation, *Me voici donc seul sur la terre,* "So here I am, alone on the earth." In this mood Rousseau declares that he is prepared to ignore the rest of the human race completely. "Everything exterior to me is henceforth foreign to me. In this world I no longer have neighbors, or fellows, or brothers. I am alone on the earth as if on a strange planet onto which I have fallen." He even, in a sort of parody of Enlightenment behaviorism, claims to regard humans as soulless robots, "mechanical beings that act only by outside impulses and whose actions can be calculated only by the laws of motion."

Nevertheless, the *Reveries* are for the most part thoughtful and even cheerful, and they are expressed with exceptional eloquence. As a whole they represent a genuinely new form, sometimes narrative, sometimes essayistic, sometimes analytical. It has been suggested that each of the ten "promenades" has a distinctive musical tonality, within which it develops a series of internal variations. In previous usage "reverie" meant idle daydreaming at best and delusion at worst. A 1771 dictionary defines the word as "ridiculous imagination" and "anxieties and cares that preoccupy the mind." But Rousseau helped create a positive valuation for an openness to experience that was more immediate and profound because it bypassed conscious thought. As a French writer comments, the word *promeneur,* with its suggestion of taking a walk or stroll, is too purposive. "Wanderer" might be the best term. In fact, he developed much of the book during the course of his rambles, when he would jot down unconnected thoughts on the backs of playing cards that he carried for that purpose.

At various points the *Reveries* comment on the *Confessions,* or go beyond. The inexpiable crime against Marion comes back, and provokes a subtle discussion of the many shades of gray between fiction and lying. *Vitam impendere vero* is no longer a simple ideal, and Rousseau says,

"The 'Know Thyself' of the temple at Delphi was not such an easy maxim to follow as I believed when I wrote my *Confessions.*" The very notion of self-knowledge, which had once seemed so straightforward, was growing murky. "What am I, myself? That is what still remains to be discovered."

At times Rousseau even approaches articulating the now-familiar concept of unconscious motivation. He describes realizing that he had begun to avoid going past a certain corner because a nice little boy would always ask him for money there, and he analyzes the implications with remarkable insight: "That's what I discovered on reflection, for until then none of it was distinctly in my thoughts. This observation has made me recall a multitude of others that convince me that the true and original motives of most of my actions are not as clear to me as I long supposed." There is a striking parallel in a story told by Freud, who realized that he was repressing the location of a familiar store because it was in the neighborhood of a kindly patron to whom he was in debt.

Above all, the *Reveries* are about memory in a new sense: not the factual reconstruction of past actions, but the recovery of states of being that live on deep in the imagination. The high point of the book, accordingly, is a return to the idyllic time on the Île de Saint-Pierre, evoking poetically the pleasure made possible by immersion in nature. Rousseau had to borrow from Italian the term for the delicious "doing nothing" that he enjoyed there, since the French language has no word for it (neither does English, of course): "Precious *far niente* was the first and foremost of those pleasures. I wanted to taste it in all its sweetness, and everything I did during my stay there was but the delicious and necessary occupation of a man who has given himself up to idleness."

Calvinism taught that idleness was a sin, and Enlightenment liberalism emphasized the value of labor. A disquieting passage in Adam Smith's *Wealth of Nations,* published at the very time when Rousseau was writing the *Reveries,* deplores "the habit of sauntering and of indolent careless application" that distinguishes the laborer who turns from one task to another from the modern factory worker who does one single thing nonstop all day long. As time went on, and as Smith's theory became a cornerstone of the modern economy, Rousseau's attitude started to look more and more attractive to many people. The message of the Enlightenment was that competition is the key to existence, the engine that drives everything forward. Rousseau did believe in work — he told Bernardin that it was "a divine gift to mankind" — and he kept constantly busy on projects of his own choosing, but he also insisted that knowing how to do nothing should be the ideal. Or at least not doing things under duress, as he says in the *Reveries:* "I have never believed that man's freedom consists in doing what he wants, but in not doing what he doesn't."

His own experience, of course, demonstrated the potential cost. To contrast him once more with that other runaway apprentice who achieved fame, Benjamin Franklin held that we can do anything we want, but only by creating an attractive social persona, imprinting it through habit until it becomes second nature, and using it to get other people to cooperate. For Rousseau there was only one nature, the one that was betrayed when civilization was invented, and he held that by honoring it we can be true to our own authentic being. But the cost was isolation.

Rousseau had long believed that natural man enjoyed the *sentiment de l'existence* in all its fullness; in the *Reveries* he talks about how an individual person might recover it. The Enlightenment sought to turn science into technology "and thus render ourselves," as Descartes had written earlier, "the masters and possessors of nature." For Rousseau nature was a mother, not a technological challenge — "Taking refuge with the common mother, I sought to hide in her arms from the attacks of her children" — and what he wanted was fresh air that could blow away the constraints of society. At times he felt an almost mystic oneness with nature, as when he floated at random in a little boat on the Lac de Bienne, but that could happen only when he let go of his thinking self and became a simple organism at home in its environment. For this, reverie was a liberating technique.

Later generations increasingly valued the deepening consciousness of self attained when thinking was stilled and memories could come surging back; in Wordsworth's words,

> They flash upon that inward eye
> Which is the bliss of solitude.

Even among the ambitious and self-driven philosophes in Rousseau's own day, such a state of feeling could seem attractive. It was Diderot, not Rousseau, who wrote almost longingly in the *Encyclopédie* about a "delicious repose" in which the mind ceases to think, pleasure spreads through the body, time seems to stop flowing, and one is aware only of "the sweetness of one's existence."

The final and never finished book of the *Reveries* was begun on Palm Sunday of 1778, fifty years to the day from Rousseau's first glimpse of Mme de Warens. Her memory had never ceased to haunt him. "Ah, if only I had been as sufficient for her heart as she was for mine! What peaceful and delicious days we would have passed together!" But it was not so much Mme de Warens whom he was recreating in imagination, as his own youthful existence during "that one brief time in my life when I was completely myself . . . when I was loved by a kind and gentle woman, I did what I wanted to do, and I was what I wanted to be." In reverie he could regain the security of a beloved child, and an idealized nature could assume the role that Maman once played. Gaston Bachelard says in *The Poetics of Reverie* that psychoanalysis affirms the mythology of "the solitary state of the essentially orphan child who, in spite of everything, is at home in the original world and loved by the gods." Rousseau was just such a lonely orphan, and the primitivism of the *Discourse on Inequality* was his intellectualized version of that condition. At Les Charmettes and on the Île de St. Pierre he believed — in retrospect at least — that he succeeded in living it.

Visitors in these final years continued to find Rousseau surprisingly cheerful, for as he told Bernardin, "I was never happy until the moment when I had given up all hope." This statement probably implied a general retreat from the world, but there was a specific reference as well. In the *Reveries* he mentions that a recent event, "equally sad and unforeseen," had dispelled any remaining rays of hope and had left him reconciled to his fate. The likeliest guess is that he meant the sudden death of the prince de Conti in August 1776. Although they had been completely out of contact for six years, Conti remained a highly visible symbol of resistance to royal absolutism, and reformers still hoped that he might join a new administration. It has been plausibly suggested, therefore, that Rousseau looked forward to the day when Conti would come to power and dismiss the still-outstanding warrant of the parlement of

Paris, rehabilitating his reputation at last. Conti's death put an end to any such hope.

On October 24, 1776, two months after Conti's death, a strange accident befell Rousseau, interesting above all for the reflections he drew from it. He was making his way along a narrow street, on his way home from a long day's walk, when a nobleman's carriage came hurtling toward him, flanked by a huge, galloping Great Dane. He was unable to dodge in time, the dog bowled him over, and he fell hard on the cobblestone street, bleeding profusely and unconscious. The carriage never slowed down, but passersby hurried to help him, and after he revived he was so bewildered by the concussion that he had no idea what was going on, or even that he was hurt. When he got home, however, Thérèse cried out in horror at his mangled appearance, and it was some time before he recovered.

Bernardin described the dog as "one of those Great Danes which the vanity of the rich causes to run through the streets in front of their carriages, to the misfortune of people on foot," something that would have aroused Rousseau's political resentment in earlier times. In a discourse on economics he had written bitterly, "Fifty honest pedestrians, going about their own business, will be crushed rather than delay the carriage of an idle fool." Corancez added that the dog belonged to the baron de Saint-Fargeau and that it was dashing along "with the speed of a rifle bullet." When Corancez visited the next day he was horrified by Rousseau's appearance, with badly swollen face and strips of paper covering his wounds from nose to chin. He was relieved, however, to find that Rousseau didn't interpret the incident with his usual paranoia. "I found with great pleasure that he excused the dog, which undoubtedly he would not have done if it had been a man; he would inevitably have seen in this man an enemy who had long meditated the blow. He saw the dog simply as a dog 'which,' he said, 'tried to take the right course to avoid me, but wanting to act on my own behalf, I did the opposite. He did better than I, and I was punished for it.'" When the dog's owner found out who had been injured, he offered financial compensation, but Rousseau refused it.

What is most memorable about the incident is the imaginative use Rousseau made of it in the *Reveries*. He was undoubtedly remembering a passage in Montaigne's *Essays,* written two hundred years before, that curiously anticipated his own experience. Montaigne was thrown from a horse, and when he returned to consciousness he had no idea what had happened, except for hazy thoughts that seemed to drift in from someplace outside. Rousseau's account is fuller, and deserves to be quoted at length.

> Night was beginning to fall. I perceived the sky, some stars, and green leaves. This first sensation was a delicious moment. I was conscious of myself only through this. I was being born into life in that instant, and it seemed to me that I filled up all the objects I perceived with my frail existence. Entirely absorbed in the present moment, I remembered nothing; I had no distinct notion of my individuality, nor the slightest idea of what had just happened to me; I didn't know who I was or where I was; I felt no pain, or fear, or uneasiness. I watched my blood flow just as I would have watched a brook, without imagining that this blood belonged in any way to me. I felt, throughout my whole being, a ravishing calm, and every time I remember it I can find nothing comparable in all the activity of familiar pleasures.

For Rousseau, this incident was a turning point in showing the meaning of the present moment. He had always been haunted by the past and obsessed by the future; now he was immersed in a state of being in which he literally had no past. By the lights of the psychology of the day, indeed, he was no longer anyone at all, since people were defined entirely by the coherence of their memories. Whatever you could remember was who you were; conversely, what you could no longer remember had ceased to be part of you. But according to Rousseau's intuition he was at last truly himself, no longer deformed by the influence and expectations of other people, unable even to attach any significance to them.

From this point on, however, Rousseau's health began to decline, and very likely he had sustained some neurological damage. "Over a long period of time," Corancez recalled, "I noticed a striking alteration in his physique. I often saw him in a convulsive state that made his face unrecognizable, and his expression was truly frightening. In that state his gaze seemed to embrace his surroundings and his eyes appeared to see everything at once, but they saw nothing. He turned himself on his chair and put his arm over the back, and suspended like that, this arm had an accelerated movement like the pendulum of a clock." According to modern medical interpreters, the symptoms probably point to epileptic seizures.

By the beginning of 1778 life in the Paris apartment was getting too difficult to manage. The weary climb up the stairs was daunting, Rousseau's hand was too shaky to keep up music copying, and Thérèse complained constantly of ill health. (Mme Delessert, visiting from Lyon, commented that Thérèse was suffering from "the vapors" as a consequence of going through menopause.) With their income declining, the Rousseaus would have to accept help from some rich friend or admirer, and they began to consider various possibilities. Some places that would otherwise have been attractive were too far away, for travel now seemed virtually impossible. When a nobleman offered a country retreat near Lyon, Rousseau thanked him but explained that both he and Thérèse were too ill for a journey of that kind and that he felt death near at hand. "You are relighting, Monsieur, an almost extinguished wick, but there's no more oil in the lamp, and the least breath of air may extinguish it forever." When Moultou, with whom he had broken during the time at Môtiers, happened to pass through Paris in May 1778, Rousseau gave him most of his papers, including the second part of the *Confessions,* for safekeeping and eventual publication.

The solution came from a certain marquis de Girardin, an admirer who, like others, had made Rousseau's acquaintance through the stratagem of bringing music to copy, and who now proposed that Rousseau and Thérèse come to live at his château of Ermenonville, twenty-five miles north of Paris. A mutual acquaintance assured Rousseau that Girardin would be a considerate host, and on May 20 he abruptly departed, not bothering to inform Bernardin or Corancez. A few days later Thérèse joined him, and they settled down comfortably in a guest ouse near the grand château, sheltered by trees and next to a moat filled with water.

Girardin had developed extensive gardens in the style of Julie's Elysée; there were a few temples and monuments of the kind favored at the time, but mostly an invitingly natural landscape in which cows and sheep wandered freely. Rousseau was enchanted, went for plant-collecting strolls with a young son of Girardin's as his assistant, and seems to have thought less than usual about dying. He sent to Paris for books on

ROUSSEAU BOTANIZING

An aquatint by Frédéric Mayer showing Rousseau at Ermenonville, rather elaborately dressed for walking in the country, holding flowers that are presumably destined to be pressed in one of his *herbiers*. Behind him is the house in which he would soon die. An engraving made from this portrait was widely reproduced.

grasses, mosses, and mushrooms, and even talked about resuming work on *Daphnis and Chloe* and *Émile and Sophie*. When a visitor remarked one day that men are wicked, he responded with his fundamental axiom, "Men are wicked, yes, but man is good." That evening there was a concert in the château, and he accompanied on the pianoforte his own setting of the Willow Song from Shakespeare's *Othello*.

The next day Rousseau took his customary early morning walk and returned for café au lait with Thérèse. He was about to go over to the château for a music lesson with Girardin's daughter when alarming symptoms suddenly overcame him. He complained of tingling on the soles of his feet and a sensation like cold water trickling down his spine, along with chest pains. These were followed by a headache so violent that he complained his skull was bursting, and when he fell to the floor shortly afterward, Thérèse was unable to revive him and went for help. Nothing could be done. Rousseau was dead on July 2, 1778, four days after his sixty-sixth birthday.

Rumors soon spread that Rousseau had killed himself, either by poi-

HOMAGE TO ROUSSEAU

A rock by the lake at Ermenonville (to the left in this 1788 picture, and no longer visible today) was inscribed with the Italian verses that Saint-Preux scratched into the cliff at Meillerie, and an eighteenth-century guidebook to the garden suggested the appropriate response: "'How different,' I will be told, 'are these objects here from those mountains soaring into the clouds, those rocks disappearing into air, those fir trees old as the earth!' I agree; but this is their tableau in miniature. Imagination, which transported you to those places consecrated by the prose of Rousseau, can enlarge these too, and you will be at Ermenonville no longer." When Rousseau himself first beheld this scene, according to his host, Girardin, "I saw his eyes fill with tears, and I felt at that moment with what sensitivity his heart recalled the delights of his country and the pure happiness of his youth."

son or with a pistol, but an autopsy by five doctors found the cause to be massive cerebral bleeding. They diagnosed the attack as a stroke, but modern opinion inclines to believe that he was suffering the consequences of repeated falls, including perhaps the accident with the Great Dane. It is known that he had alarming attacks of vertigo during his last weeks in Paris. During the autopsy, incidentally, no trace was found of the malformation that Rousseau was sure would explain his urinary troubles.

Girardin arranged to have the body embalmed, and the great sculptor Jean-Antoine Houdon hurried from Paris to take a death-mask impression. Rousseau was interred in a lead-lined coffin and buried at

DEATH MASK OF ROUSSEAU
At the news of Rousseau's death,
the famous sculptor Houdon
hastened to Ermenonville to
make the death mask.

midnight, with appropriate ceremony, on a little island known as the Isle of Poplars in the ornamental lake of the château. "Ermenonville belongs to Girardin no more," Rousseau's doctor wrote the next day; "it is Rousseau who has taken possession of it for eternity."

Thérèse stayed on for a while at Ermenonville, and the next year she formed a relationship with Girardin's valet, an Englishman named John Henry Bally, who hoped to share in her income from Rousseau's books. She was fifty-eight and he was thirty-four. Not much money ever came in, and she was living in extreme poverty when she died in 1801 at the age of eighty in the nearby village of Plessis-Belleville. It is a sad story, but she honored Rousseau's memory to the end. A visitor long afterward was led to her unmarked grave by an old woman who remembered that Thérèse always spoke affectionately of Rousseau. "He is buried in the lake at Ermenonville, because he was not of our religion. It seems that he wrote books. Alas, poor woman, that did her so much harm! She told me she was forced to flee with him, where I don't know.

ROUSSEAU'S TOMB ON THE ISLE OF POPLARS

Girardin replaced a temporary tomb with this impressive monument in the form of a Roman altar, designed by the painter Hubert Robert. A bas-relief by Jacques-Philippe Lesueur shows a mother nursing her infant while reading *Émile*. Figures of Eloquence and Music flank the scene, a civic crown accompanies Rousseau's *vitam impendere vero* motto, and an inscription reads: HERE REPOSES THE MAN OF NATURE AND OF TRUTH. In this view a new generation of poplars is in place, and Girardin's imposing château (today a hotel) can be seen in the distance.

In spite of that she wasn't unhappy with him; she always said he was a very good man."

Immediately after Rousseau's death Thérèse was reported to have said, "If my husband is not a saint, who will ever be one?" Streams of admirers began to visit the tomb at Ermenonville, and in 1794, when he had indeed become a sort of secular saint of the French Revolution, his remains were transferred to the recently completed Panthéon in Paris with immense pomp. "The moon that shed its pale and colorless light," according to the official report of the occasion, "gave this procession the aspect of those ancient mysteries whose initiates were pure or washed

◄ REVOLUTIONARY ALLEGORY

This 1792 assemblage of revolutionary symbols suggests what the radicals made of Rousseau, whose stern and intense gaze is mirrored in the all-seeing eye of Providence (which also appears on the American one-dollar bill). The twin flags are inscribed *République Française* and *Amour de la Patrie;* Rousseau taught loyalty to fatherland — as in the French anthem, *Allons enfants de la patrie* — rather than the Enlightenment ideal of citizenship of the world. The Egyptian obelisk, a Masonic symbol of permanence, is inscribed with a triangle, the word *égalité,* and a legend declaring that courage establishes republics and virtue preserves them. The red cap of liberty is raised above a column made of staves whose strength is increased by being bound together, the ancient Roman "fasces," from which fascism later took its name; the words *force, vérité, justice, union* are emblazoned on the column. Next to it a tree of liberty has been planted, and in the background a soldier with a cannon defends the truncated column of "regeneration of morals," with "rights of man and of the citizen" at its base.

---

clean of their faults." Especially notable was a delegation from his native city marching with a banner that read "Aristocratic Geneva proscribed him, a regenerated Geneva has avenged his memory." It might have gratified his sense of irony that his handsome wooden tomb in the crypt, a relief to the eye in a sea of stone, directly faces Voltaire's. And above, beneath the great dome, a monument in Rousseau's honor stands opposite one that honors his *frère ennemi* Diderot.

In the generations that followed, Rousseau's influence continued to spread, and not just among people who knew his books. Romanticism, with its emphasis on originality, imagination, and oneness with nature, was profoundly in his debt. The growing recognition that governments should reflect their people's will, together with the conviction that social inequality is intrinsically unjust, have profound roots in his thought. The concept of childhood as a crucially formative stage of development is Rousseauian at its heart. And psychoanalysis, searching for hidden foundations of the self, carries forward the quest that he launched in the *Confessions.*

Rousseau never wanted to found a system, and he didn't. His mission was to expose the unreconciled conflicts that make human life so difficult and that conventional systems of politics and education and psychology try to iron out. At Mme d'Houdetot's house in the days of their intimacy, he once took a peach from the bottom of a pyramid of fruit, upon which the whole pile fell down. "That's what you always do with all our systems," she commented; "you pull down with a single touch, but who will build up what you pull down?" By pulling down, he challenged later generations to build up again in new ways, and his style of questioning has become inseparable from our culture. "The friends of Rousseau," one acquaintance remarked, "are as though related to each other through his soul, which has joined them across countries, ranks, fortune, and even centuries." Many people who have barely heard of him are, at a deep level, friends of Rousseau.

The places remain where Rousseau's restless spirit once made a temporary home. The house of Les Charmettes still stands. So do the woods of Montmorency where he exchanged hot guilty kisses with Mme d'Houdetot; the Petit Montlouis where he brought *Émile* and *The Social Contract* to completion; the house at Môtiers in Switzerland from which he was driven by a hail of stones; and the Île de Saint-Pierre where he responded to the hypnotic lapping of the waves. Perhaps the most moving view of all is from the quiet Weaver Hills, above the remote hamlet of Wootton, where he collected plants while anguishing over imagined betrayals by former friends. It was a bitter time for Rousseau, and for Thérèse too. Yet it was there that the *Confessions* took form, transmuting remembered pain and happiness into a vision of the growth of an individual spirit. For all its wrong turnings and disappointments, Rousseau's life was deeply exemplary. His faithfulness to his own most vital impulses meant a lifelong struggle to break free from the chains of society, including the glittering ones forged by his own successes. The heart of his message is proclaimed at the beginning of the *Confessions:* there will never be another Jean-Jacques Rousseau. Yet in revealing himself to us, he holds up a mirror in which we can see our resemblance, because the same is true of every one of us. In our individuality, we are each in our own way his *semblables,* and he shows how his quest can become our own.

Timeline of Rousseau's Life

1712 Jean-Jacques Rousseau born in Geneva, 28 June, to Suzanne and Isaac Rousseau; after his mother dies on 7 July, his aunt Suzon cares for him.

1718 Moves with his father, aunt, and older brother to Coutance in the artisans' quarter of Saint-Gervais.

1722 After his father leaves Geneva to avoid arrest, boards with the pastor Lambercier in the village of Bossey.

1725 Apprenticed to the engraver Ducommun.

1726 His father remarries in the town of Nyon.

1728 At sixteen, abandons his unfinished apprenticeship and runs away from Geneva; meets Mme de Warens in Annecy; goes to Turin (capital of the Savoie) to convert to Catholicism, and holds low-level jobs there; is strongly influenced by a wise priest, the abbé Gaime.

1729 Returns to Annecy and moves in with Mme de Warens.

1730 Spends a year wandering, attempting to be a music teacher in Lausanne and Neuchâtel.

1731 Brief and disappointing stay in Paris; returns to Mme de Warens, now living in Chambéry, and begins an eight-month employment as a clerk in the land survey office.

1734 Death (probably by suicide) of Claude Anet, Mme de Warens's steward and lover, who has been obliged to share her with Rousseau.

1735 Begins intermittent residence in a country house at Les Charmettes.

1737 At twenty-five, reaches the Genevan age of majority and recovers part of his modest inheritance; journeys to Montpellier to seek a cure for imagined health problems.

1738   Returns to Chambéry and finds his place taken by another young man, Wintzenried; lives alone at Les Charmettes and reads widely.

1740   Takes a position as tutor to the young sons of M. de Mably in Lyon, where he comes into contact with Enlightenment ideas.

1742   Moves to Paris at the age of thirty, hoping for a career as a musician.

1743   Takes a post as secretary to the French ambassador in Venice, the comte de Montaigu, and develops a passion for Italian music; because of Montaigu's incompetence, he takes on much of the embassy's work.

1744   Discharged by Montaigu, returns to Paris and develops a close relationship with Diderot, who becomes an intellectual mentor, in a circle that includes d'Alembert and Condillac.

1745   Forms lifelong alliance with Thérèse Levasseur, aged twenty-three (Rousseau is turning thirty-three); composes an operatic ballet, *The Gallant Muses,* but fails to get it produced.

1746   Birth of the first of five children, all of whom are consigned to a foundling home; takes a secretarial job with Mme Dupin.

1747   Death of Rousseau's father, whom he has not seen for many years.

1749   Writes articles on music for the projected *Encyclopédie* edited by Diderot and d'Alembert; on the road to Vincennes to visit Diderot, imprisoned for subversive writings, he conceives the idea of the *Discourse on the Sciences and Arts.*

1750   The *Discourse* wins first prize from the Dijon Academy, is published, and brings fame at the age of thirty-eight.

1752   Rousseau's opera *The Village Soothsayer* is performed at court to great acclaim; a comedy written years earlier, *Narcissus,* is also produced.

1753   Publication of *Letter on French Music,* which becomes the center of a controversy on the respective merits of French and Italian music.

1754   Visits Geneva and reconverts to Protestantism to regain citizenship; sees Mme de Warens for the last time.

1755   Publication of a second discourse, *On the Origin of Inequality,* that confirms Rousseau's originality as a thinker.

1756   At the invitation of Mme d'Épinay, moves with Thérèse to the Hermitage, at La Chevrette near Paris; begins work on the novel *Julie, or the New Héloïse.*

1757   Largely platonic affair with Mme d'Houdetot ends in recriminations; also breaks with Mme d'Épinay, her lover Grimm, and Diderot.

1758   Moves to Montlouis in the village of Montmorency; *Letter to d'Alembert on the Theater* defends Genevan mores (and earns Voltaire's enmity).

1759   Develops a close friendship with the duc and duchesse de Luxembourg and often stays in the Petit Château on their estate.

1761   Publication and immense success of *Julie, or the New Héloïse.*

1762   Publication of *The Social Contract* and *Émile, or Education,* which are immediately condemned in Paris and Geneva on religious and political grounds; when an arrest warrant is issued, Rousseau flees France. Settles with Thérèse in the village of Môtiers near Neuchâtel, under the protection of the Maréchal Keith; develops a keen interest in botany with new friend Du Peyrou.

1763   Renounces Genevan citizenship in disgust over political developments there; notoriety as religious freethinker is exacerbated by *Letter to Christophe de Beaumont.*

1764   A trenchant critique of Genevan politics, *Letters Written from the Mountain,* alarms conservatives throughout Europe; Voltaire's anonymous *Sentiment of the Citizens* reveals the secret of Rousseau's abandoned children.

1765   Protestant ministers organize a campaign against Rousseau, and he is driven from Môtiers when his house is stoned; after a brief idyllic stay on the Île de Saint-Pierre, he is ordered to leave.

1766   Journeys to England with David Hume and settles with Thérèse at Wootton, Staffordshire; begins work on the *Confessions;* becomes convinced that Hume is plotting against him and writes a long accusatory letter that Hume makes public.

1767   In a state of panic, returns to France, where the arrest warrant of 1762 is still in force; takes an assumed name and lodges in a château at Trye under the protection of the prince de Conti; Du Peyrou visits but is also suspected of treachery.

1768   Overwhelmed by paranoia, leaves Trye and moves to Lyon, then Grenoble, and finally Bourgoin in eastern France; goes through a form of marriage (not legally valid) with Thérèse after twenty-three years with her.

1769   Grim winter at the farm of Monquin near Bourgoin; nearly completes the *Confessions.*

1770   Resumes his real name and moves to Paris to confront his enemies, who fail to appear; supports himself by copying music; becomes reclusive but forms a lasting friendship with Bernardin de Saint-Pierre, with whom he collects plants in the countryside outside Paris.

1771   Attempts to rehabilitate his reputation by giving readings of the *Confessions* but is ordered by the police to stop.

1772   Begins a new attempt at self-justification, *Dialogues: Rousseau Judge of Jean-Jacques,* which he works at intermittently.

1776   Tries in vain to deposit the *Dialogues* manuscript in Notre-Dame cathedral; abandons hope of rehabilitating his much-maligned reputation; begins an unfinished final work, *Reveries of the Solitary Walker;* is knocked unconscious and incurs lasting damage when a huge dog runs him over in the street.

1778   In failing health, accepts the marquis de Girardin's invitation to live at his château at Ermenonville outside Paris; dies there of cerebral bleeding on July 2 at the age of sixty-six. He is buried on the Isle of Poplars in an ornamental lake.

1780   *Dialogues* published.
1782   First half of the *Confessions* published.
1789   Remainder of the *Confessions* published.
1794   Rousseau's remains transferred with great pomp to the Panthéon in Paris.
1801   Death of Thérèse, in extreme poverty.

Notes

Abbreviations

As mentioned in the introduction, translations from French (and occasionally from German) are my own unless otherwise indicated.

The following works are identified by abbreviations:

Annales	*Annales de la Société de Jean-Jacques Rousseau* (Geneva, 1905–)
Bernardin	Jacques-Henri Bernardin de Saint Pierre, *La Vie et Ouvrages de Jean-Jacques Rousseau,* ed. Maurice Souriau (Paris: Cornély, 1907)
C.C.	*Correspondance Complète de Jean-Jacques Rousseau,* ed. R. A. Leigh, 52 vols. (Geneva: Institut et Musée Voltaire, 1965–1971; Oxford: Voltaire Foundation, 1971–1998)
Corr. Litt.	Friedrich Melchior Grimm, *Correspondance Littéraire, Philosophique et Critique,* ed. Maurice Tourneux (Paris: Garnier, 1877–1882)
Cranston	Maurice Cranston, three-volume biography: *Jean-Jacques: The Early Life and Work* (New York: Norton, 1982); *The Noble Savage* (Chicago: University of Chicago Press, 1991); *The Solitary Self* (Chicago: University of Chicago Press, 1997)
Dictionnaire	Raymond Trousson and Frédéric S. Eigeldinger, *Dictionnaire de Jean-Jacques Rousseau* (Paris: Champion, 1996)
Guéhenno	Jean Guéhenno, two-volume biography: *Jean-Jacques Rousseau,* trans. John and Doreen Weightman (London: Routledge, 1967)
Mémoire	Raymond Trousson, *Jean-Jacques Rousseau: Mémoire de la Critique* (Paris: Presses de l'Université de Paris–Sorbonne, 2000)
O.C.	Jean-Jacques Rousseau, *Oeuvres Complètes,* ed. Marcel Raymond et al., 5 vols. (Paris: Gallimard, Bibliothèque de la Pléiade, 1959–1995)
Trousson	Raymond Trousson, two-volume biography: *Jean-Jacques Rousseau: La Marche à la Gloire* and *Jean-Jacques Rousseau: Le Deuil Éclatant du Bonheur* (Paris: Tallandier, 1988–1989; reissued in 2003 in single-volume format as Jean-Jacques Rousseau, but my references are to the two-volume version)

Introduction

2   "It took Kant": Jean Starobinski, *Jean-Jacques Rousseau: Transparency and Obstruction,* trans. Arthur Goldhammer (Chicago: University of Chicago Press, 1988), p. 115 (adapting a phrase by Eric Weil).

"I would rather": *Émile* II, *O.C.* 4: 323.

3   "I found in myself": *Lettres à Malesherbes,* no. 3, *O.C.* 1: 1140.

"no one can write": *Ébauches des Confessions, O.C.* 1: 49.

"the 'Know Thyself'": *Rêveries* IV, *O.C.* 1: 1024.

1. The Loneliness of a Gifted Child

7   "I was born in Geneva . . . my misfortunes": *Confessions* I, *O.C.* 1: 6–7.

"He has not been shown": *Émile* IV, *O.C.* 4: 505.

8   "A son who quarrels": Rousseau to the marquis de Saint-Brisson, 22 July 1764, *C.C.* 20: 315.

he thought his father: *Confessions* VII, *O.C.* 1: 339 (Isaac Rousseau died in 1747 at the age of seventy-five, but Jean-Jacques believed he was sixty.)

9   Didier's descendants became: a comprehensive account of Rousseau's antecedents is given by Eugène Ritter, *La Famille et la Jeunesse de J. J. Rousseau, Annales,* vol. 16 (1924–1925); the material in this section is drawn from this volume. There is also a good summary in Cranston, vol. I, chap. 1.

"and heaven blessed": *Confessions* I, *O.C.* 1: 6.

10   Vincent Sarrasin, interest in the theater: Ritter, *La Famille,* pp. 68–83.

average marriage age: see Daniel Roche, *France in the Enlightenment,* trans. Arthur Goldhammer (Cambridge: Harvard University Press, 1998), pp. 183, 491; and Anne-Marie Piuz, *A Genève et Autour de Genève aux XVIIe et XVIIIe Siècles: Études d'Histoire Economique* (Lausanne: Payot, 1985), p. 18.

11   Suzanne brought 6,000 florins: Ritter, *La Famille,* pp. 103–4.

"the greatest vagabonds": *Corr. Litt.* 4: 77 (1 Feb. 1759). On Rousseau's wandering relatives, see François Jost, *Jean-Jacques Rousseau Suisse: Étude sur sa Personnalité et sa Pensée* (Fribourg: Editions Universitaires, 1961) 2: 18; and Ritter, *La Famille,* pp. 101–2.

Constantinople was a long way: Trousson 1: 29.

"shining the torch,": Ritter, *La Famille,* p. 117.

impromptu poem . . . French diplomat: *Confessions* I, *O.C.* 1: 7.

wealthy godfather . . . "on Thursday": Ritter, *La Famille,* pp. 103–4, 125, 11.

12   "I don't know . . . everyone around me": *Confessions* I, *O.C.* 1: 8, 10.

"a maiden lady . . . poor aunt Suzon": ibid., pp. 12, 61.

dictated a letter . . . another letter: 5 Dec. and 27 Dec. 1764 (the second letter is from Charlotte Bolomey, who presumably wrote the first at Suzanne's dictation), *C.C.* 22: 169, 297.

"Dear aunt, I forgive": *Confessions* I, *O.C.* 1: 8.

13   "It is through her": Rousseau to Madeleine-Catherine Delessert, ca. Apr. 1774, *C.C.* 39: 234.

"the good Jacqueline": Ritter, *La Famille,* pp. 122–23.

"I often say": 22 July 1761, *C.C.* 9: 70. Jacqueline was sixty-five at the time.

increasingly pressed for cash: Cranston gives the financial details: 1: 23.

14 such pilgrims as Stendhal: Bernard Gagnebin, *Album Rousseau* (Paris: Gallimard, 1976), pp. 11, 17.

Two men out of every ten: Louis Binz, *Brève Histoire de Genève* (Geneva: Chancellerie d'État, 1981), pp. 36–38; Alfred Dufour, *Histoire de Genève* (Paris: Presses Universitaires de France, 1997), pp. 90–91.

un homme du peuple: Ébauches des Confessions, O.C. 1: 1150; "those important persons": *Émile* III, *O.C.* 4: 457.

"A Genevan watchmaker": letter to Théodore Tronchin, 26 Nov. 1758, *C.C.* 5: 241.

"Even the lower class" . . . works of Locke and Montesquieu: William Coxe, *Sketches of the National Political and Civil State of Swisserland* (1789); John Moore, *A View of Society and Manners in France, Switzerland and Germany* (1779); both quoted by Mavis Coulson, *Southwards to Geneva: 200 Years of English Travellers* (Gloucester: Alan Sutton, 1988), pp. 21, 23.

had more political agitators: Helena Rosenblatt, *Rousseau and Geneva: From the First Discourse to the Social Contract* (Cambridge: Cambridge University Press, 1997), p. 31.

"a gang of bandylegged": *The Travel Diaries of William Beckford of Fonthill,* ed. Guy Chapman (Cambridge: Constable, 1928), p. 319. Beckford's account of the Salève excursion cannot be dated precisely but may have been written in 1777.

15 "a puffy, shapeless, bucolic": Cranston 1: 326.

"but soon our interest . . . cure me of": *Confessions* I, *O.C.* 1: 8. Rousseau's complicated relationship with his father is perceptively explored by Claire Elmquist, *Rousseau: Père et Fils* (Odense: Odense University Press, 1996).

16 "My first and best": *Ébauches des Confessions, O.C.* 1: 1160.

"Constantly occupied": *Confessions* I, *O.C.* 1: 9; "my master and comforter": letter to Mme d'Épinay, 26 May 1754, *C.C.* 2: 265; knew Plutarch by heart: Bernardin, p. 116.

minority of the total population: Piuz, *A Genève et Autour de Genève,* p. 13; and Roche, *France in the Enlightenment,* pp. 167–68, 176, 179–80, 194.

17 No Rousseau was ever elected: Ritter, *La Famille,* pp. 52–53.

Rousseau grew up believing: details from Louis J. Courtois, *Enfance Faubourienne ou Jean-Jacques à Coutance* (Geneva: Jullien, 1933), p. 6; and Pierre-Paul Clément, *Jean-Jacques Rousseau: De l'Éros Coupable à l'Éros Glorieux* (Neuchâtel: Le Baconnière, 1976), p. 394n.

"A sovereign that never": quoted by Marcel Raymond, "Rousseau et Genève," in *Jean-Jacques Rousseau,* ed. Samuel Baud-Bovy et al. (Neuchâtel: La Baconnière, 1962), p. 226.

induced to publish the *Edicts:* Barbara Roth-Lochner, "De la Réforme à la Révolution," in Claude Lapaire et al., *Liberté, Franchises, Immunités, Us et Coutumes de la Ville de Genève* (État et Ville de Genéve, 1987), p. 79.

"the virtuous citizen": dedication to the *Discourse on Inequality, O.C.* 3: 118.

"Today there is more": *citoyen,* in the *Synonymes Français* of the abbé Girard (1736), as cited in Rousseau's *La Nouvelle Héloïse,* ed. Henri Coulet (Paris: Gallimard, 1993), 1: 511n.

18 "Most of them gathered": *Lettre à d'Alembert , O.C.* 5: 123–24.

20 "Never did he . . . only my son": *Confessions* I, *O.C.* 1: 7.

"I recognized him": Marcet de Mézières in 1754, quoted by Ritter, *La Famille,* p. 160.

"a man of pleasure": *Confessions* II, *O.C.* 1: 61.

"took up the life": *Confessions* I, *O.C.* 1: 9.

"at the request": quoted by Alexis François, "Encore la Famille de Rousseau," *Annales* 31 (1946–1949): 254–57.

"I scarcely saw": *Confessions* I, *O.C.* 1: 9.

"The child knows": *Émile* IV, *O.C.* 4: 500.

"I remember that": *Confessions* I, *O.C.* 1: 9–10.

21 "I would be only": *Julie* I.lxiii, *O.C.* 2: 176. The relevance of this passage to the incident with François is noted by Kamilla Denman, "Recovering *Fraternité* in the Works of Rousseau: Jean-Jacques' Lost Brother," *Eighteenth-Century Studies* 29 (1995–1996): 191–210; see also Clément, *De l'Éros Coupable,* chap. 2.

"My father, my aunt": *Confessions* I, *O.C.* 1: 10.

"Rousseau and his father": Raymond Trousson and Frédéric S. Eigeldinger, *Jean-Jacques Rousseau au Jour le Jour: Chronologie* (Paris: Champion, 1998), p. 14.

"Is there any being": *Julie* V.iii, *O.C.* 2: 569.

22 "that if he had been": *Rêveries* IV, *O.C.* 1: 1036–37.

"our children are dear": *Julie* IV.i, *O.C.* 2: 399.

"indifferent to everything": *Émile* IV, *O.C.* 4: 505. The absence of affection between Émile and the tutor who takes the place of his father is explored by Elmquist in *Rousseau: Père et Fils,* chap. 17.

"I remember the pounding heart": *Émile* IV, *O.C.* 4: 689.

a disastrous quarrel: the details are given by Ritter, *La Famille, pp. 131–37.*

23 "Why are you laughing": Bernardin, p. 40.

2. The End of Innocence

25 Bossey: the village is mentioned in *Émile* II, *O.C.* 4: 369.

a formal investigation: Ritter, *La Famille,* pp. 143–48; and Pierre-Maurice Masson, *La Religion de Jean-Jacques Rousseau,* 3 vols. (Paris: Hachette, 1916), 1: 21–23.

26 servant was dismissed: *Confessions* I, *O.C.* 1: 16.

"an only son": ibid., p. 10. On the fate of Rousseau's brother see *O.C.* 1: 1238n3.

"as gentle . . . annihilate us": *Confessions* I, *O.C.* 1: 13.

"because, separated": *Émile* II, *O.C.* 4: 385.

"and all the petty . . . none of it": *Confessions* I, *O.C.* 1: 12–13.

27 "I can still see": ibid., p. 21.

"raised with gentleness . . . deserted me": *Rêveries* III, *O.C.* 1: 1013.

"No matter who opened": Masson, *La Religion de Rousseau* 1: 28; and on Genevan religious practices, pp. 5–10.

"When I hear": "Unité de Mélodie," in *Dictionnaire de Musique, O.C.* 5: 1143.

28 "When I happened": *Confessions* I, *O.C.* 1: 14.

"If I had to depict": *Émile* IV, *O.C.* 4: 554.

"he treats as stupid": Masson, *La Religion de Rousseau* 1: 34.

"far from getting bored": *Confessions* II, *O.C.* 1: 62.

"flustered, but . . . neighboring room": *Émile* II, *O.C.* 4: 385–86.

"I was never scared": letter to Pierre-Laurent de Belloy, 12 Mar. 1770, *C.C.* 37: 323; Rousseau had already said something similar in *Confessions* XI, *O.C.* 1: 566.

29 "I found in the pain": *Confessions* I, *O.C.* 1: 15.

One writer suggests . . . Another observes: Georges-Arthur Goldschmidt, *Jean-Jacques Rousseau, ou, l'Esprit de Solitude* (Paris: Phébus, 1978), p. 170; Philippe Lejeune, *Le Pacte Autobiographique* (Paris: Seuil, 1975), pp. 65–66.

"The second time": *Confessions* I, *O.C.* 1: 15.

police report: cited by Patrick Wald Lasowski, "La Fessée ou l'Ultime Faveur," *Magazine Littéraire,* special issue on Rousseau, Sept. 1997: 30.

As Philippe Lejeune suggests: *Le Pacte Autobiographique,* pp. 70–75.

"To be at the knees": *Confessions* I, *O.C.* 1: 17. On the historical usage of *jouissance,* see *Le Robert Dictionnaire Historique de la Langue Française* (Paris: Robert, 1998) 2: 1925.

30   "I had an affection": *Ébauches des Confessions, O.C.* 1: 1157.
"who would believe": *Confessions* I, *O.C.* 1: 15.
as Pierre-Paul Clément suggests: *De l'Éros Coupable,* chap. 9.
"Is Jean-Jacques' posterior": quoted by Georges May, *Rousseau* (Paris: Seuil, 1985), p. 8 ("*Le postérieur de Jean-Jacques est-il le soleil de Freud qui se lève?*").
"the derrière . . . perhaps even more": *Confessions* I, *O.C.* 1: 22.
"I couldn't look at": ibid., p. 16. The Petit Sacconex area lies just beyond the Saint-Gervais neighborhood, where Rousseau lived with his father and aunt, and it would have been unlikely for him to go there from Bossey.

31   Lejeune remarks: *Le Pacte Autobiographique,* p. 83.
Clément notes: *De l'Éros Coupable,* p. 73.
"Almost fifty years": *Confessions* I, *O.C.* 1: 19–20.
We happen to know that Gabriel Bernard: François, "Encore la Famille," pp. 249–50.
"Devoid of all . . . to lie": *Émile* II, *O.C.* 4: 321, 336.

32   "shouting at the top . . . Caesar was at thirty": *Confessions* I, *O.C.* 1: 24.
an enterprising cabinetmaker: *Dictionnaire,* p. 91.
"he would either be": L. C. F. Desjobert, *Journal de ma Tournée et de mon Voyage en Suisse,* reporting what he heard from the pastor Montmollin at Môtiers, *C.C.* 26: 374. Some years earlier Rousseau and Montmollin had had a bitter fight, but Montmollin was proud of the confidences Rousseau had once shared with him, and there is no reason to disbelieve this story.

33   "but afterward embraced": *Lettre à d'Alembert, O.C.* 5: 103.

34   "My uncle": a version of this statement is in *Confessions* I, *O.C.* 1: 25, but the phrase "to console herself for her husband's infidelities" appears only in the draft known as the Neuchâtel manuscript: *Annales* 4: 36.
"I gave myself": *Confessions* I, *O.C.* 1: 27.
as indeed he refused: *Confessions* I, *O.C.* 1: 25.
"She permitted herself . . . *tic tac Rousseau*": *Confessions* I, *O.C.* 1: 27. The Pléiade editors believe that *tic tac* means spanking, but another editor has found provincial expressions of the time that imply a less specific kind of teasing: Rousseau, *Confessions,* ed. Jacques Voisine (Paris: Garnier, 1964), p. 29.

35   "all my senses": *Confessions* I, *O.C.* 1: 28.
"They have nothing": draft version of the *Confessions* account, *O.C.* 1: 1247n.
The contract survives: *O.C.* 1: 1209–10.

36   Historians have ascertained: Conrad André Beerli, *Rues Basses et Molard: Genève du XVIIIe au XXe Siècle* (Geneva: Georg, 1983), pp. 248–52.
A Swedish traveler: ibid., pp. 332–34.
"What first strikes": *Lettre à d'Alembert, O.C.* 5: 85.
"a charming situation": *Discourse on Inequality, O.C.* 3: 115.

37   roosters could be heard: Piuz, *A Genève et Autour de Genève,* p. 9.
"tarnished all": *Confessions* I, *O.C.* 1: 30.
he never found time: ibid., p. 24.
"I must have had": ibid., p. 31.
"died in the arms": ibid., p. 7.
Apprentices throughout Europe: see Robert Darnton, *The Great Cat Massacre, and Other Episodes in French Cultural History* (New York: Basic Books, 1984), chap. 2.

38   "His strength is not": *Rousseau Juge de Jean-Jacques* II, *O.C.* 1: 818.
"I believed I was stealing": *Confessions* I, *O.C.* 1: 35.
"great human desert": Lejeune, *Le Pacte Autobiographique,* p. 138.

"I judged that": *Confessions* I, *O.C.* 1: 34–35.

"I fancy his harsh": Benjamin Franklin, *The Autobiography and Other Writings,* ed. Kenneth Silverman (London: Penguin Books, 1986), p. 21.

39   "mortal hatred . . . fits and starts": *Discourse on Inequality, O.C.* 3: 145, 128.

"the little gourmand . . . buy a thing": *Confessions* I, *O.C.* 1: 37.

"Good and bad alike . . . modest disposition": *Confessions* I, *O.C.* 1: 39–41.

40   "I reached my sixteenth year": ibid., p. 41.

intensive religious observances: as Masson remarks, *La Religion de Rousseau* 1: 11.

"a space enclosed": Chevalier de Jaucourt, in *Encyclopédie* XVII (1765): 279.

"an accursed captain": *Confessions* I, *O.C.* 1: 42. That Minutoli liked to close his gate half an hour early is reported in a draft version of the *Confessions.* The date of Mar. 14 can be deduced from a later reference to Palm Sunday, which came a week after this event (*O.C.* 1: 1252–53).

"the sinister and fatal": *Confessions* I, *O.C.* 1: 42.

"Free and my own": ibid., p. 45.

41   "I would have spent": ibid., p. 43.

as Marcel Raymond says: *Jean-Jacques Rousseau: La Quête de Soi et la Rêverie* (Paris: Corti, 1962), p. 15.

"I have never really": *Rêveries* VI, *O.C.* 1: 1059.

3. "I Desired a Happiness of Which I Had No Idea"

43   "He was a boy": *Confessions* I, *O.C.* 1: 42.

"lodging with farmers": *Confessions* II, *O.C.* 1: 46.

45   "Many years later": Bernardin, pp. 103–4.

"I was content": *Confessions* II, *O.C.* 1: 45.

gained numerous converts: F. Vermale, *Jean-Jacques Rousseau en Savoie* (Chambéry: Librairie Dardel, 1922), p. 13.

"a sort of missionary": *Confessions* II, *O.C.* 1: 47.

pamphlet of Pontverre's: Masson, *La Religion de Rousseau* 1: 21–22, 40, 46.

"they made me recall": *Confessions* I, *O.C.* 1: 63.

46   "I saw a face . . . talk with you": *Confessions* II, *O.C.* 1: 49.

"Without being": *Confessions* II, *O.C.* 1: 48; bad teeth: *O.C.* 1: 1256n; "horrible teeth": *Dialogues* II, *O.C.* 1: 777.

47   "A rather timid": *Julie,* Appendix 2: "Sujets d'Estampes," *O.C.* 2: 762.

"she had a tender": *Confessions* II, *O.C.* 1: 49–50.

"blonde, with a sweet . . . devout woman": "Sujet d'Estampes," *O.C.* 2: 761.

48   "In all of the pictures": to François Coindet (a friend who was supervising the illustrations), 5 Nov. 1760, *C.C.* 7: 295.

"a lot of heart": Trousson 1: 83.

49   sent other converts: Vermale, *Rousseau en Savoie,* p. 29.

"It is a series": Trousson 1: 58.

"These gentlemen saw": *Confessions* II, *O.C.* 1: 55.

50   "the said act": *O.C.* 1: 1211.

roads were more like rural trails: Daniel Roche, *France in the Enlightenment,* p. 44.

"Young, vigorous": *Confessions* II, *O.C.* 1: 57–58.

51   almost three weeks: Émile Gaillard, "Jean-Jacques Rousseau à Turin," *Annales* 32 (1950–1952): 56–57.

Walpole and Gibbon: Edward Pyatt, *The Passage of the Alps* (London: Robert Hale, 1984), pp. 56–59.

"the court of Turin": Addison, *Remarks on Italy* (1705), in *The Miscellaneous Works of Joseph Addison,* ed. A. C. Guthkelch (London: Bell, 1914), 2: 197.

"The houses are of brick": Gray, letter to Richard West, 16 Nov. 1739, *Correspondence of Thomas Gray,* ed. Paget Toynbee and Leonard Whibley (Oxford: Clarendon Press, 1935), 1: 127.

"For anyone like myself": Giovanni Agnelli of Fiat, quoted in *L'Express,* 13 July 2000, p. 50.

52   still there today: the great door opened on the Via della Torri, which today is No. 9 Via Porta Palatina. The Confraternity sold the building, which had become too expensive to keep up, in 1873: Gaillard, "Rousseau à Turin," p. 58.

"four or five . . . sometimes met mine": *Confessions* II, *O.C.* 1: 60–61.

53   The registry: Gaillard, "Rousseau à Turin," pp. 58–60.

"Feeling that I was": *Confessions* II, *O.C.* 1: 66.

not yet been confirmed: Masson, *La Religion de Rousseau,* 1: 36.

"Still a child": *Rêveries* III, *O.C.* 1: 1013.

54   "something sticky . . . offenses of my sex": *Confessions* II, *O.C.* 1: 67–69.

"In the hospice": F. C. Green, *Jean-Jacques Rousseau: A Critical Study of His Life and Writings* (Cambridge: Cambridge University Press, 1955), p. 22.

"buggered me": Haydn Mason, *Voltaire: A Biography* (Baltimore: Johns Hopkins University Press, 1981), pp. 20, 52–54.

55   *"Can maledit"*: *Confessions* II, *O.C.* 1: 67.

modern editors comment: *O.C.* 1: 1265.

it has been suggested: Bernard Gagnebin, "Vérité et Véracité dans *Les Confessions,"* in *Jean-Jacques Rousseau et son Oeuvre: Problèmes et Recherches,* ed. Jean Fabre et al. (Paris: Klincksieck, 1964), pp. 11–12.

"Giovanni Giacomo Franco Rosso": quoted by Gaillard, "Rousseau à Turin," who gives a full account of the documentary evidence, pp. 62–71; see also Masson, *La Religion de Rousseau* 1: 50–51.

56   it has been suggested: Ritter, *La Famille,* pp. 164–65; see also Ronald Grimsley, *Jean-Jacques Rousseau: A Study in Self-Awareness* (Cardiff: University of Wales Press, 1961), p. 27n.

"They advised me": *Confessions* II, *O.C.* 1: 70.

"that excellent . . . voluptuous frugality": ibid., pp. 71–72, 1265.

"We all slept": ibid., p. 71.

57   "my little story . . . piquant brunette": ibid., p. 73.

"With avid eyes": ibid., p. 74.

"but there was a mirror": ibid., p. 75.

"If I had the temerity": ibid., p. 1160.

58   "Speak . . . has to offer?": *Émile* V, *O.C.* 4: 745–46.

"for ever panting": Keats, "Ode on a Grecian Urn."

59   "that little boy": *O.C.* 1: 79.

"Nothing I have felt": ibid., pp. 76–77.

"My restless . . . at one's pleasure": *Confessions* III, *O.C.* 1: 108–9.

"I am persuaded": *Émile* IV, *O.C.* 4: 662.

60   "Her life had been": *Confessions* II, *O.C.* 1: 83.

the comtesse's will: Gaillard, "Rousseau à Turin," pp. 81–96. The identity of the comtesse de Vercellis and her family was obscure until Gaillard searched the Turin archives and tracked down her marriage contract and will.

61   "She judged me less": *O.C.* 1: 82.

"They showed her": ibid., p. 85.

"One can find": Lejeune: *Le Pacte Autobiographique,* p. 54.

62   mirror image: Starobinski: *Transparency and Obstruction,* p. 122.
"a little ribbon": *Confessions* II, *O.C.* 1: 60.
"The presence of everybody": ibid., p. 86.

63   "He made me feel": *Confessions* III, *O.C.* 1: 91.
"I have a loving soul": ibid., p. 92.

64   "The good priest": *Émile* IV, *O.C.* 4: 606.
"To protect the young": ibid., p. 562.
"I was restless": *Confessions* III, *O.C.* 1: 88.
"What they saw": ibid.

65   "a big man . . . long time": ibid., pp. 89–90.
much commentary: see especially the virtuoso interpretation by Jean Starobinski, *La Relation Critique* (Paris: Gallimard, 1970), pp. 98–154.
"that air of softness . . . notice I was there": *O.C.* 1: 94.

66   It has been suggested: there was a Solaro family tradition to this effect; see Gaillard, "Rousseau à Turin," p. 113.
"This was one": *O.C.* 1: 96.

67   "I hate the great": *Lettres à Malesherbes, O.C.* 1: 1145.
"He took me outside": *Émile* IV, *O.C.* 4: 565.

68   "I remembered with delight": *Confessions* III, *O.C.* 1: 99.

4. Rousseau Finds a Mother

69   "There, you're home . . . abandon him.": *Confessions* III, *O.C.* 1: 113, 103–4.

70   "A change in mood": *Émile* IV, *O.C.* 4: 490.
calling her Maman: *O.C.* 1: 1280n.
Mme de Warens became: except where otherwise noted, information and quotations are drawn from Albert de Montet, *Madame de Warens et le Pays de Vaud* (Lausanne: Georges Bridel, 1891); and François Mugnier, *Mme de Warens et J.-J. Rousseau* (Paris: Calman Levy, 1891).

71   "seized by a violent passion": her husband's account is printed in full in *C.C.* 1: 266–91.

73   "She left her family": *État des nouveaux convertis auxquels on a distribué la moitié de la charité faite par sa Sainteté au mois d'août 1732,* quoted by Masson, *La Religion de Rousseau* 1: 63.

74   "abandoned a great . . . awash in tears": to père Claude Boudet, 19 Apr. 1742, *C.C.* 1: 146–47.
"For her, the principle": Cranston 1: 70.
wrote his own account: Conzié to an unknown correspondent, ca. 1786–1787, *C.C.* 1: 292–93.

75   Claire feels relief: *Julie* IV.ii, *O.C.* 2: 407.
"When she was pondering": *Confessions* III, *O.C.* 1: 107.
"That's quite a lot": *O.C.* 1: 105.

76   "It has the lake": Jean and Renée Nicolas, *La Vie Quotidienne en Savoie aux XVIIe et XVIIIe Siècles* (Paris: Hachette, 1979), quoting the prosecutor Barfelly, pp. 139, 141.
"You meet with nothing": to Philip Gray, 25 Oct. 1739, *Correspondence of Thomas Gray,* 1: 124.
"I was born": *Le Petit Savoyard, ou la Vie de Claude Noyer* (ca. 1756), *O.C.* 2: 1200.
"She was the tenderest . . . a thousand times": *Confessions* III, *O.C.* 1: 106–7.
"I was always in fear": *O.C.* 1: 1280.

77 "and even the floor . . . swallowed it": *O.C.* 1: 108.
"If some new . . . suck them": ibid., p. 110.

78 "I would recover": ibid., p. 112.
"Despite what my exterior": ibid., p. 113.

79 "a good little man . . . charming woman": ibid., p. 117.
"What was strongly . . . someone else's": ibid., pp. 118–19.

80 "not so much to forbid": *Julie* VI.vi, *O.C.* 2: 668. On the unlikelihood of Gâtier's disgrace, see *O.C.* 1: 1289–90.
"Let us think": Jean-Joseph Turretini, *Sermon sur le jubilé de la Réformation établie il y a deux cents ans* (1728), quoted by Jean-Louis Leuba, "Rousseau et le Milieu Calviniste de sa Jeunesse," in *Jean-Jacques Rousseau et la Crise Contemporaine de la Conscience,* ed. Leuba et al. (Paris: Beauchesne, 1980), pp. 28–29.
"Allow me to send": 5 Oct. 1743, *C.C.* 1: 198.

81 "So far as I can": *O.C.* 1: 121. Rousseau's testimonial of 1742 is in *C.C.* 1: 146–51.
faute de mieux: O.C. 1: 1291.

82 "In the various . . . cathedral steps": ibid., pp. 122–23.
"Bantering, playful . . . like an oracle": ibid., p. 125.

83 "I turned the corner": ibid., p. 129.

84 Scholars have combed: ibid., pp. 1293–94.
"without however giving": Comte Annibale Maffei to Comte Louis-Ignace de Foglizzo, 24 July 1730, *C.C.* 1: 301.
"Word has reached me": François Mitonet to count de Foglizzo, 31 July 1730, ibid., p. 303.
"the secret of our": Victor-Amédée II to Maffei, 2 Sept. 1730, ibid., pp. 310–11.

85 "When she pushed": *Confessions* IV, *O.C.* 1: 134. *Contrepointière* is defined in *O.C.* 1: 1298.
"No no, you don't . . . stage for a girl": *O.C.* 1: 135–36.

86 "I climbed . . . offended": ibid., pp. 137–38.
"some youthful folly": ibid., p. 135.
"Not a single": ibid., p. 138.

87 The records show: ibid., pp. 1296–97.

5. *A Year of Wandering*

88 "I couldn't imagine": *Confessions* IV, *O.C.* 1: 144.

89 "my good father . . . my duty": *O.C.* 1: 145.
"In spite of": May/June 1731, *C.C.* 1: 12. In this letter Rousseau mentions having had no communication with his father, presumably since the meeting in Nyon a year before.
"A father's heart": *Julie* I.lxiii, *O.C.* 2: 175.

90 "I badly needed": *O.C.* 1: 146.
A fragmentary letter: *C.C.* 1: 1–2.

91 "together with the bass": *Confessions* IV, *O.C.* 1: 148–49. The music historian is Michael O'Dea, *Jean-Jacques Rousseau: Music, Illusion and Desire* (London: Macmillan, 1995), p. 12.
"Everyone congratulated me": *O.C.* 1: 149.
interprets the ghastly concert: Starobinski, *Transparency and Obstruction,* pp. 59–61.
"I was called": *O.C.* 1: 150.

92 "During this trip": ibid., p. 152.
"I went to Vevey": ibid., p. 152.

no fatted calf: Trousson 1: 106.

93   "I was gradually": *O.C.* 1: 153.
"I didn't ask for anything": ibid., p. 154.
"That was the only": ibid., p. 156.
"The cashier will pay": ibid., p. 1303n.

94   Bishop Bernex: mentioned in a letter from Rousseau to Comte Joseph Piccone, 5 Mar. 1739, *C.C.* 1: 93.

95   "Be assured . . . anything base": May/June 1731, ibid., pp. 7–9.
"The misfortunes . . . pressing crisis": May/June 1731, ibid., pp. 12–14.

96   "with myself . . . old hats": *O.C.* 1: 159.
Voltaire compared it: *Candide,* chap. 22. Details on Paris in this paragraph are drawn from Jean Chagniot, *Nouvelle Histoire de Paris: Paris au XVIIIe Siècle* (Paris: Hachette, 1988), pp. 171–81, 217–39.

97   "The *grands timides*": Gaston Bachelard, *L'Eau et les Rêves* (Paris: Corti, 1942), p. 218.
"Never have I . . . seek it": *O.C.* 1: 162–63.

98   "So you believed . . . depicted him perfectly": ibid., p. 161.

99   "that inextinguishable": ibid., p. 164.
"What does all": Alphonse Callery, quoted ibid., p. 1309n.
"and didn't stop": ibid., p. 166.

100   "where the most appalling": ibid., p. 168.
"It had been very hot": ibid., pp. 168–69.
"for I was as skinny": ibid., p. 170.

101   "She was neither . . . grand emotions": ibid., p. 171.

102   "Never has a flat": ibid., pp. 172–73.
"a blue chasm": William Wordsworth, *The Prelude* (1805 version), book XIII, lines 56–59.
"Without speaking": *O.C.* 1: 173.

6. In Maman's House

104   "doorkeepers of the Alps": Christian Sorrel et al., *Histoire de Chambéry* (Toulouse: Privat, 1992), p. 10; other details on Chambéry are from Nicolas, *La Vie Quotidienne,* pp. 139–40, 144–47, 153.

105   a female laborer: her name was Marie Gay; the date was Feb. 1734 (Nicolas, *La Vie Quotidienne,* p. 52). Information on literacy: ibid., pp. 313–18.

106   "No more garden": *Confessions* V, *O.C.* 1: 176.
"*chez moi*": *O.C.* 1: 176.
"In Annecy": ibid., p. 196.
"the fertile years": Ritter, *La Famille,* p. 15.

107   aunt was mother superior: Mugnier, *Mme de Warens,* p. 9n.
"She was of middle . . . their integrity": Conzié, letter to an unknown correspondent, ca. 1786–1787, *C.C.* 1: 293–94.
"Although he was as young": *O.C.* 1: 201.

108   "I didn't dare": ibid., pp. 177–78.
cadastre, the land registry: on these reforms, see Roche, *France in the Enlightenment,* pp. 27–33.
"the closed field": Georges Daumas, "Rousseau à Chambéry," *Annales* 33 (1953–1955): 220–25.
"Reflection joined": *O.C.* 1: 179.

109   "Occupied eight hours": ibid., p. 188.

"the smallest duties": first *Lettre à Malesherbes, O.C.* 1: 1132.

"in everything imaginable": *Rêveries* VI, *O.C.* 1: 1053.

Erik Erikson writes: in numerous books, notably *Young Man Luther* (New York: Norton, 1958); *Identity, Youth, and Crisis* (New York: Norton, 1968); and *Gandhi's Truth* (New York: Norton, 1969).

"I will have few": *O.C.* 1: 178.

110   *"Qui bien chante"*: ibid., p. 187.

he told a friend: Bernardin, p. 57.

111   "I have decided": 29 June 1732(?), *C.C.* 1: 16.

"one hardly knows": Nicolas, *La Vie Quotidienne,* pp. 190–91.

"and after having been": *O.C.* 1: 186.

112   "persecuted the late": père Antoine Belfils to his erstwhere ally père Bonaventure Jorand, quoted by Georges Daumas, "En Marge des *Confessions,*" *Annales* 33 (1953–1955): 218; on Canevas, see pp. 210–11.

"There I was . . . it is Chambéry": *O.C.* 1: 188.

"with impossible names": Trousson 1: 122.

"the most beautiful": *Confessions* V, *O.C.* 1: 190.

"but if you still see": undated letter, perhaps written in 1734, probably to Catherine-Françoise de Challes, *C.C.* 1: 22.

113   "that sometimes attracted": *O.C.* 1: 189.

"But instead": ibid., p. 192.

"the very model . . . herself understood": ibid., pp. 190–91.

"The novelty": ibid., p. 194.

114   "she always believed": ibid., p. 198.

"For the first time": ibid., p. 197.

"What a dream": Hippolyte Buffenoir, *Les Charmettes et Jean-Jacques Rousseau* (Paris: Paul Cornau, 1902), pp. 11–12.

"was totally without": Cranston 1: 109.

"a sexually promiscuous": Grimsley, *A Study in Self-Awareness,* p. 102.

115   "since she wasn't": *O.C.* 1: 197.

"One can well believe": Olivier Marty, *Rousseau de l'Enfance à Quarante Ans* (Paris: Debresse, 1975), p. 139.

"With Maman my pleasure": *Confessions* VI, *O.C.* 1: 253–54.

"The need for love . . . in the act": *Confessions* V, *O.C.* 1: 219.

116   "I don't know . . . to her happiness": ibid., p. 201.

"on the fifth day": ibid., p. 205.

it is easy to imagine: Clément: *De l'Éros Coupable,* p. 187. The inaccessibility of *génipi* in March was first noted by Mugnier, *Mme de Warens,* p. 119.

117   One curious incident: *Julie* I.xliii–xliv, IV.x.

"all the worse . . . truly lactified": letter probably dated 13 Aug. 1733, *C.C.* 1: 20; R. A. Leigh notes that Rousseau apparently invented the word *lactifié.* The illness is mentioned in *Confessions* V, *O.C.* 1: 184.

118   "After the death": to Claude Boudet, 19 Apr. 1742, *C.C.* 1: 149.

a notebook still exists: mentioned by Leigh, *C.C.* 1: 25n.

"I ardently pray": letter of 18 Dec. 1734, *C.C.* 1: 314. The events of 1734 are recounted by Mugnier, *Mme de Warens,* chap. 5.

"this aberration . . . on her part": *C.C.* 1: 26–27.

119   "For six months": ibid., p. 24.

"Since she has nothing": ibid., p. 109 (probably written in 1739).

120   "This baroness": ibid., p. 293 (written in 1786 or 1787).

"It's true that . . . without its use": ibid., pp. 29–31.

121 "that we are miserable": *La Liturgie ou la Manière de Célébrer le Service Divin dans l'Église de Genève* (1743), quoted in Leuba, "Rousseau et le Milieu Calviniste," p. 42.

"I avow that": Mugnier, *Mme de Warens,* p. 11.

"devout almost in the manner": *Rêveries* III, *O.C.* 1: 1013.

this belief would undergird: Starobinski, *L'Oeil Vivant,* pp. 155–61.

street in front of the seminary: Léandre Vaillat, *La Savoie* (Paris: Perrin, 1912), p. 321.

"I passed two": *O.C.* 1: 218.

122 "No matter how reserved": ibid., p. 212.

Gabriel Bagueret: his colorful career is summarized by Leigh, *C.C.* 1: 36.

123 "Feeling myself": *O.C.* 1: 221.

"I became completely . . . ceasing to be": ibid., p. 222.

"I intend to beg:" *C.C.* 1: 32.

124 "but as isolated": *O.C.* 1: 224.

7. The Idyll of Les Charmettes

125 A lease survives: Georges Daumas, "L'Idylle des Charmettes est-elle un Mythe?" *Annales* 34 (1956–1958): 83–105; on the farm products and livestock: *Dictionnaire,* p. 134.

127 "perfectly free": *Rêveries* X, *O.C.* 1: 1099.

"Here begins . . . single moment": *Confessions* VI, *O.C.* 1: 225–26.

128 "No longer able": *O.C.* 1: 227.

doctors were not plentiful: Nicolas, *La Vie Quotidienne,* p. 41.

129 "This accident . . . least bored": *O.C.* 1: 228, 235.

"As a sick man": to Mme d'Épinay, 26 Mar. 1757, *C.C.* 4: 200.

"Doubting that I": *O.C.* 1: 231.

"read and reread": *Confessions* VI, *O.C.* 1: 232.

"After having known": Bernard Lamy, *Entretiens sur les Sciences,* ed. François Girbal and Pierre Clair (Paris: Presses Universitaires de France, 1966), p. 65.

130 "I no longer thought": *O.C.* 1: 232.

"The joy with which": ibid., p. 233.

"I have always taken": ibid., pp. 233–34.

"to the author . . . sensual pleasure": ibid., pp. 236–37.

"It is probable": ibid., p. 1350n.

131 "Maman, Maman . . . not yet visited": ibid., pp. 244–45.

Jean-Samuel-Rodolphe Wintzenried: the available materials are reviewed in *O.C.* 1: 1361–62; *C.C.* 1: 89–90; and *Dictionnaire,* pp. 943–44.

"He was as noisy": *O.C.* 1: 262.

132 "ruinous projects": Conzié, letter to unknown correspondent, ca. 1786–1787, *C.C.* 1: 294.

"He has wit": memorandum of 1757 by the *intendant général,* quoted by Mugnier, *Mme de Warens,* pp. 419–20.

"Never have the purity . . . the one I love": *O.C.* 1: 264–66.

"a sudden and complete": ibid., p. 263.

"What a *bouleversement*": *Confessions* I, *O.C.* 1: 19.

133 "The abstinence": *Confessions* VI, *O.C.* 1: 266.

"for his lodging . . . Roman Church": *O.C.* 1: 1212–13.

134 "he often talked": *Confessions* V, *O.C.* 1: 215.

"shut up in my inn": 24–26 July 1737, *C.C.* 1: 44–45.

"she received it": *Confessions* VI, *O.C.* 1: 247.

135 "who used to call . . . state secrets" *O.C.* 1: 216–17.

"We regarded": Madeleine Jacquéry to Rousseau, 28 July 1762, *C.C.* 12: 121. Rousseau seems not to have responded to this letter.

136 *malade imaginaire: Confessions* VI, *O.C.* 1: 258.

"a mass of coagulable lymph": Matthew Baillie, *The Morbid Anatomy of Some of the Most Important Parts of the Body* (London, 1793), p. 14.

"Allow me, Madame . . . do otherwise": 13 Sept. 1737, *C.C.* 1: 48–49.

137 Jacobites were well known: see Clément, *De l'Éros Coupable,* p. 155; the implications of Rousseau's alias are interestingly explored in Geoffrey Bennington, *Dudding: Les Noms de Rousseau* (Paris: Galilée, 1991).

138 "*Voilà* Mme de Larnage . . . experiencing pleasure": *Confessions* VI, *O.C.* 1: 249, 253–54.

"She had given me": ibid., p. 252.

"a budding passion": Fénelon, *Les Aventures de Télémaque,* ed. Jeanne-Lydie Goré (Paris: Garnier, 1968), book VI, p. 174.

his exhibitionism: Starobinski, *L'Oeil Vivant,* p. 107.

139 "The echoing . . . thinks of everything": *O.C.* 1: 256.

"At an inn": Bernardin, p. 52; see also *O.C.* 1: 256–57.

"regarded me": Bernardin, pp. 47–48.

140 "Montpellier is a large": to Jean-Antoine Charbonnel, 4 Nov. 1737, *C.C.* 1: 61.

"I don't love": to the marquis de Mirabeau, 31 Jan. 1767, *C.C.* 32: 84.

"The food . . . understand me": 23 Oct. and 4 Dec. 1737, *C.C.* 1: 53–59, 63–64.

141 "For the first": *O.C.* 1: 260.

"I went upstairs": ibid., p. 261.

142 "Since the name": ibid., p. 265.

"Monsieur the château-keeper": Cranston 1: 135.

"enacting the role": ibid., p. 140; the legal document, dated 24 Oct. 1739, is reprinted in *C.C.* 1: 316.

"Madame, receive": *O.C.* 2: 1122.

"Since you have settled": 3 Mar. 1739, *C.C.* 1: 88.

"the most tender . . . the bitterness": 18 Mar. 1739, ibid., pp. 98–99.

143 "Ah, if only": *Rêveries* X, *O.C.* 1: 1098.

"Why was it not": *Émile et Sophie* I, *O.C.* 4: 895; Clément, *De l'Éros Coupable,* p. 188.

"To read while eating": *Confessions* VI, *O.C.* 1: 269.

"I don't know why": *O.C.* 1: 242.

144 "While reading . . . one's time": ibid., pp. 237, 239, 234.

"Men of genius": Bernardin, p. 149.

145 "It seemed to me": *O.C.* 1: 238.

"A diagram would make": 20 Sept. 1738, *C.C.* 1: 79.

pet-en-l'air: O.C. 1: 241.

"the 'me' is hateful . . . hate themselves": Pascal, *Pensées,* nos. 455, 451, 468, in the numeration of Léon Brunschvicg.

"and if Maman . . . was not difficult": *O.C.* 1: 243.

146 "a Catholicism": Nicolas Bonhôte, *Jean-Jacques Rousseau: Vision de l'Histoire et Autobiographie: Étude de Sociologie de la Littérature* (Lausanne: L'Age d'Homme, 1992), p. 210.

throw it into the fire: *Confessions* VII, *O.C.* 1: 293.

"set to music": *O.C.* 2: 1163, 1906n; *C.C.* 1: 48n.

The Orchard: O.C. 2: 1123–29.

"stale and colorless": Jean-Louis Lecercle, *Rousseau et l'Art du Roman* (Paris: Librairie Armand Colin, 1969), p. 42.

147 "I tell you frankly . . . diversions": *C.C.* 1: 72.

"In Praise of the Monks": *O.C.* 2: 1120–22.

composed a morning prayer: *O.C.* 4: 1034–39.

French chargé d'affaires: *C.C.* 1: 93–95 (also in *O.C.* 1: 1214–17).

148 "I left my fatherland": *C.C.* 1: 93–94 (also in *O.C.* 1: 1218–20).

"that accursed trip": 3 Mar. 1739, *C.C.* 1: 88.

implausible proposal: ibid., pp. 96–97.

8. Broadening Horizons

149 "rescue him": 22 Aug. 1740, *C.C.* 1: 124–25.

"I will try to deserve": Apr. 1740, ibid., p. 120.

150 "with all my heart": 25 Apr. 1740, ibid., pp. 121–22.

"a town without a history": Maurice Garden, *Lyon et les Lyonnais au XVIIIe Siècle* (Paris: Flammarion, 1975), pp. 351, 63, 352. The table on p. 180 indicates that in 1789 60 percent of the workers were in the textile trades, and nearly half of those in silk.

151 wrote one to a member: "Épître à M. Bordes," *O.C.* 2: 1132.

"I don't care": *Émile* III, *O.C.* 4: 477.

"noble and generous . . . best-acting of men": *Confessions* VII, *O.C.* 1: 281, 280.

"I was a base child . . . on my account": *O.C.* 2: 1139–40.

"He was glimpsing": Guéhenno 1: 111.

152 "good-looking . . . learning a thing": *Confessions* VI, *O.C.* 1: 267.

"I could see": ibid., p. 268.

153 "Nothing is more . . . affects me at all": *O.C.* 4: 13, 31, 10, 21.

154 "a certain very nice": *O.C.* 1: 269.

"I'm not surprised": Bernardin, p. 115.

Barbarus hic: O.C. 2: 1890.

"Displaced by fate": "Pour Madame de Fleurieu," ibid., p. 1133.

155 "which I got bored": *O.C.* 1: 268.

"She had nothing": *Confessions* VII, *O.C.* 1: 282. The reference to Mlle Serre at eleven (Rousseau remembered her as being fourteen) is in *Confessions* IV, *O.C.* 1: 171.

"I understand": *C.C.* 1: 103–6.

156 "I embrace you": 5 Dec. 1764, *C.C.* 22: 170.

"jeunesse égarée": C.C. 1: 106n.

"To Fanie": in a letter to Conzié, 14 Mar. 1742, *C.C.* 1: 144–45.

long letter thanking: to Conzié, 17 Jan. 1742, ibid., pp. 132–39.

157 "Wit only comes": Bernardin, p. 5.

158 "When he would go": Trousson 1: 104.

"Nothing is more": *Émile* II, *O.C.* 4: 342–43.

"ugly street": *Confessions* VII, *O.C.* 1: 282.

159 "It appears to us": quoted in Elisabeth Badinter, *Les Passions Intellectuelles,* 2 vols. (Paris: Fayard, 1999, 2002), 1: 225.

160 "You must courageously": quoted in Guéhenno 1: 123.

"knew better how": quoted in Arthur M. Wilson, *Diderot* (New York: Oxford University Press, 1972), p. 16.

"thickset, with a build": reminiscence of Jean-Nicolas Dufort, comte de Cheverny, referring to an incident in 1768, quoted in Wilson, *Diderot,* p. 543.

161 walk through a hall of mirrors: Alain Grosrichard, "Où suis-je? Que suis-je: Ré-
flexions sur la question de la *place* dans l'oeuvre de Jean-Jacques Rousseau à partir
d'un texte des *Rêveries,*" in *Rousseau et Voltaire en 1978: Actes du Colloque International de Nice* (Geneva: Slatkine, 1981), p. 356.

"brilliant in imagination": André Morellet, *Mémoires de l'Abbé Morellet,* ed. Jean-
Pierre Guicciardi (Paris: Mercure de France, 1988), p. 58.

"He speaks with a warmth . . . black and blue": quoted in Wilson, *Diderot,* pp. 630,
695, 632.

"the first bomb": quoted in *The New Oxford Companion to Literature in French,* ed.
Peter France (Oxford: Clarendon, 1995), p. 845.

162 "He had the look ": Wilson, *Diderot,* p. 350.

"I have a mask": Diderot, *Salon de 1767,* ed. Jean Seznec and Jean Adhémar (Oxford:
Clarendon, 1963), p. 67.

163 "He meditates deeply": Jacob Jonas Björnstahl to Carl Christoffer Gjörwell, 1 September 1770, *C.C.* 38: 95.

"Does it wound you": Antoine Bret, manuscript, "Anecdotes sur Rousseau," transcribed by A. C. Keys, *Annales* 32 (1950–1952): 184.

"Man strives": *Salon de 1767,* in *Oeuvres Complètes de Diderot,* ed. J. Assézat (Paris:
Garnier, 1876), 11: 127.

frères ennemis: Jean Fabre, "Deux Frères Ennemis: Diderot et Jean-Jacques," in
Lumières et Romantisme, 2nd ed. (Paris: Klincksieck, 1980), pp. 19–65.

"Since the musicians": *Confessions* VII, *O.C.* 1: 288–89.

"*entrée* into a wealthy": ibid., p. 291.

"First silence": Voltaire, *Candide,* chap. 22.

164 Saint-Preux describes Julie: *Julie* II.xiv-xv.

"entirely undistinguished": Giacomo Casanova, *History of My Life,* trans. Willard
Trask (New York: Harcourt, Brace & World, 1966), 2: 223, 8: 249.

"One has to have": *Lettres sur les Ouvrages et le Caractère de J.-J. Rousseau,* ed. Marcel
Françon (Geneva: Slatkine Reprints, 1979), p. 42.

"biting and satiric": *Julie,* Seconde Préface, *O.C.* 2: 21.

"Woe to him . . . claim to pity": *Julie* II.xvii, *O.C.* 2: 248, 256, 252, 250, and II.xxvii,
O.C. 2: 303. Coulet gives eighteenth-century examples of the phrase *gens de l'autre
monde* in his edition of *La Nouvelle Héloïse* 1: 513.

165 "When I saw her . . . with my eyes": *Confessions* VII, *O.C.* 1: 291–92.

"Open your eyes": Trousson, who quotes the poem (1: 182), believes it to be authenti-
cally Rousseau's, though that is not certain.

"I have learned": 9 Apr. 1743, *C.C.* 1: 182.

166 "He was one of the worst": Louis de Bachaumont, *Mémoires Secrets pour servir à
l'Histoire de la République des Lettres en France depuis 1762,* 26 Feb. 1769, in Pierre-
Paul Plan, *J.-J. Rousseau Raconté par les Gazettes de son Temps* (Paris: Mercure de
France, 1912), p. 96.

"even if Mme Dupin": *Confessions* VII, *O.C.* 1: 293.

"heroic ballet . . . amours of a poet": ibid., p. 294.

9. The Masks of Venice

168 "I have a good opinion": Louis-Gabriel-Christophe de Montaigu to Pierre-François,
comte de Montaigu, 29 June 1743, *C.C.* 1: 187.

"For many years": ibid., p. 188.

169 "to see my poor Maman": *Confessions* VII, *O.C.* 1: 295.

"his trip to Chambéry": Mugnier, *Mme de Warens,* p. 216.

"I have been charmed": Jonville to Montaigu, 26 Sept. 1743, *C.C.* 1: 196.

170 "even though since": 21 Sept. 1743, ibid., p. 194. Leigh's note (pp. 195–96) summarizes the financial crisis.

"Two days after": Montaigu to the abbé Pierre-Joseph Alary, 15 Aug. 1744, *C.C.* 2: 50.

"If he had never": Guéhenno 1: 140.

"secretary to the embassy": Rousseau wrote to Mme de Warens that she should use this title when addressing letters to him, 5 Oct. 1743, *C.C.* 1: 198.

translated into code: described in *O.C.* 3: ccl–ccli.

171 "The clerk for foreign": J.-G. du Theil's clerk to Montaigu, 28 Nov. 1743, *C.C.* 1: 215; *Confessions* VII, *O.C.* 1: 304.

"I am irritated": Montaigu to L. G. C. de Montaigu, 19 Nov. 1743, *C.C.* 1: 210.

Rousseau was quick: ibid., p. lv.

173 "The senator turned . . . sister Camille": *Confessions* VII, *O.C.* 1: 302.

"It is perhaps": ibid., p. 306.

"the very innocent": ibid., p. 305.

"at one o'clock": the abbé Nauti to Rousseau, 30 Dec. 1743, *C.C.* 1: 221.

"a fabulous": Henri Zerner, unpaginated preface to Philippe Monnier, *Venise au XVIIIe Siècle* (Brussels: Complexe, 1907; reprint, 1981).

174 "More than a disguise": Monnier, *Venise,* p. 34.

"I have altered": to the comtesse de Montaigu, 23 Nov. 1743, *C.C.* 1: 213.

"a breath of . . . their bodies": Johann Wolfgang von Goethe, *Italian Journey 1786–1788,* trans. W. H. Auden and Elizabeth Mayer (New York: Pantheon, 1962), pp. 88, 75, 71, 68.

"while listening . . . awakened me": *O.C.* 1: 314.

"A type of song": "Barcarolles," in *Dictionnaire de Musique, O.C.* 5: 650.

175 "The sound of their voices": Goethe, *Italian Journey,* p. 77.

"What an awakening . . . awakened me": *O.C.* 1: 314.

always vocal melody: Madeline Ellis, *Rousseau's Venetian Story: An Essay upon Art and Truth in Les Confessions* (Baltimore: Johns Hopkins University Press, 1966), p. 122.

"Come, Sophie": *O.C.* 1: 315.

"Brilliant illumination": "Fragment d'une Épitre à M. B[ordes]," *O.C.* 2: 1145. The Pléiade editors (pp. 1897–98) date the poem to Apr. 1744 and identify the singer as Caterina Aschieri, known as Cattina.

"A little Mass": Monnier, *Venise,* p. 28; the story about the three convents was reported by Charles de Brosses (ibid., p. 201).

176 "but not with the kind . . . her scruples": *O.C.* 1: 317.

plausibly suggested: Jacques Borel, *Génie et Folie de J.-J. Rousseau* (Paris: Corti, 1966), p. 84. See also D. Bensoussan, *La Maladie de Rousseau* (Paris: Klinckgieck, 1974), p. 46.

"Whoever you may be": *O.C.* 1: 320.

Montaigu's own helpful suggestion: *C.C.* 2: 38n.

"Her large black eyes . . . I obeyed": *O.C.* 1: 318–19.

177 "Women who can be bought": *Confessions* I, *O.C.* 1: 36.

"I endure their caresses": *Confessions* VII, *O.C.* 1: 320.

"her sleeves . . . *studia la matematica*": ibid., pp. 320–22.

178 one-eyed choir girl: Christopher Kelly, *Rousseau's Exemplary Life: The Confessions as Political Philosophy* (Ithaca: Cornell University Press, 1987), pp. 172–83.

"True love is always modest": *Julie* I.50, *O.C.* 2: 138.

"Never will you . . . wear it out": *Julie,* appendix, "Les Amours de Milord Édouard Bomston," *O.C.* 2: 753, 760.

179 "Might this not be": *O.C.* 1: 1401.
more women were on their backs: Charles de Brosses, quoted in Trousson 1: 200–201.
"he thinks only": quoted in Trousson, 1: 197.
"unworthy mother . . . its protectors": *Confessions* VII, *O.C.* 1: 323.

180 "I had opportunities . . . sense of the word": *Confessions* IX, *O.C.* 1: 404–5.

181 "he always had three": Bernardin, p. 44 (citing "a person worthy of trust" who was familiar with Montaigu).
"A chair at one end": Montaigu to the abbé Alary, 15 Aug. 1744, *C.C.* 2: 50–51.
"was almost like": Guéhenno 1: 139.

182 "I began to laugh": *O.C.* 1: 312.
"like a bad valet": Montaigu to Alary, 15 Aug. 1744, *C.C.* 2: 50.
"I shall return": to J.-G. du Theil, 15 Aug. 1744, ibid., p. 48.
"Is there anything worse": to Du Theil, 11 Oct. 1744, ibid., p. 67.

183 "The justice and uselessness": *O.C.* 1: 327.
some servants protested: Le Blond, letter of 13 Sept. 1749, quoted in *O.C.* 3: 1844n.

10. A Life Partner and a Guilty Secret

184 "by Switzerland": from Thomas Birch, *Life* of Boyle (1744), quoted in Edward Pyatt, *The Passage of the Alps* (London: Robert Hale, 1984), p. 51.
unscrupulous adventurer: Montaigu to the abbé Chaignon, 10 Oct. 1744, *C.C.* 2: 65.

185 "I drank your health": Vincent Capperonnier de Gauffecourt to the abbé Chaignon, 12 Sept. 1744, *C.C.* 3: 417.
"Duvillard went to find": *Confessions* VII, *O.C.* 1: 324.
"Taking an excursion": *Confessions* I, *O.C.* 1: 29.
"Everyone agreed": *Confessions* VII, *O.C.* 1: 325.

186 "He didn't have . . . senses to be born": ibid., pp. 327–29.
"Rousseau was unhappy": Stendhal, letter to his sister Pauline, 12 July 1804, *Correspondance,* ed. H. Martineau and V. del Litto (Paris: Gallimard, 1962), 1: 128.
"my poor brother . . . Adieu, Maman": 25 Feb.–1 Mar. 1745, *C.C.* 2: 73–77.

187 "The first time . . . looking for anyway": *Confessions* VII, *O.C.* 1: 330–31; Thérèse's birth certificate, which survives in Orléans, shows that she was born 21 Sept.1721: Charly Guyot, *Plaidoyer pour Thérèse Levasseur* (Neuchâtel: Ides et Calendes, 1962), p. 19.

188 "the supplement": *Confessions* VII, *O.C.* 1: 332. Starobinski was the first to expose the ambiguities here, in *Transparency and Obstruction,* p. 179; they became the focus of an extended analysis by Jacques Derrida, *Of Grammatology,* trans. Gayatri Spivak (Baltimore: Johns Hopkins University Press, 1976), pp. 141–64. See also *O.C.* 1: 1407n.
"dangerous supplement": *Émile* IV, *O.C.* 4: 663.
"From the moment": *Confessions* IX, *O.C.* 1: 414.
"By engaging himself": Clément: *De l'Éros Coupable,* p. 229; the parallel with Marion is noted on pp. 224–25.

189 "Not only was Marion": *Confessions* II, *O.C.* 1: 84.
lower-class mistresses: see Darnton, *Great Cat Massacre,* pp. 165–67.
"He had a Nanette": *Confessions* VII, *O.C.* 1: 346.

190 *lieutenant-criminel: Confessions* VIII, *O.C.* 1: 353.

"became almost my own": *Confessions* VII, *O.C.* 1: 333.

"He could see": Morellet, *Mémoires,* p. 115.

"a little, lively, neat": Boswell's diary for 3 Dec. 1764, in *Boswell on the Grand Tour: Germany and Switzerland,* ed. Frederick A. Pottle (New York: McGraw-Hill, 1953), p. 220. (The conversation in French is translated by Pottle; Leigh gives the original in *C.C.* 22: 355.)

"The windowsill served . . . for each other": *Confessions* VIII, *O.C.* 1: 353–54.

191 "Often in Switzerland": *Confessions* VII, *O.C.* 1: 332.

"I made up my mind": ibid., p. 345.

192 newborns back in Chambéry: Nicolas, *La Vie Quotidienne,* p. 119.

"in a wooden box": quoted from the original admissions records by Léon Lallemand, *Histoire des Enfants Abandonnés et Délaissés* (Paris: Picard, 1885), p. 157. My account of the Enfants Trouvés relies on Lallemand, pp. 131–217, and on Camille Bloch, *L'Assistance et l'État en France à la Veille de a Révolution* (Paris: Picard, 1908), pp. 57–120.

"the tomb of maternal": Académie de Châlons (1777), quoted by Bloch, *L'Assistance,* p. 119.

193 Joseph Catherine Rousseau: *O.C.* 1: 1421–22.

letter to Mme de Francueil: 20 Apr. 1751, *C.C.* 2: 142–44.

194 "Oh! as to that": quoted in *O.C.* 1: 1417.

"a spotless fidelity": to the duchesse de Luxembourg, 12 June 1761, *C.C.* 9: 15.

"since the children": *Journal Encyclopédique,* 30 Apr. 1791, reprinted in *C.C.* 2: 310.

195 Thérèse later remembered four: after Rousseau's death, the marquis de Girardin tried unsuccessfully to trace the children and seems to have heard from Thérèse of "four children" (Henri Laliaud to Girardin, 16 Oct. 1779, *C.C.* 44: 54).

"will weep long": *Émile* I, *O.C.* 4: 263.

"Never for a single": *Confessions* VIII, *O.C.* 1: 357.

11. A Writer's Apprenticeship

196 "I have resolved": to Daniel Roguin, 9 July 1745, *C.C.* 2: 83–85.

"if you are in trouble": undated reply, ibid., p. 86.

197 described by a . . . specialist: D. Paquette in *Dictionnaire,* p. 633.

"This work is so mediocre": *O.C.* 2: 1051.

"I can say that": *Confessions* VII, *O.C.* 1: 294–95.

they could barely look: Jean Francois Marmontel, *Mémoires,* ed. John Renwick (Clermont-Ferrand: Bussac, 1972), 1: 97–105.

198 "I was struck": Jean Philippe Rameau, *Erreurs sur la Musique dans l'Encyclopédie* (1755), quoted in *O.C.* 1: 1409.

"Nourished since childhood": *Avertissement* to *Les Muses Galantes, O.C.* 2: 1051.

"If he ever did": Diderot, *Le Neveu de Rameau,* in the Pléiade *Oeuvres,* ed. André Billy (Paris: Gallimard, 1951), p. 399.

one contemporary said he looked: Chabanon and Piron, quoted in Daniel Paquette, *Jean-Philippe Rameau, Musicien Bourgignon* (Saint-Seine-l'Abbaye: Éditions de Saint-Seine-l'Abbaye, 1984), pp. 87, 91.

199 "Lovely fire . . . jealous rivals": *O.C.* 2: 1061, 1060.

"I have never seen . . . fighting them": to J.-B. du Plessis, 14 Sept. 1745, *C.C.* 2: 87.

"an old musician's fear": Paquette, *Rameau,* p. 52.

"and not only does": *Essai sur l'Origine des Langues,* chap. 14, *O.C.* 5: 416.

200 "For fifteen years": Rousseau to Voltaire, 11 Dec. 1745, *C.C.* 2: 92.
"I well know": Voltaire to Rousseau, 15 Dec. 1745, ibid., p. 94.
"gratuities accorded": *O.C.* 1: 1411.
"Two months of labor": Charles Malherbe, quoted ibid.

201 "returned home": *Confessions* VII, *O.C.* 1: 337.
"symbolic death . . . objects of hatred": Jean Starobinski, introduction to Rousseau, *Essai sur l'Origine des Langues* (Paris: Gallimard, 1990), p. 14.
French music was more moving: *Lettre sur l'Opera Italien et Français, O.C.* 5: 255.
calling himself a "disciple": Claude Varenne, 17 Oct. 1747, *C.C.* 2: 95–101.
"In considering the desperate": undated notes collected under the title "Mon Portrait," *O.C.* 1: 1129.

202 "much gaiety": ibid., p. 342.
"He is full of compliments": *Les Contre-Confessions: Histoire de Madame de Montbrillant,* ed. Georges Roth, rev. Elisabeth Badinter (Paris: Mercure de France, 1989), pp. 450–51.
"At about this time": *O.C.* 1: 339.
"Coming home . . . conquered myself": ibid.

203 M. Tavel: Tavel to J.-F. Hugonin, 17 Mar. 1746, *C.C.* 2: 288.
"All of her letters": *O.C.* 1: 339.
"As for myself": 17 Oct. 1747, *C.C.* 2: 102.

204 "Time slipped away . . . from their blows": *Confessions* VII, *O.C.* 1: 340.
"might help me to find": autumn 1735, *C.C.* 1: 30.
"he had in his employment": George Sand, *Histoire de ma Vie* (Paris: Lecou: 1854), 1: 129.

205 "manual labor": Anicet Sénéchal, "Jean-Jacques Rousseau, Secrétaire de Madame Dupin," *Annales* 36 (1963–1965): 207.
she admitted as much: *Confessions* III, *O.C.* 1: 116–17.
"But tell me": reported by Olivier de Corancez, "Mémoires de J.-J. Rousseau," in *Mémoires Biographiques et Littéraires,* ed. Mathurin de Lescure (Paris: Firmin-Didot, 1881), p. 278.
"was like myself": *Confessions* VII, *O.C.* 1: 347.

206 "a very clever boy . . . modern intellectual": Darnton, *Great Cat Massacre,* pp. 180, 168.
"conversations with that virtuous": "Fragment Biographique" (probably written 1755–1756), *O.C.* 1: 1115.
"his gaiety": quoted in Badinter, *Les Passions Intellectuelles* 1: 259.

207 "These little weekly dinners": *Confessions* VII, *O.C.* 1: 347.
"Nothing is more dissimilar . . . less changeable than I": *Le Persifleur, O.C.* 1: 1108, 1110.
"Few well-regarded books": *Émile* IV, *O.C.* 4: 674.

209 "He had a harpsichord": *Confessions* VIII, *O.C.* 1: 352.
Rousseau even convinced himself: *Confessions* II, *O.C.* 1: 59.
"was keeping a young . . . laugh or cry": *Confessions* VIII, *O.C.* 1: 354–55.
"Plato and Jean-Jacques": Diderot, *Jacques le Fataliste,* in the Pléiade *Oeuvres,* p. 658.

210 "Let him who will regret": Voltaire, *Le Mondain,* in *Mélanges,* ed. Jacques van den Heuvel (Paris: Gallimard, 1961), pp. 203–4.
"mortal poison": *Julie* I.li, *O.C.* 2: 141.
"Pretty Frenchwomen": Rousseau to Pierre-Alexandre Du Peyrou, 4 Nov. 1764, *C.C.* 22: 6.
"For two or three hours": Antoine Bret, manuscript memoirs, *C.C.* 2: 311.

12. The Beginnings of Fame

212   "You see, Monsieur": *Confessions* VIII, *O.C.* 1: 350.

"I beheld a different . . . that of drunkenness": ibid., p. 351; *Lettres à Malesherbes* II, *O.C.* 1: 1135.

"Madmen, what have": *Discours sur les Sciences . . . , O.C.* 3: 14.

Diligent scholarship: R. Galliani, "Rousseau, l'Illumination de Vincennes, et la Critique Moderne," *Studies on Voltaire and the Eighteenth Century* 245 (Oxford: Voltaire Foundation, 1986): 403–47.

213   "I had placed myself": Augustine, *Confessions,* trans. R. S. Pine-Coffin (Harmondsworth: Penguin, 1961), VIII.7, p. 169.

"I was a prisoner . . . in soul": Marmontel, *Mémoires,* 1: 204.

214   "I developed a contempt": *Lettres à Malesherbes* II, *O.C.* 1: 1135.

as rakes did: Diderot, *Le Neveu de Rameau, Oeuvres,* p. 395.

"his thought is always": Georges Poulet, *Studies in Human Time,* trans. Elliott Coleman (Baltimore: Johns Hopkins University Press, 1956), p. 186.

Greek aphorism: made famous by Isaiah Berlin, *The Hedgehog and the Fox: An Essay on Tolstoy's View of History* (New York: Simon & Schuster, 1953).

"I have turned . . . forgetting a lot": *Confessions* III and VIII, *O.C.* 1: 114, 352.

215   "In crowning the work": "Compte rendu de la séance du 23 août 1750," *C.C.* 2: 297. A full survey of the Dijon Academy can be found in Marcel Bouchard, *L'Académie de Dijon et le Premier Discours de Rousseau* (Publications de l'Université de Dijon, Paris: Société des Belles Lettres, 1950).

216   called the autocritique: Mark Hulliung, *The Autocritique of Enlightenment: Rousseau and the Philosophes* (Cambridge: Harvard University Press, 1994).

"Suspicions, offenses": *Discours sur les Sciences. . . , O.C.* 3: 8–9.

"Even while government": *O.C.* 1: 6–7.

"If only he had lived": *Ébauches des Confessions, O.C.* 1: 1160.

217   "This admirable portrait": Rousseau to Maurice Quentin de La Tour, 14 Oct. 1764, *C.C.* 21: 255.

"the Cato and Brutus": Diderot, *Essai sur le Peinture, Oeuvres,* ed. Billy, p. 1134.

"This discourse . . . scandalous effrontery": *Journal et Mémoires du Marquis d'Argenson,* quoted in Benoît Mély, *Jean-Jacques Rousseau: Un Intellectuel en Rupture* (Paris: Minerve, 1985), pp. 61–62.

218   "My adversaries' . . . at the root": "Fragment Biographique," *O.C.* 1: 1115.

Diderot wrote: "*la philosophie s'avance à pas de géant, et la lumière l'accompagne;*" "*la saine philosophie, dont les lumières se répandent partout . . . ,*" from "Bramines" and "Capuchon," in *Encyclopédie,* cited by Roland Mortier, *Clartés et Ombres du Siècle des Lumières* (Geneva: Droz, 1969), pp. 30–31.

"The satyr, says": *O.C.* 3: 17. Rousseau found the story in Plutarch and seems to have misinterpreted it (*O.C.* 3: 1247n).

219   "There they esteem": Diderot, *Salon de 1765,* ed. Else Marie Bukdahl and Annette Lorenceau (Paris: Hermann, 1984), p. 231.

"heavy but good food": Morellet, *Mémoires,* p. 130.

"One could see mistrust": Marmontel, *Mémoires,* 1: 109–10.

"I found all": *Émile* IV, *O.C.* 4: 568 (the Savoyard vicar).

"the livery of philosophy": *Corr. Litt.* 5: 103 (15 June 1762).

"Can one look": *Rêveries* III, *O.C.* 1: 1016.

"dogmatically established": Morellet, *Mémoires,* p. 131.

"They laughed at": Edward Gibbon, *Memoirs of My Life,* ed. Betty Radice (Harmondsworth: Penguin, 1984), p. 136.

220 "Je suis bon encyclopédiste": quoted in Wilson, *Diderot,* p. 152.

"Their philosophy is": *Rêveries* III, *O.C.* 1: 1016.

"They're joking": *Mémoires et Correspondance de Mme d'Épinay* (Paris: Volland, 1818), 2: 65.

inventory of his wardrobe: *C.C.* 2: 304–9.

221 "an attack of colic": to Mme de Warens, 26 Aug. 1748, ibid., p. 108.

"'My son,'": *Émile* IV, *O.C.* 4: 499.

"reminded me": *Confessions* VIII, *O.C.* 1: 359.

222 Rousseau seized his chance: *Confessions* I, *O.C.* 1: 38–39.

"had no recollection": Sand, *Histoire de ma Vie* 1: 27n.

"I applied all": *Confessions* VIII, *O.C.* 1: 362.

"to pass the rest": *Rêveries* III, *O.C.* 1: 1014.

"saying to myself": *Confessions* VIII, *O.C.* 1: 363.

The portable watch: Roche, *France in the Enlightenment,* p. 88.

"We thus see": as reported by Mme de Graffigny to François-Antoine Devaux, 28 Feb. 1753, in English Showalter, *Madame de Graffigny and Rousseau: between the two Discours* (Oxford: Voltaire Foundation, 1978), p. 75.

223 "As we went in . . . no matter who": Iselin, *Pariser Tagebuch 1752,* 10 and 14 June 1752, *C.C.* 2: 315–17.

"I will earn": Rousseau to the marquise de Créqui, ca. Nov. 1752, ibid., p. 201.

"No more of that rabble": "Épitre à M. de l'Étang, Vicaire de Marcoussis," *O.C.* 2: 1152.

"The earth produces": Rousseau to Mme Francueil, 20 Apr. 1751, *C.C.* 2: 143.

224 "One sees the actresses": *Julie* II.xxiii, *O.C.* 2: 285.

"He has a very delicate": written by Lenieps on a blank page of Rousseau's *Dernière Réponse, C.C.* 3: 321.

Rousseau slunk away: *Confessions* VIII, *O.C.* 1: 377.

225 "I'm sure that": *O.C.* 1: 379.

"You were wrong": Pierre Jélyotte to Rousseau, 20 Oct. 1752, *C.C.* 2: 197.

"with a warmth": *O.C.* 1: 381.

"the least imposing": Corancez, "Mémoires de J.-J. Rousseau," p. 278.

226 "Thus was our philosopher": J. Dusaulx, *De Mes Rapports avec J. J. Rousseau* (Paris: Didot, 1798), p. 28.

"One cannot imagine": comments by d'Holbach, reported by Guinguiné, *O.C.* 1: 1444–45.

"Hurry up and find": Charles-Pierre Coste d'Arnobat, "Doutes d'un Pyrrhonien Proposés Amicalement à J.-J. Rousseau," *Mémoire,* pp. 104–5.

"From a technical": *Dialogues* I, *O.C.* 1: 682.

227 "I saw him almost": *Confessions* VIII, *O.C.* 1: 398.

"*The Village Soothsayer*": quoted in *O.C.* 2: xci.

"You should know": from an 1809 memoir, quoted by Leigh, *C.C.* 2: 198n.

"People spoke . . . to recover these": anonymous report to Joseph d'Hémery, 30 Mar. 1753, *C.C.* 2: 328–33.

228 "At the end of a line": "Lettre d'un Symphoniste," *O.C.* 5: 277.

229 "It's for poets": *Lettre sur la Musique Française, O.C.* 5: 292.

"for it is not . . . 'being is here'": *Essai sur l'Origine des Langues,* chaps. 15–16, *O.C.* 5: 419.

"These effects": "Musique," *Dictionnaire de Musique, O.C.* 5: 924.

230   "seem national to me": Germaine de Staël, *Lettres sur les Ouvrages et le Caractère de J.-J. Rousseau,* ed. Marcel Françon (Geneva: Slatkine Reprints, 1979), p. 87.

"to a cow that gallops": *Julie:* II.xxiii, *O.C.* 2: 286n (Rousseau's footnote).

dogs barked out of tune: reported by Julie von Bondeli to J. G. Zimmermann, 8 Dec. 1764, *C.C.* 22: 194.

"I had the honor": *Confessions* V, *O.C.* 1: 185.

"I conclude that the French": *Lettre sur la Musique Française, O.C.* 5: 328.

Rousseau didn't fully grasp: see Cynthia Verba, *Music and the French Enlightenment: Reconstruction of a Dialogue, 1750–1764* (Oxford: Clarendon Press, 1993), pp. 20–29, and O'Dea, *Rousseau: Music, Illusion and Desire,* pp. 16–18.

"There was too much": Charles Burney, *A General History of Music* (London, 1789), 4: 615.

"with kicks": notes by the marquis d'Argenson, 15 Dec. 1753, *C.C.* 2: 324.

231   "As he constantly circles . . . his philosophy": Jacques Cazotte, *Observations sur la Lettre de J.-J. Rousseau au Sujet de la Musique Française* (1753),in *Mémoire,* p. 103.

"Freedom in music": d'Alembert, *De la Liberté de la Musique* (ca. 1760), quoted in Trousson 1: 313.

"with his delicacy": *O.C.* 2: 977.

232   "How do you find": ibid., p. 983.

"When one loves well": ibid., pp. 1018, 1016.

"I forgot to tell you": Rousseau to Lenieps, 16 Jan. 1753, *C.C.* 2: 211.

"a desire to fail": introduction, *O.C.* 2: lxxxvii.

"M. Rousseau's passionate desire": *Lettres sur Quelques Écrits de ce Temps,* quoted in *O.C.* 2: lxxxix.

233   epigram of Voltaire's: quoted in Wilson, *Diderot,* p. 197.

"What is at stake . . . my century": preface to *Narcisse, O.C.* 2: 959, 974.

13. Rousseau's Originality

234   "I carry a source": "Mémoire à M. de Mably," *O.C.* 4: 21.

"a long and confused . . . has suited me": *Confessions* III, *O.C.* 1: 114, 116.

235   "This piece is very bad": *Discours . . . sur la Vertu du Héros, O.C.* 2: 1262.

"A *torche-cul*": Rousseau to Marc-Michel Rey, 31 Jan. 1769, *C.C.* 37: 36.

triste et grand système: preface to an unpublished "Seconde Lettre à Bordes," *O.C.* 3: 105.

"Without having any *état*": *Ébauches des Confessions, O.C.* 1: 1150.

"The manner of life": to the prince de Wurtemburg, 15 Apr. 1764, *C.C.* 19: 301.

236   "Let us begin": *Discours sur l'Origine de l'Inégalité, O.C.* 3: 132–33.

Lévi-Strauss once went: "Jean-Jacques Rousseau, Fondateur des Sciences de l'Homme," in *Jean-Jacques Rousseau,* ed. Baud-Bovy et al., pp. 239–48.

"All men naturally hate": Blaise Pascal, *Pensées,* no. 451 in the Brunschvicg numeration.

"*Amour-propre* is love": François, duc de La Rochefoucauld, *Maximes,* no. 563 (final edition, 1678).

237   "no arts, no letters": Thomas Hobbes, *Leviathan,* I.xiii.

"herding impulse": Anthony Ashley Cooper, third earl of Shaftesbury, *Characteristics of Men, Manners, Opinions, Times,* ed. J. M. Robertson (London: Grant Richards, 1900), 1: 75.

"The blood flows": David Hume, *A Treatise of Human Nature,* ed. Ernest C. Mossner (London: Penguin, 1984), II.ii.4, p. 402.

237 "I would rather be": *Émile* IV, *O.C.* 4: 325.
Julie says: *Julie* III.xviii, *O.C.* 2: 362.
238 "His imagination paints": *Discours sur . . . l'Inégalité, O.C.* 3: 144.
"The state of reflection": ibid., p. 138.
"Rousseau traced man": Henri Fuseli (or Füssli), *Remarks on the Writing and Conduct of J. J. Rousseau* (London, 1767), p. 25.
Germaine de Staël observed: *Lettres sur les Ouvrages,* p. 7.
239 "an artificial sentiment": *Discours sur . . .l'Inégalité, O.C.* 3: 158.
Ceci est à moi: ibid., p. 164.
"Mine, thine": Pascal, *Pensées,* no. 293 in the Brunschwicg numeration.
"Equality disappeared": *O.C.* 3: 171.
240 "Primitive man had": Tacitus, *The Annals of Imperial Rome,* trans. Michael Grant (Harmondsworth: Penguin, 1977), p. 132.
"the habit of living . . . happiness and innocence": *Discours sur . . . l'Inégalité, O.C.* 3: 168–70.
"new book against": Voltaire to Rousseau, 30 Aug. 1755, *C.C.* 3: 156–57.
241 "It is dreadful": *Timon* (1756), in *Mémoire,* p. 151.
"like those famished wolves": *Discours sur . . . l'Inégalité, O.C.* 3: 175–76.
"*Voilà* the philosophy": quoted ibid., p. 1339 (Starobinski, the editor of this *Discours,* comments, "Réaction de propriétaire").
"He who meditates": Diderot to the abbé Le Monnier, 15 Sept. 1755, in Diderot, *Correspondance,* ed. Laurent Versini (Paris: Robert Laffont, 1997), p. 51.
"Whoever does not": "Droit naturel," in *Encyclopédie,* cited in Trousson 1: 331.
242 "It would take a book": Trousson 1: 330.
"a state that no longer": *Discours sur . . . l'Inégalité, O.C.* 3: 123.
"As soon as you see": *Émile* II, *O.C.* 4: 309.
en lui-même . . . hors de lui: Discours sur . . . l'Inégalité, O.C. 3: 193.
"The status": ibid., p. 187.
243 "The immense echo": Jean Starobinski, introduction to *Discours,* ibid., p. xlix.
As Arthur Melzer shows: *The Natural Goodness of Man: On the System of Rousseau's Thought* (Chicago: University of Chicago Press, 1990).
"I hate servitude": "Fragments de la Lettre à Christophe de Beaumont," *O.C.* 4: 1019.
"The liberty of the individual": Sigmund Freud, *Civilization and Its Discontents,* trans. James Strachey (New York: Norton, 1961), p. 42.

14. Lionized in Geneva, Alienated in Paris

245 "more than sixty": *Confessions* VIII, *O.C.* 1: 390.
"You can verify": Mme de Warens to Rousseau, 10 Feb. 1754, *C.C.* 2: 250.
"I saw her again . . . with tears": *Confessions* VIII, *O.C.* 1: 392.
246 "In this famous man": Trousson 1: 346–47.
"I have always blamed": Conzié to an unknown correspondent, ca. 1786–1787, *C.C.* 1: 295.
"Although I'm not": Wintzenried de Courtilles to Mme de Warens, 8 Oct. 1754, *C.C.* 3: 370–71.
247 "taken to France . . . our Church": registry of the Consistory, 25 July 1754, *O.C.* 1: 1220–21.
"so generously paid back": the episode is described, and the documents quoted, in Guyot, *Plaidoyer pour Thérèse Levasseur,* pp. 49–51.

"spoke of the divinity": Brissot de Warville, *Mémoires,* ed. M. De Lescure (Paris: Firmin-Didot, 1877), p. 260 (also *C.C.* 3: 329).

"What I am hungry for": Rousseau to Vernes, 25 Mar. 1758, *C.C.* 5: 65.

"spirit filled with fire": *Confessions* VIII, *O.C.* 1: 394.

248 "This city seems": Rousseau to Mme Dupin, 20 July 1754, *C.C.* 3: 16.

as Cranston points out: Cranston 1: 340; the details of Genevan politics are very fully surveyed in his chap. 17.

249 "The people . . . pleasant smile: reminiscence by Jean Donzel, *C.C.* 3: 330.

"He preferred the company": Francis d'Ivernois, *Tableau Historique et Politique des Révolutions de Genève* (1782), *C.C.* 3: 345.

"in wanting to be noticed": notes recorded by Georges-Louis Le Sage, *C.C.* 3: 332.

"added not a little": reminiscences of Théodore Rousseau (a relative), ibid., pp. 328–29.

"We took seven days": *Confessions* VIII, *O.C.* 1: 393.

250 "I like to think": Rousseau to Rey, 29 Nov. 1761, *C.C.* 9: 284. The relationship between Rousseau and Rey is surveyed by Raymond Birn, "Rousseau and Literary Property: From the *Discours sur l'Inégalité* to *Émile*," *Leipziger Jahrbuch zur Buchgeschichte* 3 (1993): 13–37.

251 "a flock of eagles": Marie-Joseph Chénier, *Dénonciation des Inquisiteurs de la Pensée,* quoted in Daniel Roche, "Censorship and the Publishing Industry," in *Revolution in Print: The Press in France, 1775–1800,* ed. Robert Darnton and Daniel Roche (Berkeley: University of California Press, 1989), p. 13.

"Because the law": quoted in Raymond Birn, "Malesherbes and the Call for a Free Press," in *Revolution in Print,* p. 50.

"and I admit": reminiscences of J. A. C. Cérutti, *C.C.* 3: 347–48. The story was also related by Grimm, differing somewhat in details but essentially the same (cited in *C.C.* 3: 31n). The letter of condolence is lost, but is confirmed by d'Holbach's testimony as well as Rousseau's.

252 "He has written": *Journal Encyclopédique,* quoted in Trousson 1: 382.

"No one else has": *Corr. Litt.* 4: 343 (1 Feb. 1761).

253 "Voltaire wanted": Julien-Louis Geoffroy, *L'Année Littéraire* (1783), in *Mémoire,* pp. 513–14.

"Up until then": *Corr. Litt.* 5: 103 (15 June 1762).

"One has to have known": *Oeuvres* (Paris: Belin, 1821), 4: 464; in *Mémoire,* p. 284.

Elisabeth Badinter: *Les Passions Intellectuelles* 1: 453–54.

254 "to be always myself": *Confessions* VIII, *O.C.* 1: 378.

"Sincerity is the consciousness": Peter L. Berger, *Invitation to Sociology: A Humanistic Perspective* (New York: Doubleday Anchor Books, 1963), p. 109.

"Duclos says . . . in order to be": diary of the abbé Trublet (1755), *C.C.* 3: 350; Rousseau uses the terms *être* and *paraître* in the *Discours sur . . . l'Inégalité* (*O.C.* 3: 174), and the tension between them is a central theme in Starobinski, *Transparency and Obstruction.*

"The scorn . . . uprooted vanity": *Confessions* IX, *O.C.* 1: 416–17.

"The author is so preoccupied": *Lettre . . . sur une nouvelle Réfutation* [by Claude-Nicolas Lecat], *O.C.* 3: 99–100.

255 "We must have gravy": *Dernière Réponse, O.C.* 3: 79.

"I have tried to console . . . angry about it": Rousseau to the comte de Lastic, the marquise de Menars, and Mme d'Épinay, 20 and 25 Dec. 1755, *C.C.* 3: 231–38.

"The man with the butter": *Julie* V.vii, *O.C.* 2: 610, and 1713–14n.

15. An Affair of the Heart

256 he objected that he had: Rousseau to Théodore Tronchin, 27 Feb. 1757, *C.C.* 4: 162.

257 "That the State of War": *O.C.* 3: 601–12; see Maurice Cranston, "Rousseau on War and Peace," in *Rousseau and the Eighteenth Century: Essays in Memory of R. A. Leigh,* ed. Marian Hobson et al. (Oxford: Voltaire Foundation, 1992), 189–96.

"There was such a mania": Masson, *La Réligion de Rousseau* 1: 219.

"I don't believe": *Confessions* VIII, *O.C.* 1: 396.

"I left the city": *Confessions* IX, *O.C.* 1: 403.

259 "draped gracefully over": Ruth Plaut Weinreb, *Eagle in a Gauze Cage: Louise d'Épinay, Femme de Lettres* (New York: AMS Press, 1993), p. 22.

260 "walked in silence": d'Épinay, *Histoire de Madame de Montbrillant* 3: 18.

"At last my wishes": *Confessions* IX, *O.C.* 1: 403.

261 *gouvernante* . . . woman who took care: *Le Robert Dictionnaire Historique de la Langue Française* (2: 1620) finds this sense in use from 1690 onward.

"those fleeting . . . never obeyed me": *Lettres à Malesherbes* III, *O.C.* 1: 1139–41.

262 "I wouldn't know . . . wears us out": Deleyre to Rousseau, 3 July 1756, *C.C.* 4: 20–21.

263 a feminist two centuries ahead: Badinter, *Les Passions Intellectuelles* 2: 249–50.

"She had taken it": *Confessions* IX, *O.C.* 1: 411.

"Climates, seasons": ibid., p. 409.

264 "M. Rousseau believes": Jean-Baptiste Tollot to Gabriel Seigneux de Correvon, Aug. 1754, *C.C.* 3: 341.

"This proposition . . . like any other": 10 and 12 Mar. 1756, *C.C.* 3: 292, 296. Leigh quotes Mme d'Épinay's fictional reply (294–95n) and shows that whatever she actually wrote at the time must have been much milder.

"If you refuse": quoted in Badinter, *Les Passions Intellectuelles* 2: 295n.

"I am not pretty": Louise d'Épinay, "Mon Portrait," *Mes Moments Heureux* (Paris: Sauton, 1869), p. 3.

265 "Myself, the queen": ibid., p. 133.

"The bear *par excellence*": Mme d'Épinay to the marquis de Saint-Lambert, 28 Feb. 1756, *C.C.* 3: 288.

"in my emotion": *Confessions* IX, *O.C.* 1: 437.

"I felt comfortable": ibid., p. 412.

266 "I meditated . . . extravagant swain": ibid., pp. 426–27.

"All power of fancy": Samuel Johnson, *Rasselas* (1759), chap. 44.

"There are souls": "Les Amours de Claire et de Marcellin," *O.C.* 2: 1195.

"The first and gravest": "Le Petit Savoyard," *O.C.* 2: 1200.

267 "Monsieur, that is": *O.C.* 1: 436.

268 "Although I don't": ibid., p. 439.

"a forest of thick": ibid.

"She came, I saw her": ibid., p. 440.

Stendhal describes: *De l'Amour,* ed. Pierre-Louis Rey (Paris: Pocket Classiques, 1998), chap. 2, p. 31.

"to love with love": *Confessions* VIII, *O.C.* 1: 360.

269 "The last person": Charles Collé, quoted in Marty, *Rousseau de l'Enfance,* p. 399n.

270 Diderot too paid: according to Arthur M. Wilson, in all of Diderot's voluminous writings there are only two casual references to the war (Wilson, *Diderot,* p. 248).

"making a desert": *Julie* IV.iii, *O.C.* 2: 412.

"Since her mannerisms": Mme d'Épinay, "Portrait de Madame ***," *Mes Moments Heureux,* pp. 218–19.

"a hundred thousand . . . ask for a copy": Diderot to Sophie Volland, 14 July 1762 and 30 Sept. 1760, *Correspondance,* pp. 375, 236. The "Hymne aux Tétons" was actually by Jean-Pierre-Nicolas du Commun.

"love was the motive . . . person she loved": "Madame d'Houdetot jugée par Madame de Vintimille," in Hippolyte Buffenoir, *La Comtesse d'Houdetot: Sa Famille, Ses Amis* (Paris: Leclerc, 1905), pp. 84–85.

271   "Married as one": reminiscences of Mme de Rémusat, in Buffenoir, *La Comtesse d'Houdetot,* pp. 302–3.

"she changed . . . mingled together": *Confessions* IX, *O.C.* 1: 443–44.

envie rather than *désir:* Clément, *De l'Éros Coupable,* p. 125.

272   "What intoxicating . . . to stand up": *O.C.* 1: 444–45. It is accepted by Rousseau scholars, on the basis of terms he uses elsewhere, that this passage can refer only to masturbation.

"all she could see": ibid., p. 446.

"someone who has inspired": ibid., p. 463. There is some evidence that the letters were burned not by Mme d'Houdetot herself but by a niece after her death (*O.C.* 1: 1496n).

"Do you remember": Rousseau to Mme d'Houdetot, July 1757, *C.C.* 4: 225–26.

273   "No, Maman": *Confessions* VI, *O.C.* 1: 264.

using the familiar *tu:* *Confessions* IX, *O.C.* 1: 463–64.

"for the good reason": Elisabeth Badinter, preface to *Les Contre-Confessions: Histoire de Madame de Montbrillant par Madame d'Épinay* (Paris: Mercure de France, 1989), p. x. Badinter's introduction is the most balanced survey of the whole issue; her text follows Georges Roth's edition.

274   "a kind of delayed": Wilson, *Diderot,* pp 608–11; see also P. N. Furbank, *Diderot: A Critical Biography* (New York: Knopf, 1992), pp. 352–53. Mme d'Épinay's strongest defender is Weinreb, *Eagle in a Gauze Cage.*

"Know, Madame": Roth's edition of *Madame de Montbrillant* 3: 151–52.

"I said to the little": ibid., p. 147.

275   "if you could persuade": Rousseau to Mme d'Houdetot, 12 July 1757, *C.C.* 4: 227.

Saint-Lambert permitted himself: *Confessions* IX, *O.C.* 1: 462–63. The Pléiade editors place this event in the spring of 1758 (*O.C.* 1: 1464n), but Trousson and Eigeldinger in *Rousseau au Jour le Jour* (p. 88) are inclined to accept Rousseau's date of mid-July 1757.

"I can't tell you . . . forgive you": exchange of letters on 31 Aug. 1757, *Madame de Montbrillant* 3: 178–83; *C.C.* 4: 246–52 (following Rousseau's manuscript copies; also in *Confessions* IX, *O.C.* 1: 450–53).

276   "You should have listened": *Madame de Montbrillant* 3: 195.

277   "Everyone is unbearable": Rousseau to Mme d'Épinay, 6 Sept.(?) 1757, *C.C.* 4: 253–54.

"You would be doing": *Madame de Montbrillant* 3: 198.

"No, no, Saint-Lambert": Rousseau to Saint-Lambert, 15 Sept. 1757, *C.C.* 4: 258.

"Don't accuse . . . of my life": Saint-Lambert to Rousseau, 11 Oct. 1757, ibid., pp. 281–82.

278   "I dare to place": Mme d'Houdetot to Rousseau, 29 Sept. 1757, ibid., pp. 267–68.

"I won't remind": Rousseau to Mme d'Épinay, ca. 10 Oct. 1757, ibid., pp. 276–78. Rousseau later wrote on the manuscript, "This letter was never sent" (p. 280n).

"born melancholy": Mme d'Épinay to Rousseau, 26 Sept. 1757, ibid., p. 264.

279   "he granted me": *Confessions* IX, *O.C.* 1: 473.

"they often made . . . friendship ends": Rousseau to Grimm, 26 Oct. 1757, *C.C.* 4: 299–301.

280 "One might say": Rousseau to Saint-Lambert, 28 Oct. 1757, ibid., p. 311.

"This zeal to make": Rousseau to Mme d'Épinay, 29 Oct. 1757, ibid., pp. 316–17.

"You dare to talk": Grimm to Rousseau, 31 Oct. 1757, ibid., p. 323. This letter is known only from *Madame de Montbrillant,* but Leigh gives reasons for believing it to be authentic (*C.C.* 4: 324n).

281 "I withheld": Rousseau to Grimm, 1 Nov. 1757, *C.C.* 4: 325.

"So what are": Mme d'Houdetot to Rousseau, 2 Nov. 1757, ibid., p. 331.

"If I had any hope": Rousseau to Mme d'Houdetot, 3 Nov. 1757, ibid., p. 336.

"Adieu, my dear": Rousseau to Mme d'Houdetot, 4 Nov. 1757, ibid., p. 339.

282 "If one could die": Rousseau to Mme d'Épinay, 23 Nov. 1757, ibid., p. 372.

"Since you wanted": Mme d'Épinay to Rousseau, 1 Dec. 1757, *Madame de Montbrillant* 3: 278; also quoted by Rousseau in a letter to Mme d'Houdetot, 10 Dec. 1757, *C.C.* 4: 388.

"You will be pleased": Rousseau to Mme d'Épinay, 19 Apr. 1756, ibid., p. 5.

"He was a man": "Souvenirs et Remarques sur M. de Saint-Lambert par la Comtesse d'Houdetot, in Buffenoir, *La Comtesse d'Houdetot,* p. 269.

"the wisest of the French": "Testament de M. de Saint-Lambert," ibid., p. 258.

"He was alarmingly": reminiscences of baron Gaspard (or Caspar) de Voght, quoted by O. Kluth, "Lettres Inédites de Madame d'Houdetot au Baron Voght," *Annales* 28 (1939–1940): 43–44.

283 She enjoyed showing visitors: reminiscences of Mme d'Houdetot's life, *C.C.* 5: 277.

16. The Break with the Enlightenment

284 "what the French call": journal of Joseph Teleki, comte de Szek, *C.C.* 8: 360.

"For him society": Isabelle de Charrière, *Éloge de Jean-Jacques Rousseau* (1790), *Mémoire,* p. 588.

286 "half for myself": *Confessions* X, *O.C.* 1: 514.

287 "my childish frankness . . . comparison with them": Rousseau to Mme d'Houdetot, 5 Jan. 1758, *C.C.* 5: 4–7.

bade him a sad farewell: Mme d'Houdetot to Rousseau, 7 Jan. 1758, ibid., p. 9.

"Reply, *mon cher*": Mme d'Houdetot to Rousseau, 10 Jan. 1758, ibid., p. 13.

"the purest and truest": Rousseau to Mme d'Houdetot, 11 Jan. 1758, ibid., p. 17.

"I owe it": Mme d'Houdetot to Rousseau, 6 May 1758, ibid., p. 72.

288 "Although ordinary company": *Lettres à Malesherbes* I, *O.C.* 1: 1132.

"What is a sensitive": Diderot, "Rêve de d'Alembert," in *Oeuvres,* ed. André Billy (Paris: Gallimard, 1951), p. 925.

"The feelings . . . process of sorting": *Dialogues* II, *O.C.* 1: 825, 861–62.

"the soul directly irrigating": Simon Schama, *Citizens: A Chronicle of the French Revolution* (New York: Alfred A. Knopf, 1989), p. 150.

289 "He is *un honnête homme*": Mme Geoffrin to the king of Poland, 8 May 1774, quoted by Pierre de Ségur, *Le Royaume de la Rue Saint-Honoré: Madame Geoffrin et sa Fille* (Paris: Calmann Lévy, 1897), p. 315.

"two or three times": Angélique de Vandeul [née Diderot], *Vie de Diderot,* in *Oeuvres Choisies de Diderot,* ed. François Tulou (Paris: Garnier, 1908), 1: 39–40.

"the unhappy time . . . covered with mud": *Rêveries* IX, *O.C.* 1: 1092–93.

290 "If by some magic": Diderot to Sophie Volland, 15 Sept. 1760, *Correspondance,* pp. 216–21.

"There's a bit": Diderot to Étienne-Noël Damilaville, 3 Nov. 1760, ibid., p. 297.

"I have to speak": Rousseau to the marquis de Mirabeau, 25 Mar. 1767, *C.C.* 32: 239.

291 "an uncompleting man": Jacques Barzun, "Why Diderot?" in *Varieties of Literary Experience,* ed. Stanley Burnshaw (New York: New York University Press, 1962), p. 33.

292 "You have been given . . . like your own": *Le Fils Naturel* IV.i, in Diderot, *Oeuvres Complètes,* ed. Roger Lewinter (Paris: Club Français, 1970), 3: 89–90. The relevance of the comment on raising children is noted by Thomas Kavanagh, *Writing the Truth: Authority and Desire in Rousseau* (Berkeley: University of California Press, 1987), p. 148.

"Adieu, Citizen": Diderot to Rousseau, 10 Mar. 1757, *C.C.* 4: 169.

"very dry": Rousseau to Diderot, 23 Mar. 1757, ibid., p. 194.

"it pierced me": Rousseau to Mme d'Épinay, 13 Mar. 1757, ibid., p. 171.

mustard up his nose: Trousson 1: 420 (*il sentait la moutarde lui monter au nez*).

"philosophers on foot": Diderot to Rousseau, 14 Mar. 1757, *C.C.* 4: 173.

"abominable": Rousseau to Diderot, 23 Mar. 1757, ibid., p. 194.

"In our altercations": Rousseau to Diderot, 16 Mar. 1757, ibid., pp. 178, 180.

293 "Believe me": Rousseau to Mme d'Épinay, 16 Mar. 1757, ibid., p. 183.

"The Gospel commands": Rousseau to Mme d'Épinay, 17 Mar. 1757, ibid., p. 186.

"Oh, Rousseau": Diderot to Rousseau, 21 Mar. 1757, ibid., p. 191.

"Ingrate, I have never": Rousseau to Diderot, 23 Mar. 1757, ibid., p. 195.

"Corporeal friends": William Blake, *Milton,* book I, plate 4, in *The Complete Poetry and Prose of William Blake,* ed. David V. Erdman (New York: Doubleday Anchor Books, 1988), p. 98.

Diderot's modern biographers: Furbank, *Diderot,* p. 312; Wilson, *Diderot,* p. 544.

"pitilessly": *Madame de Montbrillant* 3: 169.

294 *feuillu: Confessions* IX, *O.C.* 1: 461.

"as if I had a damned": *Madame de Montbrillant* 3: 257–58. Some Rousseau scholars are inclined to believe this letter genuine (*O.C.* 1: 1509n), but Versini does not include it in his edition of Diderot's *Correspondance.*

"What a spectacle": *Discours sur . . . l'Inégalité, O.C.* 3: 192–93.

295 "this morality": *Rêveries* III, *O.C.* 1: 1022. See also Rousseau's account of the cynical code of behavior that Grimm supposedly taught Mme d'Épinay and that Diderot refused to discuss, *Confessions* IX, *O.C.* 1: 468.

"At a hundred leagues": Jean-François de La Harpe to the Grand Duke of Russia (contrasting Voltaire with Rousseau), summer 1776, *C.C.* 40: 80.

Voltaire came to believe: see Mason, *Voltaire,* pp. 73–74, 97–99; on Voltaire at Les Délices and Ferney, see pp. 119–20, 139.

296 Voltaire and Rousseau probably never met: the rather thin evidence is surveyed by English Showalter, *Madame de Graffigny and Rousseau,* pp. 27–34; see also *Dictionnaire,* pp. 930–31.

"Tell us, celebrated Arouet": *Discours sur les Sciences et les Arts, O.C.* 3: 21.

felt as far away as Chambéry: Nicolas, *La Vie Quotidienne,* pp. 330–31.

random geological event: Wilson, *Diderot,* p. 247.

"atoms tormented": Voltaire, "Poème sur le Désastre de Lisbonne," in *Mélanges,* ed. Van den Heuvel, p. 308.

297 "Should we say": *Lettre à Voltaire, O.C.* 4: 1062.

"Instead of 'all is well' . . . find that all is well": *O.C.* 4: 1068, 1075, 1074.

"Heraclitus Rousseau": *Corr. Litt.* 6: 133 (1 Dec. 1764).

Candide was written specifically: letter to the prince de Wurtemburg, 11 Mar. 1764, *C.C.* 19: 210, and *Confessions* IX, *O.C.* 1: 430 (where Rousseau claims, very improbably, that he never read *Candide*).

298 "with no fire": *Confessions* X, *O.C.* 1: 495.

"I am so sick": Rousseau to Rey, 9 Mar. 1758, *C.C.* 5: 50.

"a disinterestedness . . . feel myself worthy": *Lettre à d'Alembert, O.C.* 5: 120.

"Among my contemporaries": "Parallèle entre les deux républiques de Sparte et de Rome," *O.C.* 3: 538. This piece is undated but has much in common with the *Lettre à d'Alembert,* in which Rousseau declares his preference for Sparta over Athens, which he would repeat for the rest of his life (*O.C.* 5: 122).

299 "What is the talent": *Lettre à d'Alembert, O.C.* 5: 73.

"The actor weeps": Diderot, *Paradoxe sur le Comédien* (1773; not published until 1830), *Oeuvres,* ed. Billy, p. 1011.

300 "Jean-Jacques, aime": *Lettre à d'Alembert, O.C.* 5: 124.

"Everything good": Rousseau to Jean Sarasin, 29 Nov. 1758, *C.C.* 5: 243.

two ideologies confronted each other: see Marcel Raymond, "Rousseau et Genève," in *Rousseau,* ed. Baud-Bovy et al., p. 229.

ruling elites were committed: see Roche, *France in the Enlightenment,* pp. 82–83.

301 "interrupting their joyous": David Chauvet to Christofle Beauchâteau, 8 June 1761, *C.C.* 9: 7–8.

"The finest pleasures": Jean-Louis Mollet to Rousseau, 10 June 1761, ibid., p. 9.

"Great Rousseau": Antoine-Jacques Roustan, Aug. 1759, *C.C.* 6: 151.

"Oh, how you would change": Tronchin to Rousseau, 13 Nov. 1758, *C.C.* 5: 220–21.

"I have read M. Rousseau's": d'Alembert to Malesherbes, 22 July 1758, ibid., p. 120.

"The philosophes are disunited": Voltaire to d'Alembert, 19 Mar. 1761, in *The Complete Works of Voltaire,* ed. Theodore Besterman (Geneva: Institut Voltaire; Oxford: Voltaire Foundation, 1960–), 107: 107.

302 "The priests": Voltaire to d'Alembert, 20 Oct. 1761, ibid., 108: 41.

"I admit that": d'Alembert to Voltaire, 31 Oct. 1761, ibid., p. 78.

"I do not like you": Rousseau to Voltaire, 17 June 1760, *C.C.* 7: 136.

303 "I used to have": *Lettre à d'Alembert, O.C.* 5: 7.

"If thou hast opened": Ecclesiasticus 22: 22, in the King James version. (Rousseau cites 22: 27 in the Vulgate; the Apocrypha was included in Catholic Bibles, though not in most Protestant ones.)

"I embrace you": Saint-Lambert to Rousseau, 9 Oct. 1758, *C.C.* 5: 168.

"Diderot may have": Saint-Lambert to Rousseau, 10 Oct. 1758, ibid., p. 169.

Deleyre . . . told Rousseau frankly: Deleyre to Rousseau, 29 Oct. 1758, ibid., pp. 193–94.

"All my works": *Confessions* X, *O.C.* 1: 501.

304 "The opinion of any": "Rousseau à des gens de loi," 15 Oct. 1758, *C.C.* 5: 179.

"This man is false": "Les Tablettes de Diderot," *Mémoire,* p. 175; also *C.C.* 5: 282–83, quoting Diderot's friend J.-H. Meister, who saw him get the notes out of his desk when he wanted to refresh his memory of the quarrel.

"I had the honor": Rousseau to Duchesne, 21 May 1760, *C.C.* 7: 98.

17. Peace at Last and the Triumph of Julie

306   a quarter of a million nobles: J. M. Roberts, *The Penguin History of the World* (London: Penguin, 1995), p. 542; this figure is quite widely accepted, but Guy Chaussinand-Nogaret's exhaustive study of sources (*La Noblesse au XVIIIe Siècle: De la Féodalité aux Lumières* [Brussels: Éditions Complexe, 1984], pp. 46–47) suggests something closer to 130,000.

     "There is only one": Stendhal, *Le Rouge et le Noir,* epigraph to chapter 30.

     the Luxembourgs were wealthy: based on an assessment at the time of the duke's death in 1764; Mme de Luxembourg brought approximately 100,000 livres per year from a previous marriage. See Mély, *Un Intellectuel en Rupture,* p. 106; and Hippolyte Buffenoir, *La Maréchale de Luxembourg* (Paris: Émile-Paul Frères, 1924), p. 20.

307   "I think that if both": Rousseau to the duc de Luxembourg, 27 May 1759, *C.C.* 6: 108.

     "I will honor": *Confessions* X, *O.C.* 1: 534.

     "you would have to know": *Lettres à Malesherbes* IV, *O.C.* 1: 1144.

     "I was in the earthly": *Confessions* X, *O.C.* 1: 521.

308   "Rousseau has accepted": 5 June 1759, Diderot, *Correspondance,* ed. Versini, p. 106.

     "He broke with all": *Corr. Litt.,* 15 June 1762, *Mémoire,* p. 275.

     "Monsieur the duc": *Confessions* X, *O.C.* 1: 527.

309   "The more they have": *Émile* IV, *O.C.* 4: 537.

     "It was during . . . sometimes at mine": *O.C.* 1: 527–28.

     "He was a father . . . dying breath": Marianne de La Tour to Rousseau, 1 Nov. 1763, *C.C.* 18: 91.

     "noble souls like yours": Rousseau to Jacques-François Deluc, 29 Mar. 1758, *C.C.* 5: 68.

310   "Is it possible": Mme de Luxembourg to Rousseau, 3 Sept. 1759, *C.C.* 6: 158.

     "You haven't wanted": Rousseau to Mme de Luxembourg, 24 Jan. 1760, *C.C.* 7: 21.

     "the most charming": Mme de Luxembourg to Rousseau, 28 Jan. 1760, ibid., p. 22.

     "Your patron saint": Voltaire, *À Madame de Boufflers, qui s'appelait Madeleine,* ca. 1749, in *Complete Works* 31b: 528.

311   "She was not one": Buffenoir, *La Maréchale de Luxembourg,* p. 10.

     "She dominates": from the marquise du Deffand's correspondence, quoted ibid., p. 15.

312   "The most skillful copyist": "Copiste," in *Dictionnaire de Musique, O.C.* 5: 735.

     Morellet said: Morellet, *Mémoires,* p. 114.

     "If Rousseau had merely": Malesherbes to the comte de Sarsfeld, 28 Nov. 1766, *C.C.* 31: 223.

     "We went into . . . had been nectar": François Favre to Paul-Claude Moultou, 11 Dec. 1759, *C.C.* 6: 225.

     "A girl, or woman": journal of Joseph Teleki, comte de Szek, 6 Mar. 1761, *C.C.* 8: 360–61.

314   "Thérèse was no longer": ibid., p. 362n.

     "The third person": Casanova, *History of My Life* 5: 224. Trask's footnote indicates that the anecdote has been disputed, but it is not clear why it should be; see Yves Vargas, *Rousseau: l'Enigme du Sexe* (Paris: Presses Universitaires de France, 1997), p. 24.

"I made a dictionary": *Confessions* VII, *O.C.* 1: 332.

Côme carried out a painful probing: *Confessions* XI, *O.C.* 1: 571–72.

"Ever since I hardened": Rousseau to the marquise de Verdelin, *C.C.* 7: 58.

315   "He never in his life": Jean-Louis Lecercle, "La Femme selon Jean-Jacques," in Jean Starobinski et al., *Jean-Jacques Rousseau: Quatre Études* (Neuchâtel: La Baconnière, 1978), p. 53.

316   "No, keep your kisses": *Julie* I.xiv, *O.C.* 2: 65.

"If my ardent": *Julie* I.li, ibid., pp. 140–41.

"This slender corset that touches and embraces": *Julie* I.liv, ibid., p. 147.

"I imagined no other . . . follows it": *Julie* I.lv, ibid., pp. 148–49.

"the poison that corrupts": *Julie* I.iv, ibid., p. 39.

"Love is accompanied": *Julie* III.xx, ibid., p. 372.

317   "If I could change": *Julie* IV.xii, ibid., p. 491.

"It's not Julie": *Julie* IV.xiv, ibid., p. 509.

"It's ended": *Julie* IV.xvii, ibid., pp. 520–21.

318   "without finery": *O.C.* 2: 768.

"I get angry every time": recorded by J. H. Meister, *C.C.* 20: 127.

319   "The avid and daring": *Julie* I.xxiii, ibid., p. 82.

"I felt from the way": *Julie* V.iii, ibid., p. 559.

"Was it not your own": Bernardin, pp. 139–40.

"O my benefactor": *Julie* V.viii, *O.C.* 2: 611.

320   "What ecstasy": *Julie* I.xxxviii, ibid., p. 115.

"taking pride": *Émile* V, *O.C.* 4: 719; see the editors' note to the corresponding passage in *Julie, O.C.* 2: 1408–9.

"If I have imagined": Rousseau to Mme Boy de La Tour, 29 May 1762, *C.C.* 10: 310.

"Happier in the pleasures": *Julie,* appendix, "Les Amours de Milord Edouard Bomston," *O.C.* 2: 760.

"Big Brother in a powdered": Trousson 2: 26.

"a gentle totalitarianism": Bonhôte, *Rousseau: Vision de l'Histoire,* p. 98.

321   "Luxury nourishes": "Dernière Réponse à M. Bordes," *O.C.* 3: 79.

"recalling all . . . continual fête": *Julie* V.vii, *O.C.* 2: 603.

"if anyone happens": *Julie* V.vii, ibid., p. 609.

"moral castration": Alexis Philonenko, *Jean-Jacques Rousseau et la Pensée du Malheur* (Paris: Vrin, 1984), 2: 194.

"often she draws": *Julie* IV.x, *O.C.* 2: 465–66. The parallel with the episode in Turin is noted by the Pléiade editors, *O.C.* 2: 1606.

322   "Servitude is so unnatural . . . obliged to do": *Julie* IV.x, ibid., pp. 460, 453.

"O great being": *Lettres à Malesherbes* III, *O.C.* 1: 1141.

his gaze seldom extended: David E. Allen, *The British Naturalist* (London: A. Lane, 1976), p. 54.

323   "it makes one think": Claire-Eliane Engel, *La Littérature Alpestre en France et en Angleterre aux XVIIIe et XIXe Siècles* (Chambéry: Dardel, 1930), pp. 22–24.

"one breathes more . . . dared not sound": *Julie* I.xxiii, *O.C.* 2: 78, 77.

as a scholar comments: Daniel Mornet, *Le Sentiment de la Nature en France de J.-J. Rousseau à Bernardin de Saint-Pierre* (Paris: Hachette, 1907), p. 55.

A Polish countess: quoted by Lucien Lathion, *Jean-Jacques Rousseau et le Valais: Étude Historique et Critique* (Lausanne: Éditions Rencontre, 1953), p. 11.

324   "So, Monsieur, you can go": Marcel Raymond, introduction to Gagnebin, *Rousseau et son Oeuvre,* p. xxiii.

"Julie the devout": Rousseau to Jacob Vernes, 24 June 1761, *C.C.* 9: 27.

"A coal merchant's wife": *Julie* V.xiii, *O.C.* 2: 633; Rousseau describes the incident in *Confessions* X, *O.C.* 1: 512.

325 at least seventy editions: see Jo-Ann E. McEachern, *"La Nouvelle Héloïse:* Some Bibliographical Problems," *Eighteenth-Century Fiction* 1 (1989), 305–17; Rey reports earning 10,000 livres in a letter of 7 Dec. 1761, *C.C.* 9: 299. The complicated details of the publication of *Julie* are very fully described in Cranston 2: 244 ff.
the passions . . . burned the paper: *Journal Encyclopédique* (1 June 1761, p. 112), quoted by Mornet, *Le Sentiment de la Nature,* p. 201.
"to make virtue": de Staël, *Lettres sur les Ouvrages,* p. iv.
"Jean-Jacques Rousseau spelled": *O.C.* 2: 26–27.
seduced by characters: Arnaud Tripet, *La Rêverie Littéraire* (Geneva: Droz, 1979), p. 39.
"Whoever does not idolize": Rousseau to Pierre-Laurent de Belloy, 19 Feb. 1770, *C.C.* 37: 241.
"an author devoid": *Corr. Litt.* 15 Jan. 1761, no. 2 [not in the Tourneux edition], *C.C.* 8: 344.

326 "He carries the torch": Diderot, *Éloge de Richardson, Oeuvres,* ed. Billy, p. 1061.
lady who started reading *Julie: Confessions* XI, *O.C.* 1: 547.
"I was beyond tears": marquise de Polignac to Rousseau, 3 Feb. 1761, *C.C.* 8: 56–57. The letter is unsigned, and Leigh's notes suggest several possible writers, but the marquise de Polignac seems clearly identified by Rousseau in the *Confessions, O.C.* 1: 547–48.
"Women above all": *Confessions* XI, ibid., p. 545.

327 "If the great Rousseau": baron de Bormes to Rousseau, 27 Mar. 1761, *C.C.* 8: 280.
"How much our hearts": abbé Jacques Pernetti to Rousseau, 26 Feb. 1761, ibid., p. 178.
"A god was needed": Charles-Joseph Pancoucke to Rousseau, 10 Feb. 1761, ibid., pp. 77–79. Pancoucke's letter, together with a number of others, is discussed by Robert Darnton in "Readers Respond to Rousseau: The Fabrication of Romantic Sensitivity," in *Great Cat Massacre,* chap. 6.
"She was sleeping . . . cooler souls:" La Chapelle (not otherwise identified) to Rousseau, 23 Aug. 1764, *C.C.* 21: 58.

328 "I don't know what": Rousseau to La Chapelle, 23 Sept. 1764, ibid., pp. 179–80.
"the infinite pleasure": Buffenoir, *La Maréchale de Luxembourg,* pp. 86–87.
"Julie, my dear Julie!" *Julie* VI.xi, *O.C.* 2: 719. Julie's imprisonment in her role is emphasized by Lori J. Marso, "Rousseau's Subversive Women," in *Feminist Interpretations of Jean-Jacques Rousseau,* ed. Lynda Lange (University Park: Pennsylvania State University Press, 2002), pp. 245–76.

329 "By myself I cannot": *Julie* VI.xiii, *O.C.* 2: 743–44.
"The pupil will lose": *Prédiction tirée d'un vieux manuscrit sur La Nouvelle Héloïse* (1761), in *Mémoire,* p. 224.
"Milord proves . . . more of a philosopher": *Lettres à M. de Voltaire sur La Nouvelle Héloise ou Aloïsia de Jean-Jacques Rousseau citoyen de Genève* (1761), in *Mémoire,* pp. 240, 242.
"The author knows how": *L'Année Littéraire* (1761), in *Mémoire,* pp. 251, 256.
"Condemned to pain": anonymous writer to Rousseau, 20 Apr. 1761, *C.C.* 8: 305.

330 "O Love, in the age": Henri-Nicolas Latran to François-Antoine Devaux, 4 Oct. 1770, *C.C.* 38: 356.
"the person who desires": Leo Braudy, *The Frenzy of Renown: Fame and Its History* (New York: Vintage, 1997), p. 375.

18. Rousseau the Controversialist

331 "At the age of sixty": *Émile* II, *O.C.* 4: 306–7.

332 "Children sometimes flatter": *Émile* I, ibid., p. 265.
"I still have an old sin": Rousseau to Toussaint-Pierre Lenieps, 11 Dec. 1760, *C.C.* 7: 351. On the same day Rousseau wrote in similar terms to Mme Dupin, ibid., p. 352.
"Whoever cannot fulfill": *Émile* I, *O.C.* 4: 262–63.
"Oh, he hadn't any": James Boswell, diary for 15 Dec.1764, in *Boswell on the Grand Tour: Germany and Switzerland,* p. 258 (translated by Pottle from Boswell's record of the conversation in French).

333 "All of our wisdom": *Émile* I, *O.C.* 4: 253.
"A school is the cavern": Gibbon, *Memoirs,* p. 73.
"white paper . . . power he is": *The Educational Writings of John Locke,* ed. James L. Axtell (Cambridge: Cambridge University Press, 1968), pp. 325, 145.

334 "esteem and disgrace": ibid., p. 152.
"seeing with his own eyes": *Émile* IV, *O.C.* 4: 551.
"He is a savage": *Émile* III, ibid., p. 484.
"He is not the man": *Émile* IV, ibid., p. 549.
"I am teaching": *Émile* II, ibid., pp. 370–71.
"Everything is good": *Émile* I, ibid., p. 245.
"This book": *Dialogues* III, *O.C.* 1: 934.
"Dare I expound": *Émile* II, *O.C.* 4: 323.

335 "How rapidly we pass": *Émile* IV, ibid., p. 489.
"Even if I were": *Émile* II, ibid., pp. 301–2.
"It is easy to put": ibid., p. 350.

336 "The boy cries . . . movement of vanity": *Émile* III, *O.C.* 4: 438, 440.
age of nature lasted: the "Favre manuscript" of *Émile,* ibid., p. 60.
Starobinski does call: *Transparency and Obstruction,* p. 127.

337 "None of us is philosopher": *Émile* II, *O.C.* 4: 355.
"One must not": ibid., pp. 317–18.
"No one likes": ibid., p. 356.

338 "I see [Émile] ardent": ibid., p. 419.
"Since that time": *Émile* II (referring to Mozart's Paris visit in 1763–1764), in a copy annotated by Rousseau for a projected collected edition of his work, *O.C.* 4: 1398n.
"I know that an absolute": *Dialogues* II, *O.C.* 1: 813.
"Rather than destine": *Émile* V, *O.C.* 4: 765.
As Yves Vargas observes: *Rousseau: L'Énigme du Sexe,* pp. 57–58.

339 "We love the image": *Émile* IV, *O.C.* 4: 656.
"Let us call your future mistress Sophie": ibid., p. 657.
"Sophie, my dear": Rousseau to Mme d'Houdetot, 23 Nov. 1757, *C.C.* 4: 581. The verbal echo is noted in Trousson 2: 492n.
"At the first . . . intoxicating him": *Émile* V, *O.C.* 4: 776.

340 "Émile, take this hand": ibid., p. 813.
"She is entirely": ibid., p. 707.
"Made to obey": ibid., p. 710.
Mary Wollstonecraft: *A Vindication of the Rights of Women* (1792).

341 "A woman should reign": *Émile* V, *O.C.* 4: 766–67.

the modern sentimental family: Susan Moller Okin, "Women and the Making of the Sentimental Family," *Philosophy and Public Affairs* 11 (1982): 69–88.

"Rousseau was influential": Sarah Maza, "Women, the Bourgeoisie, and the Public Sphere," *French Historical Studies* 17 (1992): 949.

"But his wife divines": *Émile* V, *O.C.* 4: 732. The significance of this passage is emphasized by Lori Jo Marso, *(Un)Manly Citizens: Jean-Jacques Rousseau's and Germaine de Staël's Subversive Women* (Baltimore: Johns Hopkins University Press, 1999), pp. 39–42.

"We all said it": Georges Louis Leclerc, comte de Buffon, quoted in *Journal de Paris,* 30 Oct. 1778, *C.C.* 40: 187n.

"She had a weakness": Marmontel, *Mémoires* 1: 292.

342   "Inasmuch as a woman's": *Émile* V, *O.C.* 1: 721.

"I do not think": Rousseau to Frédéric-Guillaume de Montmollin (letter never sent), 14 Nov. 1762, *C.C.* 14: 40.

"What I ask": Rousseau to Moultou, 14 Feb. 1769, *C.C.* 37: 57.

Bernardin noted: Bernardin, p. 7.

343   "In any other system": *Rêveries* III, *O.C.* 1: 1019.

"I look forward": *Émile* IV, *O.C.* 4: 604–5.

"The various modes": Edward Gibbon, *The History of the Decline and Fall of the Roman Empire,* ed. J. B. Bury (London: Methuen, 1909–1914), 1: 31.

"the only man of genius": de Staël, *Lettres sur les Ouvrages,* p. 72.

344   "They speak of a God": "Mémoire à M. de Mably," *O.C.* 4: 8.

as Starobinski observes: *L'Oeil Vivant,* pp. 140–42.

"You have enjoyed": *Émile* V, *O.C.* 4: 821.

345   "Delivered from the anxiety": *Émile et Sophie,* ibid., p. 905.

à la Jean-Jacques: see *Dictionnaire,* p. 289.

"A perfect Émile": Louis-Sébastien Mercier, *Oeuvres Complètes de J.-J. Rousseau* (1788), *Mémoire,* p. 531.

346   "The truth doesn't lead": *Du Contrat Social* II.ii, *O.C.* 3: 371.

"Man is born free . . . that question": *Du Contrat Social* I.i, ibid., p. 351.

"the argument of the book": Cranston 2: 306.

347   "The English people": *Du Contrat Social* III.xv, *O.C.* 3: 430.

"Taking the term": *Du Contrat Social* III.iv, ibid., p. 404.

348   "The generality of men": *Corr. Litt.* 10: 129 (Jan. 1773, reviewing Rousseau's *Considerations on the Government of Poland).*

"He is Demosthenes": Charles Palissot, *Mémoires pour Servir à l'Histoire de notre Littérature* (1769), in *Mémoire,* p. 402.

"The laws are always": *Du Contrat Social* I.ix, *O.C.* 3: 367.

"When a man of importance": *Discours sur l'Économie Politique,* *O.C.* 3: 271–72.

heart of Rousseau's thinking: Melzer, *Natural Goodness of Man;* I am indebted also to Kelly, *Rousseau's Exemplary Life;* James Miller, *Rousseau: Dreamer of Democracy* (New Haven: Yale University Press, 1984); and Alan Bloom, "Rousseau's Critique of Liberal Constitutionalism," in *The Legacy of Rousseau,* ed. Clifford Orwin and Nathan Tarcov (Chicago: University of Chicago Press, 1997), 143–67.

"Each *me* is the enemy": Pascal, *Pensées,* no. 455 in the Brunschvicg numeration.

349   "Each one, uniting . . . common me": *Du Contrat Social* I.vi, *O.C.* 3: 360, 361.

"a monstrous democracy . . . rights are inalienable": Horace-Bénédict Perrinet de Franches to M. C. F. de Sacconay, 24 Jan. 1766, *C.C.* 28: 223.

"We hold these truths": "Declaration of Independence," July 4, 1776.

"human beings are numerators": Kelly, *Rousseau's Exemplary Life,* p. 146.

"In order that the social": *Du Contrat Social* I.vii, *O.C.* 3: 364.

350   as one writer comments: Bronislaw Baczco, "Rousseau and Social Marginality," *Daedalus* 107, no. 3 (summer 1978): 38.

"I know of nothing . . . to be slaves": *Du Contrat Social* IV.viii, *O.C.* 3: 465, 467.

351   "opium for the soul": *Julie* VI.viii, *O.C.* 2: 697.

"Most of it": *L'Année Littéraire* (1785), in *Mémoire,* p. 522.

Mercier published a book: the larger implications are explored by James Swenson, *On Jean-Jacques Rousseau: Considered as One of the First Authors of the Revolution* (Stanford: Stanford University Press, 2000).

"What truths . . . keenness of melancholy": quoted by F. G. Healey, *Rousseau et Napoléon* (Geneva: Droz, 1957), pp. 16, 23.

352   "It would have been better": quoted in Stanislas de Girardin, *Mémoires* (Paris, 1834) 1: 189.

"Seeing men of letters": Rousseau to Jacob Vernes, 29 Nov. 1760, *C.C.* 7: 332.

"I venture to ask": Rey to Rousseau, 31 Dec. 1761, *C.C.* 9: 368.

"She ought to write": Rousseau to Rey, 9 May 1762, *C.C.* 10: 235.

353   "I have a very loving . . . don't see them": *Lettres à Malesherbes* IV, *O.C.* 1: 1144.

"There is no place": Rousseau to Samuel-André Tissot, 1 Apr. 1765, *C.C.* 25: 3.

354   "Embittered by the injustices": *Lettres à Malesherbes* II, *O.C.* 1: 1134–35.

"When I was least": ibid., p. 1136.

"the torment": Malesherbes to Mme de Luxembourg, 25 Dec. 1761, *C.C.* 9: 357.

Grimm remarked: quoted in R. A. Leigh, *Unsolved Problems in the Bibliography of J.-J. Rousseau* (Cambridge: Cambridge University Press, 1990), pp. 12–13.

355   As Leigh points out: ibid., pp. 14 and 24, critiquing the standard view that derives from a 1910 article by Daniel Mornet.

"in what would be called": Malesherbes to baron de Breteuil, 27 July 1776, quoted in Mély, *Un Intellectuel en Rupture,* p. 128.

356   as Pierre Serna observes: Serna, "The Noble," in *Enlightenment Portraits,* ed. Michel Vovelle, trans. Lydia G. Cochrane (Chicago: University of Chicago Press, 1997), pp. 76–77.

"Those were mere battles": comte de Ségur, *Mémoires,* quoted in Chaussinand-Nogaret, *La Noblesse au XVIIIe Siècle,* p. 16.

Protestants . . . comprised: Roche, *France in the Enlightenment,* pp. 364–65.

"To forbid assembly . . . right to punish it": Rousseau to Jean Ribotte, 24 Oct. 1761, *C.C.* 9: 200–201.

357   "Deign, Monsieur": *C.C.* 6: 214 (also *Confessions* IX, *O.C.* 1: 531–32).

"I find the letter": Mme de Luxembourg to Rousseau, 26 May 1760, *C.C.* 7: 110.

They say that the parlement": Rousseau to Moultou, 7 June 1762, *C.C.* 11: 36.

358   "He has the *dévots*": 18 July 1762, Diderot, *Correspondance,* pp. 383–84.

"think only of pillaging": *Censure de la Faculté de Théologie de Paris* (1762), quoted in Philippe Lefebvre, "Jansenistes et Challoliques contre Rousseau," *Annales* 37 (1966–1968): 129.

Thérèse called them . . . *commères*: *Confessions* X, *O.C.* 1: 506.

A scholar who has explored the question: Lefebvre, "Jansenistes et Catholiques," pp. 131–35.

"The author . . . Palais de Justice": *Arrêt de la Cour de Parlement, C.C.* 11: 265–66.

359   "Jean-Jacques Rousseau": Rousseau to Mme de Créqui, 7 June 1762, ibid., p. 39.

"In the name of God": Mme de Luxembourg to Rousseau, 8 June 1762, ibid., p. 45.

360   "She embraced me several times": *Confessions* XI, *O.C.* 1: 583.

"she pierced the air": ibid., 582.

19. Exile in the Mountains

362 "my hand shook . . . suffers like this": Rousseau to Mme de Luxembourg, 17 June 1762, *C.C.* 11: 99.

"On reaching the territory": *Confessions* XI, *O.C.* 1: 587.

"If it's not the best": ibid., p. 586.

363 "sons of Belial": John Milton, *Paradise Lost*, I.501–2.

as critics have observed: I am especially indebted to François Van Laere, *Jean-Jacques Rousseau: Du Phantasme à l'Écriture* (Paris: Minard, 1967); and Thomas Kavanagh, *Writing the Truth*, pp. 102–23, as well as to some brief but suggestive remarks in Clément, *De l'Éros Coupable*, pp. 50–51.

"Benjamin, sad child": "Le Lévite d'Ephraïm," *O.C.* 2: 1208.

his *roguinerie*: Daniel Roguin to Rousseau, 10 July 1762, *C.C.* 12: 9.

364 "I have said": Rousseau to Frederick the Great, 10 July 1762, ibid., p. 1.

"There are few": Frederick to the duchess of Saxe-Gotha, 10 Feb. 1763, quoted in Mély, *Un Intellectuelle en Rupture*, p. 327n.

Rousseau pronounced it: after hearing Rousseau talk, his friend Bernardin wrote it as "Kheit" (Bernardin, p. 45). He knew there was an "h" somewhere, but he didn't hear it.

"All we could make . . . of popularity": Edith Cuthell, *The Scottish Friend of Frederic the Great: The Last Earl Marischall* (London: Stanley Paul, 1915), 1: 122, 143, 147.

366 "It seems he doesn't": Voltaire to Mme Denis, 24 Aug. 1751, *Complete Works*, ed. Besterman, 104: 17.

"I saw in Mylord's": *Confessions* XII, *O.C.* 1: 597.

"my friend, my protector": Rousseau to the comtesse de Boufflers, 28 Dec. 1763, *C.C.* 18: 243; Rousseau repeated the phrase in slightly altered form in *Lettres Écrites de la Montagne, O.C.* 3: 797.

"Mylord, I have": Rousseau to Keith, 8 Dec. 1764, *C.C.* 22: 185.

"I had only to cross": *Confessions* XII, *O.C.* 1: 592.

"My heart has always": Thérèse Levasseur to Rousseau, 23 June 1762, *C.C.* 11: 141.

367 *Monquer atous:* Thérèse's original spelling as transcribed by Mugnier, *Mme Warens et Rousseau*, p. 316.

Rousseau later wrote him: Rousseau to the abbé Baptiste-Philippe-Aimé Grumet, 30 Nov. 1762, *C.C.* 14: 139.

"What emotions": *Confessions* XII, *O.C.* 1: 595.

"a beautiful wild valley": James Boswell's diary for 3 Dec.1764, in *Boswell on the Grand Tour: Germany and Switzerland*, p. 220.

368 "Grand though the spectacle": Rousseau to Luxembourg, 28 Jan. 1763, *C.C.* 15: 113.

"Today, when I would": *Lettre à d'Alembert, O.C.* 5: 57.

"I believed I would": Rousseau to Luxembourg, 20 Jan. 1763, *C.C.* 15: 48.

a contemporary guidebook: Samuel Frédéric Ostervald, *Description des Montagnes et des Vallées qui font Partie de la Principauté de Neuchâtel et Valangin* (Fauché: Neuchâtel, 1766), p. 17.

"The abundance of money": Rousseau to Lenieps, 15 July 1764, *C.C.* 20: 281.

A visitor sixty years later: Pierre-François Bellot, notes on a visit in 1823, *C.C.* 26: 378–79.

inventory after their departure: 28 Sept. 1765, *C.C.* 26: 380–82.

369 "In order to have bread": Rousseau to Luxembourg, 20 Jan. 1763, *C.C.* 15: 120.

"It is not possible": François-Louis d'Escherny, quoted in Frédéric S. Eigeldinger,

"Des Pierres dans mon Jardin": Les Années Neuchâtelois de J.J. Rousseau et la Crise de 1765 (Paris and Geneva: Champion-Slatkine, 1992), p. 18.

370 When Boswell visited: *Boswell on the Grand Tour: Germany and Switzerland,* pp. 258–59 (15 Dec. 1764).

he often got up to make it: described by Julie von Bondeli to J. G. Zimmerman, repeating what she had heard from one of Rousseau's visitors, 21 Aug. 1762, *C.C.* 12: 236.

"and the whole thing": H.-C. d'Astier de Cromessière to Rousseau (writing from Carpentras), 22 Aug. 1763, *C.C.* 17: 177.

"She called me": *Confessions* XII, *O.C.* 1: 601–2.

371 "because it was said": an old laundress, in an account by Ami Mallet, quoted in "Sur les Pas de J.-J. Rousseau à Môtiers-Travers," *Annales* 26 (1937): 313–14.

"It seems to me": Rousseau to Mme Boy, 9 Oct. 1762, *C.C.* 13: 184.

"In all seasons": Rousseau to Duchesne, 15 Oct. 1763, *C.C.* 18: 38.

as Frédéric Eigeldinger suggests: "Des Pierres," p. 79.

"O why was I born": Blake to Thomas Butts, 16 Aug. 180, in Blake, *Complete Poetry and Prose,* p. 733.

372 "They are intended": Rousseau to Mme Boy, 9 Oct. 1762, *C.C.* 13: 184.

"Wear under happy": Rousseau to Anne-Marie d'Ivernois, 13 Sept. 1762, ibid., p. 60. Leigh (p. 61n) says that this letter became one of the best-known passages from Rousseau's correspondence.

"I am trying to lose": Rousseau to the marquise de Verdelin, 4 Sept. 1762, ibid., p. 10.

"I thought as a man": reported by Julie von Bondeli to J. G. Zimmermann, 21 Aug. 1762, *C.C.* 12: 236.

daughter of an impoverished: von Bondeli to Zimmermann, ibid., p. 235.

"Their curious glances . . . could inhabit": Rousseau to Mme Boy, 14 Aug. 1763, *C.C.* 17: 153.

373 "I am attached": Rousseau to Montmollin, 24 Aug. 1762, *C.C.* 12: 246.

congregation saw him in tears: reported by a relative of Isabelle Guyenet, *C.C.* 13: 170n.

Montmollin even lent: Rousseau to B. C. A. Dumoulin, 16 Jan. 1763, *C.C.* 15: 42.

"Rousseau, and Rousseau alone": Henri (or Heinrich) of Prussia to the prince de Wurtemberg, 23 June 1765, *C.C.* 26: 60n.

mon fils le sauvage: Keith to Rousseau, 13 Apr. 1764, *C.C.* 19: 296.

"David will pay": Keith to Rousseau, 2 Oct. 1762, *C.C.* 13: 149.

374 "You want to give": Rousseau to Frederick II, 1 Nov. 1762, *C.C.* 14: 1.

"Let him make": Rousseau to Keith, ibid., p. 3.

Keith replied dryly: Keith to Rousseau, 3 Nov. 1762, ibid., p. 7.

"One must admit: Frederick II to Keith, 26 Nov. 1762, ibid., p. 116.

"a very great number": *Mandement de Mgr. l'Archevêque de Paris,* in *Oeuvres Complètes de J.-J. Rousseau,* ed. M. Launay (Paris: Seuil, 1967), 3: 336.

"A genuinely apostolic": anonymous writer in *L'Année Littéraire* (1785), in *Mémoire,* p. 524.

"I have been surrounded": *Lettre à Christophe de Beaumont, O.C.* 4: 963.

"What common language . . . I am nothing": ibid., pp. 927, 1007.

375 "Whatever they may": d'Alembert to Julie de Lespinasse, May 1763, *C.C.* 16: 368.

"In this piece . . . and revelation": *Corr. Litt.* 5: 290–92 (15 May 1763).

"O my dear": Moultou to Rousseau, 23 Mar. 1763, *C.C.* 15: 316.

"Get thee behind me": Antoine-Jacques Roustan to Rousseau, 8 May 1763, *C.C.* 16: 154 (referring to Matthew 16: 23, repeated in two other Gospels).

376   "struck me like": Marc Chappuis to Rousseau, 18 May 1763, ibid., p. 198.

"Rousseau is no longer": Théodore Tronchin to Jacob Vernes, 18 May 1763, ibid., p. 204.

"disposed to believe": Chambrier d'Oleyres, quoted by Charly Guyot, *Un Ami et Défenseur de Rousseau: Pierre-Alexandre Du Peyrou* (Neuchâtel: Ides et Calendes, 1958), p. 15. My account of Du Peyrou is based on Guyot's work.

377   "All of it flowed": Jacob Wegelin, *Denkwürdigkeiten von Johann Jakob Rousseau, C.C.* 18: 257, 259.

378   "To a mild countenance": Pierre Mouchon to Jeanne Mouchon, 4 Oct. 1762, *C.C.* 13: 167.

"the father of my soul": Mouchon to Rousseau, 20 Oct. 1762, ibid., p. 231.

"they make me die": Suzanne Curchod to Julie von Bondeli (the other minister was Leonhard Usteri of Zurich), 10 Oct. 1762, ibid., p. 198.

"I think only": Mouchon to Rousseau, 5 Nov. 1762, *C.C.* 14: 12.

"He was tall . . . became inseparable": *Confessions* XII, *O.C.* 1: 616.

379   "He told everyone": ibid.

A scholar who has pondered: Madeleine Anjubault Simons, *Amitié et Passion: Rousseau et Sauttersheim* (Geneva: Droz, 1972), p. 16; on the parallel with the account of Christ (in the *Lettres de la Montagne*), see p. 23.

"The reign of love": *Julie* VI.iii, *O.C.* 2: 653.

vilaine salope: Confessions XII, *O.C.* 1: 617.

"morals of the purest": Rousseau to Roguin, 18 Aug 1763, *C.C.* 17: 163.

when she was interrogated: Simons, *Amitié et Passion,* p. 37; naming her baby Jean-Jacques, p. 41.

380   "I swore solemnly": 21 Oct. 1764, *Boswell on the Grand Tour: Germany and Switzerland,* p. 150.

"a feeling heart . . . write as he has written": Boswell's letter to Rousseau, 3 Dec. 1764, as translated ibid., pp. 218–19. Pottle, the modern editor, also prints the drafts in which Boswell worked out the best way to present himself. The original French is given in *C.C.* 22: 156–57.

"a little, lively . . . world as it is": ibid., pp. 220–24. The allusion to *Julie* is to VI.viii, *O.C.* 2: 693.

381   "Day and night": Rousseau to Moultou, 18 Jan. 1762, *C.C.* 10: 40.

splitting firewood: Rousseau to Duchesne, 26 Feb. 1764, *C.C.* 19: 183.

"and I feel in every way": Rousseau to Mme de Verdelin, 30 Apr. 1763, *C.C.* 16: 129. On the rivers freezing, see Leigh's note, *C.C.* 15: 39n.

confined by snow: mentioned by Roguin in a letter to Rousseau, 1 May 1764, *C.C.* 20: 3.

"without setting foot": Rousseau to Daniel Roguin, 28 Feb. 1765, *C.C.* 24: 108.

As Leigh says: Leigh, *Unsolved Problems,* p. 11.

"I never get a virtuous": Rousseau to Malesherbes, 11 Nov. 1764, *C.C.* 22: 44.

383   "My God, Monsieur": D'Escherny's memoirs, *C.C.* 20: 322–23.

"Oh look!": *Confessions* VI, *O.C.* 1: 226.

"overwhelmed with maladies": Conzié to Rousseau, 4 Oct. 1762, *C.C.* 13: 164.

384   "to cover with flowers": Rousseau to Conzié, 5 May 1763, *C.C.* 16: 145.

"I made one friend": Rousseau to Deleyre, 3 June 1764, *C.C.* 20: 136.

"How much more": Rousseau to Mme de Luxembourg, 5 June 1764, ibid., p. 141.

"I feel Mme la Maréchale's": Rousseau to La Roche, 27 May 1764, ibid., p. 98.

"In God's name": Mme de Luxembourg to Rousseau, 10 June 1764, ibid., p. 175.

It has been calculated: Eigeldinger, "Des Pierres," pp. 167–69.

"The moment of waking": Henriette to Rousseau, 26 Mar.1764, *C.C.* 19: 245.

385 "You are a distressing": Rousseau to Henriette, 4 Nov. 1764, *C.C.* 22: 9.

it could fill a book: Jean-Jacques Rousseau and Madame de La Tour, *Correspondance,* ed. Georges May (Arles: Actes Sud, 1998).

the editor of the correspondence: ibid., p. 9.

"To write to you": Rousseau to Mme Alissan, 21 Oct. 1764, *C.C.* 21: 285.

"You have a very unhappy": Rousseau to Mme Alissan, 10 Feb. 1765, *C.C.* 23: 337.

386 "It is one of the great": "Opéra," in *Dictionnaire de Musique, O.C.* 5: 958–59.

"Several articles": Bachaumont, *Mémoires Secrets,* 10 Dec. 1767, quoted by Plan, *Rousseau raconté,* p. 90.

"If I were she . . . through you": *Pygmalion, O.C.* 2: 1228, 1231.

"These brave people": *Contrat Social* II.x, *O.C.* 3: 391.

387 As Trousson says: Trousson 2: 254.

"In the name": *Constitution pour la Corse, O.C.* 3: 943.

20. *Another Expulsion*

389 "slaves of an arbitrary": *Lettres de la Montagne, O.C.* 3: 835.

"you are merchants": ibid., p. 881.

"Our people are saying openly": François-Henri d'Ivernois to Rousseau, 21 Dec. 1764, *C.C.* 22: 262.

"I'm going to behave": Rousseau to Lenieps, 10 Feb. 1765, *C.C.* 23: 339.

"The author of *Émile*": Voltaire, *Lettre au Docteur Jean-Jacques Pansophe* (1766), in *Mémoire,* p. 359.

"to prepare for a triumphant return": Voltaire to d'Alembert, 20 Apr. 1761, *Complete Works* 107: 167.

390 "a little book": "Pierre le Grand et J.-J. Rousseau," quoted in *O.C.* 1: 1467n.

"It would never": Theodore Besterman, *Voltaire* (New York: Harcourt, Brace, 1969), p. 298.

"Let the Council": Voltaire to François Tronchin, 25 Dec. 1764, *Complete Works* 56: 230.

suggestion about communion bread: *Lettre à Christophe de Beaumont, O.C.* 4: 999; Voltaire to d'Alembert, 1 May 1763, *Complete Works* 110: 197.

he died a Catholic: John McManners, *Reflections at the Death Bed of Voltaire: The Art of Dying in Eighteenth-Century France* (Oxford: Clarendon Press, 1975), p. 22.

"We avow with grief": *Le Sentiment des Citoyens, C.C.* 23: 381.

391 "I have never exposed": Rousseau's annotated copy of the *Sentiment des Citoyens,* ibid., p. 381n, which he got Duchesne to publish.

"the most ardent": *Lettre de M. Rousseau de Genève, C.C.* 20: 102.

"I the undersigned": Jean Louis Wagnière, in a letter from Vernes to Du Peyrou (sent to him for insertion in a new edition of the *Confessions*), 9 Jan. 1790, *C.C.* 23: 384; see also *O.C.* 1: 1597n.

392 "You have shown": Deleyre to Rousseau, 16 June 1763, *C.C.* 16: 315.

"I will depict myself": Rousseau to Duclos, 13 Jan. 1765, *C.C.* 23: 100.

"Either Monsieur Rousseau": Frédéric-Guillaume de Montmollin, *Lettre à Monsieur *** rélative à J. J. Rousseau* (1765), p. 109.

"catching fire": Keith to Rousseau, 8 Mar. 1765, *C.C.* 24: 174.

393 "that he believes": deliberations of the Vénérable Classe de Neuchâtel, 13 Mar. 1765, ibid., p. 347.

"he deleted": Deleyre to the marquis de Girardin, 5 Aug. 1778, *C.C.* 5: 291.

Pury's covert goal: Eigeldinger, "Des Pierres," p. 127.

Rousseau did promise: records of the Conseil d'État, *C.C.* 25: 51n.

394 "Mlle Levasseur, whom": Jakob Heinrich Meister to Moultou, 5 Oct. 1764, *C.C.* 21: 219.

"her extreme intemperance": d'Escherny's memoirs, *C.C.* 26: 365.

Du Peyrou said: as told to J. P. Brissot, ibid., p. 358.

"They say it was less": Sarasin to Montmollin, 12 Feb. 1766, *C.C.* 28: 295.

"If you reply": Daniel Muller to Rousseau, 12 Apr. 1763, *C.C.* 16: 53–54. Muller had written to Rousseau once before, *C.C.* 13: 16–18.

inflammatory sermon, 1 Sept. 1765: summarized (but not recorded in detail) in the official investigation soon afterward: *C.C.* 26: 325–26.

395 "spoke with foaming rage": Meuron to Keith, 7 Sept. 1765, ibid., p. 313.

"I have other business": Montmollin to Martinet, 4 Sept. 1765, ibid., p. 294.

"My God, it's a quarry": *Confessions* XII, *O.C.* 1: 635.

facetious homily: reprinted in Eigeldinger, "Des Pierres," pp. 13–16.

"with a heated imagination": *Corr. Litt.* 6: 405 (15 Nov. 1765).

396 One girl who was fourteen: reported by Jean-Pierre Gaberel, *Rousseau et les Genevois* (1858), *C.C.* 26: 359.

an effigy representing him: report by David-François Clerc, 10 Oct. 1765, *C.C.* 26: 341.

"Bring me a gun . . . know anything": judicial inquiry of 5 Sept. 1765, ibid., pp. 327–28.

one of Keith's subordinates: Samuel Meuron to the graf von Finckenstein, 24 Oct. 1765, *C.C.* 27: 173.

"magic and sorcery": legal records quoted in Eigeldinger, "Des Pierres," p. 145.

397 "much like the Old Man": Keith to Samuel Meuron, 24 Sept. 1765, *C.C.* 27: 37.

still telling visitors: memoirs of L. C. F. Desjobert, describing a visit to Môtiers in 1777, *C.C.* 26: 373.

"singularly situated": *Rêveries* V, *O.C.* 1: 1040.

"You recall Robinson": Deleyre to Rousseau, 11 Nov. 1765, *C.C.* 27: 252.

Rousseau up a tree: mentioned twice, in *Confessions* XII, *O.C.* 1: 644; and *Rêveries* 5, *O.C.* 1: 1044.

399 "O nature": *Confessions* XII, *O.C.* 1: 644.

"The sound": *Rêveries* V, *O.C.* 1: 1044.

"We relaxed": ibid., p. 1045.

"so much is going on": Keith to Rousseau, 26 Oct. 1765, *C.C.* 27: 184.

"The founding of this": *Rêveries* V, *O.C.* 1: 1044.

l'Île des Lapins: for example, Johann Heinrich Weiss, *Atlas Suisse, gravée par Guerin, Eichler, et Scheurmann* (Aarau, 1786–1802), map of Lac de Neuchâtel and the Val de Travers.

400 "Monsieur Jean-Jacques . . . am not yours": Philippe-Cyriaque Bridel, *Course de Bâle à Bienne* (1789), *C.C.* 27: 329.

401 "I'm counting on": Rousseau to Roguin, 4 Oct. 1765, ibid., p. 79. The records in Berne confirm that the harvest was over by Oct. 10: ibid., p. 101n.

"with the greatest regret": Graffenried to Rousseau, 16 Oct. 1765, ibid., pp. 124–25.

Berne was under pressure: Bernard Gagnebin, "Voltaire a-t-il Provoqué l'Expulsion de Rousseau de l'Ile Saint-Pierre?" *Annales* 30 (1943–1945): 111–31. (Gagnebin concludes that Voltaire didn't work actively to have Rousseau expelled but was glad to see it happen.)

remarking gloomily: Rousseau to Guy, 1 Oct. 1765, *C.C.* 27: 55.

402 As Starobinski says: *L'Oeil Vivant,* p. 143.

Rousseau made a desperate: Rousseau to Graffenried, 20 Oct. 1765, *C.C.* 27: 147–49.

remembered his last night: Sigmund Wagner, *L'Île de St. Pierre, dite l'Île de Rousseau* (1795), ed. Pierre Kohler (Lausanne: Éditions SPES, 1926), pp. 76–78.

21. *In a Strange Land*

403 "I arrived in this town": Rousseau to Thérèse, 30 Oct. 1765, *C.C.* 27: 197–98.
"J. J. Rousseau, proscribed": reported by J. G. Zimmermann to Isaac Iselin, 13 Nov. 1765, ibid., p. 346.
"That man has made": Tronchin to Suzanne Necker, 30 Oct. 1765, ibid., p. 199.
"the gracious and glorious": Montmollin to Frederick, 12 Dec. 1765, *C.C.* 28: 39.

404 "the end of the troubles": Charles-Godefroi de Tribolet, *Histoire de Neuchâtel et Valangin* (Neuchâtel: Wolfrath, 1846), p. 169.
Rousseau told Thérèse: 4 Nov. 1765, *C.C.* 27: 217.
he was invited to conduct: anonymous Strasbourg journal, 9 Nov. 1765, ibid., p. 335.
"that I had to break": Rousseau to Du Peyrou, 25 Nov. 1765, ibid., p. 298.
Mme d'Houdetot and Saint-Lambert offered houses: Mme de Verdelin to Rousseau, 28 Nov. 1765, ibid., p. 313.
"Having weighed everything": Rousseau to Du Peyrou, 30 Nov. 1765, ibid., p. 314.
"you would find": Hume to Rousseau, 22 Oct. 1765, ibid., p. 161 (Hume's first draft in English, which he translated into French before sending).
"to throw myself": Rousseau to Hume, 4 Dec. 1765, *C.C.* 28: 17.
"and seeing absolutely": Rousseau to Guy, 7 Dec. 1765, ibid., p. 21.

405 Sauttersheim, who visited him: referred to in his later letter to Rousseau, 15 July 1766, *C.C.* 30: 87.
"I have people": Rousseau to Du Peyrou, 1 Jan. 1766, *C.C.* 28: 146.
"Rather than remaining": Jean-Pierre Crommelin to Pierre Lullin, 4 Jan. 1766, ibid., pp. 158–59.
"I know that two very agreeable": Hume to Hugh Blair, 28 Dec. 1765, ibid., p. 115.

406 "I have loved": Mme Alissan to Rousseau, 21 Dec. 1765, ibid., p. 75.
"I am not alone": Rousseau to Mme Alissan, 28 Dec. 1765, ibid., p. 111.
"After seeing you": Rousseau to Mme Alissan, 2 Jan. 1766, ibid., p. 148.
"Since it's necessary": Henriette to Rousseau, 18 Dec. 1765, ibid., p. 68.
he had to admit: Rousseau's reply to Henriette, 25 Oct. 1770, *C.C.* 38: 124.
"I do well not to give": Diderot to Sophie Volland, 20 Dec. 1765, *Correspondance,* ed. Versini, p. 576.
a cold manner: Rousseau to Du Peyrou, 30 Nov. 1765, *C.C.* 27: 314.
"He imagines himself": Hume to Mme de Boufflers, 19 Jan. 1766, *C.C.* 28: 203.

407 "a great eater": anecdotes of Alexander Carlyle, quoted by Ernest C. Mossner, *The Life of David Hume* (Oxford: Clarendon Press, 1970), p. 245.
"I threw myself": Rousseau to Hume (describing the event later on, after they had quarreled), 10 July 1766, *C.C.* 30: 29.

408 "totally desperate": Hume to John Wilkes, 16 Oct. 1754, *Letters of David Hume,* ed. J. Y. T. Grieg (Oxford: Clarendon Press, 1932), 1: 205. On Hume's accent in French, see Mossner, *Life of David Hume,* p. 214.
"Your broad perspective": Rousseau to Hume, 19 Feb. 176, *C.C.* 15: 199. Rousseau mentions in the *Confessions* (*O.C.* 1: 630) that Hume's *History* was the only work of his he had read.
"Company is naturally": Hume, *Treatise of Human Nature,* II.ii.4, p. 402.
"like a man who": Hume to Hugh Blair, 25 Mar. 1766, *C.C.* 29: 58.
"the celebrated Rousseau": Hume to Blair, 28 Dec. 1765, *C.C.* 28: 112.

"was making a raree show": Brooke Boothby, *Observations on the Appeal from the New to the Old Whigs* (London, 1792), p. 89.

Rousseau at Drury Lane: Hume to John Home, 2 Feb. 1766, *C.C.* 28: 267 and 267–68n.

409   lost bonnets and wigs: *Gazetteer and New Daily Advertiser,* 25 Jan. 1766, *C.C.* 29: 297.

"It's not as bad": quoted by Diderot to Sophie Volland, 10 Dec. 1765, *Correspondance,* ed. Versini, p. 571.

"no better than": Hume to Hugh Blair, 28 Dec. 1765, *C.C.* 28: 114.

"M. de Luze": Hume to Mme de Boufflers, 19 Jan. 1766, ibid., pp. 203–4.

"He is confoundedly weary": William Rouet to William Mure, 25 Jan. 1766, ibid., p. 225.

410   "You won't be annoyed": Boswell to Rousseau, 31 Dec. 1764, *C.C.* 22: 345.

"He has such a rage": Hume to Mme de Boufflers, 12 Feb. 1766, *C.C.* 28: 287.

"He is a true man": Keith to Rousseau, 3 Mar. 1766, *C.C.* 29: 13.

as Cranston severely observes: Cranston 3: 98.

"Yesterday morning had gone": *Boswell on the Grand Tour: Italy, Corsica, and France,* ed. Frank Brady and F. A. Pottle (New York: McGraw-Hill, 1955), p. 279.

According to the collector: he was colonel Ralph Isham, who later sold the Boswell papers to Yale University; his story is reviewed in Frederick A. Pottle, *James Boswell: The Earlier Years* (New York: McGraw-Hill, 1966), pp. 276–78, and in Leigh, *C.C.* 28: 347–50, who reprints Isham's account.

411   "a friend of the celebrated": *London Chronicle,* 11 Feb. 1766, *C.C.* 28: 297n.

"Permit me in turn": Rousseau to Boswell, 4 Aug. 1766, *C.C.* 30: 203, 204n.

"I think him one": James Boswell, *Life of Johnson,* ed. G. B. Hill and L. F. Powell (Oxford: Clarendon Press, 1934), 2: 11.

412   "The house, although small": Rousseau to Mme. de Luze, 10 May 1766, *C.C.* 29: 199.

"It's been frozen": Rousseau to Hume, 29 Mar. 1766, *C.C.* 29: 67.

"Here I am": Rousseau to Coindet, 29 Mar. 1766, ibid., p. 69.

413   "Wootton under Weaver": quoted from an early nineteenth-century guidebook by Louis-J. Courtois, *Le Séjour de Jean-Jacques Rousseau en Angleterre* (Geneva: Slatkine Reprints, 1970), p. 42.

"Rousseau in Derbyshire": *St. James's Chronicle,* 15 May 1766, *C.C.* 29: 304.

"Is there wood": Hume to William Fitzherbert, 25 Feb. 1766, *C.C.* 28: 328.

"belated and cold": Rousseau to Mme de Luze, 10 May 1766, *C.C.* 29: 198–99.

"These hills, though high": Izaak Walton and Charles Cotton, *The Compleat Angler,* ed. Howell Raines (New York: Random House, 1996), p. 276.

414   "My faculties are weakening": Rousseau to the duchess of Portland, 20 Oct. 1766, *C.C.* 31: 40.

"You'll hold conversations": Du Peyrou to Rousseau, 27 Feb. 1766, *C.C.* 28: 339.

"Mlle Levasseur acts": Rousseau to Hume, 29 Mar. 1766, *C.C.* 29: 66.

415   "She hasn't learned": Rousseau to Du Peyrou, 21 June 1766, ibid., p. 266.

"currans & raisins": Rousseau's vocabulary notes, *C.C.* 30: 3.

they remembered him afterward: *Dialogues* II, *O.C.* 1: 905.

"owd Ross Hall . . . You see": William Howitt, *Visits to Remarkable Places* (London: Longman, 1840), pp. 508–11; also in *C.C.* 33: 267–71.

416   "Just a few things": Rousseau to the marquis de Mirabeau, 31 Jan. 1767, *C.C.* 32: 83.

Starobinski comments: *Transparency and Obstruction,* p. 83.

"d'Avenport": Rousseau to Du Peyrou, 14 June 1766, *C.C.* 29: 260.

he stayed at Wootton: Davenport to Rousseau, 24 Mar. 1767, *C.C.* 32: 236; on Davenport's education and interests: J. H. Broome, *Jean-Jacques Rousseau in Staffordshire,*

1766–1767 (Keele, U.K.: Keele University Library, 1966); and Courtois, *Le Séjour de Rousseau,* pp. 50–53.

"M. Davenport does favors": Rousseau to Du Peyrou, 14 Feb. 1767, *C.C.* 32: 140.

"His vivacity": viscount Nuneham to viscountess Palmerston, 17 Sept. 1768, *C.C.* 36: 97.

They had musical evenings: *C.C.* 32: 254n.

417 "My lovely neighbor": Rousseau to Mary Dewes, 9 Dec. 1766, *C.C.* 31: 247.

"You say more": Mary Dewes to Rousseau, 17 Dec. 1766, ibid., p. 276.

"climb over rocks": Rousseau to Du Peyrou, 17 Oct. 1767, *C.C.* 34: 146.

"Never in my life": Rousseau to Du Peyrou, 8 Jan. 1767, *C.C.* 32: 30.

"The snow here": Granville to Rousseau, 16 Jan. 1767, ibid., p. 48.

"that has kept Calwich": Rousseau to Granville, 28 Feb. 1767, ibid., p. 185.

"I was well received": memoirs of Brooke Boothby, *C.C.* 33: 277.

"Are you a botanist": Howitt, *Visits to Remarkable Places,* p. 513, and *C.C.* 33: 270.

418 "This worthy man": Samuel-André Tissot to comte Alexandre de Golowkin, 22 Mar. 1765, *C.C.* 24: 277.

as Mély comments: *Un Intellectuel en Rupture,* p. 224.

"I have powerful": Rousseau to Du Peyrou, 7 Feb. 1765, *C.C.* 23: 310.

419 "absurd charge": Mossner, *Life of David Hume,* p. 523.

Louis-François Tronchin's account: reported by J. H. Meister to J. J. Bodmer, 17 Nov. 1766, *C.C.* 31: 173.

"What could I do": Hume's note enclosed by d'Alembert in a letter to J. B. A. Suard, 29 Nov. 1766, ibid., pp. 225–26n.

"The man I mentioned": Rousseau to F.-H. d'Ivernois, 31 May 1766, *C.C.* 29: 240. D'Ivernois gave Rousseau the code in a letter of 28 Apr., p. 159.

Rousseau accepted 2,400 livres: Du Peyrou to Rousseau, 8 Mar. 1768, *C.C.* 34: 190.

"Liberality is doubtless": Rousseau to Davenport, 22 Mar. 1766, *C.C.* 29: 48.

420 "An allowance made": Samuel Johnson, *Dictionary of the English Language* (1755).

"If you persist": Walpole's "king of Prussia" letter, Dec. 1765, *C.C.* 28: 345.

421 "triumvirate": Rousseau to Du Peyrou, 31 May 1766, *C.C.* 29: 237.

"measured and calculated": Rousseau to Mme de Boufflers, 20 Aug. 1761, *C.C.* 12: 217.

"his broad unmeaning face": anecdotes by Lord Charlemont in Mossner, *Life of David Hume,* p. 446.

"After supper . . . *mon cher monsieur*": Rousseau to Hume, 10 July 1766, *C.C.* 30: 35.

422 "I hope, dear Madam": Hume to Mme de Boufflers, 3 Apr. 1766, ibid., p. 90.

"I hope you have not": Hume to Hugh Blair, 25 Mar. 1766, ibid., p. 59.

"Instead of melting": Rousseau to Mme de Verdelin, 9 Apr. 1766, *C.C.* 29: 101–2.

423 "Cyclops face": Rousseau to Moultou, 28 Mar. 1770, *C.C.* 37: 350.

"Skillfully darkening": *Dialogues* II, *O.C.* 1: 782.

Bernardin on the Ramsay engraving: Bernardin, 32–33n.

Deleyre told Boswell: 8 Dec. 1766, *C.C.* 31: 243.

424 "Several times during": Rousseau to Hume, 10 July 1766, *C.C.* 30: 44.

"but there was something": Rousseau to Mme de Verdelin, 9 Apr. 1766, *C.C.* 29: 101.

"I cannot answer": Hume's footnote responding to Rousseau's account, in *A Concise and Genuine Account of the Dispute between Mr. Hume and Mr. Rousseau* (London: Becket, 1766), p. 79n.

Mély's suggestion: *Un Intellectuel en Rupture,* pp. 234–42.

"You will be astonished": Hume to Davenport, 26 June 1766, *C.C.* 29: 283.

425 a psychoanalyst observes: Silvio Fanti, "Une Lecture de J. J. Rousseau en Micro-

psychanalyse," *Bulletin d'Information de l'Association des Amis de Jean-Jacques Rousseau* 1 (Neuchâtel, 1964): 3–15.

"bad brothers": Clément, *De l'Éros Coupable,* p. 338 and passim.

"The vices of men": Rousseau to the chevalier d'Éon, 31 Mar. 1766, *C.C.* 29: 82.

"David Hume is only doing": *O.C.* 1: 1272n.

"My nights are cruel": Rousseau to Malesherbes, 10 May 1766, *C.C.* 29: 193.

426   "perfect frenzy": Hume to Davenport, 15 July 1766, *C.C.* 30: 97.

d'Holbach and d'Alembert both took care to destroy: see *C.C.* 29: 306–7.

"It won't be long": Morellet, *Mémoires,* p. 113.

"I'm warning you": Marmontel, *Mémoires* 1: 232.

"The church, the Whigs": Smith to Hume, 6 July 1766, *C.C.* 30: 17.

427   "You are too confirmed": Mme de Boufflers to Hume, 22 July 1766, ibid., p. 142; for d'Alembert and Smith, see pp. 16–17 and 19.

"to gratify some spleen": Walpole to the duchesse d'Aiguillon, 3 Nov. 1766, *C.C.* 31: 110.

"All Europe laughs": Walpole to Hume, 6 Nov. 1766, ibid., p. 120.

"I don't think anyone": *Corr. Litt.* 7: 145 (15 Oct. 1766).

"I knew these two ": Diderot, quoted by J. H. Meister to J. J. Bodmer, 27 Oct. 1766, *C.C.* 31: 87.

"the abbé Coyer": Voltaire to Bordes, 15 Dec. 1766, ibid., p. 268.

"but prejudices are": Rousseau to Mme de Boufflers, 30 Aug. 1766, *C.C.* 30: 291.

a London satirist: *The Miscellany, No. 11, by Nathaniel Freebody Esq.,* 15 Jan. 1767, *C.C.* 32: 297.

428   "Be sure that they're": Mme de Verdelin to Coindet, 24 July 1766, *C.C.* 30: 155.

"My good friends": Théodore Tronchin to Jacob Tronchin, 4 Aug. 1766, ibid., pp. 211–12.

"You are not fleeing": Keith to Rousseau, 19 Nov. 1765, *C.C.* 27: 284.

"What, Mylord": Rousseau to Keith, 8 Feb. 1767, *C.C.* 32: 119–20.

"I am old, infirm": Keith to Rousseau, 22 Nov. 1766, *C.C.* 31: 196.

429   "I don't know how": Rousseau to Du Peyrou, 28 Feb. 1769, *C.C.* 37: 61).

he left Rousseau the watch: d'Alembert, *Éloge de Keith, C.C.* 12: 289.

"I am the most unfortunate": Rousseau to Hume, 10 July 1766, *C.C.* 30: 46.

"a vulgar old kitchen maid": Boothby's reminsciences, *C.C.* 33: 277.

"I find that Mr. Davenport": Hume to Turgot, 22 May 1767, ibid., p. 82.

"her venomous tale-telling": Mme de Verdelin to Coindet, 15 June 1767, *C.C.* 33: 148.

an aged former nurse: the quarrel with Thérèse is reported by V. L. Dutens, *C.C.* 32: 252n.

surprised Davenport with a letter: Rousseau to Davenport, 22 Dec. 1766, *C.C.* 31: 295–96.

430   "The master of a house": Rousseau to Davenport, 30 Apr. 1767, *C.C.* 33: 37.

"I hope he will enjoy": Hume to Davenport, 2 May 1767, ibid., p. 41.

"I am surrounded": Rousseau to Du Peyrou, 2 Apr. 1767, ibid., p. 4.

"behaved in such a brutish": Granville to Mary Dewes, 10 May 1767, ibid., p. 53.

"his *governante* has": Davenport to Hume, 6 July 1767, ibid., pp. 199–200.

"I had some conversation": viscount Nuneham to viscountess Palmerston, 17 Sept. 1768, *C.C.* 36: 97–98. The cook sprinkling ashes is also reported by Walpole, *C.C.* 33: 287.

431   "one of the most cursed": Davenport to Rousseau, 18 May 1767, *C.C.* 33: 70.

Du Peyrou had recommended Cerjat: Du Peyrou to Rousseau, 27 Jan. 1766, *C.C.* 28: 234.

"It seems he wrote": Hume to Davenport, 9 May 1767, *C.C.* 33: 50.

members of a book club: Edmund Jessop to Rousseau, 10 May 1767, ibid., pp. 51–52; Rousseau's reply, 13 May, pp. 55–56.

wrote to the lord chancellor: Rousseau to Baron Camden, 5 May 1767, *C.C.* 33: 44.

432 "He is plainly mad": Hume to Davenport, 16 May 1767, ibid., p. 62.

paid his way by selling off silverware: told later to Corancez, *De J. J. Rousseau* (Paris, 1798), ibid., p. 280.

"I have tormented . . . middle way": Rousseau to Henry Conway, 18 May 1767, *C.C.* 33: 63–67.

"an attack of madness": Corancez, *De J. J. Rousseau,* ibid., p. 280.

"Vexed at the obstinacy": "Rusticus," *European Magazine and London Review,* Oct. 1787, in Courtois, *Le Séjour de Rousseau,* p. 299.

433 "seemingly rational": Hume to Mme de Boufflers, 19 June 1767, *C.C.* 33: 165.

"I would give half my life": Rousseau to Du Peyrou, 2 Apr. 1767, ibid., p. 5.

22. The Past Relived

434 "this infernal affair": Du Peyrou to Rousseau, 9 Dec. 1766, *C.C.* 31: 252.

"It's the past": Rousseau to Mme de Créqui, 10 May 1766, *C.C.* 29: 196.

anonymous letter: a Genevan artisan to Rousseau, Aug. 1763, *C.C.* 17: 205–21.

435 earlier writers' anecdotes of childhood: see the extracts from memoirs by the abbé de Marolles (1657) and Mme de Staal–Delaunay (1755) in Jean-François Perrin, *Les Confessions de Jean-Jacques Rousseau* (Paris: Gallimard, 1997), pp. 207–11.

"Nothing is more insipid": quoted in Besterman, *Voltaire,* p. 14.

"almost intentionally inscrutable": Wilson, *Diderot,* p. 24; Diderot's opinion of childhood, p. 28.

"One of the sweetest": Diderot to Sophie Volland, 18 Oct. 1760, *Correspondance,* ed. Versini, p. 262.

"Many readers will be": undated fragment collected under the title "Mon Portrait," *O.C.* 1: 1120.

"The course I have chosen": *Confessions* III, *O.C.* 1: 116.

436 "Who can know how much": George Eliot, *Middlemarch,* chap. 68.

"I must keep myself": *Confessions* II, *O.C.* 1: 59.

"Let the trumpet": *Confessions* I, ibid., p. 5.

"If Monsieur Rousseau": Grimm to the duchess of Saxe-Gotha, 7 Mar. 1765, *C.C.* 24: 168.

"He seems to have formed": Louis-Sébastien Mercier, *Mon Bonnet de Nuit* (1786), in *Mémoire,* p. 525.

"The book written": "To the Deists," plate 52 of *Jerusalem,* in Blake, *Complete Poetry and Prose,* p. 201.

437 "There are times": *Confessions* III, *O.C.* 1: 128.

"the anguished and contradictory": Raymond Trousson, *Jean-Jacques Rousseau: Bonheur et Liberté* (Nancy: Presses Universitaires de Nancy, 1992), p. 193.

"a psychology of rupture": Raymond, *Rousseau: La Quête de Soi,* p. 16.

"Turn your eyes inward": "A Difficulty in the Path of Psycho-Analysis," in *The Standard Edition of the Complete Psychological Works of Sigmund Freud,* ed. James Strachey (London: Hogarth Press, 1955), 17: 143.

438 "What Rousseau *really* wanted": Paul de Man, *Allegories of Reading: Figural Language in Rousseau, Nietzsche, Rilke, and Proust* (New Haven: Yale University Press, 1979), p. 285.

six hundred persons: Gagnebin, "Vérité et Véracité dans *Les Confessions,*" in *Rousseau et son Oeuvre,* p. 9.

Recent research on memory: see Jerome Bruner, "The Autobiographical Process," in *The Culture of Autobiography: Constructions of Self-Representation,* ed. Robert Folkenflik (Stanford: Stanford University Press, 1993), pp. 38–56; see also Roy W. Perrett, "Autobiography and Self-Deception: Conjoining Philosophy, Literature, and Cognitive Psychology," *Mosaic* 29 (Dec. 1996): 25–40.

"These moments would still": *Confessions* I, *O.C.* 1: 20.

439   "I loved to expand": *Rêveries* IV, *O.C.* 1: 1035.

"It's not a present": Lejeune, *Le Pacte Autobiographique,* p. 53.

"Wanting to recall": *Rêveries* II, *O.C.* 1: 1003.

"All the birds": *Confessions* IV, *O.C.* 1: 135.

"I am undertaking an enterprise": *Confessions* I, ibid., p. 5.

"It's necessary to invent": *Ébauches des Confessions, O.C.* 1: 1153.

"for when one saw": *Confessions* IV, *O.C.* 1: 141.

440   "dromomania": Emmanuel Régis, cited in Claude Wacjman, *Fous de Rousseau: Le Cas Rousseau dans l'Histoire de la Psychopathologie* (Paris: Harmattan, 1992), p. 49. Wacjman's book is a fair-minded survey of psychological studies of Rousseau.

Freud describes people: *The Ego and the Id,* trans. Joan Riviere, rev. James Strachey (New York: Norton, 1962), p. 39.

"the malady substituted": Charles Baudouin, *Psychanalyse du Symbole Religieux* (Paris: Fayard, 1957), p. 109.

441   "Persecution has elevated": *Ébauches des Confessions, O.C.* 1: 1164.

"Rends confus": Psalm 35: 1, quoted in Masson, *La Religion de Rousseau* 1: 33.

"He needs the dark": Starobinski, *Transparency and Obstruction,* p. 247.

"the grosser appetite": Gibbon, *Memoirs,* p. 104.

"The captain": ibid., p. 128.

"To conclude": Hume, "My Own Life," dated 18 Apr. 1776 (he died four months later), in Mossner, *Life of David Hume,* p. 615.

442   "He has read": Hume to Hugh Blair, 25 Mar. 1766, *C.C.* 29: 58.

"an invaluable book": *Ébauches des Confessions, O.C.* 1: 1154.

443   "Our senses show us": Rousseau to Dom Deschamps, 8 May 1761, *C.C.* 8: 320.

"Who can do more": Edmund S. Morgan, *Benjamin Franklin* (New Haven: Yale University Press, 2002), p. 146.

"that aversion": Franklin, *Autobiography,* p. 21.

445   "What will it matter": *Journal Encyclopédique* (July 1782), in *Mémoire,* p. 180.

"If the over-sincere . . . indelibly ridiculous": *L'Année Littéraire* (1782), in *Mémoire,* p. 468.

446   "a man like Rousseau": *Corr. Litt.* 13: 162 (July 1782).

"Autobiography is only": George Orwell, "Benefit of Clergy: Some Notes on Salvador Dali," *Collected Essays* (London: Secker & Warburg, 1961), p. 209.

"I am made like no one": *Confessions* I, *O.C.* 1: 5.

"The author": Lionel Trilling: *Sincerity and Authenticity* (Cambridge: Harvard University Press, 1972), p. 24.

23. *Into the Self-Made Labyrinth*

447   Guéhenno on the Nazi occupation: Guéhenno 2: 204–5.

448   "If you change your name": Conti to Rousseau, 15 June 1767, *C.C.* 33: 146.

449 "My lord, I honor": *Confessions* X, *O.C.* 1: 543.
"What! I did give": Sébastien-Roch Nicholas, known as Chamfort, *Caractères et Anecdotes,* in Chamfort, *Oeuvres* (Paris, 1812), 2: 237.

450 "Such has been the fate . . . all my heart": Rousseau to Coindet, 27 and 28 June 1767, *C.C.* 33: 177, 178.
"rather lower": Rousseau to Mme de Verdelin, 22 July 1767, ibid., p. 230.
"The root of the evil": Rousseau to Coindet, 9 Sept. 1767, *C.C.* 34: 137.
"I have no one": Rousseau to Du Peyrou, 27 Sept. 1767, ibid., p. 116.

451 "He spoke ceaselessly . . . my life": Rousseau to Conti, 19 Nov. 1767, ibid., pp. 185, 190. (This letter was not sent, but Rousseau carefully preserved it.)
"The barbarous man . . . last spark": ibid., p. 187.
Du Peyrou told Rousseau: 26 Nov. 1767, ibid., p. 208.

452 "You say you were": Rousseau to Du Peyrou, 27 Nov. 1767, ibid., p. 211.
Rousseau admitted to Coindet: 27 Dec. 1767, ibid., p. 264.
"Solitude used to be": marquis de Mirabeau to Rousseau, 15 Mar. 1768, *C.C.* 35: 201–2, responding to Rousseau's letter of 9 Mar., p. 193.
"I will never importune": Rousseau to Mme de Boufflers, 24 Mar. 1768, ibid., p. 217; Leigh (p. 217n) says that her letter of 23 Mar. is the last she is known to have written to Rousseau.

453 "I ask you": Conti to Rousseau, 8 Apr. 1768, ibid., p. 243.
"M. Rousseau's disposition": Du Peyrou to Coindet, 17 July 1768, *C.C.* 36: 19.

455 a warning from Conti: Conti to Rousseau, 24 July 1768, ibid., p. 24.
"as deep as it": Rousseau to Conzié, 28 July 1768, ibid., p. 28.
"Receive my adieux": Rousseau to A.J.M. Servan, 11 Aug. 1768, ibid., p. 30.

456 "the most important action": reminiscences of Luc-Antoine Donin de Champagneux, ibid., p. 233.
"My housekeeper": Rousseau to Moultou, 10 Oct. 1768, ibid., p. 144.
"the tender and pure": Rousseau to Henri Laliaud, 31 Aug. 1768, ibid., p. 65.

457 "Not only have they": Rousseau to Mme Delessert, 3 Sept. 1768, ibid., pp. 74–75.
The Swiss doctor: Rousseau to Samuel-Auguste Tissot: 5 Jan. 1769, *C.C.* 37: 3–5.

458 "Kings and the great . . . spite of himself": "Sentiments du Public sur mon Comte dans les Divers États qui le Composent," *O.C.* 1: 1183–84 (also *C.C.* 36: 76–78).
"a veritable ice-house": Rousseau to Mme Boy, 2 Jan. 1770, *C.C.* 37: 198.

459 "When we united . . . way whatsoever": Rousseau to Thérèse, 12 Aug. 1769, *C.C.* 37: 120–23. The letter is analyzed interestingly in Guyot, *Plaidoyer pour Thérèse Levasseur,* pp. 118–20.

460 Grimm later reported: *Corr. Litt.* 9: 91 (15 July 1770).
"The ceiling above": *Confessions* VII, *O.C.* 1: 279.
"painful in its tragic": *C.C.* 37: xxiv.

461 "Let me know": Rousseau to C. A. de Saint-Germain 26 Feb. 1770, ibid., p. 292.

462 "We drank . . . days of his life": reminiscences of Horace Coignet, *C.C.* 38: 306–7.

24. The Final Years in Paris

464 "Adieu, then, Paris": *Émile* IV, *O.C.* 4: 691.
"It was on the ninth": *Confessions* IX, *O.C.* 1: 403.
"Some days ago": Louis de Bachaumont, *Mémoires Secrets,* 1 July 1770, in Plan, *Rousseau Raconté,* p. 99.
"When half of those people": *Corr. Litt.* 9: 91 (15 July 1770).

465   "blind and stupid confidence": *Confessions* X, *O.C.* 1: 542n.

"I've returned": Rousseau to Saint-German, 14 July 1770, *C.C.* 38: 62.

he wrote to Du Peyrou: 5 Nov. 1770, ibid., pp. 126–27. Du Peyrou mentions his 1775 visit to Rousseau in a letter to Mme de Franqueville, 9 May 1779, *C.C.* 43: 262–63.

rue Plâtrière . . . familiar territory: Harumi Yamazaki-Jamin, "La Rue Jean-Jacques Rousseau," in *Études Jean-Jacques Rousseau: Rousseau et l'Exclusion* (Montmorency: Musée Jean-Jacques Rousseau, 2000–2001), pp. 245–48.

visitor who expressed surprise: Julien-Jacques Moutonnet de Clairfons, *Le Véritable Philanthrope . . . précédé d'Anecdotes et de Détails Peu Connus sur J. J. Rousseau* (1790), quoted by Madeleine Molinier, "Un Portrait de J.-J. Rousseau par un Visiteur Oublié," *Revue d'Histoire Littéraire de la France* 65 (1965): 415.

467   "I am living proof": *Rêveries* VII, *O.C.* 1: 1065.

"Doctors sometimes effect": Rousseau to the duc d'Albe, 1 Oct. 1772, *C.C.* 39: 110.

"He no longer has": *Dialogues* II, *O.C.* 1: 865–66.

"I would never have": Jacob Jonas Björnstahl to Carl Christoffer Gjörwell, 1 Sept. 1770, *C.C.* 38: 94.

spoke with a Genevan accent: Raymond, "Rousseau et Genève," in Baud-Bovy, *Jean-Jacques Rousseau,* p. 236.

rings engraved with his parents' names: noted by Björnstahl, letter to Gjörwell, 1 Sept. 1770, *C.C.* 38: 95.

"he never spoke": Bernardin, p. 39.

"Madame, does M. Rousseau": Marie-Jeanne Philipon [or Phlipon] to Marie Cannet, 29 Feb. 1776, *C.C.* 40: 39.

468   apartment on the fifth floor: visitors' recollections varied as to what floor it was, but it was definitely the fifth (see Leigh's note, *C.C.* 38: 345).

"It's not to show": reminiscences of the chevalier de Toustain, in Antoine-Joseph de Baruel-Beauvert, *Vie de Rousseau* (1789), ibid., p. 330.

"My heart was wrenched": Carlo Goldoni, *Mémoires* (1797), ibid., p. 335.

"abode of rats . . . spoken of it": prince de Ligne, *Lettres et Pensées,* ed. Raymond Trousson (Paris: Tallandier, 1989), p. 288.

"At one time my wife": Bernardin, p. 51.

"What do you have": Lebègue de Presle, quoted by Guyot, *Plaidoyer pour Thérèse Levasseur,* p. 131n.

"For me it's a labor": Bernardin, p. 65.

Rousseau's record of music copying: *O.C.* 1: 1685n.

469   "He copied . . . *cou pelé*": Corancez, *Mémoires de Rousseau,* pp. 267, 275.

"He had a dark . . . the rejection": Bernardin, pp. 31–36, 80, 90, 77, 66–67, 184.

471   "Monsieur, go": Bernardin's account as recalled by Antoine Bret, *C.C.* 38: 326.

"So you know": Björnstahl to Gjörwell, 1 Sept. 1770, ibid., p. 93.

"His health regime . . . able to capture": Bernardin, pp. 49, 165, 50–51n, 54, 110.

472   "Never has a botanist": Pierre Prévost, *Lettre sur J.-J. Rousseau* (1804), *C.C.* 40: 267.

"When one studies": Bernardin, *Harmonies de la Nature,* in *Oeuvres Complètes,* ed. Louis Aimé-Martin (Paris: Méquignan-Marvis, 1820), 8: 317.

"It's a true pedagogical": Goethe to the duke of Weimar, June 1782, quoted by Leigh, *C.C.* 39: xxviii.

473   "an opportunity to display": *Correspondance Secrète* (11 Nov. 1775), in *Mémoire,* p. 417; on the motionless pose, Bachaumont, quoted in *C.C.* 40: 29n.

"I'm enchanted": memoirs of Johann Christian Mannlich, *C.C.* 39: 337. (Leigh is somewhat skeptical of the authenticity of this letter but confirms that Rousseau admired Gluck and saw him frequently.)

arrangement of Vivaldi's *Spring: C.C.* 40: 22n.

Franklin was one of the subscribers: mentioned in Schama, *Citizens,* p. 157. The history and aesthetic qualities of the songs are discussed by Jenny H. Batlay, *Jean-Jacques Rousseau Compositeur des Chansons* (Paris: Éditions de l'Athanor, 1976).

"he sang a mediocre": Vico Millico, quoted by Guyot, *Plaidoyer pour Thérèse Levasseur,* pp. 125–126.

"He told me . . . laughter on the stairs": A. E. M. Grétry, *Mémoires ou Essais sur la Musique* (1789), *C.C.* 40: 257.

474 "What wouldn't one give": Philippe Lejeune, *Je est un Autre: l'Autobiographie de la Littérature aux Médias* (Paris: Seuil, 1980), p. 111.

"I expected a session": Claude-Joseph Dorat to the comtesse de Beauharnais, Dec. 1770, *C.C.* 38: 154–55.

"He wept . . . more unhappy": Dusaulx, *De Mes Rapports,* pp. 65, 113.

475 "little good-for-nothing . . . is a phenomenon": Condorcet, *Mémoires, C.C.* 38: 348.

"I finished . . . should be choked": *Confessions* XII, *O.C.* 1: 656.

"I think you must": Mme d'Épinay to Sartine, 10 May 1771, *C.C.* 38: 228.

476 "He would say to me": Bernardin, p. 29.

"Ah, there they are . . . or the time": Dusaulx, *De Mes Rapports,* pp. 101–2.

"I don't know when": Rousseau to Rey, 11 Oct. 1773, *C.C.* 39: 202.

477 As Leigh says: ibid., p. xxiii.

"Picture to yourself": *Dialogues* I, *O.C.* 1: 756.

478 "It was necessary": "Sujet et Forme de Cet Écrit," *Dialogues,* ibid., p. 665.

Jean-Jacques writing a dialogue: *Dialogues* II, ibid., p. 836.

"What I had to say": "Sujet et Forme," *Dialogues,* ibid., p. 664.

"His suspicious": Mercier, *Oeuvres Complètes de Rousseau* (1788), in *Mémoire,* p. 533.

479 "buried alive": *Dialogues* I, *O.C.* 1: 706.

"he could pass today": Jean-François de La Harpe to the Grand Duke of Russia, June/July 1776, *C.C.* 40: 80.

Corancez on Rousseau's cousin: *Mémoires de Rousseau,* pp. 288–89.

as Françoise Barguillet suggests: *Rousseau, ou l'Illusion Passionnée: Les Rêveries du Promeneur Solitaire* (Paris: Presses Universitaires de France, 1991), pp. 41, 68.

"Rousseau used to go": *Recueil de Lettres Secrètes, Année 1783,* attributed to Guillaume Imbert de Boudeaux, ed. Paule Adamy (Geneva: Droz, 1997), pp. 336–37.

480 "A deposit committed": *Histoire du Précedent Écrit, O.C.* 1: 978–79.

"The least that is due": *Copie du Billet Circulaire, O.C.* 1: 990.

"told me": *Histoire du Précedent Écrit, O.C.* 1: 984.

481 "*Me voici donc* . . . I have fallen": *Rêveries* I, *O.C.* 1: 995, 999.

"mechanical beings": *Rêveries* VIII, ibid., p. 1078.

distinctive musical tonality: Michèle Crogiez, *Solitude et Méditation: Étude sur les Rêveries de Jean-Jacques Rousseau* (Paris: Champion, 1997), p. 113.

"ridiculous imagination": *Dictionnaire de Trévoux,* quoted by Érik Leborgne in his edition of the *Rêveries* (Paris: Flammarion, 1997), p. 36.

As a French writer comments: Goldschmidt, *Rousseau, ou, l'Esprit de Solitude,* p. 140.

482 "The 'Know Thyself'": *Rêveries* IV, *O.C.* 1: 1024.

"What am I, myself?": *Rêveries* I, ibid., p. 995.

"That's what I discovered": *Rêveries* VI, *O.C.* 1: 1051.

a story told by Freud: *Complete Psychological Works* 6: 137–38. The patron was Josef Breuer.

"Precious *far niente*": *Rêveries* IV, *O.C.* 1: 1042.

"the habit of sauntering": Adam Smith, *An Inquiry into the Nature and Causes of the Wealth of Nations* (1776), book I, chap. 1, "Of the Division of Labour."

483 "a divine gift": Bernardin, p. 127.

"I have never believed": *Rêveries* VI, *O.C.* 1: 1059.

"and thus render": René Descartes, *Discours de la Méthode* (1637), part VI.

"Taking refuge": *Rêveries* VII, *O.C.* 1: 1066.

"They flash upon": William Wordsworth, "I Wandered Lonely as a Cloud."

484 "delicious repose . . . one's existence": "Délicieux," in *Encyclopédie,* discussed by Georges Poulet, "Le Sentiment de l'Existence et le Repos," in Simon Harvey et al., *Reappraisals of Rousseau: Studies in Honour of R. A. Leigh* (Manchester: Manchester University Press, 1980), 37–45.

"Ah, if only . . . wanted to be": *Rêveries* X, *O.C.* 1: 1098–99.

"the solitary state": Gaston Bachelard, *The Poetics of Reverie: Childhood, Language, and the Cosmos,* trans. Daniel Russell (Boston: Beacon Press, 1969), p. 133.

"I was never happy": Bernardin, p. 113.

"equally sad": *Rêveries* I, *O.C.* 1: 997.

sudden death of the prince: the evidence is surveyed in the Pléiade introduction, *O.C.* 1: lxxxiii–lxxiv, and in Fabre, "Jean-Jacques Rousseau et le Prince de Conti," in *Lumières et Romantisme,* pp. 101–35.

485 "one of those Great Danes": Bernardin, p. 49.

"Fifty honest pedestrians": *Discours sur l'Économie Politique, O.C.* 3: 272.

"with the speed . . . punished for it": Corancez, *Mémoire de Rousseau,* pp. 275–76.

486 Montaigne was thrown: Michel de Montaigne, "De l'Exercice," *Essais* II.vi.

"Night was beginning": *Rêveries* II, *O.C.* 1: 1005.

"Over a long period": Corancez, *Mémoires de Rousseau,* p. 291.

487 modern medical interpreters: Bensoussan, *La Maladie de Rousseau,* p. 50 , citing medical authorities.

"the vapors": Mme Delessert to Jean-André Deluc, 30 July 1777, *C.C.* 40: 139.

"You are relighting": Rousseau to the comte Duprat, 3 Feb. 1778, ibid., p. 194.

he abruptly departed: Bernardin, pp. 186–87; Corancez, *Mémoires de Rousseau,* p. 293.

He sent to Paris for books: reminiscences of Lebègue de Presle, *C.C.* 40: 330.

488 "Men are wicked": reminiscences of Jean Hyacinthe de Magellan, ibid., p. 323; on the concert, p. 324.

489 "'How different,'": commentary by Mérigot fils, *Promenade, ou Itinéraire des Jardins d'Ermenonville* (Paris: Mérigot, 1788), p. 51.

"I saw his eyes": Girardin, *Lettre à Sophie comtesse de ***, C.C.* 40: 337.

account of Rousseau's death: Lebègue de Presle, ibid., p. 331.

489 Rousseau's autopsy: ibid., p. 373; on the attacks of vertigo, Moultou's account, p. 315.

modern opinion on cause of death: Cecil Treip, professor of pathology, cited by Leigh, ibid., p. 374n.

490 "Ermenonville belongs": quoted by Charles Samaran, *Paysages Littéraires du Valois* (Paris: Klincksieck, 1964), p. 16.

"He is buried": reminiscences of Victor Offroy, quoted in Guyot, *Plaidoyer pour Thérèse Levasseur,* p. 192. The full story of Thérèse's last years is narrated by Guyot on pp. 135–72.

491 "If my husband is not": reported by the architect Pâris in *Récit de la Mort de Rousseau,* quoted by Masson, *La Religion de Rousseau* 2: 251.

"The moon that shed": "Rapport fait au Comité d'Instruction Publique de la Convention Nationale, 20 Vendémiaire an III" (11 Oct. 1794), *C.C.* 48: 79, and *Mémoire,* p. 599.

492 "Aristocratic Geneva": quoted in a very full description of the ceremony by J.-M. Paris, *Honneurs Publiques Rendus à la Mémoire de J.-J. Rousseau* (Geneva: Carey, 1878), pp. 66–75.

493 "That's what you": Maria Edgeworth to Mary Sneyd, 10 Jan. 1803 (recounting a conversation with the now elderly Mme d'Houdetot), *C.C.* 5: 280.

"The friends of Rousseau": Deleyre to Girardin, 5 Aug. 1778, ibid., p. 291.

Index